ACHI 2019

The Twelfth International Conference on Advances in Computer-Human Interactions

February 24 – 28, 2019

Athens, Greece

ACHI 2019 Editors

Uttam Kokil, Kennesaw State University Marietta, USA
Tomoko Ota, Chuo Business Group Co., Japan

Printed from e-media with permission by:

Curran Associates, Inc.
57 Morehouse Lane
Red Hook, NY 12571

Some format issues inherent in the e-media version may also appear in this print version.

Printed by Curran Associates, Inc. (2019)

International Academy, Research, and Industry Association (IARIA)
412 Derby Way
Wilmington, DE 19810

Phone: (408) 893-6407
Fax: (408) 527-6351

petre@iaria.org

Additional copies of this publication are available from:

Curran Associates, Inc.
57 Morehouse Lane
Red Hook, NY 12571 USA
Phone: 845-758-0400
Fax: 845-758-2633
Email: curran@proceedings.com
Web: www.proceedings.com

Table of Contents

ACHI 2019

Forward

The Twelfth edition of The International Conference on Advances in Computer-Human Interactions (ACHI 2018) conference was held in Athens, Greece, February 24 - 28, 2019.

The conference on Advances in Computer-Human Interaction, ACHI 2019, was a result of a paradigm shift in the most recent achievements and future trends in human interactions with increasingly complex systems. Adaptive and knowledge-based user interfaces, universal accessibility, human-robot interaction, agent-driven human computer interaction, and sharable mobile devices are a few of these trends. ACHI 2019 brought also a suite of specific domain applications, such as gaming, social, medicine, education and engineering.

The event was very competitive in its selection process and very well perceived by the international scientific and industrial communities. As such, it is attracting excellent contributions and active participation from all over the world. We were very pleased to receive a large amount of top quality contributions.

The accepted papers covered a wide range of human-computer interaction related topics such as graphical user interfaces, input methods, training, recognition, and applications.
We believe that the ACHI 2019 contributions offered a large panel of solutions to key problems in all areas of human-computer interaction.

We take here the opportunity to warmly thank all the members of the ACHI 2019 technical program committee as well as the numerous reviewers. The creation of such a broad and high quality conference program would not have been possible without their involvement. We also kindly thank all the authors that dedicated much of their time and efforts to contribute to the ACHI 2019. We truly believe that thanks to all these efforts, the final conference program consists of top quality contributions.

This event could also not have been a reality without the support of many individuals, organizations and sponsors. In addition, we also gratefully thank the members of the ACHI 2019 organizing committee for their help in handling the logistics and for their work that is making this professional meeting a success.

We hope the ACHI 2019 was a successful international forum for the exchange of ideas and results between academia and industry and to promote further progress in the human-computer interaction field.

We also hope that Athens provided a pleasant environment during the conference and everyone saved some time for exploring this beautiful city.

ACHI 2019 Chairs

ACHI Steering Committee
Leslie Miller, Iowa State University - Ames, USA
Uttam Kokil, Kennesaw State University Marietta, USA
Flaminia Luccio, University Ca' Foscari of Venice, Italy

ACHI Industry/Research Advisory Committee
Jacki O'Neill, Microsoft Research, India
Weizhi Meng, Institute for Infocomm Research (I2R), Singapore
Harald Milchrahm, Institute for Softwaretechnology - Technical University Graz, Austria
Steffen Scholz, Karlsruhe Institute of Technology (KIT), Germany
Ryo Ishii, NTT Corporation, Japan
Zahen Malla Osman, The National Center for Scientific Research (CNRS), France
Mohammed Korayem, Careerbuilder.com, USA

ACHI 2019

COMMITTEE

ACHI Steering Committee
Leslie Miller, Iowa State University - Ames, USA
Uttam Kokil, Kennesaw State University Marietta, USA
Flaminia Luccio, University Ca' Foscari of Venice, Italy

ACHI Industry/Research Advisory Committee
Jacki O'Neill, Microsoft Research, India
Weizhi Meng, Institute for Infocomm Research (I2R), Singapore
Harald Milchrahm, Institute for Softwaretechnology - Technical University Graz, Austria
Steffen Scholz, Karlsruhe Institute of Technology (KIT), Germany
Ryo Ishii, NTT Corporation, Japan
Zahen Malla Osman, The National Center for Scientific Research (CNRS), France
Mohammed Korayem, Careerbuilder.com, USA

ACHI 2019 Technical Program Committee

Andrea F. Abate, University of Salerno, Italy
Shameem Ahmed, Western Washington University, USA
Majed Alshamari, King Faisal University, Saudi Arabia
Popi Anastasiou, Open University, UK
David Benyon, Edinburgh Napier University, UK
Chidansh Bhatt, FX Palo Alto Laboratory Inc., USA
Christos Bouras, University of Patras and Computer Technology Institute & Press «Diophantus», Greece
Christian Bourret, UPEM - Université Paris-Est Marne-la-Vallée, France
DanaKai Bradford, Australian eHealth Research Centre | Commonwealth Scientific and Industrial Research Organisation, Australia
Michael Brayshaw, University of Hull, UK
Jan Broer, ifib - Institut für Informationsmanagement Bremen GmbH, Germany
Marcin Butlewski, Poznan University of Technology, Poland
Nan Cao, NYU Shanghai, China
Stefan Carmien, University of York, UK
Youngjun Cho, University College London (UCL), UK
Andre Constantino da Silva, Federal Institute of São Paulo – IFSP, Brazil
Patricia Cornelio, University of Sussex, UK
David Costa, Universidade de Lisboa, Portugal
André Magno Costa de Araújo, Federal University of Pernambuco, Brazil
Marco Patricio Crasso, IBM - SilverGate, Argentina
Clara Crivellaro, Newcastle University, UK
Marcelo de Paiva Guimarães, Federal University of São Paulo/ Centro Universitário Campo Limpo Paulista, Brazil
Antonio Diaz Tula, University of São Paulo, Brazil
Júlio C. Dos Reis, University of Campinas, Brazil
Rolf Drechsler, University of Bremen/DFKI, Germany

Ahmed Elkaseer, Karlsruhe Institute of Technology (KIT)/Institute for Automation and Applied Informatics (IAI), Germany
Larbi Esmahi, Athabasca University, Canada
Sascha Fagel, KV Telematik GmbH, Germany
Peter Forbrig, University of Rostock, Germany
Somchart Fugkeaw, Mahidol University - Nakhonpathom, Thailand
Andrea Gasparini, University of Oslo, Norway
Bernard Grabot, LGP-ENIT, France
Denis Gracanin, Virginia Tech, USA
Andrina Granić, University of Split, Croatia
Toni Granollers, University of Lleida, Spain
John Alexis Guerra Gómez, Los Andes University, Colombia / UC Berkeley, USA
Celmar Guimarães da Silva, University of Campinas, Brazil
Maki Habib, The American University in Cairo, Egypt
Till Halbach, Norwegian Computing Center, Oslo, Norway
Ibrahim A. Hameed, Norwegian University of Science and Technology (NTNU), Ålesund, Norway
Sung H. Han, POSTECH, South Korea
Marc Herrlich, University of Kaiserslautern (TUK), Germany
José R. Hilera, University of Alcalá, Spain
Olivier Hugues, MINES ParisTech - PSL Research University, France
Mas-Ud Hussain, Northwestern University, Evanston, USA
Francisco Iniesto, Institute of Educational Technology - The Open University, UK
Jamshed Iqbal, University of Jeddah, Saudi Arabia
Gökhan İnce, Istanbul Technical University, Turkey
Ghislain Maurice N. Isabwe, University of Agder, Norway
Ryo Ishii, NTT Corporation, Japan
Shahram Jalaliniya, Malmö University, Sweden
Angel Jaramillo-Alcázar, Universidad de Las Américas, Ecuador
Lei Jing, University of Aizu, Japan
Suhas Govind Joshi, University of Oslo, Norway
Hanmin Jung, Korea Institute of Science & Technology Information, Korea
Katarzyna Kaczmarek, Systems Research Institute - Polish Academy of Sciences, Poland
Sushant Kafle, Rochester Institute of Technology (RIT), USA
Yasushi Kambayashi, Nippon Institute of Technology, Japan
Ahmed Kamel, Concordia College, Moorhead, USA
Mahmoud Kamel Mahmoud Abdalaziz, Digitex Corporation, Egypt / Fashion Libretto Corporation, Italy
Vaishnav Kameswaran, University of Michigan, USA
Saras Karanam, Utrecht University, Netherlands
Ljilja (Lilia) Ruzic Kascak, Georgia Institute of Technology, USA
Yasaman Khazaeni, IBM Research AI, USA
Jesuk Ko, Gwangju University, Korea
Uttam Kokil, Kennesaw State University Marietta, USA
Johannes A. König, Aachen University of Applied Sciences, Germany
Mohammed Korayem, Careerbuilder.com, USA
Nataliya Kosmyna, Inria Rennes, France
Yong Ming Kow, City University of Hong Kong, Hong Kong
Neha Kumar, Georgia Tech, USA
Jiyoung Kwahk, POSTECH, South Korea

Wen-Hsing Lai, National Kaohsiung First University of Science and Technology, Taiwan
Monica Landoni, Università della Svizzera italiana, Switzerland
Caroline Larboulette, Université Bretagne Sud, France
Dagmawi Lemma, Addis Ababa University, Ethiopia
Asterios Leonidis, Foundation for Research & Technology - Hellas (FORTH) | Institute of Computer Science (ICS), Greece
Tsai-Yen Li, National Chengchi University, Taiwan
Wenjuan Li, City University of Hong Kong, Hong Kong
Yifang Li, Clemson University, USA
Flaminia Luccio, University Ca' Foscari of Venice, Italy
Sergio Luján Mora, University of Alicante, Spain
Yan Luximon, The Hong Kong Polytechnic University, Hong Kong
Zahen Malla Osman, The National Center for Scientific Research (CNRS), France
Céline Mateev, Ecole Nationale Supérieure d'Arts et Métiers, France
Weizhi Meng, Technical University of Denmark, Denmark
Daniel R. Mestre, CNRS Institute of Movement Sciences - Mediterranean Virtual Reality Center, Marseilles, France
Harald Milchrahm, Institute for Softwaretechnology - Technical University Graz, Austria
Les Miller, Iowa State University, USA
Yasser F. O. Mohammad, Assiut University, Egypt / KDDI Laboratories, Japan
Natalie Mrachacz-Kersting, Aalborg University, Denmark
Nicholas H. Müller, University of Applied Sciences Würzburg-Schweinfurt, Germany
Jaime Muñoz-Arteaga, Universidad Autónoma de Aguascalientes, Mexico
Yoshitoshi Murata, Iwate Prefectural University, Japan
Daniel Mwesigwa, Collaboration on International ICT Policy for East and Southern Africa (CIPESA), Uganda
Minoru Nakayama, Tokyo Institute of Technology, Japan
Roger Ng, Hong Kong Polytechnic University, Hong Kong
Quan Nguyen, University of Texas Medical Branch, Galveston, USA
Jacki O'Neill, Microsoft Research, India
Rita Orji, Dalhousie University, Canada
Tomoko Ota, Chuo Business Groupe, Japan
Dawid Pacholczyk, Polish-Japanese Academy of IT, Warsaw, Poland
Freddy Paz, Pontificia Universidad Católica del Perú, Peru
Marina Puyuelo, Universitat Politècnica de València, Spain
Didier Puzenat, LIRIS - University Lyon 2, France
Paul Rosenthal, University of Rostock, Germany
Cheryl Zhenyu Qian, Purdue University, USA
Rafael Radkowski, Iowa State University, USA
Karen Renaud, Abertay University, UK
Andreas Riener, University of Applied Sciences Ingolstadt, Germany
Antonio M. Rinaldi, Università degli Studi di Napoli Federico II - Napoli, Italy
Cuauhtémoc Rivera-Loaiza, Universidad Michoacana de San Nicolás de Hidalgo, Mexico
Covadonga Rodrigo San Juan, E.T.S.I. Informática - UNED, Spain
Juan Rosso, University Grenoble Alpes | CNRS, France
Ljilja Ruzic, The Center for Assistive Technology and Environmental Access (CATEA) | Georgia Institute of Technology, USA
Jaime Sánchez, University of Chile, Chile

Sandra Sanchez-Gordon, Escuela Politécnica Nacional, Ecuador
Antonio-Jose Sanchez-Salmeron, Universitat Politecnica de Valencia, Spain
Jon Sanford, Georgia Tech, USA
Danielle Santos Alves, Universidade Federal de Pernambuco - UFPE, Brazil
Diana Saplacan, University of Oslo, Norway
Steffen Scholz, Karlsruhe Institute of Technology (KIT), Germany
Trenton Schulz, University of Oslo, Norway
Yoshihiro Sejima, Okayama Prefectural University, Japan
Amando P. Singun, Jr., Higher College of Technology Muscat, Sultanate of Oman
Yan Shi, University of Wisconsin-Platteville, USA
Marie Sjölinder, RISE SICS, Sweden
Preethi Srinivas, Indiana University Center for Aging Research | Regenstrief Institute Inc., USA
Cristian Stanciu, University Politehnica of Bucharest, Romania
Ana Tajadura-Jimenez, Universidad Carlos III, Spain / University College London, UK
Hilda Tellioglu, Vienna University of Technology, Austria
Azeemsha Thacham Poyil, University of Hertfordshire, UK
David Unbehaun, UniversityofSiegen, Germany
Tommaso Venturini, INRIA / Institut Rhônalpin des Systèmes Complexes, France
Guri B. Verne, University of Oslo, Norway
Connie Veugen, Vrije Universiteit Amsterdam, Netherlands
Christian Wagner, City University of Hong Kong, Hong Kong
Michael L. Walters, University of Hertfordshire, UK
Yun Wang (Maigo), Carnegie Mellon University, USA
Primal Wijesekera, UC Berkeley / ICSI, USA
Christian Wögerer, PROFACTOR GmbH, Austria
Y. Wayne Wu, University of Illinois at Urbana-Champaign, USA
Shuping Xiong, Korea Advanced Institute of Science and Technology (KAIST), South Korea
Anbang Xu, IBM Research - Almaden, USA
Bin Xu, Cornell University, USA
Anja Zeising, ifib - Research Institute at the University of Bremen, Germany
Xiaoyi Zhang, University of Washington, USA
Fan Zhao, Florida Gulf Coast University, USA
Ye Zhu, Cleveland State University, USA

Copyright Information

Short- and Long-Term Effects of an Advanced Driving Assistance System on Driving Behavior and Usability Evaluation

Shota Matsubayashi
Institute of Innovation for Future Society (MIRAI)
Nagoya University
Aichi, Japan
e-mail: shota.matsubayashi@nagoya-u.jp

Kazuhisa Miwa
Graduate School of Informatics
Nagoya University
Aichi, Japan
e-mail: miwa@is.nagoya-u.ac.jp

Takuma Yamaguchi
Institute of Innovation for Future Society (MIRAI)
Nagoya University
Aichi, Japan
e-mail: t_yamaguchi@nuem.nagoya-u.ac.jp

Tatsuya Suzuki
Graduate School of Engineering
Nagoya University
Aichi, Japan
e-mail: t_suzuki@nuem.nagoya-u.ac.jp

Abstract—**In recent times, advanced driving assistance systems have become popular, and drivers have had more opportunities to interact with the system continually. Although the majority of earlier studies compared driving behaviors with and without systems or before and after using systems, the effect of the system has not been verified from a long-term perspective. Therefore, the present study investigates both short- and long-term effects of driving assistance systems on drivers' behaviors and usability evaluations. The results found two types of transition patterns in driving behavior and one stable pattern in usability evaluations. This indicates that there are non-uniform effects of a single driving assistance system, depending on the kinds of risk objects and driving behaviors.**

Keywords-short-term effect; long-term effect; driving behavior; usability; advanced driving assistance system.

I. Introduction

There are two popular measures to encourage drivers to adopt safer behaviors: educational measures and engineering measures [1]. Engineering measures include advanced driving assistance systems, while educational measures include driver training and safety education. As an example of engineering measures, a head-up display system provides visual guidance to drivers on the immediate required behavior. In recent times, such systems are known to directly intervene in driver behavior—for example, emergency brake systems, which decelerate a car in danger of collision with others.

Several educational measures have proven beneficial in the long term [2]. However, the effect of engineering measures, especially that of an advanced driving assistance system, is yet to be proven because of its short duration in use.

Many studies have compared driving behaviors with and without systems or before and after using systems. It is known that driver behavior shifted to both safe and risky behaviors based on the authority bestowed by intelligent speed adaptation systems after using the system [3].

As driving assistance systems become popular, drivers have more opportunities to interact with the system continually. Therefore, it is essential to consider both the short-term and long-term effects of the systems. For example, drivers' behaviors appeared to improve for six months following brief exposure to the system [4]. However, the longer the drivers interacted with the intelligent speed adaptation system, the more frequently they overrode it [5].

A few earlier studies show that subjective evaluations toward systems is related to changes in driving behaviors [6]. Similarly, from a long-term perspective, some drivers barely trusted and accepted an adaptive cruise control system when they were provided incomplete information [7]. These studies reveal the importance of measuring subjective evaluations to encourage drivers to change their driving behaviors appropriately.

Therefore, it is essential to consider both the short- and long-term effects of an advanced driving assistance system. The present study empirically verifies the effects of the system on drivers' behaviors and usability evaluations from short- and long-term perspective.

The changes in speed, margin, and evaluation scores immediately after driving with assistances are defined as "short-term effects," while the changes after one week of driving with assistances are defined as "long-term effects." If drivers can comprehend the system's intention immediately after initially driving with assistances, their driving behaviors would improve on day 1 and no changes would be observed thereafter. If drivers understand the system's intention gradually, their driving behaviors would improve gradually week after week.

Section 2 describes the experimental method and Section 3 describes the results of the experiment. In Section 4, we discuss the short- and long-term effects of an advanced driving assistance system.

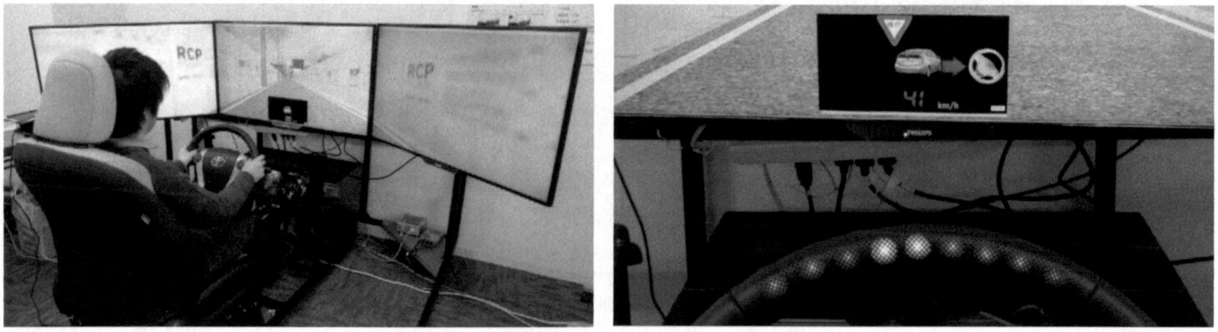

Figure 1. Driving simulator used in the experiment.

TABLE I. THR NUMBER OF RISK OBJECTS IN COURSES

Running	Intersections		Parked Cars		Pedestrians		Others
	High risk	*Low risk*	*High risk*	*Low risk*	*High risk*	*Low risk*	
Practice Running	4	2					
Pre- and Post-Running	4	2	1	1	1	1	
Running with Assistance							
Parked Cars (High Risk)	2	1	2				
Parked Cars (Low Risk)	2	1		2			
Pedestrians (High Risk)	2	1			2		
Pedestrians (Low Risk)	2	1				2	
Filler (Parked Cars)	2	1					2 (Parked cars in the opposite lane)
Filler (Pedestrians)	2	1					2 (Pedestrians in the opposite lane)

II. METHOD

A. Apparatus

We used a driving simulator equipped with a driving assistance system in an experiment (Figure 1). This system detects the potential risks that may lead to accidents, such as drivers' blind spots. Such risks are identified based on the normative behaviors of expert driving instructors. The following two driving assistance stages are employed [8] [9]:

1) Cognitive guidance: This provides information about the surrounding environment and guides the driver to brake or turn.

2) Behavioral intervention: This is an intervention in driver braking and steering behavior when cognitive guidance does not positively affect driver behaviors.

The following information is provided when cognitive guidance is given and behavioral interventions are performed. Three stimuli are provided: a beep and notification message (e.g., "Caution! A parked car") as the auditory stimuli; a slowdown icon, an arrow pointing to the left/right, and an LED light on the steering wheel as visual stimuli; and steering wheel and accelerator vibration as tactile stimuli.

The scope of the behavioral intervention (i.e., the power of braking and steering torque) depends on the status of the car and the safety region monitored by the system. Braking intervention decelerates the car to a fixed speed when crossing an intersection and passing a parked car or a pedestrian. Steering intervention autonomously operates a steering wheel, but this torque is sufficiently small; therefore, drivers can turn the steering wheel against the system's intervention. This intervention occurs when passing a parked car and a pedestrian but not when crossing an intersection.

This driving assistance system provides information about the potential risks and encourages drivers to change their behaviors if necessary. No assistance (i.e., cognitive guidance and behavioral intervention) is provided in the case of safe driving. From an educational perspective, if the drivers understand the system's intention, they are expected to adopt safer driving behaviors than before.

B. Course Settings

Approximately 1,400 meters is used as the length of the driving course utilized in the experiment. Although the course includes some intersections, participants are required to drive straight at all intersections.

Intersections without signals, parked cars, and pedestrians are arranged on the course as the risk objects, which the system can detect. Each risk object is of two different kinds, depending on their risk level.

- *Intersections:* The size of blind spots can be controlled by the height of fences near intersections—that is, high-risk intersections with high fences and low-risk intersections with low fences.
- *Parked cars:* The size of blind spots can be controlled by the size of parked cars—that is, high-risk parked trucks and low-risk parked compact cars.
- *Pedestrians:* The level of risk can be controlled by the direction of pedestrians—that is, high-risk pedestrians in the same direction as the car and low-risk pedestrians in the direction facing to the car.

The system provides more assistance toward the high-risk objects than toward low-risk objects because the system determines the amount of assistance based on the risk levels. If drivers understand the relationship between risk levels and the amount of assistance, they may adopt safer behavior by themselves.

C. Procedure

Eighteen drivers participated in four 90-minute experiments spanning four weeks, with a one-week interval between experiments. Ethic approval was granted by the Nagoya University Institute of Innovation for Future Society Ethics Committee and participants were provided with an informed consent form.

All four experiments were conducted according to the following procedure. Table 1 shows the number of the risk objects arranged in each running.

- *Practice running:* Participants were allowed to drive the course once without assistance to understand the driving simulator.
- *Pre-running:* Participants drove the course twice to measure the initial driving behavior without assistances. The course included each of two kinds of risk objects for intersections, parked cars, and pedestrians.
- *Instruction:* Participants were informed that the system encourages drivers to adopt safer driving behaviors with cognitive guidance and behavioral interventions. Participants also watched a movie on the assistances provided by the system.
- *Pre-evaluation:* Participants answered a usability questionnaire prior to using the system. This questionnaire measured six elements: effectiveness, efficiency, satisfaction, understandability, comfort, and motivation. Each element has three questions rated on a five-point scale [10].
- *Running with assistance:* During training, participants drove the six courses with assistances. To encourage participants to understand the relationship between the risk levels and the amount of assistance, either parked cars or pedestrians were arranged in each running. Two filler runnings were included in the six courses to inform participants that the system does not provide assistances unnecessarily for objects with extremely low risk. In this running, the number of intersections was reduced to half, as the length of the course was set to half the normal length. The order of the six courses was counterbalanced with a Latin square.
- *Post-running:* Participants drove the course twice, similarly as in the initial pre-running.
- *Post-evaluation:* Participants answered a usability questionnaire after using the system, similarly as in the initial pre-evaluation.

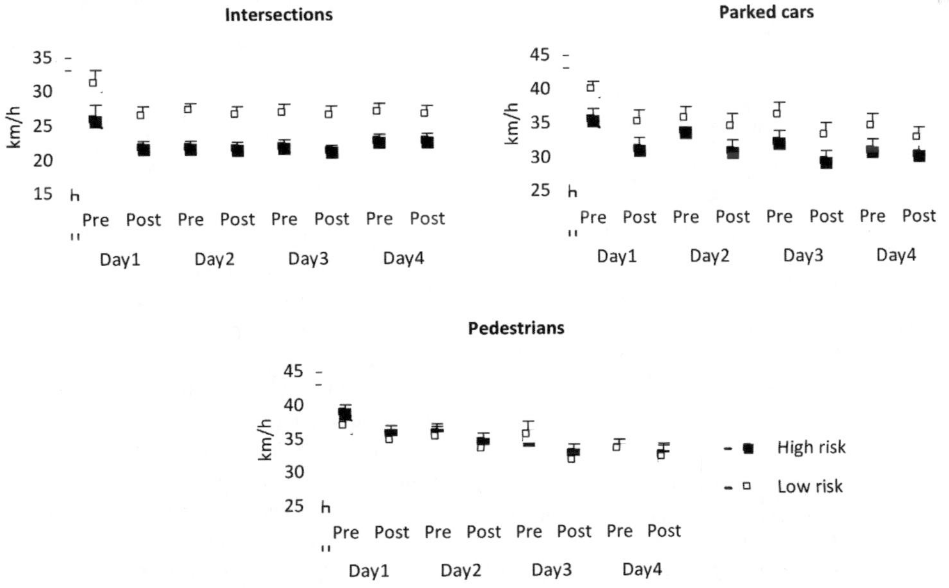

Figure 2. Transition of speed. The error bars represent the standard error of the mean.

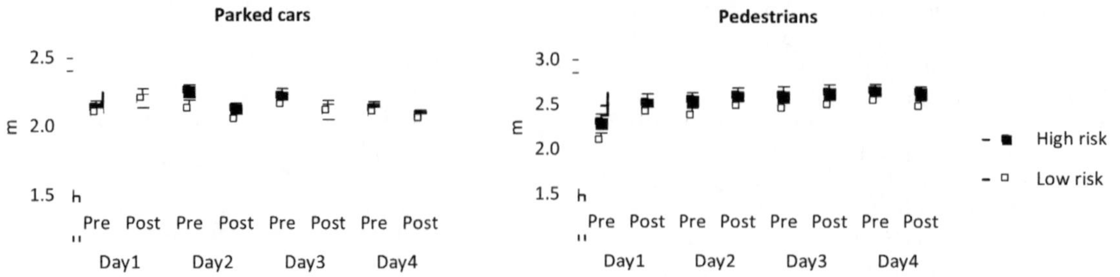

Figure 3. Transition of margin. The error bars represent the standard error of the mean.

TABLE II. SUMMARY OF ANOVA RESULTS FOR SPEED

Objects	Risk	Day (1/2/3/4)			Running (Pre/Post)		Day × Running			Effect Type
		F	*p*	*Significant pairs*	*F*	*p*	*F*	*p*	*Significant pairs*	
Intersections	High	2.98	**0.039***	1-2, 1-3	4.06	**0.059+**	4.46	**0.007***	Day1: pre-post Pre: 1-2, 1-3, 1-4	Initial short-term
	Low	2.24	**0.094+**		9.25	**0.007***	5.04	**0.003***	Day1: pre-post Pre: 1-2, 1-3, 1-4	Initial short-term
Parked Cars	High	2.21	**0.098+**		21.90	**0.001***	1.55	0.21		Short- and long-term
	Low	3.63	**0.018***	1-3, 1-4	15.93	**0.001***	1.45	0.23		Short- and long-term
Pedestrians	High	5.67	**0.002***	1-3, 1-4	11.99	**0.003***	0.85	0.47		Short- and long-term
	Low	1.89	0.14		9.34	**0.007***	0.90	0.44		Short- and long-term

*: $p < .05$, +: $p < .10$

TABLE III. SUMMARY OF ANOVA RESULTS FOR MARGIN

Objects	Risk	Day (1/2/3/4)			Running (Pre/Post)		Day × Running			Effect Type
		F	*p*	*Significant pairs*	*F*	*p*	*F*	*p*	*Significant pairs*	
Parked Cars	High	2.01	0.12		7.15	**0.016***	4.80	**0.005***	Day2, 3: pre-post Pre: 1-2, 2-4	Others
	Low	0.85	0.47		0.28	0.60	2.11	0.11		Others
Pedestrians	High	4.88	**0.004***	1-2, 1-3, 1-4	2.36	0.14	2.74	**0.052+**	Day1: pre-post Pre: 1-2, 1-3, 1-4	Initial short-term
	Low	6.12	**0.001***	1-2, 1-3, 1-4	7.09	**0.016***	5.03	**0.003***	Day1: pre-post Pre: 1-2, 1-3, 1-4	Initial short-term

*: $p < .05$, +: $p < .10$

III. RESULTS

All 18 participants of mean age 30.5 years were analyzed. The standard deviation of age was 10.1 years. We conducted 4 (Day factor: 1/2/3/4) × 2 (Running factor: pre/post) ANOVAs for the following analyses.

A. Driving Behaviors

Figure 2 shows the transitions in speed when crossing an intersection and passing a parked car or a pedestrian, and Figure 3 shows the transitions of the margin between the car and a parked car or a pedestrian. We can find two types of transition patterns in speed and margin: "initial short-term effect" and "short- and long-term effects."

1) Initial short-term effect: On day 1, short-term effects from pre- to post-running were observed, and no changes were observed thereafter. This effect appeared for speed when crossing an intersection and for margin when passing by a pedestrian. Statistically, there were significant interactions between day factor and running factor and significant differences between pre-running on day 1 and the other three pre-runnings (Tables 2 and 3).

2) Short- and long-term effects: The short-term effects between pre- and post-running as well as the long-term effects between days appeared simultaneously. Therefore, driving behavior improved gradually over four weeks. This effect appeared for speed when passing by a parked car and a pedestiran. Statistically, there were significant main effects of both day facror and running factor and no significant interaction (Table 2).

These transition patterns depended on the kinds of risk objects and driving behavior, regardless of the risk levels. The margin when passing by a parked car did not conform to these two patterns (Table 3).

B. Usability Evaluations

Figure 4 shows the transition of usability scores. We found that each of the scores is not fluctuating, with small variances. However, the ANOVA results show significant main effects for some elements. First, significant main effect of day factor for efficiency was observed ($F(3, 51) = 4.89, p < 0.005, \eta^2 = 0.05$). The score on day 1 was significantly lower than that on the other three days (day 1-2: $t(35) = 2.06, p < 0.05$; day 1-3: $t(35) = 3.50, p < 0.001$; day 1-4: $t(35) = 3.09, p < 0.005$). Second, a marginally significant main effect of running factor for understandability indicates that participants comprehend the system more in post-running than in pre-running ($F(1, 17) = 3.46, p < 0.10, \eta^2 = 0.01$). However, subjective evaluations were stable because both effect sizes were extremely small.

IV. Discussion and Conclusion

The present study empirically confirmed the short- and long-term effects of an advanced driving assistance system on drivers' behaviors and usability evaluations. As a result, we found two types of transition patterns in driving behaviors and one stable pattern in usability evaluations.

The first pattern in driving behavior, in which changes between pre- and post-running on day 1 and no changes following day 1 are observed, is interpreted as the initial short-term effect. This pattern appears for speed when crossing an intersection and for margin when passing by a pedestrian. Drivers adequately understand the potential risks immediately after an initial driving session with assistances and remember them until the next week.

The second pattern, in which changes between pre- and post-running on each day and changes between days are observed, is interpreted as the short- and long-term effects. In other words, changes between pre- and post-running on each day disappear in pre-running in the following week. This pattern appears for speed when passing by a parked car and a pedestrian. Although drivers could not adequately understand potential risks after their initial driving session with assistances, they gradually comprehend the risks after repeated runnings with assistances.

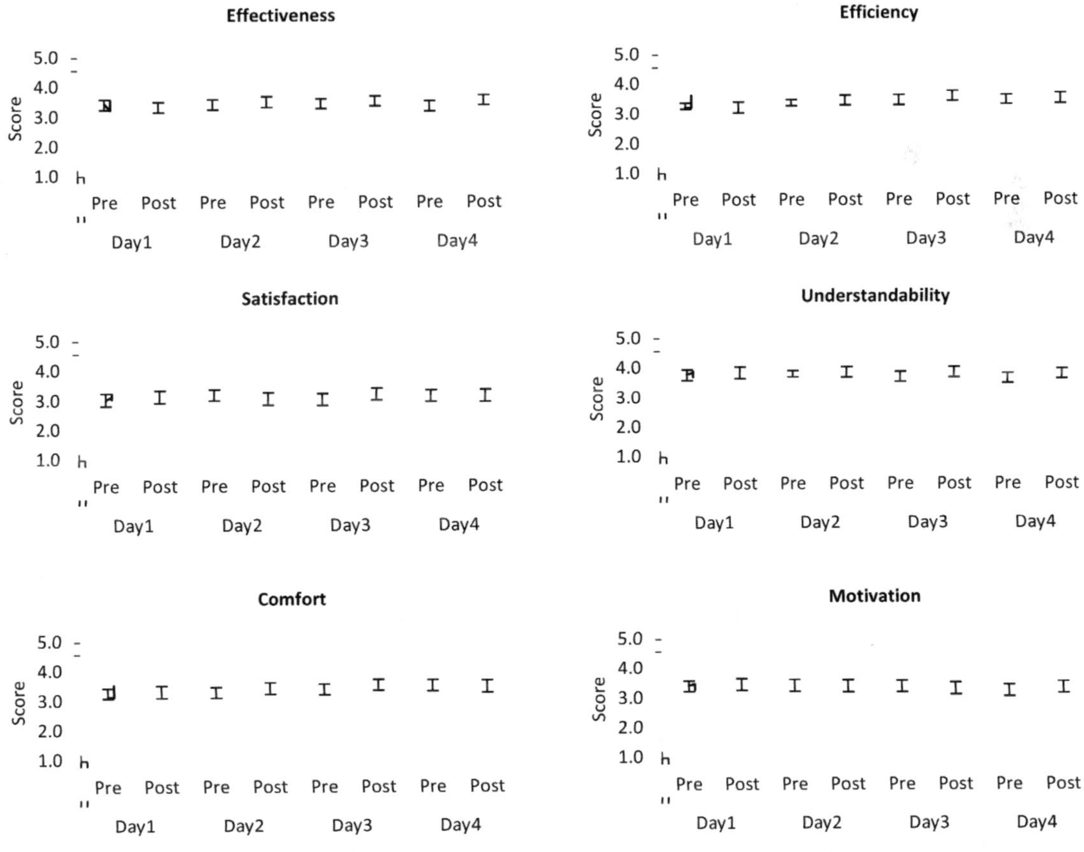

Figure 4. Transition of usability evaluation scores. The error bars represent the standard error of the mean.

What determines the type of effect that appears in driving behaviors? The study results indicate that the factor is the combination of risk objects (i.e., an intersection, a parked car, or a pedestrian) and driving behaviors (i.e., speed or margin), regardless of risk levels (i.e., high risk or low risk).

There is no steering intervention when crossing an intersection, unlike when passing by a parked car and a pedestrian. Similarly, drivers are prone to experience sudden slowdowns prompted by the system because the risk level of intersections is higher than the risk levels of parked cars and pedestrians. Such salient experiences of slowdowns in an intersection encourage drivers to learn the potential risks well, which could appear as the initial short-term effect in driving behaviors. The number of intersections is likely to influence the type of effect because more intersections are arranged than parked cars and pedestrians.

Both braking and steering interventions are conducted when passing by a parked car and a pedestrian. A pedestrian is the only object that moves autonomously in courses, unlike a parked car. Moreover, previous research using the same driving assistance system shows that the change in margin between the car and a pedestrian after running with assistances was larger than that in the margin between the car and a parked car [6] [11]. Therefore, drivers could easily understand the potential risks that a pedestrian might run right in front of the car. Drivers might increase the margin between the car and a pedestrian, which could appear as the initial short-term effect in driving behaviors.

The present study revealed that there is no uniform effect of a single driving assistance system and it depends on the kinds of risk objects and driving behaviors. Although we used only engineering measures in the experiment, it would be more beneficial to use both engineering and educational measures, such as training, in order to encourage drivers to adopt safer behaviors in real life.

ACKNOWLEDGMENT

This research was supported by the Center of Innovation Program (Nagoya-COI) from Japan Science and Technology Agency, and by JSPS KAKENHI Grant Number JP16H02353.

REFERENCES

[1] T. Ishida and T. Matsuura, "Introduction to Traffic Psychology," Japan, Traffic Problem Labolatory in Enterprise Develop Center, 2017 (In Japanese, translated by the author of this article).

[2] D. L. Roenker, G. M. Cissell, K. K. Ball, V. G. Wadley, and J. D. Edwards, "Speed-of-Processing and Driving Simulator Training Result in Improved Driving Performance," Human Factors, United States, vol. 45, no. 2, pp. 218–233, June 2003.

[3] S. L. Comte, "New systems: New behaviour?," Transportation Research Part F: Traffic Psychology and Behaviour,United Kingdom, vol. 3, no. 2, pp. 95–111, June 2000.

[4] A. Ben-Yaacov, M. Maltz, and D. Shinar, "Effects of an in-vehicle collision avoidance warning system on short- and long-term driving performance," Human Factors, United States, vol. 44, no. 2, pp. 335–342, June 2002.

[5] F.Lai, M. Hjälmdahl, K. Chorlton, and M. Wiklund, "The long-term effect of intelligent speed adaptation on driver behaviour," Applied Ergonomics, United Kingdom, vol. 4, no. 2, pp. 179–186, March 2010.

[6] S. Matsubayashi et al., "Cognitive and Behavioral Effects on Driving by Information Presentation and Behavioral Intervention in Advanced Driving Assistance System," Cognitive Studies, Japan, vol. 25, no. 3, pp. 324–337, September 2018.

[7] M. Beggiato and J. F. Krems, "The evolution of mental model, trust and acceptance of adaptive cruise control in relation to initial information," Transportation Research Part F: Traffic Psychology and Behaviour, United Kingdom, vol. 18, pp. 47–57, May 2013.

[8] T. Yamaguchi et al., "Supervisory Cooperative Control and Its Verification," 2016 Society of Automoyive Engineers of Japan Annual Spring Congress (2016 JSAE), May 2016, no. 65-16S, pp. 1593–1598.

[9] T. Kamiya et al., "Experimental Verification for Cooperative Control by Supervisor," 2016 Society of Automoyive Engineers of Japan Annual Spring Congress (2016 JSAE), May 2016, no. 65-16S, pp. 1599–1604.

[10] A. Maehigashi, K. Miwa, K. Kojima, and H. Terai, "Development of a Usability Questionnaire for Automation Systems," Lecture Notes in Computer Science, Germany, vol. 9731, pp. 340–349, June 2016.

[11] S. Matsubayashi et al., "Empirical Investigation of Changes of Driving Behavior and Usability Evaluation Using an Advanced Driving Assistance System," The Thirteenth International Conference on Autonomic and Autonomous Systems (ICAS 2017), pp. 36–39, May 2017.

Enabling Sensemaking for Intelligence Analysis in a Multi-user, Multimodal Cognitive and Immersive Environment

Shannon Briggs[1], Matt Peveler[2], Jaimie Drozdal[2]
Chelsea Sun[2], Lilit Balagyozyan,
Communications[1], Computer Science[2], CISL[3]
Rensselaer Polytechnic Institute , Troy NY USA 12180
Email: briggs3@rpi.edu, email: pevelm@rpi.edu,
email: drozdj3@rpi.edu, email: sunc4@rpi.edu, email: balagl@rpi.edu

Hui Su[2]
IBM Thomas J. Watson Research Laboratory
Yorktown Heights NY USA 10598
email: huisuibmres@us.ibm.com

Abstract— **This research proposes a user interface design for a collaborative, multimodal, multi-user cognitive and immersive environment for intelligence analysis, informed by sensemaking theory and scenario-based design. We have created a prototype software in a cognitive and immersive environment, which is designed to facilitate the structured brainstorming process. Part of our research goal is to determine whether this environment will better enable sensemaking compared to traditional pen and paper tools.**

*Keywords- **HCI; immersive environment; intelligence analysis; sensemaking; scenario-based design; multimodal interaction***

I. INTRODUCTION

The intelligence community needs software which can help them to make sense of the information they are receiving through their work as analysts. The research in this paper addresses an important aspect of how technology and the ever-increasing availability of massive amounts of data [1] impact the national security domain, specifically how intelligence analysts are challenged when sorting through information, gathering evidence, and proposing hypotheses. According to Hutchins et. al, "currently available technology is not always effective in helping the analyst assimilate the huge amount of information that needs to be synthesized." [1]

Previous software for intelligence analysis has been discarded because of two major factors: the barrier of use of the software is too high, or the software does not meet the needs of the analyst. Our research takes a different approach to conceptualizing and designing software for analysts. We are developing software that will support analysts' sensemaking by integrating educational and training materials that are already used by analysts in their own domain, such as those described by Beebe and Pherson [2] or Hall and Citrenbaum [3]. We believe that this will create a more accessible interface and will provide affordances that are already familiar to the user base. Providing analysts with a tool that provides a similar interface has proven to have some success with analysts as users, as has been discussed by Smallman [4]. Our team is focusing on the structured analytic technique of brainstorming and how we can leverage the cognitive process to create a digital tool.

Through the lens of scenario-based design, we integrate the intended users' cognitive processes into the development of our software; to do this, we will adopt cognitive tools, such as the brainstorming tool, and techniques already utilized by intelligence analysts [2], to create a cognitive and immersive environment that supports multiple users and multimodal interactions in a way that is useful for intelligence analysis. By leveraging the capabilities of the cognitive and immersive room, we are aiming to reduce cognitive load inherent in intelligence analysis. The specific research questions formulated for this stage of our research are: 1.) How can we leverage brainstorming tools to expedite the foraging process as described by Pirolli and Card [5], and 2.) How can we utilize multimodal, multi-participant input to address cognitive load ? Our application of structured analytic techniques (which can be seen in Figure 2) is a new approach to the development of digital tools and software for intelligence analysis.

This paper will review historical trends among capabilities in previously released software and will suggest an application of sensemaking theory, participatory design, and scenario-based design to strengthen development of our software's capabilities. The framework for our research is based on the intelligence analysis sensemaking process (see Figure 1) as explained by Pirroli and Card [5]. Thorough integration of the respective iterative loops of foraging for information and sensemaking will also inform how a user interface and the system tools should support the intelligence process.

We propose that our software should be informed by direct feedback from analysts, scenario-based designs derived from existing structured analytic techniques, and associated resources that are currently used by intelligence analysts for training purposes, such as the tradecraft primer created by the CIA [6]. This is a novel approach to conceiving and designing software for intelligence analysis, as most existing software does not draw from the structured analytic techniques that we propose to build as a digital system. For future work, we will conduct user studies to determine the digital tool's utility and usability, as well as more in-depth studies to examine if it successfully enables the sensemaking process.

In Section 2 of this paper, we discuss previous literature in the following fields: state of the art of software developed for intelligence analysis, literature in sensemaking, user modelling, scenario-based design, and previous work in electronic brainstorming tools. In Section 3 of this paper we discuss our software and how we implemented user centered features informed by our research. In our final section, Section 4, we discuss limitations of our research, future work, and our conclusions.

II. LITERATURE REVIEW

This section covers literature discussing state of the art technologies for intelligence analysis, sensemaking theories, user modelling, and scenario-based design.

A. *State of the Art*

Wright et al. [7] introduce Sandbox, which is the successor to the analysis tool nSpace. Their paper explains human information interaction capabilities, such as 'put this there' cognition, automatic process model templates, gestures for fluid expression of thought, assertions with evidence, and scalability metrics. The authors use cognitive task analysis to identify a number of techniques used by analysts. The authors take note of the use of Post-its by analysts in order to organize and sort ideas. The authors translated this into a feature called MindManager, which employed concept map strategies to allow diagrammatic visual representations. The activities the software is designed to support are visual thinking and working with evidence. They designed the software to be flexible to adapt to different types of analysts and analytical styles. The software also incorporates a source attribution and context function. Another interesting feature is that the software can provide automatic evidence fitted to templates of analytic framework.

Pioch and Everett [8] describe the Polestar intelligence analysis toolkit, which is one of the earliest software suites designed for intelligence analysis. Polestar included a snippet view of texts, where users could highlight and drag text to the portfolio view for later analysis. This portfolio view also records metadata about the text. Polestar also included a way to start knowledge structuring, such as a wall of facts similar to the sticky-note exercise taught in intelligence analysis classes. This software included a timeline feature, to allow analysts a way to visualize relationships in data. Polestar included an argument tree editor, allowing analysts to structure and formulate hypotheses in a visual fashion. The dependency viewer allowed users to trace back where a document or object was found in the dependency network.

Eccles et al. [9] explore part of intelligence analyst' process of using narration to make sense of events of interest and how the authors, themselves, use a software system called GeoTime to map geo-temporal events for easier access. The authors discuss the major features of GeoTime: the space-time pattern finding system, the theory behind which is that it relieves the analyst from effort of searching for common patterns and events. The second part of the system relies on visual annotations, which takes the visual information and appends relevant information. The final part of the software is a text editor that allows analysts to make relevant comments on the found information. GeoTime uses a collaborative environment but also emphasizes a data-aware object, where annotations are embedded in time and space, so these become a new piece of information connected to the found information. GeoTime is also interested in allowing analysts to work on a meso-level, such as behavioral trends, events, and plots, rather than an individual unit.

Keel [10] introduces E-Wall, which is a visual analytic environment design to support remote sensemaking. It is designed around object focused thinking, where information is represented as an object, and users construct semantic relations between them. The E-wall layout is designed to allow users to collaborate while working on information and to allow users to manipulate data in object-like chunks. The E-Wall uses two computational agents to manage information flow, and infers relationships among data types, and another that evaluates databases and suggests data to the user. The E-Wall allows users to navigate large amounts of data independently and minimizes the need for verbal interaction. Our research anticipates that communication between users is an important part of the collaborative process and therefore our tool integrates deliberate periods of interaction among users to collaborate on theories.

Rooney et al. [11] discuss INVISQUE (an abbreviation of INteractive VIsual Search and QUery Environment), a tool that allows searching, automated clustering of data, automated entity extraction, and manual manipulation of data on an infinite canvas. Users can initiate a search to look for articles related to a topic or create clusters of their own. The authors here discuss the way that users would group documents in a way that had semantic meaning to them, that the software would not have been able to infer and then group. The authors use Pirolli and Card's sensemaking model, along with Klein's Data/Frame extension. The software we are developing has superficial similarities to INVISQUE, however we propose a more structured method that is aligned with the formalized structured analytic technique of brainstorming to encourage analysts to develop topic ideas and clusters before they seek for more data. This should allow for users to experience a more focused search for data during the foraging process.

Jigsaw is another piece of software designed for intelligence analysis. Gorg et al. [12] discuss the capabilities of the software in their article. Jigsaw is designed to support the sensemaking activities surrounding collecting and organizing textual information by intelligence analysts. The Jigsaw system is designed to provide visualization for different perspectives on information in documents and it supports evidence marshalling through a Shoe Box view. The earliest version of the software focused heavily on visual representation of relationships between entities but did not provide any kind of text analysis. One of the major findings of creating this software was that software functions cannot replace the reading of reports. Repeated careful reading of selected texts tended to be the preferred method to understand the information in texts. As a result, the Jigsaw system incorporated the ability to summarize and cluster similar important text information. From there, the software used packages such as GATE, LingPipe, the OpenCalais system, and the Illinois Named Entity Trigger, to import data from documents.

Murdock and Roth [13] use the lens of Pirroli and Card's sensemaking theory to examine a map-based prototype system called Basic Ordnance Observation Management System (BOOMS), developed at the Penn State GeoVISTA center. The aim of the paper is to explore how visuo-spatial contexts and maps contribute toward the intelligence analysis understanding of the events in their field. The authors focus on the capabilities of the software and how it offers users context to understand details concerning specific events within a one-year time period. The authors use sensemaking to model the technical concerns that must be addressed for technology that is used for gathering information. The mapping software is interactive and includes a structured top down navigation system. The aim of the software is to be able to provide insight for operational and policy decision makers through pattern finding abilities in the software.

Petersen et al. [14] discuss the software CrimeFighter, an analysis tool designed for criminal investigators. The authors introduce the concept of applying sensemaking to counter terrorism and criminal networks, and a software tool called CrimeFighter Investigator. The challenges outlined in the article concerning criminal investigation are also relatively similar to challenges in intelligence analysis. Several specific elements are information volume, information complexity, and information sharing. The authors discuss the capabilities of the software, and how they support the investigation process. The authors describe how the history function helps to allow for revisiting and revising the information in the software for further consideration. The software also has some prediction features possible, which are supported by social network analysis, decision making, and hypothesis making. The tool also has a storytelling feature, which allows for the grouping of elements of the investigation on the timeline that seem related to the analyst.

Chung et al. [15] discuss VisPorter, a collaborative text analytics tool aimed toward allowing sensemaking in a collaborative environment. The software is meant for multi-user engagement and the designers focused on different elements such as haptic touch, lighting, and to explore how people forage for information to share hypotheses. The VisPorter software includes the Foraging tool, which contains the document viewer and the concept map viewer, and the Synthesis tool, which allow users to share information found individually with the foraging tools. Some of the features included in this software was gesture-based interaction, with an example of someone with a small display flipping a document off the left side of their device, and having it be shared and dropped on the right side of a synced large display. Our brainstorming software is situated in an immersive environment that also uses multimodal input on an immersive display that allows multiple users to collaborate, but our software recognizes users' body frames and allows users to interact with the system using only physical gestures. We anticipate this should allow users to spend more cognitive energy on analysis than on interacting with the system.

Benjamin et al. [16] describe the capabilities of an analytic software tool called DIGEST. Its main capabilities are extracting data from text, such as sentiments, social influence, and information flow structures; the tool also has exploratory data analytics, and finally it uses the stored results to create various knowledge products. After the data collection and processing stage, where analysts can configure the tool to collect data on specific topics, the tool develops a template for information reporting. Finally, the analyst can populate the template with the information the tool has collected. The analyst can choose what information they want included, as well as add any of their own insights to the product.

While several features of our software have been present in the software discussed above, the underlying concept for all of our features is to enable human collaboration during sensemaking; by applying the intended users' domain knowledge to our software development we hope to achieve create a cognitively more accessible product. The process that we are proposing of retrospectively consulting and integrating educational materials into the software design is novel for this problem. This novelty is partly due to the fact that the users' requirements as intelligence analysts might be too rigorous for a generic brainstorming software to be useful; to address this special user need, we are implementing the structured brainstorming process developed by intelligence analysts. The specific process for this tool is a structured analytic technique called brainstorming, where a group of analysts record salient pieces of data on sticky notes and creates topic groups from these notes. Our software design is using a blended approach of interviews and integration of source material from the intelligence analysis domain.

B. Sensemaking theory

Sensemaking theory is well represented in human-computer interaction studies on user interface design for intelligence analysis [5][7]–[9][11][13][14][17]–[22]. Pirolli and Card introduce the concept of the sensemaking process in intelligence analysis as a cognitive schema operating on expert level behavior [5]. Given this assumption, the authors also prelude their article with the understanding that expertise and experience will form a series of behavioral patterns that will inform how the intelligence analysts behave.

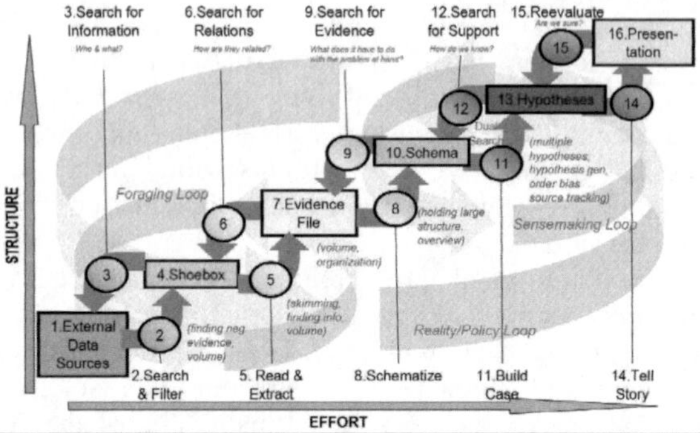

Figure 1 The sensemaking process and leverage points for analyst technology as identified through cognitive task analysis *[5]*.

The authors state that analysts would restructure incoming information to fit previously built organizational formats, to aid in planning, evaluation, and reasoning. Pirolli and Card posit that the intelligence process can be divided into two loops: 1) the foraging loop, where analysts seek out and sort information, and 2) the sensemaking loop, where analysts pinpoint the best evidence, and building a mental model from the evidence. Our digital tool is intended to facilitate this process, more specifically, the foraging loop.

C. User modelling

We have studied structured analytic techniques in educational materials that were created for use in the intelligence analysis field. These techniques include but are not limited to: brainstorming, what-if analysis, and multiple scenario generation [6]. We are transforming these techniques into digital tools for our cognitive immersive environment. Currently, while there are many digital tools and software that have been created for the intelligence analysis domain, few of these tools use structured analytic techniques in their design or operation, or they fail to account for the user in system designs [23]. Gotz et al. [24] detail the intelligence analysis process, conducted an experiment concerning intelligence analysis, behavioral modeling, and user interface implications. Based on their findings, the authors argue for a flexibility in computer tools available to analysts, as analysts have a varied method of collecting and recording information. One of their final conclusions is user interface design should have some amount of user centered design and modelling, because analysts create information models when none are present, and they expressed appreciation when the models were available [24]. Perhaps the most well-known structured analytic tool that has been transformed into a digital tool is the Analysis of Competing Hypothesis tool, initially created by Richard Heuer [25].

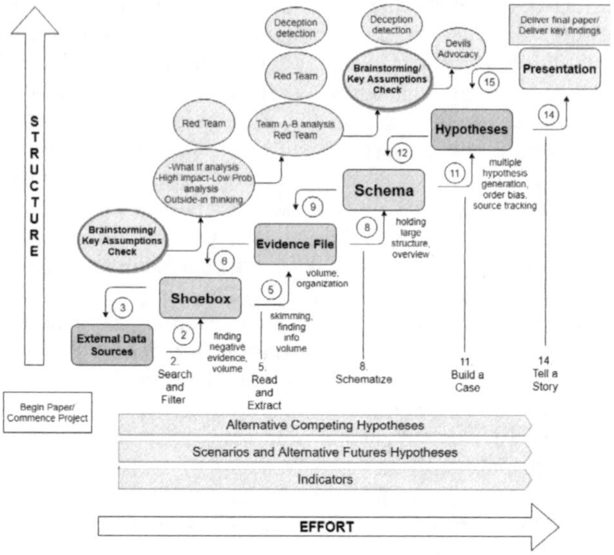

Figure 2 Pirolli and Card's sensemaking model with structured analytic techniques superimposed

One challenge in successfully creating a digital tool for intelligence analysis is identifying the specific information demands of the operations analysts use to support their work. We consult intelligence analysis training materials, manuals, and final products, such as briefs, to understand the steps taken by analysts when conducting intelligence analysis.

As structured brainstorming is a standard structured analytic technique in the sensemaking process, we are developing a digital tool in a cognitive and immersive environment for brainstorming in the intelligence analysis domain. We aim to create an environment that will facilitate sensemaking during the brainstorming process, and therefore it is imperative that we understand how analysts identify important evidence, discuss ideas, and how they interact with each other as a team in order to identify how to proceed with analysis. As mentioned above, our research team conducted several pen and paper brainstorming sessions and observed brainstorming sessions conducted in an intelligence analysis class at a local university, using direct feedback from analysts and integrating material from the domain.

The structured brainstorming process is explained in Beebe and Pherson's 2014 book, "Cases in intelligence analysis" [2]. The process begins with a group of analysts reading a document individually and then recording pieces of evidence they find most salient on sticky notes. After a predetermined amount of time, the recording portion of the brainstorming process ends, and the group puts their sticky notes up on a wall or other surface. After the notes are put up, the group members rearrange the notes into topic groups, initially with no discussion. Lastly, the group discusses the emerging topics to determine which are most relevant to their project. We have created a user model off of this process using the principles of scenario-based design, which are discussed below section D. Scenario based design.

The practice of examining users' work routines to construct a model of how software should be developed for the user base is known as scenario-based design [26]. There are established benefits of scenario based-design, as it examines and seeks to model the real-world processes undergone by the users. The core concept is to examine how people use technology and then to more deeply examine how technology impacts or shapes their activities. Another feature of scenario based design is applying user scenarios for interface and technology design in order to mold the technology to the users' needs and situation [26].

The scenario-based design process is intended to examine the potential stakeholders, as well as develop claims about the current practices of the potential users, which will inform how user scenarios are developed. Once the user analysis is developed, it is utilized in design analysis. Design analysis focuses on user activities, information design, and interaction scenarios. These are all developed, further shaped, and informed by information on the projected user and their needs and use of the software. Usability claims and analysis are also reiterated during design analysis. Then, a prototype is prepared, where more specific usability specifications are developed and programmed. The process of reshaping the software to reflect user needs is re-iterated as necessary. However, the process that we are proposing of retrospectively consulting and integrating educational materials into the software design is novel for developing software for intelligence analysis.

E. Electronic brainstorming tools

Electronic sticky notes are not uncommon in digital brainstorming literature. Previous works have looked at the use of sticky note tools in group and collaborative settings [27] and in remotely mediated group work, as well as, how sticky notes can be used to define affinity groups in collaborative work [28]. Jensen et al. [29] compare the use of traditional analog sticky notes to a digital sticky-notes tool, and concludes that the digital sticky notes were superior in terms of increased note interaction, clustering, and labelling. Existing digital sticky note tools can be found in examples such as Discusys [28], ECOPack [30], Padlet [31], and Quickies [32].

More closely aligned to the focus of our research, a sticky-notes brainstorming tool known as RAMPARTS has been designed for criminal investigations. The study by Wozniak et al. [33] found that "...RAMPARTS spatial awareness decreased task completion time when compared to a paper-based system, without any adverse effect on task completion time compared to a tabletop, and without increasing perceived cognitive workload" [33]. Investigating task completion time and spatial awareness aspects will be important to consider for future user testing with our own software, in order to determine if our digital tool will be able to enable sensemaking during intelligence analysis.

III. Implementing user Centered Features

This project seeks to extend existing research by incorporating scenario-based designs into the software interface, as informed by sensemaking theory. We are using a blended approach of including direct feedback from former analysts at a local university, as well as cognitive analytic techniques created by the domain experts [2][3]. Intelligence analysis classes are available in some universities, and they often teach techniques that widely used in the intelligence domain. We conducted several of our own pen-and-paper brainstorming sessions and observed an intelligence analysis class at a local university to better understand the methods used in the field of intelligence analysis. These sessions further motivated the behavior and capabilities of our software.

In order to enable sensemaking for analysts, we have taken the pen-and-paper brainstorming exercise as described by Beebe and Pherson [2] and implemented it into an immersive, digital tool that can be used collaboratively in a multi-user context. The research project will incorporate feedback from analysts, both through direct feedback and user studies, and is currently informed by documents from the training and educational literature that has been produced by the intelligence field. The goal of integrating training and educational materials into the software capabilities and interactions is to make the tool accessible to a majority of the users, as they will have had previous exposure to these materials in their domain experience. Furthermore, it is important for our tool to support human interactions individually and as a group, and enable fluid manipulation of the users' ideas as sticky notes to reduce cognitive effort and bias.

We use the Pirolli and Card sensemaking notational model (Figure 1) to develop the structure and behavior of our software. This model depicts the cognitive tasks completed by intelligence analysts, and it includes a foraging phase and a sensemaking phase. The brainstorming tool is informed by the foraging phase from Pirolli and Card's model to allow analysts to search, discover, and filter information during the shoebox phase. The tool is also derived from structured analytic techniques already in use by intelligence analysts. Our hypothesis is that the software should be informed by cognitive processes that intelligence analysts undergo during the intelligence process, as well as the cognitive analytic tools currently used by intelligence analysts. It is imperative to leverage these techniques to create a useful and usable cognitive, immersive environment.

The sticky notes brainstorming tool is situated in a cognitive immersive environment in the Cognitive Immersive Systems Lab (CISL). This environment is comprised of a 360-degree panoramic display that stands at 14 feet tall. The brainstorming tool is comprised of a personal view and a global view to accommodate individual and group brainstorming. We have integrated verbal and gestural commands into the software that equate with the actions in the analog brainstorming exercise, and we have enabled a personal view and a global view (see Figure 4). We believe informing the software with techniques already familiar to the user will create a more usable interface [4], and will enable sensemaking during the analysis process.

Digital sticky notes are created and edited on the personal view with a personal device, such as a laptop or a tablet. Then, the personal view is synced to a web server, allowing notes to transfer to the global view. The personal view includes an area to create new notes that are only shown within the personal view, an uncategorized area where notes can be sent to the blank space on the global view, and an area that reflects all of the other created categories and notes of the session. Our personal view (see Figure 3) is accessed through a web browser, allowing it to work on a wide variety of devices. Users can send notes from the personal view to the global view by tapping on a note and then tapping into the uncategorized area.

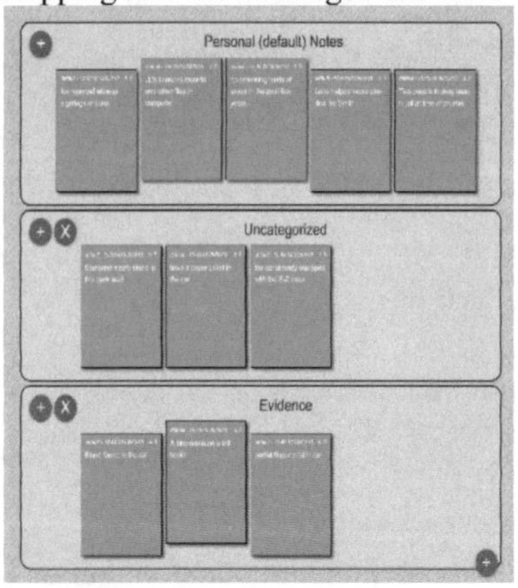

Figure 3 Personal view of sticky notes brainstorming tool.

Once notes are on the shared screen, users can discuss with each other and interact with the global and personal views (see Figure 3) to create categories from their ideas.

The cognitive and immersive system is equipped to handle gestural commands and verbal commands, either separately or in tandem for multimodal interactions. The technologies that enable multi-user input are Kinects [34], which are used to detect body frames and spatial information. This information allows users to make gestural commands as input to the system. Lapel microphones allow multiple users to give verbal commands to the system. The system output is projected via five projectors onto the 360-degree screen. The system can also speak to users through a synthesized voice. This environment creates an immersive and interactive workspace for analysis.

In order to support a cognitive and immersive environment, we enabled verbal and gestural commands for the user to interact with the global view of the system. Verbal commands relayed through the lapel microphone currently consist of: 1) Create note, 2) Edit note, 3) Delete note, 4) Move note, 5) Create category, 6) Rename category, 7) Add note to category. Gestural commands are recognized by the Kinect sensors [34]. The gestures recognized by the global view in the brainstorming environment are pointing to select a note, grasping with a hand to pick up a note, and releasing a hand to drop a note elsewhere on the screen.

Additionally, the system is able to handle a multimodal approach of input allowing a combination of verbal and gestures to make up a command, such as a user pointing at a note and saying, "Delete that note." These technologies enable multimodal interactions which we hypothesize will help reduce the cognitive load of analysts, which has been documented in previous work through interviews with analysts and experiments involving intelligence analysts [1] [33][35]–[37].

Figure 4 User interaction with point/select system in brainstorming tool.

The interactions between the global view and the personal view are designed to be faithful to the structured analytic brainstorming process, and to match the sensemaking process outlined by Pirolli and Card. Analysts create notes solitarily before they share the notes with the group, and then spend time discussing the shared notes as a group. To facilitate collaboration, our technology allows multiple users to interact with the global view at the same time.

IV. CONCLUSION AND FUTURE WORK

This paper has introduced our sticky notes brainstorming tool, as informed by cognitive tools from intelligence analysis, which is aiming to better enable sensemaking for analysts. The underpinnings for our research are brought in from sensemaking theory, scenario-based design, and user modelling research on intelligence analysis, and considers prior research in electronic sticky notes. Our prototype tool, situated in CISL, is comprised of a personal view accessible on personal devices, and a global view that is projected onto a screen viewable by all users. We have integrated multimodal input for the system through gestural and verbal commands.

We have found that designing software for intelligence analysis has presented a number of challenges, which has informed the limitations of our current research. The accessibility of the intended user is generally less than other user groups, as by nature of their work they cannot divulge sensitive information. Similarly, accessibility of accurate and relevant source material to inform the design of the software has been challenging for the reason discussed above. On a more technical note, the range of input we are enabling in a multimodal environment is in a conceptual phase, and we are designing and carrying out user studies to understand the potential impact on users.

For future work, we will conduct user studies to examine the usability and utility of the brainstorming tool. We use Pirolli and Card's sensemaking theory and notational model [5] to understand how their representation of how the cognitive tasks of intelligence analysis might be supported by the brainstorming tool in our cognitive immersive environment. Our tool will be used to run mock intelligence exercises to determine if it can produce results that will be considered useful to an analyst. Failure or success will be determined by how many unique ideas are generated during the brainstorming session, the quality of the ideas, the length of the session, how many topic clusters are generated, and the perceived quality of the discussion. Based on future user studies with our tool, we can identify modifications to create a more usable product for the user base. If the software is more usable with these modifications, and returns useful information, then we can determine that including educational and training materials is a necessary step in designing the software. Our first user study will compare the actions and interactions between groups using traditional pen and paper tools compared to our digital brainstorming tool. The subject pool will be college students. We will do multiple rounds of studies and will improve the tool capabilities and user interface after each round. A future user study will include former intelligence analysts as subjects in order to give us domain specific feedback for the tool.

Our prototype of a digital brainstorming tool is motivated by a scenario-based design, as well as, existing intelligence analysis resources and materials Future work includes creating more personalized experiences for users, developing and researching new gestures and multimodal interactions, and extending the tool to other structured analytic techniques (see Figure 2).

REFERENCES

[1] S. G. Hutchins, P. Pirolli, and S. Card, "Use of Critical Analysis Method to Conduct a Cognitive Task Analysis of Intelligence Analysts," *Proceedings of the Human Factors and Ergonomics Society Annual Meeting*, vol. 47, no. 3, pp. 478–482, Oct. 2003.

[2] S. M. Beebe and R. H. Pherson, *Cases in Intelligence Analysis: Structured Analytic Techniques in Action*. CQ Press, 2014.

[3] W. M. Hall and G. Citrenbaum, *Intelligence analysis: How to think in complex environments: how to think in complex environments*. ABC-CLIO, 2009.

[4] N. W. Warner, C. A. P. Smith, and M. P. Letsky, *Macrocognition in Teams: Theories and Methodologies*. CRC Press, 2017.

[5] P. Pirolli and S. Card, "Sensemaking processes of intelligence analysts and possible leverage points as identified through cognitive task analysis," in *Proceedings of the 2005 International Conference on Intelligence Analysis, McLean, Virginia*, 2005, vol. 6.

[6] "A Tradecraft Primer: Structured Analytic Techniques for Improving Intelligence Analysis." American Psychological Association, 2009.

[7] W. Wright, D. Schroh, P. Proulx, A. Skaburskis, and B. Cort, "The Sandbox for Analysis: Concepts and Methods," in *Proceedings of the SIGCHI Conference on Human Factors in Computing Systems*, New York, NY, USA, 2006, pp. 801–810.

[8] N. J. Pioch and J. O. Everett, "POLESTAR: collaborative knowledge management and sensemaking tools for intelligence analysts," in *Proceedings of the 15th ACM international conference on Information and knowledge management*, 2006, pp. 513–521.

[9] R. Eccles, T. Kapler, R. Harper, and W. Wright, "Stories in GeoTime," *Information Visualization; Thousand Oaks*, vol. 7, no. 1, pp. 3–17, Spring 2008.

[10] P. E. Keel, "EWall: A Visual Analytics Environment for Collaborative Sense-making," *Information Visualization*, vol. 6, no. 1, pp. 48–63, Mar. 2007.

[11] C. Rooney, S. Attfield, B. L. W. Wong, and S. Choudhury, "INVISQUE as a Tool for Intelligence Analysis: The Construction of Explanatory Narratives," *International Journal of Human–Computer Interaction*, vol. 30, no. 9, pp. 703–717, Sep. 2014.

[12] C. Görg, Z. Liu, N. Parekh, K. Singhal, and J. Stasko, "Jigsaw meets Blue Iguanodon - The VAST 2007 Contest," in *In IEEE Symposium on Visual Analytics Science and Technology*, 2007.
[13] M. J. Murdock, R. E. Roth, and N. V. Maziekas, "The Basic Ordnance Observational Management System: geovisual exploration and analysis of improvised explosive device incidents," *Journal of Maps*, vol. 8, no. 1, pp. 120–124, 2012.
[14] R. R. Petersen and U. K. Wiil, "CrimeFighter Investigator: Integrating synthesis and sense-making for criminal network investigation," *Security Informatics*, vol. 2, no. 1, p. 10, 2013.
[15] H. Chung, C. North, J. Z. Self, S. Chu, and F. Quek, "VisPorter: facilitating information sharing for collaborative sensemaking on multiple displays," *Personal and Ubiquitous Computing*, vol. 18, no. 5, pp. 1169–1186, 2014.
[16] P. Benjamin, K. Madanagopal, M. Erraguntla, and D. Corlette, "Distributed Information Gathering, Exploration and Sensemaking Toolkit (DIGEST)," in *Proceedings on the International Conference on Artificial Intelligence (ICAI); Athens*, Athens, United States, Athens, 2016, pp. 449–455.
[17] C. Baber, S. Attfield, G. Conway, C. Rooney, and N. Kodagoda, "Collaborative sense-making during simulated Intelligence Analysis Exercises," *International Journal of Human-Computer Studies*, vol. 86, pp. 94–108, Feb. 2016.
[18] Y. a Kang and J. Stasko, "Characterizing the intelligence analysis process: Informing visual analytics design through a longitudinal field study," in *2011 IEEE Conference on Visual Analytics Science and Technology (VAST)*, 2011, pp. 21–30.
[19] P. E. Lehner, L. Adelman, B. A. Cheikes, and M. J. Brown, "Confirmation Bias in Complex Analyses," *IEEE Transactions on Systems, Man, and Cybernetics - Part A: Systems and Humans*, vol. 38, no. 3, pp. 584–592, May 2008.
[20] J. Paik and P. Pirolli, "ACT-R models of information foraging in geospatial intelligence tasks," *Computational and Mathematical Organization Theory*, vol. 21, no. 3, pp. 274–295, 2015.
[21] G. Park and C. A. Ntuen, "A cognitive model for human terrain information processing," in *IIE Annual Conference. Proceedings*, 2011, p. 1.
[22] B. Tomaszewski and A. M. MacEachren, "Geovisual analytics to support crisis management: Information foraging for geo-historical context," *Information Visualization*, vol. 11, no. 4, pp. 339–359, 2012.
[23] M. K. Dhami, "A Survey of Intelligence Analysts' Perceptions of Analytic Tools," in *2017 European Intelligence and Security Informatics Conference (EISIC)*, 2017, pp. 131–134.
[24] D. Gotz, M. X. Zhou, and Z. Wen, "A study of information gathering and result processing in intelligence analysis," in *IUI 2006 Workshop on IUI for Intelligence Analysis*, 2006, p. 6.
[25] R. J. Heuer, *Psychology of intelligence analysis*. Washington, D.C.: Center for the Study of Intelligence, Central Intelligence Agency, 1999.
[26] M. B. Rosson and J. M. Carroll, *Human Computer Interaction Handbook: Fundamentals, Evolving Technologies, and Emerging Applications, Third Edition*. CRC Press, 2012.
[27] C. C. Dornburg, S. M. Stevens, S. M. L. Hendrickson, and G. S. Davidson, "Improving Extreme-Scale Problem Solving: Assessing Electronic Brainstorming Effectiveness in an Industrial Setting," *Hum Factors*, vol. 51, no. 4, pp. 519–527, Aug. 2009.
[28] W. Widjaja, K. Yoshii, K. Haga, and M. Takahashi, "Discusys: Multiple User Real-time Digital Sticky-note Affinity-diagram Brainstorming System," *Procedia Computer Science*, vol. 22, pp. 113–122, Jan. 2013.
[29] M. M. Jensen, S.-K. Thiel, E. Hoggan, and S. Bødker, "Physical Versus Digital Sticky Notes in Collaborative Ideation," *Comput Supported Coop Work*, pp. 1–37, May 2018.
[30] S. Majd, A. Marie-Hélène, M. Véronique, M. Claude, and V. David, "Integration of brainstorming platform in a system of information systems," in *Proceedings of the 8th International Conference on Management of Digital EcoSystems*, 2016, pp. 166–173.
[31] "Padlet is the easiest way to create and collaborate in the world," *Padlet*. [Online]. Available: https://padlet.com/. [Accessed: 23-Dec-2018].
[32] P. Mistry and P. Maes, "Augmenting Sticky Notes as an I/O Interface," in *Universal Access in Human-Computer Interaction. Intelligent and Ubiquitous Interaction Environments*, Springer, Berlin, Heidelberg, 2009, pp. 547–556.
[33] P. Wozniak, N. Goyal, P. Kucharski, L. Lischke, S. Mayer, and M. Fjeld, "RAMPARTS: Supporting Sensemaking with Spatially-Aware Mobile Interactions," in *Proceedings of the 2016 CHI Conference on Human Factors in Computing Systems*, New York, NY, USA, 2016, pp. 2447–2460.
[34] R. Zhao, K. Wang, R. Divekar, R. Rouhani, H. Su, and Q. Ji, "An Immersive System with Multi-Modal Human-Computer Interaction," in *2018 13th IEEE International Conference on Automatic Face & Gesture Recognition (FG 2018)*, Xi'an, 2018, pp. 517–524.
[35] F. L. Greitzer and R. E. Hohimer, "Modeling Human Behavior to Anticipate Insider Attacks," *Journal of Strategic Security*, vol. 4, no. 2, pp. 25–48, Jun. 2011.
[36] B. M. Moon and R. R. Hoffman, "How Might 'Transformational' Technologies and Concepts be Barriers to Sensemaking in Intelligence Analysis?," p. 12.
[37] A. Toniolo *et al.*, "Supporting Reasoning with Different Types of Evidence in Intelligence Analysis," in *Proceedings of the 2015 International Conference on Autonomous Agents and Multiagent Systems*, Richland, SC, 2015, pp. 781–789.

Immersion as a Strategy to Facilitate Participatory Design Involving People With Intellectual Disabilities and Caretakers as Proxies

Shaping spaces for participation through contextual insight

Åsmund Dæhlen
Department of Informatics, Faculty of Mathematics and Natural Sciences, University of Oslo
Oslo, Norway
email: aasmunkd@ifi.uio.no

Suhas Govind Joshi
Department of Informatics, Faculty of Mathematics and Natural Sciences, University of Oslo
Oslo, Norway
email: joshi@ifi.uio.no

Abstract — **This paper reports from the early phase of a Participatory Design (PD) process where the goal is to design technology that involves people with Intellectual Disabilities (ID) and their caretakers as participants. The background of the study is a long-term collaboration with a local activity center for people with ID and 56 participants from this empirical context participated in this study. The presented methodological approach emphasizes immersion as a means of gaining access to and learning about the context to help identify crucial considerations for the facilitation of later PD activities. The paper presents two analyses of contextual data to reflect on how immersion as a strategy provides important insight into contextual considerations that can help shape future PD activities. Three learning outcomes are presented and discussed: involving users with ID and their caretakers as proxies, organizing long-term commitment, and lastly building on already-established forms of mutual learning.**

Keywords — ***participatory design; Intellectual Disabilities; immersion; proxy designer.***

I. INTRODUCTION

The increased attention devoted to the user perspective in the assessment of the quality of life has opened up possibilities for people with Intellectual Disabilities (ID) to involve themselves more in research activities [1]. However, including people with communicational issues due to cognitive limitations present obstacles for meaningful participation in PD. One such example is the often seen presence of alternative forms of communication, e.g., as mentioned by [2]. The background for our study is a long-term collaboration with a local activity center where the goal is to facilitate a design process where 40 people with ID and their caretakers can engage in the co-design of technology.

This paper reports from the initial phase of a Participatory Design (PD) process with users and caretakers of the activity center aiming at designing technology to support the users in their everyday activities. We consider PD appropriate as it embeds important underlying values that we believe are necessary to tackle the challenges found within our empirical context, e.g., power relations, mutual learning, and emancipation [3]. Our PD process emphasizes immersion as a strategy to gain the necessary contextual insight to facilitate future PD activities. We report from our initial phase where we have immersed ourselves in the context to help identify important considerations. This study involves 56 participants, including users with ID, their caretakers, and the managerial staff. The data gathered through immersion revealed two main topics overarching all contextual factors, namely activity and communication. We used these two topics to structure our analysis of what type of contextual insight we gained through immersion, and then later use the findings to reflect on why this knowledge is necessary to facilitate a PD process involving both people with ID and proxy designers. We end the paper by presenting three concrete learning outcomes: (1) the PD process should facilitate for the participation of caretakers as proxies; (2) the PD process should be organized as a long-term commitment; (3) the PD process should be built on top of already established forms of mutual learning. We discuss the implications of these three learning outcomes by summarizing why we advocate immersion as a strategy on how to gain the contextual knowledge necessary to facilitate a PD process involving people with ID and their caretakers as design proxies.

Throughout this paper, the word *user* describes someone using a facility or service. This notion derives from people being users of healthcare systems or services [4]. Linguistically, it also represents a neutral word that allows the caretakers to talk about people with ID without stigmatizing or revealing specific details about the users in everyday communication. We attempt to distinguish this notion from users in a design process by describing the latter as end-users rather than users.

This paper is structured as follows. We give an introduction of related work in Section 2, while Section 3 outlines our research methodology, empirical context, and the specific methods of inquiry. Section 4 presents the results from our empirical work. We end the paper in Section 5 by introducing three implications of our approach, as well as discussing the significance and relevance to ongoing discussions concerning design for people with ID.

II. Related Work

Previous studies have explored the use of proxies in the context of PD involving both adults and children with ID (e.g., [2] and [5]). Brereton et al. [5] present the initial use of proxies as an important step towards realizing requirements, imagining possibilities, and ensuring successful inclusion of people with ID into the process of design after design. There are other examples of successful inclusion of people with ID in specific phases of design, e.g., [6]. Putnam & Chong [7] seek to gather information on software and technology use for people with autism through surveys directed at adult proxies, as well as some adults living with autism. Blomberg & Karasti [8] present an important perspective on ethnography in PD as a means of "channeling access" to the context. Holone & Herstad [9] also stress the importance of starting the design in the practice of users.

Redhead and Brereton [10] explain how short-term methods as a means to engage in design can be ineffective for communities of people. They argue that the researchers' presence and activities are inherently academic, and might be too distant from the empirical context to understand and support local practice and interaction. Their suggestion on how to approach this challenge is by shifting from short-term to long-term commitment. A similar point is also raised by [11].

A common denominator in studies about people with cognitive impairments is the need for highly contextualized understandings of the participants and their challenges and capabilities [9][12][13]. As Holone & Herstad suggest, working with kids with disabilities requires more time to get to a "starting line" where the design process can begin [9]. Francis et al. [12] also characterize how challenges caused by highly individualized forms of communications amongst people with Asperger's and autism can be tackled with correct management of the co-design process. Brosnan et al. [14] also reflect upon PD practice, challenges related to engaging different stakeholders, and also points to pitfalls such as overlooking the value of inclusion. Finally, [13] advocates the uniqueness of each co-design study for people with cognitive and sensory impairments and the importance of understanding the context and people in-depth when adjusting the methods applied.

III. Research Method

A. Empirical context

The empirical context of our study is an activity center located in Norway for approximately 40 people with ID. Their ages range from 22-70 years with non-significant differences in gender distribution. The impairments range from mild to profound mental capabilities, but also extend to physical challenges as people may have bodily configurations that also complicate autonomous functioning. To support each person's cognitive and physical capabilities, their everyday activities are individually tailored and organized to maximize the sense of autonomy. For some people, this requires one-on-one assistance from caretakers, while others can work in groups or even without any direct assistance. The caretakers' background ranges from non-related or lacking a higher education to domain-specific competencies such as social workers, social educators, teachers, and ergotherapists.

The everyday dialogue between the people and their caretakers is highly contextualized (see, e.g., Figure 1). Certain users can only communicate when using a limited and tailored vocabulary; however, the caretakers rely on many forms of non-verbal communication, most of which are directly tied to the context, e.g., objects, places, activities, and routines found at the activity center. Examples of such non-verbal forms of communication include icons, signs, physical gestures, and photographs. The activity center offers a wide range of both educational and recreational activities for the users such as therapeutic activities (e.g., music and light therapy), ludic activities (e.g., games and audiobooks), creative activities (e.g., painting and sewing), and physical actives (e.g., swimming and field trips).

Figure 1. Illustrations being used as an alternative form of communication

B. Methodology

The methodological approach of this study is Participatory Design (PD) – a worldview that emphasizes the inclusion of the people who will eventually use the technology in the design process as equal co-designers [3]. Central principles of PD include mutual learning, co-construction, and having a say [3], and our approach attempts to create a space for engagement supporting these principles while simultaneously allowing us to design technologies for and with users with ID. One of the central challenges in our long-term PD process is to support co-creation and autonomy without necessarily demanding participation from users in all phases and activities.

Our approach relies on immersion as a strategy to build up enough contextual knowledge about the users, their lives and everyday activities, to represent their voices in activities where they are not interested in, or unable to, participate themselves. We see the PD process as a use-oriented design cycle that requires familiarity with both the real-life problem situation and the practice [3] before moving to elicitation of needs and requirement descriptions. As such, we use this paper to argue for immersion as a necessary component in studies involving proxy designers engaged on behalf of users with an ID, especially when representing the users' voices in the design of technology intended to support them with their everyday goals and activities.

Immersion in our context draws on ethnographic traditions and practices. More precisely, we align our view on immersion with Crang and Cook's intersubjective perspective [15]: *"participant observation should not be to separate its 'subjective and 'objective components, but to talk about it as a means of developing intersubjective understandings between the researcher and researched"* (p. 37). We position ourselves as such due to the embedded emphasis on mutual learning in PD [16], and our argument is that the contextual knowledge gained through immersion during the earlier stages of a long-term PD process is vital to the facilitation of later design activities. Thus, the results, findings, and discussions of this paper revolve around how non-users engaged as proxy designers can better connect with the everyday world of the users and actively change it and create new knowledge through immersive participation.

The long-term commitment of the study was conducted on a weekly basis, where one of the researchers worked on a volunteer basis at the activity center. This means working closely with the proxies and the users of the activity center, engaging in everyday activities, learning about their different means of communication and lives in general. The nature of the communicational difficulties faced by the users means that the proxies were very important in bridging an apparent gap of knowledge that was required to have meaningful interactions with some of the users.

On an everyday basis the employees are working together in bridging their differences in knowledge and ask each other questions about how to perform specific tasks or activities. The care-workers are proxies to the users because they continuously try to mediate their wants and needs and facilitate for a workday which carries meaning in some way.

C. *Research methods*

This paper presents the results from the initial phases of our long-term PD process and the data involved was gathered through six research methods throughout four months. Our activities involved 56 participants, including users with an ID, their caretakers, managers, and researchers. Table 1 presents an overview of the six research methods and the participants involved in each activity.

TABLE 1. OVERVIEW OF THE RESEARCH METHODS

#	Research method	Participants
A	Participatory inquiry	30 users and 15 employees
B	Contextual observation	Researcher
C	Diary journaling	Researcher
D	Explorative workshop I	2 researchers and 1 design expert
E	Interviews	Manager
F	Explorative workshop II	6 Employees

1) *Participatory inquiry*

One of the researchers in this study immersed himself into the context by taking on the role as a volunteer caretaker, receiving formal training and introduction similar to the training provided to all other caretakers. While the researcher still works part-time at the activity center in this voluntary role, the data presented in this paper originates from the first four months of work, which equals approximately 100 working hours. The goal of this immersive activity was to gain knowledge through first-hand experience of the context and the users we are designing for and with in our study. The methods of inquiry included observations and shadowing of colleagues and users during everyday activities, their interaction with technology, as well as their means of communication. The data produced from this activity consisted of notes, photographs, and mind maps.

2) *Contextual observation*

The purpose of the observation was to capture important contextual concerns in a medium suited for later design activities where participants might not possess verbal communication skills. As such, the data was documented in the form of photographs. 50 suitable photographs that described important contextual relationships related to everyday activities, interaction between people, and technology were selected. Most of these photographs were taken after working hours to ensure that the researchers' presence did not disrupt or interfere with the users' activities. Examples of relevant contextual concerns include technologies (e.g., audio systems, massage chairs, and light projectors), objects used in activities (e.g., instruments, games, and drawings), and places of interest (e.g., sensory rooms, resting places, and creative spaces).

3) *Diary journaling*

After each full day of volunteer work, an entry was written in an elicitation diary describing the activities and communication challenges encountered. Important events, major issues, and concrete examples of situations requiring contextual insight constituted the main content of the diary. Similar to the contextual observation, most of the diary entries were produced after working hours or in the absence of users as the goal was to allow everyday activities to progress as normal despite being the subject of investigation. Throughout four months, 18 journal entries were written down, ranging from a couple of sentences to a couple of pages.

4) *Explorative workshop I*

To explore design opportunities in the context of technology intended to support users with ID in their everyday activities, we engaged one researcher and one design experts in an explorative workshop. During the workshop, we presented data from the previous activities such as photographs, mind maps, and transcribed interviews as the basis for a discussion of how we can facilitate future design activities in our PD process. Furthermore, both researchers conducted an individual objective coding on the same data set, which later served as the basis for a reflection of the insight gained through immersion and how contextual knowledge directly affected our interpretation of the same set of data.

5) *Interviews*

An important part of the immersive approach was facilitating easier access to both contextual and domain knowledge which included in-depth details about the capabilities of each person who used the activity center. One of the main sources of information was ten semi-structured interviews with the manager of the activity center revolving around practical and organizational issues that were relevant to our facilitation of a PD process including both the users and their caretakers. These interviews revealed opportunities and limitations for participation, e.g., insight into the working schedule of the caretakers, as well as suggestions on suitable caretakers who could fit the role as proxy designers in later stages of our PD process. Each interview lasted between 30-60 minutes and was scheduled throughout the four months depending on the manager's availability.

6) *Explorative workshop II*

The final activity in our initial phase of the PD process was a second explorative workshop conducted with six caretakers at the activity center during a morning meeting. The goal of this workshop was to compare how the caretakers as potential proxy designers understood the everyday activities and communication challenges found within their own work context with issues we had identified. We also used their in-depth knowledge of users and everyday activities to facilitate a group discussion on how to scaffold the PD process around existing routines and preferences to best support our underlying PD principles, i.e., mutual learning, co-construction, and having a say.

IV. Results and Analyses

The data gathered through the six activities outlined in the last subsection consisted of diary entries, transcribed interviews, observation notes, discussion summaries, mind maps, individual data coding from workshops, and photographs. From the data, we identified two recurring topics that were common across all the activities and mentioned by all participants, both users and non-users, namely *activity* and *communication*. These two topics also embody most of the underlying issues that were discussed during the two exploratory workshops. As such, we used these two overarching topics to help us structure our analysis of whether immersion could contribute to any deeper insight to help facilitate the future activities of our PD process.

A. *Results*

1) *Activity*

The empirical context is an activity center, and as such, there was an intrinsic emphasis on activities. Both the caretakers employed at the activity center and the users with ID who used it shared an activity-centric focus. Already during the first participatory inquiry, we registered that the caretaker training revolved heavily around daily routines and how different users engage in activities. Concerning how to engage the caretakers as proxy designers in our PD process, the manager who was interviewed explained that the availability of these caretakers was highly related to their work schedule, which in turn revolved around activities. This point was also raised during the first exploratory workshop where the participants believed it would be easiest for both caretakers and users if the PD process were structured around activities.

From the users' perspective, we registered through the diary entries that most of their autonomy, as well as the sense of pride and accomplishment, were related to both the activity and the context in which it took place. One of the reasons behind selecting activity as a common denominator was that users who engaged in activities experienced a multitude of personal reactions and rewarding sensations based on their particular capabilities and background. We also learned during the second exploratory workshop that the participation in activities was itself an important catalyst for the users' sense of mastery. In some cases, the act of carrying out an activity was of greater importance to the user than the purpose or end-goal of the activity. The photographs from the contextual observation complemented this point by revealing that most of the equipment present at the activity center was not intended at problem-solving, but rather as means to enable engagement in activities without necessarily having a fixed end-goal. Finally, we made multiple observations of how successful participation depended on the activity's ability to acknowledge the user's vulnerability, e.g., sudden urges to use bathroom facilities.

2) *Communication*

One of the main challenges when working for and with people with ID is facilitating communication. Previous studies have discussed the need for compensating strategies (e.g., [2]). This is especially important to our PD process and the emphasis on mutual learning. In our empirical context, we found multiple examples of how the activity center compensated for the lack of verbal communication skills. One such example was the labeling of the shelf shown in Figure 1, where photographs rather than text communicated different activities.

Another prominent example was the users' individual daily diaries where the caretakers registered all entries and then communicated a summary back to the user. In later situations, the diary itself became a means of non-verbal between the user and the caretaker. The caretakers who participated in the second exploratory workshop also described how being heard and seen was vital to the users' motivation. Most forms of communication were self-developed and internalized by the different users and the contextual activity at hand. As such, one of the contextual insights gained through the participatory inquiry and the elicitation diary entries was instances of different, but highly specific, combinations of gestures and speech employed by the users to communicate with their caretakers. To facilitate a proper dialogue where the users can communicate choices and selections, understanding these varying forms of communication is a necessity for all parties. In the most extreme cases that we observed, some users rely completely on the caretakers' ability to interpret their language, or lack thereof, as well as the caretakers' ability to reduce the dialogue to questions that the user can answer with a simple yes or no by using their bodies.

B. Analysis

We identified two recurring topics in our data, namely activity and communication, and we wanted to use these two topics to structure our analysis. While the emphasis on these two topics emerged from the empirical data itself, they align well with the goal of our overarching PD process, i.e., designing technology that supports people with ID in their everyday activities. The embedded nature of creating spaces for co-construction and mutual learning in PD also depend on our ability to facilitate communication between participants. As such, we used these two topics to structure our analysis. Figure 2 illustrates how the analysis included multiple people and different types of data.

1) Inter-rater reliability analysis

In the first analysis, we wanted to analyze to what degree our immersion strategy actually provided contextual insight. The individual coding of the same data set performed by the two researchers in the first exploratory workshop yielded a total of 64 overlapping first-order codes shared by the two coders. The data included in this analysis consisted of photographs, observation notes, elicitation diary entries, and documents from the activity center.

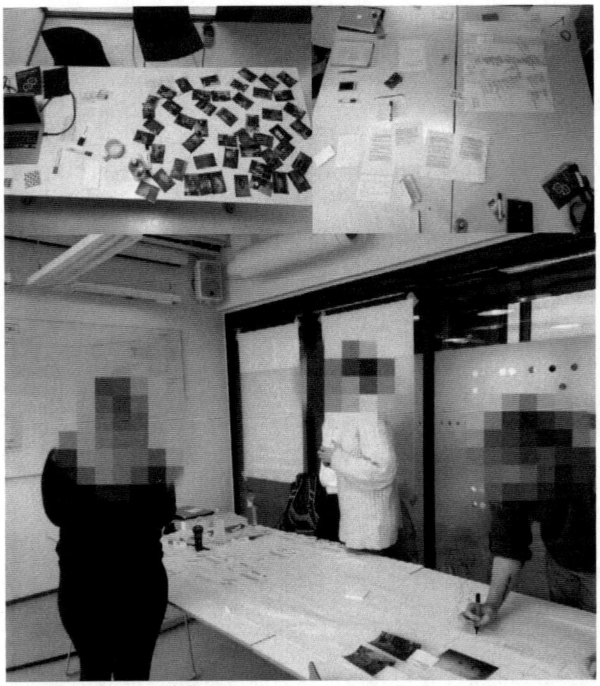

Figure 2. Examples of raw data (top row) used in the analysis (bottom row)

We compared these two sets of individual codes to examine how a researcher without contextual knowledge of the users and their everyday lives identified opportunities and challenges relatively compared to the researcher who had gained contextual knowledge through 100 hours of in-situ volunteer work during the participatory inquiry. More precisely, we wanted to use the inter-rater reliability between these two coders to examine whether the researcher without any contextual knowledge rated each code similar to the researcher who had immersed himself into the context. To study the consensus, both coders individually labeled each of the 64 codes as either activity or communication. We then used Cohen's kappa to determine the exact level of agreement between the two coders. The result of the cross tabulation is outlined in Table 2, where Researcher A represents the immersed researcher while Researcher B represents the researcher without any contextual knowledge.

TABLE 2. ANALYSIS OF INTER-RATER RELIABILITY

		Researcher B		
		Communication	Activity	Total
Researcher A	Communication	21	7	28
	Activity	12	24	36
	Total	33	31	64

From the table, we can see that both researchers divided the number of codes between the two topics fairly equally: Researcher A labeled 28 codes as communication and 36 codes as activity, while Researcher B labeled 33 codes as communication and 36 codes as activity. However, there were large discrepancies in which codes that were labeled under each topic. The coders agreed on 21 of the 64 codes (32.8 %) as examples of communication and 24 of the 64 (37.5 %) as examples of activity. However, the level of inter-rater reliability was still only moderate, $\kappa = .409$ (95 % CI, .189 to .629), $p < .001$. As such, we see that the two researchers had a different understanding of the latent meaning behind similarly identified codes in the same data set.

2) Thematic analysis

During the second analysis, we conducted an inductive thematic analysis of all the data gathered over four months to elicit themes related to our two topics activity and communication. The goal was to use the themes to summarize and exemplify the type of contextual knowledge that was accessible through our emphasis on immersive participation. To structure our inductive thematic analysis, we followed the procedure presented by Braun & Clarke [17], and used the two topics activity and communication as the overarching topics to tie together the different emerging themes. The preparation consisted of transcribing relevant audio recordings from workshops, annotating photographs, and a systematic structuring of all elicitation diary entries and notes from the participatory inquiry. We categorized the data into 40 first-level codes that constituted the lowest level of patterned responses and opinions. The codes were collated into 15 categories that were organized as four main themes. We ended our thematic analysis by mapping out the relationships between the different categories and themes, and by relating them to our overarching analytic topics activity and communication. Figure 3 illustrates the categories and themes identified. We omitted the 40 first-level codes as they were all collated into the 15 categories outlined in the figure.

Figure 3. The result of the thematic analysis

V. FINDINGS

A. *Contextual insight gained through immersion*

Table 3 presents a summary of the four themes identified in the data during the thematic analysis: meaning, practice, choices, and routines. These four themes represent the type of contextual insight gained through our immersive PD approach; the two former themes relate to activity as an overarching topic while the two latter relate to communication. The table also lists the source methods for each of the themes along with key quotes or observations. The four identified themes are examples of higher-order issues that we have separated to highlight the different types of contextual insight gained through immersion, as well as to demonstrate the variety of relevant considerations. As such, the themes are not four separate and independent examples of insight, but rather four overarching themes that represent a set of overlapping and intertwined factors.

Meaning outlines an understanding of the meaning bearers for the users. P*ractice* describes the context and the various kinds of work and activities carried out at the activity center. *Choice* describes the challenges the users and employees face during decision making, as well as how they are resolved in situations involving different cognitive capabilities. *Routine* defines how we can understand the role and implications of the daily routines within the everyday lives of the users.

B. *The distribution of difference in understanding*

The four themes and the underlying categories from the thematic analysis were also used to assess whether the differences in interpretation between researchers with and without contextual knowledge pertained to specific themes or created divergence across all themes. The 64 codes used to assess the level of agreement between the coders in the inter-rater reliability were compared to the 40 first-order codes used to structure the thematic analysis, and the differences were visualized. Figure 4 combines the four themes with the analysis of inter-rater reliability to demonstrate how the differences in understanding of contextual factors were distributed across all themes and underlying categories. The white circles indicate a similar understanding for all underlying codes; the striped-colored circles indicate disagreements in only some of the underlying codes; and the grey circles indicate disagreements in all underlying codes, i.e., the whole category itself.

As we can see in Figure 4, the differences between the two coders were distributed across all four themes, as well as 11 of the 15 underlying categories. For instance, the two coders interpreted the whole theme of *routine* very differently, including all underlying categories. In other cases, the differences in interpretation of first-order codes did not propagate as the clusters of codes were identified and collated. One such example would be *profession*, where only one out of several codes was read differently without affecting the affiliated theme. As such, the contextual knowledge gained through immersion was not limited to certain aspects of activity or communication but pertained to most categories branching out of the four themes.

Stimuli is another example of how contextual knowledge created a divergence between the coders.

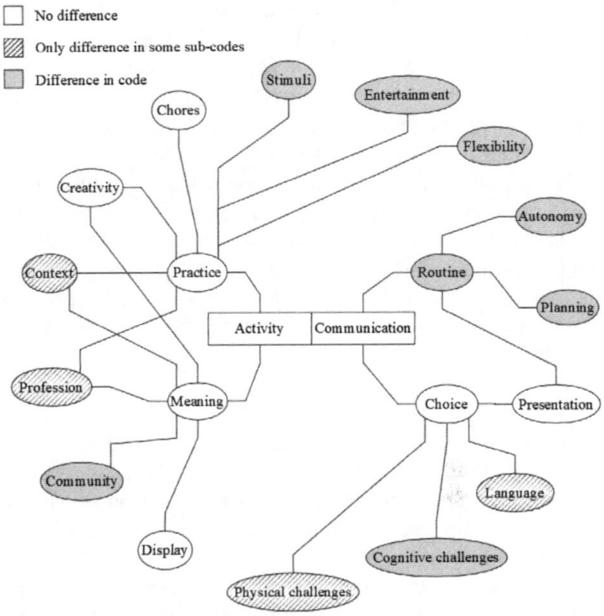

Figure 4. Distribution of difference in coding between the two researchers

TABLE 3. OVERVIEW OF THE FOUR THEMES AND MAIN FINDINGS

Theme	Main findings	Source	Key observations and quotes
Meaning *(Activity)*	• Meaning emerges through the context in which the activities take place. • The company of the caretaker can affect the way in which meaning emerges.	[A], [C], [F]	Users have individually tailored activities and contexts to situate specific kinds of meaning *"Examples of meaning bearer are social relations, safety, predictability, well-being, change of environment, learning and acknowledgment."* (caretaker, [F])
Practice *(Activity)*	• The practice involved in activities varies between users. • Activities need to be flexible regarding duration.	[A], [C], [E]	*"Some activities require 1-on-1 assistance depending on the individuals involved and the context in which it is carried out."* (diary entry, [C]) *"During the first day, I had to end an activity with a user because I was requested to help with something else"* (diary entry, [C])
Choices *(Communication)*	• Presentation of choices must be tailored to both the user and the context. • Limited language and cognition skills inhibit the presentation of choices.	[A], [B], [C]	*"The user was presented with two alternatives, which I later discovered was a rather restricted choice considering the user's capabilities"* (field note, [A]) Representations of choices often require non-verbal forms of communication (see Figure 1, [B])
Routines *(Communication)*	• Structure and daily routines affect the users' ability to participate. • Routines promote autonomy by facilitating learning over time.	[A], [C], [F]	*"For some users, it is a crisis to have a day off as it breaks routines"* (caretaker, [F]) *"One user was frustrated when I communicated that I had to leave early because it disturbed some of the users' routines"* (diary entry, [C])

For the researcher with contextual knowledge, this code was considered an in-vivo code referring to a specific activity, while the researcher without contextual knowledge understood it as a matter of communication rather than activity. We saw similar differences with *physical challenges*; the researcher with contextual knowledge referred to communication challenges with this code as most users relied on bodily gestures to communicate, while the researcher without contextual knowledge saw this as a challenge related to participation opportunities in activities.

We argue that this distribution of the difference in understanding creates highly different outlooks for the facilitation of an inclusive and tailored PD process involving users with ID and their caretakers as proxy designers.

VI. DISCUSSION

In the immersive nature of our PD process, taking on the role as a volunteer caretaker has us given the possibility to create and embed mutual learning in the context on the premise of the users and caretakers. We have used the contextual knowledge gained to analyze the importance of our presence and the type of insight it may provide. We end the paper by introducing three concrete learning outcomes that we believe can inform the next stages of our own PD process. We also use these three learning outcomes to structure our discussion and argue what these outcomes signalize in a broader context relevant to other PD practitioners working with users with ID.

A. The PD process should facilitate for the participation of caretakers as proxies

The use of proxies has been discussed in previous studies, e.g., as a way to help researchers learn about the goals of the end-users [7]. However, we argue that the caretakers specifically constitute appropriate proxies due to their ability to break down language barriers (as seen in [2]) that may prevent equalized power relations. Throughout the immersive process the proxies have been vital in bridging communicational gaps and is best exemplified by cases where the users have mixed forms of communication, using hand signs, body language and words to express themselves where either contextual knowledge, like having read the users diary(some of the ID keep a diary), or having the care-workers explicitly tell you what they think the users are communicating.

Balancing the power relations is a common challenge found within PD [3][5]. The caretakers' presence during design activities also increases the researchers' chances to successfully facilitate a space for mutual learning by supporting non-verbal and contextual forms of communication. This allows the users to express themselves, make choices, and be properly understood. Being able to speak your native (to the context) language in the design process can avoid issues of "model monopoly" and expand the universe of discourse [3]. Facilitating an arena that allows the users to practice collaborative working skills was seen as highly dependent on the presence of the caretaker in our study, and other studies are suggesting that this factor is often overlooked [14]. We also want to shed light on considerations related to the management of the design process [12], and advocate the use of caretakers to help lower the threshold for participation as they know how to initiate design discussions without disrupting ongoing everyday activities. One such instance is when the care-workers has approached the researcher during workhours to discuss topics of interest.

A final related topic not addressed in this paper but relevant to the balance of power relation is the inclusion of contextual probes [6][18] as another way to circumvent users finding themselves in a "passive role" [19] due to communication barriers.

B. The PD process should be organized as a long-term commitment

Identifying the appropriate point of departure in a PD process demands contextualized knowledge [9]. However, we argue that contextual insight over time contributes to mutual learning by allowing time and space to identify enough examples of the uniqueness of each situation being symbiotically shaped by the users, the context, and the caretakers' intimate knowledge of the situations. As such, we argue that long-term engagement is a way to converge on the uniqueness of each situation [13], as well as a way to avoid communities rejecting opportunities for collaboration due to short-burst facilitation [10]. Furthermore, we saw from our empirical context that committing to long-term engagement also contributed to both respect and trust [9], and the development of social relationships and skills [7]. This gave the activity center more time to familiarize themselves with our academic practice, which may be unfamiliar to certain communities [10].

Finally, we also advocate long-term presence as a means to support "channeling" the access to the context and the co-inhabitants' needs [8], which we argue is not a static matter, but rather something *"[...] continually in the making through everyday contestations among neighbors, relatives, colleagues and the material world they co-inhabit."* [20, p. 15].

C. The PD process should be built on top of already established forms of mutual learning

One core concept of PD is to enable participants to take control over their futures by affecting the technology that will help shape it [3]. Technology intended to support vulnerable users carries a responsibility of not affecting the users' everyday lives in a negative manner, for instance through use or even the inability to use. One such example is stigmatization through technology, which has previously been reported within our empirical context. [21] discusses the importance of not disrupting the sense of feeling "normal" for people with ID through technology that separates them from the rest of the world. Similar challenges have been reported in other demographics as well, e.g., PD involving older adults [22].

As such, we argue that immersion offers a chance to learn about everyday activities where people with ID and their caretakers already have established mutual learning through their everyday activities. We argue for building on top of established means of communication, which may also contribute to the participants accessing a sensation of mutual learning quicker [7], as well as taking more ownership of the design process and its outcomes [23]. Scaffolding the PD process around existing routines and habits allows for easier participation for caretakers who find themselves in a busy work environment. This may also reduce misunderstanding as caretakers more familiar with the individual users can assist the researchers in their interpretation of non-verbal forms of communication [24]. The researchers' knowledge of the context has allowed us to facilitate on top of already established arenas like using the "morning meeting" to conduct the *Explorative workshop II*.

VII. Conclusion

In this paper, we have reported from the early stages of a long-term collaboration with an activity center for people with ID. The PD process involved both the users and their caretakers as proxy designers. We argue for immersion as a strategy to gain contextual knowledge. The paper describes how underlying values of PD in combination with our immersive emphasis helped us identify examples of contextual insight that can inform future PD activities. We involved a total of 56 participants throughout four months. The data was gathered through six research methods, including participatory inquires, contextual observation documented through photographs, journal entries, explorative workshops, and interviews. The data was subject to two sets of analysis. The first analysis compared the level of agreement between one researcher with contextual knowledge and one researcher without, and the second analysis consisted of an inductive thematic analysis structured around two recurring topics (activity and communication). We ended the paper by presenting and discussing three concrete learning outcomes: (1) the PD process should facilitate for the participation of caretakers as proxies; (2) the PD process should be organized as a long-term commitment; and (3) the PD process should be built on top of already established forms of mutual learning.

References

[1] J. Perry and D. Felce, "Initial findings on the involvement of people with an intellectual disability in interviewing their peers about quality of life," *J. Intellect. Dev. Disabil.*, vol. 29, no. 2, pp. 164–171, Jun. 2004.

[2] J. L. Boyd-Graber *et al.*, "Participatory design with proxies: developing a desktop-PDA system to support people with aphasia," in *Proceedings of the SIGCHI Conference on Human Factors in Computing Systems*, 2006, pp. 151–160.

[3] T. Bratteteig, K. Bødker, Y. Dittrich, P. H. Mogensen, and J. Simonsen, "Organising principles and general guidelines for Participatory Design projects," *Routledge Handb. Particip. Des.*, p. 117, 2012.

[4] M. K. Bahus, "bruker," *Store norske leksikon*. [Online]. Available from: https://snl.no/bruker 2018.10.19

[5] M. Brereton, L. Sitbon, M. H. L. Abdullah, M. Vanderberg, and S. Koplick, "Design after design to bridge between people living with cognitive or sensory impairments, their friends and proxies," *CoDesign*, vol. 11, no. 1, pp. 4–20, Jan. 2015.

[6] M. Dawe, "'Let Me Show You What I Want': Engaging Individuals with Cognitive Disabilities and Their Families in Design," in *CHI '07 Extended Abstracts on Human Factors in Computing Systems*, New York, NY, USA, 2007, pp. 2177–2182.

[7] C. Putnam and L. Chong, "Software and technologies designed for people with autism: what do users want?," in *Proceedings of the 10th international ACM SIGACCESS conference on Computers and accessibility*, 2008, pp. 3–10.

[8] J. Blomberg and H. Karasti, "Positioning ethnography within participatory design," *Routledge Int. Handb. Particip. Des.*, pp. 86–116, 2012.

[9] H. Holone and J. Herstad, "Three Tensions in Participatory Design for Inclusion," in *Proceedings of the SIGCHI Conference on Human Factors in Computing Systems*, New York, NY, USA, 2013, pp. 2903–2906.

[10] F. Redhead and M. Brereton, "Growing local participation through long term design," in *Proceedings of Participatory Innovation Conference 2012*, 2012, pp. 1–4.

[11] N. Moraveji, J. Li, J. Ding, P. O'Kelley, and S. Woolf, "Comicboarding: using comics as proxies for participatory design with children," in *Proceedings of the SIGCHI conference on Human factors in computing systems*, 2007, pp. 1371–1374.

[12] P. Francis, S. Balbo, and L. Firth, "Towards co-design with users who have autism spectrum disorders," *Univers. Access Inf. Soc.*, vol. 8, no. 3, pp. 123–135, Aug. 2009.

[13] N. Hendriks, L. Huybrechts, A. Wilkinson, and K. Slegers, "Challenges in doing participatory design with people with dementia," presented at the Proceedings of the 13th Participatory Design Conference: Short Papers, Industry Cases, Workshop Descriptions, Doctoral Consortium papers, and Keynote abstracts - Volume 2, 2662196, 2014, pp. 33–36.

[14] M. Brosnan, S. Parsons, J. Good, and N. Yuill, "How can participatory design inform the design and development of innovative technologies for autistic communities?," *J. Assist. Technol. Hove*, vol. 10, no. 2, pp. 115–120, 2016.

[15] M. Crang and I. Cook, *Doing ethnographies*. Sage, 2007.

[16] T. Robertson, T. W. Leong, J. Durick, and T. Koreshoff, "Mutual learning as a resource for research design," in *Proceedings of the 13th Participatory Design Conference: Short Papers, Industry Cases, Workshop Descriptions, Doctoral Consortium papers, and Keynote abstracts-Volume 2*, 2014, pp. 25–28.

[17] V. Braun and V. Clarke, "Using thematic analysis in psychology," *Qual. Res. Psychol.*, vol. 3, no. 2, pp. 77–101, 2006.

[18] H. Hutchinson *et al.*, "Technology probes: inspiring design for and with families," in *Proceedings of the SIGCHI conference on Human factors in computing systems*, 2003, pp. 17–24.

[19] P. Börjesson, W. Barendregt, E. Eriksson, and O. Torgersson, "Designing Technology for and with Developmentally Diverse Children: A Systematic Literature Review," in *Proceedings of the 14th International Conference on Interaction Design and Children*, New York, NY, USA, 2015, pp. 79–88.

[20] J. Halse, Ed., *Rehearsing the future*. Copenhagen: The Danish Design School Press, 2010.

[21] P. K. A. Havgar, "Designing for Intellectual Disability: Combining User-Centered Design and Research through Design," *Master Thesis Univ. Oslo 2016*, 2016.

[22] S. G. Joshi, "Emerging ethical considerations from the perspectives of the elderly," presented at the CaTaC'14: Culture, Technology, Communication: Celebration, Transformation, New Directions, Oslo, Norway, 2014, pp. 186–203.

[23] C. Bigby, P. Frawley, and P. Ramcharan, "Conceptualizing Inclusive Research with People with Intellectual Disability," *J. Appl. Res. Intellect. Disabil.*, vol. 27, no. 1, pp. 3–12, Jan. 2014.

[24] L. C. L. de Faria Borges, L. V. L. Filgueiras, C. Maciel, and V. C. Pereira, "Customizing a Communication Device for a Child with Cerebral Palsy Using Participatory Design Practices: Contributions Towards the PD4CAT Method," in *Proceedings of the 11th Brazilian Symposium on Human Factors in Computing Systems*, Porto Alegre, Brazil, Brazil, 2012, pp. 57–66.

Empirical Heatmap Decomposition — A Fresh Look on Gaze Behavior

Saad Al-Baddai
Chair of Information Science, and CIML Group
Regensburg University
Regensburg, Germany
Email: saad.al-baddai@ur.de

Karema Al-Subari
and Elmar Lang
Institute of Biophysics
Regensburg University
Regensburg, Germany

Barbara Ströhl
and Bernd Ludwig
Chair of Information Science
Regensburg University
Regensburg, Germany

***Abstract*—The motivation for analyzing a person's gaze behavior stems from the eye-mind-hypothesis that correlates the observation of content by viewing it with its cognitive comprehension. A standard approach to quantitative analysis of gaze behavior is to analyze so called heatmaps generated by an eye tracker. This technical process is subject to noise. In order to compensate it, state-of-the-art eye tracking software smooths raw data using linear filters. In this paper, we present an alternative method based on interpolation. We provide empirical data that our method reproduces the actual gaze behavior more precisely. Furthermore, we introduce *Empirical Heatmap Decomposition* (EHD) to cluster eye movements into classes of similar frequency and amplitude. For evaluation, we present an analysis of gaze data that illustrates how EHD can uncover details in the observed gaze behavior that state-of-the-art heatmaps do not visualize.**

***Keywords*–Empirical Mode Decomposition; Eye tracking; Gaze Behavior; Sifting process**

I. INTRODUCTION

Understanding the gaze behavior of users while they read multimodal documents containing text, as well as images, graphics, or sketches is of vital interest for anybody engaged in designing digital content, e.g., of web pages, electronic product catalogs, or search engine result pages. This understanding is of particular importance if the digital content is to be generated automatically and in real-time as necessary for, e.g., interactive web pages, digital guides for sightseeing or museums. For these applications it is crucial to ensure that all content is perceived by the users immediately and provides positive user experience and joy of use.

A. Fixations and Saccades

For empirical investigations of the user behavior in situations as sketched above, eye tracking is a state-of-the-art method for monitoring the gaze of users. The reading and comprehension of text has been investigated using eye tracking, e.g., by [1], [2]. The analysis of the gaze data allows to reconstruct in which way, in which order, with which velocity, and in which regions of the digital content users view the presented material. From these observations, it can be concluded how users process the observations cognitively. As reported by [3], eyes could be attracted by some part of a visual scene and fixate these parts — named *Areas of Focus* (AoFs) — for a longer period. The process of identifying AoFs, based on the duration of eye fixations, can help in advanced analyses of gaze behavior [4], among others in the analysis of so called distractors: Assuming that regular patterns for reading text do exist, how do images or even animated material (e.g., videos on a web page) influence and — in particular — disturb the comprehension of the presented text? This question was investigated — among others — by [5]. The authors report empirical results that pictures, and in particular those that are unrelated to the topic of the text, distract and slow down the standard reading behavior. A similar observation has been made by [6]. Unrelated material when included in the presented digital content provides negative user experience and leads to reading patterns that are significantly different from the standard ones. The authors even use this observation to construct an algorithm that predicts whether a user struggles with the displayed content due to the presence of distractors.

While these results are highly relevant for the purposes mentioned before, it has to be noted that most analyses of gaze are based on heatmaps for fixations and plots for saccades that visualize all movements at once. However, eye movements differ

- in their speed and
- in the fixation duration

between subsequent movements [1], [2], [6]. However, only few researchers develop mathematical models for a quantitative analysis of such types of gaze (e.g., [7]).

This fact is quite astonishing as in other research areas (e.g., in medical image processing), it is common practice to decompose raw data using transformations (e.g., Fourier or Wavelet) in order to identify different causes for observations in a data set. More recently, a more more data driven approach called Empirical Mode

Decomposition (EMD) was pioneered by [8]. Based on an interpolation approach, EMD proved to reveal the characteristics of the textures in raw data sets more transparently and intuitively. As an elaboration of EMD, [9] applied Green's functions [10] for the interpolation problem (GiT-BEMD) in order to avoid artifacts and the immense computation load in the decomposition process that presented a major problem to the original version of EMD. GiT-BEMD works in real time and can therefore be used in real-time applications.

B. Gaze Decomposition

GiT-BEMD (as will be explained later) is interesting for gaze analysis as it provides an "all-in-one solution" for processing gaze data: While the standard EMD applies interpolation for separating sources in the signal, GiT-BEMD provides a substitute for linear filtering of raw gaze data. State-of-the-art commercial eye tracking software such as SMI's BeGaze applies Gaussian filters to reduce noise (see BeGaze Manual V 3.4, 2014, p. 204). However, this approach is problematic as the Gaussian kernel may blur away interesting data points. Recently, as an alternative, other filters, e.g., Savitzky-Golay filter [11], have been employed in eye-tracking area [12]–[14]. They are based on regression while GiT-BEMD interpolates data points and in this way tends to preserve original data as perfectly as possible.

C. Contribution

Even if we will provide data later that GiT-BEMD outperforms filters used in state-of-the-art software, adding the interpolation approach to smoothing gaze data is a side contribution of the present paper. Our main focus is on decomposing the smoothed signal. To the best of our knowledge, this is the first paper that investigates the value of decomposition methods to the analysis of gaze data. The algorithmic solution we developed is intended to be part of an open source tool box for analyzing eye tracking data. Similar other tool boxes have been implemented so far: *eSeeTrack* that focuses on the analysis of patterns of sequential gaze recordings [15], or *i*map [16] [17] which analyzes and compares eye movements under different conditions, iComp [18], ILAB [19], or GazeAlyze [20]. None of them however decomposes eye tracking data and therefore GiT-BEMD is an innovative extension to existing toolboxes.

To present our results, in Section II we introduce our empirical setup. Then we introduce the GiT-BEMD method in detail. In Section III we apply GT-BEMD on gaze data and provide first empirical results highlighting the performance of the new approach in Section IV. In Section V, we draw conclusions of the approach's impact on theoretical and practical issues of eye tracking for gaze and viewing analysis.

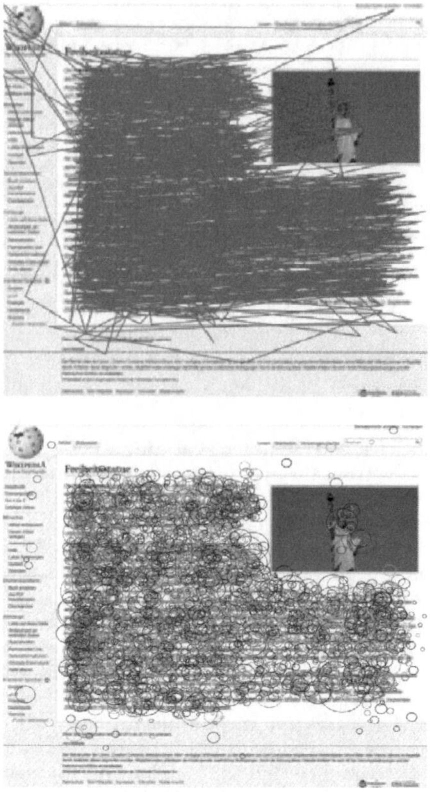

Figure 1. *Left*: Actual eye movement of participants during reading a Wikipedia page (scan paths observed by the eye tracker). *Right*: Fixations at the start and end point of a scan path (circle radius corresponds to the average fixation time)

II. SCENARIO

As [5], [6], we were interested in the effect of images on the reading behavior. An example of the digital content we investigated is the Wikipedia page in Figure 1. In particular, we wanted to know whether images that illustrate the textual information support the memorability of the digital content. According to the eye-mind-hypothesis [21], the gaze duration correlates with the cognitive processing time and depth of the perceived content. So it was surprising that participants mentioned details of an image on the Web page even if in the BeGaze heatmap no fixations on the image were registered (see Figure 4 left for an example).

In order to deeper analyze the collected gaze data and understand whether the described phenomenon was an artefact of the BeGaze's method to generate heatmaps, we applied four different methods on the same data set:

- The first method is the same as used by SMI's BeGaze analysis tool: the raw data is smoothed with a Gaussian filter.

- The second method is based on EMD: after Gaussian filtering, the data is decomposed using EMD (see [9]). It produces three heatmaps. Each of them groups fixations that are similar in terms of frequency and amplitude.
- The third method is GiT-BEMD without decomposition (and therefore analogous to the first method).
- The fourth method is GiT-BEMD including decomposition (analogous to the second method).

Our hypothesis is that EMD and GiT-BEMD reveal the gaze behavior more precisely than pure filtering. In order to measure the effect of the decomposition, we compute those areas of neighboring pixels in which all pixels have an average fixation time higher than to be expected under the assumption of a uniform probability distribution for fixations over the whole digital content. This is an unsupervised way to identify AoFs (area of focus). Using this notion, our hypothesis can be stated quantitatively. The decomposition based methods are more precise than pure filtering if they

- detect significantly more AoFs and
- in each detected AoF, identify more pixels fixated longer than chance (i.e., with probability higher than $1/\text{pixels in image}$)

than the pure filtering methods. Before presenting in Section IV the results using the unsupervised metric, in the next section we introduce the mathematical foundations of our approach and the empirical data we used to analyze the performance of GiT-BEMD to detect AoFs.

III. METHOD

We collected gaze data using an SMI RED 250mobile eye tracker at 250 Hz. In a controlled lab experiment, BA students of an introductory course to information science were asked to read a Wikipedia page presented to them for two minutes. They knew in advance that they had to answer fact retrieval questions about the page's content afterwards. We randomly chose 10 data sets from the described experiment to test the GiT-BEMD method.

A. Smoothing Heatmaps

The raw data produced by an eyetracker contains a list of subsequently fixated pixels during recording eye movements. Saccades can be calculated as difference vectors of subsequently fixated pixels. Due to noise caused by technical constraints of the eyetracker, for each fixated pixel in the raw data there is a certain chance that the observed fixation is a artifact. To account for this issue, raw data is smoothed. As already discussed above, the standard way to smoothing in commercial eyetracking software is Gaussian filtering that essentially is a linear operation on data windows to compute a weighted average from all pixels in the window. A major disadvantage of averaging is that isolated peaks in a window are blurred away. While this effect is even welcome in image processing, in the analysis of gaze data important fixation are eventually discarded leading to an erroneous reconstruction of the actual gaze behavior.

As an alternative, GiT-BEMD instead of averaging data locally, interpolates data globally. In this way, smoothing is achieved by spline interpolation. Smoothing then basically aims at finding the smoothest envelope surface passing through a grid of irregularly spaced extrema (i.e., the fixation count or duration of pixels from the raw data; see [9], [22], among others). The boundary value problem for a spline that interpolates fixated pixels can be stated with appropriate conditions for the spline's derivatives [23]. The resulting system of equations can then be solved using the family of Green's functions [10]. An envelope surface that fulfills all stated conditions can be expressed as

$$s(\mathbf{x}) = \sum_{n=1}^{N} w_n \Phi(\mathbf{x}, \mathbf{x}_n) \tag{1}$$

In this formula, $\mathbf{x}_u$ denotes any point where the surface is unknown, $\mathbf{x}_n$ represents the n-th recorded fixation, $\Phi(\mathbf{x}, \mathbf{x}_n)$ is the Green's function and w_n is the respective weight in the envelope representation. Calculating $s(\mathbf{x})$ for all pixels finally generates a smoothed heatmap.

An envelope surface is constructed in two steps: the first step estimates the weights $\mathbf{w} = [w_1 \quad w_2 \ldots w_P]$: The surface values $[s(\mathbf{x}_1), \ldots, s(\mathbf{x}_N)]^T \equiv \mathbf{c} = [c_1, c_2, \ldots, c_N]^T$ are known in a total of N pixels $\mathbf{x}_n$. Employing (1) for each of the known points $\mathbf{x}_n$, a linear system of N equations is obtained:

$$\mathbf{G}\mathbf{w} = \mathbf{c}$$

where n-th row of matrix $\mathbf{G}$ is the evaluation of the Green function $\Phi(\mathbf{x}_n, \mathbf{x}_m), m = 1, 2 \ldots N$. We solve the equation for the weights $\mathbf{w} = \mathbf{G}^{-1}\mathbf{c}$.

Corresponding slopes s_m in directions $\hat{\mathbf{n}}_m$ can be obtained by evaluating the relations

$$s_m = \sum_{m=1}^{N} w_m \nabla\Phi(\mathbf{x}_m - \mathbf{x}_n) \cdot \hat{\mathbf{n}}_m \qquad m = 1, \ldots, N.$$

The second step estimates the interpolating envelope surface: Using the weights $\mathbf{w}$, the value $s(\mathbf{x}_u) \equiv c_u$ of the envelope surface can be estimated at any point $\mathbf{x}_u$ by solving (1), which can be re-written as

$$c_u = \mathbf{w}^T \mathbf{\Phi}. \tag{2}$$

The vector $\mathbf{\Phi} = [\Phi(\mathbf{x}, \mathbf{x}_1) \; \Phi(\mathbf{x}, \mathbf{x}_2) \; \ldots \; \Phi(\mathbf{x}, \mathbf{x}_N)]^T$ contains the Green's function values of all distances between the N data constraints and the considered location.

GiT-BEMD implements the concept of smoothing

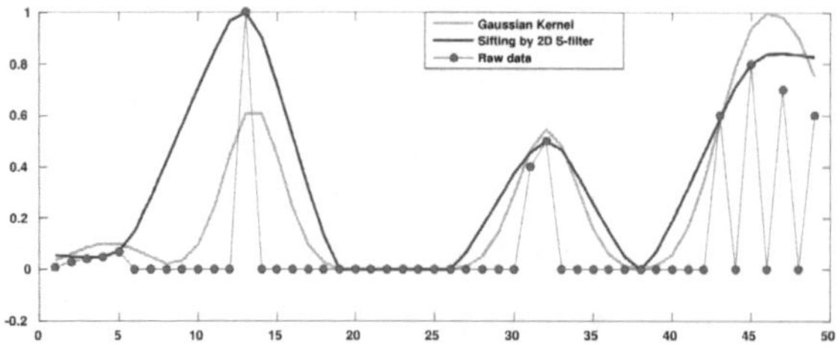

Figure 2. The effect of Gaussian smoothing and the S-filter in 1D. The y axis shows normalised fixation durations.

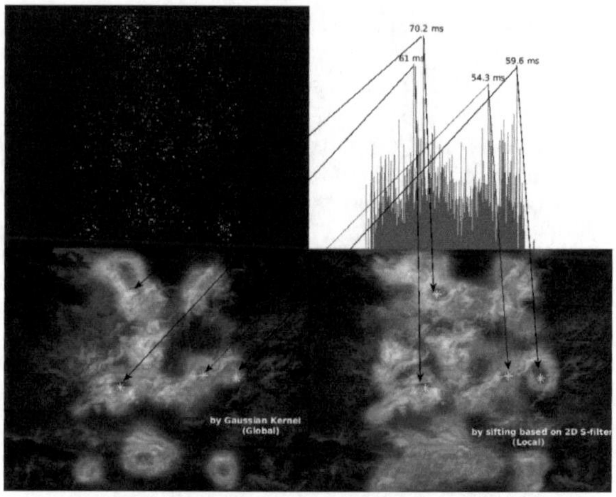

Figure 3. Effects of Gaussian smoothing and the GiT-BEMD. *Top left:* map of actual fixations. *Top right:* some fixation durations. *Bottom left:* Gaussian smoothing. *Bottom right:* GiT-BEMD

described above with one extension: As eyetracking data normally is sparse (i.e., for many pixels there is no fixation at all), adding white noise is required to decrease the computational load of building an envelope surface by interpolating from the extracted extrema. Without added noise, zero crossings would be considered as local minima and maxima that actually do not exist. After a surface has been constructed by applying the described concept, the artificially added noise can be ignored and does not disturb the further analysis.

Figure 2 illustrates the approach and shows a first comparison to Gaussian smoothing. It is easy to see that the GiT-BEMD aims to actually interpolate the raw data points while the Gaussian smoothing calculates sort of a "compromise". This is true for regions where a few pixels have many fixations as in the case of the leftmost extremum. Such situations are typical for eyetracking data and therefore we conclude that GiT-BEMD has the potential to outperform Gaussian smoothing.

For the two dimensional case, the same effect is illustrated in Figure 3. In the top left, one can see the (sparse) map of actual fixations while in the top right for some examples the fixation durations are plotted. Some extrema are given explicitly. The map in the bottom left illustrates how Gaussian smoothing influences the relevance of these extrema while on the right the map computed by GiT-BEMD is displayed. It is obvious that Gaussian smoothing tends to build large prominent regions (as the 70.2 ms) when the neighbors of a pixel show similarly high fixation durations. On the other hand, isolated pixels such as the 59.6 ms are "smoothed away" and considered as noise. GiT-BEMD however preserves large, but also detects small regions.

B. Decomposition of Heatmaps

Gaze data is produced by eye movements of different velocity and fixations (i.e., eye movements with velocity $v = 0$) of different durations. Therefore, it is reasonable to separate the gaze data into several components for movements of similar velocity (i.e., frequency) and analyze the durations (i.e., amplitudes). Such separations are common and well-known algorithms for their computation are Fourier or Wavelet transforms. However, as with Gaussian smoothing, Fourier or Wavelet transforms are classical approaches, but not suited optimally for eyetracking data. Instead, the GiT-BEMD decomposes data by constructing a series of surface envelopes for a given data set. In essence, EHD iteratively applies the GiT-BEMD smoothing explained above on the raw data without adding any artificial noise. Once a surface function has been constructed, it gets subtracted from the initial data, and the procedure is repeated on the pixelwise difference. In this way, EHD can decompose a heatmap $H(m, n)$ into several component heatmaps. This kind of decomposition can be computed effectively by using a so called sifting process [8], [24]–[27] as follows:

$r_{-1}(m,n) := H(m,n)$;
$k := 0$;
while $r_{k-1}(m,n) \neq 0$ *or* $r_{k-1}(m,n)$ *is not monotone* **do**
  $i := 0$;
  $I_{k,i}(m,n) := r_{k-1}(m,n)$;
  while $I_{k,i}(x)$ *has non-negligible local mean* **do**
    $U(m,n)$ is a cubic spline through all local maxima of $I_{k,i}(m,n)$;
    $L(m,n)$ is a cubic spline through all local minima of $I_{k,i}(m,n)$;
    $\text{mean}_{k,i}(m,n) := \frac{1}{2}\left(U(m,n) + L(m,n)\right)$;
    $I_{k,i}(m,n) := I_{k,i}(m,n) - \text{mean}_{k,i}(m,n)$;
    $i := i + 1$;
  end
  $\text{IMF}_k(m,n) := I_{k,i}(m,n)$;
  $r_k(m,n) := r_{k-1}(m,n) - \text{IMF}_k(m,n)$;
  $k := k + 1$;
end

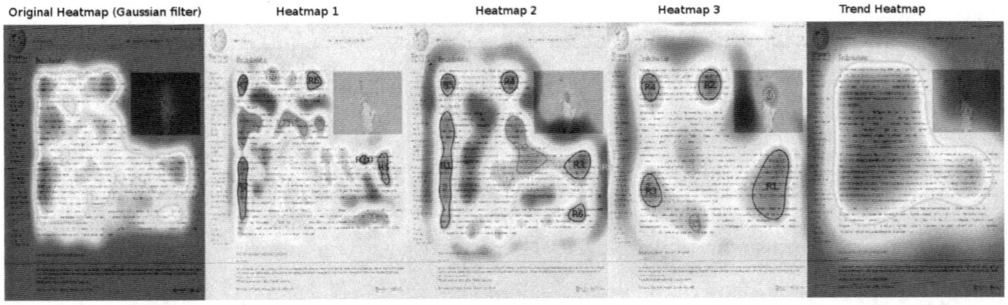

Figure 4. Heatmap (Gaussian smoothing) Components 1, 2, and 3 extracted by EHD. Boundary lines surround detected AoFs.

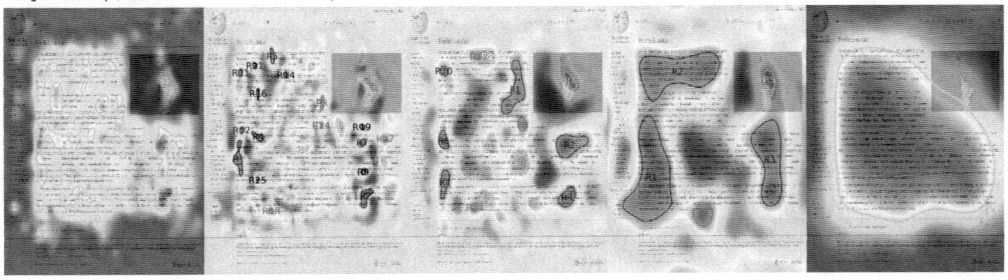

Figure 5. Heatmap (GiT-BEMD). Components 1, 2, and 3 extracted by EHD. Boundary lines surround detected AoFs.

The result of this process is the following decomposition of the original heat map $H(m, n)$ into the approximative decomposed heatmap $\hat{H}(m, n)$:

$$\hat{H}(m, n) = \sum_{j=1}^{k} \text{IMF}_j(m, n) \tag{3}$$

Note that $\hat{H}(m, n)$ depends on the parameters and stop criteria. For any $\hat{H}(m, n)$, in each extracted component $\text{IMF}_j(m, n)$ different AoFs can be detected.

IV. Evaluation

In this section, we will present an example which can illustrate the efficiency of the approach we are advocating in this paper. In our Wikipedia experiment, we are interested in analyzing the reading behavior. In particular, we want to know whether test persons fixate the image that is a distractor for reading the text. This issue has been investigated already in previous work [5], [6], as outlined in the introduction.

A. Baseline: State-of-the-Art Eyetracking Software

In Figure 1, one can observe that there are fixations on the statue of liberty, but not many. We use this data as ground truth in our evaluation. We first normalize all fixation durations to the interval $[0; 1]$. While the average duration on the whole Wikipedia page is 0.55, the highest duration in the area of the statue of liberty is 0.1869 and the fixated pixels are quite isolated in comparison to the pixels in the text area. However, as we know from the post-test-questionnaires, all test persons remembered the statue on the page although they could not know about the image as the page was designed just for the experiment imitating a Wikipedia page. Therefore, according to the eye-mind hypothesis, the test persons must have seen the image. This is in line with the fixations in the raw data, but contradicted by the results of the BeGaze filtering. It becomes obvious that state-of-the-art heatmaps eventually provoke researchers to draw wrong conclusions.

B. Smoothing by Interpolating raw data

However, as can be seen in Figure 4 on the left, after Gaussian smoothing there is no AoF detected in the area of the statue as the highest fixation duration is lower than elsewhere and the surrounding pixels do not contribute fixations. So, the information is regarded as noise and discarded even if the area must have been fixated. GiT-BEMD's output is shown in Figure 5. Here, AoFs are detected (see the areas enclosed by a green line). In order to analyze this intuitive observation systematically, for each of the ten test persons, we computed the number of pixels fixated longer than by chance (i.e., their fixation duration is 0.5 or more) and how many of them had still a duration of 0.5 or more after filtering. In an ideal heatmap, the difference between both numbers should be 0. However, for Gaussian smoothing the difference is 19.7 while for GiT-BEMD it is 6.9 on average over all 10 trails. The difference between both averages is significant ($p < 0.01$): Even without applying EHD, GiT-BEMD better preserves fixation details while still reducing noise in the raw data.

C. Decomposition of Heatmaps

The benefit of the new EHD can be understood when considering the three components displayed in the middle of Figure 4. They are ordered from high to low velocity of the eye movements. Component 2 in the middle already highlights relevant fixations on the statue's head. However, they are not significant as other areas in this component (see the bounding lines around the named AoF). Component 3 then reveals a significant AoF on the head when only slow eye movements are considered. We conclude that EHD allows us to identify different for of gaze behavior caused by the nature of the observed object: Recognizing text requires many fast movements while identifying a known object by retrieving it from memory can only be achieved by slow movements scanning an AoF in detail.

EHD provides an even more exact analysis (see Figure 5): significant AoFs are found in all three components. The new approach is obviously more reliable in detecting as many actual fixations as possible. This claim can be backed by statistics: in component 1 (fast eye movements) the difference between actual and detected fixations is -1.7 for Gaussian smoothing and -30.0 for GiT-BEMD ($p < 0.001$). Independently of the filter used, EHD detects more fixations than could be expected assuming the same chance for each pixel. Note however, that in this component the fixation duration is very low. Consequently, pixels can be fixated longer than by chance relatively easily. This component therefore gives an overview of the parts of the page the test persons fixated while scanning the complete digital content superficially. For component 2 (average velocity of eye movement) the differences are 12.7 and -13.8. Gaussian smoothing again detects fewer fixations ($p < 0.001$) and now already misses fixations that are relevant actual fixations. Finally for component 3 the difference for Gaussian smoothing is 16.2, while for GiT-BEMD it is 5.9. Again, Gaussian smoothing misses more fixations, however in this component the difference is no longer significant ($p = 0.07687$). In this component, slow movements in particular during reading the text are observed. Saccades are short and therefore the Gaussian kernel removes fewer fixations as noisy compared to both other components. The comparison of the trend of both approaches reveals no significant differences (25.7 vs. 24.3 with $p = 0.7872$).

Tab. I summarizes the comparison of both approaches. The row *Original* provides evidence that the third method outperforms the first one as hypothesized earlier in Section II. The columns *Gaussian* and *GiT* indicate that the fourth method is superior to the second.

TABLE I. NUMBER OF DETECTED AoF PER COMPONENT

Heatmap	p-value	Gaussian	GiT	
Original	$p < 0.001$	7.70	20.50	$***$
Component 1	$p < 0.001$	29.10	57.40	$***$
Component 2	$p < 0.001$	14.7	41.2	$***$
Component 3	$p < 0.01$	11.20	21.50	$**$
Trend	$p > 0.05$	1.70	3.10	

V. Discussion

In this paper, we presented EHD as an approach to decompose gaze heatmaps according to the velocity of eye movements. We showed that the approach can be implemented effectively and even works in real-time — an interesting fact for pervasive computing. We validated the approach by analyzing gaze data from an experiment in which users had to read a simulated Wikipedia page and after the were tested which objects on the page they could remember. For a quantitative evaluation, we applied an unsupervised approach to detect AoFs. We chose this metric, as it does not require an expert to label AoFs. In our view, in this way we could avoid biases stemming from the expert's valuation of the digital content. Assuming instead that each pixel has the same chance to attract the focus of test persons, therefore enables a fairer evaluation of different methods to analyze gaze data. In future work, we will measure the effects of EHD by comparing the ability of test persons to recall certain details of the digital content and correlate their performance with the results produced by each analysis method. Assuming the eye-mind hypothesis to be valid, better recall performance o content must correlate statistically with a higher probability of the respective AoF to have been viewed.

The evaluation results show that EHD outperforms commercial state-of-the-art software packages for gaze behavior. It can identify AoFs which are not present in the heatmap if raw data is smoothed only, but not decomposed. Furthermore, EHD can distinguish different types of gaze behavior. Depending on the speed of the eye movement and the duration of fixations, EHD detects different AoFs. Therefore, EHD allows us to better understand how persons perceive content and in which chronological order they process it cognitively.

VI. Future Work

In the future, we will compare GiT-BEMD filtering to regression approaches such as the Savitzky-Golay filter [11] and continue the comparison with the state of the art in order to implement new toolboxes for gaze data analysis which we will make available to the public and use ourselves to investigate human reading behavior.

REFERENCES

[1] T. Vo, B. S. U. Mendi, and T. Gedeon, Gaze Pattern and Reading Comprehension. Berlin, Heidelberg: Springer Berlin Heidelberg, 2010, pp. 124–131.

[2] D. Fahey, T. Gedeon, and D. Zhu, Document Classification on Relevance: A Study on Eye Gaze Patterns for Reading. Berlin, Heidelberg: Springer Berlin Heidelberg, 2011, pp. 143–150.

[3] A. Poole and L. J. Ball, "Eye tracking in human computer interaction and usability research: Current status and future prospects," In C. Ghaoui (Eds.), Encyclopedia of human computer interaction, 2005, pp. 111–219.

[4] D. D. Salvucci, "An interactive model based environment for eye-movement protocol analysis and visualization," In Proceedings of the Symposium on Eye Tracking Research and Applications, 2000, pp. 57–63.

[5] D. Beymer, P. Z. Orton, and D. M. Russell, An Eye Tracking Study of How Pictures Influence Online Reading. Berlin, Heidelberg: Springer Berlin Heidelberg, 2007, pp. 456–460.

[6] V. Navalpakkam, J. Rao, and M. Slaney, "Using gaze patterns to study and predict reading struggles due to distraction," in CHI '11 Extended Abstracts on Human Factors in Computing Systems, ser. CHI EA '11. New York, NY, USA: ACM, 2011, pp. 1705–1710.

[7] R. Rosenberg and C. Klein, "The moving eye of the beholder: Eye tracking and the perception of paintings," in Art, Aesthetics, and the Brain, J. P. Huston, M. Nadal, F. Mora, L. F. Agnati, and C. J. C. Conde, Eds. Oxford: Oxford University Press, 2015, ch. 5, pp. 79–108.

[8] N. E. Huang, Z. Shen, S. R. Long, M. L. Wu, H. H. Shih, Q. Zheng, N. C. Yen, C. C. Tung, and H. H. Liu, "The empirical mode decomposition and Hilbert spectrum for nonlinear and non-stationary time series analysis," Proc. Roy. Soc. London A, vol. 454, 1998, pp. 903–995.

[9] S. Al-Baddai, K. Al-Subari, A. Tomé, J. J. Solé-Casals, and E. Lang, "A green's function-based bi-dimensional empirical mode decomposition," Information Sciences, vol. 348, 2016, pp. 305–321.

[10] Y. Melnikov, , and M. Melnikov, Green's Functions: Construction and Applications, ser. De Gruyter studies in mathematics. De Gruyter, 2012.

[11] S. J. Orfanidis, Introduction to Signal Processing. Englewood Cliffs, NJ: Prentice Hall, 1996.

[12] H.-K. Ko, D. M. Snodderly, and M. Poletti, "Eye movements between saccades: Measuring ocular drift and tremor," Vision Research, vol. 122, 2016, pp. 93–104.

[13] W. Dai, I. Selesnick, J.-R. Rizzo, S. J. Rucker, and T. Hudson, "A nonlinear generalization of the savitzky-golay filter and the quantitative analysis of saccades," Journal of Vision, vol. 17(9), 2017, pp. 1–15.

[14] S. Al-gawwam and M. Benaissa, "Robust eye blink detection based on eye landmarks and savitzky-golay filtering," Information, vol. 9(4), 2018, pp. 1–11.

[15] H. Y. Tsang, M. Tory, and C. Swindells, "eSeeTrack-visualizing sequential fixation patters." IEEE Transactions on Visualization and Computer Graphics, vol. 16(6), 2010, pp. 953–962.

[16] R. Caldara and S. Miellet, "iMap: A novel method for statistical fixation mapping of eyemovement data," Behavior Research Methods, vol. 43, no. 3, 2011, pp. 864–878.

[17] J. Lao, S. Miellet, C. Pernet, N. Sokhn, and R. Caldara, "imap4: An open source toolbox for the statistical fixation mapping of eye movement data with linear mixed modeling." Behavior Research Methods, 2016, pp. 1–17.

[18] J. Heminghous and A. T. Douchowski, "iComp: A tool for scanpath visualization and comparison," in Proc.of the 3rd Symposium on Applied Perception in Graphics and Visualization, 2006, pp. 152–152.

[19] D. R. Gitelman, "ILAB: A program for post experimental eye movement analysis," Behavior Research Methods, Instruments, & Computers, vol. 34, no. 4, 2002, pp. 605–612.

[20] C. Berger, M. Winkels, A. Lischke, and J. Hoppner, "GazeAlyze: a MATLAB toolbox for the analysis of eye movement data." Behavior Research Methods, vol. 44, 2012, pp. 404–419.

[21] M. A. Just and P. A. Carpenter, "A theory of reading: from eye fixations to comprehension." Psychological review, vol. 87, no. 4, 1980, p. 329.

[22] P. Wessel and J. M. Becker, "Interpolation using a generalized green's function for a spherical surface spline in tension," Geophysical Journal International, vol. 174, no. 1, July 2008, pp. 21–28.

[23] P. Wessel and D. Bercovici, "Interpolation with splines in tension: A green's function approach," Mathematical Geology, vol. 30, no. 1, 1998, pp. 77–93.

[24] N. E. Huang, M. L. Wu, S. R. Long, S. Shen, w. Qu, P. Gloersen, and K. Fan, "A confidence limit for the empirical mode decomposition and Hilbert spectral analysis," The Royal Society, 2003, pp. 2317–2345.

[25] Z. Wu and N. E. Huang, "A study of the characteristics of white noise using the empirical mode decomposition method," Proceedings of the Royal Society of London. Series A: Mathematical, Physical and Engineering Sciences, vol. 460(2046), 2004, pp. 1597–1611.

[26] ——, "Ensemble Empirical Mode Decomposition: a noise-assisted data analysis method," Adv. Adaptive Data Analysis, vol. 1(1), 2009, pp. 1–41.

[27] Z. Wu, N. E. Huang, and X. Chen, "The Multidimensional Ensemble Empirical Mode Decomposition Method," Adv. Adaptive Data Analysis, vol. 1, 2009, pp. 339–372.

Down the Rabbit Hole:

Five Hedonic and Pragmatic Facets of Audience Engagement in Playable Stories

Daniel Echeverri
School of Design
The Hong Kong Polytechnic University
Kowloon, Hong Kong
email: 17901330r@connect.polyu.hk

Huaxin Wei
School of Design
The Hong Kong Polytechnic University
Kowloon, Hong Kong
email: huaxin.wei@polyu.edu.hk

***Abstract*— This paper presents an exploratory study that relates hedonic and pragmatic aspects of audience engagement to playable stories on different interactive media. Eighteen participants discussed their individual experiences with three different interactive adaptations of Lewis Carrol's *Alice in Wonderland*. The paper illustrates the initial findings of how *fun, attraction, excitement, satisfaction,* and *frustration*, as facets of audience engagement, are shaped by different attributes that are related to the affordances of each medium.**

Keywords-Playable Stories; Interactive Narrative; User Engagement; Hedonic Experience; Play

I. Introduction

This work in progress aims to explore the attributes that shape audiences' experience with playable stories, by mapping out the relations between engagement dimensions with attributes of the narrative media. This study is driven by a larger research that seeks to identify possible methods of interaction that can be applied to a model intended for playable interactive narratives. In it, the participants played with one of three interactive adaptations of *Alice in Wonderland*. Each represented a different mode of interaction: hypertext, touch-based and naturally tangible. This paper intends to present a structure that explores the relationship between different facets of audience engagement and medium-specific attributes of interactive narratives. Most of the published work in regards to engagement in interactive narratives, especially games and video games, has been grounded in quantitative methods (see [13] for details). Nonetheless, Ijsselsteijn et al. [7] argue that gaming experiences are so experientially rich that by just measuring engagement and involvement, other dimensions such as fun are left out of the traditional metrics. Additionally, Boyle et al. [2] note that in most studies of this type, the attention is placed on usability factors instead of the enjoyment of the game itself. Using an alternative and complementary approach that relies on semi-structured interviews, this paper intends to present instead an account of a study grounded on emotional and subjective aspects of a playable narrative experience. This paper is organized in the following way: Section 2 will introduce briefly the key concepts and related works relevant to the study as well as its procedures. Section 3 will present the findings, illustrating some attributes explored in the paper with statements from some of the participants. Finally, Section 4 will discuss the conclusions and future work of the study.

II. Related Works and Background

A. *Concepts and Literatre*

Playable Stories, a primordial component of this study, is defined by Ryan [19] as the narratives in which the audience observes the evolution of the story world, focusing on aesthetic pleasure, and free play. User engagement, on the other hand, can be characterized by the depth of someone's investment when interacting with a system and the context of the experience [11][15]. For example, Chapman [3] talks about *engagement* as something that draws, attracts and holds a person's attention, while Laurel [8] mentions playfulness, and sensory integration. Other concepts involved are *flow*, where there is intrinsic motivation, sustained focus, and loss of awareness, as well as *play*, as something that encourages learning, creativity, an urge to satisfy needs and a sense of competition or collaboration [4][17].

One of the most cited studies of user engagement is the User Engagement Scale (UES) originally developed by O'Brien and Toms and further revised by O'Brien et al. [11][12]. Among many adopters of UES, Wiebe et al.'s [22] adapted the Scale specifically for engagement in video game-based environments, which is highly relevant to this work. In their framework, which incorporates O'Brien & Toms's and Hassenzahl et al.'s theories, user engagement dimensions are classified into two categories: hedonic and pragmatic [6]. Hedonic aspects include pleasure, aesthetics and novelty, whereas pragmatic aspects include usability and whether the user would want to use it again. For games, it is commonly believed that user engagement is mainly driven by hedonic rather than pragmatic qualities [22]. These aspects were further developed into a four-factor model of User Engagement that considered [11]:

- **Aesthetic Appeal:** related to the perceived attractiveness and visual appeal of the medium.
- **Focused Attention:** describes the feeling of absorbed in the interaction and losing track of time during the experience.
- **Perceived Usability:** the affect, either positive or negative, experienced because of the interaction and the degree of control and effort.
- **Reward:** associated also to *Satisfaction* [22], it describes the success of the interaction, the curiosity, and interest in the medium while having fun with it.

B. Study Procedure

Our first study covered eighteen individual sessions with the same number of participants from The Hong Kong Polytechnic University, including eleven Ph.D. students, four undergraduates, and three academic staff. Only one was a native English speaker, while the rest were non-native speakers from Europe, South East Asia and Mainland China. Ten were women; eight were men, all between 20 to 35 years old. The participants were based on a convenience sample recruited through a mass email as well as posters placed across different other departments on campus. Before each session, the participants were asked to complete the Common European Framework (CEFR) Can-Do self-assessment grid. This self-assessing tool allows the participants to categorize themselves as language speakers in three groups A (basic), B (independent), C (proficient) and 2 levels respectively. Each level describes the learner abilities in terms of reading, listening, speaking and writing the language [21]. One participant categorized himself as a beginner, eight as independent and nine as proficient English speakers. The purpose of this initial assessment was to single out problems caused by language abilities during the experiment.

At the beginning of the session, participants were asked to pick from a closed bag a piece of paper that contained the name of the adaptation they were going to interact and play. The chosen adaptations were Matthias Conrady's hypertext version *Allice Falling*, Emmanuel Paletz's *The Alice App* designed for touch-based tablet devices and Robert Sabuda's movable book *Alice's Adventures in Wonderland* (Figure 1). All participants read and interacted specifically with *Down the Rabbit Hole*, the first chapter of the *Alice in Wonderland* story, which appeared across all adaptations. Although the textual details of this chapter differ and might marginally influence the results, the three adaptations cover the same plot and characters with little to no changes in the narrative itself. Once finished, the participants completed a slightly varied version of the aforementioned UES questionnaire. Our survey contained 29 of the of the original 30 questions outlined by O'Brien et al. [12]. The

Figure 1. Media used in the study. **Left:** Matthias Conrady's *Alice Falling*. **Center:** Emmanuel Paletz's *The Alice App* **Right:** Robert Sabuda's *Alice's Adventures in Wonderland*.

discarded question –PU8 in the UES– addressed a matter associated to productivity and not applicable to interacting with a playable narrative. The session concluded with a semi-structured interview partly inspired by Fullerton's suggested list of general postgame questions for playtesters that focus on the experiential aspects of the game [5]. Other questions invited participants to elaborate on the reward and aesthetic appeal attributes from the UES, to ensure the interview to cover a wide range of emotions and experiences. All the sessions were video and audio recorded for a total of 12 hours worth of material. The duration of each session was, on average, 40 minutes; out of those, 5 minutes were dedicated to the Can-Do statements, 12 minutes for the participants to read and interact with the story, 5 minutes to complete the UES and 13 minutes for the semi-structured interviews.

Each session was later transcribed and grouped based initially on the medium the participants interacted with. Following Smith's *Shared Experiences* [20], each collection of interviews was analyzed and coded, later grouped into themes and then connected as clusters. The analysis of the information gathered was done through an inductive approach. Considering that our primary interest was to look at emotional and affective responses of the participants, the primary themes identified were mainly drawn from the key moments when participants were discussing their affective experiences:

- **Fun:** *pleasure without purpose. Framed in two types: solipsistic where every individual gets to define their version of fun, and consensual, where fun involves physical pleasure, abandonment, and debauchery* [10].
- **Attraction**: *object-based emotions or (appealing-ness)* It *concerns the person's attitudes and relative to their predispositions to like or dislike certain aspects* [14].
- **Excitement**: a positive emotional state that consists of *high levels of pleasure and arousal [18].*
- **Satisfaction:** framed *as the pleasure or contentment one feels when s/he performs a required or desired action and experiences the result* [9].
- **Frustration:** is a *phenomenon that happens from the struggle to fulfill a will or particular goal* [1].

The first four aspects are classified as hedonic experiences while frustration as a pragmatic one. Although frustration can be classified also as a hedonic experience, the Perceived Usability attribute of the UES focuses specifically in frustration and other cognitive aspects of the experience [12] [22]. Considering these themes, the statements of each medium (hypertext, touch-base, and tangible) were grouped based on the attributes above. Only then, they were coded initially and organized. Some of the statements were placed across several attributes as they described different phenomena. There were statements that were split into separate entries due to their length and their theme, as sometimes the participants expressed multiple ideas in a single sentence.

III. FINDINGS

This section focuses on the qualitative findings from the exploratory analysis of the interview results, which concern the emotions and experiences perceived and discussed by the participants. Based on the language and comprehension criteria established for this study, the contributions from seventeen out of the eighteen participants were considered suitable. The excluded participant scored himself as A1 in his language proficiency assessment and his overall narrative comprehension was substantially lower compared to the other participants. The remaining participants presented an acceptable level of language proficiency –equal or above B1 in the self-assessment, and an adequate comprehension of the narrative –being able to recall key events in the story. Gender or age of the participants were not an excluding parameter of this study.

The interview findings aim to establish a relationship and a hierarchy between the experiences observed and the medium's affordances that induced them. These affordances are mostly experiential and their supporting attributes or features are of hedonic nature (Figure 2). This can be explained by Pucillo and Cascini's [16] characterization for experiential affordances, which are enabled by a product's hedonic features to contribute to users' basic psychological needs.

The UES results, on the other hand, showed a comparative tendency among the three media on the four dimensions of engagement. For example, participants report higher scores in Focused Attention and Reward for the naturally tangible story (i.e., the movable book). Nevertheless, as the sample size was small, the current study findings weigh more on the interview than the UES questionnaire results.

A. *Fun*

The participants who played with the hypertext adaptation stated that the narrative ambiguity originated their sense of fun. This was most likely instigated by the plot, usually dependent on the adapting author, the navigational position of the hypertext, and certain interactive elements available to the audience. The feeling of uncertainty stimulated their imagination, with the support of such visual stimuli as animation or changes in text color and shape. Regarding this, Participant *5A stated: "I deliberately... when was like: Do cats eat bats? It didn't stop looping [...] I kept trying not to press anything and [to] see what happens."*

In the touch-based tablet adaptation, fun was derived from the sense of feeling curious and anticipation about what happens in the narrative, with the support of dynamic elements that generate sound or motion. Because of the medium's perceptible nature, manipulation is also essential to foster fun; sometimes it can be exploratory, while in other cases it can have a diegetic effect. Participant *6B mentioned "I was quite curious, like when I saw... when it started there was the key basically.... and it fell down when I tested... so it made me expect in every page some kind of animation, so I was just checking if there was anything."*

In the naturally tangible narrative instead, the dynamics of motion and manipulation of three-dimensional objects contributed to the sense of ludic play, which was reported to have nurtured

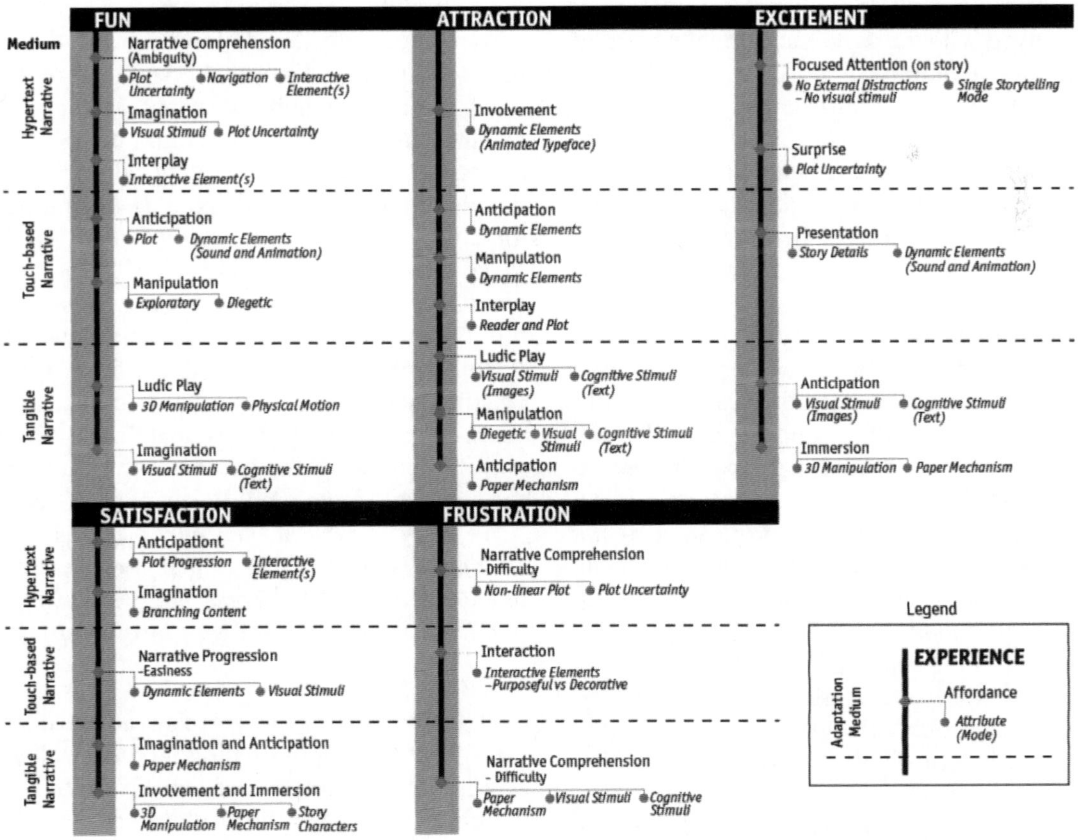

Figure 2. Attributes and modes between the experiences observed and the medium's affordances that induced them.

their imagination. This was also grounded in the different visual (images) and cognitive (text) stimulus of the experience. The latter especially, not only in the narrative itself but also for example, on the labels placed in the mechanisms that entice to act upon them. Participant *2C stated, "It's kind of like... you can have the playable thing to match what is happening in the story"* Only the participants that interacted with this medium mentioned being able to "play" with the story, while those that experienced the hypertext and touch-based narratives described the experience as being just fun but never mentioned the idea of ludic play. Although all narrative media offered a way of playing with the story, it seems that the sense of play develops better and is more rewarding in media that allow direct, three-dimensional manipulation.

B. *Attraction*

The second hedonic facet is the sense of attraction that entices audiences to interact with the narrative. In hypertext narratives for example, feeling involved with the dynamic elements seemed to be the most attractive affordance. This is particularly true with animated typeface that entailed the reader acting on it before moving forward in the story, for example Participant 1A expressed: *"I need[ed] to chase the words... like the "Cats eat bats" [...] when the first sentence is popping out, I need to chase it... yeah, chasing something."*

Due to its manipulable nature, the different dynamics embedded in the touch-based narrative were the most attractive affordances, especially when several elements stimulated the participant's curiosity, which sets up their anticipation. About this, Participant 2B said, *"I was just turning a page, and I noticed that when I was trying to turn the page, there were some movements, so that made me curious that, while in the previous pages I did not do that... so that made me curious that there might be a purpose."* This also led to interplay between the reader and the plot. In some cases, it had a purpose like seeing how the character grew, while in other cases it turned into exploratory free play with the interactive elements.

In the naturally tangible narrative, the images and the text in the book were cognitive and visual stimuli to support play and manipulation that has a diegetic effect in the story. The participants expressed that the ingenuity of the medium –as having functional paper mechanisms– raised their curiosity with the experience. For example, Participant *4C* noted that *"... once you started seeing all these different elements and characters, the story starts taking shape and it all happens in your mind as you read."*

C. *Excitement*

Feeling excited changes the way an audience engages with a narrative. The participants expressed that in the hypertext narrative, it was the curiosity and the anticipation or surprise of an outcome coming from an uncertain part in the plot that generated excitement in them. Another essential affordance of excitement in this medium is the ability to focus on the story; probably due to the lack of external distractions such as images and a single storytelling mode.

In contrast, excitement was the least discussed in touch-based narratives, perhaps because the participants were already familiar with this mode of interaction and did not feel novel or foreign. There were cases in which the participants highlighted excitement from the dynamic elements of the narrative such as the moving images and other details of the story. Participant *3B* mentioned about this: *"...see there is a picture of a British king there... little details like that... I'm not sure everyone would pick that...but I appreciated that."*

In the naturally tangible narrative, the images of the movable book along with the texts of the story, acted as visual and cognitive stimulus, to fuel the sense of curiosity and anticipate the next. Playing and manipulating the paper mechanisms intensify the sense of immersion. Participant *4C* concluded, "*You don't know what the next page will give you, so there is a sense of... unexpected... something unexpected, [...] like, something folded shows up... you flip it, and you discover more detail[s]*".

D. *Satisfaction*

The process of engagement is not exclusively linear, but a series of looping moments. Satisfaction seems to be mostly derived from that looping experience. In the case of the hypertext narrative, the sense of contentment was constructed by the plot progression based on specific actions on a branching point in the narrative or acting through one of the interactive elements. In both cases, this was motivated by anticipating the outcomes. This cause-effect factor also nurtured imagination, as the participants had to create mental images of what was happening in the story. For example, according to participant *5A "When there is some underlying hidden text... for example what she thinks, it's not bulky at the very start, but when you read it you want to know what she thinks, that's why you click on it. And then it says what she is thinking."*

The visual features of the touch-based narrative allowed the participants to feel that the medium augmented the narrative and their imagination through different dynamic elements on the screen. These elements also eased the readers understanding of the text and what they thought the writer intended to tell. This was especially important to the participants with lesser second-language skills.

In the naturally tangible narrative, evidently, the sense of satisfaction comes from the cognitive stimuli of manipulating the paper mechanisms that produced movement and inspired their imagination and curiosity. Contrasting the other media, satisfaction was usually discussed from a more expressive standpoint as the participants felt happy and involved with the story and the characters. This also developed a sense of immersion as the plot progressed. For example, Participant 5C highlighted *"...and when we see some pop-up images like [the] big forest... although we are not in the forest, it made me feel like we are there... it's so huge it made me feel like I'm part of it... I'm part of Alice's story."*

E. Frustration

This experience is directly connected to the pragmatic qualities of user engagement. It is worth discussing as interesting statements were collected regarding frustration. It appears that the non-linear nature of the hypertext narrative is one of the main sources of frustration, especially when feeling uncertain about the plot position and the expectations on functional factors as well as the plot itself. Seemingly, the frustrations in hypertext narratives came from a series of chained factors that unfolded into a single struggle. In the other media however, they were isolated moments.

The most prominent concern on what makes the experience of the touch-based narrative frustrating was to tell those purposeful and functional interactive elements apart from those that appear to be decorative. Compared to the other media, ironically, what was frustrating to the participants on the naturally tangible narrative were the same distinctive features that generated fun and excitement: the paper mechanisms. These frustrations were visual—overwhelming images and colors, cognitive—text that was hard to engage with or understand because of the mechanisms, and dynamic—urge to play with the mechanisms overcoming the need to read.

F. Child's (and adult's) Play

One interesting observation, although not directly related to the experiences discussed, was a general consensus on the generational view of the story; namely, a certain sense of bending the generational appropriateness of the story was continually mentioned across the all media. For example, one participant mentioned that compared to a regular book, the movable one was too delicate for children, although for her being an adult felt it was ok to manipulate. Other participant stated that the story was told mostly to children, but that the medium made it more relatable to adults. One final participant argued that as an adult she does not get to engage with this type of narratives regularly and that although it was for children, its child-like aspects made her feel good.

IV. CONCLUSSION AND FUTURE WORK

This work-in-progress paper presented the initial findings from an exploratory study that identified five hedonic and pragmatic facets of user engagement in the context of playable stories. The preliminary findings provided a comparative account of how people engage with different but related narrative media and how this engagement relays their emotions into their own subjective experiences.

The initial findings also provided a promising structure to associate the affordances and their supporting medium-specific attributes to varied facets of audience engagement. Such affordances as ludic play, immersion, imagination, or manipulation lead to free play and pleasure as experienced in the unfolding of the narrative and in some cases, physically unleashing the storytelling spectacles. These findings, after validation, will help researchers and designers better harness the power of different interactive media to craft playable stories with more intended hedonic experiential effects.

As mentioned earlier, the scale of the current study-in-progress is not large enough to provide clear quantitative tendencies or a fully reliable interpretation during the exploratory data analysis. The next round of the audience study will increase the sample size and refine the procedure in order to reach more reliable findings. For example, considering the generational bias towards *Alice in Wonderland* as shown among our participants, we may, if possible, employ a second story example that is more adult-oriented to complement findings through *Alice*. Collecting data from more media can also help reveal new affordances or attributes. With more valid quantitative results complemented with interview results, we will potentially be able to interpret better the patterns emerged from them, as well as provide insights into the subtle differences between the engagement of users of a system, game, or software and audiences of a playable story, as well as the cause behind these differences. This presents an interesting opportunity to contribute further to the limited amount of theory available on playable stories.

ACKNOWLEDGMENT

We thank all the participants who were involved in our study. We also thank Dr. Jeffrey C. F. Ho for his valuable insights and suggestions along the research process. Finally, we thank the reviewers for their valuable input in the refinement of this paper.

REFERENCES

[1] A. Amsel and J. Roussel, "Motivational properties of frustration: I. Effect on a running response of the addition of frustration to the motivational complex.," *Journal of experimental Psychology*, vol. 43, no. 5, p. 363, 1952.

[2] E. A. Boyle, T. M. Connolly, T. Hainey, and J. M. Boyle, "Engagement in digital entertainment games: A systematic review," *Computers in Human Behavior*, vol. 28, no. 3, pp. 771–780, May 2012.

[3] P. Chapman, "Models of Engagement: Intrinsically Motivated Interaction with Multimedia Learning Software.," M.A. Sc Thesis, University of Waterloo, Ontario, Canada, 1997.

[4] M. Csikszentmihalyi, *Flow: the psychology of optimal experience*, 1st ed.. New York: Harper Perennial, 1991.

[5] T. Fullerton, "Chapter 9: Playtesting," in *Game design workshop: a playcentric approach to creating innovative games*, Third Edition., Boca Raton, FL, US: A K Peters/CRC Press, 2008, pp. 294–295.

[6] M. Hassenzahl, S. Diefenbach, and A. Göritz, "Needs, affect, and interactive products – Facets of user experience," *Interacting with Computers*, vol. 22, no. 5, pp. 353–362, Sep. 2010.

[7] W. IJsselsteijn, Y. De Kort, K. Poels, A. Jurgelionis, and F. Bellotti, "Characterising and measuring user experiences in digital games," in *International conference on advances in computer entertainment technology*, Salzburg, Austria, 2007, vol. 2, p. 27.

[8] B. Laurel, "Dramatic Interactors: Collaboration, Contrainsts and Engagement," in *Computers as theatre*, Second Edition., Addison-Wesley, 2013, pp. 139–145.

[9] M. A. Mahmood, J. M. Burn, L. A. Gemoets, and C. Jacquez, "Variables affecting information technology end-user satisfaction: a meta-analysis of the empirical literature," *International Journal of Human-Computer Studies*, vol. 52, no. 4, pp. 751–771, 2000.

[10] A. McKee, "What is Fun?," in *FUN!: What Entertainment Tells Us About Living a Good Life*, Springer, 2016, pp. 29–40.

[11] H. L. O'Brien and E. G. Toms, "The development and evaluation of a survey to measure user engagement," *Journal of the American Society for Information Science and Technology*, vol. 61, no. 1, pp. 50–69, Jan. 2010.

[12] H. L. O'Brien, P. Cairns, and M. Hall, "A practical approach to measuring user engagement with the refined user engagement scale (UES) and new UES short form," *International Journal of Human-Computer Studies*, vol. 112, pp. 28–39, Apr. 2018.

[13] R. P. de Oliveira, D. P. de Oliveira, and T. F. Tavares, "Measurement Methods for Phenomena Associated with Immersion, Engagement, Flow, and Presence in Digital Games," *Proceedings of SBGames*, pp. 127–135, Sep. 2016.

[14] A. Ortony, G. L. Clore, and A. Collins, "Factors Affecting the Intensity of Emotions," in *The cognitive structure of emotions*, Cambridge university press, 1990, pp. 59–83.

[15] C. Peters, G. Castellano, and S. de Freitas, "An exploration of user engagement in HCI," in *Proceedings of the International Workshop on Affective-Aware Virtual Agents and Social Robots*, 2009, p. 9.

[16] F. Pucillo and G. Cascini, "A framework for user experience, needs and affordances," *Design Studies*, vol. 35, no. 2, pp. 160–179, Mar. 2014.

[17] L. P. Rieber, "Seriously considering play: Designing interactive learning environments based on the blending of microworlds, simulations, and games," *ETR&D*, vol. 44, no. 2, pp. 43–58, Jun. 1996.

[18] J. A. Russell, "A circumplex model of affect.," *Journal of personality and social psychology*, vol. 39, no. 6, p. 1161, 1980.

[19] M.-L. Ryan, "From Narrative Games to Playable Stories: Toward a Poetics of Interactive Narrative," *Storyworlds: A Journal of Narrative Studies*, vol. 1, pp. 43–59, 2009.

[20] J. Smith, M. Jarman, and M. Osborn, "Doing Interpretative phenomenological analysis," *Qualitative Health Psychology*, pp. 218–240, 1999.

[21] N. Verhelst, P. Van Avermaet, S. Takala, N. Figueras, and B. North, *Common European Framework of Reference for Languages: learning, teaching, assessment*. Cambridge University Press, 2009.

[22] E. N. Wiebe, A. Lamb, M. Hardy, and D. Sharek, "Measuring engagement in video game-based environments: Investigation of the User Engagement Scale," *Computers in Human Behavior*, vol. 32, pp. 123–132, Mar. 2014.

Spatial Note System Using Virtual Agent to Enhance Family Connection

Puxuan Qu

Graduate School of IPS
Waseda university
Fukuoka, Japan
Email: qpx1995331@outlook.com

Jiro Tanaka

Graduate School of IPS
Waseda university
Fukuoka, Japan
Email: jiro@aoni.waseda.jp

Abstract—**The pace of life is becoming faster. As a result, some people are too busy to communicate with their families. In this paper, we propose an Augmented Reality (AR) system using smartphone. The system allows us to leave emotional notes in the real environment using Virtual-Agent. The crucial part of the system focuses on the emotional short voice message exchange with the Virtual-Agents. Spatial note system is based on two parts, one is the virtual agent services and the other is the AR system. The virtual agent services allow users to make a voice message by recording user's voice. Then, a Virtual-Agent with the appropriate facial expression is generated. User can also change the facial expressions as he likes. There are 4 emotions of the virtual agents: happy, sorrow, angry and calm. Each emotion has 4 levels to express. The AR system will detect planes from the smartphone view of the real world. Users can put the Virtual-Agent anywhere on a plane.**

Keywords–Augmented Reality; Virtual Agents; Emotional Notes

I. INTRODUCTION

Some people are too busy to communicate with their families. When parents are busy with their work, the children are studying at school. It is also difficult for children to chat with their parents in their home because their parents return home late in the evening.

The best way to enhance the family connection is to provide the means which will increase the communication between children and parents. We try to find a way for both children and parents to share each other's life without taking up their time.

Message exchange will be an appropriate method in sharing information. The current ways of exchanging messages are:

1. Leaving a sticky note at home. This approach makes it easy for others to understand what the user wants to express because the notes are placed in the real world. One drawback is that these notes can easily be lost.
2. Sending a message in LINE using smartphone. In this case, users can read messages instantly, regardless of time and place. It also delivers the true voice of the user. But on the other hand, Messages are completely separated from the real world.

So, we propose an Augmented Reality (AR) system using smartphone. Our system can leave emotional notes in the real environment. The crucial part of the system is that we focus on the emotional short voice message exchange using the Virtual-Agent. Our system allows users to make voice message by recording user's voice. Additionally, the system can detect the emotion, i.e., calm, happy, angry or sorrow, from their voice. Then, the system generates a Virtual-Agent with the appropriate facial expression. Users can place the Virtual-Agent anywhere they want in the real world by using their smartphones. This mechanism can help families start small conversations, talking about daily life without facing each other.

AR is a new technology to make computer interfaces invisible and enhance user interaction with the real world [1]. AR allows the user to see the real world, with virtual objects superimposed upon or composited with the real world. Therefore, AR supplements reality, rather than completely replacing it. Ideally, it would appear to the user that the virtual and real objects coexisted in the same space [2]. AR is a direct or indirect live view of a physical, real-world environment whose elements are augmented by computer-generated perceptual information, ideally across multiple sensory modalities, including visual, auditory, haptic, somatosensory, and olfactory [3].

In computer science, a virtual agent is a computer program that acts for a user or other program in the agent context. Agents are colloquially known as bots. They can be embodied as software, such as chat bots [4]. Virtual agents can be autonomous and can also work with other agents and personnel [5].

II. GOAL AND APPROACH

The goal of this research is to create a useful and novice system that helps busy families share, communicate and exchange information.

In this paper, we propose Spatial Note System using AR and Virtual Agent. With the help of this system, family members can exchange information, share feelings, discuss topics, and eventually, strengthen family connection and keep good relationships

Through this system, we can:

1. Put messages into real environment to create environment-supportive messages (like sticky notes),
2. Make messages compelling so that it won't be ignored (like sticky notes),
3. Leave messages based on the real voice (like LINE), and
4. Make messages convey emotions to improve empathy.

So, we propose an Android AR system that uses Virtual-Agent to leave emotional notes in space to enhance family connection

Figure 1. Family member A gets home, he can leave a voice message using smartphone and put the emotional voice message in the real environment.

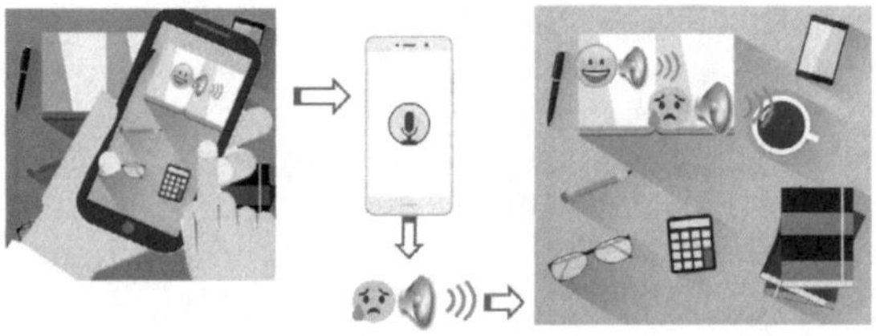

Figure 2. Family member B gets home, he can see that message. And after listening message of A, B leave back a new one.

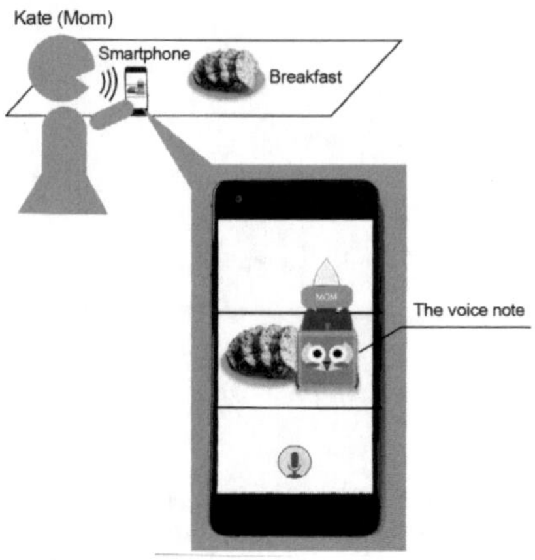

Figure 3. Mom leaves notes in the morning to her daughter about breakfast.

and convey emotions. The crucial part of the system focuses on the emotional short audio message exchange with Virtual-Agent.

Spatial note system allows the user to create a voice message by recording the user's voice. The following is an example of how the system works. In Figure 1, when a family member A returns home, he can use smartphone to leave a voice message and put the emotional voice message in the real environment. In Figure 2, when other family member B gets home, he can see that message. And after listening to the message of A, B can figure out what A means and what A feels. And then B can leave a new message. Additionally, the system can detect the users' voice after recording and then generate a Virtual-Agent with the appropriate facial expression. These facial expressions express user's emotions. The virtual agents can detect four main emotions from the user's voice, they are calm, happy, angry and sorrow. Users can use a smartphone to place Virtual-Agent anywhere they want.

III. Spatial Note System

In this section, we introduce the usage scenario of the system and explain how to use this system.

A. Usage Scenario

- Notes-leaving Scenario: Mom prepares a delicious breakfast in the morning for the family and eats with her husband. Before she leaves, she puts her daughter's breakfast on the table. The daughter is still sleeping. She then leaves a voice note to her daughter using the spatial note system in her smartphone. She said:" I bought your favorite bread, please remember eat it all, mom loves you!" Then she uses the smartphone to put the note on the table near the breakfast. The note is represented by a smiling virtual agent and can be seen through smartphone camera. The usage scenario is shown as Figure 3. After that, the parents leave home to go to work.
- Responding Scenario: After daughter gets up, she knows that her parents are out. She sees the breakfast on the table. When she walks near the table, there is a new note alert on her phone. She turns on the spatial note system in the smartphone to see that note. When she turns on the phone's camera and holds the phone towards the breakfast, a smiling virtual agent appears on the table. She finds that her mom left her a note, so she clicks on the agent to listen. After hearing what her mom said, she records a new note with the words "Thanks mom, the bread is delicious, but it is too much." She puts this new note next to her mom's note, responding to her mom, shown as Figure 4. Finally, she goes to school.

B. System Overview

Spatial note system is based on two parts, one is the virtual agent services and the other is the AR system (see Figure 5). The virtual agent services allow users to make voice messages by recording user's voice. A virtual agent with the appropriate facial expression is then generated to express the user's emotions. User can also change facial expressions according to his own preferences. Virtual agents have four emotions: happy, sorrow, angry and calm. Each emotion has 4 levels to express. The AR system can detect planes in the real environment through the camera of the mobile phone. Users can put the Virtual-Agent anywhere on a plane using the AR system.

C. Role Classification

In general, there are three types of roles in the family, i.e., Mom, Dad and Child, as shown in the Figure 6. Communication happens between two of them. Once the user chooses one of the roles, she/he will enter the role's interface. It is important to categorize different roles when using the system. Without this feature, it will be difficult to identify who is the note sender and who will be the note receiver. The users of

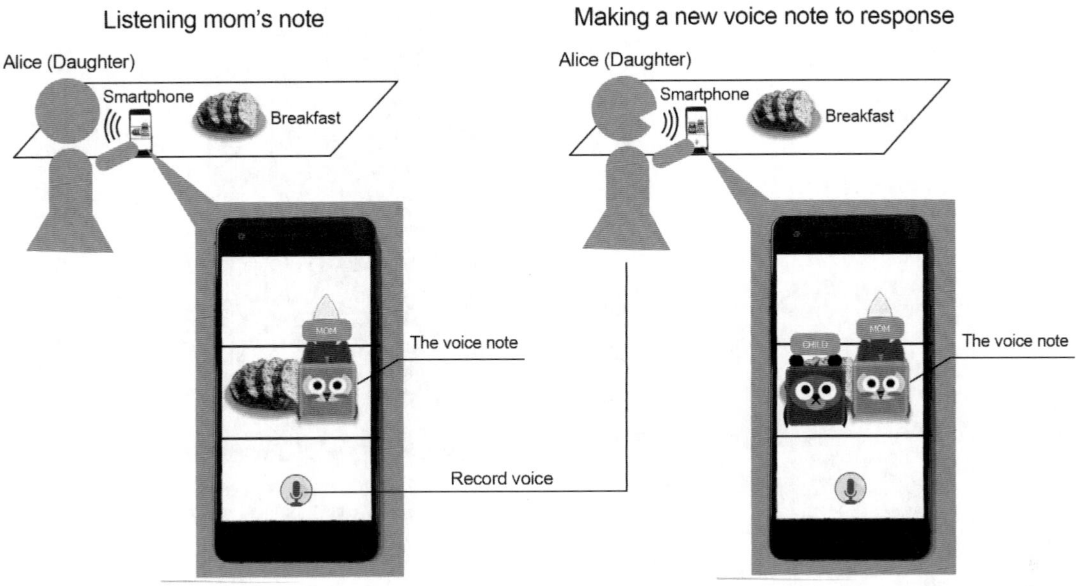

Figure 4. Daughter responds her mom about the breakfast when she gets home.

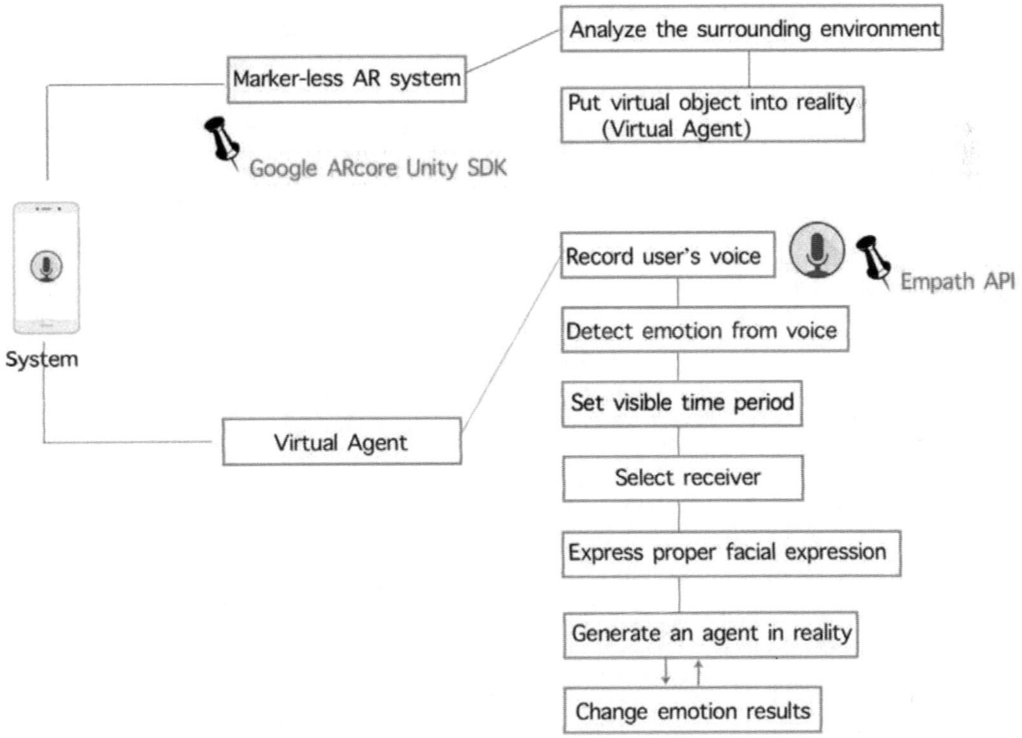

Figure 5. Spatial note system is based on two parts, one is the virtual agent services and the other is the AR system.

Figure 6. From left to right: Mom, Dad, Child.

Figure 7. Mom got a new note from daughter, and from left to right is : before listening to the new note, after listening to the new note.

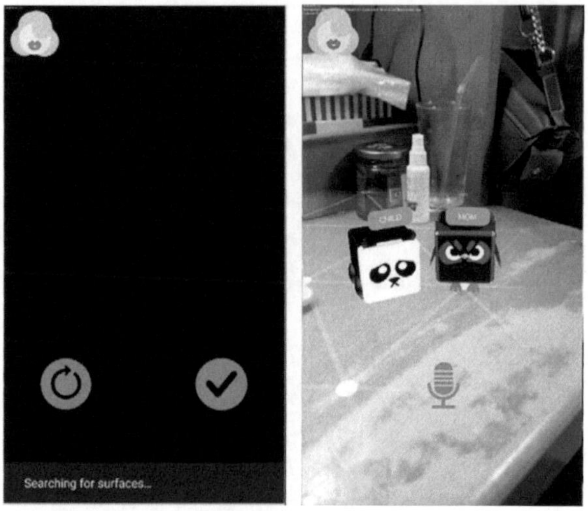

Figure 8. From left to right: Recording voice, system generate mom's virtual agent as voice note and mom puts it near the daughter's.

different roles can communicate with each other and content can only be seen by the addressed user. It is also possible to send messages to all members.

D. New Notes Alert

Once a family member A leaves a note to another family member B, the family member B will receive a new notice. Specifically, in the role's interface, a figure will appear in the lower right corner of the role icon, indicating that several notes left for him have not been heard. When the user finds a new note in the real world and listens, the number in the lower right corner of the icon is decremented by 1. The figure in the lower right corner of the roles icon disappears when the user hears all new notes. This is to remind users not to forget any messages left to him and remind user to reply to the message.

E. Checking New Notes and Listening

Users can hold smartphones to find new notes at home, and if found, the virtual agent will appear on the screen, users can click the virtual agent and listen to the voice notes left by the other family members, as shown in Figure 7.

F. Making Voice Notes

1) Environment scanner: The system uses ARCore [6]. In addition to identifying key points, ARCore can detect flat surfaces, such as tables or floors, and estimate the average illumination of the surrounding area. The combination of these features allows ARCore to build its own understanding of the world around it. ARCore's understanding of the real world allows users to place objects, notes or other information in a way that integrates seamlessly with the real world. Users can place a napping kitten at the corner of the coffee table or annotate a painting with the artist's biography. This is the fundamental part of putting virtual agent into reality.

2) Recording Voice and Emotion Detection: User can click the Record button to start recording the voice. The user presses stop button after completing the sentence. The Record button is always displayed on the main page, so user can leave a message by recording voice anytime, anywhere. When recording a voice note, the system can perform voice emotion recognition. When the user records his voice to leave a note, the system will call the Empath API [7] and get the emotion detection results. The Empath API recognizes emotion by analyzing physical properties of user's voice, such as pitch, tone, speed and power. It can detect emotion in every language. After the user records his voice and the system completes emotion detection, the spatial virtual agent with the emotional facial expression will be displayed at the location selected by the user. Figure 8 shows the interfaces of voice recording and virtual agent. If the user presses the virtual agent for a long time, emotion results interface will be displayed. Emotional outcomes include 4 emotions, such as calm, angry, happy and sorrow. Each emotion has 4 levels, a little, much, very much and extreme. They are represented by 4 different emojis. Figure 9 shows the images of emotion detection interface. In the interface, there are 4 emotion elements and their values, which are detected from the user's voice. The level of emotion is determined by the energy value, which is also given from Empath API. For the emotional elements, each element is measured independently from speech. The detected values vary from 0 to 50. Only one element will be selected, and this element determines the final emotional outcome.

3) Emotion Result Change: Users can change emotional outcomes by clicking the virtual agent on the detection interface, which can change emotional outcomes and emotion

Figure 9. Emotion Detection Result.

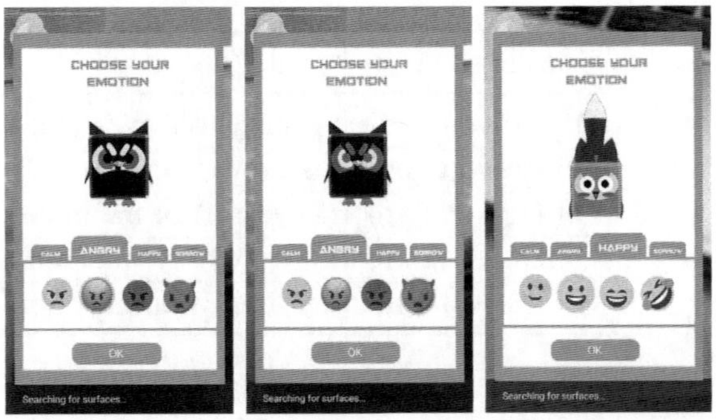

Figure 10. Emotions changes from left to right: a little angry, extremely angry, a little happy.

levels. Selecting different emotional levels will change the facial expression of the virtual agent. The Figure 10 shows the change of the emotion.

4) Visible Time Setting and Receiver Setting: The user can decide how long this agent exists after being listened to. Options include 1 hour, 4 hours, 8 hours and 24 hours. User can also decide who can receive notes, individuals or entire families. If the user only sends notes to an individual, the notes can only be seen by the recipient, not anyone else. But if the user chooses the entire family, then all family members can see that note.

IV. Preliminary Evaluation

We conducted a preliminary user study to verify whether users can communicate more with their family by using our proposed system and assess the usability of the system. We asked 3 families to do the experiments.

A. Participants

As shown in Table 1 and Table 2, in order to assess the usability and efficiency of using our system, we plan to recruit 3 families from friends, each with 3 participants. A total of 3 children participated, aged between 22 and 24, with 6 parents, aged 49 to 52. All participants have a general knowledge of computers, and have experience using smartphones.

TABLE I. Subject Demographic Information of Children.

Elements	*Description*
Participants	1 male, 2 females
Age	22-24; Mean: 23
Profession	Students

TABLE II. Subject Demographic Information of Parents.

Elements	*Description*
Participants	3 males, 3 females
Age	49-52; Mean: 51
Profession	Working in company

B. Method

One family consists of 3 persons, so there are two cases.

a) Sending a message to a person

b) Sending a message to all members, i.e., two persons.

The method we use for evaluation is described in the following 6 steps:

1. Each participant will be required to send 10 a) messages (5 messages per person) and 5 b) messages for practice.

2. Each participant will be asked to listen to messages and reply, if needed.

3. Each participant will be required to change emotion at least once.

4. Each participant will be asked to use the application to leave notes in their home to exchange information for at least 1 day.

5. Each participant is asked to fill a questionnaire survey after finishing their tasks. Each participant needs to write down the number of messages he/she wrote today and answer 5 questions about using the system. The answer is from 1 to 5 (1 = very positive, 5 = very negative).

Question	1	2	3	4	5
Q1:Do you think it is easy to leave a message?	3				
Q2:Do you think it is easy to find messages and listen?	1	2			
Q3:Do you think it is correct of the emotion detection result?	2	1			
Q4:Do you think it is easy to change emotion?		3			
Q5:Do you think your family connection is enhanced by using this system?	3				

Figure 11. Answers Statistics of Investigative Questions from Children.

Question	1	2	3	4	5
Q1:Do you think it is easy to leave a message?	4	2			
Q2:Do you think it is easy to find messages and listen?	1	2	3		
Q3:Do you think it is correct of the emotion detection result?	2	2	2		
Q4:Do you think it is easy to change emotion?		1	5		
Q5:Do you think your family connection is enhanced by using this system?	1	3	2		

Figure 12. Answers Statistics of Investigative Questions from Parents.

These question are:

- Do you think it is easy to leave a message?
- Do you think it is easy to find messages and listen?
- Do you think it is correct of the emotion detection result?
- Do you think it is easy to change emotion?
- Do you think your family connection is enhanced by using this system?

C. Results

After collecting the results given by the participants, the evaluation of using the spatial note system to enhance family connection can be carried out.

The Figure 11 shows all the answers from children. There are 3 participants chose Grade 1 in Q1, which means that they all thought that it was easy to leave a message. In Q2, 1 child chose Grade 1 (very easy) and 2 children chose grade 2 (easy). In Q3, 2 children chose grade 1 (correct) and 1 child chose grade 2 (almost correct). In Q4, 3 children chose grade 2 (easy) and in Q5, 3 children chose grade 1 (very much).

The Figure 12 shows all the answers from parents. There are 4 participants chose grade 1 in Q1, which means that they thought it easy to leave a message and 2 participants chose grade 2 (easy). In Q2, 1 participant chose grade 1 (very easy) and 2 participants chose grade 2 (easy) and 3 participants chose grade 3 (normal). In Q3, 2 participants chose grade 1 (correct), 2 participants chose grade 2 (almost correct) and 2 participants chose grade 3 (normal). In Q4, 1 participant chose grade 2 (easy) and 5 participants chose grade 3 (normal. In Q5, 1 participant chose grade 1 (very much), 3 participants chose grade 2 (much) and 2 participants chose grade 2 (normal).

Overall, we received positive feedback through the preliminary user study.

V. Related Work

With the popularization of the AR, more and more researchers determined themselves in proposing new method, new idea in AR. AR enables the direct or indirect view of the physical, real-world environment whose elements are augmented by computer.

Rekimoto et al. [8] presents a system called CyberCode. The CyberCode is a visual tagging system based on a 2D-barcode technology and provides several features not provided by other tagging systems. CyberCode tags can be recognized by cameras, and can determine the 3D position of the tagged object as well as its ID number.

Bace et al. [9] proposed a novel wearable ubiquitous method which is described as ubiGaze to augment any real-world object with invisible messages through gaze gesture that lock the message into the object. Mistry et al. [10] presents WUW-Wear Ur World, which is a wearable gestural interface that allows projecting information out into the real-world.

Nassani et al. [11] proposed a system called Tag-It. It is a wearable system that allows people to place and interact with 3D virtual tags placed around them.

Tonchidot [12] proposed Sekai Camera, an augmented reality application that allows users to share tags for any place on the planet based on GPS.

Tarumi et al. [13] proposed an overlaid virtual system called SpaceTag. The SpaceTag system is a location-aware information system and an augmented reality system because it attaches information to real space. In this system, the virtual world consists of virtual architectural objects and virtual creatures.

VI. Conclusion and Future Work

In this paper, we addressed the family communication problems of modern families. In order to solve these problems, we have proposed an AR system using smartphone. The system allows us to leave emotional notes in the real world using Virtual-Agent.

We have assumed 3 kinds of people, i.e., Dad, Mom and Child, in our system. Our system runs on the smartphones of each family member. Our system consists of two parts, one is the virtual agent services and the other is the AR system. The virtual agent services allow the user to make a voice message by recording the user's voice. Then, a virtual agent with an appropriate facial expression will be generated to express the user's emotions. User can also change the facial expressions according to his own preferences. There are 4 emotions, i.e., happy, sorrow, angry and calm. Each emotion has 4 levels to express. The AR system can detect planes in the real environment through the camera of the smartphone. User can put the Virtual-Agent anywhere he wants in the real world using the AR system.

Through this system, family members can exchange information, share feelings, discuss topics and keep good relationships. For the note-making user, he can make any notes he wants in the real world and easily convey his emotion to other users. For the note-receiving user, he can freely choose whether to hear it according to the facial expression of the agent. He can understand the feelings of note-making user by looking at the agent's facial expression intuitively.

In the preliminary evaluation part, we conducted an experiment to evaluate the usability of our system. We asked volunteers to use the system in their homes and asked them to fill the questionnaires to give us feedback. We have collected and analyzed their answers.

There exists several things that need to be done, such as making the emotions of the virtual agents more accurate, and also adding place to store all the notes left by users. Virtual agents can have more facial expressions in the future. In short, using AR to create more vivid virtual agents will be the focus of our future work.

Acknowledgment

The authors deeply thank Boyang Liu for his comments and support for refining this paper.

References

[1] M. Billinghurst, A. Clark, and G. Lee, "A survey of augmented reality," Foundations and Trends® in Human–Computer Interaction, vol. 8, no. 2-3, 2015, pp. 73–272.

[2] R. T. Azuma, "A survey of augmented reality," Presence: Teleoperators & Virtual Environments, vol. 6, no. 4, 1997, pp. 355–385.

[3] P. Schuettel, "The concise fintech compendium," Fribourg: School of Management Fribourg/Switzerland, 2017.

[4] J. Gratch, N. Wang, J. Gerten, E. Fast, and R. Duffy, "Creating rapport with virtual agents," in International Workshop on Intelligent Virtual Agents. Springer, 2007, pp. 125–138.

[5] A. L. Baylor, "Promoting motivation with virtual agents and avatars: role of visual presence and appearance," Philosophical Transactions of the Royal Society B: Biological Sciences, vol. 364, no. 1535, 2009, pp. 3559–3565.

[6] J. Glover, Unity 2018 Augmented Reality Projects: Build four immersive and fun AR applications using ARKit, ARCore, and Vuforia. Packt Publishing Ltd, 2018.

[7] E. Fast, B. Chen, and M. S. Bernstein, "Empath: Understanding topic signals in large-scale text," in Proceedings of the 2016 CHI Conference on Human Factors in Computing Systems. ACM, 2016, pp. 4647–4657.

[8] J. Rekimoto and Y. Ayatsuka, "Cybercode: designing augmented reality environments with visual tags," in Proceedings of DARE 2000 on Designing augmented reality environments. ACM, 2000, pp. 1–10.

[9] M. Bâce, T. Leppänen, D. G. De Gomez, and A. R. Gomez, "ubigaze: ubiquitous augmented reality messaging using gaze gestures," in SIGGRAPH ASIA 2016 Mobile Graphics and Interactive Applications. ACM, 2016, p. 11.

[10] P. Mistry, P. Maes, and L. Chang, "Wuw-wear ur world: a wearable gestural interface," in CHI'09 extended abstracts on Human factors in computing systems. ACM, 2009, pp. 4111–4116.

[11] A. Nassani, H. Bai, G. Lee, and M. Billinghurst, "Tag it!: Ar annotation using wearable sensors," in SIGGRAPH Asia 2015 Mobile Graphics and Interactive Applications. ACM, 2015, pp. 12:1–12:4.

[12] B. Butchart, "Architectural styles for augmented reality in smartphones," in Third International AR Standards Meeting, 2011, pp. 1–7.

[13] H. Tarumi, K. Morishita, M. Nakao, and Y. Kambayashi, "Spacetag: An overlaid virtual system and its applications," in Multimedia Computing and Systems, 1999. IEEE International Conference on, vol. 1. IEEE, 1999, pp. 207–212.

Use of Smart Speakers by Elderly in Home Environment

Jeongyun Heo
Departments of Smart Interaction Design
Kookmin University
Seoul, Korea
e-mail: yuniheo@kookmin.ac.kr

Wan Chul Yoon
Department of Industrial and Systems Engineering
KAIST
Daejeon, Korea
e-mail: wcyoon@kaist.ac.kr

Abstract—**Digital technologies have permeated everyday life; however, the digital literacy of the elderly population is low compared with that of other generations. This is not only due to their difficulty in adapting to newer technologies, but also due to psychosocial barriers. Smart speakers use audio to interact with elderly users. With natural language commands, the psychosocial barriers for elderly individuals are expected to become lower with regard to new technology. To understand the usage and acceptance of smart speakers, we conducted observational studies of the elderly in their home environments. The results show that smart speakers are helpful at overcoming psychosocial barriers to new technology, which will motivate the elderly to learn how to use new technology.**

Keywords-smart speaker; digital divide; voice interaction; conversational model; technology acceptance;

I. INTRODUCTION

Korea has officially been classified as an "aged society," with 14.3 percent of its population 65 years or older [1]. The United Nations (UN) categorizes societies based on age of the population: when the proportion of people 65 or older exceeds 7 percent, the society is classified as aging; a figure of 14 percent is an aged society and 20 percent is a super-aged society [2].

With advances in technology, it is difficult to imagine life without technology. Using technology in our daily lives is not an option, but a mandatory tool for survival in modern society. However, the digital literacy of the elderly population is low compared with that of other generations [3][4]. The isolation of elderly citizens from digital technology has become an important social issue [5]. This issue is attributable to the difficulty faced by the elderly in adapting to technology, as well as to psychological barriers they have toward new technology. One key way of reducing this psychological barrier is to provide an easy trial. Smart speakers provide intelligent assistance via voice control technology. They can play music, turn on lights, provide weather information, provide food-ordering services for products such as milk, and answer questions. Given that communication is natural for humans, the elderly are more likely to adopt a system involving verbal communication. In this sense, verbally interacting with smart speakers may help reduce the psychosocial barriers of the elderly toward technology.

The research questions guiding this study are as follows:

1. Is there a gap between technology usage and the intention to use technology among elderly people?
2. What underlying fears and concerns do the elderly have in relation to digital technology?
3. Can overcoming psychological barriers by using voice-first technology be helpful in changing elderly attitudes toward digital technology?

The remainder of this paper is organized as follows: In section II, we discuss the progress made in current studies and the issues highlighted by them. In section III, we introduce and discuss the research method in detail. In section IV, we present and discuss the results. Finally, in section V, we provide our conclusions and scope of future work.

II. RELATED WORK

Many studies on the digital divide have been conducted [3]-[6]. It is often reported that older adults are unaware of many existing digital technologies and might lack necessary knowledge [6]-[8]. In addition, increased technology accessibility does not necessarily lead to actual technology use and adoption. Older adults are slower to adopt new technologies than are younger adults, and they have higher anxiety with regard to the use of computers, resulting in reduced use of technology [9]. It is said that "gerontechnology" invokes negative attitudes with regard to the acceptance of new technology [10]. Cognitive deficits and low self-efficacy of older adults also significantly reduce their ability to use new technology [11].

The digital divide can be measured based on three aspects: accessibility to technology, level of digital skill, and level of usage [12][13]. Based on one government report [13], elderly people in Korea have a technology accessibility of 89.9 %. Hence, technology accessibility is not the main cause of the digital divide, at least in Korea. However, digital skills and usage levels are relatively low among the elderly compared to younger people in Korea. The level of digital skill among the elderly in Korea is 41.0 %. Increasing digital skills is a key to reducing the digital divide among the elderly.

Some researchers have extended the definition of the digital divide to the gap in digital skills [12]. This is also known as a second-level digital divide. Perceived usefulness, ease of use, and user satisfaction with the ease of use influence decisions of the elderly to use new technology [7][11][14]. The difficulty in learning how to use the technology could decreases, if elderly individuals are motivated to use new technology [15]. Confidence in using technology is also a result of their attitudes toward technology [7][16]. Technological self-efficacy is the belief in one's own ability to use new technologies [16]; it has been a major barrier to technology adoption among the elderly [4][6][7][16]. They have had little chance to integrate digital technologies into their daily lives; therefore, their belief in their ability to use such technologies, called self-efficacy, could be lower than that of younger generations.

It is clear that new information and communication technologies (ICTs) have the potential to improve the quality of life and social inclusion of the elderly. Hence, it is important to determine and address the psychosocial barriers with respect to the use of technology among the elderly.

III. Research Method

In this section we discuss the research method in detail.

A. *Project Overview*

Three different types of research approach were used to understand the usage behavior and technology acceptance of the smart speaker: surveys, in-depth interviews, and observational ethnography. This mixed method research, which combines quantitative and qualitative methods, is a well-established theoretical empirical method [17]. The strengths of one method can overcome the weaknesses in the others, and the combination of the three methods can yield a greater insight than one alone.

Surveys were used to obtain a general understanding of an issue from subjects such as the experience of using a digital device, usage behavior, and attitude toward digital technology. In-depth-interviews were conducted with eight elderly citizens from among those who participated in the survey to obtain a deeper understanding of the issue. Finally, observational ethnographic research was conducted in the home environment of participants for two weeks. All the studies were conducted from June to November 2018.

The participants included elderly people who participate in computer classes for elderly citizens, which are provided as a public service in Korea. The participants must meet three criteria to be a part of the study. First, they had to be over 60 and possess basic but not strong skills with regard to the use of ICTs such as computers and smart phones. Second, they had limited motivation to learn about new technologies. Third, to ensure representativeness, they had to form a homogeneous sample. Overall, the sample consisted of middle-class individuals who are socially well-connected to digital technologies.

B. *Survey to Understand Usage Behavior*

The survey was taken by 86 adults between 60 and 80 years of age, with an average age of 72 years. The ratio of males to females was close to 1 (44 women, and 42 men). The respondents answered 28 questions on printed material via face-to-face instruction. The questionnaires consisted of questions about demographics, level of ownership of digital devices, usage level, usage frequency, and experience of using smart speakers. The results show that the majority of the survey participants had access to digital technology such as computers, laptops, and smartphones, and that they use them on a daily basis. The participants also showed strong interest in smart speakers; however, this was not sufficient for them to buy smart speakers.

C. *In-depth Interviews with Smart Speaker*

In-depth interviews were conducted for eight subjects (three females and five males). These subjects were recruited from a previous survey, as they showed a strong interest in using smart speakers. The interviews lasted for 1.5 h and consisted of two phases. The first phase involved a semi-structured interview, in which the questions were focused on the level and frequency of usage of digital devices, intention to continuously use such devices, attitude toward buying a smart speaker, and how much they were willing to pay for it. The second phase involved tasks with smart speakers. As an exit question, the participants were asked what kind of features they would want to have in the future in smart speaker technology. The interview sessions were audio-recorded and transcribed. In general, participants expressed a positive feeling about the experience of verbally interacting with the smart speaker.

D. *Ethnography in Home Environment*

Among those who participated in the survey and expressed a high level of interest in the daily use of smart speakers, five participants took part in an ethnography study. These participants underwent a prior-interview, and a short class on how to use smart speakers before they began using the devices at home. They were given task lists and a template for a self-diary. Telephone interviews were conducted twice a day to determine their usage behavior. Video-cameras were not used because the main focus of this research was to determine whether using smart speakers would change the attitude of the elderly toward adopting digital technology. Fig. 1 shows an example of the self-diary given to the participants.

IV. Results

We now present the results of our study for each of the aforementioned factors affecting usage of smart speakers among the elderly.

A. *Gap Between Accessibility and Actual Usage*

Based on the survey, the majority of the survey participants were easily able to access digital technology such as computers, laptops, and smartphones. Sixty four percent of the participants used digital technology daily. However, they did not separate their personal use from that of their family. For example, during the in-depth review, participants who reported they could use Wi-Fi revealed that they had trouble connecting to Wi-Fi networks. Some participants who owned smart pads or smart speakers reported that they could not use those devices. Smartphone usage was found to be limited to using messaging services, checking the weather, and taking photos. Only a few participants could use features such as food-ordering services, money transfer services, and public transport information services.

B. *Lack of Information About New Technology*

Most elderly participants reported that they learned to use new technology from family and friends. Some participants reported that asking for assistance reduced their feeling of independence. Some reported that they were taking ICT classes so as to not bother family members. Some participants expressed the fear of being hurt by those with bad intentions such as those who engage in voice phishing. They expressed the need for appropriate and trustworthy channels for delivery of new information. They also found the recommendation features in the self-diary helpful.

C. *Perceived Emotional Friendliness*

During the two weeks when smart speakers were used at home, all five participants experienced emotional feelings toward the smart speaker. As shown in Table I, the common emotions were comfort, interest, and friendliness. The lack of recognition accuracy or insufficient features were also perceived emotionally. They perceived it as a childlike personality traits rather than evincing any negative feeling toward it. The possibility of smart speakers being used as a talking companion was considered.

TABLE I. EXPRESSIONS USED FOR EMOTIONAL FEELINGS

Emotional Expression	Related Sentences Collected
Comfortable	"It is easier to use." "It is easier and more comfortable than a smartphone. Just talking to a smart speaker works." "I could use it simultaneously while doing other tasks." "It reads my Kakao talk message. It is convenient." "It is useful because it works from a distance."
Interesting	"I am curious about how this device will evolve." "The advertisement piques my interest regarding the smart speaker."
Friendly	"It makes me smile when it says thank you." "It feels like a friend, or family." "It reacts to me." "Using the smart speaker is a joyful experience. I am considering buying it." "It is good to use when you are alone." "When the smart speaker says a monophonic expression, it is lovely." "I am enjoying listening to the guitar playing through the smart speaker." "I feel like it smiles at me."
Childish	"It only has simple knowledge." "It is not smart enough. Sometimes it does not understand what I am saying especially for long and complex sentences." "My expectation was too high; however, it remains useful." "It appears like a 10-year-old child."

The findings of the study are as follows: 1) older adults in this study were easily able to access digital technology; however, their actual usage was limited. Participation in computer classes can be a good indicator of usage motivation. 2) The barriers to using digital technology are a lack of instruction or guidance, lack of knowledge, lack of confidence, and economic issues. 3) Most participants had positive experiences using smart speakers in their homes. They found them easy to use, and they were eager to share their experience with their family and friends. It appears that this positive experience was helpful in improving their self-efficacy. Finally, participants reported that smart speaker had an emotional friendliness.

Our findings suggest that all five participants in the ethnography study were willing to learn to use a smart speaker and eager to adopt new technology. Some even suggested starting classes on how to use smart speakers and provided ideas for new features for the smart speaker.

V. CONCLUSION AND FUTURE WORK

The results show that smart speakers are helpful in reducing psychosocial barriers among the elderly toward new technology, and are perceived as an emotional companions. The comforts of using this technology and the emotional benefits could be ways to increase digital inclusion and self-efficacy among the elderly.

Although this study yielded some important findings, there are some limitations. The sample included only senior citizens enrolled in public ICT classes. These adults may be different from those in the larger community. In addition, the sample for observation may be too small to generalize the findings. However, the major purpose of this study was to obtain a deeper understanding of the use of technology among the elderly by using smart speakers. Smart speakers have the potential to become more popular in promoting the use of ICTs among the elderly.

In the future, we will develop a theoretical framework for further study based on the findings and insights gained from this study. In addition, the possibility of increasing the sample size to enable generalization will be considered.

ACKNOWLEDGMENT

We thank the Ministry of Education and National Research Foundation of Korea for supporting this research as part of the "Leaders in Industry-university Cooperation +" Project. We would also like to thank the district council of Jong-Ro-Gu, Seoul, Korea for allowing us to recruit senior citizens from ICT classes for our survey.

REFERENCES

[1] 2018 Statistics on Elderly, Statistics Korea. [Online]. Available from: http://kostat.go.kr/portal [retrieved: 01, 2019]

[2] World Population Agwing 2017, UN. [Online]. Available from: http://www.un.org/en/development/desa/population/publications/pdf/ageing/WPA2017_Highlights.pdf [retrieved: 01, 2019]

[3] M. A. Tyler, "Connected Older Adults: Conceptualising their Digital Participation," Journal of Literacy and Technology, vol. 15, no. 2, pp. 200–215, 2014.

[4] B. Niehaves and R. Plattfaut, "Internet adoption by the elderly: Employing IS technology acceptance theories for understanding the age-related digital divide," European Journal of Information Systems, vol. 23, no. 6, 2014, pp. 708–726, doi:10.1057/ejis.2013.19.

[5] P. Khosravi, A. Rezvani, and A. Wiewiora, "The impact of technology on older adults' social isolation," Computers in Human Behavior, vol. 63, 2016, pp. 594–603, doi:10.1016/j.chb.2016.05.092.

[6] A. Quan-Haase, K. Martin, and K. Schreurs, "Interviews with digital seniors: ICT use in the context of everyday life," Information, Communication & Society, vol. 19, no. 5, 2016, pp. 691–707, doi:10.1080/1369118x.2016.1140217.

[7] T. L. Mitzner, J. B. Boron, C. B. Fausset, A. E. Adams, N. Charness, S. J. Czaja et al., "Older adults talk technology: Technology usage and attitudes," Computers in Human Behavior, vol. 26, no. 6, 2010, pp. 1710–1721, doi:10.1016/j.chb.2010.06.020.

[8] N. Selwyn, "The information aged: A qualitative study of older adults' use of information and communications technology," Journal of Aging studies, vol. 18, no. 4, 2004, pp. 369–384, doi:10.1016/j.jaging.2004.06.008.

[9] S. J. Czajaet al, "Factors predicting the use of technology: Findings from the center for research and education on aging and technology enhancement (CREATE)," Psychology and Aging, vol. 21, no. 2, 2006, pp. 333–352, doi:10.1037/0882-7974.21.2.333.

[10] S. Yusif, S. Jeffrey, and H-B. Abdul, "Older people, assistive technologies, and the barriers to adoption: A systematic review," International Journal of Medical Informatics, vol. 94, 2016, pp. 112–16, doi:10.1016/j.ijmedinf.2016.07.004.

[11] H. Alvseike and K. Brønnick, "Feasibility of the iPad as a hub for smart house technology in the elderly; effects of cognition, self-efficacy, and technology experience," Journal of Multidisciplinary Healthcare, vol. 5, 2012, pp. 299–306, doi:10.2147/jmdh.s35344.

[12] J. van Dijk, "Digital Divide Research, Achievements and Shortcomings," Poetics, vol. 34, no. 4-5, 2006, pp. 221–35, doi:10.1016/j.poetic.2006.05.004.

[13] The Report on the Digital Divide 2017, National Information Society Agency, NIA-RER-C-17004.

[14] B. D. Carpenter and S. Buday, "Computer use among older adults in a naturally occurring retirement community," Computers in Human Behavior, vol. 23, no. 6, 2007, pp. 3012–3024, doi:10.1016/j.chb.2006.08.015.

[15] H. Kim, J. Heo, J. Shim, M. Kim, and S. Park, "Contextual Research on Elderly Users' Needs for Developing Universal Design Mobile Phone," Universal Acess in Human Computer Interaction. Coping with Diversity. UAHCI 2007. LNCS 4554, 2007, pp. 950–959, doi:10.1007/978-3-540-73279-2_106.

[16] H. Y. S. Tsai, R. Shillair, S. R. Cotten, V. Winstead, and E. Yost, "Getting Grandma Online: Are Tablets the Answer for Increasing Digital Inclusion for Older Adults in the U.S.?," Educational Gerontology, vol. 41, no. 10, 2015, pp. 695–709, doi:10.1080/03601277.2015.1048165.

[17] J. W. Creswell and V. P. L. Clark, Designing and Conducting Mixed Methods Research, 3rd ed., Los Angeles: SAGE Publications, Inc., 2017.

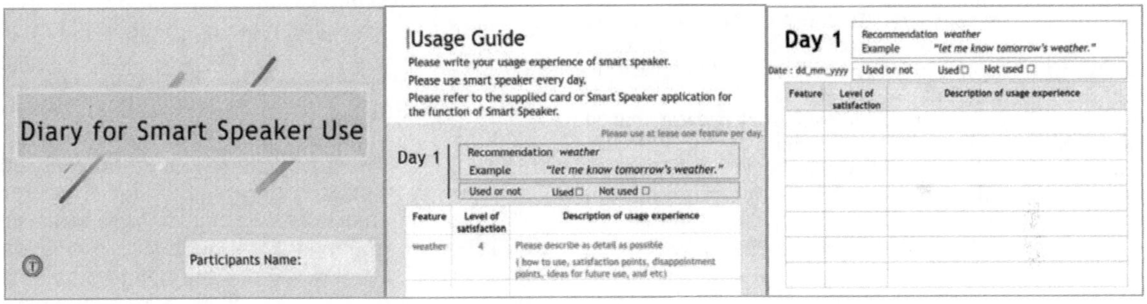

Figure 1. Example of self-diary given to participants (translated into English).

The Use of Digital Tools in Training to Real Estate and Building Sectors – a Study from French University

Bourret Christian – Meyer Claudie
Université Paris Est Marne-la-Vallée (UPEM) – Dicen-idf – Ifis., France.
e-mail: christian.bourret@u-pem.fr
e-mail: claudie.meyer@u-pem.fr

Drapier Thomas
Lycée François Mansart
Val de Marne, France
e-mail: thomas.drapier@ac-creteil.fr

Abstract - **This paper presents an analysis of two complementary evolutions, in work situations in the real estate and building sectors, using new digital tools such as the ones based on digital tablets. It concerns a bachelor degree in individual home building and new interactions in master degrees, mixing and integrating real estate and Information and Communication Technologies (ICTs) around the innovative Univcamp device. The latter promotes new real estate services with interactions between different actors in action-research situations. These evolutions correspond to a new approach of the French Universities, in particular the University Paris East Marne-la-Vallée and its component units Ile-de-France Services Engineering Institute (IFIS) and Information and Communication Devices in the Digital Era in Ile-de-France (DICEN idf). They support a specific way of apprenticeship training with the use of a new intermediation artifact between students and companies, the e-booklet. This work may help to develop a specific observatory space from work situations in an action-research perspective to promote a new "ideas integrator" interface between universities and companies. This interface will also allow observing evolutions of professions facing the challenges of new digital uses, corresponding to new skills, at first in real estate and building sectors.**

Keywords - pedagogic innovations; interactions; apprenticeship; digital tools; skills; data

I. Introduction: General Context

ICTs strongly impact all our digital society and particularly companies and universities. Today Universities are not only producers of knowledge but also act to develop new skills for students, so they may work more efficiently in the companies, by introducing specific way of apprenticeship with particular organization and pedagogical approaches: sandwiches courses, use of an intermediation and traceability tool - the e-booklet. This new approach is particularly developed at the University of Paris East Marne-la-Vallée (UPEM) with strong partnerships with other learning organizations and companies. The synergy challenges between training and research fields have also become essential, particularly the challenge of innovation, through association of one or more partners to Universities. In our case, in the UPEM, the teaching side is provided by the IFIS – *Institut Francilien d'Ingénierie des Services* while the DICEN idf – *Dispositifs d'Information et de Communication à l'Ere Numérique en Ile-de-France* is the Research team, located in the CNAM (*Conservatoire National des Arts et Métiers*), in the IFIS institute in UPEM and for some other researchers at Paris Nanterre University.

ICTs also question all our society. They change all the working conditions, especially with new digital and intermediation tools (tablets, etc.), access to information and new uses of data (especially big data). The integration of young people of the "Y Generation" also constitutes an important challenge for the companies in their new ways to cooperate with older employees (older than 50 years).

In this working paper, we propose to analyze these evolutions using case studies with students of two complementary degrees in the Building or Real Estate sectors: the Bachelor degree of Building of Individual Homes (CCBMI) and the Master degrees of Innovation Management in Real Estate (MIPI) and Digital Tools (MITIC). It is important to note that digital tools considerably change relations with customers with the idea of services co-production between all the stakeholders.

This work is a first step to introduce, through Univcamp device, CCBMI Bachelor, and the e-booklet artifact mediator, different ways to develop a specific observatory space from work situations in an Action Research perspectives to promote a new "ideas integrator" interface between university and companies. This interface will also make it possible to observe evolutions of professions in the face of the challenges of new digital uses, corresponding to new skills, first in real estate and building sectors.

After the introduction (section I), in a first step, we present the evolutions of the French Universities through the case of UPEM (section II) whose specificity is to bet on the apprenticeship. In a second step, we outline our scientific position, our goals and the methodology used (section III). Then, we show the specificity of the two degrees corresponding to this study. We also outline the challenge of ICTs for the considered companies and the importance of new ICTs tools (tablets) as levers of changes for better efficiency, developing new interactions with customers but also for new co-operations between employees (CCBMI) and for new interactions area for the Master degrees (Univcamp) (section IV is dedicated to results and section V to discussion). We also point out the importance of the e-booklet as an interactive tool (section VI). In a conclusive part (section VII), we will give some perspectives for our future work.

II. Training In UPEM, Real Estate and Building, ICTs and Skills Challenges

Universities do not only produce general knowledge but try to train their students for specific jobs with specific skills. In France, it is particularly the case of the University Paris East Marne-la-Vallée (UPEM). More than 25 % of its students are trained through apprenticeship. They are students with job contracts with companies. In UPEM, IFIS is much involved in this specific training way with 600 apprentice students.

In different degrees, for apprentice students, the skills approach has become essential. It is not only a question of acquiring knowledge but also of acquiring professional skills in work situations (in a "learning by doing" way). With this in mind, a system of professional references built with professional advice provides the pedagogical frameworks for these professional diplomas.

This is particularly the case of two different degrees in the Real estate and Building sectors: a Bachelor degree of Manager Building of Individual Houses - *Conducteur de Chantier Bâtiment en Maison Individuelle* (CCBMI) and Master degree of Innovation Management with two coordinated options in Real Estate Management - *Management, Innovation de Services et Patrimoine Immobilier* (MIPI) and in Digital Tools Integration - *Management, Innovation de Services et Technologies de l'Information et de la Communication* (MITIC). We particularly focus on tutored projects (a supervised work in a work situation) around the new use of tablets in the building sector in the Bachelor degree proposed with a partnership with Individual Houses Building Federation and François Mansart School. We also analyze the specificity of the Univcamp training / research relationship or interaction space born from a collaborative history initiated in these masters in 2006 to foster exchanges between students, business professionals and local community actors in the sectors of ICTs and real estate around new services designed and prototyped by students. It also finds its source in the construction of Sandbox, a collaborative space imagined in 2011 and realized in 2014 by the students of MIPI and MITIC, with their professors and some services of the university, as the first collaboration space of a French university, then extended to other IFIS degrees.

The family home construction market accounts for 135,000 operations per year in France. The profession played an essential role for the creation of the CCMI bachelor, expressing the lack of qualified personnel able to meet its requirements with both technical and management profiles: building technicians, facilitators of their sub-networks and real business skills (communication / negotiation) in the relationship with customers. The main skills to be given to apprentice students are especially technical: construction right and uses, management of sub contactors (coordination aspects), technical control of the construction, communication (negotiation) and relations with consumers and neighbors in the construction area, management of the construction budget of the individual house, etc. Until yesterday, largely absent in the construction of family homes, the uses of digital tools (especially tablets) are now strongly emerging, they also constitute an major challenge for the companies. We try to analyze new digital uses (tablets) in the essential economic sector of the building of individual houses [1].

In the MIPI and MITIC Master courses, Univcamp has built an ecosystem set up in its current form in 2012. Univcamp develops a cross-reflection on the collaborative society of tomorrow and especially on the use of ICTs devices in the real estate sector around innovative services imagined by students [2].

In these two degrees (bachelor and master), we particularly focus on the new Information and Communication challenges in companies around the development of new digital tools. We outline the idea of companies becoming "Digital Ecosystems", i.e. being considered as systems built by the interactions between all their actors and new uses of information with new digital tools such as tablets or smartphones, etc.

It also provides an opportunity to analyze the divided identity of the "Y generation" and its interactions with that of older workers, with the challenge of building new collective representations to improve performance in companies. We are also taking up the new challenge of the General Data Protection Regulation (GPDR). GPDR is a regulation of the European Union constituting the reference text for the protection of personal data when using personal and sensitive data in a global context of "augmented human" and data analysis for traceability and memory purposes.

In an idea of services co-production, these evolutions also question the relations with customers, becoming more involved actors, with new relations with employees of building companies through digital interface tools.

III. Scientific Position and Methodology

In terms of scientific position, we situate ourselves at the crossroads of Information and Communication Sciences and Management Sciences, to produce knowledge for action in an Action Research (AR) approach. Action Research is a process to uncover solutions through progressive problems solving activities. This process involves investigation through activity rather than theoretical response. It is also called participatory action research [3].

We refer to a constructivist perspective of construction of the social reality by the actors themselves or Constructivism, emerging first in psychology, with the Palo Alto researchers as Watzlawick [4]. As a learning theory, constructivism explains how people might acquire knowledge and learning. It suggests that humans construct knowledge and meaning from their experiences [5]. Brown-Martin [6] distinguishes "instructionism" (transmission of knowledge) from "constructionism" (reconstruction of knowledge), or teaching versus learning. According to Noy [7], in education, constructivism is a ground practice and constant questioning. For us, this pedagogical approach promotes the participation and commitment of apprentice students in a process of empowerment by improving skills through interactions with human actors and non-human devices. It is also a way of observing changes in the companies.

We also give special importance to the approach by the "complexity". Following Morin [8] [9], "complexity" is a holistic and multidimensional thought to connect in a systemic way interacting elements (actors, socio-technical devices, etc.). Genelot [10] focuses on "managing in (and with) the complexity" with the challenge of converging different representations to build a collective meaning for the organization performance. "Complexity" converges with the idea of "reliance" at different levels (micron, meso and macro) between actors in a systemic approach. We try to understand how a social system works with actors who interact to form an ecosystem of interactions. According to Le Cardinal et al [11], we also focus on the importance of trust to better develop complex projects, particularly in information systems and communication devices.

In the field of French Information and Communication Sciences (SIC), we are following Bernard [12] at the convergence of link issues (interactions), meaning, knowledge and action, in an Action Research way to produce knowledge for action, with all the importance of interactions [13]. As outlined by Gramaccia [14], project and quality management are two main tools in a more and more digitalized society.

We also follow the specific paper of technical objects developed by Simondon [15], corresponding also to the Actor-Network Theory (ANT) and the sociology of translation, proposed by Callon [16], Akrich et al. [17]. Originally created by French researchers Latour and Callon, ANT is an attempt to understand processes of technological innovation and scientific knowledge-creation, emphasizing all surrounding factors and not only on the acts: tools, labs, cultural factors and environment, and various other technical and non-technical elements. It has been criticized to give too much importance to non-human actors [18]. We consider ANT as an interesting theory to highlight the importance of digital devices but not as an analytical tool.

Our approach to using tools, better than Human-Computer Interfaces (HCI), corresponds to Computer Supported Cooperative Work (CSCW). CSCW is a generic term, which combines the understanding of the way people work in groups with the enabling technologies of computer networking, and associated hardware, software, services and techniques [19]. We point out the specificity and ambivalence of ICTs devices, that is to say positive aspects to improve performance but also constraints and possible suffering at work (stress and burn out). It may correspond to the ambivalence of technology explained by Ellul [20].

Following Goffman, we give special importance to the notion of situation, for a long time "too neglected" [21]. We also work in an idea of "situated action" as proposed by Suchmann [22]. We favor the notions of situation, context and meaning with the idea of "interactionist and situational semiotics" as Mucchielli [23]. We also position ourselves as Carayol [24] in an approach of analysis of changes, especially induced by the ICTs in daily organizational innovation as analyzed by Alter [25]. Innovation is also important to improve skills to promote the economic development of the territories as explained by Godet et al. [26]. Following Leleu-Merviel [27], we focus on the concept of "design", particularly of jobs and skills, especially in services companies, to combine project dynamics, innovation and quality dynamics in an organizational ecosystem and on territory. We meet then the idea of competitive intelligence on a territory developed by Carayon's report [28]. As well as CPDirSIC [29], we consider "Design" as "science of project" and tool to "organize the group", an ecosystem or a territory.

Extending the approach of Putnam and Nicotera about "The Constitutive Role of Communication" for organizations [30], we propose an ICOE approach: Information (new uses of data) and Communication (interactions, mediations) for Organizing Ecosystems (organizations, territories and also work situations, etc.).

From a methodological point of view, during apprenticeship situations, we develop interviews with the main actors of these courses (universities and companies). For CCBMI Bachelor, we have also periods of participatory observations in the work situations of the apprentice students in their companies' periods with their interactions with other workers and through the use of the e-booklet.

Thus, for the CCBMI Bachelor, our case study focused on a group of 17 apprentice students from January to April 2018. We help them answer to a survey (*questionnaire*), used as a prerequisite for individual interviews. During visits to apprentice students in the workplace, the training coordinator was also able to observe some of them in their work situations (9) and was able to talk with a majority of tutors (10). The results of this study were presented at the committee meeting of this degree in September 2018, where a majority of companies' apprentice students tutors (10) and all apprentice students were present.

The Univcamp interaction device is composed of three different phases. The first phase of nearly 4 months where, following a call for proposals drafting around a central theme (2019 theme: responsible ecosystems), "caring customers" propose topics to explore related to their professional and concrete needs. The call for projects is distributed in the Master's network companies.

A work of definition and verification of compatibility with both the thematic and the university operation is carried out by a team of six teachers, who will then be university referents of the projects. The "caring customers" belong to organizations as different as SNCF (Railways) Development, the IT77 Association of the attractiveness cluster of the Seine-et-Marne department, the Digital Companies Federation (Syntec), etc,, the property management and the digital campus of the University Paris East-Marne-la-Vallée University, the University Paris-East staff of the i-site project, CROUS (Services for Students), the intercommunity of Meaux area, etc..

Then, there is a second 6-month phase, during which about 50 students will carry out 10 innovative and viable service projects. They form small groups of five or six students who deal with the problematic entrusted to each group by a benevolent customer from a user-centric approach to build a prototype and a sustainable model. Projects are designed and implemented with the help of an extended team of 10 teachers from resource classes (agile project, conflict management, design thinking, prospective) as part of a skills-based approach.

The third phase (the heart of Univcamp process), more hectic, takes place during a day of interactions between all the actors. It is centered on dissemination and collaboration. The essential link between these three phases for the success of the whole system is managed by a team of 9 teachers and teachers-researchers of the Master.

We have collected data as part of participatory observation approach. The team of 9 teachers (IFIS) took the lead role with other researchers of DICEN idf. They were helped by students to take notes. For the next years, to improve our observation of the restitution phase, we will use video recordings.

IV. FIRST RESULTS

Our observations, both in tutored projects for CCBMI Bachelor and Masters MITIC and MIPI interactions in the Univcamp device, have allowed interesting conclusions.

ICTs question all our society, changing our identities, our representations, the work conditions and our relations to information and communication, introducing an important gap between Internet natives or "Y Generation" and other people, the challenge of making them working together is particularly important for the survival of the companies.

The apprentice students of CCBMI Bachelor are "connected" people. They are especially interested in new digital uses in work situations. It is a new manner to discover their new job from their "apprentice" position. They also have a "lever" position, helping other older employees in their companies to discover these new tools and so their position is valued in a perspective of a "learning organization" (*organisation apprenante*) at two levels: training its employees but also developing their new skills especially digital ones. In this way, this approach is very appreciated by their companies, and especially by their apprenticeship supervisors. Customers are also interested because these digital tablets may favor information and knowledge sharing and, consequently, new ways of co-operation in a co-production of services approach.

The results of the survey and especially the interviews revealed different positions of apprentice students, according to their different situations of activities in the companies and their different corporate cultures. Some are very dependent on the guidance of their apprenticeship tutors (4), others have more autonomy and can take initiatives (6), others are in intermediate situations with more or less autonomy of action (7).

The answers also bring differences in the dual identity of apprentice students: at the same time students, but largely co-constructing their knowledge as employees of a company, therefore already involved in the world of business.

Our interviews and observations also outline the challenge of the digital gap (*fracture numérique*) between two generations of workers in the building companies: the young digital native workers and the older ones. This evolution changes the work relations, particularly regarding knowledge transmission and apprenticeship situations. In the past, especially in the building sector, the experience and the knowledge of older workers were very valued. The oldest passed on their knowledge to the youngest, especially in the guild or corporations companies. Now, with digital tools as tablets, in some situations, it is no longer the skill acquired by the experience that is essential but the ability to use these new digital tools. The change is important because the formerly highly valued workers (often over 50 years old) have now become partly dependent on the youngest, with virtually a reversal of markers or skills sliders. It is an interesting aspect of the ambivalence of technology [20] and its strong force in change [24] that can improve the companies' performances but can also, with new job design [27] [29], changes the old standards and hierarchies and thus possibly cause stress and suffering situations at work.

In the Univcamp device, three types of actors (students, professionals and teachers-researchers) meet to discuss the projects presentations and workshops. The debates are animated at the beginning of the morning by a jury of 6 people composed of academics and professionals. The actors are then brought to the workshops designed by the students to allow each guest to experience the innovative service on the basis of model (s), prototype (s), proof of concept(s) and numerous media communication explaining the project.

Since 2013, Univcamp device brings together, each year, more than one hundred and twenty people to imagine the society of tomorrow on such important topics as the University of tomorrow, smart and digital city, ecosystem on territories around the potential of digital and new collaborative spaces (station 2.0, workspace, telecentres, fab lab using open data, bots etc.). The format adapts year by year to the expectations of the public: from a two-days BarCamp, the event has evolved into experimental workshops around projects to test ideas and answer questions asked by benevolent customers. For the 2019 edition that we are setting up a scientific committee whose objective will be to support the publication of a collective work bringing together scientific productions around Univcamp's subjects of recent years, and thus promoting co-operations in an action research perspective.

V. DISCUSSION: BEYOND THE ICTS, THE IMPORTANCE OF THE PROBLEM OF THE USES

Real estate is tackling major challenges that are partly mediated by the issues raised by the concept of "smart city" around the idea of "smart building". The smart city promises a more intelligent urbanized world to better control the irreversible growth of cities (and therefore the evolution of territories impacted by this urbanization) with at heart the global infrastructures and logistics issues: energy management, mobility, connection of buildings, and also societal ones such as healthcare, evolution of jobs, etc. The questions also arise inside buildings with life quickly changing with digital uses: new areas, new ways of working (co-working, third places, etc.). They constitute important levers of changes in territories [25] [26] [28]. In this context, ICTs participate in the emergence of three new trends:

- Using digital tools and technology to offer new services and facilitate access to improve the quality of life and live better.
- Putting users (building occupants / city inhabitants) in the center of the problematics, integrate them, make them participate and co-create, etc.
- Creating sustainable value, considering all actors and their responsibilities with all the importance of interdependencies.

However, many digital projects at the building and city levels begin with organizational silos and transform them into digital silos. The challenge is to introduce more cross-cutting approach and network with the new digital technologies to overcome the silos (platforms, data and open data, networks etc.) It is becoming important to start from the needs of the occupants of the houses and the inhabitants of the areas. All this in a balanced way with the organizational needs and to design the new interactions between all the actors, in particular from the data deposits offered by the large-scale digital deployment (Internet of Things, data storage, silos, etc.).

We identify Univcamp as a global situation or ecosystem allowing the observation of the interactions and the CCBMI Bachelor as a favorable ground for the observation of job transformations.

In this way, we refer to the emerging idea of HDI or Human Data Interfaces in order to analyze new mediated data carried between all the human actors (and from non-human devices) and to promote new uses of these data to improve services in an interactive approach of services co-production.

For us, the constructivist approach is also an interesting way to observe the changes in the companies from the level of work situations in an attempt to tackle the invisible part or unformulated part of the work.

The key question of the uses raised by this observation can be organized into three themes for reflection as shown in the figure below:

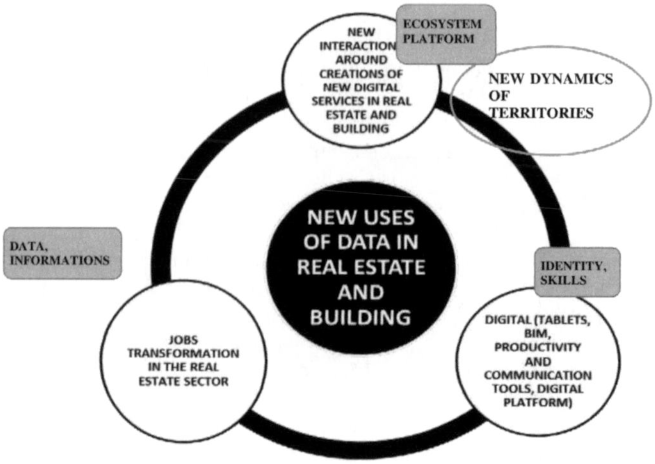

Figure 1. **An Ecosystem of Interactions Developed by New Uses of Digital Tools and Data.**

This figure is a synthesis of our analysis. It invites us to consider that a situation, consequence of the introduction of a technology, is for us the result of the information really mobilized by the actors in the situation, in relation to the questions of language, social representations, needs and skills and uses of new socio-technical devices.

VI. A POTENTIAL LEVER FOR COOPERATION IN APPRENTICES SITUATIONS, THE E-BOOKLET

In an approach based on the skills and competencies for collecting data in the workplace, we also wish, for future research, to attach particular importance to an intermediation tool in apprenticeship training: the e-booklet (*e-livret*). It is a compulsory tool to give traceability to the evolution of activities of the apprentice students during the year of their training, both in University and in companies in their work situations as analyzed by Bourret et al. [31].

Better used, the e-booklet may become an important interactions tool, focused on competencies and skills development, to show the evolution of the "employability" of the apprentice students during their training year, both in the university and in the company. It may also be an interesting support to collect new data about work in interactive situations.

More globally, for the apprentice students, the e-booklet may constitute a first step for a comprehensive skills booklet throughout their working lives, in the same way, for example, as the Electronic Health Record (EHR) for the digital health memory of all the citizens and for patient pathways including their travels or their new jobs in other countries during their lifetime.

For us, these paths represent interesting action research opportunities in a digital memory approaches to develop the traceability of our students' skills, as a first step, especially in real estate and building sectors.

VII. Conclusion: Towards An Observatory of Changes In Work Situations

Based on the promising results of Univcamp, around the Master degrees MIPI and MITIC and from the Bachelor degree CCBMI co-operations around new uses of digital tablets in the building sector, IFIS and DICEN idf wish to create an "incubator of ideas" space, as an interactions space between companies and university. It may correspond to a field of experimentation and innovation in order to analyze the changes in jobs, particularly around new digital uses. Our first steps concern the real estate and building sectors.

Its mission would be to try to respond to the societal challenges of the East of the Ile-de-France region as part of the i-site project, on the sustainable and inclusive city, central topic of the development of the UPEM University into the new one Gustave Eiffel University (January 2020), in cooperation with the French research Institute on Sciences and Technologies, Transports, Planning and Networks - *Institut Français des Sciences et Technologies des Transports, de l'Aménagement et des Réseaux* (IFSTTAR).

More globally, this interaction space aims to become a center of resources and expertise that federates the initiatives of the five Masters of the IFIS and some Bachelors (*Licences professionnelles*) for the development of new projects at two levels. First we will propose a label "incubators of ideas" for already existing initiatives as Univcamp or CCBMI Bachelor. Secondly we wish to develop new projects promoting transversal expertise between other IFIS Masters as digital tourism, quality, or healthcare and social welfare in the idea of analyzing jobs dynamics in specific ecosystems promoted by digital tools.

In this working paper, we have analyzed some of the work situations developed by new uses of digital tools, especially in the building and real estate sectors, through two complementary university degrees in a French University (UPEM) very focused on apprenticeship way of learning. This work is the first step for larger-scale works, always observing work situations of apprentice students through co-operations with their companies and discussing their feelings and their requirements, to develop their employability, that is to say to improve their skills and develop their efficiency in work situations.

IFIS Institute and Research Team DICEN idf plan also work together on a project of an observatory of job changes induced by digital tools, especially in the real estate and building sectors. We may begin with the idea of smart house or smart building linked for example to the use of Building Information Modeling (BIM) tool to an idea of Smart Building in a Smart City in a Smart Territory. It is a part of the new challenge of the UPEM in the i-site project of creation of a new federative establishment (Gustave Eiffel University) centered on the innovative, creative, integrative and sustainable city.

References

[1] C. Bourret and T. Drapier "Training in a Job Approach and Digital Uses in the Building Sector in France. The example of the Individual Houses in a French University Degree in An Apprenticeship Perspective", Proceedings, EDULEARN18 (10th annual International Conference on Education and New Learning Technologies), IATED, 2nd - 4th of July, Palma de Mallorca (Spain), pp. 2287 – 2290, 2018.

[2] C. Meyer and C. Bourret, "Developing Learning / Research Interactions in a French University from the Univcamp Device (Paris East University)", 11th Annual International Conference of Education, Research and Innovation – ICERI, Sevilla (Spain), 12 – 14th November, 2018.

[3] Available from: http://www.businessdictionary.com/definition/action-research.html/2018.12.26

[4] P. Watzlawick, The invention of reality. Contributions to constructivism / *L'invention de la réalité. Contributions au constructivisme*, Paris: Seuil, 1988.

[5] Available from: http://sydney.edu.au/education_social_work/learning_teachin g/ ict/theory/constructivism.shtml/2018.12.26

[6] G. Brown-Martin, Learning (Re)imagined. How the connected society is transforming learning, Bloomsbury Academic, 2014, 328 p.

[7] C. Noy, " Constructivism part in university studies / *La place du constructivisme dans l'enseignement universitaire* " in A. Mucchielli dir., Conference Constructivism part for communications studies / *La place du constructivisme pour l'étude des communications*, Béziers (France), pp. 225 – 238, 2003.

[8] E. Morin, Think global / *Penser global*, Paris: Flammarion, Champs-Essais, 2016.

[9] E. Morin, The seven necessary knowledges to education in the future / *Les sept savoirs nécessaires à l'éducation du futur*, Paris: Unesco, 1999.

[10] D. Genelot, Managing in (and with) the complexity / *Manager dans (et avec) la complexité*, Paris: Eyrolles, 2017.

[11] G., Le Cardinal, J.-F. Guyonnet, B. Pouzoullic and J. Rigby, "Intervention Methodology for complex problems: The FAcT-Mirror method", European Journal of Operational Research, Elsevier, n° 132, pp. 694-702, 2001.

[12] F. Bernard, "Information and Communication Sciences (ICS) : an openness and decompartementalization discipline / *Les SIC une discipline de l'ouverture et du décloisonnement*", in A. Bouzon, coord.., The organizational communication in debate Fields, concepts, perspectives / *La communication organisationnelle en débat. Champs, concepts, perspectives*, Paris: L'Harmattan, pp. 33 – 46, 2006.

[13] L. Bègue and O. Desrichard, co-dir., Treatise of social psychology. The science of human interactions / *Traité de psychologie sociale. La science des interactions humaines*, Bruxelles: De Boeck, 2013.

[14] G. Gramaccia, "Quality, project, digital : 3 symbolic variations of managerial efficiency / *Qualité, projet, numérique : 3 variations symboliques de l'efficacité gestionnaire*", in C. Batazzi coord., Communication, organisation, symbols / *Communication, organisation,*

symboles, Revue MEI n° 29, Paris: L'Harmattan, pp. 55-67, 2008.

[15] G. Simondon, The mode of existence of technical objects / *Du mode d'existence des objets techniques*, Paris: Aubier, 1958.

[16] M. Callon, Some Elements of a Sociology of Translation: Domestication of the Scallops and the Fishermen of St Brieuc Bay. In John Law (ed.), Power, Action and Belief: A New Sociology of Knowledge. London: Routledge & Kegan Paul, 1986.

[17] M. Akrich, M. Callon and B. Latour, Sociology of translation. Founding texts / *Sociologie de la traduction. Textes fondateurs*, Paris: Les Presses Mines de Paris, 2006.

[18] Available from: https://www.learning-theories.com/actor-network-theory-a/2018.12.26

[19] Available on: https://en.wikipedia.org/wiki/Computer-supported_cooperative_work/2018.12.26

[20] J. Ellul, The technique or the challenge of the century / *La technique ou l'enjeu du siècle*, Paris: Economica, 1990.

[21] E. Goffman, "The Neglected Situation", in J.J. Gumperz and D. Hymes dir., "The Ethnography of Communication", *American Anthropologist*, Washington DC, pp. 133 – 137, 1964.

[22] L. Suchmann, Plans and Situated Actions. The Problem of Human-Machine Communication, Cambridge: Cambridge University Press, 1987.

[23] A. Mucchielli, Communication & Influence. Situational approach / Communication & *Influence. Approche situationnelle*, Nice: Les Editions Ovadia, 2010.

[24] V. Carayol, Organizational communication. An allagmatic perspective / *Communication organisationnelle. Une perspective allagmatique*, Paris: L'Harmattan, 2004.

[25] N. Alter, The ordinary innovation / *L'innovation ordinaire*, Paris: PUF, 2005.

[26] M. Godet, P. Durance and M. Mousli, Unleash innovation on territories / *Libérer l'innovation dans les territoires*, Paris : Conseil d'Analyse Economique - La documentation Française, 2010.

[27] S. Leleu-Merviel and H., Boulekbache-Mazouz, Design Researches Conception processes, witings and representations / *Recherches en design. Processus de conception, écriture et représentations*, Paris ISTE Editions, 2014.

[28] B. Carayon dir., Economic intelligence, competitiveness and social cohesion / *Intelligence économique, compétitivité et cohésion sociale*, Paris : La Documentation française, Available from: http://www.ladocumentationfrancaise.fr/rapports-publics/034000484/index.shtml, 2003.

[29] CPdirSIC (Permanent conference of lab directors in ICS / *Conférence Permanente des Directeurs / trices de laboratoires en SIC*), Researches Dynamics in Information and Communication Sciences / *Dynamiques de Recherches en Sciences de l'Information et de la Communication*, Paris, 2018.

[30] L. L. Putnam and A.M. Nicotera, Building Theories of Organization. The Constitutive Role of Communication, New York and London: Routledge, 2009

[31] C. Bourret, K. Fraoua, R. Eppstein, and B. Simon, "Knowledge construction and sandwiches trainings : reflections elements on monitoring lifelong leraning and skills around the new role of Universities in France / *Construction de connaissances et formations en alternance : éléments de réflexions sur le suivi des acquis de formation et des compétences tout au long de la vie autour du nouveau rôle des Universités en France*", Proceedings X[th] international ISKO (International Society for Knowledge Organization,) Strasbourg, November 2015, Chevry-Pebayle E. dir, Paris : ISTE Editions, pp. 372 – 388, 2017.

When Bigger is Simply Better After all:

Natural and Multi-Modal Interaction with Large Displays Using a Smartwatch

Franca Rupprecht & Carol Naranjo
Computergraphics & HCI
Technische Universität Kaiserslautern
Kaiserslautern, Germany
Email: rupprecht@cs.uni-kl.de
Email: valero@cs.uni-kl.de

Achim Ebert & Joseph Olakumni
Computergraphics & HCI
Technische Universität Kaiserslautern
Kaiserslautern, Germany
Email: ebert@cs.uni-kl.de
Email: josepholakunmi@gmail.com

Bernd Hamann
Department of Computer Science
University of California Davis
Davis, US
Email: hamann@cs.ucdavis.edu

***Abstract*—Smartwatches as latest technology of smart devices offer great opportunities for intuitive and natural interaction techniques. The inbuilt sensors of the smartwatches enable consistent user interaction and hands-free, heads-up operations. The utilization and usability of wrist gestures and in-air non touch gestures has been demonstrated in several studies. In combination with Large Display Devices (LDD), smartwatches can be used as control devices in a natural and intuitive way. The most common way to interact with large display devices has been through the keyboard/mouse interaction model, which gives the user wide interaction capabilities but limits the user in his physical space. However, providing more physical space for the user in order to walk around and explore the application projected limits the number of interaction modality. Often the only interaction modality performed with LDDs that do not limit the user to a steady device are pointing gestures. Using smartwatches as control interfaces for LDDs unfetters users from a steady control technology, as already demonstrated with, e.g., the Microsoft®PowerPoint smartwatch enhancement. Users are able to start presentations and switch to the next or previous slide by a simple button touch. But smartwatches offer a much higher potential as control devices of LDDs. More recently, there has been an increasing adoption of natural communication means, such as speech, touch or non-touch gestures (in-air gestures) for interacting with digital devices. Thus, in this paper we describe the design and utilization of a multi-modal interaction interface based on a smartwatch combining the input modalities: (1) touch gestures, (2) non-touch gestures, and (3) speech. In a user study, we employed the interface to different fields of application and discuss critically the suitability of the technology. It can be said, bigger is simply better after all.**

***Keywords*–smartwatch; human-computer interaction; multi-modal interaction; large display device; speech input.**

I. Introduction and Related Work

By the mid of 2017, we have access to a wide variety of inter-connected devices that communicate with their surroundings and expand interaction possibilities. For example, smartwatches have embedded sensors and decent processing units, and they have been considerably improved and become broadly available. Despite the increase of power from these ubiquitous devices, the amount of information they can display and the input capabilities via touch gestures are defined by their display sizes and are therefore limited. In spite of the small and usually poor displays on smartwatches, big-screen Televisions (TVs) and display monitors are becoming cheaper and more prevalent. As a result, display technologies are becoming less expensive as well, and there has been a steady increase in the use of the large screen displays. Using large screen displays for just viewing or public display purposes has never be a problem with researches suggesting they are very beneficial for data exploration, collaboration, and data organization [1]. Interacting with them (efficiently) has been a key problem, with several researches looking into different ways to improve interaction with large screens. Currently, one of the most prevalent way of interacting with large display is still through touch-screen interaction [2]. Touch-screen interaction in large displays suffers from a lot of shortcomings, some of which are: difficulty to reach extreme corners of the screen; privacy of input; arm fatigue due to distances between buttons, occlusion from the finger performing the touch input [3]. Additionally, the utilization of large screen metaphors in head-mounted-displays as presented in [4] requires eyes-free, natural, and intuitive interaction techniques as it is simply not possible to touch this virtual screen.

Due to the problems encountered with touch-screen interaction with large displays, several researches explored the possibilities of touch-less / remote interaction devices. Ardito et al. [2] reported 34% of surveyed paper were focused on interaction with large displays using a remote device. These devices interact with large displays mostly through wireless protocols, such as Bluetooth, Wireless Fidelity (Wi-Fi), infrared, Short Message Service (SMS), etc. Lots of research efforts have been put into this technique of interaction, employing different devices, such as smart-phones, Wiimote, etc.; however, the smartwatches are often overlooked and underutilized, despite being easily accessible.

Over the past few years, smartwatches embedded with sensors and decent processing units have been undergoing improvements in technology and sales (adoption). According to Statista [5], about 75 million smartwatches where sold in 2017. Therefore, it is noticeable that these wearable devices are becoming widely available with an adoption rate and predicted to grow even further in the coming years.

Despite the increase in processing power and capabilities of these portable devices, the amount of information that can be displayed is highly limited by the screen sizes. However, smartwatches are fitted with processing power, sensors, and input possibilities, such as touch screens, microphones, heart rate monitors, etc. These sensors and input devices can be exploited to interact with these large display devices using natural modalities of interactions, such as tilt, touch, non-touch gestures and speech. When combining these modalities appropriately with the right user interfaces, they can create novel interaction modalities other than touch-screen displays or desktop interaction models.

Technologies for large-screen displays and smartwatches have limitations, and the lack of capabilities of one device can be compensated by the capabilities of another (display/screen-estate vs. sensors). The possibilities for natural interaction to be achieved with these devices has been explored, see [6] for example. The sensors and input capabilities of the smartwatch can be exploited to support the interaction with large-display devices, using natural interactions, such as touch, gesture or speech. Speech enhances overall interaction capabilities enormously. The use of speech is often the easiest, most natural way to interact with other humans but also computers [7]. In many of today's systems, using speech and gestures is supported in the user interface, creating a concerted and more natural user interaction [8]. Such natural interaction enables innovative interaction possibilities, going far beyond those offered by a remote control or desktop interaction model. Previous work covered the aspects of body movement gestures (non-touch gestures) [9], which will be enhanced in this work with the most natural way of interaction: speech.

In this paper, an approach for fusing multiple interaction modalities, such as speech, touch-gesture, and non-touch gestures by using a smartwatch for user interaction with large display devices is introduced in Section 2. In Section 3, we investigate in depth the concepts of multi-modal interaction and speech recognition within different usage contexts.

We first present concepts of multi-modal interaction and speech recognition in a general manner. Subsequently, we demonstrate the adaptation and utilization of these concepts in a first prototype system for three different scenarios. Therefore, we explain the system implementation in Section 4. The system is evaluated within a user study, in Section 5, in order to document the benefits or shortfalls offered by the combination of the various input modalities. Afterwards, we will critically discuss the suitability of such interfaces in different fields of application and make suggestions of suitable setups for these different kind of scenarios. In Section 6, we will discuss the conclusion and give suggestions for further work.

II. Multi-Modal Interaction

The term multi-modal interaction refers to the combination of several (multi) natural methods of communication for the purpose of interacting with a system. Natural modalities of communication are, amongst others, gesture, gaze, speech, and touch [10]; thereby making it more intuitive to untrained users. This interaction interface allows a user to employ their skilled and coordinated communicative behavior to control systems in a more natural way. Hence, multi-modal systems incorporate different modalities.

Modality refers to the type of communication used to convey or acquire information. It is the way an idea is expressed or the manner in which an action is performed [11], and it defines the type of data exchange. The state that determines the way information is interpreted in order to extract or convey meaning is referred to as *mode*. For example, gesture modality can provide data that can be interpreted into different modes of communication, such as *tilt* or *shake*. When multiple modalities are in use, it is paramount to fuse them in a way that is most suitable and natural.

Central to this concept is the ability to combine data perceived by the user, *fusion*. While on the output end, multiple channels (mostly independent of one another) can also be used to convey information, which is called *fission*.

In multi-modal systems, the decision to fuse or not to fuse the data from different modalities depends on the suitability of the intended usage of the data. The absence of multi-modal fusion is called *independent* multi-modal interaction whereas the presence is termed *combined* [11]. Combination of audio from two microphones or a microphone-array for a stereo effect can be said to be fusion. Fission on the other hand, is the splitting and dissemination of information through several channels [12], used for outputting information in more immersive ways. This could be the transmission of text, speech, vibration feedback, and audio cues concurrently, to allow a more accurate interpretation.

III. Concept of a Multi-Modal Interaction Interface

In order to provide a proof-of-concept of multi-modal interaction system using a smartwatch and speech, we had to fully understand the general concept and explore its feasibility. Research papers, such as [13] for example, provide insight into multi-modal interaction, guiding us to determine viability of some of our envisioned approaches.

A. Modes of interaction.

As multi-modal systems become more prevalent, new and novel ways of interacting with systems are continuously being discovered and improved, techniques, such as gaze, smile, gesture, speech, and touch, amongst others, are not uncommon in modern studies in Human Computer Interaction (HCI). The modes of interaction for our implementation are chosen in order to get the most potential out of the smartwatch as main interaction device, keeping in mind the common capabilities embedded on it as well as the restrictions of size and limited processing power.

1) Speech Input: The use of speech as an interaction modality is not a new technique in HCI. Actually, it has gone through numerous evolutions to attain the level of stability it presently supports today, with some systems almost enabling free form communication. Several speech based interaction systems exist today ranging from software based speech input systems (e.g., Siri) to dedicated standalone devices (e.g., Xperia Ear). Although speech has proven very useful for hands-free interaction, it can, however, be hindered by problems, such as ambient noise, privacy, and limited support for accents. Numerous *Software Development Kits* (SDKs) have been developed from research projects aiming to improve the process of speech recognition and analysis. They can be classified into two main categories: online and offline analysis. The online based analysis engines leverage powerful cloud architecture for speech recognition thereby offloading processing from the device, which serves as input interface. Some examples of popular *Application Programming Interfaces* (APIs) are: Google Speech API [14] or Microsoft's Bing Speech API [15]. Offline analysis engines allow analysis from within the system/application without the need of a network connection,

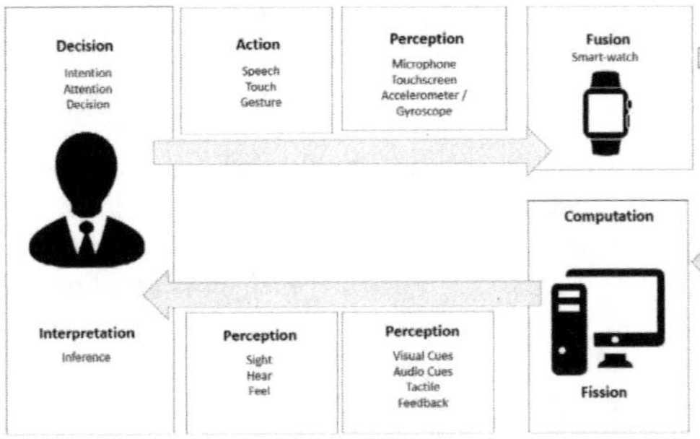

Figure 1. Multi-modal interaction system. The main components are a smartwatch and a large display enabling speech, touch, and gesture modalities perceived by the system through microphone, touchscreen, accelerometer, and gyroscope. Visual and audio cues, as well as tactile feedback are perceived by the user due sight, hear, and feel.

an example is CMU Sphinx open source speech recognition [16].

2) Gesture Input: Gestures used as interaction modes, adds more meaning to interaction with systems or interfaces, by empowering users to achieve goals in more natural ways that current modalities, such as mouse and keyboard does not allow [17]. Gesture input allows more natural communication modes, such as pointing, body movement, tilt, shake, etc. to interact with systems. A popular example is movement tracking with Kinect camera [18], which uses a RGB camera, depth sensor and a microphone array for acquiring user's complete body interaction and voice commands. Another popular gesture based input interface is the Wii remote control [19], which enables numerous ways of interacting with systems using gesture and movement [20]. Most mobile phones and smartwatches of recent age, come equipped with sensors that can be used to easily detect gestures of various forms which can range from a mere shake, down to imitation of steering wheel tilt for racing mobile games.

3) Touch Input: Touch is the most common input method for smart devices [21]. However, smartwatches compared to common smart devices have an even smaller form factor and are worn on a wrist, which demands a reconsideration of common smart device input techniques. Touch is more difficult on smartwatches, which typically have small screens, exacerbating the fat finger problem [22] and no multi-touch capabilities. Therefore, touch input on smartwatches should be designed in a way that even inaccurate touches are successful, i.e., very precise touch points (e.g., too small buttons) should be avoided, but at the same time, a good distribution of User Interface (UI) elements on the smartwatch's display can accelerate the task completion.

B. Interaction model.

An overview of the interaction model is shown in Figure 1, based on the multi-modal interaction concept, showing the main components needed to achieve the desired level of interaction capabilities. The figure emphasizes which modalities are used to support a user in the decision making process. We designed and implemented a smartwatch application that enables users to interact with large display devices, allowing users to interact with a Personal Computer (PC) using the provided combination of interaction modalities, i.e., speech, tilt gesture, and touch. Since the smartwatch is completely separated from the display or PC, one wants to communicate with, a system architecture is needed that enables transfer of user interaction data and interpretation of this data on the receiving large-display. In order to capture speech, gesture, and touch input, the smartwatch must have a microphone, gyroscope, accelerometer, and touch screen. Further, the smartwatch must be capable of communicating with the PC using a wireless network, requiring the smartwatch to have its own board and a Wi-Fi communication chip.

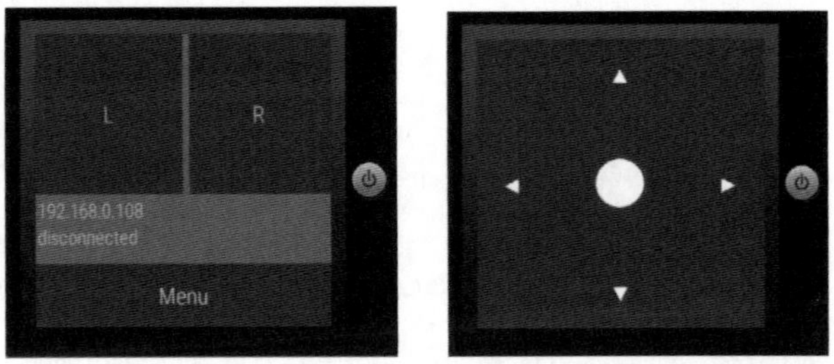

(a) Watch UI for mouse/keyboard mode (b) Watch UI for game controller mode

Figure 2. Watch User Interface for different modes

C. Application scenarios.

Multi-modal interaction can be used in many contexts, ranging from navigating a map on a white-board for controlling a robot, or navigating on a smartwatch menu. However, a "near-perfect" interaction paradigm used in one context could be inappropriate in another context; different contexts have different requirements in terms of precision and responsiveness [23]. We propose and implement two concepts to suit better different case scenarios: Free form and Tailored.

Concept A: Free Form The first category of prototypes were geared towards providing total freedom of usage to users, i.e., the input device will appear as a non customized input device, thereby appearing as an alternative to both keyboard and mouse; and also game controller. For this category the watch exists as a prototype considered suitable for "Windows, Icons, Menus, Pointing" (WIMP) and video games thereby existing as a direct substitution. The UI for the mouse/keyboard mode and the game controller-mode are shown in Figure 2.

Concept B: Tailored for Productivity According to the *productivity* category in the survey provided by Ardito et al. [2], this category refers to interfaces and interaction techniques customized for specific applications. In this mode, the UI will be created and interaction capabilities are adapted to specific use cases. We explored two use cases in our work: a data-exploration application (a common use for large displays) and a navigation game.
To better suit users' preferences, the device will provide options for customizations based on preference, such as sensitivity, inverted axis, or orientation. To support our targeted scenarios well, the application provides two options: toggling orientation to match wrist-use mode and air mouse hand-held mode in which the watch is simply hold in the hand in analogy to the usual smartdevice usage.

D. Gesture implementation.

Two classes of gestures are handled by our prototype, (1) tilt and (2) face-down. Users are alerted to calibrate the app to detect their watch's central position, used as reference point for interpreting sensor data. In order to support the tilting functionality, the data from the IMU sensors are combined and processed to obtain the updated rotation in the world coordinate system. The procedures `getRotationMatrix` and `getOrientation` of Android SDK's SensorManager are used. The procedure `getRotationMatrix` returns the rotation matrices in an orthonormal basis system[24].
The rotation matrix resulting from this process is passed on to the `getOrientation` of the `SensorManager`, returning angular vector data (in radian) as an array of `Azimuth`, `Pitch`, and `Yaw` values. This data is converted to degrees and normalized before sent to the server.
The tilt implementation was changed by using the **rotation vector**, which greatly simplifies the process, as we merely need to subscribe one sensor. The rotation vector represents the orientation as a combination of angle and axis in which the device is rotating, described as an angle θ around axis (x,y,z) [25]. The coordinate system, however, remains the same. Also, we implemented the hand flick gesture into the final system in order to perform **next**, **previous** or **toggling** through a list.
The **face-down gesture** relies on the use of gravity data. The desired effect is achieved when gravity readings are mainly in z-axis direction, with values being $v \leq -9.0m/s^2$ and readings close to 0 in the other two axis-directions. The face-down gesture is only used in this first prototype to enable listening for speech interaction. Before issuing a speech command, a user must twist the watch, forcing it to face down towards the floor, invoking the listening module and causing the watch to vibrate indicating readiness for speech input. We considered different methods to determine a very good solution for speech recognition. *Shake-to-Speak* is an operational mode where the smartwatch is quickly shaken in any direction to activate the speech listener. Another solution for the speech listening module is to continuously listen to all spoken words. Both approaches lead to many false positives and require high computation times. Using a dedicated gesture to wake up the listening module is less resource-intensive than listening continuously, and a dedicated gesture-based approach also produces less false positives.

E. Touch-Track-pad.

Furthermore, we enhanced the touch input modalities with touch-track input in order simulate mouse movements and pan activities. This could be applied by tracking finger touch movements and its velocity across the screen.

F. Speech implementation.

Several speech recognition engines were considered. The CMU pocket sphinx was adopted in this prototype, mainly due to its light-weight form and portability. Speech processing is done off-line. Two types of speech recognition were implemented, *keyword-targeted translation* and *free-form speech* for typing. Free-form speech recognition is made possible through dedicated keywords. Text synthesized from speech is transmitted as normal text in a JSON format to the server.

IV. SYSTEM IMPLEMENTATION

A. Architecture

For the implementation of our concept, we adopted a *component-based architecture*. The overall system was divided into two separate components. The system uses a *smartwatch app* component, included in the smartwatch module, and a *server* component, part of the large display module that is executed on the PC end. Both components only transmit to one another but do not rely on each other for processing capabilities, as computations and data transformations are done locally in both components.

1) Smartwatch application: For the development of the smartwatch application, the Sony smartwatch 3 [26], called SWR50 in the following, was used. The SWR50 is equipped with a microphone, Wi-Fi, and an Inertial Measurement Unit (IMU) with accelerometer, gyroscope and magnetometer, making it suitable for our purposes. It also runs the Android Wear O.S 1.5, which enables direct socket communication to help reducing latency. As shown in Figure 3, the app depends on data provided by the O.S' Sensor Manager.

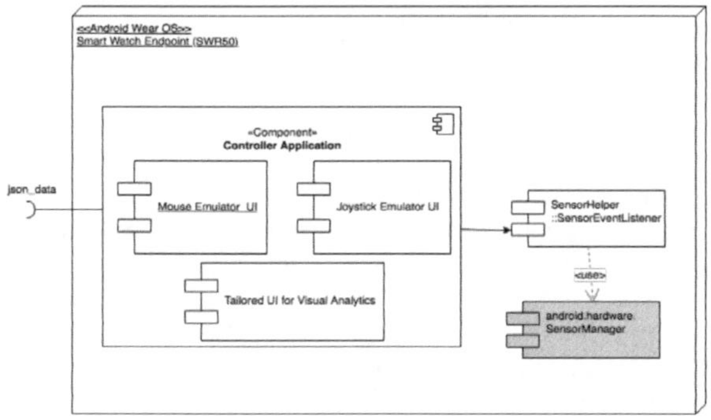

Figure 3. Smartwatch app and explicitly accessed system APIs (red).

2) Large Display Device: The large display is controlled from a Windows machine, where a *server application* is deployed to receive and interpret the data sent from the smartwatch in order to execute the intended action(s). On the same machine,it is deployed the corresponding dedicated application for the case of the tailored scenario.

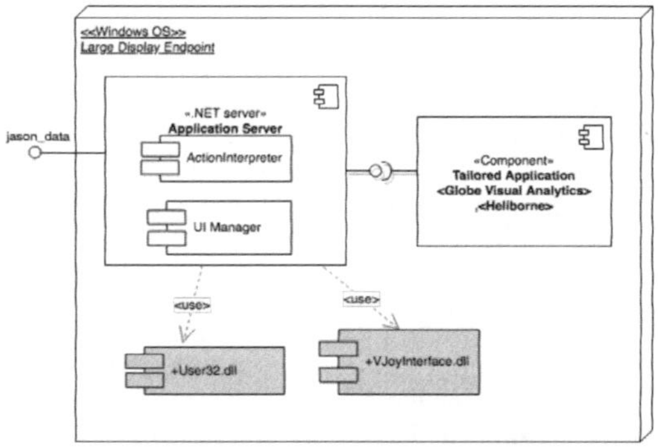

Figure 4. Large display components

a) Server application: The server application is implemented using the Microsoft .NET framework. It interprets the data from the smartwatch and decides what actions to execute. The server enacts the user's intention through the appropriate dependencies for the Windows Operative system, see in Figure 4. The server UI see in Figure 5 was designed in a straightforward manner to provide useful capabilities, including axis inversion, speed-of-mouse control and a drop-down box that allows a user to switch between three contexts to support a specific scenario via an appropriate mode. The three modes are: *mouse mode, key navigation mode*, and *game controller mode*.

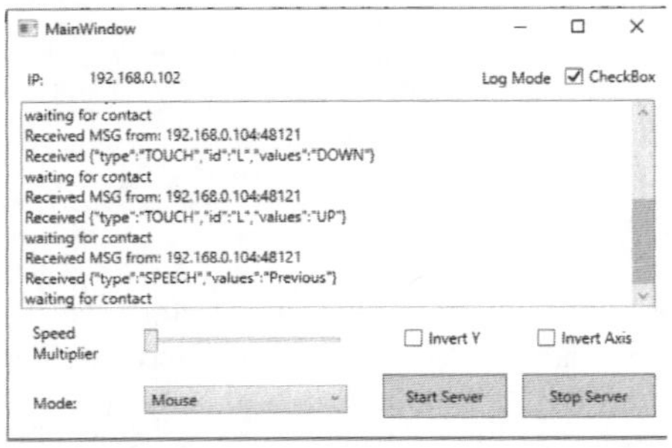

Figure 5. User Interface of the server application. The received data packets from the smartwatch are displayed for debugging purposes.

In *mouse mode*, mouse movement is simulated by tilting the smartwatch in the corresponding direction. Angular tilt data of smartwatch motion is mapped to mouse velocity. Hence, a steep tilt causes the mouse to move at high speed. In *keyboard mode*, speech is used as text input and the keyboard's cursor keys are simulated by mapping tilt angle and direction of smartwatch motion. In *controller mode*, the server acts as a feeder to the Vjoy controller, interpolating the angular values from tilt data to match an analog stick axis. This mode imitates a virtual joystick's movement, mimicking a controller analog stick with the smartwatch's tilting motions.

b) Communication Protocol: Communication between the smartwatch application and the server is enabled by a User Datagram Protocol (UDP) socket connection. Although UDP lacks reliability and congestion control, it is energy-efficient [23]. Furthermore, due to the absence of reliability logic and status packets (ACK/NACK), a high throughput and low latency can be ensured. Regarding our system, packet loss can be tolerated for our gesture data-based approach, but a lag would be detrimental for a smooth user experience. The data sent to the server is serialized as JSON since it is a light protocol that also helps in reducing the load in communication.

V. User Study

We presented two different applications covering examples for data exploration and immersive navigation, which are adequate applications to demonstrate large display interaction. Participants performed 18 tasks in total, whereby we measured their success rates in order to determine the systems effectiveness. Afterwards, surveys and interviews about usability and user satisfaction were carried out.

A. Study setting

7 university students participated in the study (undergraduate and graduate students, 21-29 years old; 5 were male and 2 female; 3 participants had experience with wearable devices and 3 participants are using speech commands frequently). In order to measure the usability and adaptability of the setup we followed the taxonomy of tasks for large display interaction, according to Foley [27]. Thus, the following task types are realized in both applications: (1) Position, (2) Orient, (3) Select, (4) Path, (5) Quantify, (6) Text. If we can demonstrate that all tasks types according to the task taxonomy are applicable in an adequate way, it can be stated that the system is usable and adaptable for large display interaction.

B. Case 1: Visual analytics - Data exploration around the globe over the years

The visual analytic application is based on the Unity3D-Globe provided by Aldandarawy [28]. A 3D globe showing the worlds population is centered on the screen, as shown in Figure 6. Area's population values are discrete data sets shown as color-coded bars attached to the country/area. The height of the bar and the color denotes the amount of population.

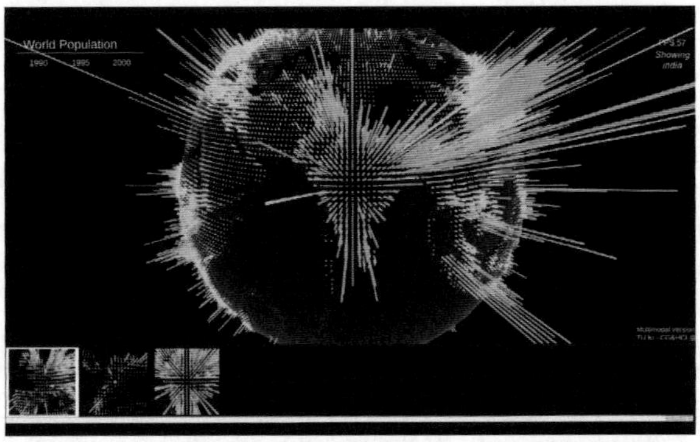

Figure 6. Unity3D-Globe application controlled with multi-model interaction techniques.

TABLE I. CASE 1: ACTION MAPPING.

No.	Action	Interaction	Task type
1	Rotate globe	Touch	Position, Orientation
2	Change data per year	Touch & Gesture	Select
3	Zoom in/out	Speech	Quantify
4	Get specific data	Speech	Text
5	Take a screenshot	Speech	Select
6	Change the mode	Gesture	Path

TABLE II. SPEECH COMMANDS FOR DATA EXPLORATION APPLICATION.

Command	Action
"Go to <Country name>"	Locate the globe to the desired location
"Zoom in" / "Zoom out"	Zoom in or zoom out in the current location
"Capture"	Take a screenshot of current location
"Remove"	Remove selected screenshot

The application is initially created for a mouse/keyboard setting but could be easily enhanced for improved interaction technology. The stated task types are mapped to the following actions inside the application as shown in Table I. The integrated speech commands are listed in Table II.

C. Tasks for Case 1

Users are given a labeled world map and a list of country names. At the beginning, users were asked to perform simple navigation tasks in order to explore the control capabilities. In the next step, users were asked to use the learned interaction techniques in order to explore the data. The following tasks had to be performed:

Control exploration phase:

1) Rotate the globe in all directions (watch control - touch & tilt).
2) Show the data for the year 1995 (watch flickering in year mode).
3) Zoom in and out (voice control).
4) Locate and view each of the countries (alternate voice and/or watch control), capture the view in few locations (voice control).
5) Remove a selected capture (voice control).

Data observations:

1) Observe the population growth in Hong Kong from year 1990 to 2000.
2) Capture the view of the current location.
3) Compare the population between Europe and Asia in the year 2000 using captures.
4) Remove existing captures (voice control).
5) Compare the population between France, Colombia, and India in the year 2000 using captures.

D. Case 2: Immersive navigation - Heliborne

The application for immersive navigation (see in Figure 7), called Heliborne [29], is also initially created for mouse/keyboard setup but could be enhanced for improved interaction technology. The application is a simple helicopter simulator controlled with multi-model interaction techniques provided by the smartwatch. Heliborne is a helicopter combat game that simulates combats and terrains, helicopter and gunships from 1950 to modern day machines. It is not a real helicopter flight simulator game, but a flight game with flight physics toned down to a control scheme make flying and playing simple and fun. Although complex maneuvers may still require some degree of expertise, the basics can be easily picked up and enjoyed.

Figure 7. Heliborne – a helicopter simulator controlled with multi-model interaction techniques.

The stated task types are mapped to the following actions inside the application as shown in Table III and linked with the speech commands listed in Table IV.

E. Tasks for Case 2

Users have a print out copy of the map in the application, highlighting specific locations. Analog to the first application, introductory users were ask to perform simple navigation tasks

TABLE III. CASE 2: ACTION MAPPING.

No.	Action	Interaction	Task type
1	Raise Altitude	Speech	Quantify
2	Reduce Altitude	Speech	Quantify
3	Control flight direction	Touch & Tilt	Position
4	Move Camera	Touch & Gesture	Orientation
5	Fire/Stop Fire	Speech & Touch	Select
6	Roll left/right	Touch & Speech	Position, Quantify
7	Switch Weapon	Flick wrist	Selection
8	Select gun	Speech	Selection

TABLE IV. SPEECH COMMANDS FOR IMMERSIVE NAVIGATION APPLICATION.

Command	Action
"Go up" / "Go down"	Raise/reduce altitude of the helicopter
"Enough"	Clears previous command
"Bank left" / "Bank right"	Role the helicopter left/right
"Open fire"	Starts fire
"Give me guns"	Selects gun as weapon
"Give me rockets"	Selects rockets as weapon

in order to explore the control capabilities. In the next step, users were asked to use the learned interaction techniques in order to explore the simulation world and to perform combined tasks. The following tasks had to be performed:

Control exploration phase:

1) Raise/Reduce altitude of the helicopter (voice control).
2) Control helicopter in all directions (watch control).
3) Move the camera in left/right direction.
4) Roll left/ right (touch and voice control).
5) Select a gun and fire (voice control & flickering).

Simulation world observation:

1) Visit the camp located around longitude 6.8 and latitude 35; count the number of Silos in that settlement. (From the starting point behind you).
2) Visit the other camp located around longitude 6 and latitude 45; count the number of silos situated there.
3) Travel to the rendezvous point at longitude 4.8 and latitude 65: locate the orange signal, destroy as much of the surrounding structure around the location as you can, before landing.

F. Procedure

Conducting the whole experiment took about 45 minutes per participant. We determined 5 minutes to introduce the setups and basic interfaces. Then the participants carried out the tasks described underneath. Before each task, the concept and input modalities have been introduced and exemplary demonstrated. The participants were asked to get familiar with the corresponding device before the actual tasks have been conducted (10 minutes per application).
After the task execution session, we conducted a survey and interview. The survey included 5 aspects listed in Figure 9. During the interview, we asked for the reasons for their ratings. We also asked about general usability issues and solicited detailed feedback about the system and the experience of multi-modal interaction with the smartwatch.

G. Results

1) Effectiveness: In order to measure the effectiveness of the system, we measured the users' success rate of each task performance. The averaged success rates defines the total accuracy value of the executed tasks. The effectiveness value is calculated by multiplying the success rate with the normalized task difficulty. Table V summarizes the accuracy and effectiveness results for both demonstrated applications.

TABLE V. ACCURACY AND EFFECTIVENESS VALUES OF BOTH APPLICATIONS.

Application	Tasks	Accuracy	Effectiveness
Visual analytics	10	96.25	95.17
Immersive navigation	8	82.5	76.73

2) User Acceptance: For the user acceptance, the descriptive statistic values mean, median, and standard deviation based on 5 point likert scale are calculated. In total, we asked 21 questions, covering the usability aspects Suitability, Learnability, Controllability, Error Tolerance, and Attitude toward using the technology, as described by Venkatesh et al. [30]. The Boxplot in Figure 8 shows the distribution of the collected user acceptance measures sorted per asked question.

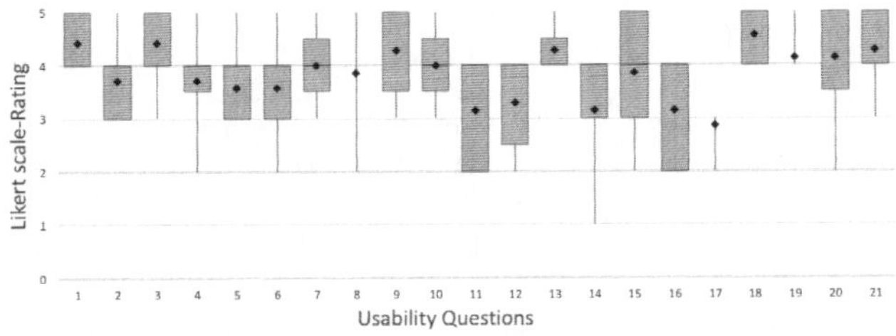

Figure 8. Boxplot displays the data distribution of the usability measures.

The average acceptability over all questions is 3.81, showing a quite good result. From direct feedback with the user, an overall satisfaction was stated, the subjects felt that learning the system was easy, using the system was fun, and the system would make their work more interesting. Users mentioned not having the feeling of complete control over the scene but also stated that it would be easy to become skillful in using the system. The attitude toward using the technology has an average value of 4.28, higher than the suitability value with 4.07, and the controllability with 3.71 in average. Table VI summarizes the acceptability measures per usability category, which are visualized in Figure 9.

TABLE VI. AVERAGE RATING OF USABILITY CATEGORIES.

Usability categories	Average rating
Suitability	4,07
Learnability	3,71
Controllability	3,71
Error Tolerance	3,28
Usage attitude	4,28

3) Quantitative Assessment: As described in [31], the qualitative results of the assessment provide a performance quantification basis that results in a scalar usability value U.

The aim of this evaluation was to proof that the system is suitable for those kinds of applications and large display interaction. Thus, the usability categories suitability and users attitude towards using the system was more important implicating the association of a higher weight in the usability score calculation. As we focused less on evaluating the quality of the implemented tasks, as well as the interaction techniques

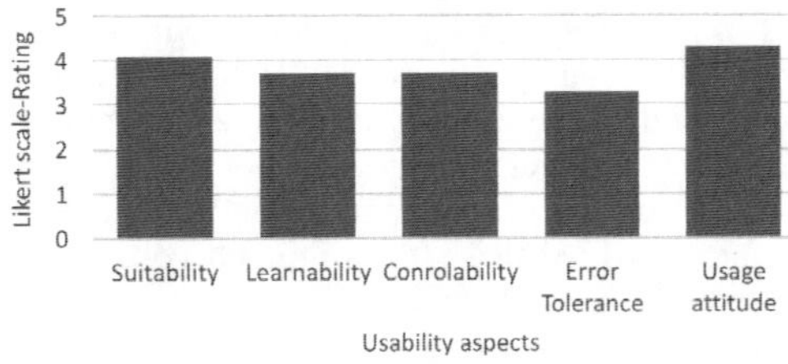

Figure 9. Average user ratings of usability categories from questionnaire.

TABLE VII. WEIGHTS AND SCORING OF USABILITY CATEGORIES TO CALCULATE USABILITY SCORE U OF THE SYSTEM.

Category	(1)	(2)	(3)	(4)	(5)
$w(s)$	0,3	0,1	0,2	0,1	0,3
$v(s)$	1	0,66	0,78	0,66	1
$w(s) \cdot v(s)$	0,3	0,06	0,15	0,06	0,3
$\sum$			0.8905		

themselves, the categories error tolerance and learnability are less weighted. Table VII summarizes the weights and scoring of each usability category, leading to a satisfactory overall usability score of $U = 0.8905$.

H. Discussion

We could demonstrate that all interaction task types according to the task taxonomy are applicable in an adequate way. It can be stated that the system is usable and adaptable for large display interaction. The visual analytics application, compared to the immersive navigation application, incorporates less degree of freedom, making the control easier. As expected, the accuracy value of the visual analytics application (96.25 %) is higher than the form of the immersive navigation application (82.5 %). Analog observations are found for the effectiveness value (95.17 % vs. 76.73 %). Thus, the first application shows very good results; implying suitability of the system for this kind of task. The immersive navigation application, however, was in total more difficult. It could be observed that the control techniques felt less cumbersome towards the end of the evaluation. After executing the interviews, it is to expect that the effectiveness of the system with this kind of applications will increase after a longer training phase as users felt they could become easily skillful at using the system.

We could prove that multi modal interaction realized with the use of a single smartwatch is usable for exploration tasks and adaptable as large display interaction. With overall satisfactory user feedback and an usability score of 0.8905 over 1, the presented system demonstrates a more natural and novel way of interaction.

As mentioned in the title of this paper, we will critically discuss the suitability of such interfaces in different fields of application. Although, it could be shown that the utilization of a smartwatch as control interface is usable for these kind of tasks, it is still to discuss if the smartwatch is really suitable in these or other scenarios.

In the case of controlling a Virtual Reality-scene (VR-scene), using the device motion sensors of smartphones is a quite common approach. The smartphone is simply tilted in the direction of movement and the tilting angle is transferred to the virtual control object. Hereby, the smartphone is held in the hand. The smartwatch, however, is attached to the wrist. Tilting gestures in all 3 Degrees Of Freedom (DOF's) is limited due to the physical constraints of the human forearm and thus, higly unnatural. Accordingly, handling of tilting with smartphones feel natural and intuitive, but not with the smartwatch. Although, usable in general and commonly applied as flick gesture, are this kind of small non-touch gesture not suitable for controlling VR-scenes.

Bigger scalled non-touch gestures, like circling the arm or swiping using the complete arm, fit to controll a VR-scene (see [9]). These kind of gestures, however, need more time than small and quick movements like tilting. But, on the contrary, bigger or longer gestures lead to longer reaction time and thus are not suitable in competing applications and VR games.

Horak et al. [32] presented enhanced exploration capabilities by the combination of a smartwatch and an interactive large display within information visualization applications. This kind of interaction does not require quick reaction time or even different DOF's. As such, the watch acts as filtering technique, while the large screen is giving the overview of the investigated dataset. Getting additional information on the smartwatch is again higly limited while larger scaled smartdives as smartphones and tablet pc's are commonly used in that kind of scenario that bring a higher degree of information presentation and interaction capabilities.

Smartwatches, however, can enhance the efficiency of collaborations arising in design, simulation or data analysis, including visualization, as presented in [33]. Additional to smartdevices, the smartwatch is used to give at-the-glance information without distracting from the actual tasks and collaborations. Using the smartwatch as an alternative to the used smartdevices would decrease the quantity and quality of information presentation and interaction capabilities.

Following, although smartwatches constitute an hand free alternative for controlling applications on large displays, the limitations of the technology is omnipresent and bigger scaled devices seem to be more suitable and powerful. Concluding, either bigger gestures (mid-air gestures) with the utilization of the smartwatch, bigger time frames for computation (no competing scenarios) or even bigger scaled hand-held devices are more promising for further trends. Leading to the teasing statement in the title that bigger is simply better after all.

VI. Conclusion and Future Work

The combination of touch gestures, non-touch gestures, and speech leads to a more natural and novel ways of interaction. Speech interaction as the most natural way of interaction enhances the range of common interaction techniques significantly. Together with touch- and non-touch gesture a wide range of natural and intuitive interaction capabilities are provided. The lightweight and portability of a smartwatch makes it very convenient to handle and fuse all the modalities into one single system. Based on first prototype combining touch, non-touch gestures, and speech as interaction techniques performed with a smartwatch we could improve the system for better performance and usability. The results are described and incorporated. The performed user study of the final system provided some useful ways of combining speech, gesture, haptic, and touch interaction modes with a smartwatch, showing an effectiveness value of 95.71 % and 76.73 %. As such, the system is suitable and adaptable as efficient interaction techniques for controlling large displays. We could gather overall satisfactory user feedback resulting in an usability score of 0.8905. Following, the presented system demonstrates more natural and novel way of interaction for large displays and in general. In further work, we will work on a system that allows to easily link application-functionality with input modalities. Therefore, we will provide a gesture library for smartwatches basing on the device motion data. Further one, we will enhance existing systems like IN^2CO [34] with these kind of input modalities and will investigate the usability of such an enhanced system.

Acknowledgment

This research was funded by the German Research Foundation (DFG) as part of the IRTG 2057 "Physical Modeling for Virtual Manufacturing Systems and Processes."

References

[1] L. Lischke and et al., "Using smart phones for large-display interaction," in Proceedings of the 2015 International Conference on Interactive Tabletops & Surfaces, pp. 501–504, 2015.

[2] C. Ardito, P. Buono, M. F. Costabile, and G. Desolda, "Interaction with large displays: A survey," ACM Computing Surveys (CSUR), vol. 47, no. 3, p. 46, 2015.

[3] B. Badillo, D. A. Bowman, W. McConnel, T. Ni, and M. Silva, "Literature Survey on Interaction Techniques for Large Displays," Oct. 2006. [Online]. Available: http://eprints.cs.vt.edu/archive/00000925/

[4] A. Schneider, D. Cernea, and A. Ebert, "Hmd-enabled virtual screens as alternatives to large physical displays," in Information Visualisation (IV), 2016 20th International Conference, pp. 390–394. IEEE, 2016.

[5] Statistia. Smartwatch unit sales worldwide from 2014 to 2018 (in millions). [Online]. Available: https://www.statista.com/statistics/538237/global-smartwatch-unit-sales/

[6] J. Rekimoto, "Tilting operations for small screen interfaces," in Proceedings of the 9th annual ACM symposium on User interface software and technology, pp. 167–168. ACM, 1996.

[7] C. I. Nass and S. Brave, Wired for speech: How voice activates and advances the human-computer relationship. MIT press Cambridge, MA, 2005.

[8] R. Bolt, "Put-that-there: Voice and gesture at the graphics interface," in ACM Computer Graphics 14, 3, pp. 262–270, 1980.

[9] F. A. Rupprecht, A. Ebert, A. Schneider, and B. Hamann, "Virtual reality meets smartwatch: Intuitive, natural, and multi-modal interaction," in Proceedings of the 2017 CHI Conference Extended Abstracts on Human Factors in Computing Systems, pp. 2884–2890. ACM, 2017.

[10] A. Jaimes and N. Sebe, "Multimodal human–computer interaction: A survey," Computer vision and image understanding, vol. 108, no. 1, pp. 116–134, 2007.

[11] L. Nigay and J. Coutaz, "A design space for multimodal systems: Concurrent processing and data fusion," in CHI '93 Proceedings of the INTERACT '93 and CHI '93 Conference on Human Factors in Computing Systems, pp. 172–178, 1993.

[12] A. E. Ali, "Multimodal interaction," Mar. 2011. [Online]. Available: https://www.slideshare.net/Abd0/multimodal-interaction-an-introduction

[13] M. Turk, "Multimodal interaction: A review," Pattern recognition letters, vol. 36, pp. 189–195, 2014.

[14] Google Developers, "Google cloud speech api documentation," Jan. 2018, (Accessed on 01/30/2018). [Online]. Available: https://cloud.google.com/speech/docs/?hl=en

[15] Microsoft, "Microsoft speech service," Jan. 2018, (Accessed on 01/30/2018). [Online]. Available: https://docs.microsoft.com/en-us/azure/cognitive-services/speech/home

[16] CMUSphinx Group, "Cmusphinx open source speech recognition," Jan. 2018, (Accessed on 01/30/2018). [Online]. Available: https://cmusphinx.github.io/

[17] S. Bhandari and Y.-K. Lim, "Exploring gestural mode of interaction with mobile phones," in CHI'08 Extended Abstracts on Human Factors in Computing Systems, pp. 2979–2984. ACM, 2008.

[18] Microsoft, "Kinect for windows sensor components and specifications," 2018, (Accessed on 01/24/2018). [Online]. Available: https://msdn.microsoft.com/en-us/library/jj131033.aspx

[19] ERP – Enterprise Resource Planning, "Nintendo wii specifications," 2018, (Accessed on 01/24/2018). [Online]. Available: http://www.tech-faq.com/nintendo-wii-specifications.html

[20] M. Schreiber, M. von Wilamowitz-Moellendorff, and R. Bruder, "New interaction concepts by using the wii remote," in 13th International Conference on Human-Computer Interaction, pp. 261 – 270. Springer-Verlag Berlin, Heidelberg, 2009.

[21] X. Chen, T. Grossman, D. J. Wigdor, and G. Fitzmaurice, "Duet: exploring joint interactions on a smart phone and a smart watch," in Proceedings of the SIGCHI Conference on Human Factors in Computing Systems, pp. 159–168. ACM, 2014.

[22] D. Schmidt, J. Seifert, E. Rukzio, and H. Gellersen, "A cross-device interaction style for mobiles and surfaces," in Proceedings of the Designing Interactive Systems Conference, pp. 318–327. ACM, 2012.

[23] S. Carrino, A. Péclat, E. Mugellini, and O. A. Khaled, "Humans and smart environments: A novel multimodal interaction approach," in ICMI '11 Proceedings of the 13th international conference on multimodal interfaces, pp. 105–112, 2011.

[24] Google Inc., "Sensor manager," Jun. 2018. [Online]. Available: https://developer.android.com/reference/android/hardware /SensorManager.html

[25] Google. Motion sensors. Portions of this page are modifications based on work created and shared by the Android Open Source Project and used according to terms described in the Creative Commons 2.5 Attribution License. [Online]. Available: https://developer.android.com/reference/android/hardware /SensorManager.html

[26] Sony Mobile Communications Inc., "Smartwatch 3 swr50 specifications," Jan. 2018, (Accessed on 01/30/2018). [Online]. Available: https://www.sonymobile.com/global-en/products/smart-products/smartwatch-3-swr50/specifications/

[27] J. D. Foley, V. L. Wallace, and P. Chan, "The human factors of computer graphics interaction techniques," IEEE computer Graphics and Applications, vol. 4, no. 11, pp. 13–48, 1984.

[28] A. Aldandarawy, "Unity3d-globe," Dec.2017, (Accessed on 12/31/2017). [Online]. Available: https://github.com/Dandarawy/Unity3D-Globe/blob/master/README.md

[29] Jet Cat Games Interactive Entertainment, UAB, "Heliborne – helicopter combat game," Jan. 2018, (Accessed on 01/18/2018). [Online]. Available: http://www.jetcatgames.com/

[30] V. Venkatesh, M. G. Morris, G. B. Davis, and F. D. Davis, "User acceptance of information technology: Toward a unified view," MIS quarterly, pp. 425–478, 2003.

[31] P. Mayring, "Qualitative social research," A guide to qualitative thinking, vol. 5, 2002.

[32] T. Horak, S. K. Badam, N. Elmqvist, and R. Dachselt, "When David Meets Goliath," Proc. 2018 CHI Conf. Hum. Factors Comput. Syst. - CHI '18, pp. 1–13. [Online]. Available: http://dl.acm.org/citation.cfm?doid=3173574.3173593 Apr. 2018.

[33] F. A. Rupprecht, G. Kasakow, J. C. Aurich, B. Hamann, and A. Ebert, "Improving collaboration efficiency via diverse networked mobile devices," Journal on Multimodal User Interfaces, vol. 12, no. 2, pp. 91–108, Jun 2018.

[34] F.-A. Rupprecht, B. Hamann, C. Weidig, J. C. Aurich, and A. Ebert, "IN2CO - A Visualization Framework for Intuitive Collaboration," in EuroVis 2016 - Short Papers, E. Bertini, N. Elmqvist, and T. Wischgoll, Eds. The Eurographics Association, 2016.

Workarounds in the Use of ERP System in SMEs

A Case Study from Automotive Industry in Norway

Shegaw A. Mengiste
University of South-Eastern Norway: School of Business
Department of Business, History and Social Sciences
Horten, Norway
e-mail: sme@usn.no

Viggo Holmstedt
University of South-Eastern Norway: School of Business
Department of Business, History and Social Sciences
Horten, Norway
e-mail: vh@usn.no

***Abstract*— ERP systems constitute an important solution for most business enterprises. They are robust and effective in what they actually do, but can be hard to tweak for the special needs of Small and Medium Enterprises (SMEs). Alongside the professional use of Information technology (IT) through an ERP system, we therefore often find in-house solutions developed by creative or even ingenious individuals. Those workaround solutions become, however, usually non-standard, silo-prone and less robust than configured standard systems usually are. Sometimes, an in-house system becomes too dependent on individuals continued workplace presence. Sometimes a workaround is obviously ineffective, as when an individual has to take notes manually from one system window, only to feed the notes into a form belonging to another system. We caught interest in the investigation of those kinds of imbalances of IT exploitation, and picked a SME in Norway to execute our research.**

Keywords-workarounds; ERP system; workarounds, Automotive industry; SME.

I. INTRODUCTION

Enterprise Resource Planning (ERP) systems, such as SAP are systems that automate and integrate business processes. There is a general consensus that investments in such systems can have a profound impact on improving work process flow [1], in improving access to integrated data across functional units, and in better transparency at enterprise level [2][3].

There are differences in terms of what firms gained from such investments. While some firms achieved impressive benefits, others have had trouble in gaining the benefits and values they expected from their investment [4]. There also are studies that demonstrated ERP system implementation failures. For example, Alonini et al. [5] reported higher failure rates for ERP projects; Kwahk et al. [6] stated 90% of ERP implementations are late or over budget, and the success rate of ERP systems implementation is only about 33% [6][7].

Other studies conducted on ERP implementation also identified distinguishing differences between large enterprises and small & medium enterprises (SMEs). As Zach [8] indicated, SMEs represent fundamentally different environmental context from large enterprises, with a number of distinctive characteristics such as: market orientation, culture, structure, and ownership type [9]. According to a study in Europe, SMEs constituted 98.8% of the almost 19 million enterprises in the 27 EU countries' non-financial business economy (Eurostat, 2008). With the growing impact of SME in job creating and the associated social impact, ERP vendors are moving their attention to the SME market, and several SMEs are implementing ERP systems to leverage business performance [10]. However, despite the development of midrange and less complex ERP systems mainly intended for SMEs, ERP system implementation remains a challenge for many SMEs [11] [12] [44].

SMEs have been challenged by constraints of limited resources, limited Information Systems (IS) knowledge, and lack of Information technology (IT) expertise in adapting, implementing and maintaining IT/IS systems in general and ERP systems in particular [13]. Due to such limitations, compared to bigger enterprises, SMEs might have greater difficulties in overcoming an ERP implementation failure [14][44]. Despite the need to study and analyze the post-implementation impacts of ERP systems using different units of analysis, much of the existing ERP research focuses on the implementation process and gives insight on critical success factors for ERP implementation [15]. In particular, as Haddara et al. [16] indicated, extant research provides only scarce findings about the effect and characteristics of post-implementation of ERP systems in SMEs (e.g., [15][17]. More specifically, although there are calls for a deeper understanding of workarounds and their impacts in IS implementations [18], the issue of post-implementation workarounds for ERP systems has often been ignored by current literature. The term Workarounds can be defined as alternative procedures employed by users to accomplish a task in response to a misfit between computer-based and existing work processes [19]. As such, it is important to recognize the distinguishing characteristics of SMEs and consider how these influence the ERP implementation issues faced by SMEs operating in different contexts. The deployment of ERP systems can bring about unintended consequences that can lead to resistance and workarounds by users [20]. When a new ERP system is implemented, users may encounter hindrances in workflow caused by various factors including poor process design, complex system functionality, poor user interface, inadequate user training, and lack of proper user guides [15].

In this study, we focus on workarounds because of a misfit between the new ERP system implemented and the new systems being used to support daily tasks and work processes in a medium sized automotive industry. The study tries to address the existing gap in literature by examining a case study of a problematic ERP implementation, where users had to use the system nevertheless to perform their daily tasks. The study particularly tries to contribute to this research void by exploring both the intermediate and corporate impacts of a problematic ERP implementation in an automotive manufacturing plant in Norway. The end-users in the different functional units (even at the executive level) of the plant were forced to use the system despite the many flaws and incompleteness they observed in their daily tasks.

The paper is organized as follows: Section II gives a brief background about the company (Kongsberg Automotive), while section III presents the theoretical framework on workarounds and IS implementation. Section IV is about the research approach and method, while section V presents the findings. In section VI, we present the discussion and concluding remarks.

II. COMPANY BACKGROUND

KA is a global organization operating in different countries, and in Norway in different cities. This study addresses the experiences, challenges, and workarounds in implementing and using an ERP system in a plant situated in one of the cities of Norway.

At the time of the interviews, KA had been using the SAP R/3 ERP system since 1996. KA uses SAP to manage financial transactions, requirements planning, inbound and outbound logistics including stock piece registration, and management tasks.

We approached the Hvittingfoss Plant at Kongsberg Automotive Company to conduct the present case study. The Hvittingfoss Plant is situated in Norway, while Kongsberg Automotive as a whole has thirty production facilities worldwide. They produce powertrain systems and chassis related products for both heavy and light duty commercial vehicles, and many related products. Kongsberg Automotive employs 10 000 workers in 18 countries. Annual revenues are roughly 1 billion EUR in 2018 according to Q2 reports. The revenues have slightly but steadily risen during 2016 and 2017.

The factory at Hvittingfoss produces gearshift- and clutch actuation systems, chassis roads and gearbox components and related products. Thus, the plant is a part of the business segment Powertrain & Chassis. They also have a driver control unit, and a distribution department situated in Raufoss. The factory hall is equipped with some robots and some manually operated units. The Hvittingfoss plant started up in 1976 and now employs around 140 people.

III. THEORETICAL FRAME: WORKAROUNDS AND IS IMPLEMENTATION

The notion of workarounds in the context of IS implementation has often been treated as a form of resistance from the end-users and a significant hindrance to system designers and developers in meeting the objectives of the system [21]. However, there is also literature that addresses workarounds from the perspective of accommodation to misfit [22], [23]. Gasser [23] posits that a misfit would typically exist because tasks can change in unforeseen but important ways when a new information system is introduced in organizations. Hence, users see workarounds as a response when a task is in particular not supported in the desired manner due to the misfit between computing and work processes, rather than a resistance to the new system. In this way, workarounds are performed with the intention to complete tasks, extend functionality, and evade designed limits that are embedded into the new system [19]. According to Gasser [23], such readjustment of work practices and tasks is often performed to accommodate the misfit and is classified into three types of strategies, i.e., Augmenting, Working around, and Fitting. Table I provides a description of the three workaround strategies:

TABLE I. STRATEGIES TO ADAPT MISFITS ADOPTED FROM [23]

Strategy	Definition	Example
Augmenting	Undertaking additional work to make up for the misfit	Having to print and submit a form manually though online submission was already performed due to unreliability of the system
Working around	Intentionally using computing in ways for which it was not designed or avoiding its use and relying on an alternative means of accomplishing work	Calling a purchasing officer to request purchase instead of entering request through system due to tedious process of filling up details
Fitting	The activity of changing computing or changing the structure of work to accommodate for the computing misfit	Improving the user interface of the system to address usability issues faced by users

The use of workarounds by end-users can also be conceptually linked to Orlikowski's notion of 'interpretive flexibility' [24], which extends HCI aspects to the relationship between human, organization and technology. As such interpretive flexibility can be manifested and influenced by several attributes including: the characteristics of the material artefact (e.g., hardware and software), the characteristics of the human agents using it (e.g., experience, motivation), and the characteristics of the context where the technology is used (e.g., social relations, resource allocations, task assignments).

In this paper, we would like to use the concept of workaround to explore how end-users assign their own meanings and interpretation to the functions of the ERP system in response to the misfit and changes encountered between work processes and the new system implemented. The three types of strategies developed by [23] are also used as initial categories to identify the different accommodation misfits in our case study. In order to complement [23] strategies for accommodation of misfits, we used [25] perspective of workarounds based on IS evolution. They suggested that organizational routines and IT/IS constantly evolve and when there are shortcomings in existing IS, ad hoc adjustments (or workarounds) can occur in two dimensions, i.e., process or IT/IS. Such gradual changes to process and IT/IS are termed by McGann & Lyytinen [25] as process embellishment and IT modification respectively. Process embellishment is a stage in the IS evolution whereby current ineffective processes are improved through leveraging the routines supported by the system and are extended for use across the organization. Whereas, IT/IS modification refers to the change in IT systems where ad hoc IT improvisations are integrated into current systems to improve alignment with current processes [25].

IV. RESEARCH APPROACH

This section presents the broader research approach and the specific data collection and analysis techniques applied to collect data relevant for the study.

A. *Interpretive case study*

As a research approach, we adopted an interpretive case study approach [26]. In interpretive studies, researchers try to understand phenomena by examining the meanings that participants assign to them, within particular social or organizational contexts [28][26][27]. Besides, the interpretive case study approach is appropriate because one can study IS in their natural setting, it allows answering 'how' and 'why' questions, and it is also appropriate when few previous studies in the same area have been carried out [29]. Similarly, in this paper, we adopt the interpretive approach to collect rich data about the context where managers, engineers, and supervisors daily interact with an ERP system, to understand their choices and rationale for the actual use of the system, and how misfits in the ERP system and their interests addressed. In interpretive studies in Information Systems in particular, neither technologies nor human exert direct causal impact [30]. Rather, outcomes are results of the interplay of computing infrastructures, and objectives and preferences of different social groups [31].

B. *Data Collection approach*

As Walsham [26] pointed out, the primary data sources in interpretive studies are interviews. The data collection for this research has been conducted through face-to-face semi-structured interviews with employees in a medium-sized automotive company. Ten interviews with engineers, operation managers, and CEO carried out between February and March 2017 at the company's premises. All interviews were voice recorded and transcribed. We took notes during the interview. The profile of the persons interviewed is presented in the following table.

TABLE II. RESPONDENTS TO THE INTERVIEW

classification	#	operational responsibility
Plant manager	1	CEO
Engineer	3	Various operations
Supervisor	6	Foreman, hour registration

The interviewees were asked some open-ended questions, but they were free to elaborate on their own thoughts and reflections whenever necessary. When there are digressions, the researchers (both are the authors of this paper) then adapted the questioning, in order to make the interviewees elaborate more on their views and ideas.

C. *Data Analysis*

For data analysis, we configured assisting tools (AT) and NVivo software [38]. We used the AT for transcribing activities, the NVivo software for coding and classifying. NVivo is a specialized tool for qualitative research [32].

Only two interviewees did not consent to audio recording in English, so we had to rely on handwritten notes. Apart from those two, most data collection is from audio interviews in English. We will therefore discuss some HCI and similar aspects of AT supported audio transcription related to our contextual approach to the audio analysis.

While transcribing audio was, both interesting and demanding, it is also resource consuming. Many researchers outsource the transcribing activities to professionals. Other researchers use Voice Recognition (VR) software [39], to keep better control over interpretations. In some practical investigation designs, researchers prefer to conduct the entire transcription process themselves, to perform interpretations based on their special knowledge and familiarity with the domain under investigation. To achieve the same level of control, while utilizing a more recent technology of VR, we developed ATs (assisting tools) to help us with the transcription.

For the interviewing, we first used dedicated sound recorder equipment, then an iPhone. We found the sound quality to be equal in each setup, the phone being easier to operate in overall use. We produced more than two hours of interviews of varying audio and speech quality. The quality varied mostly because we did not protect our environment against sudden irrelevant sounds that ruined potentially important fragments of the speech. The varying noisy environments in the plant is a contextual condition we should have considered. The variation in quality also pertained to execution of native English language. The most difficult to interpret and transcribe was surprisingly native English speech. The Norwegian interviewee's English was deliberately spoken and therefore in fact the easier to interpret.

To overcome some challenges and even make transcribing a little more interesting, we created artifacts of ATs to utilize the Google Speech API. We selected the API after having investigated several others, except older VRs. Google's speech API builds upon AI/ML trained for quite many different languages as well as several English native and exported dialects.

In practical use, we found that the API worked best if we fed it with chunks of speech of five to seven minutes duration at a time. We used the GoldWave software to section the recordings, and applied a numbering scheme to keep track of the chunks. After the automatic transcription, human audio perception and interpretation refined and edited the transcription into a satisfactory state. The editing process demanded high concentration and a considerable amount of time. Some parts of the audio were indeed difficult to interpret, and the process inferred interesting observations in terms of audio perception. You can interpret visual images very differently dependent of how you keep staring at them. We observed that speech fragments could behave likewise. Once we had edited a specific transcription fragment correctly, the correct perception of the same fragment became just as easy as it was incomprehensible before. The observation is very similar to the famous Yannie-Laurel phenomenon. A technological approach to the phenomenon suggests that shifts in pitch would infer different interpretations [41]. The phenomenon demanded an AT with HCI considerations, such as being easy to configure for re-listening and re-pitching of sound fragments.

What we constructed was an AT for producing an automatic text suggestion for a chunk of speech, with controllers to play parts of the speech repeatedly (A-B playback) or from an A-position, and with symbols to mark audio positions directly in the transcription text under improvement. The AT had facilities for adjusting the A and B positions in very fine steps after initial settings, as well as each symbol's audio positions. Text styling helped visualizing what parts of the text that was already good, and what parts remained incomprehensible, as well as yet unexplored text fragments. A pitch change tool operated A-B sequences playback. Each of those facilities proved invaluable for refined interpretation. The method was to let some incomprehensible fragments rest for a while, and then revisit them repeatedly. The various facilities to revisit and repeat fragments actually helped us transfer many fragments from incomprehensible to good.

The AT published xml-coded fragments continuously and unobtrusively, as well as comprehensive word and web content from the transcription text in progress. We used Altova XML Spy to construct useful and relevant XML schemas to support the system design. Likewise it was important to let the AT be able to switch between both interview files and chunks within the files. The AT even had to save the work in progress both risk-free and continuously. The importance of the unobtrusiveness stems from the need to avoid wearing out the human resource, and leave the greatest possible amount of capacity to the transcription, and audio perception capacity. It also stems from the need to maximize concentration on the interpretation, which is only possible when the tools don't distract the interpreter. In short, the AT must keep the workflow intact. In the field of system development and fault detection tools, Fichman et al. [33] convey that any interruption generated by an automated tool forces a developer to context-switch away from her primary objective. Even very good tools remain unused if they disturb the workflow too much. [42].

We constructed the domain AT in order to utilize the Google Speech API. The API reads the audio and deliver text. Google's APIs also have pricing plans. Google offers a resource of around 300 days and an amount of money to use on Google APIs in general. We spent only a trifle amount of the money, and almost 100 days, development and AT testing included.

The method for transcribing interviews shortly outlined here was not time saving. The reason is the parallel development of the AT and investigation of other relevant assisting technologies. Even if we primarily performed the development to better understand the content of the audio interviews, it quite naturally contributed to insight in several technical and perceptional fields, which we consider a collateral reward.

The transcription and note composition phase produced three text files. Our method used NVivo, which is why we will mention a few example findings here. We let NVivo import the three files so we could begin the analysis. From NVivo we conducted the labelling and classification of findings in the interviews. Examples of main labels identified by NVivo are subsystems and ATs, user's wishes and missing facilities statements, and labels like business processes and stock management statements. Categories of interviewees and various corporate departments are among main classifications from NVivo operations.

V. CASE DESCRIPTION & ANALYSIS

The section presents findings of our exploration on the workarounds in the customization, implementation and use of ERP systems in a medium sized automotive company in Norway. Our findings revealed that during the initial stage of customization and implementation, there was an effort by the vendor and the IT department at the head office of KA to address the local needs of the different functional units. One of the supervisors, who was there at the time of the system implementation, reported no resistance from the users on the new system. The challenge was complexity of the system to learn and master most of the functionalities in a short period. He stated the following:

> *"Everyone was willing to learn and use the new system. There was a good motivation from all staff members. The problem was the difficulty to learn too much in a short period of time."*

Despite the difficulty to learn the new system by most of the staff members, the management insisted that no matter how difficult to learn and no matter how long it took to learn, using the new system was set to be mandatory.

According to the CEO, the motive for introducing SAP at KA was initially to achieve integration and manage all its operational activities. In our interview with the manager of the plant, we realized that there are several other applications that are also in use by different units of the company. Some of them are the following: a strategic planning tool that gives strategic information about customer's volumes projections over a period of time, a human resource (HR) system called Zalaris mainly used for staff time registration, an automated invoice handling system, and a web portal to support aftermarket customers. A maintenance system is also used for different security and maintenance related tasks such as emergency lights, fire detection, diesel monitoring.

One of the biggest challenges of ERP systems is their complexity and the rigidity of some of the modules to customize to local requirements. In principle, ERP systems are customizable, but there are features that you can't customize. Those features are designed to be standard for some industries like pharmaceutical, retail. Asked about if the existing ERP system fits well to the needs and requirements of the plant, the plant manager stated the following:

> *"SAP is a complex system! It's very, very complex. In most of the cases, we end up with something that's not really what we want, because we are tied to reusing SAP. We have to do it the SAP way. If we want to do warehouse management in SAP it has to be done the SAP way, not our own way. That creates gaps in using the system to address some specific local needs at the plant. In our case, the system fails to support some of the operational tasks, and this forced us to use some additional applications like MS Excel to prepare production plan or in some cases do things manually like the time punching to register how many hours employees work. "*

When the company initially introduced the ERP system, the head office's IT department selected, customized and implemented it in collaboration with the local SAP vendor. However, follow up support that emerge from local plants was not sufficient. As the plant manager noted:

> *"IT is a centralized service; so I don't have an IT department here. I also do not know if there is any IT strategy at the company level. We requested on several instances about our needs and limitations of the SAP system to address our needs. "*

In our interview, we have also noticed that there were some smaller applications developed on top of SAP over the years to address emerging local demands even without the knowledge of the head office of the IT department at the head office. We asked why it is difficult to integrate the applications to the ERP system and if they are worried about future silo systems running at different units without sharing data and process outputs. The manager gave the following answer:

> *"... In fact I informed the IT department at the head office about the problems we encounter on the existing systems and the new applications we are using. But, you know, at the end of the day either somebody needs to come and give me some support and fix these things for me, or I need to find someone else to do things. I do know that we have had a small application done for recording machine downtime, and measuring it. That was done by a guy in Drammen. It never was completed. But it was sort of semi operational. »*

Asked about why they use MS Excel to analyze data generated by the SAP system, one of the engineers replied:

> *"When we produce parts, all our working hours from the production is filled in SAP interface. You can also register all parts produced in the SAP system. You can display that data in SAP. But, you can't do anything with that data. You can't work with them. You can't divide them on different lines, you can't present them in graphs...»*

Another engineer also stated the following:

> *"Since we had the Excel system which is more useful to my tasks, I have never used SAP for data analysis or presentation. I have only used it in Excel. But, still SAP is needed to register the numbers which will give the figures for analysis. "*

We also have come across during our interviews that there are some processes and tasks that are still done manually. Registering the time sheet for non-permanent staff is still handled manually. Check-in (punching-in) system for regular employees is done manually. Lack of a planning system to project new part-time employees needed in the plant is also identified as one problem. Stock management for internal housekeeping and warehouse stock tracing are also not currently supported by the SAP system. Though all the parts coming to the plant are registered into SAP system mainly to communicate with the accounting department and finalize payment of invoices for the parts ordered. After registration, the parts will be distributed to the two warehouses and they will be sorted manually. There is no system to trace those parts once they are dispatched to the warehouses and assembly lines. Lack of stock trace system has been identified as one of the main problems by all the people we have interviewed. According to one of the operations supervisors, there are about 11000 different incoming parts that are currently in use by the plant. Once they arrived they will be shelved and the job of tracing parts when they are needed is currently done manually. This is what the supervisor stated:

> *"...stock management is a disaster... this is the biggest problem for the department. If customers make complaints about parts we have to manually search the item using part number on the shelf and get the details afterwards. This took too much resources, too much workload on staff doing it, and so many errors."*

We asked why traceability is a problem and why it is difficult to use SAP to address this challenge. The answer was simply:

> *"SAP doesn't support it as there is no any module in SAP to support this task. While SAP was implemented this was not included as part of the requirements as there was no an issue of traceability at that time."*

Stock management is also problematic and is not supported by the SAP system. As one of the supervisors in this section noted the principle of FIFO can't be applied mainly due to lack of a system that can help to identify which item is old and which item is new. The plant has a rule to use old batch before new batches, but it has become very difficult to apply this rule as it is problematic to sort manually which parts are new and which are old just by using their 6 digits part numbers. The supervisor concluded:

> *"We have to have a system that supports our internal housekeeping"*

Planning or projecting number of new part-time employees that are needed in the coming months is an important managerial duty of plant. To address this need, different departments are using MS Excel to project the different categories of people (with their skill and knowledge) at departmental and/or monthly basis. The estimation is made by breaking down the hours for the work or material to be produced divided by the weeks needed to produce the material(s). But, doing this task using MS Excel is problematic as error checks are time consuming. Manual data registering to Excel sheet is hard and error prone. It requires skills to configure Excel for planning and forecasting. As the head of the logistics department stated:

> *"we can not plan future jobs in SAP. We are currently using Excel by copying some data from the SAP system. This is a double work and at times cumbersome."*

Human resource department also uses a different system for individual appraisal and performance management. The foremen use the Zalaris tool for hour registration and over-time work registration. There is also the automatic invoice handling system Workflow in use.

Integrating new demands to existing SAP system is a challenge. Demands could come from new requirements. It is difficult to integrate the new demands to the system that was implemented some 20 years ago. There are also SAP standards to respect. So, as some of the supervisors explained to us, it is now becoming a common practice that new customized applications are in use to address internal demands and requirements. This creates a silo system where different smaller applications are running at different units even without any integration and sharing of data. This will compromise the consistency and reliability of data generated by those units.

VI. CONCLUSION

What we have found to be true for the SME plant under study is that its IT activities apply to several of the strategies and references in our theoretical frame. Several findings support that fact. The plant is therefore likely to be in the same situation as many other SMEs globally, which makes us interested in identifying and solving problems with software misfits.

When the management level first introduces a main ERP system like SAP in a location, we can appreciate corporate expectations to employees to learn and begin to use the system as soon as possible. Likewise, we can easily understand the social and profession related stress felt by each individual. Even if some of the misfits were present already at the implementation stage, they could easily be overlooked, and maybe deemed as improper to pinpoint since the management level has already completed the planning phase.

We will therefore conclude that an implementation of ERP often starts out with misfits and missing tools. We also found evidence for the widening of the gap between services and needs as time passes. The evolution of the plant and even the enterprise as a whole go through several phases and changes over time. The customers, for instance, become increasingly aware of materials leading to health issues, which makes it important to store and retrieve information about specific stock details, not to mention the stock relocation itself. The missing possibilities to trace parts is a main theme in the findings, and therefore identifies a severe gap between enterprise implementation of SAP and the specific needs of the plant or the company at large.

From our findings, we have evidence that there are SAP standards to respect. We must further consider how the long and solid almost 50 years of history influence the SAP core code and the SAP framework. The system was born in Germany around 1972; several years before the introduction and general use of object orientation as a method of system development. Much later, developers found object oriented code easy to maintain and reuse, at least in contrast to older types of code bases [34]. We argue that the SAP system implemented for KA in 1996 consisted of code core and frameworks that were hard to change. We further argue that the implementation still is hard to refurbish. This infers the assumption that SAP is hard to accommodate to fill demand gaps [35], and therefore forces other strategies.

The strategies applied for filling the gap in our study were actually at least two of our three-fold Gasser adoption list [23]. The one we did not find was the Fitting Strategy. The Augmenting Strategy is relevant when the supervisors have to fill in hour registration manually. The supervisors and plant manager used the data in HR software, invoices reference, and even to assess performance with key performance indicators. A KPI is to assess the time taken to produce standard components. Our findings reveal that both supervisors and plant manager deem hour registration as time waste in the form they practice it. It is obvious that several other services, like those just mentioned, would benefit from augmented integration in the core system, to reduce augmenting personnel strategy. The KPI just mentioned would demand data flow between standard, or historical, timing measures for the producing of parts and the actual hour registrations.

The Working Around Strategy is, however, the dominant strategy in the SME under study. Individuals in the company needed several electronic services that were missing from SAP. Competent individuals then developed several ATs (assisting tools) which the plant manager referred to as query tools. The versatile Excel tool accepts data to the purpose of organizing, analyzing and graphing for use in for example periodic staff meetings. These tools are in several ways essential for executing important business processes.

During the years after the implementation of SAP, purchasing officers have acquired several OTS workstation tools or web based systems. We found systems like Zalaris, Amigo, Mitrol, Workday and Workflow, all of which being part of important business processes. We also found specialized tools for detecting machine downtime, and tools that addressed prioritized wishes like registering of parts locations. Each of those systems have unique user interfaces, and seldom respect best practices or HCI principles. They therefore demand resources to learn, which after a while infers resistance to stop using, even if the headquarter eventually suggests better software. We do not argue that individuals would explicitly deny using new software, only that it is likely to disturb the individual's existing workflow and routines. In some cases, temporary employees create system solutions for specific areas, like part-location registration. The importance of documentation and maintenance becomes critical once that individual leaves premises.

A more problematic characteristic is that most workaround systems also usually create silos and duplicated information captured in varying data formats. Such data sets are sometimes hard to interchange or use in any other systems, at least without resource demanding modifications. We are also aware of the dangers of duplicated data sets that may differ over time, inferring risks to business processes in the organization. The risks are for example faulty decision base caused by erroneous data sets and wrong information. With workarounds like those mentioned here, suppliers of workaround systems should take extra care to observe possibilities of singular data origins, that is, avoiding duplication of data.

From our findings, we also realized that the nature of task structure contributed to the post-implementation workarounds and shadow systems that are developed in response to the changes in work practices and the long-term implications of organizational processes. By task structure we are referring to the complexity of the task, the amount of discretion or autonomy allowed to perform the task [36], and the degree of interdependence among other groups to accomplish the task [37]. A good example from our case on task structure complexity related workaround is the check-in or punching-in system, which is currently performed manually. This task structure is complex and very difficult to automate by using conventional ERP systems. The company considered to let a device monitor the time tracking of part time employees. There are automated time tracking systems in the market that KA can use to automate its time-tracking tasks. Such systems can offer real-time access to data, ensure efficiency, and provide the company and its employees an advanced and alternative solution to the existing manual time-tracking processes. In our exploration, we observed that the strategies adopted by different groups to deal with the limits of the ERP system contributed for new workarounds and new shadow systems to the ERP system. Integrating the new application to the old ERP system would require costly customization that is also the cause of all the new shadow systems developed over a period of 20 years.

Our main contribution lies in providing empirical evidence and insights on post-implementation complexities and challenges of an ERP system, the workarounds carried out by users of the system, and the impact on the overall performance and efficiency of the organization. By doing so, we underscored the importance of workarounds in IS implementation to create viable organizational processes [43]; provide empirical evidence on the impact of workarounds in IS use; and explore how workarounds are actually re-enacted by end users.

REFERENCES

[1] M. C. Boudreau, & D. Robey, "Organizational transition to enterprise resource planning systems: theoretical choices for process research," Paper presented at the Proceedings of the 20th international conference on Information Systems.

[2] P. Besson, & F. Rowe, "ERP project dynamics and enacted dialogue: perceived understanding, perceived leeway, and the nature of task-related conflicts," ACM SIGMIS Database: the DATABASE for Advances in Information Systems, 32(4), 47-66, 2001.

[3] S. Newell, J. C. Huang, R. D. Galliers, & S. L. Pan, "Implementing enterprise resource planning and knowledge management systems in tandem: fostering efficiency and innovation complementarity," Information and Organization, 13(1), 25-52, 2003.

[4] T. F. Gattiker, & D. L. Goodhue, "What happens after ERP implementation: understanding the impact of interdependence and differentiation on plant-level outcomes," MIS quarterly, 559-585, 2005.

[5] D. Alonini, R. Dulmin, & V. Mininno, "Risk management in ERP project introduction: Review of the literature," Information & Management, 44(6), 547-567, 2007.

[6] K-Y. Kwahk, & J-N. Lee, "The role of readiness for change in ERP implementation: Theoretical bases and empirical validation," Information & Management, 45(7), 474-481, 2008.

[7] Z. Zhang, M. KO. Lee, P, Huang, L, Zhang, x. Huang, "A framework of ERP systems implementation success in China: An empirical

study," International journal of Production Economics, 98(1), 56-80, 2005.

[8] O. Zach, "ERP Implementation in small and Medium sized Enterprises," Phd Disseration. University of Agder, Faculty of Economics and Social Sciences, Department of Information Systems, 2012.

[9] K. Y. Wong, & E. Aspinawall, "An empirical study of the important factors for knowledge-management adoption in the SME sector," Journal of Knowledge management, 9(3), 64-82, 2005.

[10] H. M. Beheshti, C. M. Beheshti, "Improving productivity and firm performance with enterprise resource planning," Enterprise Information Systems, 4(4), 445-472, 2010.

[11] R. Malhotra, & C. Temponi, "Critical decisions for ERP integration: Small business issues," International Journal of Information Management, 30(1), 28-37, 2010.

[12] D. L. Olsen, & J. Staley, "Case study of open-source enterprise resource planning implementation in a small business," Enterprise Information Systems, 6(1), 79-94, 2012.

[13] P. Poba-Nzaou, & L. Raymond, "Managing ERP system risk in SMEs: a multiple case study," Journal of Information Technology, 26(3), 170-192, 2011.

[14] I. Ignatiadis, &J. Nandhakumar. "The effect of ERP system workarounds on organizational control: An interpretivist case study," *Scandinavian Journal of Information Systems, 21*(2), 2009.

[15] E. Hustad, & D. H. Olsen, "Critical Issues across the ERP Life Cycle in Small-and-MediumSized Enterprises: Experiences from a Multiple Case Study,". Conference on ENTERprise Information Systems / ProjMAN 2013 - International Conference on Project MANagement / HCIST 2013 - International Conference on Health and Social Care Information Systems and Technologies.

[16] M. Haddara, & O. Zach, "ERP systems in SMEs: A literature review, " 44th Hawaii International Conference on System Sciences (HICSS), IEEE, p. 1-10, 2011.

[17] W. J. Orlikowski, & J. Yates, «ICT and organizational change: a commentary," The journal of applied behavioral science, 42(1), 127-134, 2006.

[18] P. Koopman, & R. R. Hoffman, "Work-arounds, make-work, and kludges," *IEEE Intelligent Systems, 18*(6), 70-75, 2003.

[19] L. Lapointe, & S. Rivard, "A multilevel model of resistance to information technology implementation," MIS Quarterly, 461-491, 2005.

[20] E. H. Ferneley, & P. Sobreperez, "Resist, comply or workaround? An examination of different facets of user engagement with information systems," European Journal of information systems, 15(4), 345-356, 2006.

[21] J. Gasparas, & E. Monteiro, "Counteracting Forces in Implementation of Is-Enabled Global Business Processes,". Paper presented at the 17th European Conference on Information Systems, Verona, Italy, 2009.

[22] L. Gasser, "The integration of computing and routine work,". ACM Transactions on Information Systems (TOIS), 4(3), 205-225, 1986.

[23] W. J. Orlikowski, "The duality of technology: Rethinking the concept of technology in organizations," Organization science, 3(3), 398-427, 1992.

[24] S. T. McGann, & K. Lyytinen, «The improvisation effect: a case study of user improvisation and its effects on information system evolution," ICIS 2008 Proceedings, 209.

[25] G. Walsham, "Interpretive case studies in IS research: nature and method," European Journal of Information Systems, 4(2), 74-81, 1995a

[26] G. Walsham, "The emergence of interpretivism in IS research," Information Systems Research, 6(4), 376-394, 1995b.

[27] W. J. Orlikowski, & J. J. Baroudi, "Studying information technology in organizations: Research approaches and assumptions," Information Systems Research, 2(1), 1-28, 1991.

[28] I. Benbasat, D. K. Goldstein, & M. Mead, "The case research strategy in studies of information systems," *MIS quarterly*, 369-386, 1987.

[29] S. Sahay, "Implementation of information technology: a time-space perspective," Organization studies, 18(2), 229-260, 1997.

[30] M. L. Markus, & D. Robey, "Information Technology and Organizational Change: Causal Structure in Theory and Research," Management Science, 34(5), 583-598, 1988.

[31] E. Welsh, "Dealing with data: Using NVivo in the qualitative data analysis process," Paper presented at the Forum Qualitative Sozialforschung/Forum: Qualitative Social Research, 2002.

[32] C. Sadowski, J. Van Gogh, C. Jaspan, E. Söderberg, & C. Winter, "Tricorder: Building a program analysis ecosystem," Paper presented at the Proceedings of the 37th International Conference on Software Engineering-Volume 1, 2015.

[33] R. G. Fichman, & C. F. Kemerer, "Adoption of software engineering process innovations: The case of object orientation," MIT Sloan Management Review Magazine, 34, 7-7, 1993.

[34] G. Gable, & G. J. Stewart, "SAP R/3 implementation issues for small to medium enterprises, ". AMCIS 1999 Proceedings, 779-781, 1999.

[35] J. R. Hackman, "Work redesign and motivation," Professional Psychology, 11(3), 445-455. 1980.

[36] D. Strong, O. Volkoff, & M. J. Elmes, "ERP systems, task structure, and workarounds in organizations," AMCIS 2001 proceedings. 204.

[37] P. Bazeley & K. Jackson, K. "Qualitative data analysis with NVivo,"Sage Publications Limited, 2013.

[38] J. F. Anderson, "Transcribing with Voice Recognition Software: A New Tool for Qualitative Researchers," Qualitative Health Research, 8(5), 718-723. doi:10.1177/104973239800800511

[39] J. Bailey, J. "First steps in qualitative data analysis: transcribing," Family Practice, 25(2), 127-131. doi:10.1093/fampra/cmn003.

[40] R. Gutman, R. "Why Laurel Sounds Like Yanny," 2018.

[41] L. Layman, L. Williams, L., & R. S. Amant, "Toward reducing fault fix time: Understanding developer behavior for the design of automated fault detection tools," Paper presented at the Empirical Software Engineering and Measurement, 2007. ESEM 2007.

[42] European Commission (EC). Eurostat Regional Yearbook 2008.

[43] C. Ciborra. "The Labyrinths of Information: Challenging the Wisdom of Systems, Oxford," Oxford, Oxford University press, 2002.

[44] X., Hongjiang et al. "The Challenge of Implementing an ERP System in a Small and Medium Enterprise – A Teaching Case of ERP Project Management." Scholarship and Professional Work - Business. 213, 2011.

A Planning Pipeline for Large Multi-Agent Missions

Meghan Chandarana
Autonomous Integrated Systems
NASA Langley Research Center
Hampton, VA, USA
meghan.chandarana@nasa.gov

E. L. Meszaros
Dept. of Egyptology and Assyriology
Brown University
Providence, RI, USA
e.l.meszaros@brown.edu

B. Danette Allen
Autonomous Integrated Systems
NASA Langley Research Center
Hampton, VA, USA
danette.allen@nasa.gov

Abstract—**In complex multi-agent applications, human operators are often tasked with planning and managing large heterogeneous teams of humans and autonomous vehicles. Although the use of these autonomous vehicles broadens the scope of meaningful applications, many of their systems remain unintuitive and difficult to master for human operators whose expertise lies in the application domain and not at the platform level. Current research focuses on the development of individual capabilities necessary to plan multi-agent missions of this scope, placing little emphasis on the integration of these components in to a full pipeline. The work presented in this paper presents a complete and user-agnostic planning pipeline for large multi-agent missions known as the HOLII GRAILLE. The system takes a holistic approach to mission planning by integrating capabilities in human machine interaction, flight path generation, and validation and verification. Components - modules - of the pipeline are explored on an individual level, as well as their integration into a whole system. Lastly, implications for future mission planning are discussed.**

***Keywords*–pipeline; multi-agent; mission planning; human-machine interaction; validation and verification.**

I. Introduction

As autonomous robotic vehicles grow increasingly ubiquitous, their use in applications like search and rescue and science data collection increases. As a result, the expertise of human operators shifts from that of system level domain experts to that of application level experts. In complex multi-agent missions these application level experts are human operators who are tasked with planning and managing heterogeneous teams of agents composed of humans, Uncrewed Aerial Vehicles (UAVs), ground rovers, etc. The use of autonomous vehicles as tools increases the ability of operators to perform tasks that are beyond their current capabilities, yet these tools remain difficult to operate as they are based on unintuitive existing systems. Fixing this, however, requires the generation of a user-agnostic and comprehensive mission planning tool that allows for intuitive mission specification by any human operator.

Prior research has focused on optimizing or instantiating many individual components of this mission planning pipeline, but often fails to take into account the components as a whole and their integration into a complete pipeline. Existing work on this topic is also published across a number of different disciplines, making the process of integrating these individual components more difficult. This project focuses on the need for a cohesive pipeline that unifies individual components, allowing for successful and trusted mission planning by human operators in multi-agent teams. By demonstrating the feasibility of a full pipeline, this work innovates on advancements made to individual components.

This paper evaluates the full pipeline by which a human operator would plan a mission and define objectives, thereby allowing the system to interpret this into actionable directions. The current instantiation of this pipeline is HOLII GRAILLE: Human Operated Language Intuitive Interface with Gesture Recognition Applied in an Immersive Life Like Environment. By presenting individual components, this paper proposes a system capable of both mission planning and supervisory control during execution. We specifically focus on UAV mission planning where operators are tasked with defining vehicle flight paths.

Current research in to the development of individual components necessary to build a mission planning pipeline are outlined in Section II. Planning tools and methods for eliciting desired information from human operators are examined as a necessary component of an optimal mission planning pipeline (Section III). Different modalities of interaction are also considered for accurately capturing the intent of mission specification and general usability. A planning tool aid for determining mission parameters, such as swarm size, is outlined in Section IV. The captured data are then fused with dynamic environmental information to produce an accurate and flyable plan, as described in Section V. Section VI presents how flight paths are displayed to the human operator using virtual or augmented reality tools, allowing for iterative modification and verification methods. Once plans have been fully verified, agents can leverage established behaviors to carry out the prescribed goals. To realize a fully successful system performance, all of these individual components must partner synergistically for the creation of a cohesive mission pipeline, or the HOLII GRAILLE of mission planning systems. The full pipeline is tested on a scaled-down indoor mission in Section VII, and its implications are further discussed in Section VIII. Suggestions for continued research efforts that build upon this holistic design are considered in Section IX.

II. Background & Related Work

Current research efforts in multi-agent planning primarily focus on the low level vehicle planning. These methods range from manual interfaces that require human operators to explicitly define the paths of each vehicle individually to fully autonomous interfaces that calculate the vehicle trajectories automatically using mission parameters. Common autonomous planning frameworks include Markov Decision Processes (MDPs) [1], game theoretic frameworks [2] and integer programming frameworks [3], and typically use reward functions to shape the solution.

In addition to vehicle path planning, numerous research efforts have focused on mission planning interfaces. A large number of these choose to adopt gesture and speech input modalities. These modalities are used to mimic natural human-human communication patterns and thereby reduce operator workload [4]. Cauchard et al. showed that human operators prefer to interact with autonomous agents in the same way they would with another human [5]. Ng and Sharlin explored a gesture interface for collocated vehicles [6]. In [7] and [8], users defined flight paths directly using a speech-based and 3D spatial interface respectively. Gesture-based interfaces often rely on full body movements [9] or static hand poses to program by demonstration [10]. Bolt et al. use a multimodal interface to manipulate a graphical user interface [11]. Suárez Fernández et al. designed a flexible multimodal interface framework which allowed users to choose the input modality based on their application [12]. These methods failed to examine how multimodal interfaces could be adapted for multi-agent mission planning. In addition, previous methods failed to explore more simplistic, unmounted sensors for gesture input.

Further focus has been placed on verifying and validating autonomous systems, which can often be difficult due to complex and non-deterministic behavior. Emphasis has been placed on ensuring the safety of not just the individual components of a system but their intricate interactions as well, further complicating the process [13]. Kamali et al. describe a method of verifying models of a system's behavior and interactions to complement a model checker algorithm to verify a system [14]. Li et al. developed a game theoretic approach to modeling autonomous vehicles for verification [15]. With the spread of autonomous systems, any methods for verification and validation have focused on incorporating measures of trust and trustworthiness as well. Though not explicit certification measures, aspects of trust inform how well the system will be utilized by human operators and are therefore crucial for evaluation. Lyons et al. lament that current verification and validation techniques do not take trust and trustworthiness into account, making them outdated at best [13]. One method for improving trust and working toward more robust verification and validation methods is through explainable AI (XAI), where efforts are made to ensure the explicability of outputs from complex systems [16].

Despite extensive research in multi-agent path planning algorithms, interfaces, and verification and validation techniques, little emphasis is placed on the design of a complete planning pipeline. Individual components are built without the full pipeline in mind. As a result, the complexities and additional requirements of pipeline integration are often neglected.

III. Human Machine Interaction

To effectively plan large scale multi-agent missions (i.e., large number of agents), human operators must begin by specifying both the high level mission objective(s) and necessary vehicle specifications (e.g., vehicle flight paths and/or collaborative behavior). Regardless of what the mission is and what tools are being exploited to carry it out, the system design must address two basic questions: how will necessary information be requested from the user, and through what means will the user be allowed to provide that information? These questions must be addressed in order for the eventual mission to be a success, but they can be addressed at an abstract level, regardless of how the multi-agent mission is instantiated.

The methods by which operators provide information to the system have been the focus of much second-wave human/computer interaction research, and available options are as varied as they are ubiquitous, ranging from touch-interfaces on smart phones and voice recognition on electronic assistants to simple point-and-click computer interfaces. Recent research suggests that using intuitive interfaces that make use of natural communication techniques helps to increase usability. Making an operator learn not just how to use a system but how to interact with that system in order to use it adds an additional barrier to use. Intuitive user interfaces often eschew the metaphorical interfaces with which many users are now familiar, such as the point-and-click and even the touch interfaces. Such interfaces provide a metaphorical extension of the finger or hand into the metaphorical desktop/page/window structure of the computer. As computing systems have evolved, this underlying metaphor has remained constant [17]. A switch to intuitive methods of communication that rely on human/human interaction models should relieve the user of extra training.

Figure 1. Human operator using the multimodal interface to define a mission.

Most current research, however, focuses on natural language as a way of tapping into intuitive human/human communication strategies. Verbal and even gestural interfaces are examined for their ability to allow operators to talk to systems in an intuitive manner. More intuitive, however, are multimodal interfaces that allow for a combination of different input types [18]. Combining different input modalities allows a system to account for characteristics that are difficult to identify with one modality of input – vehemence, intonation, sarcasm, etc.

The HOLII GRAILLE project used a multimodal interface comprised of speech and gesture modalities [19][20][21]. Users were able to provide necessary information by communicating to the system as they would another human counterpart, augmenting gestural information with spoken details and vice versa (Figure 1). Human operators used gesture inputs to specify the shape of trajectory segments, while speech inputs defined additional geometric information (e.g., length, radius, height). The gesture interface used a Leap Motion controller relying on three infrared cameras to track the motions of the user's palm. Users gestured over the controller in a set of defined motions that represented flight path segments. Simultaneously, operators voiced their commands into a headset, providing additional distance information to augment the gestured trajectory. These commands were translated into text using the CMU Sphinx speech recognition software and interpreted into additional flight data. All trajectory segments were then combined by way of the fused gesture and speech input data (Section V). This multimodal approach allowed HOLII GRAILLE a means of error checking; whenever data from the speech and gesture interface provided conflicting information, the system was able to determine identify and compensate

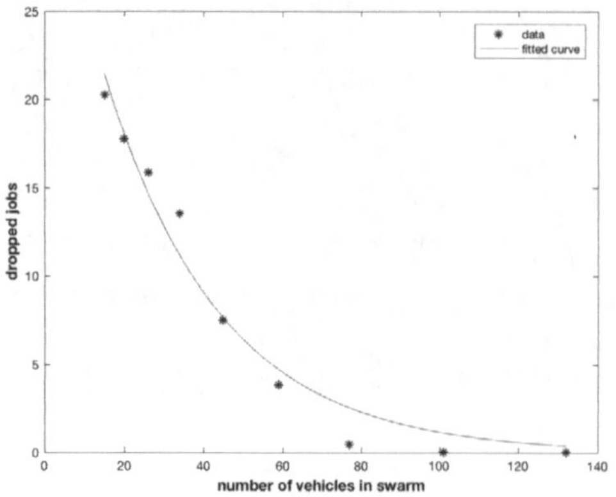

Figure 2. Example of predicted relationship between swarm size and the expected number of dropped jobs.

for the problem [21]. Future iterations of such multimodal interfaces can examine confidence levels in data coming from each interface in order to dynamically determine which one to trust in the case of discrepancy, and incorporate additional communication modalities within the multimodal interface.

IV. Mission Planning Tools

When planning large multi-agent missions, human operators are often tasked with defining additional system parameters such as the number of vehicles (i.e., the swarm size). In many multi-agent – swarm – missions, vehicles must service jobs of various types as they are sensed. For a myriad of applications these jobs must be immediately serviced or risk negative consequences. For example, failing to inspect a compromised bridge after a natural disaster may limit the evacuation routes out of a city. To successfully service the jobs, a small group of vehicles must break off from the main group for a specified amount of time. Each job type requires a different number of vehicles and service time to complete it. Typically, the expected job types and their associated resource requirements are known by the operator. However, in general, only the expected number of jobs of each type is known and not the explicit locations. This uncertainty poses an extremely challenging planning problem to human operators. Therefore, mission planning tools that can provide a predictive model of the steady state system performance must be developed. These models, when used as a reference, will allow human operators to effectively find a balance point in the complex trade-offs between mission parameters such that the desired system performance is met.

One method for modeling complex multi-job type missions is to leverage algorithmic queuing theory. If we assume that the swarm is analogous to a pool of servers, then the sensed jobs can be thought of as arriving customers. In this case, since the swarm itself is moving and the jobs are stationary, the arrival rate for jobs of each job type is simply the expected time between sensing new jobs of that type. Assuming a constant search velocity, the time is equated to the expected average distance between jobs. Jobs are assumed to be randomly and uniformly distributed throughout the search area and thus arrive according to a Poisson distribution. The steady state performance of the system can then be analyzed using an M/M/k/k queuing system, where there are k servers (i.e., vehicles in the swarm) and the allowed size of the queue is k (i.e., if not enough vehicles are left in the swarm to service a job the job is dropped). In [22] we show that the M/M/k/k model is able to accurately model multi-job type missions.

An M/M/k/k model is used to find the relationship between swarm size and expected number of dropped jobs given a set of job types and their associated parameters (i.e., required number of vehicles for service and service time). Figure 2 shows an example of the predicted relationship. The blue points show the analytical solutions, while the red line indicates the fitted curve. Depending on the application area, operators define different cost values associated with various parameters of the mission (e.g., vehicle cost, dropped job cost, etc.). These cost values allow operators to pinpoint where along the trade-off curve they should be to accomplish their desired system performance. By incorporating these prediction models as planning tools, systems like HOLII GRAILLE can reduce the workload on their operators while simultaneously improving overall system performance.

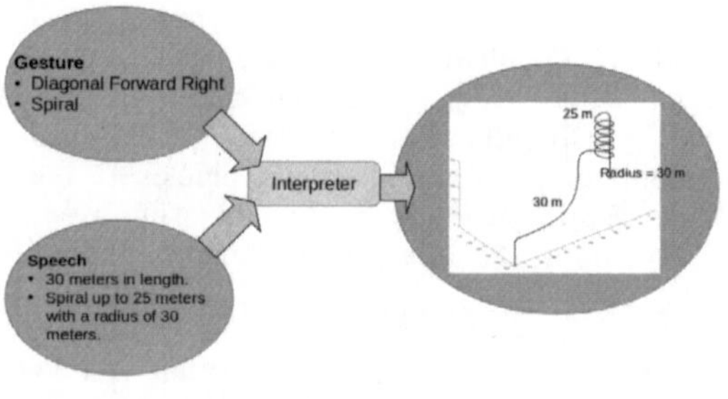

Figure 3. Example data that is fused together using the interpreter module.

V. Mission Generation

Once a human operator has defined the mission objectives and parameters, the planning pipeline is tasked with using the high level mission specifications to define the low level vehicle commands required to successfully complete the mission. This is accomplished in two stages. First, all inputs given by the human operator are interpreted and fused together (Section V-A). The fused data is then sent to a trajectory generation module which uses the general mission specifications pertaining to the flight path to generate smooth and flyable (i.e., realizable with the vehicle controller) trajectories (Section V-B).

A. Interpreter

An interpreter module is used to fuse the gesture and speech data together for each trajectory segment that is defined using the multimodal interface. This is done by first synchronizing the data from the two input modalities. The data input order is preserved from each source by way of a stacked priority queue. Matched shape and geometric data are then paired by popping data off of their respective queues at the same time (Figure 3).

In HOLII GRAILLE's current instantiation of the interpreter module, when conflicting data is received from the gesture and speech inputs the priority queue framework allows the system to choose which input to take as true. This eliminates the possibility of any conflicting data being sent to the trajectory generation module. Future iterations of the interface can produce confidence values associated with the recognition of each input. The interpreter module would then use the confidence values to make a more informed choice

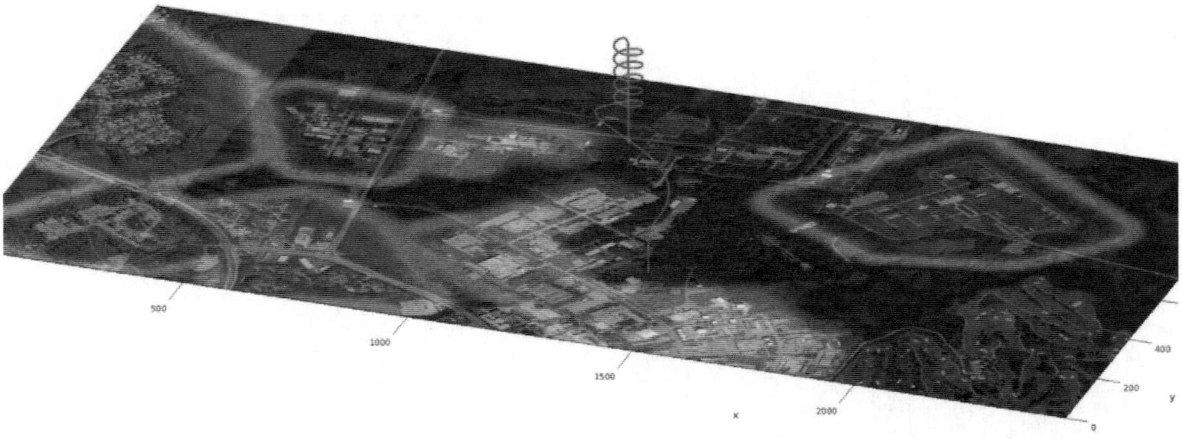

Figure 4. Example trajectory generated using human operator input combined with the expected risk map of the mission environment.

between the conflicting inputs. A weighted combination of the two inputs can also be used to improve overall system interpretation accuracy. If additional clarifying information is needed from the operator, the validation and verification step can be used to prompt the operator for this information. For example, if a conflict arises and the gesture input is chosen as the correct input, an operator may need to input the geometric information with the speech interface again so that the data collected matches the trajectory segment type that was defined using the gestures.

B. *Trajectory Generation*

Once the input data for each segment is fused together by the interpreter module, the trajectory generation module is then able to use the data to define the control points required to represent the segment with a Bézier curve. Each Bézier curve is a polynomial whose first and last control points are the start and end points of the curve. Therefore, the complete flight path is built in a piecewise manner by placing the individual curves in such a way as to ensure that the last point of the first curve is the same as the first point of the next curve. This also ensures at least C^0 continuity across the final combined curve. By extension C^1 and C^2 continuity can be guaranteed by placing the first and last two or three control points of each Bézier curve aptly. The details of this method for generating full piecewise Bézier curves is detailed by Mehdi et al. in [23].

In addition to generating realizable flight paths with guaranteed continuity, the HOLII GRAILLE framework leveraged known risk maps of the mission environment to ensure trajectories defined by human operators maintained a minimum risk level. If need be, the trajectory generation module modifies human operator generated flight paths to ensure that the level of risk for the mission stays below an allowed threshold. The risk maps used included areas with varying levels of risk (Figure 4). Risk values are shown as a color gradient from red to green. Red areas indicate no fly zones, while green areas represent areas of low risk. Blue areas on the map indicate no risk areas. A flyable trajectory with acceptable risk is shown in magenta. In this example mission, the human operator designed a trajectory which moved a UAV diagonally to a new point of interest and then moved the UAV in an upward spiral so that ozone measurements could be taken at varying altitudes over an area of interest. The trajectory generation module modified the diagonal segment to curve around the higher risk area shown in green.

Figure 5. User models the VR headset used for verification and validation.

VI. Validation and Verification

After the interface collects information and the necessary trajectories are calculated, the final stage in the pipeline is validating and verifying the results. Displaying the developed flight path against a map of the environment and terrain can help the user evaluate whether obstructions have been properly avoided, and incorporating risk information about the environment allows the user to visualize if further avoidance measures should be implemented. A critical aspect of a functioning full system pipeline is the ability for the user not only to verify mission plans but, if necessary, to adjust them. Displaying collected and calculated information back to the user allows them an opportunity to correct for any errors and adjust for any new knowledge to be added into the system.

The HOLII GRAILLE pipeline displayed the calculated flight path through Virtual Reality (VR). Donning an Oculus headset and controllers, users were able to view the flight path in relation to the geographical environment, as well as risk maps, ensuring that the flight path stays within necessary physical parameters (see Figure 5). Moreover, the VR environment allows the flight path to be viewed from many different angles not limited to standard physical constraints. Similar functionality could be gained using augmented reality (AR), allowing the user to view the simulated flight path against

Figure 6. Human operator modifying vehicle trajectory using the VR headset in the verification and validation step [24].

a backdrop of reality, though this method requires physical presence in the geographical location of the mission. For ease and extension of use, VR was chosen in favor of AR modeling methods.

Ideally, VR environments also allow for easy and intuitive manipulation of the calculated flight path. Interacting with parameters of the mission as if they were physical objects within a shared environment means that the user can grab, pull, push, and stretch elements of a flight path in order to alter them, mirroring the gestural input modality used with the initial system interface (Figure 6). Not only does such manipulation make use of effective VR interactive strategies (see [25]) but it also allows for a continuation of input modality across the mission planning pipeline. Reliance on intuitive interaction strategies increase the general usability of this verification and validation system and suggest a potential broad user base for the end product.

VII. Results

The HOLII GRAILLE pipeline incorporates all of these individual components, generating the first complete pipeline for full mission management. To demonstrate its value, an indoor scaled-down demonstration of resulting trajectory formed using the complete HOLII GRAILLE pipeline was conducted (Figure 7). In the demonstration a human operator used the multimodal interface to define a desired trajectory and mission for the a UAV vehicle. The data was then sent to the interpreter module, which fused the data together. The trajectory generation module then utilized the risk map and the fused data to build a smooth and realizable flight path for the vehicle. After the flight path was created, the human operator was able to review the flight path using the VR headset. Once the operator had verified and accepted the generated trajectory, it was sent to the controller on board the vehicle.

During the demonstration, the risk map was projected using two overhead projects on the ground. A quadcopter was used to fly the scaled-down flight path over the projected environment – being sure to stay clear of the high risk areas. The flight path followed by the vehicle is shown in magenta. This demonstration indicated the value of a full, integrated pipeline, allowing non-expert users to easily take all the actions necessary to put autonomous vehicles to use.

Figure 7. Scaled-down demonstration of a complete mission generated using the complete HOLII GRAILLE pipeline.

VIII. Discussion

Each individual component of the HOLII GRAILLE pipeline was designed with the human operator and full integration in mind. In doing so, the inputs and outputs of each component were easily identified. This also provided guidance on the internal design of the components. Additionally, by considering the human machine interaction from the start the system as a whole can push towards an increased level of trustworthiness with the human operator. HOLII GRAILLE may provide a path forward for increasing the usability of UAVs in critical domains as well as for establishing the basis for trust in and trustworthiness of these systems.

The HOLII GRAILLE pipeline is mission application agnostic, thereby allowing human operators to interact with the system in the same way regardless of their mission's objectives. The ease-of-use of the multimodal interface establishes a baseline for future execution interfaces. While this initial pipeline focuses on relatively straightforward mission specifications, the HOLII GRAILLE pipeline provides an initial design that can be modified in future iterations for more complex mission management. The interaction framework can be leveraged to develop mission modification capabilities. These execution interfaces will rely on the design and implementation of appropriate monitoring strategies that reduce the operator's overall workload [26]. In addition, for applications like search and rescue, to realize successful multi-agent missions on autonomous platforms additional behaviors, such as small team deployments, must be developed [27].

IX. Conclusion and Future Work

Having established a need for an intuitive, usable, and successful mission management tool, this paper discusses HOLII GRAILLE as one example of a full pipeline tool. With individual components working to increase usability and transparency of information, this mission management tools can work toward increasing successful interaction between application level experts and machines, as well as leading toward increased human operator trust in the system. By creating the pipeline from verified or verifiable components, the mission management tool provided a way to increase the overall trustworthiness of the system.

Future instantiations of a VR validation environment could make use of persistent simulations that continue to process information even when the user is not currently logged in [28]. Such a persistent environment could continue to recalculate risks, update information on weather, and process input from other users that would all contribute to an accurate modelling environment for the developed UAV flight path. Moreover, this environment does not have to rely on local information only and can incorporate data from a distributed network of users and inputs, further broadening the user base and increasing access to flight path verification and validation [24]. With location-agnostic multiple user access, more users can be involved in the process of ensuring the flight path is fit and making modification if necessary.

Lastly, future iterations must take into account how the system lets the user know what information it needs. While methods of information elicitation were not examined as part of the HOLII GRAILLE pipeline, understanding how to elicit information from a human operator was looked at as part of the HINGE project [29]. While information elicitation is a moderately nascent focus for investigation, it is often incorporated in studies focused on situated human computer interaction and should be a focus for future pipeline iterations [30] [31].

Building upon these areas can allow future pipelines to address the management of more complicated missions. While HOLII GRAILLE provides an example multi-agent mission planning pipeline, future work focusing in these areas can help improve usability and lead to increased mission success.

ACKNOWLEDGMENT

The authors would like to thank the additional members of the HOLII GRAILLE team – Angelica Garcia, Lauren Howell, Jeremy Lim, and Javier Puig-Navarro – as well as the members of the Autonomy Incubator who contributed to the project.

REFERENCES

[1] C. Guestrin, D. Koller, and R. Parr, "Multiagent planning with factored mdps," in Advances in neural information processing systems, 2002, pp. 1523–1530.

[2] G. Arslan, J. R. Marden, and J. S. Shamma, "Autonomous vehicle-target assignment: A game-theoretical formulation," Journal of Dynamic Systems, Measurement, and Control, vol. 129, no. 5, 2007, pp. 584–596.

[3] D. Bertsimas and R. Weismantel, Optimization over integers. Dynamic Ideas Belmont, 2005, vol. 13.

[4] L. Borin and J. Edlund, "Language technology and 3rd wave hci: Towards phatic communication and situated interaction," in New Directions in Third Wave Human-Computer Interaction: Volume 1-Technologies. Springer, 2018, pp. 251–264.

[5] J. R. Cauchard, J. L. E, K. Y. Zhai, and J. A. Landay, "Drone & me: an exploration into natural human-drone interaction," in Proceedings of the 2015 ACM International Joint Conference on Pervasive and Ubiquitous Computing. ACM, 2015, pp. 361–365.

[6] W. S. Ng and E. Sharlin, "Collocated interaction with flying robots," in 2011 RO-MAN. IEEE, 2011, pp. 143–149.

[7] M. Quigley, M. A. Goodrich, and R. W. Beard, "Semi-autonomous human-uav interfaces for fixed-wing mini-uavs," in Intelligent Robots and Systems (IROS). Proceedings. 2004 IEEE/RSJ International Conference on, vol. 3. IEEE, 2004, pp. 2457–2462.

[8] N. Li, S. Cartwright, A. Shekhar Nittala, E. Sharlin, and M. Costa Sousa, "Flying frustum: A spatial interface for enhancing human-uav awareness," in Proceedings of the 3rd International Conference on Human-Agent Interaction. ACM, 2015, pp. 27–31.

[9] S. Waldherr, R. Romero, and S. Thrun, "A gesture based interface for human-robot interaction," Autonomous Robots, vol. 9, no. 2, 2000, pp. 151–173.

[10] J. Lambrecht, M. Kleinsorge, and J. Krüger, "Markerless gesture-based motion control and programming of industrial robots," in Emerging Technologies & Factory Automation (ETFA), 2011 IEEE 16th Conference on. IEEE, 2011, pp. 1–4.

[11] "Put-that-there: Voice and gesture at the graphics interface," vol. 14, no. 3. New York, NY, USA: ACM SIGGRAPH Computer Graphics, 1980, pp. 262–270.

[12] R. A. S. Fernández, J. L. Sanchez-Lopez, C. Sampedro, H. Bavle, M. Molina, and P. Campoy, "Natural user interfaces for human-drone multi-modal interaction," in Unmanned Aircraft Systems (ICUAS), 2016 International Conference on. IEEE, 2016, pp. 1013–1022.

[13] J. B. Lyons, M. A. Clark, A. R. Wagner, and M. J. Schuelke, "Certifiable trust in autonomous systems: Making the intractable tangible." AI Magazine, vol. 38, no. 3, 2017, pp. 37–49.

[14] M. Kamali, L. A. Dennis, O. McAree, M. Fisher, and S. M. Veres, "Formal verification of autonomous vehicle platooning," Science of Computer Programming, vol. 148, 2017, pp. 88–106.

[15] N. Li et al., "Game theoretic modeling of driver and vehicle interactions for verification and validation of autonomous vehicle control systems," IEEE Transactions on control systems technology, vol. 26, no. 5, 2018, pp. 1782–1797.

[16] N. Alexandrov, "Explainable ai decisions for human-autonomy interactions," in 17th AIAA Aviation Technology, Integration, and Operations Conference, 2017, p. 3991.

[17] S. A. Brasel and J. Gips, "Tablets, touchscreens, and touchpads: How varying touch interfaces trigger psychological ownership and endowment," Journal of Consumer Psychology, vol. 24, no. 2, 2014, pp. 226–233.

[18] E. L. Meszaros, M. Chandarana, A. Trujillo, and B. D. Allen, "Compensating for limitations in speech-based natural language processing with multimodal interfaces in uav operation," in International Conference on Applied Human Factors and Ergonomics. Springer, 2017, pp. 183–194.

[19] M. Chandarana, E. L. Meszaros, A. Trujillo, and B. D. Allen, "Analysis of a gesture-based interface for uav flight path generation," in Unmanned Aircraft Systems (ICUAS), 2017 International Conference on. IEEE, 2017, pp. 36–45.

[20] E. L. Meszaros, M. Chandarana, A. Trujillo, and B. D. Allen, "Speech-based natural language interface for uav trajectory generation," in Unmanned Aircraft Systems (ICUAS), 2017 International Conference on. IEEE, 2017, pp. 46–55.

[21] M. Chandarana, E. L. Meszaros, A. Trujillo, and B. Danette Allen, "Natural language based multimodal interface for uav mission planning," in Proceedings of the Human Factors and Ergonomics Society Annual Meeting, vol. 61, no. 1. SAGE Publications Sage CA: Los Angeles, CA, 2017, pp. 68–72.

[22] M. Chandarana, M. Lewis, K. Sycara, and S. Scherer, "Determining effective swarm sizes for multi-job type missions," in Intelligent Robots and Systems (IROS), 2018 IEEE/RSJ International Conference on. IEEE, 2018.

[23] S. Mehdi et al., "Bézier curves for safe cooperative atmospheric missions with multiple heterogeneous uas," in 16th AIAA Aviation Technology, Integration, and Operations Conference, 2016, p. 4229.

[24] B. N. Kelley, R. A. Williams, J. L. Holland, O. C. Schnarr, and B. D. Allen, "A persistent simulation environment for autonomous systems," in 2018 Aviation Technology, Integration, and Operations Conference, 2018, p. 4015.

[25] S. Jang, J. M. Vitale, R. W. Jyung, and J. B. Black, "Direct manipulation is better than passive viewing for learning anatomy in a three-dimensional virtual reality environment," Computers & Education, vol. 106, 2017, pp. 150–165.

[26] P. Walker, "Improving operator recognition and prediction of emergent swarm behaviors," Ph.D. dissertation, University of Pittsburgh, July 2017.

[27] M. Chandarana, M. Lewis, K. Sycara, and S. Scherer, "Decentralized method for sub-swarm deployment and rejoining," in Systems, Man, and Cybernetics (SMC), 2018 IEEE International Conference on. IEEE, 2018.

[28] B. D. Allen, "Serious gaming for building a basis of certification for trust and trustworthiness of autonomous systems," in 2018 Aviation Technology, Integration, and Operations Conference, 2018, p. 3844.

[29] E. L. Meszaros et al., "Evaluating communication modality for improved human/autonomous system teaming," in 2019 AIAA Science and Technology Forum and Exposition. AIAA, 2019.

[30] R. Banerji, "De-instrumentalizing hci: Social psychology, rapport formation, and interactions with artificial social agents," in New Directions in Third Wave Human-Computer Interaction: Volume 1-Technologies. Springer, 2018, pp. 43–66.

[31] Y. Candau, T. Schiphorst, and J. Françoise, "Designing from embodied knowing: Practice-based research at the intersection between embodied interaction and somatics," in New Directions in Third Wave Human-Computer Interaction: Volume 2-Methodologies. Springer, 2018, pp. 203–230.

Remote Shoulder-to-shoulder Communication Enhancing Co-located Sensation

Minghao Cai and Jiro Tanaka

Graduate School of Information, Production and Systems
Waseda University
Kitakyushu, Japan
Email: mhcai@toki.waseda.jp, jiro@aoni.waseda.jp

Abstract—**In this paper, we propose our mobile remote communication prototype between two users in separated environments – a remote user goes to a shared environment with mobile augmented reality setup and a local user stays indoor immersing in a virtual reality view to this shared environment. It realizes a kind of remote shoulder-to-shoulder communication, which simulates that the users go shoulder-to-shoulder with viewing independence and bidirectional gesture communication, and the major target is to enhance a shared co-located sensation. We also introduce our preliminary evaluation used to test the system usability and user performance.**

Keywords–Remote communication; Co-located Sensation; Viewing independence; Gesture communication.

I. Introduction

In recent years, remote communication is extensively used at work or in daily life to increase productivity and to improve the performance of the instant communication. It allows users from the different locations to communicate and collaborate together as a team. It is a cost-effective way that can truly help users to get an instant solution for any type of problem [1].

Although commercial remote conferencing technologies are cost-effective and more immersive than traditional phone calls with only voice, most of these systems mainly provide a mere capture of both user's face and limited transition in terms of body language or the reference of ambient, which also act as a great source of information. When facing a physical collaborative task or conversation with context related to the surroundings, existing technologies offer limited ways for users to achieve effective gestural communication, as they tend to focus on face-to-face experiences. When users want to describe the objects or directions in the scene or showing operations, using the hand gesture would be more understandable than mere voice.

Another problem is derived from the camera used for real-time video capture. When using telecommunication systems with smartphones or tablets, users tend to switch between the front and back camera or they might place the device in a fixed position in order to have a wild range of capture. In most cases, people have to take the camera and move around in order for the remote person to perceive the entire scene. Such constraints make it difficult for users to get a common perception or feel like staying together.

In this paper, we propose a solution with a prototype providing a mobile and immersive remote *Shoulder-to-shoulder Communication* between a local user and a remote user who are in different places. This type of communication can enhance a co-located sensation during the remote communication.

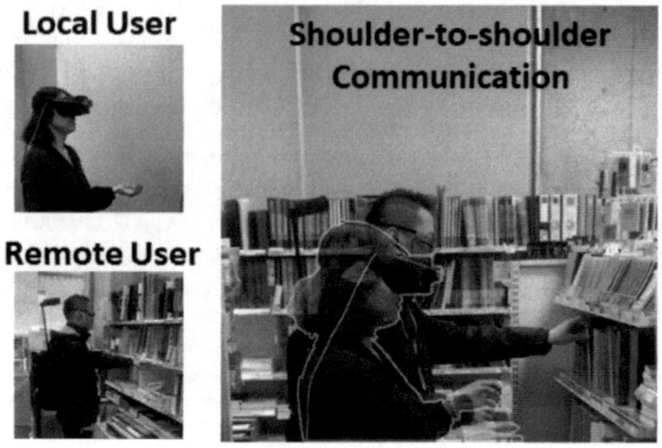

Figure 1. Remote Shoulder-to-shoulder Communication

The prototype is designed to be used by two users in different places (Figure 1). For convenience, we refer to the user who goes to a remote environment that would be shared as the remote user, and the other one who is staying in a local indoor workspace and remotely viewing the shared world as the local user, even though the roles may well be reversed. We try to offer both users a shared feeling that they are going shoulder-to-shoulder together with gesture communication. Wearing a Head-mounted Display (HMD) with a Virtual Reality (VR) experience, the local user perceives the remote environment with viewing independence, while the remote user wears a see-through smart glasses getting augmented reality (AR) experience.

The main contributions of this work are: (1) the implementation of the hardware prototype including the mobile setup for the remote user and wearable setup for the local user, and (2) the software system supporting virtual and augmented reality spatial interaction between two users, and (3) a preliminary evaluation carried out to test the usability of our prototype.

In Section II, we introduce the related works. In Section III, we introduce our system design. In Section IV, we introduce our implementation. In Section V, we introduce the preliminary evaluation. In Section VI, we discuss the difference between our should-to-shoulder communication design and traditional remote communication design. In Section VII, we draw our conclusion to this work.

II. Related Work

Currently, it is not unusual to get an instant contact with commercial video conferencing systems (e.g., Skype, Cisco WebEx Conferencing). Most of these systems provide remote communication with a face capture from disparate locations, however, they do not allow users to reference a common physical ambient or share a co-presence feeling. Some previous researches have tried to address this limitation with different approaches [2] including projecting interface [3], virtual reality interface [4].

Several pieces of research have spent effort on remote video communication techniques which aim to realize a remote collaborative work among users in separated places [5][1]. Some of these works tested depth sensors to extract and analyze body motions and interactions to support users to work in the same media space.

Hand gesture has been shown as an irreplaceable part for conversation, as it is treated as a cognitive visible awareness cue and provides rich context information that other body cues cannot reveal, which contributes significantly to a recipient's understanding [6][7]. Over the past several years, some researchers have paid attention to support gestural interaction in the shared media space with different approaches. A study confirmed that over a third of the users' gestures in a collaborative task was performed to engage the other users and express ideas [8]. Kirk et al. [9] demonstrated the positive effect of gestures and visual information in promoting the speed and accuracy in remote collaborative activities. Another work by Fussell et al. [10] demonstrated that users tend to rely more on visual actions than on speech in the collaborative work.

Previously, we built a remote sightseeing prototype supporting gestural communication to realize a gesture communication between two separated users [11][12]. It investigated providing users with an approach to achieve a spatial navigation and direction guidance during mobile sightseeing. The positive evaluation results of this work encourage us to support a mid-air gesture interaction for improvements of users' interactions in remote collaborations.

III. System Design

The system design consists of the following main aspects:

- A Shoulder-to-shoulder viewing independence
- B Shoulder-to-shoulder Gesture Communication
- C Tele-presence of the Local User's Head Motions
- D Virtual Pointing Assistance

A. Shoulder-to-shoulder Viewing Independence

To capture and share the real-time remote environment, we choose a new generation camera that provides a high-resolution video with a range of 360°in both horizontal and vertical. Different from previous view sharing systems that usually put the camera on the remote user's head or cheek [13], this camera is fixed to one of the remote user's shoulder with the help of a steel support. The real-time 360°video is streamed back to the local side via the Internet and displays in the head-mounted display wore by the local user.

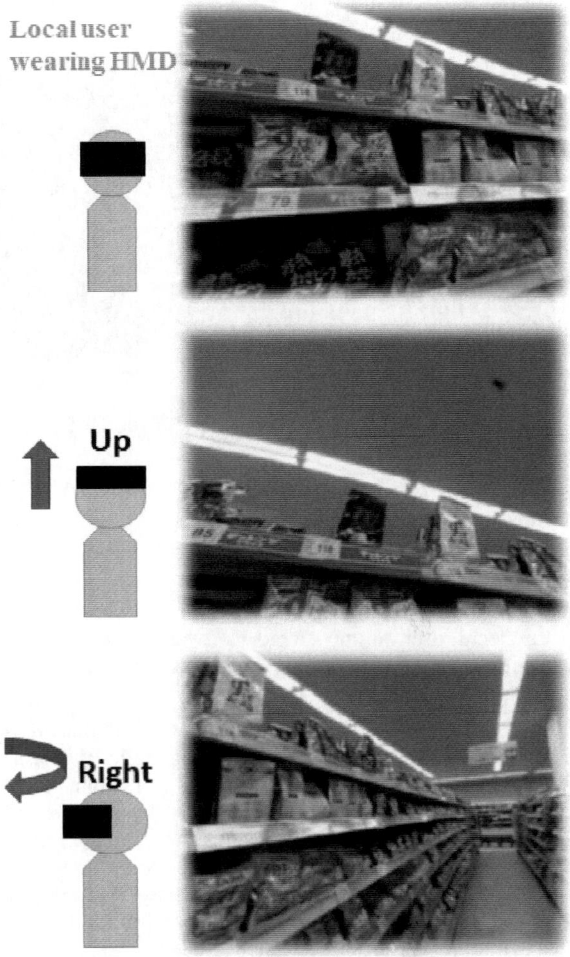

Figure 2. Independent control of the viewing direction for the local user

Since the camera fixed to the shoulder, its orientation is preventing from being influenced by the remote user's head motions. The local user is supported with independent control of viewing direction which can be simply manipulated by head movements. As shown in Figure 2, the local user simply turns the head and naturally changes the viewpoints. Through this design, the local user immerses in the virtual remote world, perceiving a sensation that personally standing next to the remote user and seeing the scene.

B. Shoulder-to-shoulder Gesture Communication

In our system, we provide users an approach to achieve a bidirectional gesture interaction during the mobile communication. On one hand, a shoulder-looking capture of the hand gestures of the remote user is included in the local user's virtual viewing. On the other hand, a pair of virtual hands based on the depth-based recognition reappearing the local user's gestures in the remote user's field of view.

1) Remote Gestures to Local User: As we have introduced in Section III-A, the local user has a 360°independent viewing of the remote world with a perspective by the remote user's

Figure 3. The local user's field of view: the remote user is making gestures

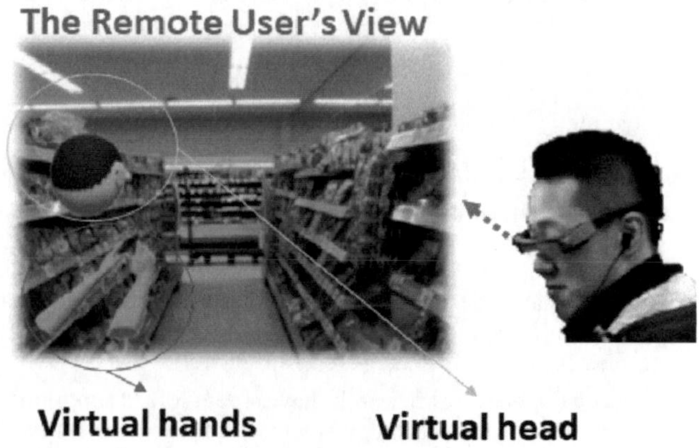

Figure 4. The remote user's field of view: the local user is making gestures. Red circle shows the virtual hands and yellow circle shows the virtual head representing the local user

shoulder. This design allows the local user to see the remote hand gestures, as well as the profile face. As shown in Figure 3, the local user simply looks leftward, and directly see the remote partner performing hand gestures with an object (opening a notebook).

2) Local Gestures to Remote User: One of the important contributions of this system is reappearing the local user's hand gestures in the remote world, as the local user is in a physically separated environment. We implement the hardware to extract the user's hand motion and the software to render it in the remote user's see-through smart glasses. Being considered as an accuracy and convenient way, depth-based recognition has been used to in current researches for hand motion extraction [14][15]. A depth sensor is attached to the front side of the local user's HMD to extract a fine 3D structure data of both hands in real time. The local user can perform hand gestures without any wearable or attached sensors on the hands, which improve the freedom of hand motions and comfort. The system extracts the raw structure data with almost 200 frames per second with the help of the Leap Motion SDK [16]. We construct a pair of 3D hand models including palms and different finger joints. This pair of 3D hand models is matched with the latest hand structure data. Then, the current reconstructed hands are sent to the remote side via the Internet and rendered in the remote user's AR smart glasses, as an event to update the previous hands. Therefore, once the local user makes hand gestures, the models change to match the exact same ones, almost simultaneously appearing in the remote user's field of view (Figure 4).

C. Tele-presence of the Local User's Head Motions

As we aim to enhance a co-located sensation by improving the interaction between users, we try to help the users easily tell where the partner is looking at. It would improve the efficiency of communication when the user tries to join in the same field of view so as to find out some common interesting points or make some discussion. As we introduced in Section III-A, the local user can easily tell the remote user's viewing direction in the virtual scene. Because the local user is in a physically separated environment, we construct a virtual head model to show his/her head motions in the remote user's view.

Figure 5. The remote user's view: Pointing cue for instructions

A motion tracking sensor is used to extract the head motion which is used to rotate the virtual head model. The model presents on the left side of the vision, showing the remote user's precise facing direction (see Figure 4).

D. Pointing Assistance

Previous research has shown that utilizing a finger pointing assistance can benefit the cooperation and instruction between users especially when spatial information is involved in conversations [5].

In our shoulder-to-shoulder communication system, we allow the local user to use a pointing assistance with fingers. The user performs a freehand pointing gesture to use a virtual 3D arrow showing specific direction information in the remote user's view. This 3D arrow is treated as a spatial cue assisting a navigation or selection task during the communication (see Figure 5).

Our system uses a heuristic approach for the gesture recognition. Using the depth sensor, our system can keep

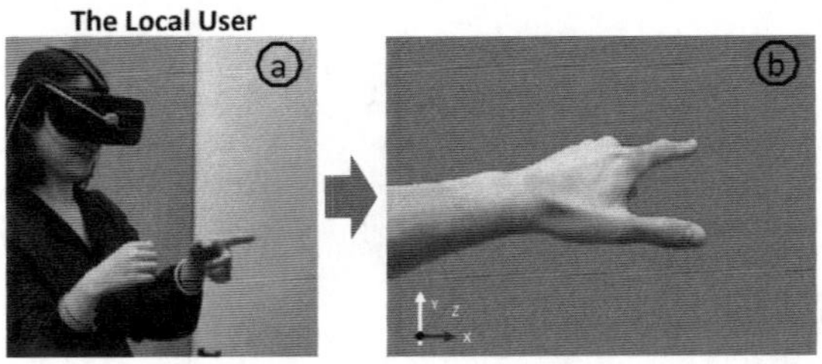

Figure 6. (a): The local user makes a pointing gesture (b): a zoomed in view of the pointing gesture

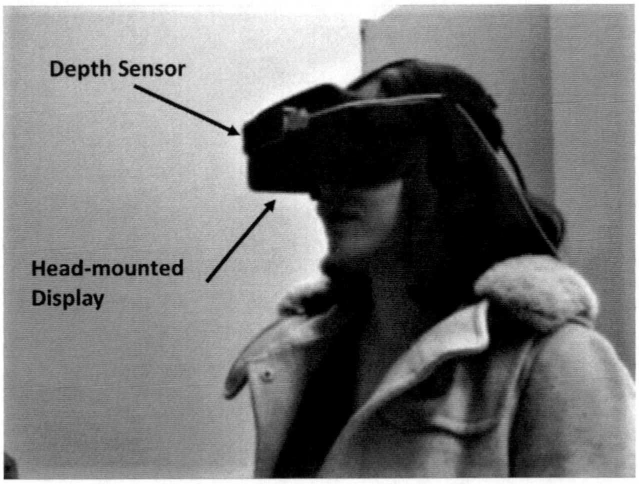

Figure 7. The remote user's wearable device: a head-mounted display with a depth sensor attached to its front side

tracking the 3D structure of the user's hands including different finger joints and extract both the 3D position and orientation of the local users fingers. Our system requires no calibration or precedent training. To activate the pointing technique, the user extends only the thumb and index finger and keeps the angle between them larger than the set threshold (see Figure 6).

IV. Implementation

Our system's hardware includes two parts: the local user side and the remote user side.

A. Local User's Side

The equipment in local user's side include the wearable devices and a desktop PC (see Figure 7). The desktop PC (Intel Core i5, RX480 Graphics Card, 8GB RAM) placed on the local user side is used to analyze data and engine the core system. We use Unity engine to render and process the incoming data from both remote and local side, as well as to generate GUI for both users. The headset we chose as the local user's head-mounted display uses a pair of low persistence OLED screens, providing a 110 field of view [17]. A point tracking sensor is used to provide a full 6 degree of freedom rotational and positional tracking of the head movements. For hand motion tracking, the depth sensor we used is light enough and introduces a gesture tracking system with sub-millimeter accuracy [18]).

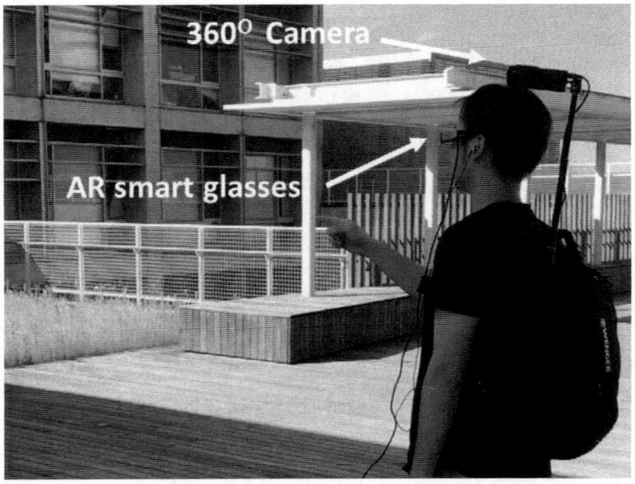

Figure 8. The remote user's field of view: the local user is making gestures. Red circle shows the virtual hands and yellow circle shows the virtual head representing the local user

B. Remote User's Side

The integrated wearable device in remote user's side consists of an AR smart glasses, a 360°camera, and a notebook computer (see Figure 8). The AR glasses presents a semitransparent display on top of the physical world while allows the user to view the physical world clearly. It packs with a motion-tracking sensor to detect the user's facing direction and a wireless module to exchange information with the local user's side via the Internet. It also provides an audio output with an earphone. The camera is connected to a notebook computer over USB (1280x720 15fps) to generate a live stream to send the live video data to the desktop PC on the local user side with Real Time Messaging Protocol (RTMP). The streaming uses H.264 software encoder.

V. Preliminary Evaluation

We carried out a user study for preliminary evaluation. The purpose is to investigate how the shoulder-to-shoulder viewing affects the remote communication experience, especially with hand gesture communication.

A. Participants

In this study, we recruited eight participants in our departments (between 21 an 27 years old). All participants had regular level computer skills. They were divided into four pairs. Each pair had two roles: a local user and a remote user.

B. Task and Procedure

In each pair, one participant played the role of the local user, while the other one played the role of the remote user. Before the experiment, our researchers explained how to use the system and the participants were allowed to practice for 10 minutes. The whole experiment took about 40 minutes for each group.

The environment of user study involved an indoor workspace for the local user and a department store where the remote user stayed.

TABLE 1. QUESTIONNAIRE

Q1. Did you observe interesting things independently?
Q2. Did you find it easy to tell your partner's viewing direction?
Q3. Did you feel gestural communication useful?
Q4. Did you feel the operation is easy enough to learn and use?
Q5. How much did you feel co-located with your partner together during the test?

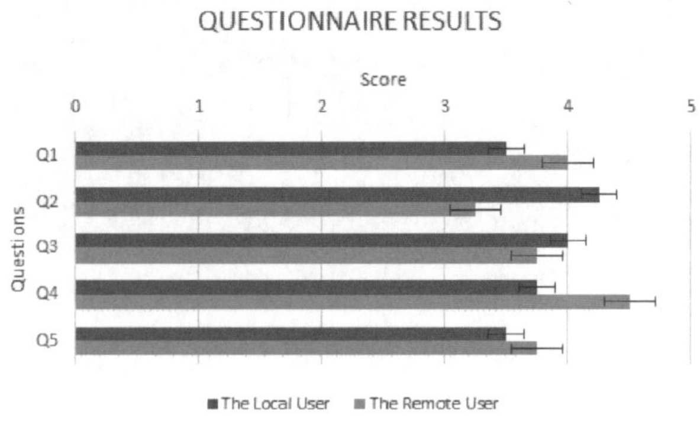

Figure 9. Questionnaire results

The study task was joint shopping in a department store to find out a product that could interest both participants (such as a pencil box). In each pair, both participants were allowed a free voice communication supported by Internet IP phone call. The remote participant walked around and communicated with the local partner, and the local participant participated in the shopping via remote communication. The subsystem in local user's part was connected to the cabled Internet, and the remote user's subsystem used a wireless connection (LTE).

After each experiment, all four pairs of participants were asked to fill out a questionnaire including to get the user feedback. The participants graded each question with 5-point Likert Scale (1 = very negative, 5 = very positive).

C. Results

Table 1 shows the questions of our questionnaires. We calculated the average score of each question in each group. Figure 9 shows the results. The results were divided into two groups–the local user's group and the remote user's group.

Question 1 – *Did you observe interesting thing independently?* was used to test whether our system could provide the users with viewing independence. According to the results, it was clear that both users could have independent control of viewpoint in the remote view sharing.

Question 2 –*Did you find it easy to tell your partner's viewing direction?* indicated that the users could be aware of the partner's attention condition easily which provides the possibility to join in the same scenery for further communication.

Question 3 – *Did you felt gestural communication useful?* was used to judge the practicability and effectiveness of the hand gesture communication through our system. It indicated that both the local user and the remote user found performing gestures to transmit their intentions was useful.

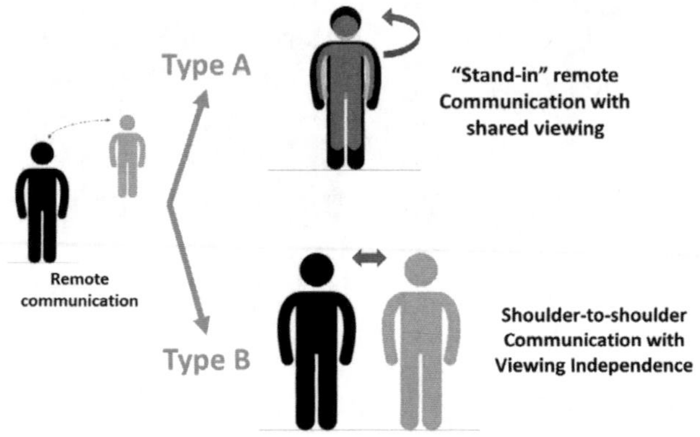

Figure 10. Comparison between two types of remote communication

Question 4 – *Did you felt the operation is easy enough to learn and use?* was used to evaluate the ease and usability of our system. The result suggested that both users generally found it was effortless to achieve communication with our system.

In Question 5 – *How much did you feel co-located with your partner together during the test?* we aimed to investigate the overall performance and user experience. It demonstrates that, during the remote communication, both users perceived a certain extent of co-located sensation.

In the results of Q3, both users gave positive scores. So, we confirmed that users could perform gestures to transmit their intentions and achieve a mutual smooth communication. During the communication, users used mutual gesture interaction as a nonverbal body cue.

From the results of Question 3, we also observed that the participants who played the role of local users graded slightly higher than their partners who played the role of the remote user. This difference means an incomplete equivalence of the gesture communication that benefits the local users more. After further communication with the participants in some post-task interviews, we found it was probably because the remote users could use hand gestures (such as touching, squeezing or grasping) to actually interact with physical objects.

In this evaluation, all participants successfully finished the tasks. In each pair, the local participant and the remote participant could reach an agreement and pick up a target object after discussion. Each user were aware of their partners during the task, which provides users with a close connection. We confirmed that both users could enjoy the communication experience and generally receive a certain level of co-located feeling.

VI. Discussion

In this section, we discuss the difference between our should-to-shoulder communication design and traditional remote communication design. We also describe some potential applications.

A. Shoulder-to-shoulder vs First-person Perspective

In traditional view sharing designs, which usually are found in previous Computer-Supported Cooperative Work (CSCW) [4], the local user mostly perceives the remote venue with the same field of view of the remote user. With such sharing of first-person perspective (FPP) of the content, the remote user acts more like a "stand-in" of the local user rather than a communicating partner (see Figure 10-Type A). It might lead to misunderstanding and limits the natural communication between users. By contrast, our shoulder-to-shoulder communication simulates a shoulder-to-shoulder togetherness, which provides both users with more independence and let them could focus more mutual interaction (see Figure 10-Type B). This could enhance a co-located sensation, which is also supported by our user study results.

B. Possible Applications

Our shoulder-to-shoulder communication design can be used in a variety of applications where remote collaboration is useful. For example, in the use of remote maintenance or remote instructions of industrial operations, the local users would be an expert to guide a worker who would be the remote user in a shared workspace. Or, the local users would be people with physical inconveniences who have to stay in the hospital or other comfort environments try to have virtual sightseeing with a remote user who might be friends or relatives.

VII. Conclusion

In this paper, we introduced our design and implementation of a shoulder-to-shoulder communication prototype which aimed to enhance a co-located sensation between two users in separated environments. This prototype supported users with viewing independence and bidirectional gesture communication. We also described our user study to investigate the system usability and user performance. The results demonstrated both users could effectively transmit instructions relating to the physical world and could achieve a smooth remote collaboration, and finally could receive a certain degree of co-located sensation. In the future work, we plan to the apply our prototype to different scenarios and perform further evaluations.

References

[1] S. Hunter, P. Maes, A. Tang, K. Inkpen, and S. Hessey, "WaaZam ! Supporting Creative Play at a Distance in Customized Video Environments," Conference on Human Factors in Computing Systems, 2014, p. 146.

[2] K. Tajimi, N. Sakata, K. Uemura, and S. Nishida, "Remote collaboration using real-world projection interface." 2010, pp. 3008–3013.

[3] P. Gurevich, J. Lanir, B. Cohen, and R. Stone, "Teleadvisor: a versatile augmented reality tool for remote assistance," in Proceedings of the SIGCHI Conference on Human Factors in Computing Systems. ACM, 2012, pp. 619–622.

[4] S. Kasahara and J. Rekimoto, "JackIn head: immersive visual telepresence system with omnidirectional wearable camera for remote collaboration," Proceedings of the 21st ACM Symposium on Virtual Reality Software and Technology, vol. 23, no. 3, 2015, pp. 217–225.

[5] R. S. Sodhi, B. R. Jones, D. Forsyth, B. P. Bailey, and G. Maciocci, "BeThere: 3D Mobile Collaboration with Spatial Input," Proceedings of the SIGCHI Conference on Human Factors in Computing Systems - CHI '13, 2013, pp. 179–188.

[6] C. Goodwin, "Gestures as a resource for the organization of mutual orientation," Semiotica, vol. 62, no. 1-2, 1986, pp. 29–50.

[7] S. W. Cook and M. K. Tanenhaus, "Embodied communication: Speakers gestures affect listeners actions," Cognition, vol. 113, no. 1, 2009, pp. 98–104.

[8] J. C. Tang, "Findings from observational studies of collaborative work," International Journal of Man-machine studies, vol. 34, no. 2, 1991, pp. 143–160.

[9] D. S. Kirk and D. S. Fraser, "The effects of remote gesturing on distance instruction," in Proceedings of th 2005 conference on Computer support for collaborative learning: learning 2005: the next 10 years! International Society of the Learning Sciences, 2005, pp. 301–310.

[10] D. Gergle, R. E. Kraut, and S. R. Fussell, "Action as language in a shared visual space," in Proceedings of the 2004 ACM conference on Computer supported cooperative work. ACM, 2004, pp. 487–496.

[11] M. Cai and J. Tanaka, "Trip together: A remote pair sightseeing system supporting gestural communication," Proceedings of the 5th International Conference on Human Agent Interaction, 2017, pp. 317–324.

[12] M. Cai, S. Masuko, and J. Tanaka, "Gesture-based mobile communication system providing side-by-side shopping feeling," Proceedings of the 23rd International Conference on Intelligent User Interfaces Companion, 2018, pp. 2:1–2:2.

[13] G. A. Lee, T. Teo, S. Kim, and M. Billinghurst, "Mixed reality collaboration through sharing a live panorama," in SIGGRAPH Asia 2017 Mobile Graphics & Interactive Applications. ACM, 2017, p. 14.

[14] H. Karam and J. Tanaka, "Finger click detection using a depth camera," Procedia Manufacturing, vol. 3, 2015, pp. 5381–5388.

[15] J. Amores, X. Benavides, and P. Maes, "Showme: A remote collaboration system that supports immersive gestural communication," Proceedings of the 33rd Annual ACM Conference Extended Abstracts on Human Factors in Computing Systems, 2015, pp. 1343–1348.

[16] Leap Motion, "Leap Motion's SDK," Retrieved: January 2019. [Online]. Available: https://developer.leapmotion.com/documentation/

[17] Oculus, "Oculus Rift," Retrieved: January 2019. [Online]. Available: https://www.oculus.com/

[18] Leap Motion, "LEAP MOTION," Retrieved: January 2019. [Online]. Available: https://www.leapmotion.com/

The Impact of Player Experience on Enjoyment in Tablet Gaming

Uttam Kokil
College of Humanities and Social Sciences
Kennesaw State University
Marietta, GA 30060, USA
E-Mail: ukokil@kennesaw.edu

***Abstract*—In the field of human computer interaction design, player experience and game enjoyment components have not been clearly differentiated and they have often been used to indicate the same entity. To disentangle the two components, this study sheds light on the relationship between player experience and enjoyment in the domain of tablet gaming. This study emphasizes mainly on the analysis and findings portion by empirically illustrating that positive player experience was associated with a higher level of game enjoyment, whereas participants with negative player experience revealed their enthusiasm was dampened during gameplay, yet enjoyment was perceived to be somewhat enjoyable. In sum, game mechanics must produce a balance between positive and negative player experiences for the player to feel rewarded.**

Keywords-player experience; tablet gaming; game enjoyment.

I. Introduction

Game enjoyment is a terminology commonly used in the domain of gaming, yet its connotation is often unclear and vague with respect to player experience [1]. This knowledge gap leads to an investigation of the relationship between player experience and game enjoyment. In this study, it is hypothesized that positive player experience entails a higher level of enjoyment during mobile gameplay. In addition, the lack of understanding concerning the effect of positive and negative player experience on game enjoyment has given rise to the research objective of this study. Different types of games are designed to deliberately elicit specific kinds of emotions.

Studies on player experience have shown that both positive and negative emotions lead to a positive player experience [2] [3]. For instance, it has been found that although a player elicits acute negative emotions during game activity, this may often give rise to a satisfying experience, adding to the overall game enjoyment [4][5]. Positive player experience is defined by the optimum level of enjoyment one derives during gameplay [3], as measured by the *Presence Involvement Flow Framework* (PIFF) instrument [6]. It has been discussed that negative affect can give rise to an "engaging player experience" [7][8]. It has also been shown that boredom and frustration states of the player can potentially lead to a negative player experience. Boredom occurs when the player's skills surpass the challenge, and frustration occurs when the player's skills do not meet the challenge [9][10]. On the other hand, tension and frustration add to the game challenges, factors necessary for an overall game play experience [11]. Apathy is a condition of low skill and low challenge. If game challenges exceed the player's skill, it will give rise to anxiety. Keeker et al. [12] explained that negative emotions are purposely built into games. These negative emotions are often trailed by positive emotions, after the challenges are surpassed, which give rise to a pleasurable experience [2].

In other domains, components such as perceived enjoyment, concentration, and perceived control have been exhibited to induce flow experience when it concerns purchase behaviors of online shoppers [13] and the use of instant messaging [14]. Non-immersive games can also lead to negative emotions such as anxiety, thereby generating a negative player experience [15]. Minimal research work has been done to examine the effect of negative player experience, also termed as negative frustration, in games [15] [16]. Game enjoyment is an important component of player experience; therefore, it becomes essential to understand the relationship between game enjoyment, positive and negative player experiences, among other confounding factors like emotions and flow. The purpose of the study is to disentangle the concept of the two components, player experience and game enjoyment, to obtain clearer definitions. The aim is to examine the effect of positive and negative player experience on game enjoyment during gameplay. The rest of this paper is organized as follows. Section II briefly describes the literature review. Section III justifies the methods, including the instruments used. Section III explains the data inspection procedures. Section IV explains the data inspection procedure. Section V elucidates the analysis and findings. Section VI provides a brief discussion and Section VII concludes the paper.

II. Literature Review

The complexity of the game enjoyment phenomenon makes it challenging to measure as there are multiple direct and indirect constructs associated with it [17]. Those constructs (e.g., game flow, emotion, affect, engagement, motivation) have been used in game research studies to evaluate game enjoyment experience from different methods such as behavioral, psychological, and physiological perspectives. The focus on player experience research has been mostly geared towards positive experience while mentally taxing or distressful experiences are largely absent from the game literature [8]. Both negative and mixed player experiences are essential, the developments leading to such cumulative positive experiences are still unclear [18]. In fact, a positive experience may occur in situations where both negative and positive emotions are elicited simultaneously thereby intensifying the entire experience or it may occur when positive emotions overcome negative ones [19]. In the gameplay context, only a few studies have been conducted to understand the transformational phenomenon of negative emotions into positive ones [20].

III. METHODS

A first-person shooter iOS game with three levels was developed for the iPad. One hundred and eleven participants were invited to play the FPS iOS game on an iPad for 15 minutes. In order examine the effect of positive and negative player experience on game enjoyment, two validated survey questionnaires PIFF [6] and Game Experience Questionnaire (GEQ) [21] were used to gather quantitative data for assessing player experience and game enjoyment, respectively following game play. The PIFF instrument comprises of two major constructs namely *adaptation* and *flow*. *Adaptation* is sub-divided into *presence* and *involvement*. Flow has two sub-categories - *emotional* and *cognitive* evaluation. The following constructs were adapted from the GEQ instrument in particular *positive affect*, *negative affect*, *flow* and *challenge*. The player experience (PX) data were split into positive and negative PX based on the median value of 2.0 reported from the dataset. This implies that on a scale of 1–5, PX mean values greater than 2.0 were considered positive PX, whereas mean values of 2.0 or less were categorized into the negative PX group. In addition to PIFF and GEQ, the Self-Assessment Manikin (SAM) [22] questionnaire was used to measure subjective emotions. was administered after each game level was completed to evaluate valence and arousal of participants. The average values for valence and arousal were reported. A challenge-skill survey was administered to determine the channel of experience of participants following gameplay.

IV. DATASET INSPECTION

This section explains how the data collected by the above PX and GEQ instruments were first inspected. Player experience (PX) data were dichotomized into two groups (low PX and high PX). An informal analysis of the dataset using boxplots showed that there were no extreme outliers (Figure 1).

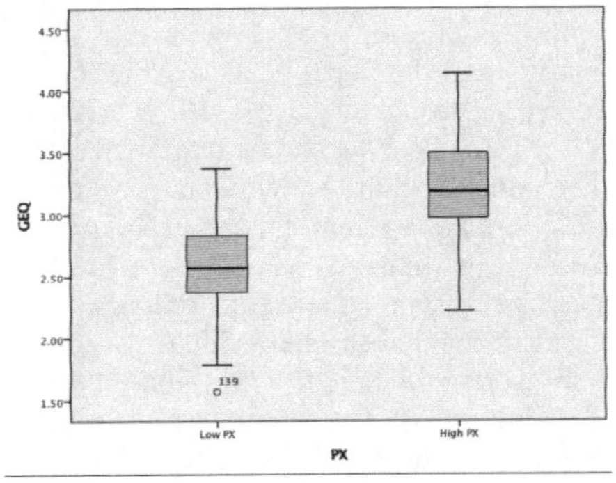

Figure 1. Low and high player experience boxplots

- The sample size of the high PX group (n=65) was larger than that of the low PX group (n=46), and they both appeared to be normally distributed, without extreme skewness. The assumptions of linear regression analysis were verified.
- There was a linear relationship between the independent and the dependent variable as reflected by the scatterplots below in Figures 2 and 3, respectively.
- The residuals of GEQ dataset were normally distributed, as illustrated in the histogram below (Figure 4).
- There was independence of observations, as determined by the Durbin-Watson statistic [34]: 1.712 for GEQ_positive and 1.854 for GEQ_negative. Values close to 2.0 indicate that observations are independent.
- There were no extreme outliers.
- The residuals of the regression line were for both GEQ_negative and GEQ_positive were normally distributed. The mean and standard deviation approximated to zero and one, respectively.
- The data showed signs of homoscedasticity as the variance of the errors (residuals) were constant across all the values of the independent variable.

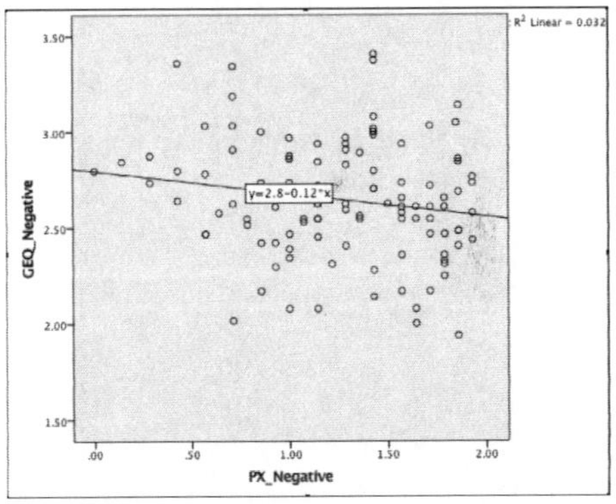

Figure 2. Scatterplot of negative PX and GEQ

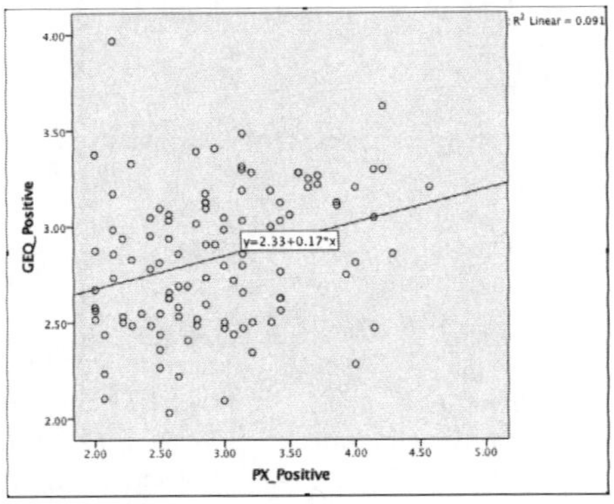

Figure 3. Scatterplot of positive PX and GEQ

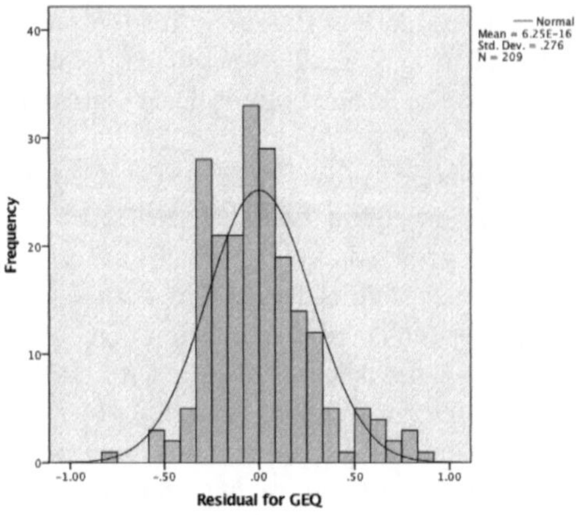

Figure 4. Histogram of GEQ Residuals

V. Analysis and Findings

It was confirmed that mean values of positive player experience (μ=3.21±0.031) and negative player experience (μ=2.50±0.038) were statistically significantly different from each other.

To examine the hypothesis, a regression analysis was conducted between (i) positive player experience and game enjoyment (ii) negative player experience and game enjoyment.

(i) Regression Analysis between positive player experience and game enjoyment

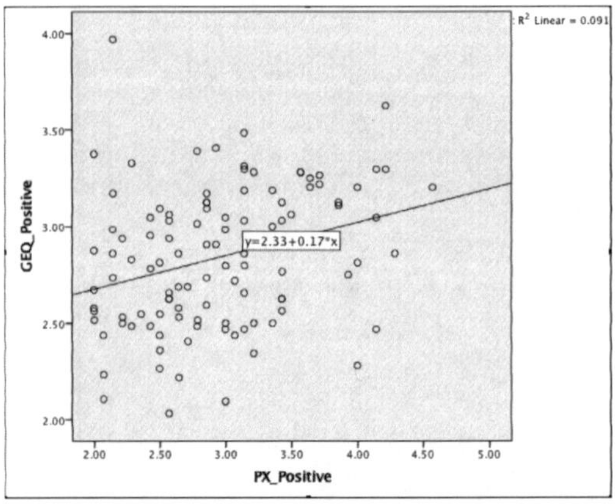

Figure 5. Scatterplot of GEQ_positive vs. PX_positive

A regression test was used to predict game enjoyment (GEQ) from the independent variable, positive player experience group (PX_positive). Positive player experience significantly predicted game enjoyment, F (1,107) =10.741, $p < 0.05$, $R^2 = 0.091$'. There was a moderate, significant and positive relationship between the explanatory variable PX_positive, and the dependent variable, GEQ, with a Pearson's coefficient of r = 0.302. The guidelines provided by Cohen (1988) were followed for the coefficient value r (0.1< \r\ < 0.3: small correlation; 0.3< \r\ <0.5: moderate correlation; \r\ > 0.5: large correlation). It was deduced that positive player experience had an impact on game enjoyment. The Scatter plot (Figure 4) shows a positive correlation between the explanatory variable (PX_positive) and the dependent variable (GEQ_positive), as the value of game enjoyment can be predicted using the equation, as in

$$y=2.33 + 0.17*x, \qquad (1)$$

where y = GEQ_positive and x = PX_positive. It is inferred from the scatterplot (Figure 4) that higher values of game enjoyment are associated with higher level of positive player experience.

(ii) Regression Analysis between negative player experience and game enjoyment

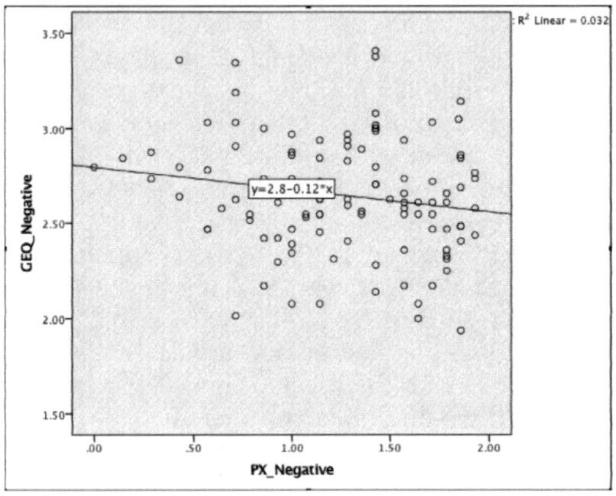

Figure 6. Scatterplot of GEQ_negative vs. PX_negative

A regression analysis was used to predict game enjoyment (GEQ_negative) from the independent variable, negative player experience group (PX_ negative). Negative player experience significantly predicted game enjoyment, *F* (1,111) =3.679', $p<0.05$, $R^2=0.032$'. There was a weak, significant (borderline significant $p=0.058$) and negative relationship (as expected) between the explanatory variable PX_ negative, and the dependent variable, GEQ_ negative, with a Pearson's coefficient of r = -0.179'. It is deduced that higher values of negative player experience are associated with lower values of game enjoyment. The slope of the graph in Figure 5 suggested that the level of game enjoyment decreased as participants felt more negative player experience during gameplay. As predicted, the regression analysis revealed that higher values of positive player experience were associated with higher values of game enjoyment (Figure 5). The findings also confirmed that as negative player experience increased, the level of game enjoyment experienced by participants decreased (Figure 6). Since the relationship between negative PX and game enjoyment attained a borderline significant level of $p=0.058$, it was considered that a relationship between the two variables exist, with a negative gradient. This explains that as negative player experience increases, the level of game enjoyment drops.

VI. Discussions

The dataset gathered from the PIFF instrument [6] to measure player experience (PX) was dichotomized into two groups, negative PX and positive PX based on the median value reported. An experience can be considered either positive or negative [23]. Player experience in this study is defined as a holistic interpretation of the meaningful experiences participants acquire as a result of product interaction [24]. It is tantamount to Norman's [25] three levels of emotional design theory whereby the reflective level has a symbolic connotation, signifying the feelings and thoughts after using a product.

The results of the hypothesis support that positive player experience gives rise to a higher level of enjoyment whereas negative player experience decreases the enthusiasm of the players, thereby diminishing the degree of game enjoyment. There is evidence of a significant correlation between reflective level (player experience) and game enjoyment. Researchers have related enjoyment in digital games as a pleasurable experience resonating with hedonic values, which triggers our mood and synchronizes our emotional responses [26][27][28].

In this study, a number of participants who self-reported negative valence (displeasure) and high arousal during gameplay using the Self-Assessment Manikin [22] instrument also experienced a moderate level of game enjoyment. This is in line with the explanation provided by game researchers that the development of negative emotion often arises during a challenging activity and is trailed by a "positive emotional spike" [2] (p. 1023) when this challenge is overcome by the players [12][29] and furthermore the sensation of suspense and followed by relief is experienced [36]. Hence, the enjoyment can originate from both positive and negative emotions, a phenomenon felt as player experience. Even though negative emotions can give rise to game enjoyment, it is found that positive player experience induces relatively higher level of game enjoyment.

On the other hand, negative player experience may originate during the following events: a player does not experience the activity challenging enough during gameplay that can match individual skill level; a player is not fully absorbed or immersed in the game [21]. In addition, "attention focus" is another factor that relates to the degree a player is absorbed in a game [32]. If a game is perceived to be difficult to play, it causes negative frustration among game players, leading to negative player experience. Not every game player experiences flow or arousal during game play. Besides flow, there are other channels of experience such as anxiety, apathy, and arousal [33]. Each channel was established based on the ratio of skill and challenge that each participant reported. Transiting into the boredom and apathy channels of experience may have led to a negative player experience [33]. The findings from the challenge-skill questionnaire empirically reports a relatively low mean value for perceived game enjoyment when participants transited into the boredom (μ=2.708) and apathy (μ=2.604) channels, as compared to arousal (μ=2.796) and flow (μ=3.111). This indicates that both *flow* and arousal states can yield in optimal experience in the case of a first-person shooter game. Conversely, game technology can also act as a barrier, provoking negative affect among novice and intermediate level players, especially if they cannot accomplish certain goals adequately, thereby diminishing the degree of perceived game enjoyment. The new contribution of the hypothesis empirically demonstrates that positive player experience is associated with a higher level of game enjoyment whereas negative player experience subdues the intensity of game enjoyment.

VII. Conclusion And Future Work

This study has empirically provided evidence that positive player experience contributes to a relatively higher level of game enjoyment, which in turn can result into flow or optimal experience. Similarly, a deep level of engagement during gameplay can lead game players into the arousal channel. Negative frustration should be minimized as it can trigger negative player experience during gameplay. On the other hand, both positive and negative emotions play significant roles in game play as they both give rise to a positive player experience, leading to game enjoyment. Therefore, a balance between positive and negative experience may contribute to a rewarding gameplay. Future work could benefit from mixed methods research by employing both qualitative and quantitative methods to understand the balance of positive and negative emotions on player experience. In addition, a clear definition of negative player experience is mandated in the domain of touch screen gaming and additional research is mandated on its associated components. It is important to obtain deeper understandings on the dynamics of negative player experience and the portion of it that can be turned into positive experience to derive optimal game enjoyment.

Acknowledgment

The author thanks Katherine Taylor for editing the paper.

References

[1] E. D. Mekler, J.A. Bopp, A. N. Tuch, and K. Opwis,"A systematic review of quantitative studies on the enjoyment of digital entertainment games," In CHI 2014 Proceedings of the SIGCHI conference on Human Factors in Computing Systems, 26 April-01 May 2014, pp. 927-936.

[2] R. L. Hazlett, "Measuring emotional valence during interactive experiences: Boys at Video Game Play," Proceedings of CHI 2006 - Novel Methods: Emotions, Gestures and Events, 22-27 April 2006, pp. 1023–1026.

[3] J. A. Bopp., E. D. Meckler, and K. Opwis, "Negative Emotion, Positive Experience? Emotionally Moving Moments in Digital Games," Proceedings of the 2016 CHI Conference on Human Factors in Computing Systems, 7-12 May 2016, pp. 2996-3006.

[4] A. Bartsch, P. Vonderer, R. Mangold, and R. Viehoff, "Appraisal of emotions in media use: Toward a process model

of meta-emotion and emotion regulation," Media Psychology, vol. 11(1), pp.7–27, 2008.

[5] C. Jäger and A. Bartsch, "Meta-Emotions," Grazer Philosophische Studien, vol. 73, pp. 179–204, 2006.

[6] J. Takatalo,"Psychologically-based and content-oriented experience in entertainment virtual environments," Ph.D. Thesis, University of Helsinki, 2011.

[7] M. Montola, "The positive negative experience in extreme role-playing," Nordic DiGRA Proceedings of the 2010 International DiGRA Nordic conference: Experiencing games: games, play and players, 16-17 Aug 2010,vol. 9, ISSN 2342-9666., pp. (n/d).

[8] M. Birk, I. Iacovides, D. Johnson and R. Mandryk, "The False Dichotomy between Positive and Negative Affect in Game Play," Proceedings of the CHIPLAY'15 Annual Symposium on computer-human interaction in play, pp. 799-804.

[9] J. M. Hektner, J. A Schmidt, and M. Csikszentmihalyi, Experience Sampling Method: Measuring the quality of everyday life. Thousand Oaks, CA: Sage publications, 2007.

[10] D. D. Reese, "Introducing Flowometer: A CyGaMEs Assessment Suite Tool. In Gaming and Cognition: Theories and Practice from Learning Sciences, R. van Eck, Ed. Hershey, PA: Information Science Reference (IGI Global), 2010, pp. 227–254.

[11] K. M. Gilleade and A. Dix, "Using Frustration in the Design of Adaptive Videogames," Proceedings of the 2004 ACM SIGCHI International Conference on Advances in computer entertainment technology, 03–05 June, 2004, pp. 228–232.

[12] K. Keeker, R. Pagulayan, J. Sykes, and N. Lazzaro, "The untapped world of video games," Proceedings of the CHI 2004 Extended Abstracts on Human Factors in Computing Systems, 24–29 April, 2004, pp. 1610-1611.

[13] M. Koufaris, "Applying the Technology Acceptance Model and Flow Theory to Online Consumer Behavior," Information Systems Research, vol. 13, issue 2, pp. 205-223, 2002.

[14] Y. Yan, R. M. Davison, and C. Mo, "Employee creativity formation: the roles of knowledge seeking, knowledge contributing and flow experience in Web 2.0 virtual communities," Computers in Human Behavior, vol. 29, issue 5, pp. 1923–1932, 2013.

[15] C. Jennett, et al., "Measuring and defining the experience of immersion in games," International Journal of Human Computer Studies, vol. 66, pp. 641-661, 2008.

[16] A. Nylund and O. Landfors, "Frustration and its effects on immersion in games," Master's thesis, Umeå University, Sweden, 2015.

[17] E. Matthews, G. Matthews, and J.E. Gilbert, " A framework for the assessment of enjoyment in video games," M. Kurosu (Ed.), HCI 2018, LNCS 10903, pp. 460–476, 2018.

[18] E.D.Mekler, S.Rank, S.T.Steinemann, M.V. Birk, and I.Iacovides, "Designing for emotional complexity in games: The interplay of positive and negative affect," CHIPLAY'16 Extended Abstracts, Austin, TX, USA, 16–19 October.

[19] S.Fokkinga and P. Desmet, "Meaningful mix or tricky conflict? A categorization of mixed emotional experiences and their usefulness for design," Proc of the 8th International Design and Emotion Conference, pp. 1–14, 2012.

[20] T.Marsh and B. Costello, "Experience in serious games: between positive and serious experience," Proceedings of the Serious Games Development and Applications, pp. 255–267, 2012

[21] W. IJsselsteijn, K. Poels, and Y. A. W. de Kort, "The Game Experience Questionnaire: Development of a self-report measure to assess player experiences of digital games," Eindhoven: TU Eindhoven. Technical Report, FUGA Deliverable D3.3., 2008.

[22] N. M. Bradley and P. Lang, "Measuring emotion: the self-assessment Manikin and the Semantic Differential," Journal of Behavior Therapy and Experimental Psychiatry, vol. 1, pp. 49-59, 1994.

[23] S. Steinemann, "Positive and Negative Experiences in Games for Change - Does Feeling Bad Make You A Better Person?" Presented at CHI PLAY 2015 Workshop on the False Dichotomy between Positive and Negative affect in Gameplay, London, United Kingdom.

[24] J. Forlizzi and K. Battarbee, "Understanding experience in interactive systems," Proceedings of the 5th conference on Designing interactive systems: processes, practices, methods, and techniques, 01–04 August 2004, pp. 261–268.

[25] D. Norman, Emotional Design: Why We Love (or Hate) Everyday Things. New York, NY: Basic Books, 2004.

[26] T. Grodal, "Video games and the pleasures of control," in Media entertainment: The psychology of its appeal, D. Zillmann and P. Vorderer, Eds. New Jersey: Lawrence Erlbaum Associates, 2000, pp. 197-212.

[27] L. Reinecke and S. Trepte, "In a working mood? The effects of mood management processes on subsequent cognitive performance," Journal of Media Psychology, vol. 20, pp. 3-14, 2008.

[28] B. De Schutter and J. A. Brown, "Digital Games as a Source of Enjoyment in Later Life," Games and Culture, vol. 11, pp. 28–52, 2016.

[29] N. Ravaja, T. Saari, M. Salminen, J. Laarni, and K. Kallinen, "Phasic emotional reactions to video game events: A psychophysiological investigation," Media Psychology, vol. 8, pp. 343- 367. 2006.

[30] C. Klimmt, "Dimensions and Determinants of the Enjoyment of Playing Digital Games: A Three-Level Model," Digital Games Research Conference, Utrecht University, 2003, pp. 246-257.

[31] T. Zhou and Y. Lu, "Examining mobile instant messaging user loyalty from the perspectives of network externalities and flow experience," Computers in Human Behavior, vol. 27, issue 2, pp. 883-889, 2013, 2011.

[32] E. Brown and P. Cairns, "A grounded investigation of game immersion," Proceedings CHI 2004 Extended Abstracts on Human Factors in Computing Systems, 24–29 April, 2004, pp.1297-1300.

[33] K. Poels., Y. de Kort, and W. A. IJsselsteijn, "It is always a lot of fun! Exploring Dimensions of Digital Game Experience using Focus Group Methodology," Proceedings of ACM Futureplay 2007, 15–17 Nov 2007, pp. 83–89.

[34] J. Durbin and G. S. Watson, "Testing for Serial Correlation in Least Squares Regression II," Biometrika, vol. 38, pp. 159 – 178, 1951.

.

Designing an Information Technology Based Voting Solution for Persons with Visual Impairment in Sri Lanka

Madhuka De Silva, Thushani Weerasinghe, Kapila Dias
University of Colombo School of Computing
University of Colombo
Colombo, Sri Lanka
desilvamadhuka@gmail.com, taw@ucsc.cmb.ac.lk, gkad@ucsc.cmb.ac.lk

***Abstract*— Sri Lanka currently uses a paper-based voting system for conducting elections. In this system, voters with special needs have to depend on the assistance of another to mark the vote. Addressing this issue, the present study used the design science approach and attempted to create a voting solution for visually impaired voters. First, two focus group interviews were held with a sample group of visually impaired individuals with voting rights and election-related authorities and professionals. Finding of this initial data gathering identified two categories of interactions: (1) interactions for navigating and (2) interactions for selecting. Considering the capabilities and preferences of the sample, a prototype was designed together with the sample of visually impaired voters at a design workshop. The interfaces and design features were based on multimodality and universal design guidelines. Thus, two interfaces were designed using touch interfaces and buttons. A prototype with the interfaces was subjected to user evaluation. Feedback received for the prototype could be interpreted as that the voters with visual impairment prefer to use this multimodal voting solution if it is further improved in terms of layouts in the interfaces and flow of the interactions.**

Keywords-Electronic Voting; Visual Impairment; Accessibility; Privacy; Usability.

I. INTRODUCTION

Around 253 million people in the world live with vision impairment [1]. In Sri Lanka, about a million people with visual impairment have the right to vote, which is 5.1% out of the total population [2]. Persons with disabilities face immense challenges in realizing their voting rights despite the vast technological advancements taking place. Internationally, rapid progress is being made to ensure the persons with visual disabilities are given equal opportunities to exercise their democratic right of voting. For instance, United States has passed Help America Vote Act 2000(HAVA Act) [3], and Section 49N in The Conduct of Elections Rules, 1961 of India [4], has provided provisions to enable voters with different disabilities to vote. However, according to Elections (Special Provisions) Act [5] in Sri Lanka, it is allowed for a proven person with a disability (an eligible individual adhering to the stated requirements by the act) to be accompanied by someone who is capable of viewing a ballot paper, and mark the choice upon the preference of the voter [6]. Given that everyone deserves to vote privately and independently, it is doubtful that the prevailing polling process in Sri Lanka caters to the requirements of visually impaired voters. Skepticism arises as to whether the assisting personnel will maintain the secrecy of the vote and whether he will not breach the visually impaired voter's trust in casting the vote.

This research is an approach to design and propose an effective voting solution with the intention of addressing the difficulties faced by voters with visual impairments in Sri Lanka. The research question aimed to solve by this research is, "*What are the systems and interface design features required to provide a fruitful effective voting experience for the Sri Lankans with visual impairment*?". These features should enable an independent and accessible vote, which supports to maintain the secrecy of the vote.

Initially, interviews were conducted with the aim of understanding the context and requirements. Results from the interviews were analyzed. Subsequently, a set of design features were listed based on the knowledge which was obtained by the interviews conducted and the previously conducted literature review [7]. Afterward, a prototype was created, which is capable of demonstrating the listed design features. Moreover, a design workshop was conducted using the prototype to obtain feedback and suggestions from the voters with visual impairment. The results from the design workshop were used to improve the design features further. The remaining sections of the paper are organized as follows. Section II explains how the existing voting systems were analyzed in order to identify voting design features that support voters with visual impairment. Section III describes how the research was conducted while Section IV analyses the data and presents the results. Section V, VI and VII describes the solution design and results of the design workshop. Section VIII discusses the results and finally, Section IX concludes this paper.

II. BACKGROUND AND RELATED WORK

Various voting systems are utilized all over the world and a preliminary study was conducted through a literature review on the existing voting systems that support voters with visual impairment [7]. Table I shows the summary of the review conducted.

Paper-based voting systems provide advantages such that ease of understanding for the voter and default verification of accuracy due to the vote being directly caste by the voter. These systems are still being used by different countries even though they have not supported individuals who have visual impairments for independent voting [8] unless optical scanning or tactile methods are incorporated.

TABLE I. SUMMARY OF REVIEW OF EXISTING VOTING SYSTEMS

Topic	Findings
Design features relevant to accessibility	Tactile features • Buttons • Rotation dials • Sleeves with punched holes Touch features • Single/Double tap • Slide rule Multimodal features • Combining tactile, touch and/or voice input
Design features relevant to privacy	Security aspect • Cryptography-based solutions Interface aspect • Accessible interfaces • Screen off feature
Design methodologies	Design principles & guidelines • User Centred Design (UCD) • Universal Design (UD) Evaluation models • Unified Theory of Acceptance and Use of Technology (UTAUT) • ISO usability standards • System Usability Scale (SUS)

Most of the systems provide Braille buttons [9], but Braille literacy varies context wise. For instance, in Sri Lankan context, according to the statistics reported in 2003, 71% of visually impaired persons had some sort of schooling [10] but most were unable to use the Braille knowledge later on in their lives. Further, a study conducted in 2015 revealed that only 41% of the individuals who know Braille could use it [11]. In this backdrop, promoting Braille ballots is unsuccessful and unfair. Thus, it is important to have other modes of input and navigation, providing blind voters with the flexibility to choose a method they prefer. Catering this need, multi-modality concept and the 2nd universal design principle of Flexibility in Use [12] has been adhered. One such example is Prime III [13], an open source, multimodal ballot marking. For a completely blind voter, the accessible mode of interaction is the buttons with voice-based instructions. However, it has only 90% accuracy within an SNR (Signal to Noise Ratio) of 1.44 [14]. Additionally, in Prime III, a poll worker has to initiate the voting system and let the voter begin the voting process. Thus, it is being dependent on the assistance of poll worker while having space for voter coercion. Another system that adheres to the multimodal concept is Universal ballot design interfaces that provide two ballots, 'Quick ballot' and 'EZ ballot' [15]. In EZ ballot design, voting is made accessible to blind voters by adding slide rule [16] interaction design feature in the touch interface. Evaluations report that this slide rule is less familiar to blind voters and is poor unnatural interaction [17]. However, EZ ballot also has design issues, such as an accidental touch on unintended spaces and spending excessive time touching inactive areas due to lack of guidance on the touch interface [17].

In terms of ensuring the privacy of the vote, the majority of voting systems consider it as only a security aspect. Few systems (e.g., AVC Edge, AutoMARK VAT) have addressed interface level privacy by turning off the screen when a blind voter uses the system but the voters are not pleased by this feature [9].

In designing an information system, the best practice is to follow the guidelines. However, there is a lack of information and available evidence on how voting systems were designed. Only a few instances have been reported of design methodologies that have been followed. Among those voting systems, User-Centered Design (UCD) guidelines and Universal Design (UD) guidelines were followed for designing features, and System Usability Scale (SUS) has been used for evaluating those features more frequently. These standards and guidelines are to be applied across large domains where "they do not address functional issues since they cannot account for the intended users, activities, and goals of a product" [18]. Thereby even if using guidelines is a proper way to initiate designing a voting system, user feedback should be obtained both during the design process and after the design is finalized, similar to prototyping techniques [18].

III. RESEARCH METHODOLOGY

The present research aims to design a solution to support blind voters and it falls under the use-inspired design science [20]. Design Science is fundamentally a problem-solving paradigm [19] which has its roots in engineering and sciences of the artificial intelligence. The research was conducted following a methodology based on the design science research process (see Figure 1) by Offermann et al. [21].

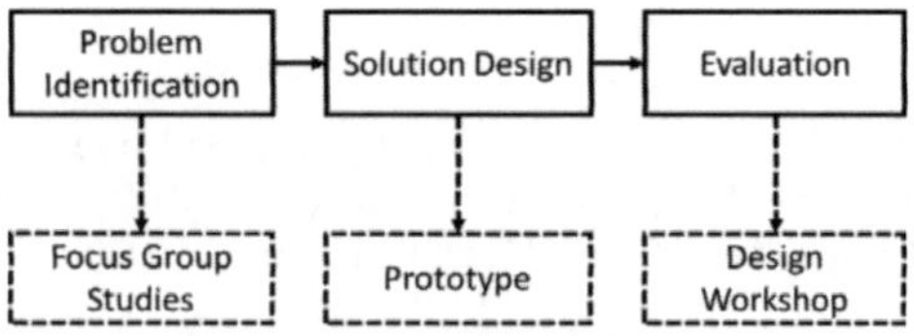

Figure 1. Research Model

In order to identify and solve the research problem, three studies were conducted. Two studies were performed by conducting interviews with two different focus groups. The results obtained from the initial two studies were used to design the ballot interfaces. The final study was based on a design workshop, which captured the interactions of visually impaired voters by providing a software prototype.

A. *Focus Group Studies*

Focus group interviews were conducted with two different groups. One group consisted of individuals from the election authority and election professionals. The other group consisted of voters with visual impairment.

Under the first focus group, one of the key people interviewed was the National Inclusion and Program Advisor of IFES (International Foundation for Electoral Systems) of Sri Lanka who has more than one year of experience in the relevant field. Also, she has worked as an independent consultant in disability rights, access, and inclusion for more than eleven years. Moreover, Additional Commissioner of Elections (Local Authorities) of Sri Lanka was interviewed. Semi-structured interview questions were used to obtain best-suited and more elaborated responses.

Later on, a group of voters with visual impairment were interviewed with the intention of understanding different types of individuals who the voting solution should be focused on. A questionnaire was constructed in a structured format. Succeeding, an expert evaluation was obtained for the questionnaire from the National Inclusion and Program Advisor of IFES. Here the information was gathered related to demography, level of visual impairment, usage of technology-based tools, usage of assistive tools, different literacy levels, and opinions on electronic voting. A sample group of nine (9) potential voters with visual impairments from the Sri Lankan Council for the Blind were selected by convenience sampling because reaching blind persons from all locations was not feasible. Further, it was convenient for the person who faced the interviews to reach a place of closer proximity. Before conducting all the interviews, consent was obtained from the participants ensuring the confidentiality of the information provided. Interview transcripts and notes were stored in MS Excel sheets. The collected data was analyzed and explained using appropriate illustrations.

B. *Conducting a Design Workshop*

After conducting interviews and gaining insights, the blind voter's journey in the voting process was identified as a sequence of steps in the proposed system. The solution was designed incorporating the identified design features and the prototype was created based on the designed solution. The design considerations of the prototype were discussed with the voters with visual impairments.

IV. Results and Findings of Focus Group Studies

The data collected from the interviews with election team (authorities and professionals) and our sample of voters with visual impairments were analyzed separately.

A. *Interviews with Election Team*

As explained in *Methodology Section*, the first set of focus group interviews conducted with election authorities and election professionals, contributed to understanding identifying the laws and procedures to be followed at elections and how elections are conducted. Elections in Sri Lanka consist of three major consecutive steps: (1) voter verification, (2) voting and (3) counting the votes. Voter verification takes place in three sub-steps where the polling officials check for a valid standard identification card, a valid polling card and verify whether the voter has not voted previously in the same election by any indelible ink left in the little finger. Once the verification is successfully completed, the voter is supplied with a ballot paper and is allowed to reach the voting precinct. Once the voter reaches the precinct, he or she marks the ballot and submits the folded ballot paper to the ballot box. Once the voting period is over, the counting process takes place and the results are announced. Voting in the election procedure is further divided into more steps based on the type of the election held. There are five types of elections taking place in Sri Lanka: presidential, parliamentary, provincial, local authorities, and referendum. Although several types of elections exist, there are only two - main variations among the election types: elections that require a vote for a particular political party only, and which both political party and candidate (preferential voting) required to be voted.

According to interviews held, there is no report of any research conducted for designing a new voting solution, which supports voters with visual impairment in Sri Lanka. However, all are looking forward to a change from the existing paper-based voting system to an electronic voting system, in the near future. In terms of supporting the voters with visual impairment, their opinion was that a digital voting system is the only solution to exercise the equal voting rights. Even though the existing law addresses only the paper-based voting system, according to election officials, actions will be taken to introduce an electronic ballot.

Election authorities expect features to ensure privacy, accuracy, and trustworthiness in a general electronic voting system. However, for a voting system, which supports voters with visual impairment, main concerns are to possess features that ensure accessibility and usability. Additionally, more features were mentioned, such as the ability to vote in a preferred language due to multi-ethnicity in Sri Lanka, clearness and preciseness in voting instructions on how to vote, a simpler solution that can address a long list of political parties and candidates without consuming a significant time to vote.

B. *Interviews with Voters with Visual Impairment*

The second set of focus group interviews were conducted with voters with visual disabilities. These interviews were contributed to identifying the demography, skills, and experience. Participant ages were in the range of 18 years to 67 years (Table II), where the average participant age was nearly 42 years (SD:17).

TABLE II. Demography and Blind Context of the Focus Group

Demography and blind context			
Age (years)	***Gender***	***Became blind at age (years)***	***Blind category***
18	Male	Birth	Total blind
21	Male	7	Partially blind
35	Female	23	Partially blind
37	Male	9	Partially blind
38	Male	Birth	Total blind
47	Female	43	Partially blind
53	Female	Birth	Partially blind
63	Female	Birth	Partially blind
67	Female	4	Total blind

Among the participants, three were totally blind and the remaining majority of participants were partially blind or have low vision with some slight variations in sight. It is observed that the age at which they have started experiencing a visual impairment is varied as shown in Table II.

Among the participants, the majority were literate in Braille (Table III) but when their preference of using Braille was questioned, 88.8% disliked. The reasons for the dislike were described as the continuous touch of Braille which causes fatigue in hand muscles, complexity in learning braille, and lack of teachers to provide Braille education. With the evolvement of new technologies, they prefer more to listen than reading in Braille.

TABLE III. BRAILLE LITERACY OF THE FOCUS GROUP

Strongly knows	55.5%
Fairly knows	11.1%
Slightly knows	22.2%
Does not know	11.1%

Moreover, experience in using mobile phones or Automatic Teller Machines (ATM), is considered a potential to use an electronic voting solution with ease implying that similar interfaces are incorporated [8]. Thus, participants were questioned of whether they have prior experience in using digital devices, such as an ATM, a computer, or mobile phones as shown in Table IV. All of them had some sort of experience in using these devices. Further discussions led to the understanding of their familiarity in using inbuilt accessibility tools, such as Talkback (by Android), Screen readers in computers.

TABLE IV. IT LITERACY OF FOCUS GROUP

Digital device/equipment	
ATM	11.1%
Computer	22.2%
Mobile phone with basic features	44.4%
Mobile phone with touch interface	66.6%

Participants were asked what functionalities they have used in mobile phones and how they have accessed those functionalities as the majority of participants were familiar in using mobile phones (Table V).

TABLE V. FUNCTIONALITIES AND INTERACTIONS USED IN MOBILE PHONES

Mobile phone functionality	Interaction	Percentage
Calling	Tap (Single/double tap)	66.6%
	Slide rule	33.3%
Messaging/typing	Tap (Single/double tap)	22.2%
	Slide rule	77.7%
Play music	Tap (Single/double tap)	88.8%
	Slide rule	11.1%
Using calculator/typing	Tap (Single/double tap)	22.2%
	Slide rule	77.7%

Participants who had prior experience in using smartphones were familiar with both interaction types found in smartphones which provide accessibility: Using single/double tap, and slide rule [16]. Moreover, usage of 'Slide Rule' was questioned because it was used in a previous study to design ballots for voters with visual disabilities. It is a one-finger scan and lift finger interaction [22]. They preferred slide rule for typing purposes like messaging and using a calculator. Moreover, they preferred tapping for selecting and navigating purposes like calling and playing music. When they were questioned further about their preferences, a majority of 83.3% liked the tapping (single/double tap) interaction over slide rule interaction. Some reasoned out stating that it is since the tap selections provide a way to confirm the selection made whereas few stated that tap selections felt intuitive and natural. Further, some explained that unintended selections are caused when the finger is dragged and released (Slide Rule).

Relevant to using touch interfaces, contradicting opinions were made where one participant mentioned the inconvenience to scan over the touch screen, which is time-consuming. Few others had opposing ideas stating that they prefer using touch phones because of the inbuilt or installable accessibility features.

Among the participants, 44.4% (Table IV) had the experience of using mobile phones with keypads. They explained that for navigation in menus, they are using the arrow buttons. For dialing numbers or typing messages, they memorize the keypad structure and the embossment mark on the number five on the keypad supports identifying the key locations. Irrespective of the experience of using mobile phones which only have keypads (not smartphones), every participant explained that it would be better if it is affordable. Thus, tactile buttons are used to design the voting solution. Two participants stated that a feature should be facilitated with the ability to change the color contrast.

V. DESIGN OF THE SOLUTION

Design of the solution is explained in detail through sub-divided sections of the voter's journey as design decisions and features, and interaction techniques.

A. *Voter Journey*

The journey of the voter with visual impairment starts when the voter wears the headphone as indicated in Figure 2. Thereafter, the audio instructions are initiated to play. At first, the voter is instructed to choose the preferred language. After the language selection, the voter is acknowledged about the 'settings' button by stating the options available that can be modified: language preference, audio volume, audio speed, and color contrast.

Succeeding the fact, the system directs the voter to the voting instructions. If the voter chooses to listen to the voting instructions, an approval from the voter is taken to make sure that he/she is ready to vote after playing voting instructions. After getting the approval the voting list is displayed mentioning the number of political parties/ candidates with the number of pages.

The voter can select the preference by pressing the appropriate button and confirm the vote. The system acknowledges the voter about the successful completion of the voting and requests the voter to replace the headphone. If the voter does not select any, the system replays the list automatically.

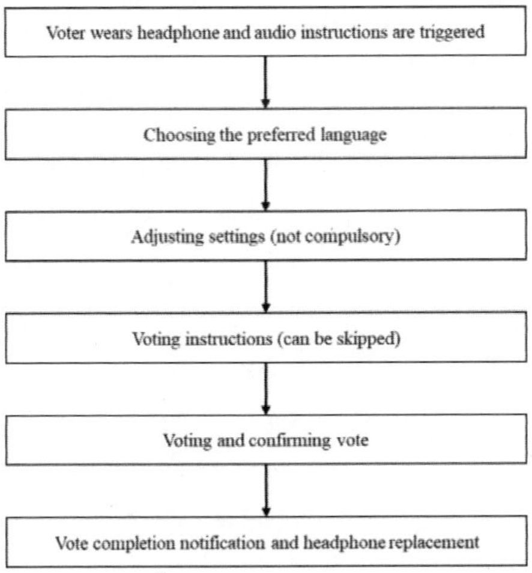

Figure 2. Flow chart of the journey of a voter with visual impairment

B. *Design Decisions and Features*

Table VI summarizes the design decisions and features of the suggested voting solution to support voters with visual impairment.

TABLE VI. DESIGN FEATURES AND JUSTIFICATIONS

Design feature	Justification aligning Universal Design (UD) Principles
Having button controls with unique features	*UD Principle 4: Perceptible Information* Satisfying both sub-principles in UD, buttons are with different shapes and colours are used as a tactile input because then, it is easily understood by persons with visual disabilities by feeling the shape of the button. Having differently shaped buttons also helps to guide the voter with instructions. Shapes and colors of the buttons based on the EZ control keypad [23].
To do a selection either of • Press 'select' • Touch the hole	*UD Principle 2: Flexibility in Use* Voters are given two methods of doing selections/voting. They can choose their preferred method.
Voting by listening to the list of political parties/candidates and press the 'select' within the given time interval	*Principle 3: Simple and Intuitive use* *Principle 6: Low Physical Effort* Here the complexity of voting is maintained by the simple press of a button while listening to audio clips. Also, it does not require high physical effort.
Voting by single tap/ double tap on the touch interface	*Principle 3: Simple and Intuitive Use* Voters being familiar with single tap/double tap interaction due to their experience in using smartphones.
Tactile sleeve with punched holes on top of the touch interface	*Principle 6: Tolerance for Error* Tactile sleeve acting as guidance for voters that would avoid touching unintended areas and less prone to errors that were reported in an existing voting system, which have touch interfaces [17].

Table VI explains the justifications for these features and how the Universal Design guideline has been followed.

C. *Voting Interfaces and Interaction Techniques*

A voting interface with both touch and buttons was designed based on the results obtained from the initial focus group interviews and previous literature review study (Figure 3). However, the findings of the interviews informed that there was a difficulty of scanning the whole touch screen in terms of using touch phones. Voting systems previously designed based on touch interfaces have also reported many issues due to the accidental touch [17]. Thus, a tactile sleeve was designed to act as guidance as shown in Figure 3. It shows that a tactile transparent sleeve with holes placed on top of the touch interface.

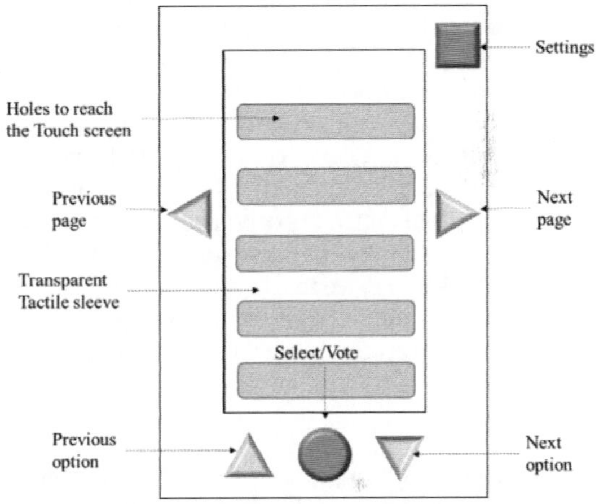

Figure 3. Voting interface with the tactile sleeve

As shown in Figure 3, the voter with visual impairment can vote using either the touch interface or using the buttons.

1) Using Touch Interface: In the touch interface, tap interactions on the holes in the tactile sleeve can be performed for both navigation and selection. The political parties or the candidates are listed on the voting page. When a hole is tapped once, the relevant political party/candidate is announced. If the voter requires to vote, the relevant hole has to be double tapped. Hense, the voter is asked to confirm the vote by tapping twice again throughout the audio instructions. Here, the transparent sleeve with holes is used as a guide to reduce the inconvenience of touching unintended areas and screen areas that have no response.

2) Using Button Interface: In the button interface, next option, previous option, next page, previous page, and settings buttons are used for navigation and select button (circular green) is used for selections as shown in Figure 3. Next option button and previous option button are used to navigate the previous and next political party/candidate.

The political parties or the candidates are announced through audio recordings. After each political party/candidate, there is a pause allowing the voters to cast their vote. If the voter prefers the particular political party/candidate, the voter should press the green circular button as indicated in Figure 3. Otherwise, the voter can wait till the system announces the next political party/candidate or press the yellow triangular button on the bottom right side. After a voter presses the green circular button, the voter is asked to confirm the vote by again pressing the same button.

VI. DESIGN WORKSHOP

The design workshop was conducted to obtain user feedback on the suggested voting interfaces by providing a prototype.

A. *Procedure*

A sample of eight persons was selected. There were four representing Sri Lankan blind council and four students from the University of Colombo in the sample. A pre-survey questionnaire was answered by the participants. Further, a set of six activities were conducted where each participant was allowed to attempt each activity a maximum of three times. After three attempts the participant was instructed to carry out the next activity. Observations were noted down during the activities and feedback was obtained after each activity. However, after obtaining the consensus of the participants, video recording was carried out for further study of observations.

B. *Prototype*

The prototype was built using MS PowerPoint slides to show the necessary content, a laptop with a touch interface, a tactile sleeve made out of rigifoam, rubber buttons and wireless headphone to play audio instructions as shown in Figure 4.

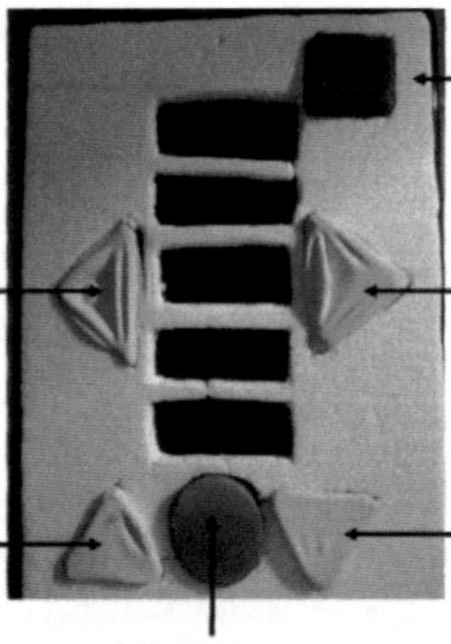

Figure 4. The prototype of the voting interface

The voting list was constructed using country names and the symbols show the animals used by the countries to represent their nation. A sample set of audio instructions were recorded by three voices and was subjected to expert evaluation by a voice expert from Sri Lankan Broadcasting Corporation. Furthermore, before using the voice clips in the prototype, the necessary modifications were made in the instructions considering how the speakers should convey the instructions. Figure 4 shows how the tactile sleeve appears when the screen is off. The feedback and observations of using the prototype are identified in three categories: touch interface with the tactile sleeve, button interface, and audio instructions.

C. *Participants*

Participant's ages were in the range of 20 years to 74 years (Table VIII), where the average participant age was around 40 years (SD:20).

TABLE VII. DEMOGRAPHY AND BLIND CONTEXT OF FOCUS GROUP

Demography and blind context					
Age (years)	***Gender***	***Became blind at age (years)***	***Blind category***	***Smartphone experience***	***Single tap/double tap vs Slide rule***
20	Female	Birth	Total blind	Yes	Tap
25	Male	10	Total blind	Yes	Slide rule
25	Female	15	Total blind	Yes	Tap
28	Male	Birth	Partially blind	Yes	Tap
33	Male	17	Partially blind	Yes	Tap
47	Female	43	Partially blind	Yes	Tap
67	Female	4	Total blind	Yes	Tap
74	Male	10	Total blind	Yes	Tap

Among the participants, three participants were partially blind and the remaining majority of participants were totally blind. All the participants had the experience of using smartphones.

VII. RESULTS AND FINDINGS OF DESIGN WORKSHOP

The results have been analyzed to find the effectiveness of button and touch interactions and the audio instructions.

A. *Button Interface:*

In the **first activity**, the participants were instructed to find the buttons one by one. Figure 5 shows how the participants were able to locate the buttons. All the participants were able to recognize the 'select' button, 'next' button, and 'previous' button in their first attempt. However, the 'next page' button and 'previous page' buttons were not identified by 88% of the participants in any of the attempts. Also, only 25% of the participants were able to identify the 'settings' button in the first attempt and the remaining participants were able to identify it at the second attempt. Most of the participants who identified the 'settings' button in the second attempt, pressed the 'next page' button mistakenly in the first attempt. One of the participants stated that 'I did not think that this device has that much length. So, I did not take my hand that far'.

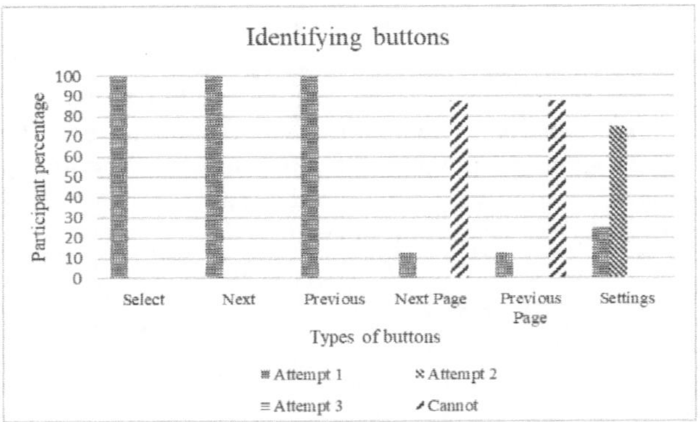

Figure. 5 How the focus group identified buttons

Another participant with partial blindness mentioned that contrast of yellow color of triangular buttons and green color of the circular button is not sufficient and that it confuses the user.

The **second activity** was to identify the function of the buttons. The button functions were described to the participants and they were asked to press the correct button relevant to a particular function. For instance, in order to identify the 'settings' button, the participants were instructed "Press the button required to navigate to Settings" The instructions were provided to try out all the buttons: select, next, previous, next page, previous page, and settings. All the participants were able to identify the 'select' button and the 'settings' button at the first attempt but several attempts were made to identify other buttons as shown in Figure 6.

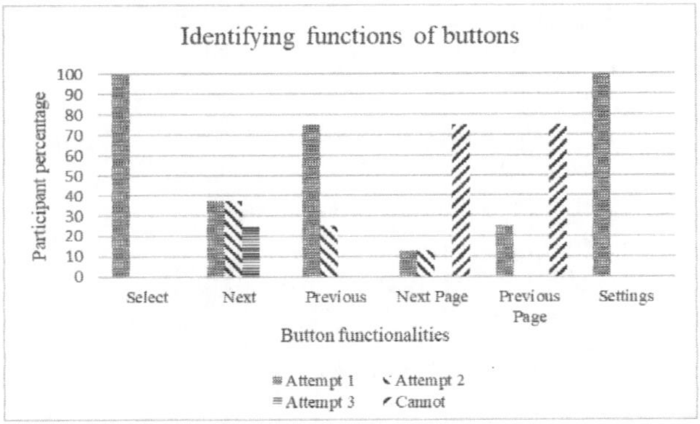

Figure 6. How the focus group identified functions of the buttons

63% of the participants could not figure out the 'next' button in the first attempt. It was observed that they pressed the 'previous' button when they were asked to press the 'next' button. Even though they made several attempts to identify the 'next' button, they easily identified the 'previous' button (triangular button on the bottom left).

Only 25% of the participants were able to identify the 'next page' button and the 'previous page' button. The remaining 75% of the participants pressed the 'next' and 'previous' button instead of pressing 'next page' and 'previous page' buttons respectively. Some participants stated that having pages and navigating through pages is uneasy for them.

Some stated that the space between buttons should be increased and few suggested that the button shapes can be easily identified if the button sizes are reduced up to an extent. The majority stated that shapes are unique and that they can figure out what they are while few suggested that it would be better to have a mark on the triangular shaped buttons to differentiate between previous and next functions.

B. *Touch interface with the tactile sleeve:*

In the **third activity**, the participants attempted to identify and touch the five holes on the tactile sleeve from the bottom to the top (1st hole, 2nd hole, 3rd hole, 4th hole, 5th hole). All the holes were identified by the participants but the attempts at which the holes were identified varied slightly as shown in Figure 7.

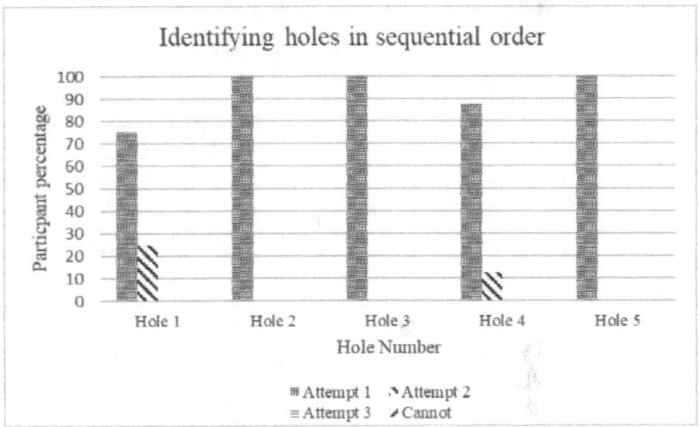

Figure 7. How the focus group identified holes in sequential order

All the participants identified the 2nd, 3rd and 5th hole at the first attempt. 75% of the participants identified the 1st hole in the first attempt but 25% identified it in the second attempt. One of the participants who could not attempt correctly in the first attempt stated that "I could not figure out where the holes started".

The **fourth activity** was to identify and touch the holes in a random order (2nd hole, 4th hole, 3rd hole, 5th hole, 1st hole). Similarly, as in Activity 3, the participants were able to identify all the holes in different attempts. All the participants were able to identify the 5th hole or the last hole. It was noted that the 4th hole was identified correctly in several attempts as in Figure 8 but identifying the 3rd hole showed a greater success. The participants explained that identifying 3rd hole was easier since they knew where the 4th hole was located.

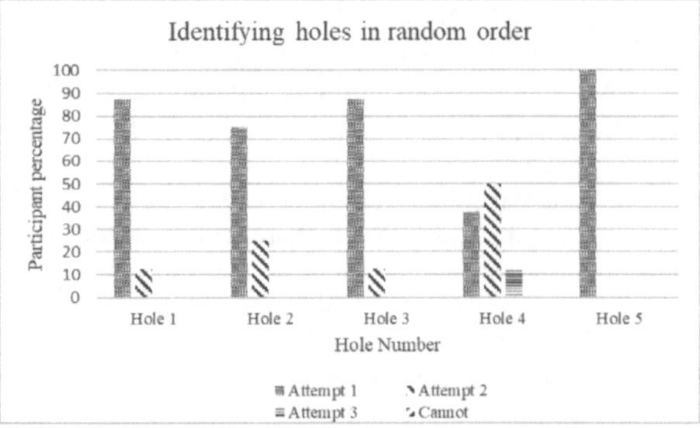

Figure 8 How the focus group identified holes in random order

Similar to the results of the third activity, the participants responded commenting that the starting hole of the device was not easily identifiable.

In the **fifth activity**, the participants attempted to vote for the instructed political party. The objective behind this activity was to identify their ability to perform single tap and double tap with the touch interface as shown in Figure 9. Here, the participants were asked, 'What is the political party represented by the 1st hole?".

They are expected to perform a single tap on the 1st hole, which resulted in playing an audio clip that announced the political party represented by it. Only 50% were able to do a single tap correctly at the first attempt while 12.5% were unable to perform. It was observed that they performed a double tap instead of a single tap.

Thereafter, the participants were asked to vote the same political party and they were expected to double tap to vote. This was successfully performed by all participants at their first attempt.

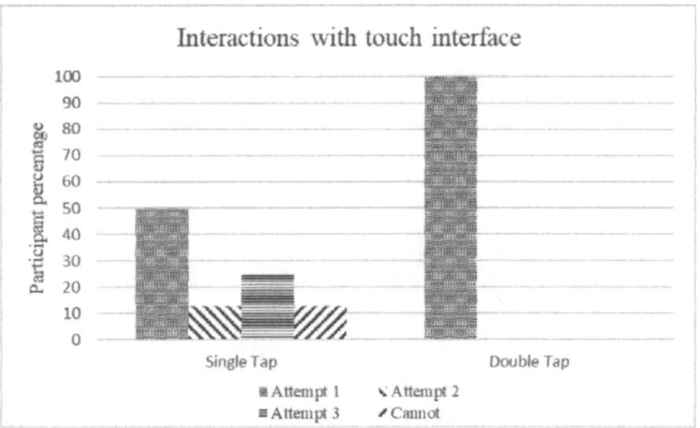

Figure 9. How focus group performed interactions with the touch interface

It was observed that all the participants were having the grip on the device by their left hand and were pressing the buttons only with their right hand. The same observation was made in how they used the tactile sleeve.

C. *Audio instructions*

Finally, it was required to find a suitable time interval, which acts as the maximum waiting time for a voter's response to a given audio instruction. For this purpose, as the **sixth activity,** the participants were asked to press the 'select' button when a particular political party is played by the audio clips. These clips were played with 3 seconds, 4 seconds and 5 seconds time intervals.

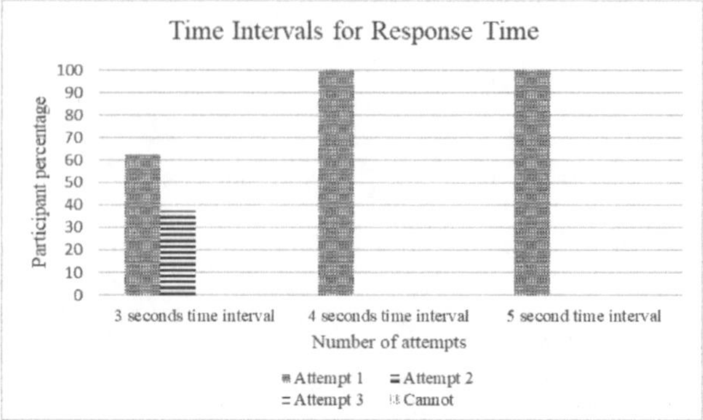

Figure 10. How the focus group performed at different time intervals for response time

All the participants were able to vote within 4 seconds and 5 seconds time intervals in the first attempt but only 62% were able to vote within 3 seconds time interval in the first attempt (Figure 10). From the feedback received, 62% mentioned that 3 seconds were sufficient but remaining stated that at least 4 seconds time interval is required.

D. *Preferences*

Participants were asked to choose their preference between the two methods of suggested voting

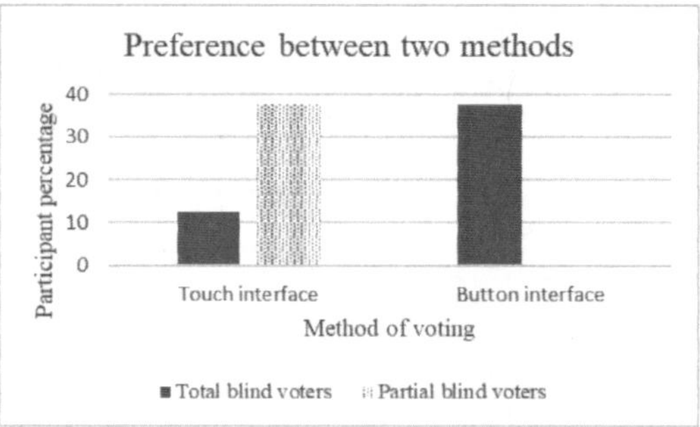

Figure 11. Participant preference on using the two methods and their blind category (percentage wise)

It was observed that the partial blind voters preferred more in using the touch interface with the sleeve and total blind voters preferred more in using buttons interface (see Figure 11). Participants who preferred the touch interface explained that it helped them to touch the appropriate places without having to touch the whole screen. Participants with total blindness suggested that the touch interface design can be further improved if some guidance is presented to track the holes instead of having to guess or remember the locations of the holes. It was observed that participants required more space on the tactile sleeve without buttons, where they can rest their hand. It was stated that the sizes of the holes are sufficient but the space between holes required to be increased. Two participants stated that having five holes is familiar to them and another participant stated, "it is not hard to identify 5 holes. 5 is easy. I think I can figure out even more".

VIII. DISCUSSION

From the interviews conducted with voters with visual impairment, it was understood that almost everyone had some sort of experience in using mobile phones. However, their experience in using different types of mobile phones varied. The majority (66%) had the experience of using smartphones but there were persons who had only the experience of using a basic mobile phone with buttons or keypads. Thus, in order to interact with the voting system, voters should be provided with several modes such that they will choose the most familiar mode, which is bringing in the multimodality concept for voting. The availability of more than one way to navigate or use the system is accommodating the 2nd Universal Design principle of Flexibility in Use [12]. Few systems are designed based on this concept whereas certain challenges remain that needs to be addressed. As mentioned earlier in the introduction section, voice-based voting is claimed accurate only within certain environments with respect to sound distortions. Thus, it leads to the discussion of tactile (using buttons) voting and touch-based voting.

Tactile voting is facilitated by a button interface, which has buttons in different shapes that are uniquely identifiable in different locations satisfying the underlying 4th universal design principle of Perceptible Information [12]. Button shapes and colors were designed similar to the EZ control keypad, which is used by some existing voting systems as an assistive tool [23]. Based on the evaluation and feedback by the focus group users of the design workshop it was discovered that colors have to be refined because some blind persons have difficulties with respect to color contrast. Additionally, this shows that solely depending on color is also not sufficient. Thus, different shapes were used to improve the uniqueness of the buttons. According to the prototype results, 'next' and 'previous' buttons were identified by trial and error even after providing instructions. Thus, those buttons should be placed together, giving a natural intuitive feeling of going up and down rather than placing on the right hand. Although it was attempted to make the buttons easily identifiable by keeping the buttons in different locations, results showed it was inconvenient for the blind voters. For an instance 'settings' button was far away for the participant to approach. Thus, buttons should be placed at close proximity. Next page and previous page buttons made less sense to the participants. They considered the 'next' button as 'next page' and 'previous' button as 'previous page' button. Instead of going through pages, the suggested approach is to consider a single page, which can be scrolled down from 'next' option after every five political parties/candidates. This is more intuitive as it is more similar to the paper-based voting, where only a single long ballot paper is provided for voting in the Sri Lankan context. In existing voting systems with touch interfaces [17] some inefficiencies were reported and identified as in the literature: accidental touch, vote-changing errors, unfamiliar touch interaction, tapping inactive areas. These inefficiencies can be reduced by allowing voters to reach only the active areas in the touch interface by the support of a transparent tactile sleeve with holes aligned with voting options. Thus, to mark the preference, the voter can listen to the voting list announced via the audio sequentially and vote for the desired by pressing button controls or tapping on the screen. Prototype evaluation results informed that users are capable and prefer to use the tactile sleeve. However, it was observed that some participants used trial and error in tracking the holes. Thus, improvements have to be made by including a feature as a guide to track the holes, so that they do not require to remember the holes or guess.

In the present study, in order to interact with the touch interface, tapping method was used instead of 'Slide rule' [16]. The slide rule was not considered since it could be less natural for blind voters [17]. This consideration confirmed the findings of the interview and the workshop pre-survey. Even though a single tap is performed when using smartphones to listen to a description, prototype results showed that majority of the blind persons are familiar with double tap more than a single tap. But there were also some participants who were familiar with a single tap gesture. Thus, in order to listen to a description or make any kind of selection (selecting settings options, vote, confirm, etc.) tap can be allowed, where no restriction is placed. As in here, after any tap gesture (single or double), a description of the selected area is described and the voter is asked to tap (single or double) again if it is required to be selected.

IX. CONCLUSIONS AND FUTURE WORK

The focus group studies with authorities ensured that there is a necessity of having an accessible voting solution designed which supports the persons with visual impairment in their voting process. Henceforth, it was reported that no research has been conducted in Sri Lanka with regard to this requirement.

The focus group study with the sample of voters with visual impairment showed that they are familiar with the touch interfaces as they have experience in using smartphones. Equally, some showed their interest in using keypads. These findings resulted in designing a multimodal voting solution incorporated with Universal Design principles. The prototype was tested through a design workshop.

However, the interfaces were tested only for the voting step and no other steps such as language selection, adjusting settings, etc. Also, the full comprehensive system was not developed in this stage but has to be created after making necessary improvements reported in this paper. After implementing a full solution, comprehensive evaluation method should be used such as System Usability Scale or following ISO Usability Standards.

REFERENCES

[1] "Vision impairment and blindness," *World Health Organization*, 2017. [Online]. Available: http://www.who.int/en/news-room/fact-sheets/detail/blindness-and-visual-impairment. [Accessed: 10-Jan-2019].

[2] Department of Census and Statistics - Government of Sri Lanka, "Census of Population and Housing 2012," 2012.

[3] "Help America Vote Act," *US Election Assistance Commission*. [Online]. Available: https://www.eac.gov/about/help-america-vote-act/. [Accessed: 10-Jan-2019].

[4] "The Conduct of Elections Rules," *Indian Elections Commission*, 1961. [Online]. Available: https://indiankanoon.org/doc/197923052/. [Accessed: 10-Jan-2019].

[5] *Sri Lanka - Elections (Special Provisions) Act, No. 28 of 2011*. Sri Lanka, 2011.

[6] "Blind Can Cast Their Vote," *Sunday Leader*, 2013.

[7] M. De Silva, T. Weerasinghe, and K. Dias, "A Review on Design Features of Electronic Voting Systems supporting Voters with Visual Impairment," *International Journal of Software Engineering and Applications, in press.*

[8] D. P. Tokaji, "The Paperless Chase: Electronic Voting and Democratic Values," *Fordham Law*, vol. 73, no. 4, 2004.

[9] D. Burton and M. Uslan, "Cast a Vote by Yourself," 2002. [Online]. Available: http://www.afb.org/afbpress/pubnew.asp?DocID=aw030603. [Accessed: 10-Jan-2019].

[10] R. Karunaratne, "Providing a good education to blind students in your country - Why and how?," *Sundaytimes.lk*, 2008. [Online]. Available: http://www.sundaytimes.lk/081005/Plus/sundaytimesplus_17.html. [Accessed: 10-Jan-2019].

[11] D. Weerakkody, "DAISY Implementation in Sri Lanka," *Dinf.ne.jp*. [Online]. Available: http://www.dinf.ne.jp/doc/english/resource/srilanka.html. [Accessed: 10-Jan-2019].

[12] B. R. Connell *et al.*, "The Principles of Universal Design," 1997. [Online]. Available: https://projects.ncsu.edu/design/cud/about_ud/udprinciplestext.htm. [Accessed: 10-Jan-2019].

[13] J. E. Gilbert *et al.*, "Universal access in e-voting for the blind," *Universal Access in the Information Society*, vol. 9, no. 4, pp. 357–365, 2010.

[14] F. Jackson, A. Solomon, K. McMullen, and J. E. Gilbert, "To Start Voting, Say Vote: Establishing a Threshold for Ambient Noise for a Speech Recognition Voting System," *Procedia Manufacturing*, vol. 3, no. Ahfe, pp. 5512–5518, 2015.

[15] S. Lee, X. Xiong, L. E. Yilin, and J. Sanford, "EZ ballot with multimodal inputs and outputs," *Proceedings of the 14th international ACM SIGACCESS conference on Computers and accessibility - ASSETS '12*, p. 215, 2012.

[16] S. K. Kane, J. P. Bigham, and J. O. Wobbrock, "Slide Rule: Making mobile touch screens accessible to blind people using multi-touch interaction techniques," *Proceedings of the 10th international ACM SIGACCESS conference on Computers and accessibility (Assets '08)*, pp. 73–80, 2008.

[17] S. Lee, "Designing Ballot Interfaces for Voters with Vision Disabilities," *CHI EA '14 CHI '14 Extended Abstracts on Human Factors in Computing Systems*, pp. 933–938, 2014.

[18] S. J. Laskowski, M. Autry, J. Cugini, W. Killam, and J. Yen, "Improving the usability and accessibility of voting systems and products," *NIST Special Publication 500-256*, no. 202, pp. 1–92, 2004.

[19] P. Antonelli, R. Mathew, A. Hevner, S. Chatterjee, and I. Series, "Design Science Research in Information Systems," pp. 9–23, 2010.

[20] T. C. Reeves, J. Herrington, and R. Oliver, "Design Research: A Socially Responsible Approach to Instructional Technology Research in Higher Education," *Journal of Computing in Higher Education*, vol. 16, no. 2, pp. 96–115, 2005.

[21] P. Offermann and E. R. Platz, "Outline of a Design Science Research Process," 2009.

[22] S. "Tina" Lee, Y. E. Liu, L. Ruzic, and J. Sanford, "Universal Design Ballot Interfaces on Voting Performance and Satisfaction of Voters with and without Vision Loss," *Proceedings of the 2016 CHI Conference on Human Factors in Computing Systems - CHI '16*, pp. 4861–4871, 2016.

[23] "EZ Access," *National Institute on Disability and Rehabilitation Research*. [Online]. Available: http://www.trace.umd.edu/ez. [Accessed: 10-Jan-2019].

Progress Indicators in Web Surveys Reconsidered — A General Progress Algorithm

Thomas M. Prinz, Raphael Bernhardt, Jan Plötner, and Anja Vetterlein
Course Evaluation Service, Friedrich Schiller University Jena
Jena, Germany
e-mail: {Thomas.Prinz, Raphael.Bernhardt, Jan.Ploetner, Anja.Vetterlein}@uni-jena.de

Abstract—**The inclusion of a progress indicator seems to be a simple part during the construction of a web survey. This paper shows that this is only true for linear surveys and does not hold true for surveys with adaptivity (branches). Therefore, we introduce a general model, which fits almost any kind of survey. Based on this model, the difficulties of progress computation are shown. As a solution, this paper proposes a general equation and algorithm to compute the progress dynamically. This algorithm predicts the number of remaining items for each page. Since the remaining items depend on the actual path through the survey, the algorithm was generalized by a so-called selection operator allowing different prediction strategies. With the help of this algorithm, it is possible to compare different strategies for a given survey and to select the best one. In examples, two prediction strategies are introduced which estimate either the most or the least remaining items. The paper concludes with a comparison of both strategies showing that the choice of the best prediction strategy is not trivial and depends highly on the structure of the survey.**

Keywords–Progress Indicator; Computation; Adaptive Surveys; Web Surveys; Questionnaire Model.

I. INTRODUCTION

Most web surveys use Progress Indicators (PIs) to give the participants feedback about the degree of completion. Such a feedback should motivate the participants to complete the survey and, therefore, consequently reduce the break-off rates [1][p. 146]. Usually, a PI shows the progress of a task between its start and its completion. It is common practice to calculate the progress in percentage and use 0% at its start and 100% at its end. The *current* progress is a number between both values.

A PI seems to be a simple feature during the construction of a web survey in which not much time and resources should be invested. For *linear* surveys this is obviously true — a linear survey has no adaptivity, all questions have a specific order, and this order is the same for each participant. But the computation of the progress is difficult for surveys with *adaptivity* (branches). In such surveys, a simple computation approach produces *jumps* [1] in the progress since some questions are not shown to each participant. Sometimes those jumps are large and could be demotivating and perceived as untrustworthy by the participant. But the progress feedback should be truthful to the subjective sense [2, p. 757]. For this reason, we need a trustworthy calculation for those complex surveys.

Since there are a lot of survey tools currently on the marked, comparing their PI approaches seemed to be a good basis for a general progress calculation in complex surveys. However, either those tools explicitly do not support PIs in complex surveys like *Survey Monkey* [3], or their approaches remain guarded: the consideration of other survey tools does not help.

The Ph.D. thesis of Kaczmirek [1] is the best starting point for the development of such an algorithm to the authors' knowledge. In his thesis, he developed the attempt of a PI computation approach for complex surveys, which unfortunately has not garnered a lot of attention in research. One reason could be the neglect to describe his approach in a concrete algorithm with a formal model.

We have developed a formal model for questionnaires used in our own survey tool Coast [4]. The model is based on mathematical graphs, which help to understand the structure of a survey and create the possibility to apply well-known algorithms of graph theory as shown in previous work [5]. Based on this model, this paper defines a general algorithm for the computation of the progress in surveys. This algorithm allows arbitrary strategies to handle complex questionnaires and compare them. As an example, this paper formalizes the two proposed strategies of Kaczmirek (used in its Ph.D. thesis) — using the maximal and minimal number of remaining items. A comparison of both strategies shows that choosing the best strategy for a given questionnaire is not trivial. As a result, the proposed strategy of Kaczmirek — taking the minimum of remaining items — should be taken with caution. There is the need for more research for defining more prediction strategies and for choosing a best fitting strategy for each survey.

This paper considers current PI research at first (Section II). In Section III, our questionnaire model is introduced, which is based on mathematical graphs. Afterwards, the general algorithm for computing the progress is derived in Section IV. In Section V, this algorithm is used to explain the two PI computation approaches of Kaczmirek. Furthermore, both approaches are compared and the difficulties of selecting the right approach are shown. The paper closes with a conclusion and a look into future work (Section VI).

II. STATE OF THE ART

Human-Computer Interaction (HCI) has considered PIs for a long time. It focuses on the duration of a task and how PIs help the user to be aware of that duration. A result is that people prefer to have a PI in comparison to not having one and that the perceived duration depends on the progress speed [6][7]. Harrison et al. found out that a user suggests a task runs faster if the PI is faster at the end of a task [8].

However, PIs in web surveys are different from those classic PIs in HCI. Villar et al. state that the tasks in web surveys are usually longer, and that the user can influence the PI and has to focus on the task. Furthermore, users of classic computer tasks want the goal of the progress, e. g., transferred money, loaded files, etc.; whereas web survey participants do not necessarily have an interest on the result. Because of those differences, PIs in web surveys should be considered with another focus as PIs in classic HCI [2].

In 1998, Dillman et al. defined some principles for the design of a web survey. These principles include PIs with less implementation costs [9]. Some years later, Conrad et al. considered different speeds of PIs for the first time: 1) *constant*, 2) *fast-to-slow*, and 3) *slow-to-fast* speeds [10]. The speed of a PI varies if there is a difference between the *displayed* and the *true* progress. The *true* progress is the progress when the remaining number of questions would be known at each point. If the difference of the displayed to the true progress is always positive, the displayed progress runs faster at the beginning and has to become slower at the end (fast-to-slow). If the difference is always negative, the displayed progress is slower at the start and becomes faster at the end (slow-to-fast).

The work of Conrad et al. was the first consideration of a divergence between the displayed and the true progress. It is especially interesting since they take notice of a correlation between the break-off rates and the speed of the PIs. It seems to be that a slow-to-fast progress is more discouraging and causes a higher break-off rate. On the contrary, a fast-to-slow progress seems to encourage the participants to finish the survey. These results were supported by Matzat et al. [11] and succeeding studies of Conrad et al. [12]. Villar et al. combined all those studies in a meta-analysis. Their results were: 1) For most studies, the decrease of break-offs is significant when showing a fast-to-slow PI instead of having none. 2) The break-off rates increases significantly for most studies if a slow-to-fast PI is applied. 3) It poses an ethical problem if the speed of the PI is manipulated on purpose in order to deceive the participants. Sometimes, however, the varying speed is not deceptive if it tries to accurately mirror the true progress [2]. A study about 25,000 real world surveys seems to state the contrary, i. e., that the PI has no effect on the break-offs [13].

Although there are a lot of studies considering the differences in PI speeds, there is missing research, which consider, *how* to compute the progress accurately. This question becomes important especially for surveys with high adaptivity. To the best knowledge of the authors, the thesis of Kaczmirek [1] is the only published work, which tries to answer this question. In one of his studies, he explains that a simple computation approach produces jumps and, therefore, he introduced a new *dynamic* strategy, which converges more to the true progress. A little study in his thesis suggests that the application of his dynamic approach does lead to less break-offs as the simple approach.

A problem of all progress computation approaches in adaptive web surveys is the logical lack of knowledge, which "*path*" through the survey a participant takes. Therefore, the true progress is only known *after* the participation. Kaczmirek [1] proposes two strategies to predict the remaining number of pages (and therefore the path): either the 1) maximum or the 2) minimum number of remaining pages is taken for the calculation. In a little study in his thesis, the break-off rates of the minimum are less than those of the maximum approach. This corresponds to the results of Villar et al. since the minimum strategy is similar to a fast-to-slow and the maximum approach is similar to a slow-to-fast PI. However, instead of manipulating the progress speed by design, Kaczmirek is not deceptive as he does it to approximate the true progress as good as possible.

III. Questionnaire Model

It is important to know how surveys are structured for the definition of an algorithm for the computation of the progress. Since surveys are like computer programs, the structure can be described precisely as a *directed graph*. A *directed graph* (or *digraph*) $G = (N, E)$ consists of a set $N = N(G)$ of *nodes* and of a set $E = E(G)$ of *edges*. E forms a set of ordered pairs, $E \subseteq N \times N$ [14, pp. 432]. The sets $\triangleright n$ and $n\triangleleft$ describe the sets of all incoming and outgoing edges of a node n, respectively, i. e., $\triangleright n = \{(n', n) \in E\}$ and $n\triangleleft = \{(n, n') \in E\}$.

Since nodes are connected by edges, it is possible to travel from one node to another node via a sequence of edges. Such a sequence of edges is called a *path*. In a digraph $G = (N, E)$, a sequence $W = (n_0, \ldots, n_m)$, $m \geq 0$, of nodes, $n_0, \ldots, n_m \in N$, is a *path*, if each node of the sequence is connected via an edge to the next node in the sequence: $\forall\ 0 \leq i < m$: $(n_i, n_{i+1}) \in E$ [15, p. 1180]. A path is called *acyclic* if all nodes on the path are pairwise different. A digraph is *acyclic* if each of its paths is acyclic. Otherwise, the digraph contains a loop and is cyclic. A digraph is *connected* if its undirected pendant (adding an edge (a, b) for each edge (b, a)) has a path between each two (different) nodes [16, S. 547].

In our model, a survey is an elicitation that uses a *questionnaire* as measurement method. Such a questionnaire consists of *items* [17, p. 18]. An item is a concrete question sometimes with some answer possibilities. In almost all questionnaires, more than one item is presented in sequence. Mostly, they are grouped thematically on *pages*.

Definition 3.1 (Page): A *page* $S = \{i_1, i_2, \ldots\}$ (S for sheet of paper) is a set of items $i_1, i_2, \ldots$.

It is known from test theory that the structure of a questionnaire influences the measurement results [18, S. 68 ff.]. For this reason, a questionnaire cannot be defined only using a set of pages since this set is unsorted. We have to define an order of the pages. From our experience, it is promising to describe the structure of a questionnaire as an acyclic, connected digraph:

Definition 3.2 (Q-Graph): A *Q-graph* Q is an acyclic, connected digraph $(\mathbb{S}, \mathbb{E})$ with a set of pages $\mathbb{S}$ and a set of *edges* $\mathbb{E}$ connecting the pages. A Q-graph Q has exactly one page without any incoming edges, the *start page*, and exact one page without any outgoing edge, the *end page*.

The previous definition describes the *structure* of a questionnaire as a Q-graph. From a detailed described Q-graph, a

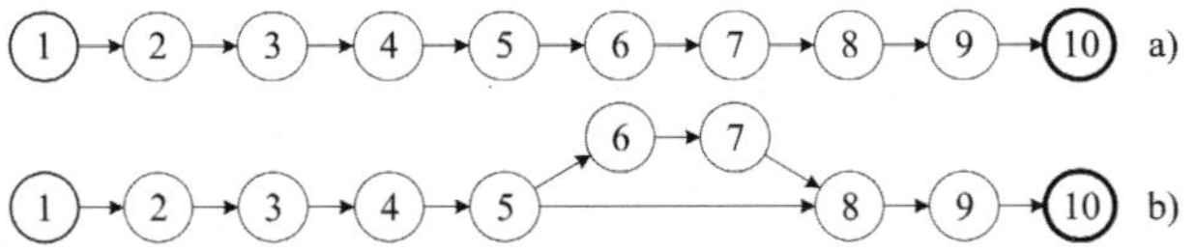

Figure 1. A linear *a)* and non-linear *b)* Q-graph

web survey can be automatically derived [4]. However, this derivation is not part of this work due to the lack of space.

IV. A General Progress Algorithm

In the last section, a Q-graph described the structure of a questionnaire as a graph. The complexity of the computation seems to depend on the complexity of the describing Q-graph. The Q-graph can be either simple or complex.

A. Simple Case

Sometimes, a questionnaire is a simple sequence of pages without any adaptivity and filters. Its Q-graph is, therefore, a chain of pages as illustrated in Figure 1 *a)*. More formally, each page (except the end page) has exactly one outgoing edge. Such a Q-graph is called *linear* in the following.

In the case of a linear Q-graph Q, it is possible to assign a position to each page depending on its distance back to the start page: the start page gets position 1, the first page after the start page gets position 2, etc. Finally, the end page has position $|\mathbb{S}(Q)|$. We write S_t for the page on position t.

If a participant is on a page S_t of a Q-graph, then there are two interesting moments regarding the progress: 1) the moment the participant *reaches* the page and 2) the moment the participant *leaves* the page. Obviously, the progress when reaching the *current* page is equal to the progress when leaving the *previous* page. It is assumed in the following, that the progress $\rho(S_t)$ on page S_t reflects the progress at the moment, the participant *reaches* the page S_t. Since, there is no previous page of the start page, the progress $\rho(S_0)$ is defined as 0 at position $t = 0$.

For example, if a participant reaches page S_7 of the Q-graph in Figure 1 *a)*, already $7/10$ of the Q-graph are processed and the progress $\rho(S_7)$ is 70%. After leaving this page, the progress is $8/10 = 80\% = \rho(S_8)$. If a participant just started a questionnaire, then the progress is $\rho(S_0) = 0\%$.

Since there is a linear association between the page position and the progress, the progress $\rho(S_t)$ on a page S_t of a Q-graph Q can be computed with:

$$\rho(S_t) = \frac{t}{|\mathbb{S}(Q)|} \tag{1}$$

This equation was proposed by Kaczmirek [1][p. 147] and he called it "*static*" calculation approach. However, it has its limitation if the progress should be computed in more precision by the number of processed items. After finishing a page S_t, $|S_t|$ items were processed ($|S_t| = |\{item_0, \ldots, item_m\}| = m$, $m \geq 0$, since a page is a set of items regarding Definition 3.1). Finishing page S_t expands the progress by a term $\frac{|S_t|}{|\bigcup_{S \in \mathbb{S}(Q)} S|}$, where $|\bigcup_{S \in \mathbb{S}(Q)} S|$ is the total number of all items of the Q-graph. This term is added to the progress of the previous page ($\rho(S_{t-1})$). It results in a general, recursive and non-recursive equation to compute the progress of a linear Q-graph with item precision:

$$\rho(S_t) = \rho(S_{t-1}) + \frac{|S_t|}{|\bigcup_{S \in \mathbb{S}(Q)} S|} = \frac{\sum_{i=1}^{t} |S_i|}{|\bigcup_{S \in \mathbb{S}(Q)} S|} \tag{2}$$

This equation cannot be simplified as long as the number of items varies from page to page. If the progress should be computed only with page precision, it can be assumed that on each page lies only one item. The formula simplifies to:

$$\rho(S_t) = \rho(S_{t-1}) + \frac{1}{|\mathbb{S}(Q)|} = \sum_{1}^{t} \frac{1}{|\mathbb{S}(Q)|} = \frac{t}{|\mathbb{S}(Q)|}$$

which is equal to the equation of Kaczmirek [1][p. 147].

B. Complex Case

Now, it is assumed, the Q-graph is non-linear (adaptive), i. e., there is at least one page in the graph, which has at least two outgoing edges (cf. Figure 1 *b)*). As a consequence, the paths throughout the Q-graph depend on the answers given by the participants resulting in multiple possible paths. Each possible path can have a different number of pages and items. Therefore, it is *not* possible any more to use the total number of pages $|\mathbb{S}(Q)|$ or the total number of items $|\bigcup_{S \in \mathbb{S}(Q)} S|$ for the computation of the progress.

Take the Q-graph of Figure 1 *b)* as an example. The total number of pages is 10. For the moment, it is assumed that each page consists of a single item and that we apply (2) for linear Q-graphs. If a participant answers the questions on the first five pages, the progress increases to $5/10 = 50\%$. If the participant takes the lower path, the path shortens to 8 pages. In this case, the participant reaches the end page with an incorrect progress of 80%. Another variant is to skip the progress of the pages 6 and 7 such that the progress finishes with 100%. But this produces a big jump in the progress, which can be misleading.

Kaczmirek proposes a *dynamic* computation of the progress in questionnaires with adaptivity. His approach considers the remaining progress and the contribution of the current page to the overall progress [1, p. 148]. His resulting equation resembles (2):

$$\rho(S_t) = \rho(S_{t-1}) + \frac{1 - \rho(S_{t-1})}{|\text{remaining pages}|}$$

The equation flattens the jumps and, furthermore, allows a dynamic changing of the number of remaining pages. Therefore, this solution allows to compute the progress for non-linear Q-graphs. However, we identified some disadvantages on the above equation:

1) The equation considers only page precision rather than item precision (except there is only one item on each page).
2) The term *remaining pages* is vague and has to be discussed in more detail.

To overcome the first disadvantage, we reformulate the equation as follows:

$$\rho(S_t) = \rho(S_{t-1}) + |S_t| \frac{1 - \rho(S_{t-1})}{|\text{remaining items}|} \quad (3)$$

This equation multiplies the number of items on the current page, $|S_t|$, and considers the remaining *items* instead of pages. The number of remaining items includes the items of the current page, $|S_t|$, as we still consider the progress at the moment when reaching a page. In other words, the term $\frac{1-\rho(S_{t-1})}{|\text{remaining items}|}$ describes the influence for a page with a single item, whereas $|S_t|\frac{1-\rho(S_{t-1})}{|\text{remaining items}|}$ describes the influence of all items on the current page on the progress. Although the progress actually depends on the current answers of the participant, the equation would become long and difficult to read. Therefore, we ignore an explicit inclusion of the current answers into the equations.

In (3), a detailed description of the *remaining items* is still missing. The difficulty of describing the number of remaining items is that it is highly dependent on the answers, a participant has already given, and in the case of future branching paths on the answers, the participant has to give in future. As it is impossible to forecast which path of the Q-graph will be taken by the participant, it is impossible to predict the remaining items accurately.

The exact number of remaining items on the current page S_t depends on the remaining, individual path W to the end page. Since there may be different paths $W_1, W_2, \ldots, W_m$, $m \geq 1$, to the end page with the *same* number of remaining items, it is *not* of interest to predict the exact path to the end page rather than that number of remaining items. This remaining items prediction function rem depends on the current page S_t. The resulting equation for computing the progress in non-linear Q-graphs is:

$$\rho(S_t) = \rho(S_{t-1}) + |S_t| \frac{1 - \rho(S_{t-1})}{rem(S_t)} \quad (4)$$

Theorem 1 in the appendix of this paper shows that (4) is equal to (2) for linear Q-graphs.

C. Compute Remaining Items

While most of the last equation can be computed easily during the survey of a participant, the remaining items function rem is still challenging. In the following, let Q be a Q-graph with an end page E and S_t the current page.

Basically, there are three different situations one can encounter on each page S_t: either S_t has *a)* no successor page, it has *b)* exactly one direct successor, or it has *c)* at least two direct successors. This is illustrated in Figure 2.

In the first situation *a)*, the participant reached the end of the Q-graph. Therefore, the number of remaining items is known as it is equal to the number of items on the end page ($n = |E|$), i. e., $rem(E) = |E|$ (cf. Figure 2 *a)*).

In the second situation *b)*, the current page S_t has exactly one direct successor. If the remaining items are known for the direct successor as a, then it is also known for the current page as $a + n$, where $n = |S_t|$ (cf. Figure 2 *b)*).

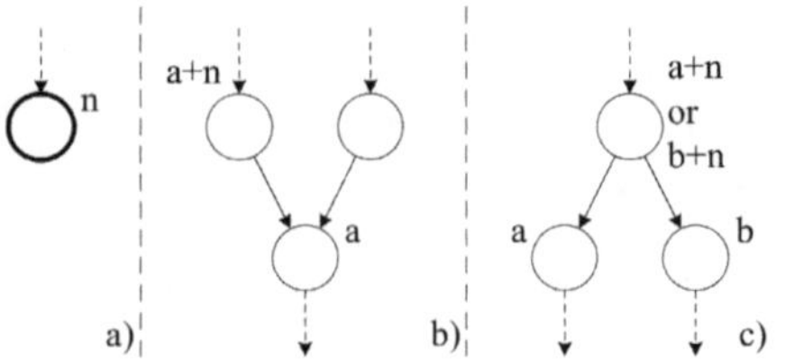

Figure 2. Three situations: *a)* no successor, *b)* one direct successor, *c)* two direct successors

In the last case *c)*, the difficulties arise since the current page S_t has at least two direct successors. Assume the remaining items on one successor is a and on the other successor is b (in the simple case of two direct successors). The current page now has either $a + n$ or $b + n$ remaining items, $n = |S_t|$ (cf. Figure 2 *c)*). The exact remaining items are only known if $a = b$. Otherwise, we have to predict, which direct successor page of S_t will be visited by the participant and, therefore, which remaining items $a + n$ or $b + n$ are taken for the computation of the progress.

For such a prediction, there are different *strategies*. For example, Kaczmirek [1] proposes two strategies: always take 1) the maximum or 2) the minimum number of remaining items. Both strategies are considered in the next section as examples. At this stage, a selection operator $\sqcup$ is introduced, which combines the solutions $a+n$ and $b+n$, e. g., $\sqcup$ can be the minimum, maximum, or another arbitrary function. The introduction of this selection operator $\sqcup$ makes it possible to define a general algorithm:

The prediction algorithm gets a Q-graph Q and a selection operator $\sqcup$ as input. We emphasize that $\sqcup$ is an *input* parameter of the algorithm and can be chosen individually.

At first, each page gets an initial value 0 as remaining items (the steps of the algorithm can be followed at Figure 3). Afterwards, the pages of the Q-graph will be put into a $work\ list$ in an arbitrary order. This work list contains all pages *without* computed remaining items. Furthermore, there is a set $visited$, which contains all *computed* pages. In a while-loop, the algorithm extracts the first page S of the work list and tries to compute the remaining items. This is only possible for S if all of its direct successors are in $visited$. The computation then follows our previous ideas corresponding to Figure 2. Otherwise, if S cannot be computed, S will be placed on the end of the work list. Finally, the algorithm terminates when the work list is empty, i. e., when each page was computed.

With Figure 3, we have found a general algorithm to compute the remaining items for each page of a Q-graph and for arbitrary strategies. Combined with (4), the progress can be calculated for arbitrary Q-graphs and selection operators allowing the comparisons of different strategies. This is explained in detail on two examples in the next section. Since the Q-graph is acyclic, the algorithm of Figure 3 always terminates. It can be easily checked, that the asymptotic runtime complexity of the algorithm depends on the $\sqcup$-operator if the pages are put topologically sorted into the work list [15, pp. 612].

```
Input: Q-graph Q and selection operator ⊔.
Output: For each S ∈ 𝕊(Q) the remaining items rem(S).
  /** Initialize **/
  for all S ∈ 𝕊(Q) do
      rem(S) ← 0
  worklist ← 𝕊(Q), visited ← ∅
  /** Iterate **/
  while worklist ≠ ∅ do
      S ← takeFirstOf(worklist)
      dirSucc ← {succ: (S, succ) ∈ S◁}
      if dirSucc ⊆ visited then
          if dirSucc = ∅ then
              rem(S) ← |S|
          else if |dirSucc| = |{succ}| = 1 then
              rem(S) ← |S| + rem(succ)
          else
              rem(S) ← |S| + ⊔_{succ∈dirSucc} rem(succ)
          visited ← visited ∪ {S}
      else
          putAtEnd(worklist, S)
```

Figure 3. General algorithm for remaining items

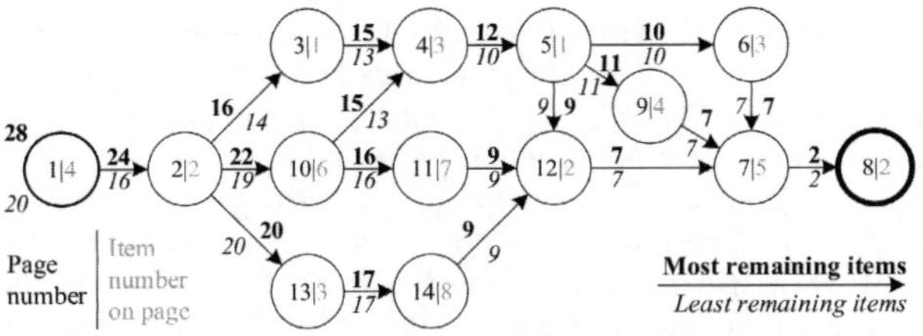

Figure 4. A sample Q-graph with page numbers (black), number of items on this page (grey), most (number above the edge) and least (number below the edge) remaining items.

V. Example Strategies

To accentuate (4) and the algorithm of Figure 3 and to show how they can be firstly used to compare arbitrary strategies, they are applied on two example selection operators in this section. Both selection operators base on the proposed strategies of Kaczmirek [1][pp. 158-159]:

1) Select the most remaining items (longest case).
2) Select the least remaining items (shortest case).

A. Most Remaining Items (Longest Case)

Taking a $\sqcup$ operator, which always selects the direct successor with the most remaining items, means that it chooses the *maximum* number of remaining items of all direct successors, $\sqcup = max$.

Figure 4 shows a Q-graph with a unique page index (the black number in the page) and the number of items on each page (the grey number in the page). Take page 5 of the Q-graph as an example. It has 1 item and three direct successors. It can be easily reconstructed that 10 items remain following the upper path (S_5, S_6, S_7, S_8). On the path in the middle, there are 11 items, and, finally, on the lower path, there are only 9 remaining items. Since the maximum of all three paths is taken, we get $1+max(10, 11, 9) = 1+11 = 12$ remaining items for page 5 following Figure 3.

TABLE I
PROGRESSES ON PATH $(S_1, S_2, S_{13}, S_{14}, S_{12}, S_7, S_8)$ FOR THE MOST, LEAST AND TRUE REMAINING ITEMS.

Progress	Most Items	Least Items	True Items
$\rho(S_1)$	14.29 %	20.00 %	15.38 %
$\rho(S_2)$	21.43 %	30.00 %	23.08 %
$\rho(S_{13})$	33.21 %	40.50 %	34.62 %
$\rho(S_{14})$	64.64 %	68.50 %	65.38 %
$\rho(S_{12})$	72.50 %	75.50 %	73.08 %
$\rho(S_7)$	92.14 %	93.00 %	92.31 %
$\rho(S_8)$	100.00 %	100.00 %	100.00 %

Applying the algorithm of Figure 3 to the Q-graph initializes each page at the begin with a remaining number of items 0. Afterwards, it puts each page in the work list. For the sample Q-graph, the work list contains the following pages in a perfect order: $(S_8, S_7, S_6, S_9, S_{12}, S_5, S_4, S_3, S_{11}, S_{10}, S_{14}, S_{13}, S_2, S_1)$. In this order, each page only has to visited once, since when a page S occurs, then all successor pages occurred before (this can be simply checked by comparing the order with the Q-graph). The algorithm computes the number of remaining items with max as selection operator. This results in the number of most remaining items of Figure 4 (numbers *above* the edges), where this number for a page is annotated on its incoming edges.

If our dynamic equation (4) is used with these values, the progress on each page can be computed. Please note, the progress depends on the visited path. For example, if the path $(S_1, S_2, S_{13}, S_{14}, S_{12}, S_7, S_8)$ is taken by a participant, the resulting progress can be found in the second column, "*Most Items*", of Table I. If instead of page S_{13} the participant goes to page S_3, $(\ldots, S_3, S_4, S_5, \ldots)$, the progress changes on page S_3 to $\rho(S_3) = 26.34\%$ instead of $\rho(S_{13}) = 33.21\%$ — a difference of more than 6%. Remember, the computed progress ρ describes the progress *after* finishing the current page and, therefore, the progress at the start of the next page.

B. Least Remaining Items (Shortest Case)

The determination of the *least* remaining items is similar to the determination of the most items although the selection operator is min. In this case, the values of remaining items of the Q-graph of Figure 4 change to the numbers *below* the edges in the same figure. The progresses for the path $(S_1, S_2, S_{13}, S_{14}, S_{12}, S_7, S_8)$ can be found in the third column, "*Least Items*", of Table I.

C. Comparison of Both Strategies

In the last two subsections, it was explained, how the most and least remaining items strategies work. Although the same path $(S_1, S_2, S_{13}, S_{14}, S_{12}, S_7, S_8)$ of the Q-graph of Figure 4 was considered, the progresses on the pages diverge between both approaches (cf. Table I). But is it possible to decide, which of the both strategies is the better one?

As mentioned in the introduction, we need a trustworthy calculation of the progress [2, p. 757]. There is a lot of discussion if a computed progress is trustworthy or not.

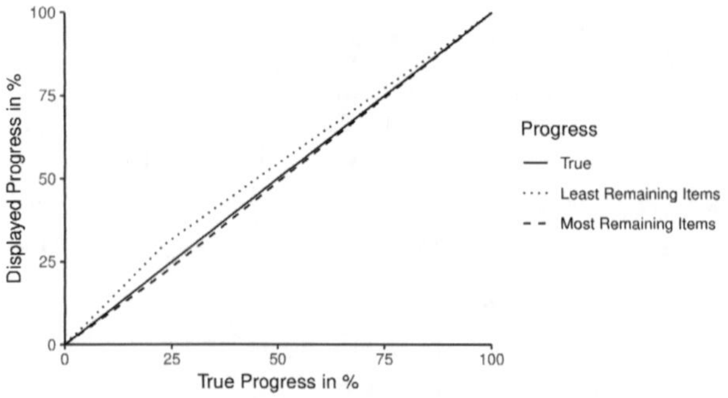

Figure 5. The *true* progress (black), the progress with least items (dotted line) and most items (dashed line)

We would argue that a computed progress is as trustworthy as it can be if the difference to the *true* progress is as small as possible. Remember, the *true* progress can only be determined *after* a participant has finished the survey, because at this point of time, we know exactly which path was taken and which was the total number of items. With this information, we can compute the *true* progress for each page easily by (2) for simple questionnaires.

Let us consider the *true* progress on each page of the previous example path. The total number of items is 26 on this path. Therefore, each item influences the progress by $1/26$ and the resulting progresses on the pages can be found in the last column, "*True Items*", of Table I.

The differences of the *true* progress on each page with the values of the computed progress with the most and least remaining items are visualized in Figure 5. The axes of the chart show the progress in percent.

The figure shows that on the least items strategy, the progress is *overestimated*, whereas on the most items approach, the progress is *underestimated*; both regarding the *true* progress. This is always true since the maximum number of remaining items is always greater or equal to the number of the true remaining items as well as the minimum number is always less or equal to the true number of items. Therefore, the progress with the least items strategy grows faster than the true progress at the beginning. The progress using the most items approach grows slower.

Considering the state of the art in Section II, the least items approach may be the better choice since there is a significant tendency in most studies that a fast-to-slow PI reduces break-offs. However, this was the consideration of one path of the Q-graph of Figure 4 only, and although the least remaining items approach fits to the hypothesis of the state of the art, it it is not sure that this approach is more trustworthy too.

As mentioned before, in our approach, a strategy (or selection operator $\sqcup$) is as trustworthy as possible if the difference between the computed progress to the *true* progress is as small as possible. In other words, the area between the computed and *true* progress should tend to be 0. In the chart of Figure 5, the area between the most items approach to the true progress is smaller than the area between the least items approach and the true progress, i. e., the most remaining items approach fits better to the *true* progress than the least remaining items approach. Remember, this is valid for the current considered path and should not be generalized. For an other path (e. g., the upper path in Figure 4), the least items approach could be the better choice.

As it was shown in this comparison, there are different arguments supporting both strategies. According to which survey and even path is given, either the most or least remaining strategy is more trustworthy. Furthermore, there could be other strategies, which fits better to a given survey than the two introduced one. Therefore, it is not easy to select the best item prediction strategy for a given survey. Furthermore, the proposed strategy of Kaczmirek [1][pp. 164-166] — taking the least remaining items — should be handled with care.

VI. CONCLUSION

Including a progress indicator in a web survey seems to be a simple part of implementation. We have shown that this is only true for linear surveys and does not hold true any more for surveys with adaptivity (branches). This paper introduced a questionnaire model, which is named Q-graph. Based on this Q-graph, the difficulties of calculating the progress in Q-graphs with branches were shown. As a solution, we propose a general equation and algorithm to compute the progress dynamically based on the ideas of Kaczmirek [1]. The algorithm predicts the number of remaining items. Since this number depends on a prediction strategy, the algorithm needs a so-called selection operator as input. This makes it possible to compare different prediction strategies in the first place. Two examples of such operators were illustrated, which estimate the most or the least remaining items. The paper concluded with a comparison of both strategies and avenues for future research.

Since it is not trivial to choose the best strategy for a given survey, it is of interest to formulate an optimization problem for the selection of a best fitting selection operator for a given survey. This should be accentuated by a case study of different Q-graphs. It is also of interest to find other selection operators, which are, for example, more intelligent by using more information about the survey. One possible idea is to check conditions in our model and to determine the resulting path for a participant as early as possible.

APPENDIX

Theorem 1: Let $Q = (\mathbb{S}, \mathbb{E})$ be a linear Q-graph. There is exact one path $(S_1, S_2, \ldots, S_m)$, $m \geq 1$, where S_1 is the start and S_m is the end page. Let I_i be the number of remaining items on page S_i. Since Q is linear, this number of remaining items I_i can be computed as follows:

$$rem(S_i) = I_i = I_{i-1} - |S_{i-1}| = I_1 - \sum_{j=1}^{i-1} |S_j| \quad (5)$$

In the case of a linear Q-graph, (4) is equal to (2):

$$\rho(S_i) \overset{(4)\,\&\,(5)}{=} \rho(S_{i-1}) + |S_i|\frac{1-\rho(S_{i-1})}{I_i} \quad (6)$$

$$=$$

$$\rho(S_i) \overset{(2)\,\&\,(5)}{=} \rho(S_{i-1}) + \frac{|S_i|}{I_1} \overset{(2)}{=} \frac{1}{I_1}\sum_{j=1}^{i}|S_j| \quad (7)$$

Proof: The proof is done by mathematical induction.
Base: Proof for $i = 1$ and $i = 2$:
$i = 1$:

$$\rho(S_1) \overset{(6)}{=} \rho(S_0) + |S_1|\frac{1-\rho(S_0)}{I_1} \overset{\rho(S_0)=0}{=} \frac{|S_1|}{I_1} \quad \checkmark \quad (8)$$

$i = 2$:

$$\rho(S_2) \overset{(6)}{=} \rho(S_1) + |S_2|\frac{1-\rho(S_1)}{I_2} \overset{(8)}{=} \rho(S_1) + |S_2|\frac{1-\frac{|S_1|}{I_1}}{I_1-|S_1|}$$

$$\overset{1=\frac{I_1}{I_1}}{=} \rho(S_1) + |S_2|\frac{\frac{I_1-|S_1|}{I_1}}{I_1-|S_1|} = \rho(S_1) + \frac{|S_2|}{I_1} \quad \checkmark$$

Step case: It is assumed that the theorem holds true for i. Proof for $i + 1$:

$$\rho(S_{i+1}) \overset{(6)}{=} \rho(S_i) + |S_{i+1}|\frac{1-\rho(S_i)}{I_{i+1}}$$

$$\overset{\text{theorem}}{=} \rho(S_i) + |S_{i+1}|\frac{1-\frac{1}{I_1}\sum_{j=1}^{i}|S_j|}{I_1-\sum_{j=1}^{i}|S_j|}$$

$$\overset{1=\frac{I_1}{I_1}}{=} \rho(S_i) + |S_{i+1}|\frac{\frac{I_1-\sum_{j=1}^{i}|S_j|}{I_1}}{I_1-\sum_{j=1}^{i}|S_j|}$$

$$= \rho(S_i) + \frac{|S_{i+1}|}{I_1} \quad \checkmark$$

■

REFERENCES

[1] L. Kaczmirek, Human Survey-Interaction. Usability and Non-response in Online Surveys, 1st ed., ser. Neue Schriften zur Online-Forschung. Cologne, Germany: Herbert von Halem Verlag, 2009, no. 6.

[2] A. Villar, M. Callegaro, and Y. Yang, "Where Am I? A Meta-Analysis of Experiments on the Effects of Progress Indicators for Web Surveys," Social Science Computer Review, vol. 31, no. 6, 2013, pp. 744–762.

[3] SurveyMonkey Inc., "SurveyMonkey: Progress Bar," Website, available: https://help.surveymonkey.com/articles/en/kb/How-can-I-add-a-progress-bar-to-my-survey, retrieved: November, 2018.

[4] T. M. Prinz, R. Bernhardt, L. Gräfe, J. Plötner, and A. Vetterlein, "Using Service-oriented Architectures for Online Surveys in Coast," in Service Computation 2018: The Tenth International Conferences on Advanced Service Computing, Barcelona, Spain, February 18–22, 2018. Proceedings, pp. 1–4.

[5] T. M. Prinz, L. Gräfe, J. Plötner, and A. Vetterlein, "Statische Analysen von Online-Befragungen mit der Programmiersprache *liQuid* (Static Analysis of Online Surveys with the Help of the Programming Language *liQuid*)," in Proceedings 19. Kolloquium Programmiersprachen und Grundlagen der Programmierung, KPS, Weimar, Germany, pp. 59–70, September 25–27, 2017.

[6] B. A. Myers, "INCENSE: A System for Displaying Data Structures," SIGGRAPH Comput. Graph., vol. 17, no. 3, Jul. 1983, pp. 115–125.

[7] ——, "The Importance of Percent-done Progress Indicators for Computer-human Interfaces," SIGCHI Bull., vol. 16, no. 4, Apr. 1985, pp. 11–17.

[8] C. Harrison, B. Amento, S. Kuznetsov, and R. Bell, "Rethinking the Progress Bar," in Proceedings of the 20th Annual ACM Symposium on User Interface Software and Technology,' 2007, pp. 115–118.

[9] D. A. Dillman, R. D. Tortora, and D. Bowker, "Principles for constructing web surveys," Social and Economic Sciences Research Center (SESRC), Washington State University, Pullman, Washington, USA, Technical Report 98-50, 1998.

[10] F. G. Conrad, M. P. Couper, and R. Tourangeau, "Effectiveness of progress indicators in web surveys: It's what's up front that counts," in Survey and statistical computing IV. The impact of technology on the survey process, pp. 1 – 10.

[11] U. Matzat, C. Snijders, and W. van der Horst, "Effects of Different Types of Progress Indicators on Drop-Out Rates in Web Surveys," Social Psychology, no. 40, 2009, pp. 43–52.

[12] F. G. Conrad, M. P. Couper, R. Tourangeau, and A. Peytchev, "The impact of progress indicators on task completion," Interacting with computers, no. 5, 2010, pp. 417—427.

[13] M. Liu and L. Wronski, "Examining completion rates in web surveys via over 25,000 real-world surveys," Social Science Computer Review, vol. 36, no. 1, 2018, pp. 116–124.

[14] G. Chartrand and P. Zhang, Discrete Mathematics, ser. 1 edn. Long Grove, Illinois, USA: Waveland Press, Inc., 2011.

[15] T. H. Cormen, C. E. Leiserson, R. Rivest, and C. Stein, Introduction to Algorithms, ser. 3. Cambridge, UK: PHI Learning, 2010.

[16] P. J. Pahl and R. Damrath, Mathematical Foundations of Computational Engineering: A Handbook, ser. 1. Auflage, F. Pahl, Ed. Berlin, Germany: Springer, 2001.

[17] J. Rost, Lehrbuch Testtheorie – Testkonstruktion (Textbook Test Theory – Test Construction), ser. Zweite, vollständig überarbeitete und erweiterte Auflage. Bern, Switzerland: Huber, 2004.

[18] H. Moosbrugger and A. Kelava, Eds., Testtheorie und Fragebogenkonstruktion (Test Theory and Survey Construction), ser. 2., aktualisierte und überarbeitete Auflage. Berlin, Germany: Springer, 2011.

Stress Detection of Human Using Heart Rate Variability Analysis Based on Low Cost Camera

Tafsut Tagnithammou
Gyrolift SAS / LISV,
University of Paris Saclay
78180 Montigny le Bretonneux, Versailles, France
Email : Tafsut.tagnithammou@gyrolift.fr

Antoine Ferszterowski
Gyrolift SAS
78180 Montigny le Bretonneux, Versailles, France
Email : antoine.fer@gyrolift.fr

Lambert Trénoras
Gyrolift SAS
78180 Montigny le Bretonneux, Versailles, France
Email: lambert.trenoras@gyrolift.fr

Eric Monacelli
LISV, Univ, Versailles Saint-Quentin-En-Yvelines,
University of Paris Saclay
78000, Versailles, France
Email: eric.monacelli@uvsq.fr

Abstract— **The article presents a non-contact solution to a stress detection. Computer human interfaces must be able to consider human's emotions. Being able to detect a stressful situation has several applications: Secure and assist Computer -Human Interfaces, telemedicine, driving assistance. This capacity allows to detect the user's state and improve the interface 's performance. We proposed a method based on a stress classification system with a sensor in contact and we compared with different classification methods based on sensors in contact. Our solution is based on a facial analysis obtained by image processing.**

Keywords-Vision; Stress; Photoplethysmography; Neural network; SVM; K-NN.

I. Introduction

Stress is a physiological response to a disturbing situation. Stressful situations can compromise not only our quality of life, but also our health, our ability to control when we are in a human-machine loop, for example man-vehicle interaction. The ability to detect a hazard is very important, but the human being is not able to objectively perceive physiological symptoms of this situation in real-time. This ability would have a lot of applications: medical, security, driving assistance, etc, and especially in the field of interactive systems. For example, for a human to be able to safely interact with new technologies (with a man-machine interface), it would mean to have the capability to detect his apprehension towards this new technology, or simply to be able to assist a novice use.

Today, there are many tools for person's stress detection. Two categories of devices can be distinguished: in-contact devices called invasive, and without-contact devices called non-invasive. Each solution may have advantages or disadvantages compared to others depending on the desired application. ElectroCardioGraphy (ECG), for example, is used for clinical applications; it measures the electrical activity of the heart to study its functioning. It can actually detect stress from variations in heart rate [1][2]. This method allows to calculate the statistical characteristics related to the intervals RR (the duration between two heart's beats) and to be able to deduce the various behaviors related to the heart (precisely to the heart rate). This solution is not adapted for an embedded application given the cost constraints and the invasiveness of this system. Electrodes are placed on the body of the person using adhesive patches to make the necessary measurements. This in-contact instrumentation is a psychological barrier since the solution is causing irritation and discomfort. There are also other solutions as Galvanic Sensor Response (GSR), which is not the subject of the article, but it is used for the test.

The purpose of this work is to show that it is possible to classify a person's stress from the physiological data captured by a low-cost camera. The main challenge of this solution is to have a sufficiently powerful system while considering the constraints related to the change of brightness of the environment especially for embedded applications and movements related to the system and the user.

The article is organized in several parts: In Section 2, we present the different solutions around the estimation of heart rate and stress. In Section 3, we describe in more detail the chain of acquisition set up to estimate the stress of a person from a camera. In Section 4, we present the evaluation protocol and the different results obtained by classification methods to build a model and the comparison between these different methods. Finally, a conclusion summarizes current findings, limitations and future work.

II. CONTEXT AND RELATED WORK

In recent years, several studies have been conducted on the use of cameras as a system for measuring cardiac activity to assess a person's stress. It is now possible to measure the fine colorimetric variations of the skin generated by the heartbeat, using a conventional camera. This process, already used by optical sensors in contact, is now exploitable using standard equipment such as the basic camera provided on laptops accessible to the public. Researchers as Poh [3], Takano [4] and Verkruysse [5] have shown that it is possible to estimate heart rate from a person’s face images. More recently, more complex solutions have been developed, not only allowing a simple estimate of heart rate, but a much more thorough analysis of cardiac activity. This analysis is based on the Heart Rate Variability (HRV), which is the study of the time’s variation between the heart’s beats. We choose to study the HRV because the set of measurements that compose it provides relatively diverse information, both in terms of cardiac activity, breathing or even the autonomic nervous system. Works like those of Bousefsaf [1], McDuff [6], Park [7] and Kaur [8] have shown that camera can be used to achieve a viable system of measurement of HRV to detect person’s stress. This is a big step forward compared to a simple estimate of the heart rate.

Several reasons led us to choose this solution. It is a non-invasive method which clearly increases the user’s comfort: the sensors in contact can generate discomfort, and even constitute a risk factor for medical applications. In addition, this solution does not require any tool to be developed, all computers are now equipped with a camera. For example, the camera used for our prototyping is a Pi camera [9]. Finally, the use of a camera allows us to perform other simultaneous processing such as example the detection of emotion from the facial expressions using the same images.

III. SYSTEM ARCHITECTURE

The objective is to show that it is possible to estimate a person’s by classifying the physiological data from processed images of a low-cost camera that is accessible to everyone for various applications. The challenge of this choice of solution is the use of a low-definition camera that can present a loss in terms of performance. We propose a chain of acquisition (presented in Figure 1), which uses a camera to classify the physiological data to estimate the stress by ensuring comfort and a non-invasive solution. We also compared this solution with the results obtained with a PPG contact sensor (PhotoPlethysmoGraphic sensor) that allows us to estimate the heart rate and to study its variability to estimate the stress of a person. The first step in our work will therefore be to create a reliable system for measuring heart rate variability from a camera. From this measurement, we can extract parameters on the variability of the heart rate, which informs us about the stress of the person. The variation in time between heart beats represents the HRV, which offers many useful measures in the study of stress.

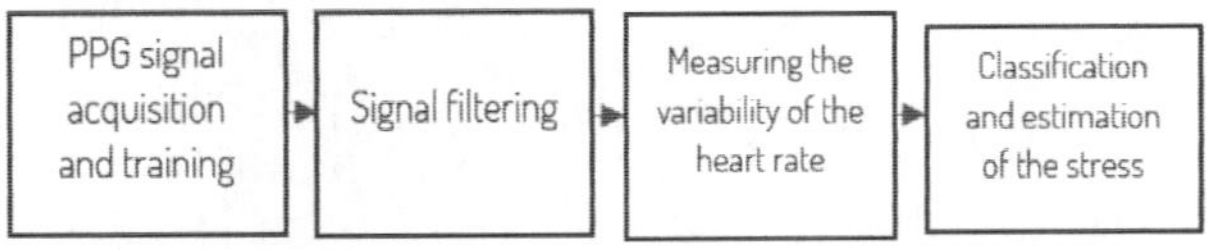

Figure 1. General method

The last step in our acquisition chain is the classification of stress indirectly through the classification of physiological data from processed images of a camera.

A. *PPG Signal Acquisition and Training*

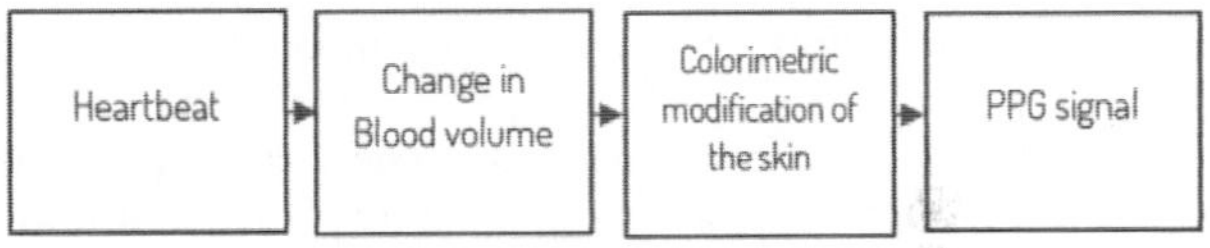

Figure 2. Principle of PhotoPléthysmoGraphy (PPG)

PhotoPlethysmoGraphy (PPG) is an optical measurement technique that allows you to observe blood volume’s variation in a non-invasive way [10].

Figure 2 illustrates the principle of PhotoPléthysmoGraphie: the cardiac activity causes fluctuations in blood volume that result in fine variations in the light reflected by the skin, and more precisely in the blood capillaries. It is this fine variation that we will seek to measure.

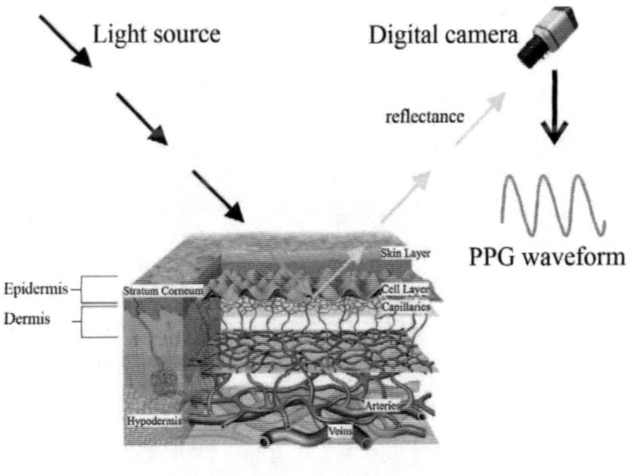

Figure 3. Description of the PPG concept [11]

As we can see in Figure 3 [11], the acquisition of a PPG signal requires two optoelectronic components: a light emitter and a light receiver. Today, cameras have become full-fledged PPG sensors, with ambient light acting as the light emitter, and the photosensitive cell matrix of the camera being the photodiode.

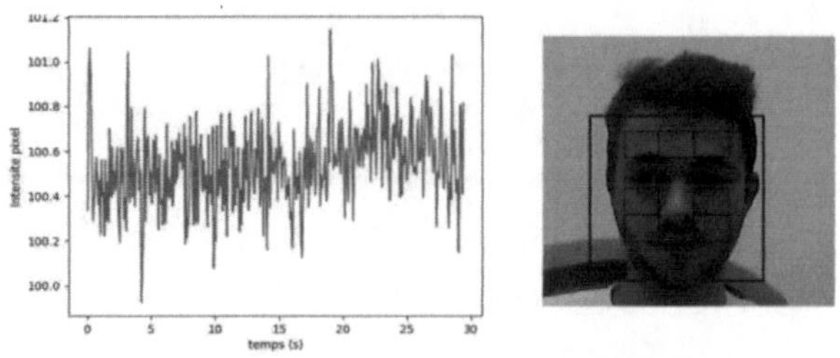

(a) **(b)**

Figure 4. PPG signal formation from the regions of interest of the face

To form the PPG signal (Figure 4a) from person's face (Figure 4b), several steps were followed:

- **Face's Detection**: This step is very important. To have a responsive and robust system it must be fast. The result of the system depends on good detection. We used the OpenCv library given the low execution time compared to other algorithms.
- **Creation of Regions of Interest (ROIs) on Face:** It is possible to define ROIs on the cheeks and the forehead (Figure 4b). This choice is to maximize the number of pixels belonging to the skin and obtain a PPG signal with minimum signal-to-noise ratio [12].
- **Chrominance Extraction *u:** We choose to use the space L*u*v more precisely the chrominance *u. This component represents the colors between red and green: wavelength interval in which photoplethysmographic variations are better observable [13].
- **Spatial Average:** Once the chrominance is extracted, we calculate the pixels' spatial of the ROIs. This average consists in summing all the pixels' intensities different from 0 and divide by this number of pixels. A point of the PPG signal represents the spatial average of a single captured frame.
- **PPG Signal Formation:** in order to have a raw PPG signal (Figure 4a), we do a normalization of the values obtained after the calculation of the spatial average as follows:

$$\dot{x}_i = \frac{x_i - \mu}{\sigma}$$

with $i \in \mathbf{N}$: number of signal's points after spatial average, σ et μ : standard deviation and mean.

A raw PPG signal is obtained at the output of the acquisition chain. We must filter it to make it more exploitable.

B. Filtering

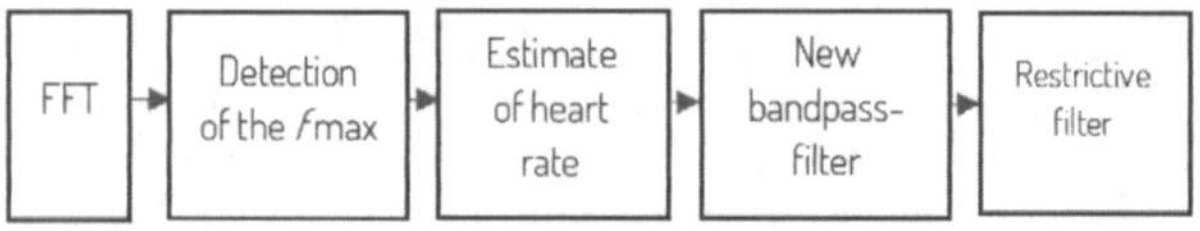

Figure 5. Signal filtering chain

Our algorithm of stress detection will be based on the study of the different peaks of the filtered PPG signal. The signal PPG is filtered in a sliding window of 30 seconds with a step of one second following the chain of Figure 5:

- After removing the continuous component, we apply a Butterworth filter with cutoff frequencies set at 0.8 Hz and 3 Hz, which corresponds to the usual heart rate in humans
- A Fast Fourier Transform (FFT) [14] is applied to determine the maximum heart rate, so we deduce the average heart rate.
- Another selective bandpass filter is applied from the average heart rate since the first filter applied does not allow to study the variability of the heart rate, we applied this second filter more restrictive to define the cutoff frequencies of the heart. filtered.

The objective of the filtering is to obtain a signal comprising distinct peaks that can be analyzed by a detection algorithm while avoiding "bad detection" as much as possible, since between each peak, there is a fixed amplitude and mean interval which eliminates any other spades that do not respect this constraint. Our algorithm of stress detection will be based on the study of the different peaks of our filtered PPG signal.

In the manner of the R-peaks of an ECG, it is possible to use the peaks of the signal PPG, which are not R-peaks indicated in (Figure 6a), but the P-peaks indicated in (Figure 6b) variability of the heart rate. The study of the variability of the heart rate via the PPG wave, is a reliable alternative and that leads to almost identical results to that of the ECG as shown [7].

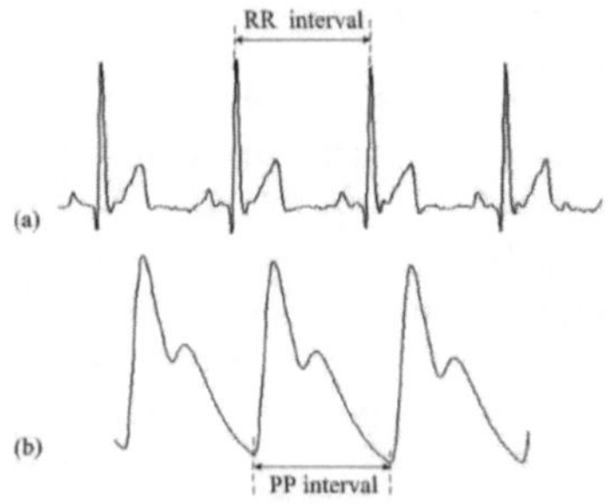

Figure 6. Analogy between R-R interval et P-P interval

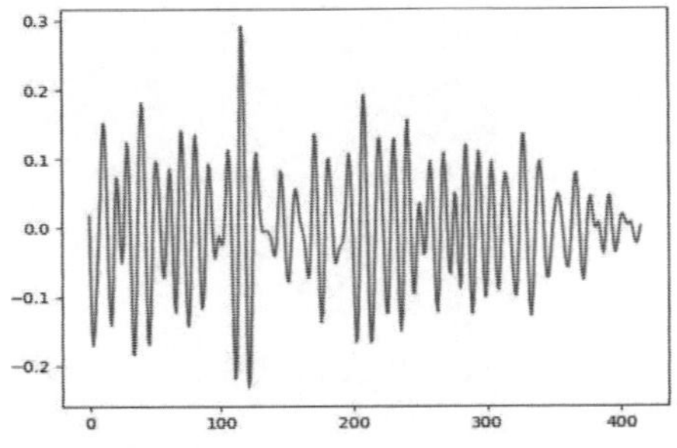

Figure 7. Filtered PPG signal

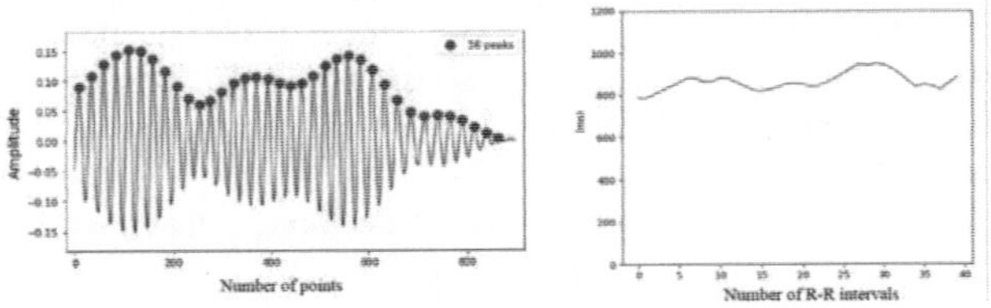

(a) (b)

Figure 8. Detection of PPG signal peaks and graphical representation of RR

The filtering method used seems adequate: The filtered PPG signal obtained (Figure 7) with the detection of the peaks (Figure 8a) corresponds to the adequate rate validated by the measurements made by a PPG sensor in contact; on the other hand the filtering is carried out in a sliding window of 30 seconds with a step of one second in parallel with the other operations: detection of the face; PPG signal extraction.

Once the R-R intervals of the filtered signal have been extracted and corrected, we have drawn the Tachogram (Figure 8b) which is the graphical representation of the R-R intervals.

C. *Heart Rate Variability and Stress*

Several studies show that heart rate variability is a marker of stress. The reference [15] shows that HRV of a person immediately drops in response to a stressful stimulus. This decrease is also observable in the case of chronic stress if we study the HRV over a longer period. The HRV presents a great informative value, it informs on the activity of the autonomic nervous system and more precisely on the balance between: The sympathetic system which helps to increase heart rate and the parasympathetic system which helps to decrease it. The reference [16] describes the autonomic nervous system which is the mechanism in charge of the regulation of stress, in the case of a stressful situation. Thus, an increase in sympathetic tone is observed together with a decrease in parasympathetic tone. Variations in sympathetic and parasympathetic tone can be seen in low frequencies and high frequencies, respectively. We will observe a decrease in high frequencies accompanied by an increase in low frequencies and therefore an increase in the ratio LF / HF in response to a stressful stimulus. We use the name Sympatho-Vagal Balance (BSV) to qualify this relation BF/HF.

It is important to note that heart rate is not a stress marker when studied in isolation. This is the interest of the HRV which has a much more informative value since it is based on the study of the variation of the time between heart beats. It is also a risk marker for many pathologies. Several studies indicate that a decline in HRV is associated with the risk of cardiovascular and coronary heart disease, hypertension and heart failure [15]. We have seen that the HRV provides information on the activity of the autonomic nervous system, vagal tone, respiration and of course the activity of the heart and its ability to adapt. That's why it can be used as a stress marker [17]. There are no normal values for the quantities of the HRV. They are modulated by a lot of parameters, including age or physical condition so they are intrinsic to each person. We choose to use 4 parameters to build our stress estimation and classification model. There are multiple combinations of parameters used to classify stress in the literature. Our choice was Beats Per Minute (BPM), Root Square of the Successive Differences (RMSSD), BSV and the Standard Deviation of all the intervals beats (SDNN). These indicators are used in recurring ways for this type of study:

- BPM: Number of beats per minute

- RMSSD: root square of squared differences of successive RR intervals which also expresses high frequency variability mainly of parasympathetic origin, modulated by respiration.

$$RMSSD = \sqrt{\frac{1}{N-1}\sum_{i=1}^{N}(RR_{diff}\,i)^\wedge 2}$$

- SDNN: standard deviation of intervals between beats

$$SDNN = \sqrt{\frac{1}{N-1}\sum_{i=1}^{N}(RR_i - \overline{RR})^\wedge 2}$$

- BSV:

$$BSV = \frac{LF}{HF}$$

However, we have chosen to limit ourselves to these 4 quantities to limit the number of input parameters of our classification model, which reduces the processing time and makes the system more responsive.

In the case of a stressful reaction, several phenomena are observable:

- An increased BSV: Increased sympathetic tone and decreased parasympathetic tone corresponding to a stressed state.

- Decreased RMSSD and SDNN: During a stressful situation, the respiratory cycle is faster, which reduces the value of the R-R intervals. Since both RMSSD and SDNN are based on these ranges, their values are also reduced.
- Increased BPM and instant heart rate

D. *Implementation of the Protocol and Creation of the Stress Classification Model*

Once our cardiac activity measurement system was defined, we began the creation of our stress classification model. Machine Learning tools are now the ones that lead to the best results in classification tasks through models that are used to predict qualitative variables like quantitative, data separation is more complex as data are separated into different groups in a more precise manner. The main constraint of this type of method lies in the need for relatively large amounts of data to build a robust "classification model". Since there is no publicly available database of measures of heart rate variability annotated as being in a stressed or unstressed state, we chose to create our own database.

1) *Test Protocol: Inducing Stress*

Our experimental protocol aims to collect cardiac activity data corresponding to stressed and unstressed states. The main difficulty is to succeed in inducing stress in a maximum of participants.

Method: Comparison between GSR + in-Contact PPG sensors and image analysis

Inclusion: After presenting the test protocol, each participant has given their consent to participate by signing a consent letter.

Test: Our test consists of three stress phases separated by relaxation phases. The chosen protocol is to broadcast a video of 6 minutes including so-called relaxation phases, as well as stress phases (Figure 9). The 6 minutes are organized in alternating phases of 1 minute. During the relaxation phases, the videos broadcast are videos of soothing natures constitute the relaxing stimulus. The videos broadcast during the stress phases correspond to the Stroop test, presented in [18]. It is common to use the Stroop test as an inducer of mild stress, which is the stressful stimulus used by Bousefsaf [13].

We chose to have participants fill out a questionnaire during the protocol, to measure their level of anxiety, in order to filter the data collected, and understand some results. Each participant had to complete the State Trait Anxiety Inventory (STAI) presented in [19] before starting the test. These psychological questionnaires also allow us to exclude some participants by correlating the GSR sensor data with the test results.

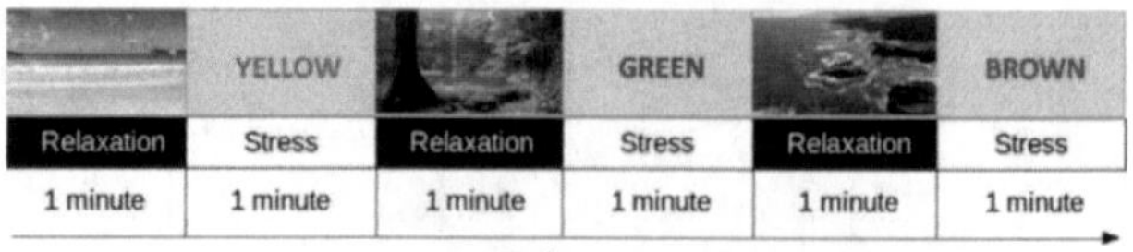

Figure 9. Stress induction test

2) *Database of Physiological Measurements*

We used data from the 15 participants. We initially had data from 21 participants. Participants 9 and 15 were excluded as they showed no evidence of physiological responses to the stressful stimulus. Finally, participants 7, 18, 19 and 22 were excluded for material reasons (sensor that breaks off during the test, etc.). We used data from the remaining 15 participants.

As shown in Figure 10, we have for each participant a set of three sensors:

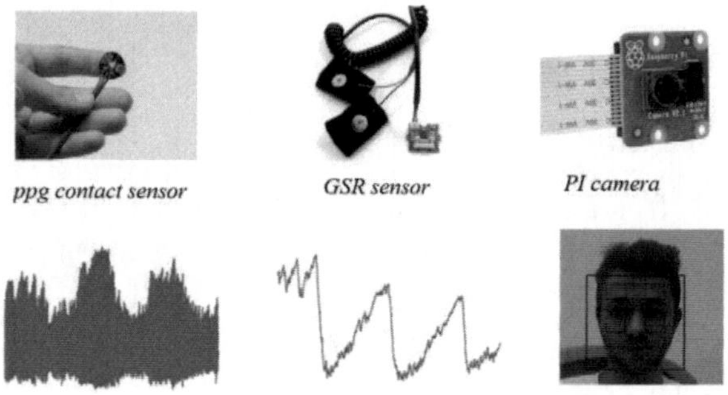

Figure 10. Test sensors

The PPG and GSR sensor to build a stress estimation model, then we will compare this model with the model established with the PI camera solution.

i. Detection Chain to Validate

- The video of the participant's face: it validates our PPG signal acquisition chain from the video, by referring to the measurements of the PPG contact sensor.

ii. Comparison Chain

- Measurements of the GSR sensor in contact: This sensor provides information on sweating of the skin, during a stressful situation, a person is supposed to have a different sweating than during a rest phase. It allows to determine if there was stress or not and therefore to select the participants to include in the training data.
- The measurements of the PhotoPlethymographic Sensor (PPG) in contact: allow to train our classification model.

iii. Validation of Learning Data

Once we have these data, we excluded participants who did not show signs of a stressful reaction, for which the GSR sensor data was used. This sensor provides information on sweating of the skin. During a stressful situation, a person is supposed to have a different sweating than during a rest phase. Our test consists of three stress phases separated by relaxation phases, the signal returned by the sensor must have (Figure 11) three separate spades, in the case where the subject has stressed.

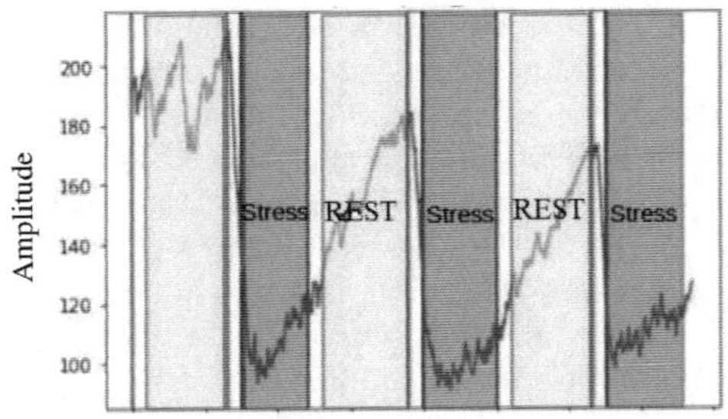

Figure 11. Representation of selected signal portions

The test consists of three stressful periods which implies that the participant should have three times a lower rate of sweating. The spectra that do not show pikes at the moments corresponding to the beginning of a stressing phase, therefore did not stress. It was therefore relatively easy to exclude the participants without any reaction, it was enough to visually grasp the data of the GSR sensor.

IV. RESULTATS & DISCUSSION

The method proceeds in two steps:

A. Step 1: Comparison of Classification Methods

This step consists in creating a reference classification model based on the physiological data of the participants coming from the PPG contact sensor. This classification model is used to validate the model created from the physiological data from the camera.

i. Description of Methods

In order to classify the data from the PPG contact sensor and annotate them, we compared three different methods. We want to generalize a classification of unknown samples from a learning database. We compare three methods of supervised learning; this choice is based on a bibliographic analysis: neural network; K-NN et SVM. These are the methods with the best results in terms of classification. The reference [18] used the KNN method and obtained a classification accuracy of 95%. Reference [19] tested the SVM and the KNN method and obtained better results with the SVM with an RBF core function, they reached the 85% accuracy. Reference [20] has shown that it is possible to classify measures of cardiac variability according to 4 levels of stress using an artificial neural network.

Neural Network (Supervised learning method): an input layer with 4 neurons which are the 4 input parameters (SDNN, BSV, RMSSD, BPM); the next three layers are hidden (the number of hidden layers is defined according to the optimal percentage of precision obtained); the last layer composed of neurons corresponding to the two outputs (stressed state; non-stressed state)

K-NN (Supervised learning method): is an algorithm based on training data that it stores in memory; it is a memory-based algorithm. This method is therefore suitable for problems with a small database. In our case, we have a few thousand samples which allows us to use this method.

SVM (Supervised learning method): This method is used for regression problems, as in our case, it can also be used for classification. It separates a dataset into two categories: using a hyperplane separator which is linear; or using a kernel function that is non-linear.

ii. Database for Classification

After acquisition of the test data, we have 1418 samples that have been split into two data sets.

Training and Validation Data: 80% samples of 1134 were used for the training and validation of the model.

Test Data: To test the model, it is necessary that the data were never injected into the model in order to evaluate the real performances of the model, 20% of the samples so 284 were used for that.

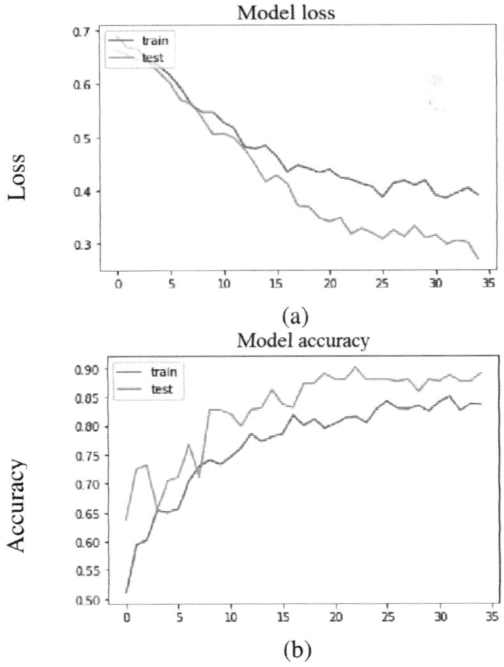

Figure 12. Neural network method

Figure 12 illustrates the performance of the model built using a neural network; the rate of loss of training and testing (Figure 13a); the training accuracy rate (Figure 13b).

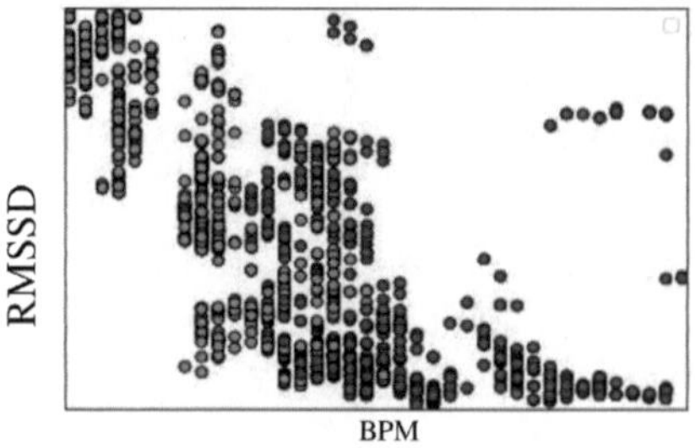

(a)

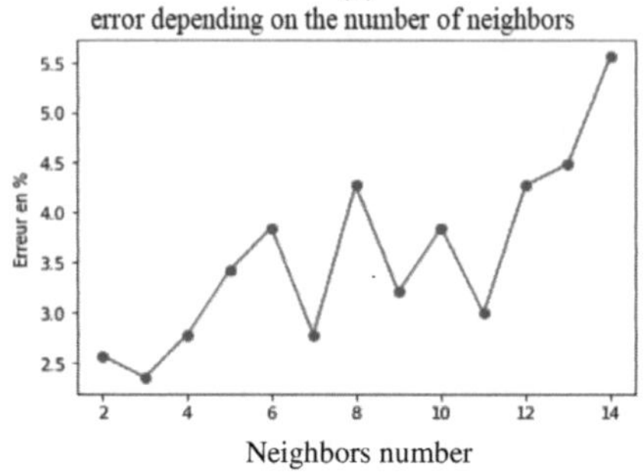

(b)

Figure 13. K-NN method

Figure 13a illustrates a classification obtained using the K-NN method, the number of neighbors is chosen which minimizes the error on the test data. It suffices to increment this hyper-parameter in a loop (Figure 14b) to determine its optimal value by visual apprehension of the curve.

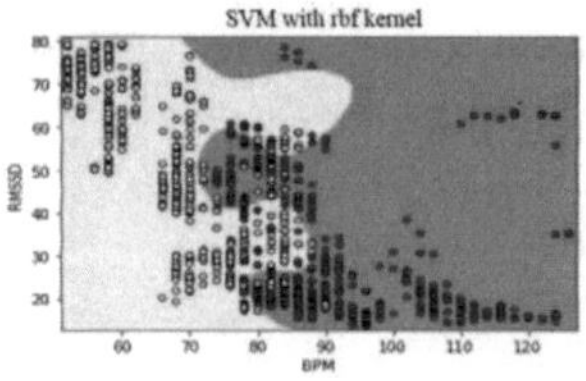

(a)

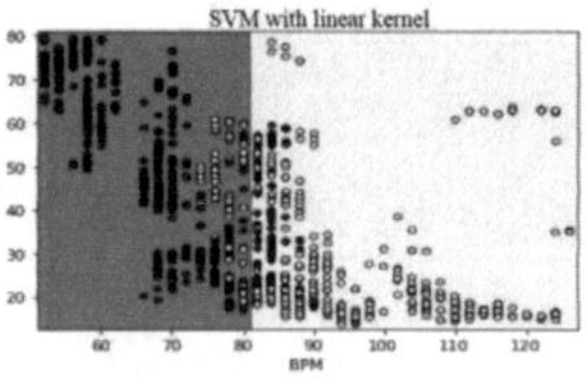

(b)

Figure 14. SVM method

Figure 14 illustrates the use of a linear SVM to classify our data (Figure 14b); and an SVM with a kernel function (Figure 14a).

iii. Discussion:

TABLE I. PERFORMANCES OF THE THREE METHODS

Algorithm	Accuracy test – data learning	Accuracy test on the second dataset
Neural network	**89,1 %**	**83,3 %**
K-NN	**97,6 %**	**77,4 %**
SVM	**97,2 %**	**75,2 %**

Table 1 summarizes the results obtained after the evaluation of the three classification methods. If we analyze the results: We note that the k-NN method is the one that presents the best classification results on the 284 samples from the learning dataset. The accuracy rate is 97.6% which is relatively high. However, this accuracy is not indicative of the performance of the algorithm under real conditions. In the test data set, measurements are almost identical to those of training, which explains why, with the k-NN method or with the SVM, it is possible to obtain such high results. That's why we have injected the second set of test data. This test database will allow us to really evaluate the performance of our models and compare them together.

We note that the neural network method presents the best classification performance on this new dataset, with an accuracy of 83.3% against 77.4% for the k-NN algorithm and 75.2% for the SVM. We can deduce that the best solution available to us the neural network solution. In fact, it has the best capacity for generalization and therefore brings us good results in real conditions.

B. Step 2: Comparison with the Non-Invasive Non-Contact model: camera

The first step made it possible to obtain the physiological data of the participants coming from a PPG sensor in contact. This acquisition was synchronized recording a video of their face. Once the classification model of the data from the contact PPG sensor is done, we will be able to analyze the quality of the acquisition chain and test our classification model only from the camera's data.

We used three classification methods to classify the data obtained from the camera; SVM; Neural network and temporal averaging method.

- Time Averaging: We made an estimate of the heart rate every second. The goal is to calculate the right heart rate estimated by choosing the one with the highest number of occurrences. In this method, the historical aspect (evolution over time) is considered to calculate the heart rate.

TABLE II. DATA CLASSIFICATION PERFORMANCE FROM THE CAMERA

Algorithm	Properly classified samples
Neural network	59,2 %
Time averaging	61,1 %
SVM	56,3 %

Table 2 shows the results of the three methods used to classify the camera dataset; 56.3% of good classification is obtained using SVM, slightly more with neural network method 59.2% and 61.1% with temporal averaging.

C. Error Calculation: Contact Model - Contactless Model

We compared the classification results obtained from the camera with the classification results obtained from the PPG contact sensor.

We used two parameters for the comparison:

- RMSE: Root Mean Square Error
- Correlation: the Pearson correlation coefficient r used to study the intensity of the link that exists between the results obtained with the model of the PPG contact sensor and the data obtained with the model of the camera.

a. Neural Network Method

TABLE III. COMPARISON OF THE NEURAL NETWORK METHOD

	RMSE	Correlation
BPM	12,057	0,37 *avec p-value <0.01
RMSSD	36,87	0,06
BSV	0,65	0,02
SDNN	28,11	0,11

b. Time Averaging Method

TABLE IV. COMPARISON OF THE TEMPORAL AVERAGING METHOD

	RMSE	Correlation
BPM	12,24	0,15 *avec p-value <0.01
RMSSD	33,4	0,05
BSV	0,7	0,04
SDNN	29,12	0,09

c. SVM Method: Injection of two second signal portions at the input of the model to predict the parameters of the HRV

TABLE V. COMPARISON OF THE SVM METHOD

	RMSE	Correlation
BPM	9,61	0,11 *avec p-value <0.01
RMSSD	43,5	0,03
BSV	1,3	0,06
SDNN	36,2	0,04

Discussion:

The results presented in Table 3, Table 4 and Table 5 correspond to the three main methods. The neural network method (Table 3) is relatively close to the temporal averaging method (Table 4). The filtering and signal processing algorithms used are strictly identical. The third method is relatively different (Table 5) since it does not require prior signal processing. The idea is simply to inject signal portions of 2 seconds into input of a classification model and the parameter to predict (BPM, RMSSD, etc.) from the sensor. The model will predict the parameter in question: the BPM, SDNN, RMSSD, BSV since the objective is to inject the raw signal from the camera without specific treatment (filtering) and to predict the heart rate with the associated HRV parameters. The most interesting results in terms of quadratic error are those obtained with the SVM method, however, the correlation rate is relatively low compared to the basic method, for BPM at least (Table 5).

The two methods to be considered are those using temporal averaging and SVM since they present more promising results. The SVM could be used more judiciously than to predict the parameters directly at the output of the model. This is a solution that was recently developed [20].

For the temporal averaging method, the histograms of the predictions show that the correct estimates are the most recurrent, however the algorithm implemented is not yet well adapted to perform a correct arbitration as to the correct estimate to be chosen when the signal is of poor quality in some areas of interest. One possible improvement would be to set up an algorithm to assign a coefficient to each estimate based on the signal-to-noise ratio (SNR) of the region of interest from which it is derived, which would be low in the case where the SNR is low and vice versa.

V. CONCLUSION AND FUTURE WORK

The objective of this work is to show that it is possible to classify the stress of a person from the physiological data captured by an accessible camera and embeddable.

The developed method allowed us to compare different methods of classification but the use of the camera as a tool for measuring cardiac activity is still in its beginnings.

To estimate the stress of a person using a sensor without contact: camera. First, we propose an acquisition chain in order to estimate the heart rate and calculate the parameters of the HRV that will be used as inputs for the stress classification model. We have put in place a test protocol to create our own database that will be used to create the stress classification model. Data acquired during this test are: sensor data in PPG contact synchronized with video recordings, and a GSR sensor.

A classification model from the PPG sensor data was created using different supervised learning methods; the method that shows the best results is the neural network method.

Then, we evaluated the performance of our acquisition chain with the camera by comparing the built classification model with the camera data.

There are many constraints brought by this tool, which today represent the main barrier to its use on embedded systems. The two main constraints are movements and light variations, constraints which are difficult to overcome even in laboratory conditions. Both are closely related since a movement will necessarily result in a change in the illumination of a person's face. These are two of these areas that we will strive to improve. Nevertheless, this solution is more accessible and especially embeddable since it is non-invasive. We will try to minimize the impact of light variations on the accuracy of our measurements. Today, light variations are one of the main challenges in computer vision on embedded systems. Since computer vision and signal processing techniques have been evolving in recent years, particularly with the advent of machine-learning tools, it is certain that the measurement of cardiac activity via the extraction of the PPG signal by a camera will improve and one day, will become a recognized alternative measurement system. It can be imagined for many applications: driver assistance, telemedicine or biometrics.

ACKNOWLEDGMENT

We wish to thank all the participant especially Fali Thamila and supervisors for their priceless help.

REFERENCES

[1] C. Maaoui and F. Bousefsaf, "Automatic human stress detection based on webcam photoplethysmographic signals," *J. Mech. Med. Biol.*, vol. 13, pp. 1–13, 2015.

[2] M. Alghatrif and J. Lindsay, "A brief review: history to understand fundamentals of electrocardiography," *J. Community Hosp. Intern. Med. Perspect.*, vol. 5, pp. 1–5, 2012.

[3] D. J. Mcduff, R. W. P. Non-, and C. Link, "Accessed Non-contact , automated cardiac pulse measurements using video imaging and blind source separation .," vol. 13, 2018.

[4] C. Takano and Y. Ohta, "Heart rate measurement based on a time-lapse image," *Med. Eng. Phys.*, vol. 29, pp. 853–857, 2006.

[5] W. Verkruysse, L. O. Svaasand, and J. S. Nelson, "Remote plethysmographic imaging using ambient light .," *Opt. Soc. Am.*, vol. 16, no. 26, 2008.

[6] D. Mcduff, S. Gontarek, and R. Picard, "Remote Measurement of Cognitive Stress via Heart Rate Variability," pp. 3–6.

[7] J. Park, "A Study on the Stress-Index Estimation Using Face Image," pp. 45–47, 2016.

[8] B. Kaur, S. Moses, M. Luthra, and V. N. Ikonomidou, "Remote Stress Detection using a Visible Spectrum Camera," *SPIE*, pp. 1–13, 2015.

[9] https://www.raspberrypi.org/documentation/usage/camera

[10] J. L. M. Id, M. X. Rocha, G. G. Vasconcelos, and J. E. V. Filho, "Advances in Photopletysmography Signal Analysis for Biomedical Applications," *sensors*, pp. 1–26, 2018.

[11] M. A. Hassan *et al.*, "Heart rate estimation using facial video : A review," *Biomed. Signal Process. Control*, vol. 38, pp. 346–360, 2017.

[12] S. Kumar, A. Prakash, and C. S.tucker, "Bounded Kalman filter method for motion- robust , non-contact heart rate estimation," *Biomed. Opt. Express*, vol. 9, no. 2, 2018.

[13] F. Bousefsaf, "Non-contact measurement of cardiac activity by analysis of the video flow from a digital camera extraction of physiological parameters and application to the estimation of stress," University of Lorraine, 2014.

[14] S. P. Singh, N. Rathee, H. Gupta, P. Zamboni, and A. V. Singh, "Contactless and Hassle Free Real Time Heart Rate Measurement with Facial Video," *J. Card. Crit. Care*, pp. 24–29, 2017.

[15] J. Marsac, "Variability of heart rate: a marker of cardiometabolic risk in public health," *Bull. académie Natl. médecine*, vol. 197, pp. 175–186, 2013.

[16] A. Ismail, "Interest of Heartbeat Variability as a Risk Marker," university of law and health of LILLE 2, 2013.

[17] H. Kim, E. Cheon, D. Bai, Y. H. Lee, and B. Koo, "Stress and Heart Rate Variability : A Meta-Analysis and Review of the Literature," *Korean Neuropsychiatr. Assoc.*, 2018.

[18] F. Scarpina and S. Tagini, "The Stroop Color and Word Test," *Front. Psychol.*, vol. 8, no. April, pp. 1–8, 2017.

[19] C. Jeunet, F. Lotte, and M. Christian, "Design and Validation of a Mental and Social Stress Induction Protocol Towards Load-invariant Physiology-based Stress Detection," in *International Conference on Physiological Computing Systems*, 2014, pp. 98–106.

[20] A. Osman, J. Turcot, and R. El Kaliouby, "Supervised Learning Approach to Remote Heart Rate Estimation from Facial Videos," in *IEEE International Conference and Workshops on Automatic Face and Gesture Recognition (FG)*, 2015, p. 6.

Introducing Augmented Reality-Ready Head-Worn Displays to Support Workers on the Shop Floor of a Car Production Line

Sebastian Felix Rauh*, Diep Nguyen*, Stephan Bolch† and Gerrit Meixner*
*UniTyLab
Heibronn University, Heilbronn, Germany
Email: *first.last*@hs-heilbronn.de
†N/PN-48E
AUDI AG, Neckarsulm, Germany
Email: stephan.bolch@audi.de

***Abstract*—In this paper, we present an approach to directly instruct workers in the quality check division of a car production line. We simulated the complete manual functional check of a car to test the possibilities of using one selected binocular optical See-Through Head-Worn Display. Furthermore, we chose one subtask to be Augmented Reality-supported to get an impression of the capabilities of this technology in this application area. Also, we tested a finger-worn input-device, representing the type of "close to the body"-input-devices. For the whole implementation we applied the Human Centred Design Approach as described in ISO 9241 - 210. We evaluated the application with four workers from the selected division. Even though we could not implement all requirements exactly as they were requested, the participants responded positively to the selected Head-Worn Display, the finger-worn input modality and the augmentation we provide.**

Keywords–Augmented Reality; Interaction Device; Head-Worn Display; Shop Floor; Production Line.

I. INTRODUCTION

Modern Head-Worn Displays (HWDs) have the power to show information directly on site where they are needed while keeping both hands free to execute tasks. Also, due to the rapid development of miniaturising high performance hardware, they have the capability to display sophisticated content when it is needed. Since the late 1980s, visually extending the real environment with virtual content is part of scientific research and also made its way into popular culture. The so-called Augmented Reality (AR) was exemplified in many areas like medicine, eLearning or user navigation. Another promising field of application is the support of workers. From the very beginning, maintenance, repair and assembly were strategically identified as key application fields of AR [1]. It also can be split up into remote support and automatic on-site support. While the first is establishing contact to an expert of the field and therefore is highly flexible, the latter is based on analysing and modelling work-flows to display supportive instructions whenever they are needed.

This automatic on-site support is less flexible as it only can access formalised knowledge, usually generated for each use case, but it especially is able to support people in work areas with low flexibility and high production rate. One prominent example of such a work area is the conveyor belt of car manufacturers, where cars are assembled and quality checks are performed. In this area we conducted our study on how AR can support workers performing quality checks after the assembly of vehicles. While AR was difficult to established with the available hard- and software, we could identify that overcoming direct interaction with the HWD (i.e., using the buttons on the HWD itself, e.g., on the glasses temple) is crucial for the success of these devices.

The work presented in this paper is structured as follows: In Section II, we present related work. In Section III, we describe the results of the analysis of the current work flow. In Section IV, we describe the implementation of the application, including the interviews conducted to validate and/or make design decisions. The results of the final evaluation are presented in Section V. In Section VI, our findings are summarised and conclusions are drawn.

II. STATE OF THE ART

Today, many AR systems are using HWDs, hand-held computers or smart phones, i.e., small devices including at least one camera and one kind of graphical display. In the context of worker support where hand-free is critical, however, HWDs are significantly advantageous. In many aspects, HWDs are similar to Head-Mounted Displays (HMDs). According to [2] the main difference is that HWDs can be put on like a normal pair of glasses while HMDs usually require the user or an assisting person to adjust the position of the display, for example via adjusting screws on the frame or head straps. Typically, HWDs function with the support from either a mobile or a wearable computer. Since the first device in 1968 [3], HMDs have gone through tremendous changes for maturation of resolution, refresh rate, Field of View (FoV), etc. The new generation of HMDs, the HWDs, are lightweight and almost like a normal pair of glasses, instead of their bulky predecessors. All of these devices come along with their own powerful computing unit, while older devices often need to be attached to a desktop-PC to be able to offer AR-features. This development is mainly based on the fast progress in the miniaturisation of high performance electronics. With the ability to function as wearable computers, modern HWDs broaden the field of application for AR, due their higher level of mobility.

Recently, car manufacturers have started supporting employees with smart glasses instead of mobile devices. For example, smart glasses now are a part of standard equipment's at Volkswagen in Wolfsburg, Germany [4]. Opel also has a virtual assistant called "Smart Helper" [5]. The importance of AR in the production environment was emphasised through the work of Meixner et al. [6] in which AR is portrayed as one of the most important technologies of user interaction evolution in future industrial environments. The AR-support offers instructions and guidelines at different levels to help users to achieve their tasks while minimising errors and increasing safety [1]. Moreover, AR also has been applied in providing remote expert support and environment interaction [7]. Rauh et al. use HWD to support workers in the quality check division of a German car manufacturer [8] displaying instructions and documentation in the Field of View rather than paper-based. The aim here was to enable any worker, independent of his/her expertise in this task to increase performance. The work showed that in general HWD have the capacity to optimise workers' performance in the selected application area. Loch et al. could show that compared to video assistance a worker supported in AR performs significantly better in terms of error rates in manual work tasks [9]. This is an important finding considering that the flexibility of a human worker is needed to be able to offer customised production services for customers.

With the specific intention of supporting workers in industrial production environments, several projects proposed designs and frameworks where AR is employed to fulfil these visions. Both projects MOON by AIRBUS Military [10] and the AR Framework for Maintenance Tasks by Re et al. [11] share similar goals of delivering 3D assembly work instructions via smart phones and tablets. Even still struggling with tracking technology and needing further development, these works have shown promising results of AR usage over productivity. In 2002, Tschirner et al. presented a welding helmet equipped with video See-Through technology to augment the welders field of view with multiple information, based on his/her current task [12]. Besides a feasibility study to assist workers while fix broke weft yarns of a industrial waving machine Kerpen et al. identified effects of the current trend of digitisation in factory environment on the worker and the portfolio of his/her tasks [13]. Among others, they predict a easier and faster access to machine related data, a higher flexibility of the work organisation and the need of increased IT-skills.

Wijesooriya et al. make use out of the increased accessibility in a prototype using AR to visualise machine status data on site [14]. Maly et al. developed an AR system for maintenance and collaboration with a robot [15]. During the ARVIKA project [16], head worn AR-based solutions for industrial applications have been developed. The project had brought AR into attention of many players across multiple areas. Related to the ambition of this work, Eissele et al. describe a system which successfully combines "multiple reality stages" (i.e., AR, Mixed Reality, Augmented Virtuality and/or Virtual Reality) to decrease assembly-time and error-rate [17]. Potentially related to the usage of a combination of multiple levels of virtual environments, according to the authors the actual strength of their system may be in highly complex tasks. Another prominent example is AR in Smart Factories (in terms of "Industry 4.0"), as described, e.g., by Paelke [18]. By using AR instructions, users without experience in the selected task were able to successfully implemented assembly tasks in down-scaled model factories. The positive outcomes of this work had encouraged further tests and investigation in a real production environment for better applications.

Aside the industrial application areas, AR shows great potential in many other areas. For example, Delft University of Technology had run a project for distributed collaboration in crime scene investigation [19]. The system allows a field investigator, equipped with a HWD, to work with an expert in distance via video stream, voice communication and a shared interactive 3D model. The work displayed promising outcomes in improving mutual understanding between investigators, fastening data exchange, as well as time management. Furthermore, medicine is another interesting domain for AR. In [20], Mentler et al. discussed several use cases in medical practice employing smart glasses. These use cases cover from triage, diagnosis to surgery. Despite the limitation of current technologies, health care experts had shown their interest for the usage of HWD.

Since AR has the power to decrease error rate and also documentation efforts, e.g., by detecting if a task was executed successfully or with errors, we believe that if this technology is introduced in the right way it can increase efficiency. In the described study we introduced a AR-ready HWD for selected work tasks and compared the direct interaction with the device (i.e., using the interaction elements on the glasses) with a clicker device (i.e., a remote control with the same buttons as the glasses). While AR turned out to be problematic due to the diminished amount of trackable features in the selected environment, feasible interaction with HWD-based systems seems to be a key feature for the users we talked to.

Figure 1. The customised layout of the Hoerbiger Smartcontrol PDA hand-held terminal as used in the described setting.

III. Analysis

We conducted the presented work on the shop floor of a German car manufacturer in the final check division of one car manufacturing line. In contrast to the assembly division, the tasks in this subsequent division require higher flexibility from the workers. Several varying automatic and manual tasks are executed, based on the car's configuration, among others to ensure the product quality. To further understand the work tasks and the environment, we analysed both as described in this section.

A. Environment

We selected the initial start-up and functional check division, which is the first subdivision of the final check division. This selection mainly is based on the fact that we already executed previous projects in this division in which we made good experiences with the flexibility of the workers. In this division, there is a greater amount of manually executed task, for which the workers need to be instructed and guided than in other divisions. Also, workers need to be mobile to execute these tasks. Finally, the workers are already instructed by a hand-held terminal, which they also use for documenting the test results. In this division, the vehicles still are on the conveyor belt. The lighting conditions, which are important for object detection in camera images, are good and consistent. For instructions and documentation of the progress Hoerbiger Smartcontrol PDA hand-held terminals (see Figure 1) are used. The unused hand-held terminals are placed on a desk, where they can be charged. Like all other important tools they are located aside the conveyor belt so workers can reach them in short walking distance.

B. Work Tasks

We selected observation and self-exploration as the methods to analyse the current work flow in this division. For observation, we watched workers while they were performing their tasks. We could ask them questions, as long as they were not interrupted in their work flow. For further questions, one employee from the technical plant support and development also was available, standing next to us. After the observation, we shifted to the rework division (located after the final check division) to experience the work on our own without risking to delay the manufacturing process or affecting the production quality by wrong performing. In this division, defects can be corrected. Due to the diversity of issues, the vehicles no longer are standing on a conveyor belt but are parked in a reworking area. We performed one exemplary functional check task flow here. In the following, the context of use and further results of this initial analysis are listed.

The workers perform manual functional checks, like verifying the bearing play of the steering wheel on each vehicle, while the vehicle is connected to an automatic functional test system. Some of the tasks of the automatic functional test system require the worker to collaborate with the system which is displayed on the hand-held device, while others are performed autonomously. Each vehicle is completely checked by one worker who shifts to check the next car when finished with the current one.

To start checking the car, initially the worker scans a bar code which among others is printed on a A4-paper attached to the windscreen. To do so, the worker pushes the scan-button of the hand-held terminal which enables its bar-code-scanner. If the scan was successful, the hand-held terminal requests the according functional checks from the back-end application and displays them in a list. To start one functional test, the worker selects it by pushing the list item on the touch screen, the hand-held terminal requests the work flow. To enable the testing system performing automatic functional checks, the worker connects the car to a test control unit which also is identified by scanning the attached bar-code. After the test control unit was identified and connected successfully, the functional test starts. In the beginning, various automatic tests are performed. This is indicated by black font colour on white background (see Figure 1). The worker is observing the automatic tests until the background changes to yellow. The systems stops performing until the worker executes the requested input (e.g., pushing a switch) or confirms that the test was performed manually by entering the result (i.e., 'OK' or 'not OK', represented by the +/- buttons in Figure 1). While automatic and manual (or collaborative) tasks alternate the worker is moving around and through the car counter-clockwise. After the last test was executed the worker removes the test control unit.

IV. Implementation

For the implementation we defined the requirements on the software solution. Afterwards we designed Mock-Ups which we validated by interviewing five (respectively four) employees of the car manufacturer. Three participants were employees working in the selected division while the other two (respectively one) were engineers of the technical plant support and development. After redesigning our Mock-Ups we developed one prototype.

A. Requirements

For developing an example application instructing the workers using AR, we concluded the following requirements as *must-have*:

a) Replacing the Hand-Held Terminal: The selected HWD shall completely replace the hand-held terminal for the selected tasks. It has to offer all the necessary features to successfully perform complete functional tests. As we aim to evaluate the general usage of AR in this environment and the user feedback, no connection to the test control unit or the back-end-system is needed. It is sufficient to simulate one exemplary functional check.

b) Hands-Free Operation: The biggest disadvantage of hand-held devices is that they blocks at least one of the worker's hand if it is not put aside. To overcome this problem, the application shall be hands-free (as long as no interaction with the device is necessary).

c) Improved Training: While previous projects mainly focused on text-based worker instructions and served as documentation system, in this project we intended to observe the capabilities of AR-ready HWD. We are aiming for using AR to support novice workers in their training phase. For demonstrating this capability some input elements from the cockpit shall be selected. The selection will be made during the development phase.

d) Ease of Operation: Using the application shall be as simple as possible and new users shall be able to use the device quickly.

e) Similar Appearance: To minimise the training phase for experienced workers, the visual design shall follow the visual design of the hand-held terminal application as long as it not requested differently by the participants in the analysis or any evaluation. The existing design shall be used as starting point and be enhanced together with the workers.

f) Bar-Code Scan: The bar-codes shall be scanned by using the HWD's camera to identify the car. As stated above, loading the work flow will be simulated.

g) Interface to Load Work-Flow Data: The application shall be able to interpret XML-based test-files to simulate different work flows.

Within this definition phase we also discussed other requirements. As the project was limited to four months we decided to classify them as *nice-to-have*. These requirements are: 1. *Saving the protocol* to be able to review the single tests. Also, they should be exportable to a computer. 2. *Configure input modalities* should be possible to reconfigure the interaction-concept. This on the one hand would enable the workers to personalise the interaction to their needs and preferences and on the other hand would simplify extending the features of the application. 3. *Offering an exchangeable work flow parser module* to ensure the application to be compatible with future plant control systems. 4. *Extending the use of AR* for more than one training scenario. This can be for example augmenting another task or also superimpose the workers' view with navigational instructions, for example, using arrows to guide them from task to task. 5. *Skilled workers should be enabled to work more independent than novice workers* by adjusting the Graphical User Interface (GUI). Therefore, the application has full access to the camera, it generally is able to detect the execution of tasks, and also to determine the skill level of each worker.

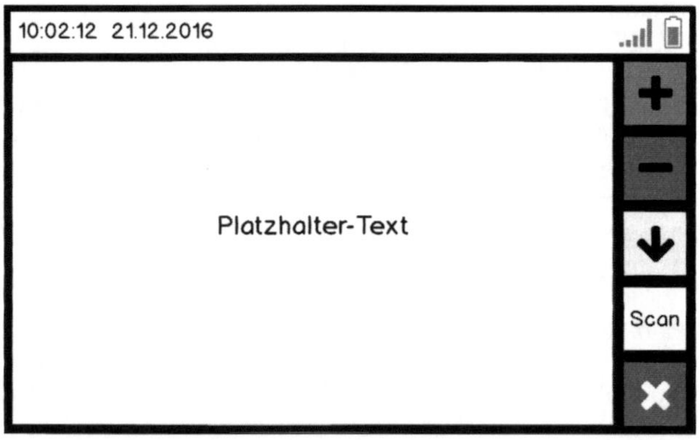

(a) The instruction screen Mock-Up. Buttons and labels follow the design of the original application.

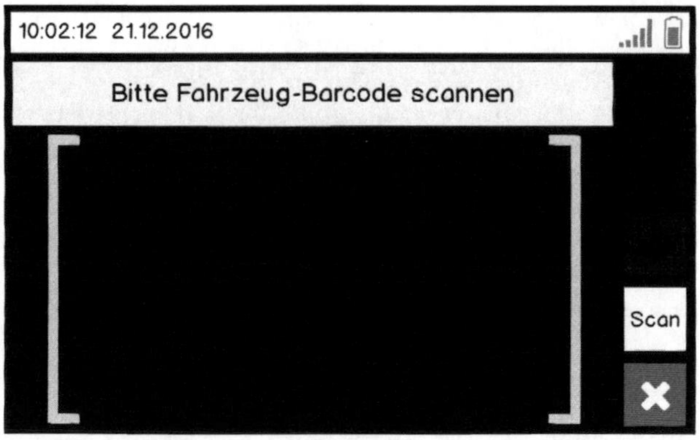

(b) The scanning screen Mock-Up. Unused Buttons are greyed out.

Figure 2. Initial Mock-Ups for both types of screens.

B. Design

Based on the analysis we identified two basic screen layouts. One for scanning tasks, and one for instruction and documentation. We decided to choose a consistent structure for both to reduce the cognitive workload when switching from the instruction screen to the scanner screen. This is based on the assumption that the worker will be able orientate himself/herself faster on two similarly structured screens.

We designed Mock-Ups of both screens as shown in Figure 2. In Figure 2 (a), the instruction screen is displayed containing five interaction elements (Buttons) on the right and a text-area ("Platzhalter-Text") for displaying instructing text. Above that area the date, time, WiFi signal strength and battery load are shown in a status-bar. The scanner screen, shown in Figure 2 (b), also contains the two required interaction elements on the right. The black area on the left is transparent and functions as viewfinder, because we plan to use the camera to scan bar-codes. Above the viewfinder-area the user is instructed to scan the vehicle's bar-code ("Bitte Fahrzeug-Barcode scannen"). On the top again there is the status-bar.

As described in the ISO 9241 - 210 Standard [21] we evaluated the Mock-Ups together with stakeholders (here: workers from the division and the engineering department), which should establish usability and ensures that we, the developers of the application, do not misunderstand the current work-flow or requests by the stakeholders. The Mock-Up evaluation was performed in a conference room located in the same building as the plant. We initially introduced the project idea and the selected HWD to each of the five participants. Also, we offered the participants to stop whenever they feel to do so and clarified that all personal data will be treated confidentially. Some of the participants already participated in a predecessor project where we evaluated the HWD Google Glass XE in the same set-up.

We prepared an icon test to validate the identification of the used icons and all other GUI-elements. The participants were asked to put on the HWD and describe all elements they can see as detailed as possible. Also, they were requested to explain what they think the element stands for. The results of icon test are listed in Table I. Except the *WiFi Signal Strength* icon all elements could be identified as expected. The high identification rate most probably results from reusing the layout of the elements from the hand-held UI.

TABLE I. RESULTS OF THE 'ICON TEST'.

Icon	*Identification Rate*
Date / Time	5/5
WiFi Signal Strength	3/5[a]
Battery Load	5/5
Text Area	5/5
Button *OK*	5/5
Button *Not OK*	5/5
Button *Repeat*	5/5
Button *Scan*	5/5
Button *Cancel*	5/5

[a] Two participants could not identify the icon correctly.

Afterwards we showed the participants 41 screens representing one possible example of a functional check. Each screen was displayed for one second and the participant was asked to stop the forwarding when he/she thinks based on this screen an active action is necessary. He/she then was asked to

TABLE II. RESULTS OF THE QUESTIONNAIRES. [a]

(a) The Mock-Up	*P1*	*P2*	*P3*	*P4*
...is well structured (++) / confusing (--).	++	++	++	++
...offers acceptable (++) / unacceptable (--) Field of View size.	--	++	++	++
...shows instruction text in sufficient (++) / insufficient (--) font size.	++	++	++	++
...does (++) / does not (--) offer all features to fulfil the task efficiently.	++	++	+/-	++
...gives sufficient (++) / insufficient (--) feedback on user input.	++	++	++	++
...does (++) / does not (--) follow a consistent interaction concept.	++	++	++	++
...can be learned in little (++) / long (--) time.	++	+	+	++
...does (++) / does not (--) allow to switch between task easily.	NS	++	+/-	NS
...does not (++) / does (--) force the user the interrupt his work.	-	+	++	-
(b) The Head Worn Display				
...simplifies (++) / impedes (--) orienting in space.	-	--	+/-	+/-
...does not (++) / does (--) show reflections above the display.	--	++	++	++
...is easy (++) / hard (--) to operate.	NS	++	+	++

[a]P = participant, NS = not specified / answer not definite.

describe which action needs to be performed. All screens were classified correctly and the necessary actions were derived.

To gather general information about the structure and appearance of the application and also about critical points (we experienced in previous projects) of the HWD, we handed out questionnaires. We used semantic differential to find out which statements the participants rather agree to. Unfortunately, participant 5 had to leave earlier due to other obligations and could not fill in the questionnaire. Hence, this evaluation phase was performed with four participants. The results, as well as the translated statements of the both questionnaires are presented in Table II. When the answer was not clear we did not count it.

Because we recognised that the first participant did not use the free text section of our questionnaire, we decided to add a short discussion about the Mock-Ups and the questionnaires to find out further details, among others that the bright white text-area stresses the eye. Participants suggested to increase transparency of the area or move the text-area to the top (similar to the scanner screen). Also, switching from near to far distance focus was experienced to result in double vision and for some participants the screen appeared blurry in the upper left corner.

All participants were very open and showed interest in the HWD. Some of them asked questions about the device or compared this experience with the one from Google Glass XE. All agreed that the AR-ready HWD ODG R-7 is more suited to the selected use case.

Based on this evaluation we reviewed our current status and decided to change the GUI-Layout as follows:

- Two participants were not able to identify the WiFi Signal Strength icon, even though this icon already is used in the GUI of the hand-held terminal. We assume that this information is of minor priority for the execution of the work tasks. Hence, we decided to not implement the WiFi Signal Strength icon.
- All five participants stated that the text-area is too big, three even experienced it as disturbing. We decided to move the text-area to the top, similar to the scanner screen (cf. Figure 2 (b)).
- Two participants stated that the upper left corner of the screen is blurry. The manufacturer offers replacement nose-pads for their HWD, which can be bought in different sizes. But still, if the device is not sitting perfectly on the nose, for example because the worker hits it unintentionally, the corners might be blurry again. We concluded that it is better to not display any information in this area. Hence, we decided to centre date, time and battery load in the status-bar.

C. Prototype

To increase to possibilities regarding AR, but also to simplify the manipulation of AR context for future use, we decided to use Unity Editor with the Vuforia AR SDK to implement the application. Another reason for this selection is Vuforia's 'native' support of the selected AR-ready HWD, which among others means that the framework has all necessary specifications to set-up a suitable scene for this particular HWD.

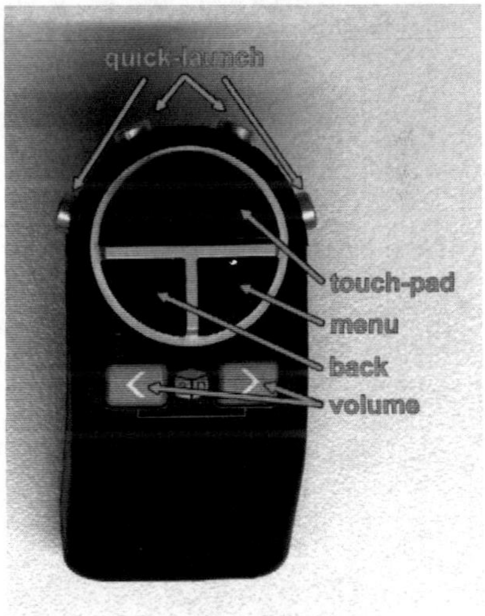

Figure 3. The Reticle Speed Mouse, a finger-worn input-device, with its standard button assignment. The size of the device is about 82 mm * 27 mm * 36 mm and can be put on one finger with the ring-strap on the backside of the device.

In previous projects, we already analysed input modalities of HWDs and their suitability for the context of a factory environment. In the selected environment, there is a moderate noise level randomly interrupted e.g., by floor-borne vehicles passing by. This prevents using voice commands without directed microphones and additional noise cancelling. Also, we did not want to intervene with the cooperative work environment by forcing the workers to talk to devices instead of communicating with the other workers from their group. Finally, most voice command frameworks use servers to analyse the spoken text and send back the transcription. This would require to enable internet access for the HWDs and therefore allow the operator of these servers unrestricted access to any voice close to the HWDs. Due to privacy and confidentiality concerns this currently is not an option.

We also evaluated hand-gesture detection frameworks and concluded that even in the selected environment with very consisted lighting conditions the tracking was too unstable to guarantee a sufficient detection rate. We assume that with a camera-technology which is able to detect depth information the tracking would be stable enough. Unfortunately, the selected HWD 'only' has a high resolution colour camera. Furthermore, non-visual gesture-tracking technologies detecting the muscle tension are available, for example the Thalmic Myo armband. Based on our experience the stability of the tracking with these technologies depends on too many variables (e.g., the skin resistance) to use it in this set-up.

Both devices (the Clicker and the HWD) offer a touch-pad (clickable), a back-button, a menu-button and buttons for increasing and decreasing volume. In addition the Clicker offers 4 quick-launch buttons and a 9-Axis Inertial Measurement Unit (IMU) for 3D gesture detection. These gestures usually require sweeping motions to be detected stably, which is not possible e.g., when sitting on the drivers seat, so we excluded this option. Furthermore, we decided to use the same five buttons on both devices. While a touch-pad click will mark a task as 'OK', clicking the back-button will mark it as 'not OK' and the menu-button will repeat the task. We assigned all buttons in the order of appearance on the GUI (top to down). As shown in Figure 3, the selected buttons on the Clicker are not labelled and as shown in Figure 4 (a) and Figure 4 (b) the labels on the HWD are not visible to the user when wearing the device. Hence, we expect that overwriting their functionality with new ones is not critical. Especially, for the back-button, which can be misinterpreted as repeat button, this is important. Furthermore, the workers will use the device with the developed application only, so they are not confronted with another assignment of these buttons.

(a) Front of the ODG R-7 with the touch-pad. Between the lenses is the camera and above a flash-led.

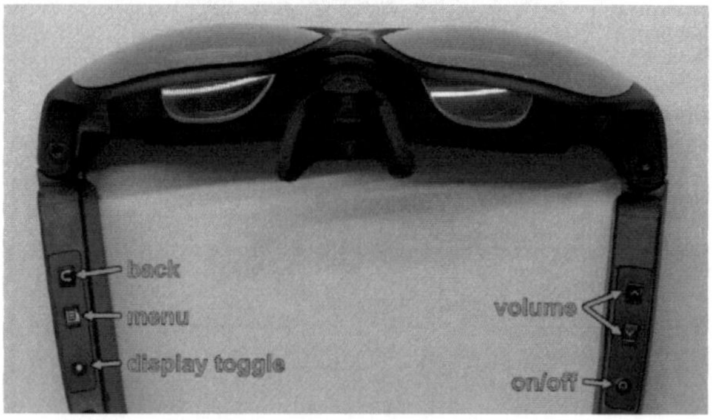

(b) Bottom view of the ODG R-7.

Figure 4. The standard button assignment of the used HWD.

(a) Initial screen. The worker is informed about the key assignment and can start the functional check by pushing the touch-pad either on the HWD or on the finger-worn input-device.

(b) Cancel screen. The worker is asked if he/she really wants to cancel. He/she can confirm by pushing the touch-pad or undo by pushing the back-button either on the HWD or on the finger-worn input-device.

Figure 5. Further Screens of the App-prototype.

Finally, we decided to work with the buttons and the touch-pad of HWD and a 'Clicker', a finger-worn input-device (cf. Figure 3). We are aware of the potential disruptive character of the Clicker, but compared to a hand-held it does not occupy the whole hand and here it serves as mean to compare direct interaction and remote interaction with the HWD.

We decided to use long click on the menu-button ('repeat') for cancelling the task (as depicted in Figure 7). Furthermore, we recognised that we never need the scan function when a functional check is performed and also do not need the mark as 'OK'/'not OK' function outside of the checks. We decided to reuse the menu-button for scanning.

TABLE III. RESULTS OF THE EVALUATION OF THE PROTOTYPE. [a]

Question	*P1*	*P2*	*P3*	*P4*
Do you understand the interaction concept of the HWD on the start screen?	no[b]	yes	yes	yes
Do you understand the interaction concept of the finger-worn input-device on the start screen?	yes	yes	yes	yes
During automatic tests: Do you see all icons and understand what they mean?	yes	yes	no[c]	yes
Can you cancel the tests by long pressing the 'repeat'-button?	yes	yes	yes	yes
AR: Do you see the green arrow?	yes	yes	yes	yes
AR: Does the arrow point on the right element?	no[d]	no[d]	no[d]	no[d]
AR: Is the arrow displayed double?	yes	yes	yes	yes
Please rank which of the devices you would prefer working with. [e]	2,3,1	3,2,1	1,2,3	3,2,1

[a] P = participant, [b] "Problems to find 'repeat'-button", [c] "Wearer of corrective glasses, Field of View of the HWD too low", [d] "Only after closing the left eye", [e] "1 = hand-held terminal, 2 = AR-ready HWD, 3 = AR-ready HWD + hand-held controller

To finish the program flow, we added two screens: One informing the workers about the key assignment and enabling them to start the tests (cf. Figure 5 (a)) and the other one to confirm cancellation of the test (cf. Figure 5 (b)).

As stated above, we also wanted to explore the potential of AR in this set-up. As a first step we selected four buttons of the dashboard (Figure 6). These have been selected, because they are standard elements of the passenger compartment. Hence, they are available in all vehicles manufactured in this manufacturing line.

We experimented with the tracking capabilities of the Vuforia Augmented Reality SDK. Our first attempt was to take a photo of the selected buttons and use it as a so called image target for the image feature detection algorithm of the SDK. Due to the mainly black appearance, we did not manage to get stable detection, even when using a high resolution camera. Second, we dismounted the whole dashboard element to scan it with the Vuforia Object Scanner Smart phone application, which generates a point cloud. Because we only needed the front of the element and we were not able to remove unneeded points we could not apply this technology as well. Last loading a 3D-Object provided by the car manufacturer currently is not possible with the selected framework. Hence, we decided to put an image target ('Vuforia-Stones') above the buttons and adjust the position of the arrow to point on each button as shown in Figure 7. We are aware that this is not an applicable solution for everyday business, but it gives an impression of what AR-support might look like in future systems.

V. EVALUATION

To evaluate the prototype, we focussed on three factors. First, we wanted to investigate if the GUI and its elements, especially those we changed, are interpreted correctly. Second, the selected input concept could not be tested with workers by now, even though it is an important factor. The focus here is on the interaction with the HWD and the finger-worn input-device and whether the introduction of the key assignment on the start screen (cf. Figure 5 (a)) is sufficient or not. Third, we simulated an actual functional check to allow testing whether the selected HWD is suitable for supporting workers. Also, we wanted to test how the workers respond on the AR support.

We simulated one functional check in the reworking area. Four workers from the initial start-up and functional check division volunteered, two of them were already participating in the design evaluation-phase. We introduced the HWD and the general usage, especially to those participants who did not work with it before, followed by the purpose of the evaluation and the planned procedure. Also, we informed the participants that all personal data will be treated confidently and that they can cancel the evaluation whenever they want.

Figure 6. The selected element of the passenger compartment: Buttons in the dashboard.

The evaluation was split in two parts. In the first part, we handed out the HWD only and asked the participants to put it on. They were asked to describe how they understand the instructions (i.e., the key assignment) shown on the start screen and then start the functional check (by pushing the touch-pad). While the automatic tests were simulated the participants were asked to describe the elements on the screen to verify that they could identify all of them correctly. When a manual or collaborative task was displayed the participants were asked to start performing it. The participants could not perform the tasks completely as they were working on a real vehicle which already was tested and set up completely. When an AR supported screen was displayed we furthermore investigated the visibility of the AR content (arrow, cf. Figure 7). In the second part, we gave the Clicker to the participants and asked them to do the test again. We did not further investigate on the GUI or the AR feature. The purpose of part two only was to experience the usage of the finger-worn input-device (representing "close to the body-interaction).

The results are listed in Table III. Summed up, we found out that the selected HWD might cause problems for spectacle wearers. This is a very common problem with this kind of devices as two glasses have to fit on each other. Especially, wider spectacle frames lead to problems. Furthermore, all participants could not instantly perceive the 3D object correctly. They saw it duplicated and on the wrong position. Based on our own experience this issue is solved after a longer period of use, when the users get used to this new experience. It is important to be aware that this also temporarily can cause eye pain, headaches and other symptoms due to the strain on the eyes, which should be taken serious. The wrong positioning also can be a result from displacing the image target slightly.

In a short discussion with each participant, directly after finishing the two parts, we asked for their impressions and points of critique. Also, we asked them for ranking which of the three possibilities they would prefer for their daily work: The hand-held terminal, the HWD or the HWD with the Clicker. The ranking is shown in Table III. Three of four participants prefer the HWD or the combination of HWD and finger-worn input-device over the Hand-held terminal. Only participant 3 prefers the hand-held terminal, most likely due to the issues he/she had with the HWD and his/her corrective glasses, which he/she emphasised in the following discussion. As in previous projects (with other HWDs) the participants pointed out that having both hands free to perform their tasks is a great facilitation. Furthermore, we got the following feedback: All participants stated that the display is too bright.

Figure 7. An overlay from an App screen-shot on a picture of the used image target ('Vuforia-Stones') attached to the vehicle's dashboard, to demonstrate what the worker sees through the HWD.

One participant suggested to not use background colours but only colouring the test white and yellow and reducing the button size. One participant suggested to move the keys to the left temple of the HWD. One participant was concerned about confusing the OS-'back'-button and the application-'repeat'-button, i.e., the key assignment. About the finger-worn input-device one participant said that might damage the car and another participant stated that pushing a button unintentionally is very likely. Two of the four participant stated that the image of the HWD dangles when walking. Also, two of the four said using the device tires the arms and puts a high strain to the nose and head, due to its high weight of about 175 g. This is why the participants doubt that they can use the HWD a whole work shift (8 h). One participant suggested to try head gestures to interact with the HWD.

VI. CONCLUSION

In this project, we developed an application for work instruction and documentation in the initial start-up and functional check division of a car manufacturing line of a big German car manufacturer. This prototype included an AR feature simplifying the guidance for the workers. We followed the Human Centred Design Approach as defined in ISO 9241 - 210 [21]. The prototype was evaluated by four participants working in this division. The aim of the project was to develop a proof-of-concept. A study with more participants is pending to gather quantitative data verifying the presented results and potentially reveal further perspectives on the prototype.

While the design of the application was easy to understand for all participants, some problems with the selected HWD occurred. Wearers of corrective glasses can be limited in the usage of this device. Also, we found out that while two-dimensional GUIs do not cause bigger problems for the users, three-dimensional objects (for the AR feature) could not be perceived adequately. All four participants stated that the selected object is not placed correctly and reported double vision. During our work with the device, we found out that these symptoms disappear when the eyes learn to focus on the objects, but this risks causing eye strain. Except one participant, who struggled with the combination of the HWD and his/her own glasses, all participants selected the HWD over the hand-held terminal. Two out of these three participants preferred input via an additional finger-worn input-device while one preferred input via the buttons of the HWD itself.

Participants who already took part in the evaluation of a HWD not capable of supporting AR in the same division stated that the AR-ready HWD is more suited for this use case. Also, even though all four participants struggled with the AR feature and limits of the selected AR framework all participants responded positively to this feature.

Furthermore, testing the finger-worn input-device gave us some insights on potentials and limits of "close to the body"-interaction in this use case: If tailored to the use case, interaction with different types of systems could be facilitated. To not disrupt work-flows the interaction either should not require any hardware to be worn, be based on hardware which can be worn unobtrusively or be in-cooperated in the workers clothes. We aim to explore this device type for use cases like the one described in this paper in future work.

REFERENCES

[1] F. Lamberti et al., "Challenges, Opportunities, and Future Trends of Emerging Techniques for Augmented Reality-Based Maintenance," IEEE Transactions on Emerging Topics in Computing, vol. 2, no. 4, 12 2014, pp. 411–421.

[2] Vuzix Corporation, "Vuzix Wins SBIR Phase II Award from the Office of Naval Research," Vuzix Corporation, Tech. Rep., 2014.

[3] I. E. Sutherland, "A head-mounted three dimensional display," in Proceedings of the December 9-11, 1968, fall joint computer conference, part I on - AFIPS '68 (Fall, part I), no. Fall, part I. New York, New York, USA: ACM Press, 1968, p. 757.

[4] Volkswagen AG. Volkswagen rolls out 3D smart glasses as standard equipment. Accessed 09/01/2019. [Online]. Available: www.volkswagenag.com/en/news/2015/11/3D_smart_glasses.htm

[5] Opel Automobile GmbH. Smart Helpers. Accessed 09/01/2019. [Online]. Available: opelpost.com/02/2017/smart-helpers/

[6] G. Meixner, N. Petersen, and H. Koessling, "User interaction evolution in the SmartFactoryKL," Proceedings of the 24th BCS Interaction Specialist Group Conference, 2010, pp. 211–220.

[7] M. Kleiber, T. Alexander, C. Winkelholz, and C. M. Schlick, "User-centered design and evaluation of an integrated AR-VR system for tele-maintenance," in 2012 IEEE International Conference on Systems, Man, and Cybernetics (SMC). IEEE, 10 2012, pp. 1443–1448.

[8] S. Rauh, D. Zsebedits, E. Tamplon, S. Bolch, and G. Meixner, "Using Google Glass for mobile maintenance and calibration tasks in the AUDI A8 production line," in 2015 IEEE 20th Conference on Emerging Technologies & Factory Automation (ETFA), vol. 2015-Octob. IEEE, 9 2015, pp. 1–4.

[9] F. Loch, F. Quint, and I. Brishtel, "Comparing video and augmented reality assistance in manual assembly," in Proceedings - 12th International Conference on Intelligent Environments, IE 2016. IEEE, 9 2016, pp. 147–150.

[10] J. Servan, F. Mas, J. L. Menendez, and J. Rios, "Using augmented reality in AIRBUS A400M shop floor assembly work instructions," in AIP Conf. Proc. 1431. the American Institute of Physics, 2012, pp. 633–640.

[11] G. M. Re and M. Bordegoni, "An Augmented Reality Framework for Supporting and Monitoring Operators during Maintenance Tasks," in Virtual, Augmented and Mixed Reality. Applications of Virtual and Augmented Reality: 6th International Conference, VAMR 2014, Held as Part of HCI International 2014, Heraklion, Crete, Greece, June 22-27, 2014, Proceedings, Part II, R. Shumaker and S. Lackey, Eds. Cham: Springer International Publishing, 2014, pp. 443–454.

[12] P. Tschirner, B. Hillers, and A. Graser, "A concept for the application of augmented reality in manual gas metal arc welding," in Proceedings. International Symposium on Mixed and Augmented Reality. IEEE Comput. Soc, 2002, pp. 257–258.

[13] D. Kerpen et al, "Effects of cyber-physical production systems on human factors in a weaving mill: Implementation of digital working environments based on augmented reality," in 2016 IEEE International Conference on Industrial Technology (ICIT). IEEE, 3 2016, pp. 2094–2098.

[14] I. Wijesooriya, D. Wijewardana, T. De Silva, and C. Gamage, "Demo Abstract: Enhanced Real-Time Machine Inspection with Mobile Augmented Reality for Maintenance and Repair," in 2017 IEEE/ACM Second International Conference on Internet-of-Things Design and Implementation (IoTDI), Pittsburgh, PA, USA, 2017, pp. 287–288.

[15] I. Maly, D. Sedlacek, and P. Leitao, "Augmented reality experiments with industrial robot in industry 4.0 environment," in IEEE International Conference on Industrial Informatics (INDIN). IEEE, 7 2017, pp. 176–181.

[16] W. Friedrich, "ARVIKA-augmented reality for development, production and service," in Proceedings. International Symposium on Mixed and Augmented Reality. IEEE Comput. Soc, 2002, pp. 3–4.

[17] M. Eissele, O. Siemoneit, and T. Ertl, "Transition of Mixed, Virtual, and Augmented Reality in Smart Production Environments - An Interdisciplinary View," in 2006 IEEE Conference on Robotics, Automation and Mechatronics. IEEE, 12 2006, pp. 1–6.

[18] V. Paelke, "Augmented reality in the smart factory: Supporting workers in an industry 4.0. environment," in Proceedings of the 2014 IEEE Emerging Technology and Factory Automation (ETFA). IEEE, 9 2014, pp. 1–4.

[19] R. Poelman, O. Akman, S. Lukosch, and P. Jonker, "As if being there," Proceedings of the ACM 2012 conference on Computer Supported Cooperative Work - CSCW '12, no. 5, 2012, p. 1267.

[20] T. Mentler, H. Berndt, and M. Herczeg, "Optical Head-Mounted Displays for Medical Professionals: Cognition-supporting Human-Computer Interaction Design," Proceedings of the European Conference on Cognitive Ergonomics, 2016, p. 26:126:8.

[21] Ergonomics of human-system interaction – Part 210: Human-centred design for interactive systems. ISO 9241-210:2010. Geneva, Switzerland: ISO, 2010.

A User Centered Design Roadmap for Researchers and Designers Working with Visually Impaired and Blind Children

Zainab AlMeraj
Information Science Department
Kuwait University
Adailiya, Kuwait
Email: z.almeraj@ku.edu.kw

Asmaa Alsumait
Computer Engineering Department
Kuwait University
Khaldiya, Kuwait
Email: asmaa.alsumait@ku.edu.kw

***Abstract*— Today, user-centered design has become an essential and successful practice to design interactive systems. With the growing acknowledgment of the importance of universal usability and the need for influencing designs, User-Centered Design (UCD) ought to be structured to adapt its methodologies to the needs and requirements of people with disabilities. This paper is preliminary research that identifies the most relevant UCD methods, needs and best practices for working with Visually Impaired and Blind (VIB) children. We start by reviewing UCD methods and identify those that are most suitable for VIB children. We then propose a UCD process for VIB children and discuss how they apply with respect to needs, requirements and abilities of VIB children.**

Keywords- User centered design; Visually impaired and blind child ; Participatory design; E-learning system

I. INTRODUCTION

User-Centered Design (UCD) is a collection of processes and techniques that emphasize putting users at the center of product design and development. It considers user's requirements, needs, objectives and feedback. The Usability Professionals Association (UPA) [1] formally defines UCD as an approach to design that grounds the process in information about the people who use the product.

According to Carr et al. [2], in User-Design users are engaged in the actual creation of their own systems in negotiation with leaders and designers; meanwhile in User-Centered Design overall control remains in the hands of designers and approval power remains with leadership. We believe that by involving users at each phase of the development process, the end product will respond to their characteristics and, therefore, provide end-users with a positive experience and better usability.

In comparison to their counterparts, children with visual disabilities have entirely different ways to structure, order, and perceive the world, assuming a singular mental model quite distinct from sighted children. Children with non-visual mental models have to cope with devices designed for children with visual mental models. Even though interactive systems designed for sighted children go through a rigorous UCD process, it does not mean that they meet the needs of non-sighted children. This is a major issue affecting both usability and accessibility. Lots of UCD research exists for VIB adults, such as those surveyed by Sahib et al. [3], however there is very little addressing VIB children [4]-[7].

This research proposes revising the UCD process to be adapted to VIB children by identifying their needs and requirements, and then highlighting appropriate methods and best practices that cater to them. The paper is organized as follows: Section II gives a review of UCD and research with children and VIB children. Section III highlights the requirements and needs of VIB children and the UCD methods most appropriate for them. Section IV proposes a refined UCD process for VIB children. And finally, in Section V, we conclude with the summary and potential future research.

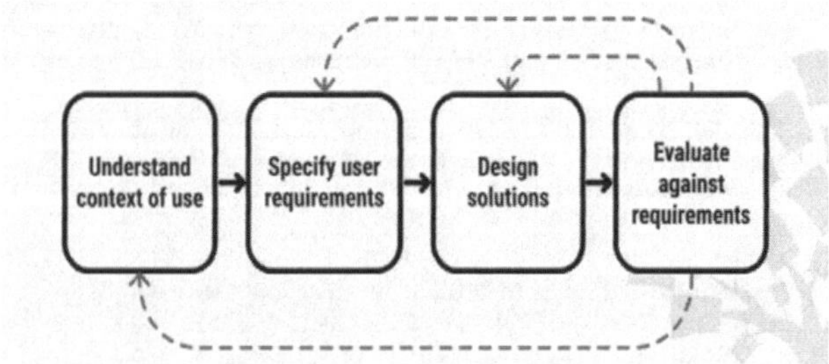

Figure 1. The Iterative Process UCD (ISO 9241-210) [47].

II. RELATED WORK

In this section we summarize methods found in literature used to implement UCD in general, with children and those used more specifically with VIB children.

A. *User Centered Design*

UCD is design that is based around real user requirements, and typically involves task analysis, prototype development with users, evaluation, and iterative design [8]. Devi et al. [9] defined UCD as a framework in which usability goals, user characteristics, environment, tasks and workflow of a product, service or process are given extensive attention at each stage of a design process.

According to ISO 9241-210, the UCD approach shown in Figure 1 takes into account the user's abilities, limitations and context in which the user operates to ensure the design of usable and accessible products [8][10]. As illustrated in Figure 1, each iteration of the UCD process involves four distinct phases. The complete process includes multiple iterations of these four phases, until evaluation results are satisfactory, and all requirements have been met:

1. Understanding the context of use: gathering requirements.
2. Requirements specification - specifying the user and organizational requirements
3. Design - Producing designs, prototypes and solutions
4. Evaluation - Carrying out user-based assessment of the site and test need satisfaction against user specific contexts.

To implement User-Centered Design a myriad of methods have been adopted. Some methods are investigative in nature (e.g., surveys and interviews) while others are generative (e.g., brainstorming) [8][10]-[12]. A summarized list of UCD methods and the UCD stage they are appropriate for are shown in the first and second columns of Table 1.

The context in which UCD methods are applied can differ depending on the target audience and system being developed. To identify several areas of interface improvement for the user interface of a Hazard Service system, Argyle et al. [13], conducted usability testing on experienced forecasting professionals via web-based tasks and a questionnaire. Meanwhile, in an attempt to maximize patient engagement Wachtler et al. [14] employed focus groups and semi-structured interviews in the design of a clinical depression prediction tool that will be incorporated into routine clinical practice. To design a preference-based family planning decision system Stevens et al. [15] used focus groups, qualitative surveys and evaluation measures. Couture et al. [16] adopted scenarios and usability testing in designing a safety-reporting tool for hospitalized patients and their family members. To enhance IoT wearable systems, Bernal et al. [17] identified contextual needs and iterative interviews to reach safer environments in energy companies. With futuristic goals in mind, Eggen et al. [18], used similar UCD methods to achieve seamless integration of user experiences in smart homes. In the following sections we explain why UCD method choices differ when the target audience is younger in age.

B. *User-centered Design with Children*

Since 2002 there has been more interest in involving children in the design process to which some have expressed as a complex process [19]-[21]. Nesset et al. [22] argue that there are more advantages than disadvantages of including children in the design process. But the issues is not *including* them, it is more to do with engaging them in the process according to Rogers et al. [23]. This engagement can take on multiple forms, each with various dimensions: user, tester, informant or design partner [24]. Schepers et al. [25] for instance, look at the role of children in participatory design as a co-designer and not just a participant. While Sims [26] looks at how children can be an advantage when incorporated in the design process of healthcare technologies.

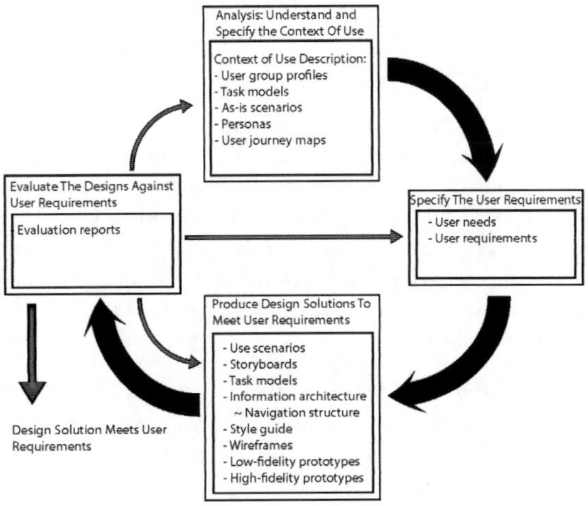

Figure 2. User Centered Design process according to ISO 9241-210.

In education through gaming, Gelderblom [27][28] finds that in spite of involving younger children in the design of a web based educational game using well-tested techniques; participatory design successfully meets the requirements. Despite not having fully developed language skills, the participation of children in UCD has been successful, encourages creativity and offers many opportunities.

C. *User-centered Design for VIB children*

It can be problematic for designers to exclusively depend on their expertise to correctly imagine the needs of a normal end user. Designers depend on UCD methods to better understand the end users' needs. Moreover, it is more challenging for the designers to make sure that they effectively understand the difficulties and obstacles VIB end user faces while interacting with interfaces. In order to create usable and accessible products for visually impaired children (VIB), it is essential to include them in all stages of the development process. Mattheiss et al. [5]-[7] highlight the problem of having many existing participatory design attempts for visually impaired adults as opposed to very few involving children. Bateman et al. [29] successfully incorporated UCD to VIB students in the design of an electrostatic haptic touchscreen, resulting in a noticeably high percentage of accuracy

The inclusionary model for involving impaired children in the design process defines different levels of involvement (user, tester, informant, design partner) as well as severity of disability [30]. The Children in the Center framework by Kärnä et al. [31] suggests the need for participation of children, families, and researchers. Some participatory design methods suggest workshops comprising of both blind and sighted people together, were sighted participants are blindfolded to experience and subsequently discuss problems blind participants have to face [4]. Mattheiss et al. [7] discussed lessons learned regarding approaches and issues with multiple UCD methods used with VIB children.

III. VIB CHILDREN'S REQUIREMENTS AND NEEDS

In a dialogue system there is almost no difference in using interfaces between sighted and VIB user. However, in case of graphical user interfaces special needs and requirements of VIB child should be considered. In this section special requirements and needs of the tools and user interface features used by VIB children are presented. Later a recommended, semantically, and blind-friendly adaptive user centered design is proposed.

A. VIB Requirements and Needs

1. Information access is sequential [32]. At any given point, VIB users perceive only a snippet of the content and often lose contextual information.
2. No rendition of graphics [33]. VIB users cannot perceive or interpret information communicated through images, color, and layout.
3. Quick information scan is not possible [34]. VIB users cannot locate goal-relevant information efficiently and easily by scanning information.
4. Keyboard-based [35]. VIB users cannot use functionality that requires mouse input.
5. Complex layouts create problems. When Web pages have a complex layout, screen readers feedback becomes ambiguous [32]. Screen-readers also mispronounce many words according to Theofanos and Redish [36] which creates comprehension problems for the VIB user.
6. Requires learning complex interface. VIB interaction requires memorizing hundreds of key commands [36]. The wide range of screen-reader functionality makes it more difficult for VIB users to remember and use appropriate functions for effective Web interaction.
7. Higher cognitive load. Cognitive resources must be split, trying to understand the browser, the screen reader, and content [36]. This leads to greater cognitive burden for VIB users on the Web [37][38].

VIB individuals are particularly dependent on their hearing and tactile senses. Adapting a graphical user interface for blind people involves some specific usability requirements:

1. The task has to be adequate given the capabilities of blind users (task adequacy),
2. The user interface has to provide a balance between the 2D access of sighted people and the 1D access of blind people (dimensional trade-off),
3. The user interface has to provide specific access to all the relevant user interface objects (behavior equivalence), for blind people
4. The user interface has to avoid losing relevant semantic information (semantic loss avoidance), &
5. The interface has to deal with a wide variation in the functionality and programming of the assistive technologies for blind people (device-independency).

B. Recommended UCD methods for VIB

The UCD framework for VIB should be dependent upon feedback gathered in the form of interviews with assistive device experts, as well as preliminary tests with visual impaired users. There is a need to select suitable UCD methods for VIB students and adapt them according to the situation (e.g., verbalization of ongoing processes in the moderation of workshops, allowing students to note down text on their devices, with assistive technology instead of posters or sticky notes). Table 1 illustrates the UCD methods, which phase they can be used, whether or not they can be used with the VIB, whether they are suitable for children and whether they are recommended for the proposed UCD for VIB children.

TABLE 1. RECOMMEBDED UCD METHODS FOR VIB CHILDREN

UCD Method	*UCD Phase*	*Suitable for VIB*	*Suitable for child*	*Recommended*
User survey questionnaire	Understanding the context of use	Y	Y	Y
Interviews	Understanding the context of use	Y	Y	Y
Contextual inquiry/interview	Understanding the context of use	Y	Y	Y
User observation/field study	Understanding the context of use	Y	Y	Y
Analyze context of use	Requirements specification	Y	Y	Y
Focus group (requirements)	Understanding the context of use/ Requirement specification	Y	M	M
Brainstorming	Requirements specification	Y	Y	Y
Evaluate existing system	Requirements gathering & specification	Y	Y	Y
Card sorting	Requirements specification	N	Y	N
Affinity diagramming	Requirements specification	N	Y	N
Scenarios of use	Requirements specification	M	M	M

Use cases	Requirements specification	N	N	N
Task analysis (analytical)	Requirements specification	N	N	N
Set usability goals	Requirements specification	Y	M	M
Storyboarding	Requirements specification	N	Y	N
Low fidelity prototype	Requirements specification	N	Y	N
High fidelity prototype	Design	Y	Y	Y
Wizard of Oz	Design	N	N	N
Conceptual models	Design	N	N	N
Participatory design	Design	Y	Y	Y
Heuristic Evaluation (HE)	Design/ Evaluation	N	N	N
Design walkthrough	Evaluation	Y	Y	Y
Usability Testing	Evaluation	Y	Y	Y

To understand why some of the UCD methods listed are recommended in VIB child research we offer the following descriptions:

1. **Participatory design with VIB children** can be challenging, as designers have to ensure their methods of communicating design ideas and feedback with users are appropriate and effective [39].
2. **Low and high fidelity prototyping** is a common way of brainstorming design ideas with users, but for VIB children visual prototyping techniques are not appropriate. Therefore, alternatives have been proposed: Brewster et al. [40] describe haptic paper prototypes that use cardboard mockups, and Miao et al. [41] describe a tactile paper prototyping approach using Braille and tactile graphic mockups.
3. **User survey questionnaires** are classic investigation tools [42]. Implementation can be based on individual comprehension level and tailored to needs using either braille-based or Web-based surveys. With the increasing uses of technology, meeting accessibility standards of web-based versions should be considered to ensure text is focused, presented correctly, and is well organized.
4. **Interviews & contextual inquiry/interviews** are powerful design and requirement gathering tools. They can be administered structured or semi-structured and adjusted to suit the VIB child's cognitive level and education. Investigations into user's environments might help elicit specific data that may otherwise not be considered [43].
5. **User observation/field study** witnessing users in specific contexts and/or environments is as powerful as contextual inquiries. By observing VIB children in action researchers can immediately identify problems with completion of specific tasks, identify frustrations while using tools and recognize things that work more efficiently. Pointers drawn from observations regardless of their numbers are key to successful design.
6. **Brainstorming.** Although tricky to implement effectively with VIB children, brainstorming sessions can result in a myriad of preferences, needs and direction for further product and application designs [44]. Sharing visuals, conveying hand gestures, and information gaps between participants are some of the concepts to keep in mind before running such sessions.
7. **Design walkthroughs** Creativity is key when attempting to run design walkthroughs with VIB children. Abate et al. [45] recommended using suitable tools to convey design and incorporating storytelling or game play into the process to keep children aware and engaged.
8. **Usability testing and evaluation** is one of the best tools to recognize problems and points of frustration for users [46]. Being in a room with a VIB child and using a master apprentice model for example, can help researchers identify needs versus extras and ease of use issues. In addition, usability testing offers the option of comparing two designs in one session, which can help reduce the number of sessions needed. However, recruitment of participants willing to sit in hour-long sessions is difficult for these evaluations.

IV. UCD PROCESS FOR VIB CHILDREN

The User-Centered Design process is made up of a set of iterative activities that result in a final design that meets all the user requirements, as shown in Figure 2. The process includes collecting feedback from the initial stages to the very end, beginning with analysis, specifying the user requirements, producing design solutions and evaluation in addition to iterative cycles of all phases until the design is complete.

However, as shown previously, when designing for VIB children it is important to modify the UCD process to cater for their needs and requirements. The proposed UCD VIB child-friendly process, shown in Figure 3, has been refined to include recommended methods from Section III.

To understand context of use during the analysis phase of working with VIB children, we recommend adopting a user survey questionnaire, contextual inquiry/interviews, or user observations and field studies.

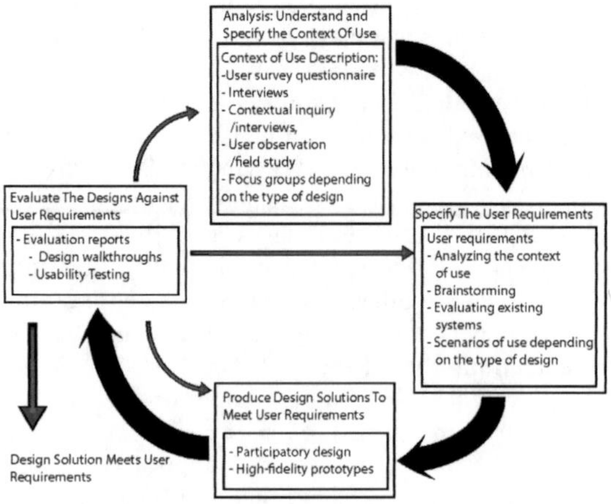

Figure 3. User centered Design adapted to a VIB Child user.

VIB children are more likely to convey opinion and ideas through speech rather than on paper, and through semi-structured interviews instead of structured ones. As for specifying user requirements, methods like analyzing the context of use, and depending on the type of design, brainstorming and scenarios of use have a higher chance of acquiring needs as opposed to other methods. Again, here we notice verbal methods are more effective in acquiring needs and requirements.

Iterative design process phase with VIB children will benefit from methods, such as participatory design and high-fidelity prototypes and heuristic evaluations only if applied by experts. Participatory design methods are popular when designing with children. The need to engage a VIB child in the design process and communicate the design ideas to them has to be in a form accessible to them. This can be achieved successfully using scenarios and dialogue interactions [3].

Once complete, the evaluation phase for VIB children includes usability testing and design walkthrough methods. Watching and listening to VIB children using design evaluation methods can be very rewarding if done correctly and with clearly set goals.

V. CONCLUSION AND FUTURE WORK

User involvement in the design process for VIB children is crucial for effective interactive interfaces. The proposed UCD process recognizes VIB child specific needs, requirements, abilities, and accordingly recommends the most suitable UCD methods. The ultimate goal is always to deliver successful systems that are easy to use and satisfy user needs and help motivate VIB child live more independently in their everyday lives. The process also ensures that the design and development teams remain focused upon the key users they are designing for, the VIB child. For future work we will conduct experiments to determine the feasibility and validity of the recommended VIB-UCD methods.

References

1. UPA Usability Professionals Association: https://uxpa.org/ [retrieved: December, 2018]
2. Carr, "User-design in the creation of human learning systems. Educational Technology Research and Development", Journal of Educational Technology Research and Development, 45(3), 5-22, 1997. DOI 10.1007/BF02299726 [retrieved: Dec, 2018]
3. N. G. Sahib, T. Stockman, A. Tombros, and O. Metatla, "Participatory design with blind users: A scenario-based approach", in: Human-Computer Interaction INTERACT, in: LNCS, vol. 8117, 2013, pp. 685–701, 2013. [retrieved: Dec, 2018]
4. M. Okamoto, "Possibility of participatory design", First International Conference on Human Centered Design HCD 2009, in: LNCS, vol.5619, pp. 888–893, 2009. [retrieved: Dec, 2018]
5. J. McElligott, and L. Van Leeuwen, "Designing sound tools and toys for blind and visually impaired children", In *Proceedings of the 2004 ACM conference on Interaction design and children: building a community* pp. 65-72, 2004. [retrieved: Dec, 2018]
6. L. Kuiper-Hoyng, R. Willems, and S. Schultz, "Involving blind children in the codesign of a Wii game", in: Paper for CHI-Sparks conference, 2011. [retrieved: Dec, 2018]
7. E. Mattheiss, G. Regal, D. Sellitsch, and M. Tscheligi, User-centred design with visually impaired pupils: A case study of a game editor for orientation and mobility training. International Journal of Child-Computer Interaction, 11, 12-18, 2017. [retrieved: Dec, 2018]
8. H. Thimbleby, "Understanding user centred design (UCD) for people with special needs", In *International Conference on Computers for Handicapped Persons*, Springer, Berlin, Heidelberg, pp. 1-17, 2008. [retrieved: Dec, 2018]
9. Kh. Rekha Devi, A. M. Sen, and K. Hemachandran "A working Framework for the User-Centered Design Approach and a Survey of the available Methods", International Journal of Scientific and Research Publications, Volume 2, Issue 4, April 2012. ISSN 2250-3153. [retrieved: Dec, 2018]
10. N. Bevan, "UsabilityNet methods for user centred design", *Human-Computer Interaction: theory and Practice*, *1*, 434-438, 2003. [retrieved: Dec, 2018]
11. K. Vredenburg, J. Y. Mao, P. W. Smith, and T. Carey, "A survey of user-centered design practice", In *Proceedings of the ACM SIGCHI conference on Human factors in computing systems*. pp. 471-478, 2002. [retrieved: Dec, 2018]
12. Y. Matas, C. Santos, F. Hernández-del-Olmo, and E. Gaudioso, "Involving teachers, parents and rehabilitation instructors in visual training for visually impaired children: A web-based approach", *International Journal of Child-Computer Interaction*, vol. *11*, pp. 83-89, 2017. [retrieved: Dec, 2018]
13. E. M. Argyle, J. J. Gourley, and Z. L. Flamig, T. Hansen, and K. Manross, "Toward a User-Centered Design of a Weather Forecasting Decision-Support Tool", Bulletin of the American Meteorological Society, Volume 98 (2), pp. 373—382, 2016. [retrieved: Dec, 2018]
14. C. Wachtler, A. Coe, S. Davidson, S. Fletcher, A. Mendoza, L. Sterling, and J. Gunn, "Development of a Mobile Clinical Prediction Tool to Estimate Future Depression Severity and Guide Treatment in Primary Care: User-Centered Design", JMIR Mhealth Uhealth. 2018 Apr; 6(4): e95. [retrieved: Dec, 2018]
15. G. Stevens, K. Z. Donnelly, R. N. Theiler, H. Washburn, E. J. Woodhams, V. Lindahl, and R. Thompson, "(Family) planning ahead: user-centered design of the birth control after pregnancy patient decision aid and protocol for delivery and evaluation", Contraception, Volume 96, Issue 4, 2017, Page 289, ISSN 0010-7824, https://doi.org/10.1016/j.contraception.2017.07.103 [retrieved: Dec, 2018]
16. B. Couture, E. Lilley, F. Chang, A. DeBord Smith, J. Cleveland, A. Ergai, Z. Katsulis, J. Benneyan, E. Gershanik, D. W. Bates, and S. A. Collins, "Applying User-Centered Design Methods to the Development of an mHealth Application for Use in the Hospital

Setting by Patients and Care Partners", Applied Clinical Informatics, Appl Clin Inform 2018; 09(02): 302-312, DOI: 10.1055/s-0038-1645888 [retrieved: Dec, 2018]

17. G. Bernal, S. Colombo, M. Al Ai Baky, and F. Casalegno, "Safety++: Designing IoT and Wearable Systems for Industrial Safety through a User Centered Design Approach", In Proceedings of the 10th International Conference on PErvasive Technologies Related to Assistive Environments (PETRA '17). ACM, New York, NY, USA, pp. 163-170, 2017. DOI: https://doi.org/10.1145/3056540.3056557 [retrieved: Dec, 2018]
18. B. Eggen, E. van den Hoven, and J. Terken, "Human-Centered Design and Smart Homes: How to Study and Design for the Home Experience?" Handbook of Smart Homes, Health Care and Well-Being, Springer International Publishing, pp. 83—92, 2017. [retrieved: Dec, 2018]
19. A. Bruckman, and A. Bandlow, "Human-computer interaction for kids", The human-computer interaction handbook. pp. 428-440L. Erlbaum Associates Inc.,2003. [retrieved: Dec, 2018]
20. W. Sluis-Thiescheffer, T. Bekker, and B. Eggen, "Comparing early design methods for children", Proceedings of IDC'07. pp. 17-24 ACM, Aalborg, Denmark, 2007. [retrieved: Dec, 2018]
21. J. A. Fails, M. L. Guha, and A. Druin, "Methods and techniques for involving children in the design of new technology for children", *Foundations and Trends® in Human–Computer Interaction*, *6*(2), 85-166, 2013. [retrieved: Dec, 2018]
22. V. Nesset and A. Large, "Children in the information technology design process: A review of theories and their applications", Library & Information Science Research, Volume 26, Issue 2, 2004, Pages 140-161, ISSN 0740-8188, https://doi.org/10.1016/j.lisr.2003.12.002 [retrieved: Dec, 2018]
23. M. Scaife, Y. Rogers, F. Aldrich, and M. Davies, "Designing for or designing with? Informant design for interactive learning environments", Proceedings of CHI'97. pp. 343- 350ACM, Atlanta, USA, 1997. [retrieved: Dec, 2018]
24. Druin: The role of children in the design of new technology. BIT. 21, 1–25, 2002. [retrieved: Dec, 2018]
25. S. Schepers, K. Dreessen, and B. Zaman, "Rethinking children's roles in Participatory Design: The child as a process designer", International Journal of Child-Computer Interaction, Volume 16, 2018, Pages 47-54, ISSN 2212-8689, https://doi.org/10.1016/j.ijcci.2017.12.001 [retrieved: Dec, 2018]
26. T. Sims, "Participatory design of healthcare technology with children", International Journal of Health Care Quality Assurance, volume 31 (1), pp. 20-27, 2018, doi 10.1108/IJHCQA-11-2016-0162 https://doi.org/10.1108/IJHCQA-11-2016-0162 [retrieved: Dec, 2018]
27. H. Gelderblom: "Designing software for young children", Proc. of IDC'04. pp. 121-122, Maryland, 2004. [retrieved: Dec, 2018]
28. H. Gelderblom, "What Children Really Contribute When Participating in the Design of Web-Based Learning Applications", Advances in Web-Based Learning -- ICWL 2017, Springer International Publishing, Cham, pages 185—195, 2017. [retrieved: Dec, 2018]
29. A. Bateman, O. K. Zhao, A. V. Bajcsy, M. C. Jennings, B. N. Toth, A. J. Cohen, and M. K. Lim, "A user-centered design and analysis of an electrostatic haptic touchscreen system for students with visual impairments", *International Journal of Human-Computer Studies*, *109*, 102-111, 2018. [retrieved: December, 2018]
30. M. L. Guha, A. Druin, and J. A. Fails, "Designing with and for children with special needs: An inclusionary model", Proceedings of the 7th International Conference on Interaction Design and Children, ACM, New York, NY, USA, pp. 61–64, 2008. [retrieved: Dec, 2018]
31. E. Kärnä, J. Nuutinen, K. Pihlainen-Bednarik, and V. Vellonen, "Designing technologies with children with special needs: Children in the Centre (CiC) Framework", Proceedings of the 9th International Conference on Interaction Design and Children, ACM, New York, NY, USA, pp. 218–221, 2010. [retrieved: Dec, 2018]
32. J. Lazar, A. Allen, J. Kleinman, and C. Malarkey, "What frustrates screen reader users on the web: A study of 100 blind users", *International Journal of human-computer interaction*, *22*(3), 247-269, 2007. [retrieved: Dec, 2018]
33. T. Armstrong, "Multiple intelligences in the classroom", ASCD 4yh edition, 2017. ISBN 978-1-4166-2509-4
34. N. Di Blas, P. Paolini, and M. Speroni, "Usable accessibility to the Web for blind users", In *Proceedings of 8th ERCIM Workshop: User Interfaces for All, Vienna, 2004*. [retrieved: Dec, 2018]
35. S. Leuthold, , J. A. Bargas-Avila, and K. Opwis, "Beyond web content accessibility guidelines: Design of enhanced text user interfaces for blind internet users", *International Journal of Human-Computer Studies*, *66*(4), 257-270, 2008. [retrieved: Dec, 2018]
36. M. F. Theofanos, and J. Redish, "Guidelines for accessible and usable web sites: Observing users who work with screen readers", *Interactions*, *10*(6), 38-51, 2003. [retrieved: Dec, 2018]
37. S. Millar, "Understanding and representing space: Theory and evidence from studies with blind and sighted children", Clarendon Press/Oxford University Press, 1994. [retrieved: Dec, 2018]
38. T.-Blanc, and F. Gaunet, "Representation of space in blind persons: vision as a spatial sense?". Psychological bulletin, 121(1), 20, 1997. [retrieved: Dec, 2018]
39. L. Nahar, A. Jaafar, E. Ahamed & A. B. M. A. Kaish (2015) Design of a Braille Learning Application for Visually Impaired Students in Bangladesh, Assistive Technology, 27:3, 172-182, DOI: 10.1080/10400435.2015.1011758 [retrieved: Dec, 2018]
40. S. Brewster and C. Magnusson, "Guidelines for haptic Lo-Fi prototyping" Proc. of the NordiCHI. Volume 102. 1483–1491, 2008.
41. M. Miao, W. Kahlmann, M. Schiewe, G. Weber, "Tactile paper prototyping with blind subjects", Haptic and Audio Interaction Design, pp. 81– 90, 2009. [retrieved: Dec, 2018]
42. V. Tadić, A. Cooper, P. Cumberland, G. Lewando-Hundt, JS. Rahi, "Measuring the Quality of Life of Visually Impaired Children: First Stage Psychometric Evaluation of the Novel VQoL_CYP Instrument",PLOS ONE 11(2): https://doi.org/10.1371/journal.pone.0146225 [retrieved: Jan, 2019]
43. M. Rastovac, J. Dolic, J. Pibernik, L. Mandić, "User-centered approach to product design for people with visual impairments", 2018. pp. 267-273. 10.24867/GRID-2018-p33.
44. C. De Oliveira, "Designing educational programming tools for the blind: mitigating the inequality of coding in schools", Masters thesis, 2017. [retrieved: Jan, 2019]
45. T. P. Abate, R. Ono, D. C. Cornelie, and K. Kowaltowski, "Tools to include blind students in school building performance assessments", Journal of Accessibility and Design for All, [S.l.], v. 6, n. 1, p. 1-25, May 2016. ISSN 2013-7087. [retrieved: Jan, 2019]
46. K. L. Kumar, and R. Owston, "Evaluating e-learning accessibility by automated and student-centered methods" journal of Educational Technology Research and Development, vol 64 (2), pp. 263—283, 2016. DOI 10.1007/s11423-015-9413-6 [retrieved: December, 2018]
47. Ergonomics of human-system integration- Part 210: Human-centered design for interactive systems (ISO 9241-210:2010) https://infostore.saiglobal.com/preview/is/en/2010/i.s.eniso9241-210-2010.pdf?sku=1441363 [retrieved: Jan, 2019]

Teaching an Alien: Children Recommending What and How to Learn

Monica Landoni
Faculty of Informatics
Università della Svizzera italiana, USI
Lugano, Switzerland
e-mail: monica.landoni@usi.ch

Emiliana Murgia
ICS Antonio Stoppani
Milano, Italy
emilianamurgia@gmail.com

Fabrizio Gramuglio
FOREVER Identity
New York, USA
fabrizio.gramuglio@gmail.com

Giorgio Manfredi
FOREVER Identity
New York, USA
giorgio.manfredi@rumbletumbleweed.com

***Abstract*—In this paper, we describe how, inspired by fiction design, primary school children are helping us to create a teachable 3D Tutor, with the appearance and personality of a friendly Alien. In line with existing literature, we assume that children enjoy learning by teaching, By making the overall process more fun, the level of children's engagement and their motivation towards it will increase. In our study, children will act as recommenders, as they are asked to prepare the lessons. They need to decide and select the material to teach and the way it is presented to the 3D Alien, to make sure s/he will have a successful learning experience. We will test the validity of these recommendations by measuring the level of engagement in children of the same age group when offered these lessons.**

Keywords- Teachable tutor; fiction design; collaborative design; teaching style.

I. INTRODUCTION

Technology is used to support teaching and learning in many ways. Here, we are working toward the design of a 3D Tutor, a friendly Alien, to act as a teachable agent to engage primary school children. Teachable agents are defined by Biswas et al. [1] as a "…computer agents that students teach, and in the process, learn themselves." Children asked to teach them are encouraged to structure their knowledge, take responsibility for its delivery and reflect upon it. These are all essential steps in the learning process. Both the social and emotional dimensions of teachable tutors are still under study. Our work contributes to this research by exploring the impact of one of its possible manifestations, that in the shape of a 3D holographic tutor.

In the first stage of this project, we involved 154 school children, attending primary 2 and aged 7-8 years, in the definition of the look and feel of their teaching tutor-agent, a friendly Alien, as in Figures 1 and 2, to design one that better satisfies their needs. Besides, given that our tutor will learn from children, we have revisited the list of qualities proposed by Buskin et al. [2] and focused on few of the most highly ranked in that study. In a previous study, we found out that for our pupils, as for the older students in that study, it is crucial that their 3D Tutor *should be enthusiastic about learning, promotes critical thinking, approachable, respectful, creative, has realistic expectations* [4]. In this paper, we explore how children can act as recommenders for other children as they are asked to prepare few lessons, i.e., decide and select the material to teach and the way it is presented to the 3D Alien, to make sure s/he will have a successful learning experience.

Figure 1. The first meeting

Figure 2. The friendly Alien

This paper starts by quickly descring in Section 2 the relevant state of the art in teachable tutors and moves on to present in Section 3 the details of our study. In Section 4, we describe how we run a focus group with a class of 16 children aged 8-9 when we examined issues related to children's preferences in learning activities. Section 5 is where we explain the activities planned for engaging children across two schools in the preparation of the lessons; to focus initially on geography as part of their school curriculum. Finally, Section 6 provides conclusions and open issues.

II. RELATED WORKS

We started from the approach defined in [8] on how co-design can help the production of active digital tutors for children and were also inspired by the work described in Herberg et al. [3] involving children in the identification of qualities for an ideal robot tutor. Particularly suitable for young children is fiction design, where "something that creates a story world… has something being prototyped within that story world, … does so to create a discursive space." [5]. Moving on to consider research on the design of teachable tutors [1], Ogan et al. [6] go on to explore their social dimension. They report on how having a friendly, equal approach, where the tutor and the child align themselves to be peers, together with being able to use informal interactions, is conducive to successful learning experiences. On the contrary, keeping a formal distance hurts the overall experience. Tanaka and Matsuzoe [7] describe an experience in using a teachable robot with primary school children. They explore three different types of teaching style such as: *direct teaching*, step-by-step, hands-on instructions given to the robot. *Gesturing*, with children moving their bodies to show a procedure to the robot. *Verbal teaching*, with children giving vocal instructions to the robot. All of them provide a significant level of closeness between children and robot by mimicking the one between parents and child. While most of the available literature reports on pro and cons of having robots to play the role of the tutor, we set out to explore an alternative, that of a 3D holographic entity. Moreover, the impact it can have on the learning by teaching process, taking place among peers.

The 3D Tutor is a 3D character animated in real-time, able to interact through different senses (touch, voice, vision) and to convey emotions together with information in lessons. By using Artificial Intelligence, the 3D Tutor can choose the right question/topic. By using Artificial Empathy, the 3D Tutor can recognize users' emotional state and engagement to react appropriately. Thus, the content is adapted to both the conditions of the student and the specific device used (mobile device, web, classroom). With the 3D Tutors, teachers can explore new ways to present subjects to students, as well as encourage students to find the learning preferences that suits them best, by fully exploiting the teaching agent paradigm. The concept of a 3D Tutor is based on that of Human-like Interaction (HLI) [3]. HLI implies the use of all dimensions of human language, not only written or verbal communication but also gestures, postures, and facial expressions.

Here we explore how this paradigm can enable children to learn from peers that act as recommenders not only of suitable, relevant and challenging material but also of fun and engaging ways to present and learn it.

III. OUR STUDY

The work described here is part of a more extensive study started one year ago and initially involving 5 (Italian) + 1 (Swiss-Italian) classes of primary school children following the same curriculum in two different schools. Children have since moved on the primary three under the supervision of the same teachers from the previous year. Two of the classes initially involved have opted out our study. Thus, we are left with 66 children and four teachers. Pupils are now practicing how to study three main subjects: history, geography, and science. Teachers have decided to focus on geography when planning activities for children to produce content for our teachable tutor. The first step we took was to run a focus group in one of the classes, to find out how aware children are of their different learning preferences.

IV. THE FOCUS GROUP

We have run an initial focus group during school hours, involving 16 children and two teachers. These stayed in class but did not take part in the discussion to let children free to express their opinions. We started the discussion by using the same fiction design trigger as in the previous year: our friendly Alien wanted to know more about our planet, maybe they could teach him. Children reacted enthusiastically, and in their discussion, they explored the following themes.

Learning preferences: Children were asked about their favorite subjects, what they liked to learn and how. Each came up with his or her favorite subjects but also with the preferred place, time and type of activities for learning. Few of them reported on the tips they were given by older siblings and parents, mostly to overcome problems with difficult subjects and in general fear and anxiety about oral and written tests. It emerged that sharing these recommendations in class made them feel more positive about their validity. Overall children felt confident about recommending what and how to learn to their Alien friend.

Differences count: two of the children pointed out we are all different and react in different ways to learning strategies. Not only children have different tastes and inclinations, but also their level of interest in the lesson presented can vary, in relation to how tired or hungry they are. They recognize that their teachers could spot these changes happening as they know them very well.

Teaching styles: not only their teachers knew them well enough to understand their level of engagement with a lesson, but they also found the best way to have them engage in it by changing the teaching style. One of the children pointed out how, when she was getting frustrated with a math exercise, her teacher turned it into a game to involve the rest of the class. Now, when the same child is asked to solve a similar exercise, she feels very confident, and this helps her to succeed.

Games for learning: children came up with many examples of how to turn an exercise into a fun game. Inspired by their favorite board games and television quizzes, they started to play with simple grammar rules they just learned and gave us a demonstration of how that worked out very well. They continued by providing examples from topics encountered in geography when describing a compass, and history, when they engaged in an impromptu story-telling session, starting from a "what if I had a dinosaur in my back garden."

Lack of participation: even if the majority of the children was enthusiastically taking part and competing to get attention, they noticed how three of them were not engaging at all in the discussion. When asked about signs of participation, children started from the eyes: bright, wide open, in contact with the speaker. Being focused and not fiddling with objects on the desk, not talking with neighbors, raising hands to contribute, were all excellent signs of engagement. Thus, we proposed two children at a time to play inspectors for the lack of these signs while the others were trying to make discussion fun.

Playing inspectors: playing inspectors proved very successful with children already engaged with the class, they seemed to enjoy that role and were extra careful in spotting every signal of disengagement.

Playing teacher: proved much harder and unfortunately, we did not see any change in the level of interest in the three children that were not involved from the start; even when the other children tried the engagement strategies their teachers had successfully used with them.

The exercise was helpful in revealing how much children were aware of the strategies and alternatives available for learning and teaching. This awareness will guide them when preparing the lessons for the teachable tutor and their peers.

We interviewed their teachers immediately afterward as they had listened to the discussion without taking an active role in it. They were impressed by the quality and variety of reflections provided by the majority of children, given they had just started to learn how to study. Teachers also confirmed how two of the three children, who were not participating in the discussion, had similar behavior in class, due to independent reasons. The third child was merely very tired for not having slept the night before. It was agreed that for future meetings, when children would prepare the lessons for the Alien, two of them, on turns, will act as inspectors.

V. Planned Activities

Together with the teachers, we have planned some activities to support children in the preparation and delivery of geography lessons. Following the fiction design approach, the process will start with a request for help sent by their Alien friend. In the message, s/he will ask children for assistance on how to use maps for finding his/her way on our planet. In particular, s/he will ask for the best path to go from A to B, using terrestrial maps. In exchange, Alien will teach children how to use space maps. Through phases of growing complexity, the students will work on a group project about how maps are made and used with local examples. Children will start focusing on the part of the city where they live, analyzing different types of maps, including the historical one. This way they will acquire enough expertise to teach the Alien how to choose and read the correct map to serve different needs. In the second phase, they will put into practice what they learned, exploring local places of interest, going around and recording everything they feel interesting for their Alien friend. They will take notes and pictures to draw a personalized map. At this point, based on the material produced, they will deliver their first lesson to their Alien friend, during a Skype session. In the third phase, they will be asked to plan a short tour in their school neighborhood, going again on the road.

Moreover, then create some VR content using VR cameras and tablets. Thus, children will set a practical activity for the Alien, e.g., draw, on the previously shared map, the path of the VR tour. The final phase will bring students and Alien to work together on designing a brand-new map answering the following question: if they were kings, how they would change the area they live to make it more children-friendly?

VI. Conclusion and Open Issues

Here, we have described the results of a focus group run with primary school children to explore their attitude toward learning and teaching. The focus group was run in preparation for the design of lessons to be prepared by children for their teachable 3D tutor, a friendly Alien. By following a fiction design approach, we will engage children in some curriculum-related activities and get them to produce material suitable for their peers. Children will also organize this material in lessons to be interesting and fun for the friendly Alien and their peers to learn. We will then measure the level of engagement these lessons generate in other children of the same age group.

References

[1] G. Biswas, K. Leelawong, D. Schwartz, and N. Vye, "The Teachable Agents Group at Vanderbilt, Learning by Teaching a New Agent Paradigm for Educational Software," Applied Artificial Intelligence, Vol. 9, issue 3-4, pp 363-392, 2005.

[2] W. Buskist, J. Sikorski, T. Buckley, and B. K. Saville, Elements of master teaching. In The Teaching of Psychology: Essays in Honor of Wilbert J. McKeachie and Charles L. Brewer, S. F. Davis and W. Buskist, eds. Mahwah New Jersey, Erlbaum, pp 27-39, 2002.

[3] J. S. Herberg, D. C. Behera, and M. Saerbeck, "Eliciting ideal tutor trait perception in robots: pinpointing effective robot design space elements for smooth tutor interactions," HRI '13, Proceedings of the 8th ACM/IEEE international conference on Human-robot interaction, IEEE Press, Piscataway, NJ, USA, pp 137-138, 2013.

[4] M. Landoni, E. Murgia, F. Gramuglio, and G. Manfredi, "Fiction Design of a 3D Tutor for and with School Children," Proceedings of the Eleventh International Conference on Advances in Computer-Human Interactions, ACHI, pp 94-97, 2018.

[5] J. Lindley, "Researching Design Fiction With Design Fiction," Proceedings of the ACM SIGCHI Conference on Creativity and Cognition, C&C15, pp 325-326, 2015.

[6] A. Ogan, et al. , "Oh, dear Stacy!": social interaction, elaboration, and learning with teachable agents," Proceedings of the SIGCHI Conference on Human Factors in Computing Systems, CHI'12, ACM, New York, NY, USA, pp 39-48, 2012.

[7] F. Tanaka and S. Matsuzoe, "Children teach a care-receiving robot to promote their learning: field experiments in a classroom for vocabulary learning," Journal of Human-Robot Interaction, Vol. 1, issue 1, pp 78-95, 2012.

[8] G. Walsh, E. Foss, J. Yip, and A. Druin, "FACIT PD: a framework for analysis and creation of intergenerational techniques for participatory design," Proceedings of the SIGCHI Conference on Human Factors in Computing Systems, CHI'13, ACM, New York, NY, USA, pp 2893-2902, 2013.

Supporting Improvisatory Story Creation for Children by Storing Their Storytelling

Yuto Suzuki, Shumpei Akahoshi, and Mitsunori Matsushita

Kansai University, Graduate school of Informatics, Japan
emails: k834596@kansai-u.ac.jp, k854371@kansai-u.ac.jp, mat@res.kutc.kansai-u.ac.jp

***Abstract*—In workshops for children participating in production activities, it is important to review not only the production activities but also completed works. However, when works are created that have no tangible shape, such as oral stories, a record of the work is needed to enable review of the works. Currently, digital devices, such as video cameras are used to record such works. However, it is difficult for children to manipulate digital devices to record and review their storytelling. Therefore, in this paper we propose a recording system that children can manipulate and use to store their own works. Based on the opinions of the designer of the workshop, we iteratively developed the system. In order to verify the usefulness of the proposed system, we conducted an evaluation experiment comparing our app with the standard iOS camera application. As a result, it was suggested that the proposed system has useful functions for recording and viewing works.**

Keywords–story creation; children; workshop; reviewing; computer interaction.

I. INTRODUCTION

There is a workshop to support children's stories. Story creation workshops aim to help children develop their imagination and expressive power by allowing them to have fun while creating stories. One example of a story creation workshop is "PeKay's Little Author Workshop"[1]. In this workshop, children freely arrange characters and text using the software "PeKay's Little Author" to complete an original digital picture book. This system was developed by Asakura. Asakura designs and implements the workshops [2]. In these workshops, the children print the completed digital picture books with a printer. Also, at the end of the workshops, the children share their digital picture books with other participants through presentations. As seen in this example, it is important not only to produce works but also to review the works produced during the workshop by allowing participants to review their completed works by themselves or by showing them to each other. By reviewing, we can acquire new consciousness and expression techniques.

In story creation workshops, it is necessary to record the works to enable them to be reviewed. At present, digital equipment such as voice recorders and video cameras are generally used. However, these digital devices have not been developed for the purpose of reviewing works produced in story creation workshops. For this reason, there arises a problem that it is difficult to easily find a desired work from a large set of recorded data in story creation workshop where work is recorded a plurality of times. Therefore, in this research, we target the story creation workshops for children, and support the review of the produced story. In this paper, we propose a recording system that considers the contents of activities by interviewing workshop designer for one workshop.

In Section 2, we introduce several examples of research that supports the creation of stories, and described the positioning of this research. In Section 3, we describe the content of "PeKay's Storytelling Picture Card Workshop" which we covered in this paper. In Section 4, we describe the design guidelines for the recording system were made by clarifying the problem of the recording of the work by the video camera in the "PeKay's Storytelling Picture Card Workshop" by interview with the designer. In Section 5, we describe the "prototype system Ver.1" and its problems. In Section 6, we describe the prototype system Ver. 2 which improved the problems of the prototype system described in Section 5. In Section 7, we describe the experiments we conducted to verify the usefulness of the proposed system. In Section 8 we describe the results and considerations of the experiment. In Section 9, we describe conclusions, including future prospects.

II. RELATED STUDIES

In this section, we introduce several examples of research that supports the creation of stories for children, and described the positioning of this research.

A. Supporting children's story creation

Many approaches have been employed to support children's story creation. Vaucelle et al. developed a doll-type system "DollTalk" that records and reproduces children's utterance contents and movements [3]. DollTalk aims to objectively review and improve the stories produced by children by allowing them to listen to their stories in a voice different from their own voices. Vaucelle et al. also developed a type of doll device called "Picture this!"[4]. In these devices, sensors and cameras are built in dolls, and by speaking using dolls and props, it is possible to create video works with simple operations. Ryokai et al. developed "StoryMat", which can create stories by recording story utterances and toy movements while children are moving toys on mats [5]. In this system, when a child plays on the mat, the previously recorded story is played as an animation. This allows children to create stories in collaboration with others. In these studies, by using dolls and props, they take the form of play seen in early childhood as a basis and support the creation of children's stories with natural flow.

Sato developed a system that allows adults and children to create stories in a way that they read stories from one another

Figure 1. PeKay's Storytelling Picture Card

Figure 2. Work example

[6]. In this system, the introductory part of a story in which the main character is in trouble is expressed with letters and text, and it is conveyed to the child by parental talk. The child arranges texts and characters and thus creates a continuation of the story, providing a solution of the problem, and tells it to the parent. Annany developed a caterpillar-type recording system called "TellTale"[7]. The system consists of five bodies and one head, each of which has the role of a recording device and a reproducing device. Recording speech individually by using the five bodies, the user can create various stories by switching the order of combination. In these studies, the goal is to cultivate the ability to think about stories and the whole composition.

Bonsignore et al. developed a mobile application called "StoryKit" that can be used to create and share stories [8]. In this system, the user can make a story using the collected images, texts, and sounds. Also, because it is a mobile application, the user can create a story while collecting photos outdoors, without being confined to one place. Furthermore, stories can be shared with other people easily by sending a URL. In this study, it is a feature that it is possible to make stories such a diary and share them with others.

B. *Position of this research*

In previous research, as a creative support for children's stories, they provide new activities through their systems. However, we support the creation of children's stories by supporting existing creation activities.

In addition, Nakae et al. are assisting in creative activities workshop by recording the activities [9]. In this research, they focus on the production process, but we focus on the created works and support reflection.

From the above, in this research the purpose is located in both "support for story creation" and "support for workshop".

III. Target Workshop

In this work, we developed a recording system that takes into consideration the activity of "PeKay's Storytelling Picture Card Workshop". Development of the system was realized through cooperation with TamieAsakura (GoodGrief Co., Ltd.) who designs and conducts this workshop. Here, we will briefly outline "PeKay's Storytelling Picture Card Workshop". The participants of this workshop are children aged 5 to 10, who create stories using "picture cards". The picture cards are divided into six genres: "character", "toy", "food", "vehicle", "place", "weather" (Figure 1). There is a total of 43 cards, including 8 character cards and 7 cards for each of the other categories. Using these picture cards, participants can create stories with the pictures functioning as prompts. The basic steps in the story creation procedure are summarized below.

1) Select a card freely.
2) Place the selected card on the desk and consider the story while changing its position.
3) Talk while presenting a card.

An example of the work created according to this procedure is shown in Figure 2. There are several possible ways to select a card. For example, besides choosing a card freely, it is also possible to randomly select a card, limit the number of cards, and so forth. Also, since one work can be made in a short time, many works are made through the workshop. In addition, the facilitator uses a video camera to record the state of utterance of the child's story, and the work is recorded in the form of a video. At the end of the workshop, as a general review, all the participants watch the work.

IV. Design Guidelines

We interviewed Asakura to determine the design guidelines for the recording system. Three interviews were conducted on March 2, May 21, and September 13, 2017. In the interview, we asked about the problem of the video camera used for the recording of the work. The results of the interviews are organized and presented below. The following three points were cited as problems. (A) Because a child moves during recording of a work, the card to be presented may not be visible to the camera. (B) When a child faces the camera, he or she should not speak shyly.(C) When viewing the work, the appearance of the child is displayed as part of the work, and this can interfere with concentrating on the content of the work. These problems are thought to be due to the fact that the facilitator is recording the story work of the child and that the presenter and the recollector are separated. Therefore, in this paper, to solve these problems, we propose a recording system for children to operate themselves and record the creation of their stories.

To implement this system, four design guidelines were set with reference to Asakura's opinions. First of all, for children, it is considered difficult to tell a full story at one time. Therefore, a story may be divided into segments and recorded in stages. Second, to enable the child to intuitively operate the system, the operation can be performed with simple interaction. Third, it is necessary to prevent extra information

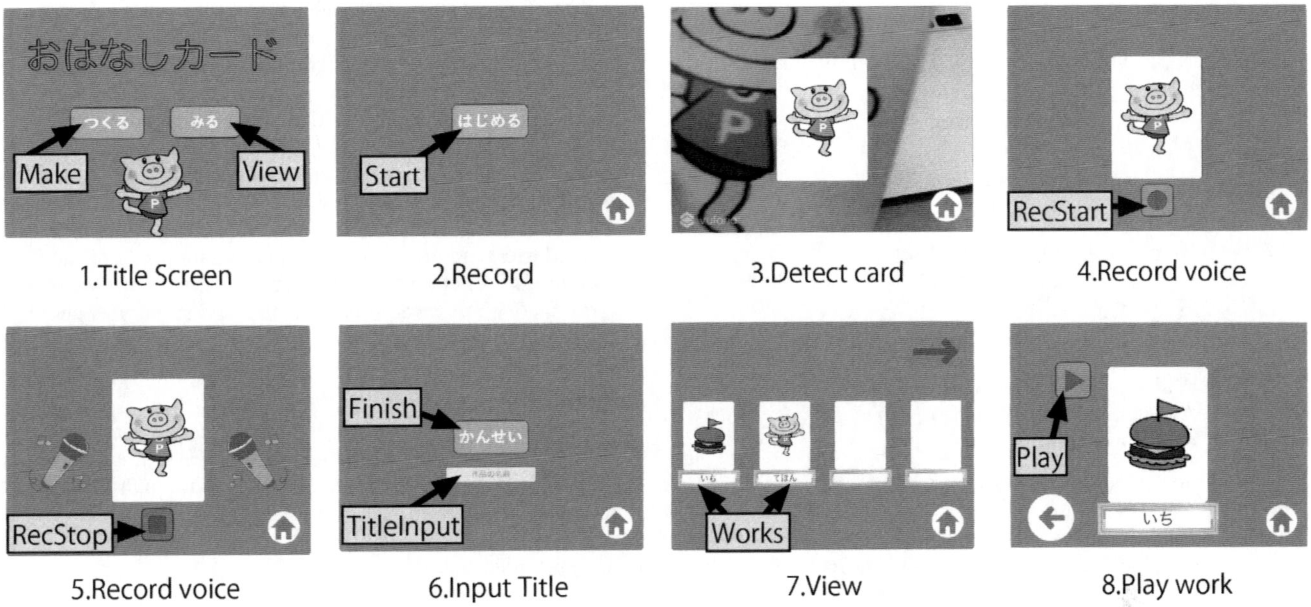

Figure 3. Prototype System Ver.1 ; When you tap Works with "1.TitleScreen", you can go to "7.View" and watch the works on images 7-8.Then, when you tap Make, you can go to "2. Record" and record the work on images 2-6.

from entering the story work, because there is a possibility that it may interfere with viewing the work intensively if the work contains extra information. The extra information here refers to information that is not related to the story, such as a part of the body of the child or the surrounding landscape. Finally, since many works are recorded, it should be easy to identify an individual work.

V. Implementation of Prototype System Ver.1

In this Section, we describe the "prototype system Ver.1" developed based on design guidelines and its problems.

A. System overview

We implemented a prototype system Ver.1 (hereinafter Ver.1) based on the design guidelines described in Section 4. To satisfy design guideline (1), the ability to divide stories and record in stages, we alternately repeat the selection of cards and the recording of sounds so that the story work is recorded in stages. To satisfy design guideline (2), according to which the operation should be able to be performed with simple interaction, all screen transitions were realized by tapping a button. In addition, regarding the card selection method, image recognition that automatically discriminates by holding the camera over the card was adopted. To satisfy design guideline (3), to prevent extra information from entering the story work, we adopted a slide show format in which images and sounds are switched correspondingly to reproduce the work. Finally, to satisfy design guideline (4), that individual works should be easily identified, we made it possible to record and display the title of each work. The above contents are organized and the functions implemented are summarized below.

- Image recognition function of the card to be used
- Audio recording function
- Work piece reproduction function in slide show format
- Title input function

Ver.1 with these functions was implemented as an iOS application on an iPad. Figure 3 shows the screen transition diagram of Ver.1. For development of the system, Unity.Ver.5.4.1f1, which can easily correspond to various platforms was used [10]. In addition, image recognition was realized by characterizing the image of each picture card and registering it as a marker using Vuforia.Ver.6.5 of SDK [11].

B. Problems of Ver.1

To clarify the problems of Ver.1, we had a discussion with Asakura. The discussion took place on November 8, 2017. We considered the following problems.

1) Operation in the horizontal screen may force the use of both hands.
2) The operation required to shift from the recording of a work to viewing will increase due to the title screen.
3) Since the number of cards that can be recorded at a time is limited to 4, the range of expression of the work is narrowed.
4) Because the story is divided for recording, there is a possibility of forgetting the contents already recorded during the recording.
5) At the time of card selection, it automatically transitions to sound recording screen at the moment of recognizing the card, which causes erroneous operation.
6) Buttons are located at the lower right or the lower left, and the hand with the terminal unintentionally touches the button, possibly causing a mistake in operation.

By improving these problems, improvement of system operability is expected. In Section 6, we will explain the prototype system Ver. 2, which incorporated improvements to address these problems.

VI. Implementation of Prototype System Ver. 2

This Section introduces the prototype system Ver.2 (hereinafter Ver. 2). In Ver.2, the following changes were made.

1) Changed the top screen to the work list.
2) Changed so that the list of works recorded on the top screen can be seen.
3) Made it possible to freely select cards to be used from 1 to 12 cards.
4) Add the previewing works function.
5) Add the redoing function Image recognition and recording.

The first change has been implemented to solve the problem clarified in the previous section "Operation on the horizontal screen may force use of both hands." This made it possible to operate the device with one hand and to have a card and a recording system at the same time. The second change has been implemented to solve the problem that "the operation required to shift from the recording of the work to the viewing will increase due to the title screen." This change made it possible to operate the system smoothly (Figure 4-1). The third change has been implemented to solve the problem that "the number of cards that can be recorded at a time is limited to 4, so the range of expression of the work becomes narrow." The fourth change was implemented to solve the problem that "because the user records the story by dividing it into parts, the user may forget the content that was already recorded in the middle of recording." With this change, it was possible to record works while confirming the contents (Figure 4-6). The fifth change was implemented to solve the problem that "it automatically transitions to the sound recording screen at the moment of recognizing the card at the time of card selection, which causes erroneous operation." The redo function allows the user to redo operations as many times as necessary until the user taps the button to select a card or start a voice recording (Figure 4-3,4).

VII. Experiment

In this section, we describe the experiments we conducted to verify the usefulness of the proposed system.

A. Outline of experiment

To verify the usefulness of the proposed system in the work record of "PeKay's Storytelling Picture Card Workshop", we compared it with the standard camera application of an iOS terminal (hereinafter referred to as "camera application"). Although the proposed system is targeted at children aged 5-10, it is expected that there will be large differences among individuals in the ability of children. Therefore, in this paper, we investigate the functionality of the proposed system by targeting students of the same university which are thought to have less differences in abilities before conducting experiments for children. For this time, we covered 6 university students, including 3 males and 3 females. Two tasks were to be carried out by the experiment participants. The first was to select cards according to three kinds of rules, and to create six works of two pieces each. The second task was to record the created works three by three, using the camera application, and Ver.2 in order. After completing the recording of the works, the participants were given a questionnaire form with question items to fill out. Also, the participants were orally asked questions about actions at the time of recording the work. To record the operation contents of the system, we obtained permission and photographed the subject's hand with a video camera. The picture cards used for the experiment were limited to 33 pictures with a high recognition rate of the image recognition function, and an iPad was used as the experiment terminal. The time required for this experiment was about one hour per person.

B. Experimental questionnaire

This subsection will briefly explain the questionnaire about the recording of the work, which was done after the experiment. First, we asked the experiment participants to respond to the questionnaire that asked the questions about the two types of recording systems. The contents of the questionnaire are presented below.

- Q1 Have you experienced any inconvenience in recording with the camera application? Yes, No
- Q2 Please tell me the reason for Q1. (Free description)
- Q3 Have you experienced inconvenience during recording with this application? Yes, No
- Q4 Please tell me the reason for Q3. (Free description)
- Q5 Did you feel that a function that can save titles is necessary? Yes, No
- Q6 Please tell me the reason for Q5. (Free description)
- Q7 Please tell me about the function that you feel is unnecessary. (free description)
- Q8 Please let me know if you have thought of any additional functions that you feel are necessary for this system. (free description)

We also orally asked questions about the conditions and procedures during the experiment. At that time, We asked all the experiment participants, "You recorded the work with two kinds of systems, which one do you like better? Why?".

VIII. Results and Discussion

This section will consider the experimental results obtained from the questionnaire from the viewpoint of the recording works, the viewing of the works, and the problems of the proposed system.

In response to the questionnaire, three of the six participants said that it is difficult to tell a whole story at once for recording using the camera application. On the other hand, regarding recording using Ver.2, two of the six participants answered that they did not experience any inconvenience because the contents were arranged by dividing and recording the story in segments. These findings suggest that the function of dividing and recording the story in parts for each card used, which was implemented in Ver.2, was able to alleviate the burden of telling the user's story at once. Also, in this experiment, both systems allowed recording to be redone. However, in the recording by the camera application, the

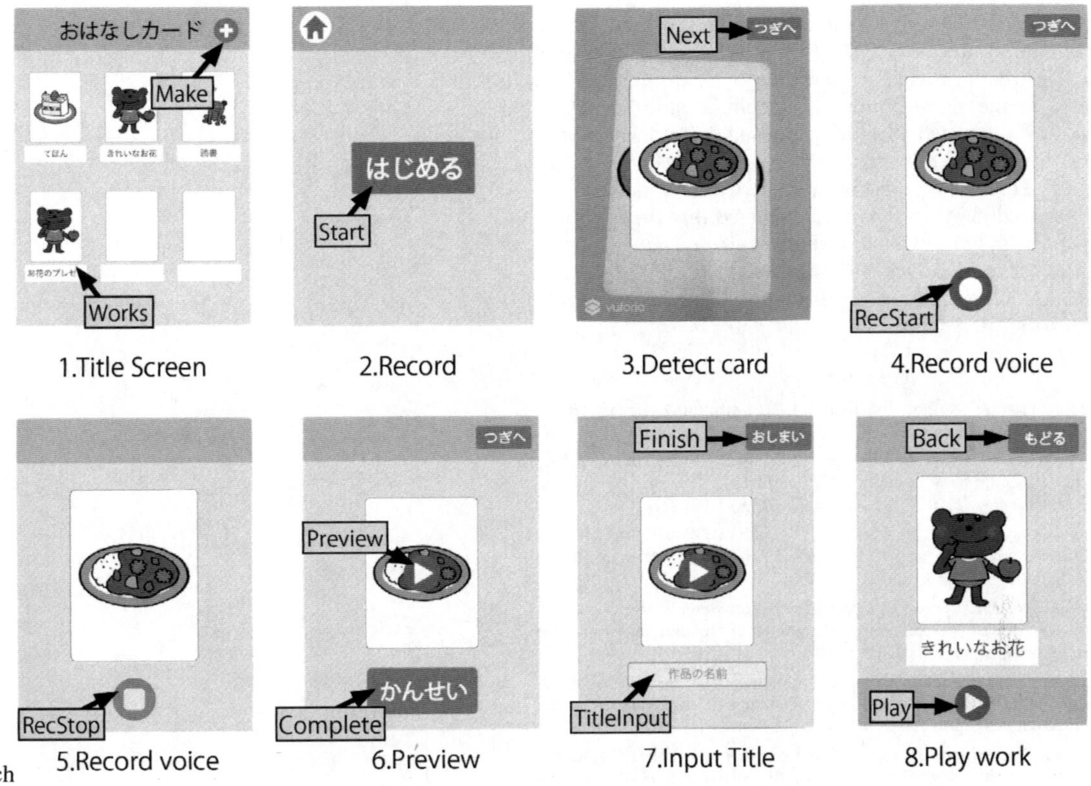

chch

Figure 4. Prototype System Ver.2 ; When you tap Works with "1.TitleScreen", you can go to "8.Playwork" and watch the work.Then, when you tap Make, you can go to "2. Record" and record the work on 2-7 images.

recording was not redone. On the other hand, in the recordings made using Ver.2, five participants re-recorded parts of their recordings, modifying their speech errors and expressions. We asked the experiment participants who redid their recordings only when using Ver.2, the reason for this. Regarding recording by Ver.2, one participant made the following comment: "I thought that I wanted to improve the quality of the work because I could re-record my voice at each stage." Regarding recording by the camera application, a participant made the following comment: "When redoing the recording of the work, it was necessary to redo the recording from the beginning of the story. When I tried recording again, I felt it was likely that I made mistakes again and compromised." These responses suggest that recording mistakes can be reduced by allowing the user to re-record parts of a story more easily when stories are divided and recorded in parts. In addition, this function was used to eliminate coughing and discontinuation, forgetting the contents of utterance, changing contents of utterance, and changing expressions in a story. Also, the number of times that the work-previewing function was used is summarized for each experiment participant, it was A: once, B: 4 times, C: 10 times, D: 3 times, E: 3 times, and F: 5 times. This function was used to check the contents of the work being recorded, and to confirm whether the recorded sound was recorded correctly.

In the viewing of the works recorded using camera application, five participants found that the appearance of hands, shadows, and screen blur interfered with the viewing quality. However, regarding the viewing of the works using Ver.2, the image and the sound switched correspondingly, so the participants had the general opinion it provided a clean impression and good viewing quality. These opinions suggest that the function of playing the work in a slideshow format is effective for viewing this kind of work. Also, in response to the title input function, five participants answered that "the title function is necessary to distinguish between works that have the same cover."

During the experiment, all of the participants made some errors in operating Ver.2, such as accidentally pushing a button, unintentionally changing the screen, and proceeding to the next screen. To address these problems, a button could be added to allow the user to return to the previous screen. Thus, the user would be able to redo a recording even in the case of an operation error.

IX. CONCLUSION

In this study, we developed a work recording system that children can operate. The system was specifically designed for participants in "PeKay's Storytelling Picture Card Workshop", in which children create stories. By referring to the opinions of the designer and provider of the workshops, we designed the system considering the activities of the workshop. As a development procedure, we interviewed the workshop provider and developed a prototype system Ver.1 based on the design guidelines identified through the interviews. In addition, we developed Prototype System Ver.2, which addressed the problems of Ver.1, which were identified by conducting discussions.

Moreover, in order to verify whether prototype system Ver.2 is an appropriate system for "PeKay's Storytelling Picture Card Workshop", we conducted an evaluation experiment of the function with the participation of 6 college students. As a result, it was suggested that the proposed system has useful functions for recording and viewing works. However, the subjects of "PeKay's Storytelling Picture Card Workshop" are 5 to 10-year-old children, and it is expected that there will be differences in system evaluation between university students and children. Therefore, we will improve the proposed system, and conduct an evaluation experiment of the system with children as the participants.

REFERENCES

[1] "PeKay's Little Author for iPad," URL: http://www.pekay.jp/pkla/ipaden [retrieved: January, 2019].

[2] T. Asakura, "Development of storybook creation software —To help nurture a Secure Base in the hearts of children—," Journal of Information Processing, vol. 2, 2011 (in Japanese), pp. 103–116.

[3] C. Vaucelle and T. Jehan, "Dolltalk: A computational toy to enhance children's creativity," CHI '02 Extended Abstracts on Human Factors in Computing Systems, 2002.

[4] C. Vaucelle and H. Ishii, "Picture this! Film assembly using toy gestures," Proceedings of the 10th international conference on Ubiquitous computing, vol. 344, 2008, pp. 350–359.

[5] K. Ryokai and J. Cassel, "Computer Support for Children's Collaborative Fantasy Play and Storytelling," Proceedings of the 1999 Conference on Computer Support for Collaborative Learning, 1999.

[6] T. Sato, "Development of Software that Supports Young Children's Narrative Productions," Proceedings of ED-MEDIA 2008–World Conference on Educational Multimedia, 2008.

[7] M. Annany, "Supporting Children's Collaborative Authoring: Practicing Written Literacy While Composing Oral Texts," Proceedings of Computer Supported Collaborative Learning Conference, 2002.

[8] E. Bonsignore, A. J. Quinn, A. Druin, and B. B. Bederson, "Sharing Stories "in the Wild": A Mobile Storytelling Case Study Using StoryKit," ACM Transactions on Computer-Human Interaction (TOCHI), vol. 20, 2013, pp. 18:1–18:38.

[9] K. Nakae and K. Tsukada, "Support System to Review Manufacturing Workshop through Multiple Videos," Proceedings of the 23rd International Conference on Intelligent User Interfaces Companion, 2018.

[10] "Unity," URL: https://unity3d.com/jp [retrieved: January, 2019].

[11] "Vuforia Developer Portal," URL: https://developer.vuforia.com/ [retrieved: January, 2019].

The Role of Physical Prototyping in Participatory Design with Older Adults

An Exploration of Form and Materials in the Design of a Robot for Older Adults

Heidi Bråthen, Harald Maartmann-Moe, Trenton Schulz
Departments of Informatics
University of Oslo
Oslo, Norway
e-mail: heidi.brathen@imv.uio.no, harald.maartmann-moe@mn.uio.no, trentonw@ifi.uio.on

Abstract— **How can older adults actively participate in the design processes of assistive robots designed for their homes? We have organized workshops with a group of older adults who worked actively with materials and physical prototyping to design a fetch robot for the home. We present the basics of the workshop materials, how the workshop was performed, and findings on the role of physical prototyping from the workshops.**

Keywords — robots; human-robot interaction; physical prototyping; older adults; participatory design

I. INTRODUCTION

Assistive technology, such as robots, is designed and implemented to help older, retired people to stay independently at home longer. In the Participatory Design tradition, one of the core values and points of origin is the ideal of democratic design of technological artefacts [1]. In this paper, we delve into how material exploration in physical prototyping workshops may facilitate the participation of older adults [2] in the design process of robots in the context of their homes.

The older adults participating in our workshops were experts on their homes and daily practices, but their expertise and interest regarding design and robot technology varied. We were interested to see if physical prototyping could enable their participation in design.

This work is part of a larger research project called Multimodal Elderly Care Systems (MECS) aimed at using robots and future sensors to help with monitoring events in the home and aid people living longer independently longer. Previous work by the MECS project includes long-term user testing of vacuum cleaner robots in the home of older adults. Some of the participants in our workshops had been part of this study [3] and thus had some experience with robots in the home. The results in terms of the design and material preferences and ideas of our participants will go into a further study in the project and be developed further in prototypes by the MECS research group. In this paper, we will review our workshops in terms of how physical prototyping and material exploration affected the level of participation.

In the next section, we outline related work on facilitation of participation when designing with older adults and robots in the home. In Section III, we describe our method: how we conducted the workshops and how we prepared and presented the samples of shapes and materials that we used. Section IV presents the results from our workshops, and in Section V, we discuss the main findings regarding what we learned from working with older adults through physical prototyping and material explorations before we conclude the paper in Section VI.

II. RELATED WORK

Participants' limited in-depth knowledge of a design project [4] may make it difficult for them to gain an overview of the possibilities in the design domain, and hence challenging to be creative within the design problem. Joshi and Bratteteig [5] suggest that elderly users should be enabled to participate in mutual learning and co-construction activities on their own terms. They describe a successful mutual learning process as the possibility for both groups to extend their creative and imaginative capacity and build on each other's ideas to design concrete artefacts. To participate on their own terms, the participants should be able to express themselves in their own language, without having to adopt the professional terminology of the design team in which they participate [5]. This may include the opportunity to show and do rather than to tell.

To express their tacit knowledge and their everyday lived practice, Brandt et al. stress the importance of being able to make things that give this practice a presence in the world. Telling about one's practice may become "generative also of that which has not yet been experienced" [6]. Physical artefacts have also proved useful in participatory design workshops to trigger unexpected and additional stories from the participants [7]. Participatory prototyping and generative tools have been central in the making activities since the beginning of participatory design [6]. Generative tools are two- and three-dimensional visual components that non-designers can use to express their ideas and dreams for future scenarios of use [6].

Robots designed to aid in the home include domestic robots such as vacuum cleaning robots and lawn mowing robots [8.] Robots have also been suggested as a form of assistive technology that can help care workers by being present in the home of older, retired people when care workers cannot. [9] What can robots do in these situations? Asking the opinion of older adults themselves, one survey found that older adults feel a robot could help in recovering from a fall or retrieving objects that were hard to reach [9]. One attempt to categorize robots targeted at older adults at home found that robots must offer something that makes the people independent and goes beyond being a tablet on wheels [10].

III. Methodology and Methods

A. *Co-construction on the participants' terms*

The goal of our workshops was to engage older adults in the co-construction of a robot. We wished to gain insight into how older adults would prefer for the robot's appearance and feel in the home, with special attention to the materials it could be constructed from, rather than realistic technical implementations.

Due to the varying degree of interest and expertise in robot technology among our participants, one of our main aims in the workshops was to explore ways to enable an exchange of ideas and expertise between the participants and the designers through telling and making. We designed a material exploration workshop featuring a variety of traditional materials to encourage the participation and co-construction on the participants' terms, visualizing some possibilities in the design domain and enabling creativity.

B. *Pilot workshop: A purpose for the robot*

We conducted a pilot workshop with one participant. This workshop took place in the home of the participant. After the pilot workshop, we adjusted the assignment to be more specific, from constructing *a robot* to constructing a robot with a dedicated purpose, a robot to fetch and carry objects. This emerged as an important theme as the pilot workshop did not proceed as expected. The materials we brought were discussed, but not explored by touching or examining them, and no prototyping was done. The procedure derailed from our plan when Patricia (not her real name) insisted on a more concrete and personally useful purpose than what we originally proposed working on: *a robot*. The derailment started a conversation about what this purpose could be. Patricia was concerned about the value of the robot, as she initially could not imagine any need for a robot in her home. After exploring this issue together, we arrived at the idea of a fetch robot that would prove to be a valuable point of departure for the following workshops.

C. *The workshops*

Subsequently, we ran two workshops in the library of an independent living facility in Norway with a total of seven participants aged 75 to 92 years old, one of whom participated in both (see Table 1).

TABLE I. OVERVIEW OF PARTICIPANTS

Activity	**Participants (P.)**			
Pilot August	P. 1 Female Patricia			
WS1 September	P. 1A Female Aimee	P. 1B Female Anca	P. 1C Female Angelica	P. 1D Female Antonella
WS2 September	P. 2A Male Bruno	P. 2B Male Basilio	P. 2C Female Brenna	P. 1D Female Antonella

In preparation for workshop one, we posted flyers in the living facility a few days prior. The posters promoting our workshop were displayed alongside other voluntary activities to avoid misusing the power of recruiting participants through independent living facilities' platforms and staff. Four inhabitants showed up to our first workshop session, and they all participated for the full length of our planned session, and, by their request, for 15 more minutes.

Exactly one week later, we held our second workshop. Two men and two women participated from beginning to end in the second session, one of which had participated in the previous session as well.

D. *Workshop Materials*

To facilitate material explorations of robot design we brought a set of materials that we believed the participants would be comfortable with, such as traditional materials commonly found in the interior design of homes, see Figure 1. We brought samples, swatch books with colour and texture samples for textiles, textile ribbons, yarn, crocheted and knitted textile samples, veneer from different woods, different self-adhesive foils and films, including aluminium foil, coloured wooden pearls, pipe cleaners, coloured paper, corrugated cardboard, acrylic glass, wooden rods, duct tape, wood glue, ordinary scissors, textile scissors, pens, marker pens/felt tip pens.

One of the things we observed in the pilot workshop was that prototyping a robot with no structural building blocks was troublesome. To minimise crafting tasks that were demanding in fine motor skills and still provide the participants with flexible choices regarding material samples, we prepared building blocks in the form of cardboard and veneer boxes and shapes to represent robot bodies and wheels. See Figure 2. We made the boxes from scratch to standardise the height of the boxes to prepare material samples that could easily be fitted onto the base boxes. We tailored the other material samples like textiles to this measure.

Figure 1. Workshop setup

Figure 2. Top: Basic shapes. Bottom: Laser cut wheels

IV. Results

A. Pilot Workshop

As mentioned in Section III.B, Patricia initially could not imagine any need for a robot in her home. We suggested that she could think about possible needs of her acquaintances. Thinking about a friend with severe tremors in her hands that made it difficult to carry coffee cups across the floor, made Patricia think of a robot that could fetch and carry items. This, in turn, made her think of her own problem with reaching things that were placed on top of tall shelves, especially the problem of dropping things that were difficult to get a hold of. She then suggested that a robot could sweep the floor after accidents with breaking objects, carry things, pour coffee and fetch things from hard to reach shelves.

Patricia wanted the hypothetical robot to be easily cleaned. She also expressed a wish for a robot that would not be camouflaged, but visible, something simple and nice, not requiring extra work, not shiny but matte. She explained that she believed that older adult participants required several repetitions of information, the possibility to try out and experience what they are being told in small steps and increments of information and task instructions to be able to follow and understand the new activity properly.

We decided to bring this concept of a fetch robot to our workshops. Considering concrete and useful purpose appeared to be a necessary step preceding prototyping.

Patricia also felt that it seemed futile for her to try and design a robot. "I can't imagine that I can make a robot. It's too utopian. I'm just grateful that someone else is taking care of building robots"

B. Workshops

Aimee shaped a prototype (Figure 3, E) with great attention to function. The robot would be waterproof so that it could wash her back and withstand spills. It would be white to match her furniture. It would nearly have the height of a human, to reach the upper cupboards. It would be round so it could navigate among all the plants in her home. Tasks came to Aimee's mind during the prototyping. The robot could also stir the sauce, empty the dishwasher, water plants, clean windows, fetch things, vacuum, carry hot and heavy cups of coffee to her chair, open bottles and lids, pour from heavy containers,

During a conversation between Aimee and Anca concerning the purpose and function of the robot, Aimee suggested that her robot could be a dancing partner, and a hairdresser as Anca had expressed a wish for this previously.

Anca embraced the suggestion of a dancing partner and hairdresser robot. She constructed long arms for the robot (Figure 3, F) that would enable it to dance and style hair.

Angelica was inspired by the challenges a friend had told her about. She then recalled that they shared one of these challenges: reaching the upper cupboards. She then fashioned a long grabbing arm with a member of our project group. The prototype (Figure 3, G) was dressed in aluminium foil and acrylic glass to represent stainless steel and glass to match her modern interior design. A green patch of fabric was carefully chosen to match her green curtains but was later disregarded because she wanted the design to be extendable to other households beyond her own. Glass would be installed in one side of the robot because she wished to see the inner workings of the robot as it worked and moved. "I think that will make it more familiar and personal, to see that it starts working when I'm calling on it", she explained. By the end of the workshop, she was proud of her design, and she told us that the experience had been fun.

Antonella constructed a prototype (Figure 3, K) with a smooth wooden exterior, represented by aluminium foil with a wood image, to represent a wooden surface that would be easy to clean. Antonella modeled edges along the top to represent a board with raised edges to keep things from falling. She also added a textile bag that would keep a pen and her glasses which she often spent time looking for. Antonella expressed satisfaction in having crafted the prototype and asked if she could also join our second workshop, which she did.

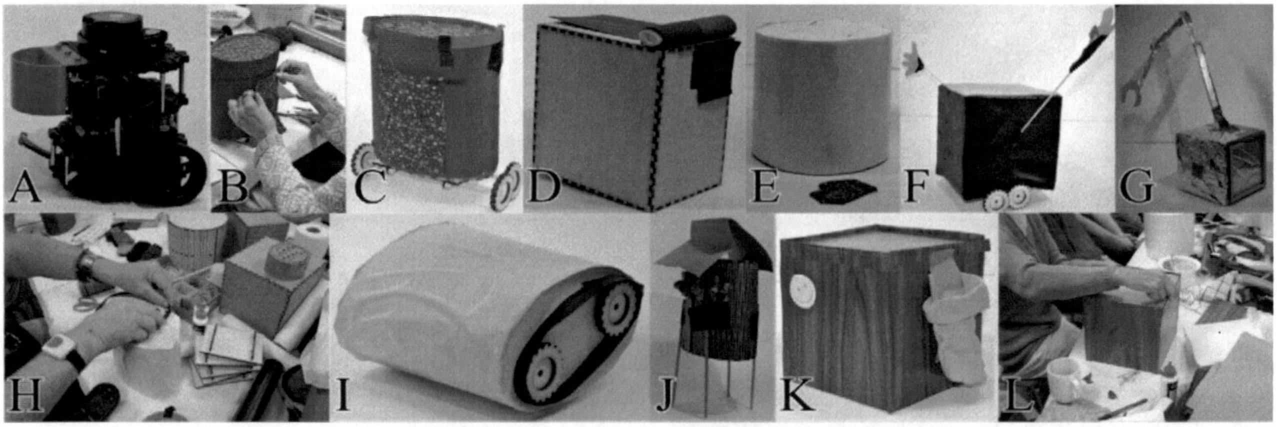

Figure 3. A: "Burger" robot with a 3D printed "backpack" for demonstration, B: Antonella, C: Antonella, D: Brenna, E: Aimee, F: Anca, G: Agelica H: Bruno, I: Bruno, J: Basilio, K: Antonella, L: Antonella

Workshop 2 had the same aim and setup as workshop 1. Here, Bruno made a prototype (Figure 3, H and I) exploring the implementation of robot locomotion. He constructed a detailed mechanical conceptual solution. It included pumping water in a tube, connected to a belt, connected to two cogwheels on the side of the robot. This could shift the center of mass to roll the robot forwards. Shifting the center of mass could also be used by the robot to "stand up", by shifting the weight to one side. This form of movement would also allow the robot to navigate tricky passages and corners in small spaces like the residents' apartments. He decided on plastic as a material, as it is common and durable. He chose the colour yellow to awaken visual interest. He said that he would lose interest if it was too dark. Yellow plastic would also match his surroundings. The yellow foil was to represent yellow plastic in the prototype. He did not wish to solve the implementation of the robot fetching things but expressed that he imagined an excavator-like arm that would stand still relative to the body of the robot.

Brenna said that the elliptical box in our kit was to slim, and too short. She did not want to have to bend to reach the objects the robot would be transporting. She pointed out that the table we were using in our workshop was at an appropriate height (70–75cm). She then chose a rectangular wooden box but expressed dislike for the sharp corners. Therefore, she rounded the corners by covering paper towels in fabric and placing it on top of the prototype (Figure 3, D) to represent rounded edges. She specified that three sides should be covered in dark green, smooth, dust repelling, easy to clean, and easy to keep clean. She commented that the boxes of wood and cardboard we brought with us were too rough, would gather dust, and be difficult to keep clean.

Antonella (who had participated in workshop 1) chose an elliptical base for the prototype (Figure 3, B, and C); she covered the base in red-purple flexible cardboard and assembled wheels for the robot prototype. She would have preferred covering the prototype in a single colour, but we did not bring enough. She further developed her design from workshop 1, and she added a pocket for her glasses and raised edges along the top to prevent things from falling down.

Basilio made a prototype (Figure 3, J) with 4 legs and a pointed top. The top could be folded down to a shelf. The side of the robot would be full of colourful lights, represented by the wooden colourful beads. The robot had a rectangular box as a base. He told us that he was fond of wood and that it was pretty. He told us that he thought it was fun and nice to participate in the workshop, he had not done anything similar previously, but he would want to do it again.

C. *Material explorations*

We noticed that the participants were not moving around the table and remained seated in their original positions through the workshop, and therefore assisted with fetching tools and materials. Some participants used wheelchairs that made moving around the table difficult. Others had pain. Some participants may also have refrained from exploring the piles and boxes of materials out of courtesy.

Some of the more successful material samples to present for the participants in terms of the extent to which the participants engaged with the samples presented to them, were textile swatch books. These consisted of equally cut pieces of textiles bundled together according to qualities and sorted by colour. These presented the participants with a chance to get an overview of the possibilities regarding textile colour and texture without engaging with large sets of materials at once. The same was true for a small collection of knitted and crochet samples, although these were larger and were not easily moved across the table. They were, however, explored by the participants who sat close by to them.

From the initial requirements formulated by the participants during their telling and making, the materials steel, aluminium, and glass was identified as missing in our samples. We did bring aluminium foil, which served as different types of metal in the prototypes, as well as one piece of acrylic glass which was reused as glass in two prototypes.

The design choice to bring ready-made basic forms, to partly prepare samples of material proved to be a good decision. Even if the samples could have been more varied in terms of sizes and forms, the partially prepared samples that fitted the basic forms helped make less demands on fine motor skills. The participants expressed a clear preference to delegating most of the physical work to us. Each participant was assisted by a researcher in many making tasks, such as cutting. Reducing cutting of fabric to one cut made it possible for some participants to do this themselves.

V. Findings

Considering how older adults may be enabled to participate actively in designing robots for the home through physical prototyping, two themes recurred in our notes from the workshops. Throughout the workshops, it was clear that the participants needed to understand the purpose, context, and function of the robot clearly before being able to generate ideas about how it should look. The participants in the subsequent workshops needed to further explore the stated purpose of the fetch robot and understand it in the context of their own lives before they could start designing the robot. They wished to reconcile the purpose with the needs of their homes and daily lives. The thought of having a robot in the perceived limited space of their apartments made them concerned whether the robot would really be useful to them. The lack of a clear purpose for the robot made it difficult, if not impossible, for the participants to start generating ideas and building a prototype.

Secondly, nearly all the participants questioned their ability to contribute to the design of robots. They felt like they did not have the right technical competence for designing robots, and they told us that it seemed futile to try to contribute new ideas to a group of researchers who were devoting their work to robot design. However, during the workshop, the participants understanding of their environment and experiences resulted in them contributing many ideas of what a robot can do in the home and what it could look like.

Regarding the method of material exploration and participatory prototyping, we found that the criteria for the choice of materials reported by the participants could be categorized broadly in aesthetic and functional concerns. The aesthetic concerns revolved around how the technology would fit into the existing and specific interior decoration of their homes. A related criterion was that the materials match current standards available in trade, that the product would match similar technology and that the materials were readily available in the production line. Several of the participants expressed concern about the functionality of the materials, especially regarding the maintainability of the robot. Most important to many participants was that the robot surface would be easy to keep clean. Some also stressed the need for visibility in terms of materials contrasting the relevant contextual material like the floor.

VI. Discussion

A. *The need for a clearly understood context and purpose for the design*

Many of our participants started out focusing on the realism of the robot design in terms of both the perceived need for and value of the robots, as well as their own ability to contribute to robot design in a meaningful way. They needed to first understand the purpose and be convinced of the value of the robot before they were willing to engage in the physical exploration. The purpose of the fetch robot seemed to be a purpose most participants could reconcile with their own needs in some way, and fetching items was also a popular suggestion in a survey among older adults [10]. We achieved this in the workshops by having a researcher pair up with each participant to explore the story of the participant. Even if the conversations went across the table between several researchers and participants, the one-to-one working pairs seemed important for the gradual development of a purpose and a context emerging from each participant. The literature emphasizes the role of physical prototyping for enabling stories about practices, understanding and mutual learning [5], [6]. We have experienced that telling and making operate in tandem and that the stories are also necessary to enable physical prototyping.

B. *Material explorations*

Our main aim with the workshop assignment was to explore the look and feel of a robot in the home, but this proved to be secondary to the purpose and value of the robot for our participants. While we could identify several criteria of choice of materials for the design of a robot in the home, as outlined under findings, these criteria often emerged during the conversation, and less so during the exploration of our material samples. The material samples were more often chosen and examined based on the aesthetic and functional requirements that emerged from the stories of the practice and the homes of the participants.

The design choices we made initially regarding what material samples to bring to the workshop and how to present them might have both limited and opened the design space in terms of new design ideas [1]. The form and positioning of the material samples and tools in relation to the participants may have influenced the extent to which any given material was explored. This suggests that the placement of samples of the available materials and tools should be given thought in the panning of physical prototyping workshops with older adults. It might have been useful to prepare samples of all available materials in small collections that the participants would be able to handle to compare the whole selection in one overview. This would imply preparing multiple equal sets of samples, and then offer to assist them in fetching larger quantities of the chosen materials as the participant reviewed the samples and got ideas for compositions. Tools should be available and placed in a handy distance so that all participants could see all the tools available to them.

C. *Creativity and technical feasibility*

While the participants started out focused on the realism of the assignment, most were able to use their imagination freely during the prototyping activity. Many of the participants developed their prototypes beyond their initial needs and requirements, such as dancing partner robot and hairdresser robot. In this phase of the design process, we were interested in the look and feel of the robots rather than the technical feasibility of the suggestions, and we encouraged creativity and fantasy in the prototyping. As we explained in our findings, Section V, several participants questioned the value of their prospective contribution to design ideas for robots. To share their expertise with us, they needed us to share our domain knowledge with them, so that they could understand the problem area and the possibilities they had in generating design ideas for robots in their homes. In the further exploration of this method, it would be interesting to introduce digital and technical components to visualise the technical possibilities and limitations of robot technology to this user group.

VII. CONCLUSION

We have reported from two workshops where we have used participatory prototyping and material explorations to facilitate participation in the design of robots for the home with older adults. Our findings suggest that while it is important to provide a context for the design of a robot at home, the development of the story about the robot in this context and in the daily life of the participants is essential to successful prototyping. A story of a robot placed into their life makes the basis for generating ideas about design. In our workshops, the activity of telling proceeded and informed the making and the material explorations. Due to the low mobility of the participants, the material exploration became more complicated, hence the presentation and forms of the material samples and tools provided in the workshops were important.

ACKNOWLEDGMENT

This work is partly supported by the Research Council of Norway as a part of the Multimodal Elderly Care Systems (MECS) project, under grant agreement 247697. We would like to thank the staff and residents at the living facility and Ingeborg, Jo Herstad, Suhas Govind Joshi, Tone Bratteteig, and Åsmund Dæhlen.

REFERENCES

[1] T. Bratteteig and I. Wagner, "Design decisions and the sharing of power in PD", pp. 29–32, 2014. Presented at the Proceedings of the 13th Participatory Design Conference: Short Papers, Industry Cases, Workshop Descriptions, Doctoral Consortium papers, and Keynote abstracts - Volume 2, ACM. doi: 10.1145/2662155.2662192.

[2] V. L. Hanson, A. Cavender and S. Trewin, "Writing about accessibility," Interactions, 22(6), pp. 62–65, 2005. doi: 10.1145/2828432.

[3] R. Soma, V. Dønnem Søyseth, M. Søyland, and T. Schulz, "Facilitating Robots at Home: A Framework for Understanding Robot Facilitation," in ACHI 2018, The Eleventh International Conference on Advances in Computer-Human Interactions, IARIA, 2018, pp. 1–6, ISBN: 978-1-61208-616-3

[4] J. Blomberg and H. Karasti, in Ethnography. Positioning ethnography within Participatory design in Simonsen, J and Robertson, T (ed.) Routledge International Handbook of Participatory Design, 2013.

[5] S. G. Joshi and T. Bratteteig, "Assembling fragments into continuous design": On participatory design with old people. Lecture Notes in Business Information Processing. ISSN 1865-1348. 223, s 13- 29, 2015. doi: 10.1007/9783-319-21783-3_2.

[6] E. Brandt, T. Binder and E. B. Sanders, in Tools and Techniques. "Ways to engage telling, making and enacting" in Simonsen, J and Robertson, T (ed.) Routledge International Handbook of Participatory Design, 2013.

[7] J. Jarke and S. Maaß, "Probes as Participatory Design Practice", *I-Com*, *17*(2), pp. 99–102, 2018. doi: 10.1515/icom-2018-0026

[8] J. Forlizzi and C. DiSalvo, "Service Robots in the Domestic Environment: A Study of the Roomba Vacuum in the Home," in Proceedings of the 1st ACM SIGCHI/SIGART Conference on Human-Robot Interaction, ser. HRI '06, New York, NY, USA: ACM, pp. 258–265, 2006. ISBN: 978-1-59593-294-5. doi: 10.1145/1121241.1121286.

[9] L. Pigini, D. Facal, L. Blasi, and R. Andrich, "Service robots in elderly care at home: Users' needs and perceptions as a basis for concept development," Technology and Disability, vol. 24, pp. 303–311, 2012.

[10] S. Bedaf, G. J. Gelderblom, and L. de Witte, "Overview and Categorization of Robots Supporting Independent Living of Elderly People: What Activities Do They Support and How Far Have They Developed," Assistive Technology, vol. 27, no. 2, pp. 88–100, 2014, ISSN: 1040-0435. doi: 10.1080/10400435.2014.978916.

Comparison of Nursing Personnel's User Experiences of Four Types of Assistive Robots: Challenges Include Knowledge and Safety Issues

Iina Aaltonen
VTT Technical Research Centre of Finland Ltd
Espoo, Finland
e-mail: iina.aaltonen@vtt.fi

Tuuli Turja
Faculty of Social Sciences
University of Tampere
Tampere, Finland
e-mail: tuuli.turja@staff.uta.fi

Marketta Niemelä
VTT Technical Research Centre of Finland Ltd
Tampere, Finland
e-mail: marketta.niemela@vtt.fi

Abstract— **The interest to employ service robots in the care context is increasing due to the aging population. Many studies have examined robot acceptance from various angles, but reports of actual robot usage and the user experiences of professional personnel are scarce. Via an online user experience questionnaire, this study targeted nursing personnel who have used assistive robots in their work. Ten statements, modified after the Almere questionnaire, concerned the respondents' acceptance of robots which they had used. Four different types of robots (robotic therapy animal; rehabilitation/recreational robot; telepresence robot; and patient lifting robot) were each covered separately. Most of the reported robot usage was with the seal robot Paro, and regular use of any robot was rare. The intentions to use and the attitudes towards each type of robot were generally positive. The patient lifting robots were most positively received regarding their usefulness, whereas the interaction with the robotic therapy animals was rated pleasant. Fewer respondents had used the rehabilitation/recreational robots and telepresence robots, which received lower scores than the others regarding many of the studied user experience aspects. In general, more knowledge is needed to make good use of the robots. Furthermore, it seems there are some concerns of the safety of using them. These results show that the initial steps towards employing robots in care work have been taken. There is a lot of underexplored ground between the simple-to-use therapy animal robots and functional patient lifting robots, and the potential and acceptance of those robots is yet to be seen. These results give a baseline for monitoring the service robot acceptance of nursing personnel based on actual robot usage.**

Keywords-human-robot interaction; service robots; acceptance; user experience; nursing.

I. INTRODUCTION

Robots have been suggested as a partial solution to tackle the challenge of aging population and the increased need for care services. For instance, it has been estimated that there will be a shortage of 380 000 caregivers by 2025 in Japan [1], and in Finland, the demand for care labor will increase by more than 100 000 persons by 2030 [2]. Robots could relieve the physical burden of care tasks (e.g., lifting and transfer of patients), increase the efficiency of care work (e.g., by improving rehabilitation of persons, or taking secondary care tasks, such as fetch and delivery tasks, from care workers) and increase the quality of life of the elderly themselves (e.g., by increasing their mobility or helping to keep in contact with their social networks) so that they would need less help from care workers.

The public opinion of robots has been studied consistently in Europe for several years. The Eurobarometer 2017 [3] shows that 61% of Europeans have a positive view of robots and artificial intelligence, and 30% a negative view (in Finland, the respective figures were 71% and 23%). On the other hand, the opinions are less positive for "having a robot to provide them services and companionship when infirm or elderly," and a comparison between the last two Eurobarometers (years 2014–2017) shows that exceedingly more people feel uncomfortable having robots perform these tasks [3]. Regarding gender differences, men have typically more positive attitudes towards robots than women [3][4] although the opposite has been reported for the seal robot Paro [5].

In the care context, the attitudes of elderly people towards service robots have been studied extensively (see, e.g., reviews [6][7]), and a lot of technical development is done towards assisting the elderly people at their homes (see e.g., reviews [8][9]). Although the views of the elderly and their relatives provide good input to the research and technical development of assistive technology, Saborowski & Kollak raised the importance of taking into account the care professionals' needs [10]. Specifically, they pointed out that new technology and robotics have started to change the relation between care workers and technology, and already the care workers need to have the knowledge to help people use assistive technology. Their interviews revealed that the care staff had encountered several technology-related issues, such as malfunctioning devices and lack of competence and training [10]. In rehabilitation context, barriers to adopt new technologies were similar [11]. On the other hand, in the rehabilitation context, the acceptance and use of new technologies was most strongly affected by the perceived usefulness of the technologies, while the effort to use them or social pressure were not significant factors. Current use of new technologies was affected by behavioral intention and facilitating conditions, such as institutional support [11].

The care personnel's general opinion towards robotics has been studied to some extent. Compared with the opinion of the general population, healthcare professionals had more negative attitudes towards robots [12]. However, the healthcare professionals would be comfortable with robots aiding in moving heavy materials, patients or other items, and in sorting and shelving [12]. In addition to those, other tasks that have been suggested for robots in the care context include laundry, food and medicine distribution, patient monitoring, help with forgetfulness and falling, motivation and activation, and companionship [13]–[15].

A literature review showed that the concerns the health professionals have regarding robots include the fear of the robot's unreliability in clinical situation, privacy of patients, unemployment, and decrease of face-to-face contact with patients [13]. In the same article, 39% of surveyed nurses thought they may need service robots at work. The reasons for needing robots was not affected by perceived high physical workload; however, aspects such as making the work lighter, increasing the meaningfulness and quality of work, and time savings affected the need for robots [13].

There are relatively few studies that have reported of the care personnel's experiences of actual robot usage at work. Focus group discussions about professional caregivers' experiences with the seal robot Paro showed that the emotional and social impact of the robot were perceived as positive, while there were difficulties in taking the full advantage of the robot due to the lack of information and availability of the robot, and the caregivers were worried about the robot's hygiene and about breaking the robot [16].

A bathtub robot was initially rejected by nursing staff due to temporal and financial investments, but it was later accepted, because it supported the staff's values on patient well-being and integrity, even though the robot did not bring significant ergonomic benefits nor save labour [17].

In the context of a mobile self-navigating greeting robot in a care-hospital, the personnel raised issues, such as the fear of making mistakes with the robot, the fear of being replaced by robots, the inability of robots to replace human care, and irritation caused by the robot's presence. On the other hand, the robot was seen as a source of support for staff and it elicited a positive atmosphere [18].

With telepresence robots, the personnel's primary concern of the elderly users' negative reactions was not realized in practice. The personnel approved that the robot enabled the residents to interact with their families remotely, and despite technical problems, the personnel believed that with adequate training and assistance, the use of the telepresence robot would be feasible in the future [19]. In two other telepresence studies, care workers experienced robot trials positively although issues, such as the privacy and integrity of the patients, and the need for common rules, were raised [20][21].

To summarize the studies related to robots in the care context, the elderly perspective is well represented in the literature, but it seems the studies on professional personnel's attitudes, needs and concerns remain on a general level and are based on expectations rather than on actual robot usage. Therefore, there is a research gap between expectations of robots and the actual usage experiences among the professionals in the healthcare sector, especially when different robots and larger user groups are considered. The aim of this paper is to compare the nursing personnel's user experiences of four different kinds of robots which they have actually used in their work (Figure 1). These results give a baseline for monitoring the acceptance of service robots by professional nurses and help us identify needs for future development, which is important if robots are to be the future co-workers of the care personnel.

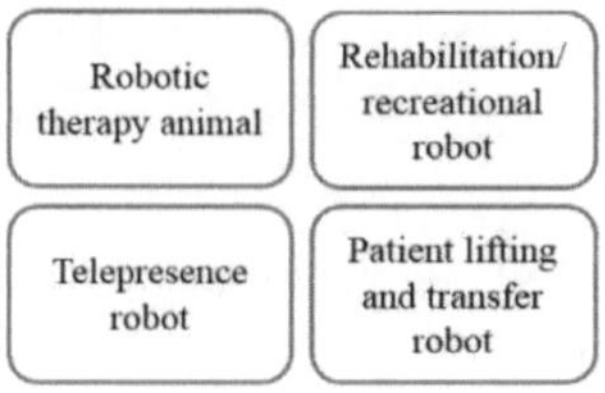

Figure 1. The four types of robots that were in the focus of this research.

The rest of this paper is organized as follows. Section II describes the methods. Section III reports the results and Section IV discusses them. Section V and the acknowledgements conclude the paper.

II. METHODS

As part of a research project concerning the use of robotics in welfare services, Finnish nursing personnel were asked to participate in an online questionnaire concerning their attitudes towards robots and their robot usage at work [12]. In addition to user experience questions, the online questionnaire included 127 general multiple-choice questions concerning demographics, occupational details, and attitudes towards technology and robotics. The online questionnaire was distributed between October and December 2016 through two major trade unions, The Union of Health and Social Care Professionals in Finland and The Finnish Union of Practical Nurses (most of the Finnish nurses are unionized [22]). The final aggregate data included the responses of 3 800 respondents who had completed at least the first page of socio-demographic information and a question concerning their interest in technology (reported elsewhere [12]). The average response time was 19 minutes. 458 respondents (12% of total) had had first-hand experience with robots, and their responses are reported in this paper.

The respondents with first-hand experience with robots (n=458) were prompted to answer a user experience (UX) questionnaire regarding each of the types of robots they had used. They were aged 19–70 (mean 46.8; standard deviation 11.46), and 95% of them were native Finnish speakers. By profession, 62% were practical nurses, 34% registered nurses, and 4% were physiotherapists, instructors, and assistants.

The UX questionnaire covered the robot usage of four different types of robots, which were introduced using generic terms and example photos as follows:

- Robotic therapy animal (image of the seal robot Paro)
- Rehabilitation/recreational robot (image of the humanoid robot Nao)
- Telepresence robot (image of Double)
- Patient lifting and transfer robot (images of RoboticBed and Riba bear).

The respondents with first-hand usage experience with any of the types of robots listed above were prompted for more questions regarding the frequency they had used the type of robot in question (used once or twice; a few sporadic times; in regular use for less than one month; in regular use for one or two months; in regular use for several months); followed by ten items concerning their user experience (5-point Likert scale, totally disagree – totally agree), adapted from the Almere questionnaire [23]. The Almere model is an extension of the Unified Theory of Acceptance and Use of Technology (UTAUT)[24], and it was developed to test the acceptance of social robots. The Almere model uses constructs (e.g., anxiety, trust, perceived ease of use) to predict the user's intention to use a robot. In the Almere questionnaire, each of the constructs is represented by 2-5 statements evaluated using the Likert scale [23].

The questionnaire items are listed in Table 1 (translated from Finnish; order reorganized to facilitate reporting). In the UX questionnaire, the questions were answered separately for each type of robot the respondents were experienced with. Compared with the Almere questionnaire, the items #1, #6 and #10 deviate most from the original items whereas the other items are mainly about re-phrasings of the original ones to suit all four types of robots and to reflect the literal translations from the Finnish language. The Almere model has two items for Trust, but they reflect trust for the robot's advice (the studied robots do not generally give advice), and therefore item #6 was generated to measure the overall perceived reliability of the robot and its safety.

Regarding the non-social robots, item #10 measures "Perceived operating friendliness" instead of "Perceived sociability" to reflect the smoothness of interaction instead of social characteristics. Moreover, the Almere item for Perceived sociability in the context of telepresence robots could have been misinterpreted to mean the interaction between two humans communicating through the robot. The UX composite variables showed good inter-item consistency: Rehabilitation/recreational robot (α = .787), robotic therapy animal (α = .846), telepresence robot (α = .819), and patient lifting robot (α = .781).

The participants were instructed to answer the questionnaire as follows: "Please answer the following questions thinking that the same robot that you are already experienced with would be taken into use at your workplace by the personnel."

There were several reasons for adapting the set of questions from the Almere questionnaire. Firstly, the number of questions had to be limited to keep the overall answering time manageable: using the whole Almere questionnaire would have made the whole online questionnaire [12] too burdensome, and therefore only ten items were included. Secondly, to the best of our knowledge, there are no human-robot interaction questionnaires available that would suit all four kind of robots. For example, many available questionnaires are targeted at the social characteristics of robots (e.g., [27]), which would not make sense in the context of telepresence or mechanoid lifting robots. The Almere construct "Social presence" was dropped for a similar reason. Thirdly, we wanted to use constructs that are compatible with technology acceptance models (e.g., [24][26]), but would reflect at least some of the characteristics related to robots specifically (e.g., safety and interaction). The Almere constructs have also been used in a review [7] and as a part of a study focusing on telepresence robots [28].

TABLE I. UX QUESTIONNAIRE FOR THE FOUR TYPES OF ROBOTS. EXCLUDING ITEM #10, THE PHRASES WERE THE SAME FOR ALL FOUR TYPES OF ROBOTS, WITH THE [ROBOT] REPLACED BY EACH TYPE OF ROBOT. THE RESPECTIVE ITEMS AND CONSTRUCTS IN THE ALMERE QUESTIONNAIRE [23] ARE SHOWN ON THE RIGHT.

#	Questionnaire item	Respective item in Almere	Construct in Almere
1	If the [robot] was available, I would use it[a]	I'm certain to use the robot during the next few days	Intention to use
2	I think it's a good idea to use the [robot]	I think it's a good idea to use the robot	Attitude towards technology
3	I think the [robot] would be useful in my job[b]	I think the robot is useful to me	Perceived usefulness
4	I think I can use the [robot] without any help	I think I can use the robot without any help	Perceived ease of use
5	Working with the [robot] would be pleasant	I enjoy doing things with the robot	Perceived enjoyment
6	I would be worried about the safety of using the [robot][c]	–	Trust
7	I think the [robot] can be adapted to what I need	I think the robot can be adaptive to what I need	Perceived adaptivity
8	I know enough of the [robot] to make good use of it	I know enough of the robot to make good use of it	Facilitating conditions
9	I would be afraid to make mistakes with the [robot].	If I should use the robot, I would be afraid to make mistakes with it	Anxiety
10	I find the {Robotic therapy animal; Rehabilitation/recreational robot} pleasant to interact with In my experience, controlling the {Telepresence robot; Patient lifting robot} goes smoothly[d]	I find the robot pleasant to interact with	Perceived sociability (Perceived operating friendliness)[d]

a. "If the robot was available, I would use it." was used in [25].

b. "I would find [.....] useful in my job" was used originally in [24][26].

c. The item reflects the Almere definition of Trust "The belief that the system performs with personal integrity and reliability".

d. Perceived sociability was replaced by "Perceived operating friendliness" for the non-social robots.

The data were fitted into the Almere model to see if the nine questionnaire items (items #2–9 in Table 1) could predict the Intention to use (item #1 in Table 1) according to the model [23]. However, the small sample size did not produce statistically significant results among all the robot types and explanatory factors. Wanting to present results separately for every robot type, we therefore focus on a descriptive analysis of the UX. Additionally, the general opinion towards robots among these respondents was asked using the same phrase as in the Eurobarometer survey ("Generally speaking, do you have a 'very positive' (4); 'fairly positive' (3); 'fairly negative' (2); or 'very negative' (1) view of robots?").

III. RESULTS

The number of respondents having used robots was a) 201 (44%) for a robotic therapy animal; b) 59 (13%) for a rehabilitation/recreational robot; c) 63 (14%) for a telepresence robot; and d) 79 (17%) for a patient lifting robot; the total number of respondents reporting of first-hand robot usage was 458 (some participants chose not to answer all questions). Figure 2 shows that most respondents had used the robots only once or twice whereas regular use was much less common.

The effect of the frequency of usage on the questionnaire items was not significant. Looking at all the robot types combined, Intention to use correlated the most with Attitude ($r=.695$; $p<.001$) and Perceived enjoyment ($r=.626$; $p<.001$). Regarding opinions towards robots in general, 61% of respondents had a positive and 26% a negative opinion towards robots, and the rest were indecisive (mean = 2.73; SD .68; scale 1–4). The user experience viewed as an aggregate variable of average questionnaire items did not correlate with age or working years of the respondent. Regarding the experiences of the robotic therapy animal, women had more positive views than men ($F(1)$ 4.546; $p<.05$). The other robot types did not show gender differences. Earlier experiences of care technologies correlated positively with the questionnaire items, yet only with the users of telepresence robots ($r = .362$; $p < .01$) and the robotic therapy animal ($r = .242$; $p < .05$).

There were big differences between the UX questionnaire data for the different types of robots (see the error bars indicating the standard error of the mean in Figures 3–5). The UX questionnaire for each robot was answered only by nursing personnel with actual user experience of the robot in question. On average, the questionnaire items (Figures 4–5) were towards the positive end of the scale except for the items for the Facilitating conditions (sufficient knowledge about the robot) and Trust (worrying about the safety) for which three types of robots received lower ratings. Overall, looking at the average of all 10 questionnaire items, the

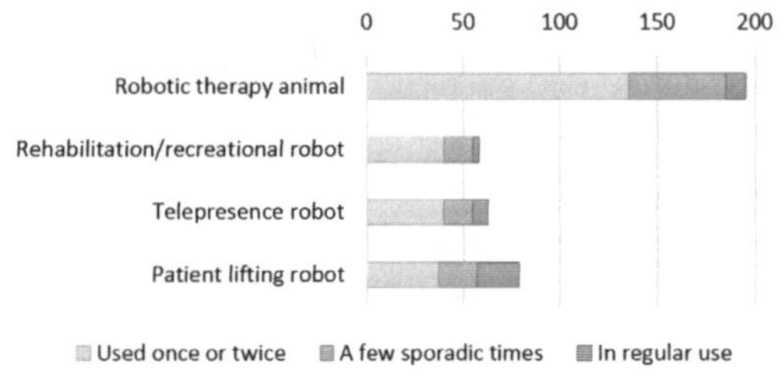

Figure 2. Number of nurses with experience of robot usage for each robot type. The legend indicates the frequency of usage.

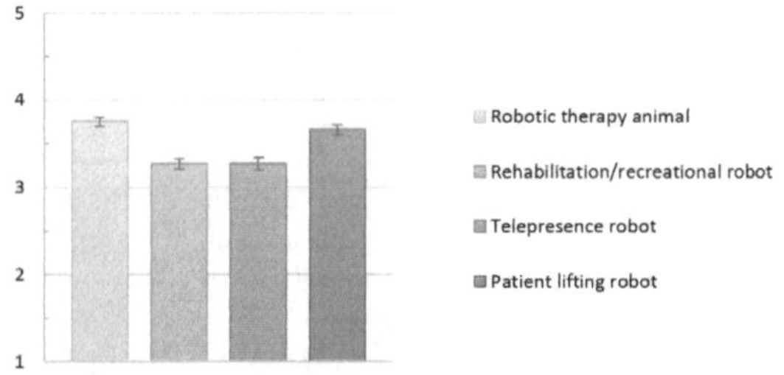

Figure 3. Average of the ten questionnaire items by robot type. Higher values indicate a more positive attitude towards robot usage (5=totally agree, 1=totally disagree).

robotic therapy animal (open field answers indicated most respondents had used the Paro seal) was most positively received, followed by the patient lifting robot (Figure 3). On the other hand, Intention to use, Attitude, and Perceived usefulness of patient lifting robots were higher than those for the robotic therapy animal (Figure 4). With the robotic therapy animal, interaction and work were rated pleasant, the robot was easy to use, and the respondents were not afraid to make mistakes with it.

The rehabilitation/recreational robot (open field answers indicated most respondents had used the Zora robot) and the telepresence robot received more cautious ratings. The respondents had less experience with these robots and they did not have enough knowledge of them. The pleasantness and smoothness of interacting and working with them was rated close to neutral, but lower than with the other two robots, and they were not considered as useful. Nevertheless, Intention to use and Attitude were positive. The responses did not identify robot brands for telepresence and patient lifting robots.

IV. DISCUSSION

The Finnish nursing personnel with actual experience of robot usage at work had a more positive attitude towards robots than the Finnish nursing personnel in general (cf. [12]). However, their attitude remains slightly more negative than the opinion of the general population in Finland (Eurobarometer data)[12]. On the other hand, the general acceptance of robots is higher in Finland than in many other European countries [3], and the Finnish nursing personnel's acceptance comes close to the recent European average. Robot acceptance at work (as opposed to the general acceptance) has been found stronger among those healthcare professionals who have used robots in their work [12], and therefore first-hand experiences with robots at work are important in molding the ground for robots in care work.

Regarding gender issues, whereas men are typically more positive towards robots than women [3][4], these results indicated higher acceptance of the robotic therapy animal among women in the care context, which is consistent with an earlier evaluation of the same robot by exhibition visitors from different countries [5].

Most of the robot usage was with a robot therapy animal, or the Paro seal. The Paro seal is easy to use, and it can help in creating a positive atmosphere toward care robots, and

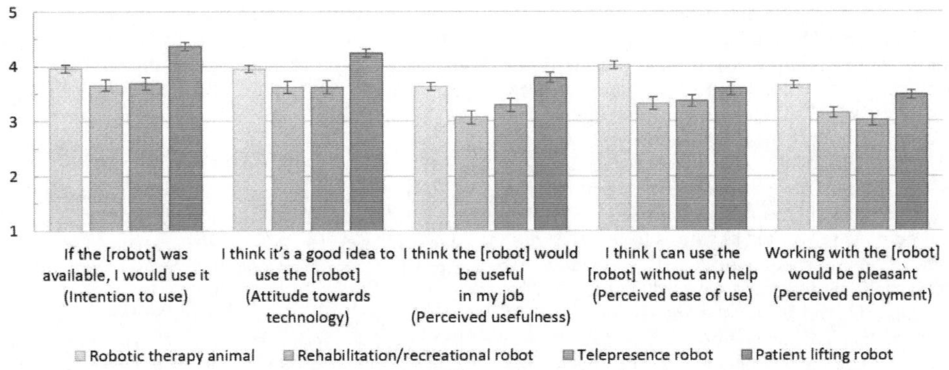

Figure 4. Mean responses to the questionnaire items #1–5. Higher values indicate a more positive attitude towards robot usage (5=totally agree, 1=totally disagree).

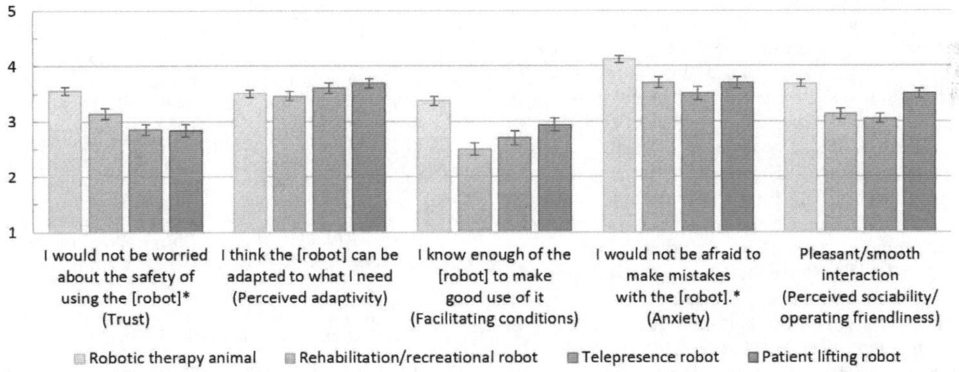

Figure 5. Mean responses to the questionnaire items #6–10. Higher values indicate a more positive attitude towards robot usage (5=totally agree, 1=totally disagree; the items marked with an asterisk * are inverted; see Table 1 for the used phrases).

therefore facilitate the adoption of other robots as well [16]. Assistive robots, however, include many more possibilities than just the social, companionship types of characteristics.

A minority of the respondents had used any robot regularly (Figure 2). Therefore, the answers may be based on projected expectations of how robots could aid the care work in the future. On the other hand, there was no significant difference between the responses of those with very little and those with regular experience of robot usage. Earlier research has shown that even meeting a robot may result in more favorable attitudes [29], although direct experiences with robots have not always affected acceptance ratings [25]. Repetitive testing for determining acceptance has been suggested [7][23], and therefore the robot UX of the nursing personnel should be monitored repetitively.

The lack of knowledge of the robots (Facilitating conditions) was clearly the aspect that needs most improvement although the evaluations for each type of robot can reflect different things. For example, using the Paro seal requires understanding of the therapeutic possibilities of the robot (see also [16]) whereas operating the Nao (or Zora) robot requires also some technical skills. Others have also raised the knowledge of how to use and adapt the technology as an important topic [10]. In this study, most of the respondents believed the robots could be adapted to their needs, but a future question is whether it is the nursing personnel or specialized persons who do the adapting, or if the robot is self-adaptive. Furthermore, the users may also have to adapt to the needs of the robots [30]. In the rehabilitation context, training needs have been identified as a barrier for using new technology, and similarly, Facilitating condition (institutional support and knowledge) has been found to be the strongest construct for current use of new technologies by rehabilitation professionals [11], and therefore the issue of knowledge should be emphasized in the future.

The nurses' low level of trust in the safety of the robots is slightly alarming, because the robots the nurses had used are presumably commercial products. On the other hand, the ratings were near the middle of the Likert scale, which can also mean that the respondents were indecisive or had mixed feelings towards the questionnaire item. Furthermore, as with the knowledge issues, safety can take different meanings with different robots, which should be examined further. For example, telepresence robots may seem wobbly and pose security and privacy issues [20], and patients may be harmed if an extremity is squeezed by the robot's joints.

The attitudes were most positive for the patient lifting robots. Additionally, the intention to use and perceived usefulness for the patient lifting robots were also higher than for other robots, which can reflect that their purpose of use can be easier to see than for the other robots. A weakness to the study design is that the respondents did not have to specify which kind of lifting robots they had used.

The UX questionnaire worked as a basis for a descriptive analysis of the different robot types. With especially the rehabilitation/recreational robots, however, the questionnaire leaves some ambiguity regarding the interaction with the robot (e.g., pleasantness of interaction, ease of use, fear of making mistakes). The questionnaire did not specifically state whether the interaction was only about the social interaction, or was the programming of the robot also considered a form of interaction. In a similar vein, the robot classification in questionnaire item #10 was done based on the presumption that the interaction with robots with social characteristics would be more natural and that they would not need "controlling" as the more mechanical robots do. Categories of physical or social assistance [31], or companion or service type of assistance [23] could facilitate in assigning the constructs. The question of who will be programming and controlling the robots, and adapting their behavior, is a relevant issue for the future working practices and education of nursing personnel on a larger scale.

The limitations of the study include the small number of the UX questionnaire items and the previously discussed ambiguity related to the questionnaire, the low frequency of use, and the uncertainty related to the extent to which the respondents had interacted with the robots. Moreover, the exact versions of the robots and the ways the robots had been used are not known, and therefore the results should not be considered as user experience evaluations of specific robot models or interfaces.

In addition to the four types of assistive robots considered in this study, there are also other robots that can support care work, such as exoskeletons, indoor logistics, and surgical robots. Compared to the robots' future tasks that have been conceived by care personnel [12]–[15], none of the latter kind of robots fulfil those needs, and neither do the robots included in this study meet those needs in full. Currently, there is little or no experiences of actual robot usage of robots that can perform those tasks, and it will be interesting to see how the acceptance of that kind of autonomous and possibly multitasking robots relate to the types of robots reported in this paper.

V. Conclusion and Future Work

This study provides a baseline for monitoring the acceptance of different types of service robots by professional nurses. Because service robots are still scarce in the health sector, these results are novel in that they show the comparison of four different types of robots and they are based on actual robot usage instead of expectations. The results showed that Finnish nursing personnel have a relatively positive attitude towards using robots in general and the robots they are most experienced with, but more effort is needed to improve the personnel's knowledge of robots, the understanding of the robots' potential use applications, and the trust towards the safety of using the robots.

Acknowledgement

Sincere thanks to all questionnaire respondents. This research is a part of the project Robots and the Future of Welfare Services 2015–2020, which is funded by the Strategic Research Council at the Academy of Finland.

References

[1] Y. Matsumoto, "Development and introduction of robotic devices for elderly care in Japan," Invited talk in IEEE ICRA 2018 Workshop on Elderly Care Robotics - Technology and Ethics (WELCARO), 2018. [Online]. Available from: https://docs.google.com/viewer?a=v&pid=sites&srcid=ZGVmYXVsdGRvbWFpbnxpY3JhMjAxOHdlbGNhcm98Z3g6MzU5ZGUxYTI0MjIyYjYxMQ [retrieved: 1, 2019].

[2] E.-L. Koponen, "Sosiaali- ja terveysalan työvoiman riittävyys nyt ja tulevaisuudessa [The sufficiency of the social and health sector workforce now and in the future]," TEM raportteja 13/2015, pp. 1–28. [Online]. Available from: https://julkaisut.valtioneuvosto.fi/bitstream/handle/10024/75078/TEMraportti_13_2015_web_27022015.pdf?sequence=1 [retrieved: 1, 2019].

[3] European Commission, "Special Eurobarometer 460 – March 2017 'Attitudes towards the impact of digitisation and automation on daily life,'" 2017.

[4] M. M. A. de Graaf and S. Ben Allouch, "Exploring influencing variables for the acceptance of social robots," Rob. Auton. Syst., vol. 61, no. 12, pp. 1476–1486, 2013.

[5] T. Shibata, K. Wada, Y. Ikeda, and S. Sabanovic, "Cross-Cultural Studies on Subjective Evaluation of a Seal Robot," Adv. Robot., vol. 23, no. 4, pp. 443–458, 2009.

[6] K. M. Goher, N. Mansouri, and S. O. Fadlallah, "Assessment of personal care and medical robots from older adults' perspective," Robot. Biomimetics, vol. 4, no. 5, pp. 1–7, 2017.

[7] S. Whelan, et al., "Factors Affecting the Acceptability of Social Robots by Older Adults Including People with Dementia or Cognitive Impairment: A Literature Review," Int. J. Soc. Robot., vol. 10, no. 5, pp 643–668, 2018.

[8] S. Bedaf, G. J. Gelderblom, and L. De Witte, "Overview and categorization of robots supporting independent living of elderly people: what activities do they support and how far have they developed," Assist. Technol., vol. 27, no. 2, pp. 88–100, 2015.

[9] P. Khosravi and A. H. Ghapanchi, "Investigating the effectiveness of technologies applied to assist seniors: A systematic literature review," Int. J. Med. Inform., vol. 85, no. 1, pp. 17–26, 2015.

[10] M. Saborowski and I. Kollak, "'How do you care for technology?' - Care professionals' experiences with assistive technology in care of the elderly," Technol. Forecast. Soc. Change, vol. 93, pp. 133–140, 2015.

[11] L. Liu, et al., "What factors determine therapists' acceptance of new technologies for rehabilitation – a study using the Unified Theory of Acceptance and Use of Technology (UTAUT)," Disabil. Rehabil., vol. 37, no. 5, pp. 447–455, 2015.

[12] T. Turja, L. Van Aerschot, T. Särkikoski, and A. Oksanen, "Finnish healthcare professionals' attitudes towards robots: Reflections on a population sample," Nurs. Open, vol. 5, no. 3, pp. 300–309, 2018.

[13] K. J. Vänni and S. E. Salin, "A Need for Service Robots Among Health Care Professionals in Hospitals and Housing Services," LNCS (including Subser. Lect. Notes Artif. Intell. Lect. Notes Bioinformatics), vol. 10652 LNAI, pp. 178–187, 2017.

[14] D. Facal, L. Pigini, M. Mast, L. Blasi, and F. I. Cavallaro, "SRS Multi-Role Shadow Robotic System for Independent Living. Deliverable D1.1. Detailed user requirements, environment definition, general guidelines on ethical concerns and SRS scenario report.," 2011. [Online]. Available from: http://srs-project.eu/sites/default/files/SRS%20247772%20DELIVERABLE%201.1.pdf [retrieved: 1, 2019].

[15] E. Broadbent et al., "Attitudes towards health-care robots in a retirement village," Australas. J. Ageing, vol. 31, no. 2, pp. 115–120, 2012.

[16] M. Niemelä, H. Määttä, and M. Ylikauppila, "Expectations and experiences of adopting robots in elderly care in Finland: perspectives of caregivers and decision-makers," ICServ Special Session: Meaningful Technologies for Seniors, Sept. 2016, pp. 1–8.

[17] K. Beedholm, K. Frederiksen, A. M. S. Frederiksen, and K. Lomborg, "Attitudes to a robot bathtub in Danish elder care: A hermeneutic interview study," Nurs. Heal. Sci., vol. 17, no. 3, pp. 280–286, 2015.

[18] D. Hebesberger, T. Koertner, C. Gisinger, and J. Pripfl, "A Long-Term Autonomous Robot at a Care Hospital: A Mixed Methods Study on Social Acceptance and Experiences of Staff and Older Adults," Int. J. Soc. Robot., vol. 9, pp. 417–429, 2017.

[19] W. Moyle, et al., "Connecting the person with dementia and family: a feasibility study of a telepresence robot," BMC Geriatr., vol. 14, no. 7, pp. 1–11, 2014.

[20] M. Niemelä, L. van Aerschot, A. Tammela, and I. Aaltonen, "A Telepresence Robot in Residential Care: Family Increasingly Present, Personnel Worried About Privacy," in The 9th International Conference on Social Robotics, ICSR 2017. Part of LNCS (including Subser. Lect. Notes Artif. Intell. Lect. Notes Bioinformatics), 2017, vol. 10652 LNAI, pp. 85–94.

[21] I.-L. Boman and A. Bartfai, "The first step in using a robot in brain injury rehabilitation: patients' and health-care professionals' perspective," Disabil. Rehabil. Assist. Technol., vol. 10, no. 5, pp. 365–370, 2015.

[22] T. Kilpeläinen, "Foreign nurses' guide to Finnish working life," Satakunta University of Applied Sciences. European Social Fund (ESF), 2010.

[23] M. Heerink, B. Kröse, V. Evers, and B. Wielinga, "Assessing acceptance of assistive social agent technology by older adults: The Almere model," Int. J. Soc. Robot., vol. 2, no. 4, pp. 361–375, 2010.

[24] V. Venkatesh, M. G. Morris, G. B. Davis, and F. D. Davis, "User acceptance of information technology: Toward a unified view," MIS Q., vol. 27, no. 3, pp. 425–478, 2003.

[25] Y. H. Wu, et al., "Acceptance of an assistive robot in older adults : a mixed-method study of human-robot interaction over a 1-month period in the Living Lab setting," Clin. Interv. Aging, vol. 9, pp. 801–811, 2015.

[26] F. D. Davis, "User acceptance of information technology: system characteristics, user perceptions and behavioral impacts," Int. J. Man. Mach. Stud., vol. 38, pp. 475–487, 1993.

[27] C. Bartneck, D. Kulić, E. Croft, and S. Zoghbi, "Measurement instruments for the anthropomorphism, animacy, likeability, perceived intelligence, and perceived safety of robots," Int. J. Soc. Robot., vol. 1, no. 1, pp. 71–81, 2009.

[28] A. Cesta, G. Cortellessa, A. Orlandini, and L. Tiberio, "Long-Term Evaluation of a Telepresence Robot for the Elderly: Methodology and Ecological Case Study," Int. J. Soc. Robot., vol. 8, no. 3, pp. 421–441, 2016.

[29] R. Q. Stafford et al., "Improved robot attitudes and emotions at a retirement home after meeting a robot," Proc. IEEE International Workshop on Robot and Human Interactive Communication, Sept. 2010, pp. 82–87.

[30] J. Forlizzi and C. DiSalvo, "Service robots in the domestic environment," Proc.The 1st ACM SIGCHI/SIGART conference on Human-robot interaction - HRI '06, March 2006, pp. 258–265.

[31] S. Leminen, M. Westerlund, and M. Rajahonka, "Innovating with service robots in health and welfare living labs," Int. J. Innov. Manag., vol. 21, no. 8, pp. 1–24, 2017.

A First Postural Tracking Using a Kinect v2 Sensor During an Immersive Wheelchair Driving Simulation

Franck Pouvrasseau, Eric Monacelli, Sébastien Charles

Laboratory of Engineering of Systems of Versailles (LISV)
University of Versailles Saint-Quentin (UVSQ)
Versailles, France
Email: franck.pouvrasseau@uvsq.lisv.fr , eric.monacelli@uvsq.lisv.fr
sebastien.charles@uvsq.lisv.fr

***Abstract*—Wheelchair simulators using virtual reality have been conceived for a better understanding of the mobility problem, and also to train people in wheelchair driving. Virtual Fauteuil is an immersive simulator equipped with a compact motion platform that reproduces physical effects like collisions, or being on slopes along the roll and pitch axis. Like most of the existing simulators, Virtual Fauteuil offers a training program, based on the performances of the user. However, a parameter is neglected for the performance evaluation, which is the posture of the user, although it affects his stability. This study focus on a light, basic and non-invasive solution for body tracking, the Kinect v2 sensor, and its implementation in the simulator Virtual Fauteuil. The experiment conducted in this paper consists in analyzing the movement of the torso when the user lives a perturbation in the simulator. This first postural evaluation has been done with 12 participants (9 males and 3 females). They were not asked to drive the wheelchair. The simulator was indeed programmed in such a manner that the avatar follows by itself a straight route composed of bumps which cause physical perturbations through the simulator. The experiment was in two sessions. During the first session, the travel was not displayed on the screen, so it means that the users lived perturbations without expecting it. During the second session, the participant lived the same travel but this time, with a visual immersion on a front screen. Perturbations are measured by investigating the rotation of the trunk compared to the rotation of the platform. Results shows that participants were more impacted by perturbation when the simulation was displayed on the screen. We also found that for the expermiment, participants were immune to trunk flexions, which means that the trunk of participants were mostly straight during disturbances. In-depth study will soon be done around the postural response of the user and on different exercises.**

***Keywords*–virtual reality; simulation; wheelchair training; rehab; postural tracking.**

I. INTRODUCTION

Wheelchair users are facing mobility problems that have different causes. Wheelchairs are a very practical solution for disabled people to recover a significant part of their mobility but it still have imperfections, that discourages people with reduced mobility. For example, wheelchairs are not adapted to all kind of terrain. In fact, public spaces have accessibility deficiencies like stairs, type of terrains, slopes etc. that make a wheelchair travel arduous. A poorly accessible route can expose the person to a loss of balance and in the worst situation to a fall from his wheelchair. In order to improve the mobility of people with reduced mobility in the broad sense, immersive simulators using Virtual Reality have been developed [1]–[6]. Indeed, wheelchair simulators can have different functions: First, it can raise able people awareness about mobility issues faced by persons with disabilities. Secondly, simulators can be an interesting tool to evaluate the accessibility and the arduousness of a route and help person to plan their trip. It also can help architects who conceive public infrastructures for the conception of their urban planning which are destined to wheelchairs accessibility. And finally, wheelchair simulators are a really valuable way to train people in wheelchair driving. Using an immersive simulator to train people to drive a wheelchair have a lot of advantages. The whole environment is configurable, which means that, for example, in the situation of a training program for a beginner, we control the type of exercises we want to train the user in. We also can regulate the difficulty, (by adding obstacles, or making the travel harder to achieve) so the simulator is always adapted to the person. Another aspect make the use of wheelchair simulators interesting. In fact, some people already experienced a traumatic experience and it repels them to use their wheelchair again. Simulators are secured. It is a comforting and attractive experience. Finally, using a simulator enable a monitoring of the performances of the user. Simulators can evaluate the performance from measured values provided by the simulator like: duration of a fixed travel, distance needed for the travel, number of collisions, etc. These functional index of performances focus on the wheelchair and its movement and neglect the user's posture. This study proposes a first method for postural tracking during a simulation. The postural tracking system has been implemented to the simulator Virtual Fauteuil [7], which has been developed in the LISV (Laboratoire d'ingénierie des systèmes de Versailles) - University of Versailles Saint-Quentin.

II. PRESENTATION OF THE SIMULATOR VIRTUAL FAUTEUIL

Virtual Fauteuil (Figure 1) is a simulator composed of a compact and easily transportable platform whose dimensions are 1.20 meter by 1 meter which can host any type of wheelchair. This platform is equipped with haptic feedback systems which enhance the immersion and the realism of the simulation (Figure 2):

- 4 Jack actuators, located at the 4 corners of the

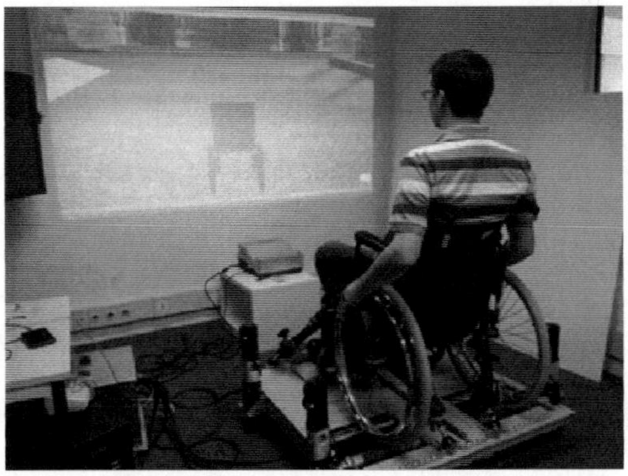

Figure 1. The simulator Virtual Fauteuil

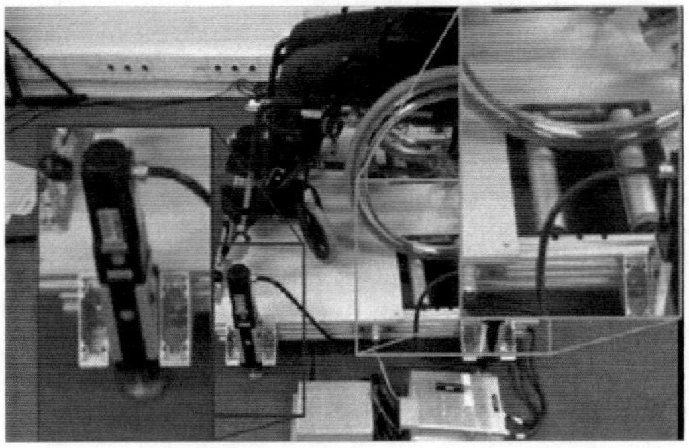

Figure 2. The two haptic feedback system of the platform. The Jack actuators in blue, and the force-feedback rolls in orange.

platform, which are used to rotate the platform in order to reproduce the sensations of going thought a slopes, or having perturbations like collisions or going down a sidewalk.

- 4 rolls on which are placed the two rear wheels of the wheelchair. Each wheel of the wheelchair is thus based on a roll in gear with an electric motorcycle-encoder and a passive roller which ensures the stability of the user. This configuration allows firstly to recover shift of the wheelchair data and thus to render the movements of the user in the virtual environment, and secondly, to send to the user's force feedback for example by simulating change of declination of the ground and/or inertial effect

The principle of the management of the haptic devices and the virtual environment is condensed in the figure 3.

A. Projection of the simulation

Simulations are conducted in a 3D virtual reality environment modeled on the Unity software. Thus, simulation can take place in any environment previously implemented in Unity or other modeling software such as Sketchup software. The projection, however, is done on one or more white front screen using a projector, or with a virtual reality helmet.
The projection of the simulation can be done in 3 different configurations, a single front view, a mixed-views display, and finally with a virtual reality headset. The mixed-views configuration offers a front view but also a top view for the visualisation near the ground in the front of the wheelchair. The mixed view also contains two lateral views.

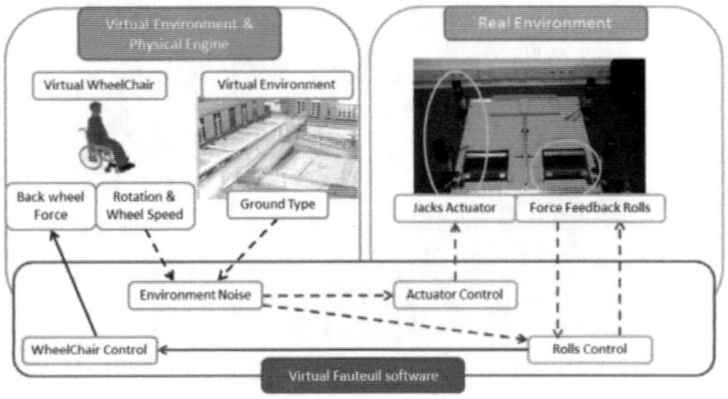

Figure 3. Communication diagram between simulator devices and the virtual environment

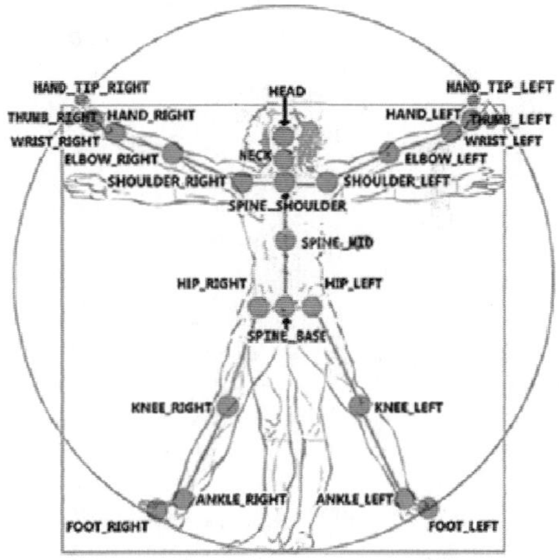

Figure 4. The 25 Joints tracked by the Kinect sensor

B. Integration of the Kinect v2 sensor to the simulator

In order to enable postural tracking during a simulation, a Kinect v2 sensor has been linked to Virtual Fauteuil. The Kinect sensor combines a RGB camera with depth sensor. Which enable to measure the spatial position of an object tracked, in this application: the body of the users. The SDK of the Kinect sensor eases the implementation to a software application such as Unity3D. As depicted on the figure 4, the Kinect sensor can track 25 joints in the user's body. This fits to a lot of cinematic models of the human body.
The framerate of acquisition of the Kinect sensor is up to 33.3 Hz. The reliability of the Kinect sensor has been the object of several studies. All these studies evaluates a great reliability [8], [9]. These experiments resulted in comparing the measures of the Kinect with the measures of another motion capture like for example the Nexus Vicon which is used as a reference.
The Kinect has two main uses in the simulator:

- Online mode: It enables to check online some criteria concerning the posture of the user. For the moment,

Figure 5. The virtual environment of the exercise used for the experiment

we focus on the lean of the trunk and the symmetric distribution of the posture in the frontal plane. Indicators are displayed during the simulation to instantly tell if the sufficiently well positioned on the sagittal and frontal planes.

- Offline mode: It is possible to record the joints position during a simulation. All the data are recorded in a .csv file. This enable postural analysis.

III. Experiments

We have conducted a series of evaluations of the postural response of users during a simulation of a simple travel. This travel results in going forward until the finish which is symbolised by a blue diamond placed at the end of the way. The straight track is composed of bumps which causes perturbation with the motion platform during the simulation as we can see on figure 5.
The subjects have been chosen to represent a large amount of morphologies. There was also an additional condition for the selection of the subjects. They necessary need to be able person, which are novice in wheelchair driving.
During these tests, the users were asked to sit on a manual wheelchair, which were placed on the motion platform. The protocol is done on two phases:

1) In a first phase, the subjects were submitted to perturbations along the roll axis due to a chaotic road. In this phase, the user is facing perturbations but he does not control the avatar. The simulation is not displayed on this phase, which means that the users will experiments perturbations due to the motion platform but they will not be able to prepare themself to face these perturbations.
2) In a second phase, the subject still does not drive the avatar, but both feedbacks, haptic and visual, are activated. The user is placed on the same simulated situation but this time with a visual immersion.

12 participants have been selected for this experiment. 9 males and 3 females. They were students whose height vary between 1m62 and 1m90 with a mean of 1m75 and their weight vary between 45 kg and 100 kg with a mean of 70.3 kg
These first analyzes only focus on the rotation of the torso of the participant in order to see how it behaves during perturbations. We focus on the sagital plane because the perturbations also took place in the sagital plane.
At first, since the kinect allow us to assume the trunk as splitted in two parts because it can measure a point located at the top of the trunk (Spine Shoulder (P_{SS}) on the Figure 6), a point located at the middle of the trunk (Spine Mid (P_{SM}) on the Figure 6) and a point located around the hips (Spine Base (P_{SB}) on the Figure 6). The trunk can then be considered in three differents parts : the lower part: the segment D_{low} between the P_{SB} and P_{SM} points, the upper part : the segment D_{up} between the P_{SS} and P_{SM} points and finally the full trunk: the segment D_{full} between the P_{SS} and P_{SB} points. .We measured the rotations of these 3 parts from the position data collected during the simulation in order to see how these three variables varies in time.
The second main study is about the comparison between the postural reaction, in and out of the visual environment to see if the visual immersion can have an impact on the behaviour of the user.
The Table I. depicts the means intercorrelations amongst the 12 participants between the three angles related to the trunk: α_{up}, α_{low} and α_{full}. Figure 7 is an example of these three angles. Rely on these results, we conclude that for these partipants, who are abled people, the perturbations had very little impact on the trunk flexion, which means that the trunk was praticly always straight.

TABLE I. THE MATRIX OF THE MEAN OF THE R COEFFICIENTS CORRELATION BETWEEN THE 3 ANGLES RELATED TO THE TRUNK. THE LOWER, THE UPPER AND THE FULL TRUNK.

r-coefficient between:	α_{up}	α_{low}	α_{full}
α_{up}	1	0.9708	0.9882
α_{low}	0.9708	1	0.9599
α_{full}	0.9882	0.9599	1

IV. Results

In order to compare the difference between the postural behaviour of the participants with and without the visual immersion, we did, as a short analysis, a comparison of the standard deviation of the rotation of the trunk with and without the visual feedback. The Figure 9 depicts the oscillation of the trunk of the participant 7 which is a representive for the others participants. The signals compared almost have an alternative and periodic pattern, in this, we use the standard deviation as an indicator of the dispersion of the signal. We suggest this hypothesis : the bigger the standard deviation is, the more the participants was perturbated.
The results (in Table II) show that standard deviation values are always bigger with the visual immersion and the maximum variation is with the participant 3 who has almost doubled his perturbation located on the trunk. We suppose that one of the reason is that, in the first case, the participant does not know when the perturbations will occur, so he may unconsciously strengthen himself to get ready, whereas, with the visual feedback, the participant is more confident because he can expect the arrival of perturbations.

V. Conclusion

This first experiment strengthen us in the idea that enabling simulators dedicated to training to track the body of the user during his simulations can lead us to a better comprehension

TABLE II. STANDARD DEVIATION (SD) OF α_{trunk} FOR EACH PARTICIPANT DURING THE NON-VISUALLY AND THE VISUALLY IMMERSIVE SIMULATION

Participants	Standard Deviation of α 1st phase : No visual immersion	Standard Deviation of α 2nd Phase: with visual immersion
1	0,0925	0,0987
2	0,0257	0,0279
3	0,0318	0,0607
4	0,0355	0,0505
5	0,0999.	0,1047
6	0,0201	0,0263
7	0,0493	0,0778
8	0,0272	0,0378
9	0,0375	0,0381
10	0,0442	0,0546
11	0,0253	0,0341
12	0,0857	0,0972

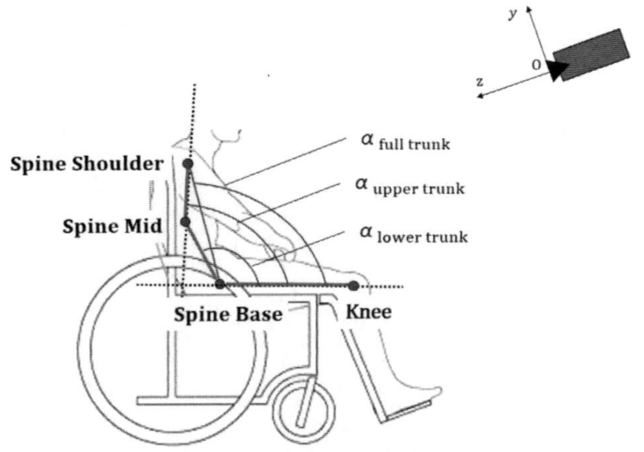

Figure 6. Joints of the body used to calculate the angle between the trunk and the thigh. From left to bottom right, Spine shoulder, Spine Mid, Spine Base , and knees

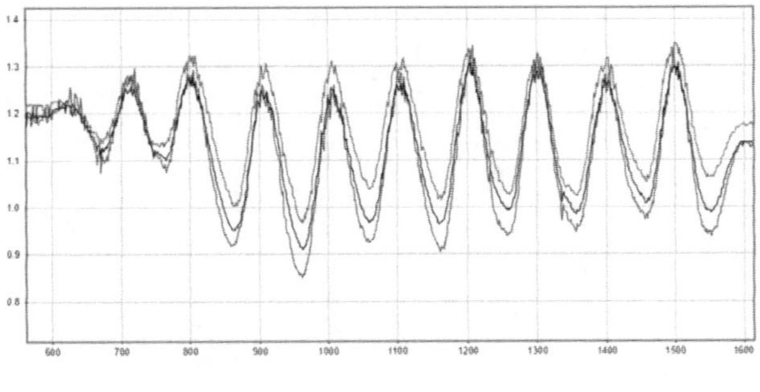

Figure 7. Oscilliation of α_{up}, α_{low} and α_{full}
In blue: α_{up}
In purple: α_{low}
In black: α_{full}
Legend : X-axis : Time (ms) Y axis(rad)

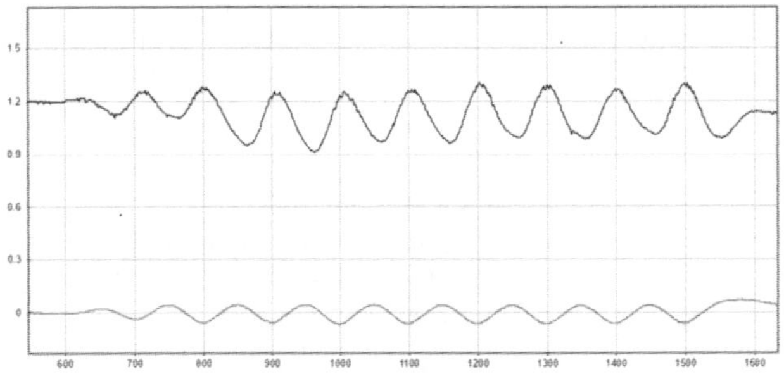

Figure 8. Oscilliation of α_{full} and $\alpha_{platform}$
In black: α_{full}
In orange: $\alpha_{platform}$
Legend : X-axis : Time (ms) Y-axis(rad)

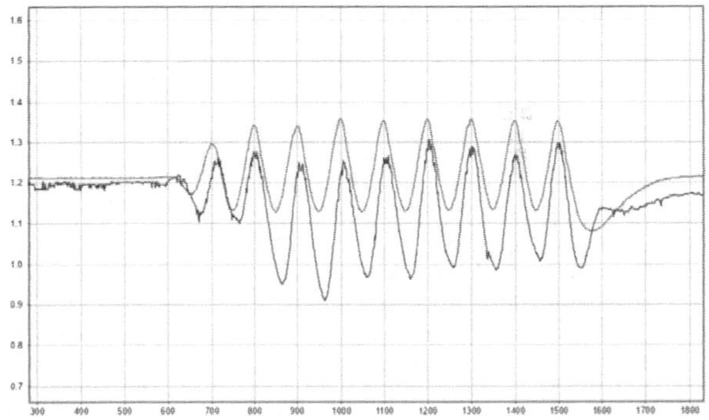

Figure 9. Oscilliation of α_{full} with and without the visual immersion
In blue: α with visual immersion

of the postural stability of wheelchair drivers. This is not the first study about the postural analysis for wheelchair users, others have been lead using different kind of sensor in contrast. Like cushion for the seat and the back rest that measure the pressure distribution and its variation [10], [11]. Some study [12], [13] has also been done with motion platforms and body tracking analysis. But to our knowledge, we are the first study that deal with postural analysis managed by a non-immersive sensor and with a simulation of an immersive driving scene. . Body tracking can highly improve the performances of most of wheelchair simulators on several points. This can also be, coupled to others sensors, a tool to analyse the stroke of wheelchairs driver in the simulator like a lot a biomechanical studies [14]–[18], but instead of ergometers, with the simulators we can make the user in a realistic situation, and the use of a simulator allow the monitoring of more variables due to the virtual environment, and the sensors.

VI. FUTURE WORK

This first preliminary study fosters us in our approach. This results is not statiscally significant yet, but next experiments will provide us better insights. In addition, new tests will be newly done in order to investigate differents leads. The first one is to determine if following a light but weekly training program on the simulator can improve the resistance of participants. In fact, we will train the same twelves participants in a period of

2 mounth and collect their performances in order to observe their evolution We also consider making tests with wheelchairs users, to see if their motor deficiency brings on new cases, and the simulator can help them as part of a training program.

ACKNOWLEDGMENT

The project Virtual Fauteuil if sponsored by the region Ile de France, in partnership with: CEREMH et EDF R&D

REFERENCES

[1] R. A. Cooper, D. M. Spaeth, D. K. Jones, M. L. Boninger, S. G. Fitzgerald, and S. Guo, "Comparison of virtual and real electric powered wheelchair driving using a position sensing joystick and an isometric joystick." Medical engineering & physics, vol. 24, no. 10, dec 2002, pp. 703–708.

[2] T. ITO, M. SHINO, T. INOUE, and M. KAMATA, "Development of a Powered Wheelchair Driving Simulator for Research and Development Use," Journal of Mechanical Systems for Transportation and Logistics, vol. 2, no. 2, 2009, pp. 90–101. [Online]. Available: http://joi.jlc.jst.go.jp/JST.JSTAGE/jmtl/2.90?from=CrossRef

[3] N. Steyn, Y. Hamam, E. Monacelli, and K. Djouani, "Modelling and design of an augmented reality differential drive mobility aid in an enabled environment," Simulation Modelling Practice and Theory, vol. 51, feb 2015, pp. 115–134. [Online]. Available: https://www.sciencedirect.com/science/article/pii/S1569190X14001865

[4] Y. Morere, G. Bourhis, K. Cosnuau, G. Guilmois, E. Blangy, and E. Rumilly, "ViEW, a wheelchair simulator for driving analysis," pp. 100–105, 2015.

[5] G. Tao and P. S. Archambault, "Powered wheelchair simulator development: implementing combined navigation-reaching tasks with a 3D hand motion controller," Journal of NeuroEngineering and Rehabilitation, vol. 13, no. 1, jan 2016, pp. 1–13. [Online]. Available: http://dx.doi.org/10.1186/s12984-016-0112-2

[6] C. S. Harrison, P. M. Grant, and B. a. Conway, "Enhancement of a virtual reality wheelchair simulator to include qualitative and quantitative performance metrics." Assistive technology : the official journal of RESNA, vol. 22, no. 1, 2010, pp. 20–31. [Online]. Available: http://www.researchgate.net/journal/1040-0435_Assistive_technology_the_official_journal_of_RESNA

[7] F. Goncalves, L. Trenoras, E. Monacelli, and A. Schmid, "Motion adaptation on a wheelchair driving simulator," in 2014 2nd Workshop on Virtual and Augmented Assistive Technology, VAAT 2014; Co-located with the 2014 Virtual Reality Conference - Proceedings, 2014, pp. 17–22.

[8] K. Otte, B. Kayser, S. Mansow-model, J. Verrel, F. Paul, A. U. Brandt, and T. Schmitz-hu, "Accuracy and Reliability of the Kinect Version 2 for Clinical Measurement of Motor Function," 2016, pp. 1–17.

[9] H. B. F. Mentiplay, "Reliability and concurrent validity of the Microsoft Kinect V2 for assessment of standing balance and postural control," Gait & Posture, 2015. [Online]. Available: http://dx.doi.org/10.1016/j.gaitpost.2015.03.005

[10] R. Aissaoui, M. Lacoste, and J. Dansereau, "Analysis of sliding and pressure distribution during a repositioning of persons in a simulator chair," IEEE transactions on neural systems and rehabilitation engineering : a publication of the IEEE Engineering in Medicine and Biology Society, vol. 9, no. 2, jun 2001, pp. 215–224.

[11] R. Aissaoui, C. Boucher, D. Bourbonnais, M. Lacoste, and J. Dansereau, "Effect of seat cushion on dynamic stability in sitting during a reaching task in wheelchair users with paraplegia," Archives of Physical Medicine and Rehabilitation, vol. 82, no. 2, feb 2001, pp. 274–281.

[12] D. Kamper, M. Parnianpour, K. Barin, T. Adams, M. Linden, and H. Hemami, "Postural stability of wheelchair users exposed to sustained , external perturbations," no. May, 1999.

[13] D. Kamper, K. Barin, M. Parnianpour, S. Reger, and H. Weed, "Preliminary investigation of the lateral postural stability of spinal cord-injured individuals subjected to dynamic perturbations," no. 1999, 2015, pp. 40–46.

[14] S. L. Soltau, J. S. Slowik, P. S. Requejo, S. J. Mulroy, and R. R. Neptune, "An Investigation of Bilateral Symmetry During Manual Wheelchair Propulsion," Frontiers in Bioengineering and Biotechnology, vol. 3, no. June, 2015, pp. 3–8. [Online]. Available: http://journal.frontiersin.org/article/10.3389/fbioe.2015.00086

[15] M. M. Rodgers, G. W. Gayle, S. F. Figoni, M. Kobayashi, J. Lieh, and R. M. Glaser, "Biomechanics of wheelchair propulsion during fatigue," Archives of physical medicine and rehabilitation, vol. 75, no. 1, 1994, pp. 85–93.

[16] W. M. Richter, "The effect of seat position on manual wheelchair propulsion biomechanics: A quasi-static model-based approach," pp. 707–712, 2001.

[17] O. J. Kilkens, A. J. Dallmeijer, A. V. Nene, M. W. Post, and L. H. van der Woude, "The longitudinal relation between physical capacity and wheelchair skill performance during inpatient rehabilitation of people with spinal cord injury," pp. 1575–1581, aug 2005. [Online]. Available: http://0.245.111.74

[18] L. H. V. V. D. Woude, C. M. V. Konlngsbruggen, A. L. Kroes, I. Kingma, C. M. V. Konlngsbruggen, A. L. Kroes, and I. Kingma, "Effect of push handle height on net moments and forces on the musculoskeletal system during standardized wheelchair pushing tasks," vol. 3646, no. October, 2017.

Assessing the Impact of Muscular Fatigue on Myoelectric Signals Using Myo Armband

Sudhir Sharma
School of Engineering and Computing
University of Hertfordshire, UK
Email: s.sharma25@herts.ac.uk

Volker Steuber
School of Engineering and Computing
University of Hertfordshire, UK
Email: v.steuber@herts.ac.uk

Farshid Amirabdollahian
School of Engineering and Computing
University of Hertfordshire, UK
Email: f.amirabdollahian2@herts.ac.uk

***Abstract*—This paper investigates the impact of muscular fatigue on myoelectric signals in order to incorporate biological feedback acquired wirelessly into a game interaction intended for rehabilitation. The study was conducted in four phases: Familiarisation, Training-1, Dumbbell exercises and Training-2 with 20 healthy participants. During the two training phases, each participant performed 5 hand gestures, each gesture was performed in 5 iterations. Each iteration lasted 5 seconds and consisted of 5 repetitions of each gesture, visually guided to last a second each. The logged data was recorded into CSV (Comma-Separated Values) files at a rate of 200Hz. In order to compare grasps before and after the fatiguing exercise, we used SVM (Support Vector Machine), using the capability to judge grasp accuracy for each phase. By comparing the grasp accuracy pre and post exercise, we found that muscular fatigue can negatively impact on gesture accuracy. The gesture accuracy detected after dumbbell exercises was significantly lower than that of the gestures performed before exercise. The data collected through subjective questionnaires also supports the results. In this study, we identified that fatigue, caused by interaction intensity and effort, can affect the accuracy of gesture detection. This has a further implication for cases where EMG (Electromyography) is used as the biofeedback involved in human-machine interactions, such as gameplay. While it is thought that more intensive interaction may benefit recovery after stroke, it is possible to optimise interactions towards reducing fatigue, for example by pacing the game difficulty based on detected level of fatigue.**

***Index Terms*—Gesture detection; fatigue; electromyography.**

I. INTRODUCTION

Humans utilise their hands to accomplish tasks, interact with their environments and also for communication via gestures. Human-computer interaction utilising hand gestures can play a significant role in this smart world. The way of interaction with devices and applications has been completely changed, smart devices use new interaction techniques such as voice commands, mimics, and gestures to communicate with humans. The hand gesture based technique is a unique approach which provides a natural way of interaction and communication [1].

In the past, researchers have used various methods such as vision-based and glove-based methods to detect hand gestures. Vision-based solutions often involve detecting the fingertips or fingers and inferring joint-articulations using inverse kinematic models of the hand and wrist skeleton [2][3]. They are susceptible to changes in illumination, rotation problem, and occlusion [4]. Glove-based methods reduce the computation time by having a direct measurement of the articulation [2] [3] of the hand and wrist joints. Glove-based techniques require the user to wear a glove, sometimes uncomfortable to wear and requiring a correct size/handedness. Also position encoders may have connection cables limiting free motion and interfere with the donning and doffing and comfort. Furthermore, gloves may impact on tactile sensations of the fingers when interacting with objects.

In our previous research, Leon et al. [5] achieved more than 90% of accuracy in gesture recognition using Support Vector Machines (SVM) while applying the technique to recordings from hand flexion and extension measured by a glove using its bending sensors. Tavakolan et al. [6] used SVM for pattern recognition of surface electromyography signals of four forearm muscles in order to classify eight hand gestures. They concluded that it was feasible to identify gestures using the four locally placed electrodes. Similarly, Wang et al. [7] used linear discriminant analysis to achieve an average accuracy of around 98% in detecting 8 hand gestures using two electrodes placed on the forearm. Using the Myo armband, researchers in our group initially achieved low accuracies using k-nearest neighbours [8] and changing the machine learning method to SVM, they achieved an overall recognition accuracy of 94.9% detecting hand and wrist gestures [9].

Similarly, in our current study, a series of dumbbell exercises were performed between two training sessions to assess the impact of muscular fatigue on myoelectric signals. This study focused on assessing gesture recognition accuracies in fatigued muscles prior to incorporating them into a rehabilitation game. While our earlier recognition results were promising, they required a training of 2.5s per gesture, repeated 25 times before a gesture could be automatically detected in 0.2s. A limitation of this approach is that incorporating such techniques in an interactive game may result in delays to gameplay due to training needed for each gesture. Hence in current study, we explore if SVM is able to perform with 1s of training data, and if such amount is suitable in detecting gestures in fatigued muscles.

The rest of the paper is organised as follows. In section II, we introduce fatigue and its potential role in machine-mediated rehabilitation. Section IV presents methodologies used for data acquisition, experiment, analysis and evaluation. Section V provides the results of the experiment with statistical analysis and section VI provides an analysis of the results. Finally, section VII draws conclusion from the work presented.

II. Fatigue

Fatigue is a common problem among stroke survivors performing physical activities for rehabilitation [10]. Stroke patients often suffer from weariness, tenderness and lack of energy, initiative, and motivation. Fatigue is a condition in which a person lacks the physical and mental energy that is perceived by the individual to interfere with usual and desired activities [11]. Staub and Bogousslavsky defined fatigue in stroke patient as a feeling of early exhaustion developing during activity with lack of energy and aversion to effort [12]. It can be differentiated into two categories, subjective fatigue, and objective fatigue [13]. The subjective fatigue corresponds to the symptom that is felt by the patient, which can be estimated by self-reported questionnaires. The objective fatigue corresponds to a decrease in measured physical or mental performance over the set duration of a task [13].

In using machine learning for fatigue detection, a study was carried out by Nourhan et al. [14] using Electromyography (EMG) electrodes to measure the muscle activity during dynamics contractions. In this work, the Myo armband device was used to assess the viability of using Myo to quantify muscle fatigue. During the experiment a set of muscle fatiguing exercises was conducted where elbow flexion and extension were performed. The acquired EMG signals from muscles were analysed and features such as Root Mean Square and Median Frequency were used as indicators of fatigue using adaptive neural networks. Results show that automating the process of localised muscle fatigue detection shows higher accuracy using supervised techniques compared to thresholding or observation techniques.

III. Machine-mediated rehabilitation and games

In the context of rehabilitation for stroke, more recent machine-mediated tools often incorporate functional activities such as grasping and manipulation of objects [5], as in daily living activities. It is believed that the repetition of these training activities influence the neuromodulation needed for re-learning and performing of the activities affected by stroke [15][16].

Studies exploring the machine-mediated rehabilitation often utilise the sensory recording from robots. These include kinematic data, such as position and orientation, that can be utilised alongside other dynamic models [17], to infer on active involvement of the patient, and also to provide input for assessing the movement performance. However, rarely these methods consider fatigue that is accumulated over the interaction time, and those studies that consider fatigue, often rely on measuring fatigue using indirect methods, such as measurement of movement error [18].

Games are seen as a good medium for practicing activities of daily living. Robot-mediated activity is often limited to worn devices that are cumbersome and heavy, and cannot be utilised for a prolonged period of time. Also, robots are often tethered to their controller and therefore it is not possible to practice exercises freely. Wireless myoelectric devices such as Myo armband offer a potential solution for receiving hand gestures and incorporating them into rehabilitation games. The study conducted by Oskoei et al. [19] focused on manifestation of fatigue in myoelectric signals during dynamic contractions produced during playing PC games. The study results show that there is a significant decline in signal frequency after a period of operation, which is linked to fatigue in the muscles [20]. This led to our research question exploring suitability of machine learning in detecting fatigue from interactions sensed using the Myo armband.

IV. Material and Methods

The Myo armband [21] depicted in Figure 1 is a gesture recognition device worn on the forearm. It enables a user to control ICT technology wirelessly using various hand/wrist motions. It is designed with 8 EMG electrodes which are placed equidistantly around the arm. The armband is built with an ARMCortex M4 processor and a rechargeable lithium-ion battery allowing it to be used while communicating via Bluetooth 4. The armband is equipped with accelerometers, gyroscope and magnetometers, and also provides haptic feedback in form of vibration. It can be worn easily without any assistance.

Fig. 1. Myo Armband from Thalmic Labs

Experiment Design: The proposed study was designed to assess gesture recognition before and after a series of fatiguing dumbbell exercises. It also focused on using shorter grasp cycles of 1 second in order to train the support vector machines for gesture recognition. This was to reduce the training time needed for in-game calibration of gestures at a later time. The experiment was designed in four phases, Familiarisation, Training-1, Dumbbell Exercises and Training-2 shown in Figure 2. Subjective fatigue was assessed using a questionnaire prior to, and after the last phase of the experiment.

The experiment protocol was approved by the University of Hertfordshire's ethics committee under the approval number

COM/PGR/UH/02741. A total number of 20 participants consented to take part in the study with their demographics presented in summary table I. As an exploratory study, a sample size of 20 was seen as sufficient to search for initial evidence for impact of fatigue on recognition accuracy. Participants sat in front of a 21" monitor, wearing the Myo armband on their dominant arm.

TABLE I. DEMOGRAPHIC DATA

Gender	Participants	Age (m ± std)
Female	6	28.5 ± 3.5
Male	14	34.2 ± 7.3

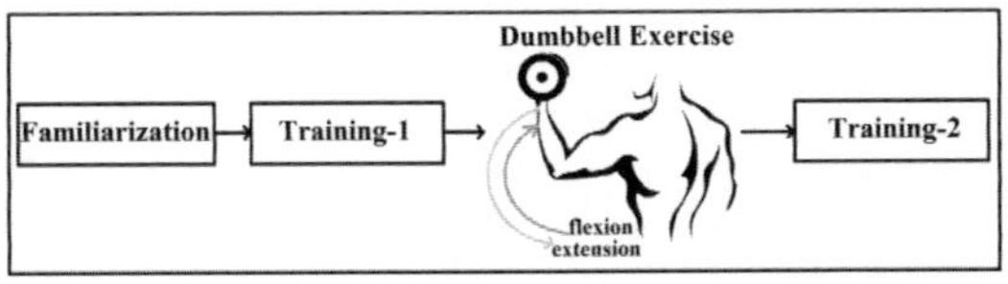

Fig. 2. Experiment Setup

Familiarisation: In this phase, participants interacted with the Myo armband and learned its operation. They performed 5 gestures shown in Figure 4, which were displayed in form of an animated image on screen (Figure 3). Each animated gesture repeated 5 times, each lasting 1 second. The familiarisation process cycled through the 5 gestures, until participants were confident in using the device.

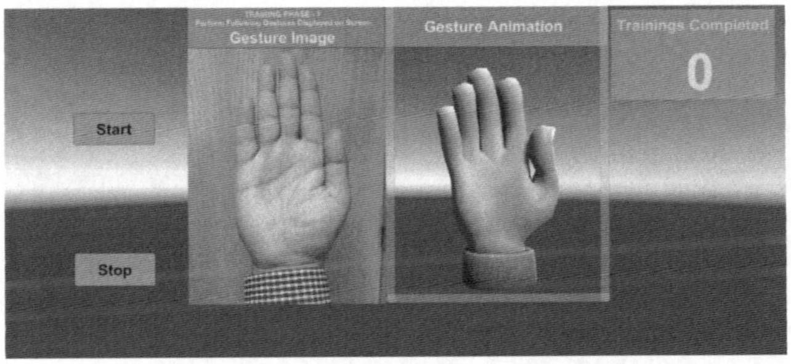

Fig. 3. Gesture image and gesture animation

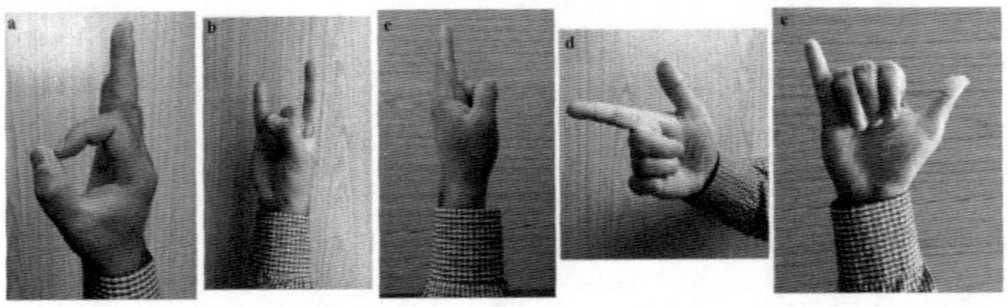

Fig. 4. Designed poses for Familiarization: (a) OK, (b) Rock, (c) Pointer, (d) Gun, (e) Phone

Training-1: During this phase, participants performed five gestures consisting of cylindrical, lateral pinch, spherical, tripod and hook grasps displayed on the screen. These gestures were randomised to appear on screen in 5 iterations. Participants were asked to perform and repeat each presented gesture 5 times as shown by the animated image on screen. The animated image timed each gesture to one second, thus 5 repetitions were expected to last 5 seconds. Based on this, each of the gestures in the list was performed 25 times, lasting approximately 25 seconds.

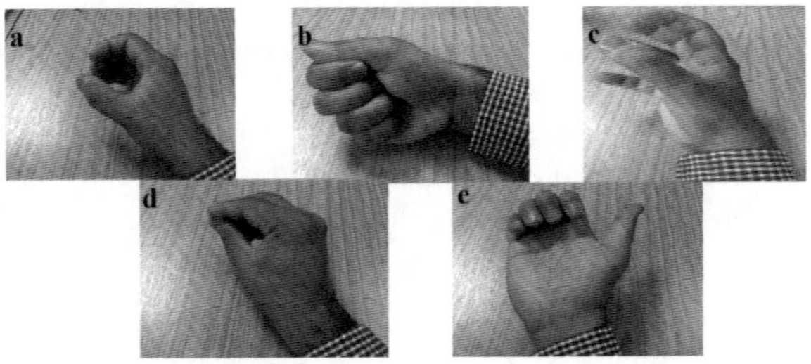

Fig. 5. Designed poses for Training-1: (a) Cylindrical, (b) Lateral Pinch, (c) Spherical, (d) Tripod, (e) Hook

Dumbbell Exercises: Next phase required performing of a series of Dumbbell exercises. During this phase, participants performed some dumbbell exercises which varied in difficulty between male and female participants, while applying a gradual increase of weight up to 10Kg for male and 7.5Kg for female participants on advise received from sport science colleagues. They performed repeated elbow flexion/extension (biceps curls) and stopped the exercise when they felt personal fatigue or tiredness.

Training-2: This phase was an exact replica of the Training-1 phase, with the only difference being that this phase occurred after the fatiguing dumbbell exercise.

Data Acquisition: Data was captured by placing the armband on the forearm making direct contact with skin. The Myo armband must be tight enough to stay in one place without losing contact with skin for better signal transmission. Data were collected at $200Hz$ sampling rate and logged into comma delimited text files. Each subject completed 2 training sessions, each training contained 5 iterations, each iteration containing 5 different gestures. Each gesture was performed 5 times making 5 repetitions. Overall, each participant performed 5 gestures under Training-1 and the same gestures under Training-2, and hence each gesture class contains 25 seconds of gesture data, corresponding with 25 repetitions of each gesture.

Feature Selection: One of the first steps to SVM analysis is the feature selection step. Oskoei and Hu showed that the waveform length (WL) feature is capable of detecting gestures with an accuracy of more than 90% [20]. Huang and Chen (1999) [22] define the waveform length as:

$$\boldsymbol{WL} = \sum_{k=1}^{N} |X_k - X_{k-1}|$$

Features were selected using $N = 40$ in the above equation. This allows to reduce 200 data samples to only 5 rows, where 40 samples are reduced to one waveform length value. These values are then used for training and recognition. The choice of N is due to research by [23] that showed 200ms of data is sufficient to detect intention in muscle EMG.

SVM Classification: The classification process involves learning features in a training set, and testing the learning using what is labeled as a recognition set. We used *libsvm* and Python libraries for this assessment.

Our earlier study had identified optimal length of training and recognition sets for testing the SVM detection accuracy. In that study, gestures were held for 5 seconds; e.g. a cylindrical gesture was produced and held, and the data from the 5-second recording was used to train the SVM engine and to recognise gestures. In our results a potential drop in some recorded accuracies were linked to the delay in perceiving an action command, before it is executed. We did not try to control the task onset using audio-visual commands or screen animation [9].

In our current study, we were concerned about the speed of gesture detection in order to have a utility for seamless gameplay. A subsequent research question was raised regarding reliability of SVM if produced gestures were maintained for a shorter time. So, here we asked our participants to repeat the gesture 5 times within each iteration while providing an on-screen animation showing the gesture start and finish, accompanied by audible signals. As a post-process, we explored different lengths of training and recognition files versus their accuracies in classification.

Model: An SVM model was constructed with three iterations $\{1,2,3\}$ from both training sets (Training-1 and 2) as *Train* and remaining two iterations$\{4,5\}$ from both training sets as *Recognition* sets. This includes 15 repetitions of each training gesture in the training set, and 10 repetitions of each gesture in the recognition set. Data in both sets are labelled with their right classification, for example $G_{12}I_4$ is labelled as the 1st gesture, 2nd repetition, 4th iteration. After recognition process, the SVM engine compares the label given by the SVM recognition, to the one being set for the data as its label, and comparing right and wrong recognitions lead to a recognition accuracy, at gesture and overall levels. We are also able to draw a confusion matrix that presents the reliability of our method. The resulting recognition accuracies are then gathered in a comma delimited text file and analysed using IBM SPSS version 25.

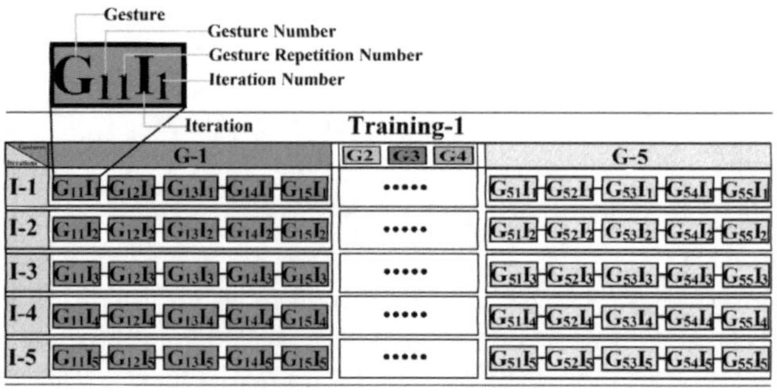

Fig. 6. The data was recorded containing 5 gestures in each iteration and 5 iterations in each Training-1 and Training-2 datasets. Each iteration consists of 5 iteration for each gesture.

V. Results

This section presents the results of the experiment analysed based on gesture accuracy along with the participant's response about fatigue before and after dumbbell exercise performance. Results shows that overall gesture accuracy was higher (52.4 ± 28.54 (m $\pm$ std)) before dumbbell exercise compared to gesture accuracy after the dumbbell exercises (30.0 ± 4.144) with statistical significance ($p < 0.01$) also graphically shown in Figure 8. The data presented in Table II shows the median accuracy for each gesture pre and post-fatigue.

Questionnaire data scored the level of fatigue on a scale of 1 to 10, 10 being most fatigued. The results show that the fatigue status of participants pre-exercise (median fatigue = 0, 0.65 ± 1.137 (m $\pm$ std)) and post-exercise (median fatigue = 8, 7.5 ± 2.1) were significantly different. ($p < 0.01$) shown in Figure 7.

TABLE II. MEDIAN ACCURACY FOR EACH GESTURE

Type	Gestures	Gesture Accuracy	
		Pre-Exercise	Post-Exercise
1	Cylindrical	52	35
2	Lateral	57	27
3	Spherical	50	27
4	Tripod	49	35
5	Hook	54	25

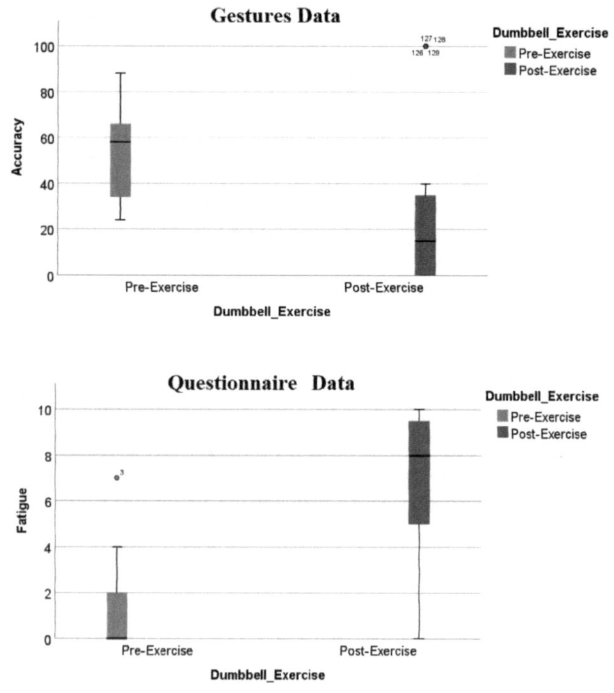

Fig. 7. Represents the impact of muscular fatigue on gesture accuracy of post-exercise compared to pre-exercise (top), and also subjective status of fatigue can be seen in post-exercise compared to pre-exercise evaluation (bottom).

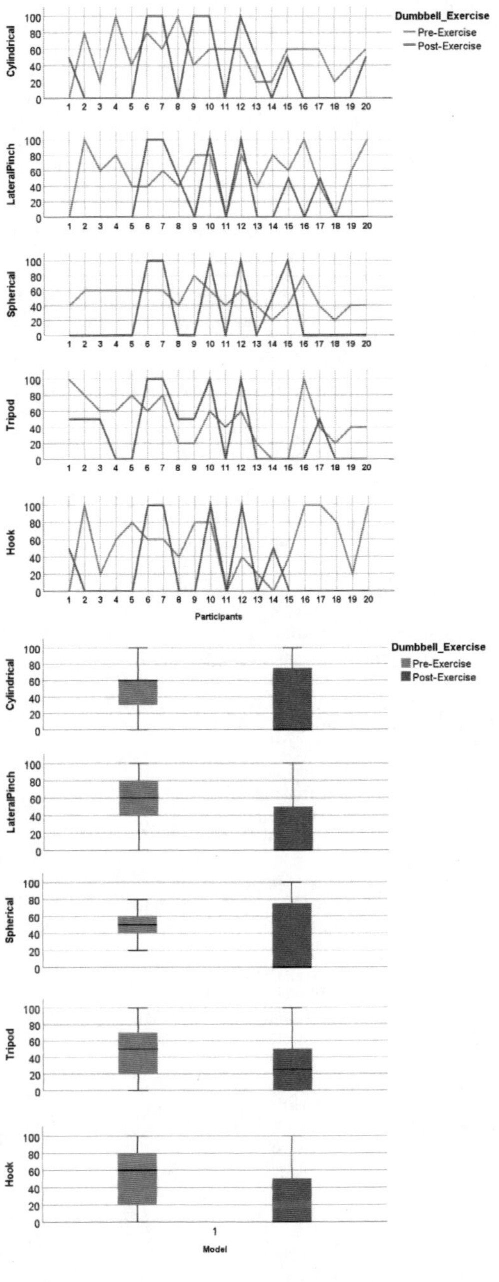

Fig. 8. Line graph on the top represents the lower gesture accuracy for post-fatigue (red line) compared to pre-fatigue (blue line), Boxplot on the bottom represents the median gesture accuracy for pre and post fatigue.

VI. Analysis & Discussion

This study was focused on the impact of muscular fatigue on hand gesture detection using myoelectric signals acquired from the Myo Armband. The result shows that muscular fatigue does affect the gesture accuracy negatively. The gesture accuracy detected after dumbbell exercises was significantly lower than that for the gestures performed before the fatiguing exercise. The data collected through the questionnaires about participants fatigue confirms the presence of fatigue in each participant. The gesture accuracy analysed separately for each of the five gestures also shows a significant reduction for each gesture performed before and after the exercise.

Observation of gesture detection accuracy pre-fatigue, compared to our earlier study shows a significant drop in gesture accuracy (reduction from 95% to 52% overall). This could be due to a number of variations between the two studies:

a) Reducing the length of training datasets for the SVM engine, from 2.5 second to only 1s in each training repetition. This was done to allow for a practical length of training data that would suit a game calibration phase. However, the drop in accuracies, pre and post-fatigue does not support using less data in training phase.

b) The current study used one gesture per second instead of a static gesture produced and maintained over 5 seconds. We intend to explore influence of these differences. We suspect that holding a gesture for a period of time greater than the amount of training data needed, allows for least variations in gesture data, while doing one gesture per second includes flexion and extension articulations that can introduce additional variability and hence, reduce recognition accuracy. We are currently assessing this using a further pilot study, thus to ensure correct choice of learning gestures and optimal parameters for best accuracies in fatigued interaction.

c) Here we used 200Hz sampling and a different reduction factor to arrive at the same waveform length, and different method to acquire the data. It could be possible that the new method to acquire the data from Myo has applied filters to the data which has negatively impacted on recognition accuracies.

The experiment was conducted with voluntary participation of 20 healthy individuals. Each participant performed 5 gestures for 5 seconds for 5 times displayed on the screen in animated form. Among all of 5 gestures, the Lateral gesture was detected with the highest accuracy 57%, Hook 54%, Cylindrical 52%, Spherical 50% and Tripod gestures was the lowest 49% shown in Table II.

In a rehabilitation scenario, it is expected that patients involved in training process will fatigue with effort and exercise intensity. Using the wireless armband may therefore offer unreliable results given the observed drop in recognition accuracy, comparing fatigue and non-fatigue conditions. In this regard, further improvements to recognition accuracy is needed, prior to incorporating our method in rehabilitation games for stroke patients.

VII. Conclusions

The objective of our analysis was to focus on hand gesture detection influenced by muscular fatigue and optimise gestures prior to incorporating them into a rehabilitation game. The conclusion drawn from this study was that muscular fatigue does significantly affect the gesture accuracy. We observed that using accuracy of recognition, it is possible to identify fatigue and non-fatigued myoelectric signals. The data collected through questionnaires about participants fatigue status support our results.

We noted a significant drop in accuracy of detection, comparing non-fatigued muscles in this study and those reported in our earlier work. It is possible that our choice of recording from a steady gesture held for 5 seconds offers a more reliable and accurate data for the machine learning. This aspect would benefit from further investigations to identify best training setups.

Our approach was intended for using the SVM classifier as an online adjustment tool for exercise intensity within a serious game designed for stroke rehabilitation. While we observed that the Myo armband is reliable with data acquisition, given the low accuracies in detecting fatigued gestures, further work is needed to improve recognition accuracies. In a rehabilitation context, patients often suffer from fatigue or are easily fatigued. Given this, more work is needed to ensure recognition accuracy remains within a reliable gameplay range.

Considering motivational factors, we remain convinced that the Myo armband or similar wireless electromyographic sensors allow for free movement in space, which does not interfere with performing activities of daily living. Hence we continue our work on EMG assessment using machine learning algorithms, thus to identify best set of learning mechanisms that could enable using the armband in a rehabilitation context.

ACKNOWLEDGMENT

The authors would like to thank the volunteers who have participated in this study contributing to our understanding of fatigue and optimal gesture detection algorithms.

REFERENCES

[1] V. I. Pavlovic, R. Sharma, and T. S. Huang, "Visual interpretation of hand gestures for human-computer interaction: A review," IEEE Transactions on Pattern Analysis & Machine Intelligence, no. 7, 1997, pp. 677–695.

[2] F. Amirabdollahian and M. L. Walters, "Application of support vector machines in detecting hand grasp gestures using a commercially off the shelf wireless myoelectric armband," in 2017 International Conference on Rehabilitation Robotics (ICORR), July 2017, pp. 111–115.

[3] A. Chaudhary, J. L. Raheja, K. Das, and S. Raheja, "Intelligent approaches to interact with machines using hand gesture recognition in natural way: A survey," CoRR, vol. abs/1303.2292, 2013. [Online]. Available: http://arxiv.org/abs/1303.2292

[4] R. Z. Khan and N. A. Ibraheem, "Comparative study of hand gesture recognition system." Citeseer, 2012.

[5] B. Leon. et. al, "Grasps recognition and evaluation of stroke patients for supporting rehabilitation therapy," BioMed research international, vol. 2014, 2014, pp. 1–14.

[6] M. Tavakolan, Z. G. Xiao, and C. Menon, "A preliminary investigation assessing the viability of classifying hand postures in seniors," BioMedical Engineering OnLine, vol. 10, no. 1, Sep 2011, p. 79. [Online]. Available: https://doi.org/10.1186/1475-925X-10-79/[accessed: 2019-01-6]

[7] N. Wang, Y. Chen, and X. Zhang, "The recognition of multi-finger prehensile postures using lda," vol. 8, 11 2013, p. 706712.

[8] F. Amirabdollahian, M. Walters, R. Heffernan, S. Fletcher, and P. Webb, "Using myoelectric signals for gesture detection: a feasibility study," 4 2017, pp. 353–358. [Online]. Available: http://www.ehf2017.org.uk/

[9] F. Amirabdollahian and M. L. Walters, "Application of support vector machines in detecting hand grasp gestures using a commercially off the shelf wireless myoelectric armband," in 2017 International Conference on Rehabilitation Robotics (ICORR), July 2017, pp. 111–115.

[10] J. L. Ingles, G. A. Eskes, and S. J. Phillips, "Fatigue after stroke," Archives of physical medicine and rehabilitation, vol. 80, no. 2, 1999, pp. 173–178.

[11] T. J. Braley and R. D. Chervin, "Fatigue in multiple sclerosis: mechanisms, evaluation, and treatment," Sleep, vol. 33, no. 8, 2010, pp. 1061–1067.

[12] F. Staub and J. Bogousslavsky, "Fatigue after stroke: a major but neglected issue," Cerebrovascular Diseases, vol. 12, no. 2, 2001, pp. 75–81.

[13] C. Lan Nguyen Hoang. et. al, "Physical factors associated with fatigue after stroke: an exploratory study," Topics in stroke rehabilitation, vol. 19, no. 5, 2012, pp. 369–376.

[14] T. Nourhan, M. Piechnick, J. Falkenberg, and T. Nazmy, "Detection of muscle fatigue using wearable (myo) surface electromyography based control device," in Information Technology (ICIT), 2017 8th International Conference on. IEEE, 2017, pp. 44–49.

[15] J. H. Carr and R. B. Shepherd, A motor relearning programme for stroke. Aspen Pub, 1987.

[16] P. Kan, R. Huq, J. Hoey, R. Goetschalckx, and A. Mihailidis, "The development of an adaptive upper-limb stroke rehabilitation robotic system," Journal of neuroengineering and rehabilitation, vol. 8, no. 1, 2011, p. 33.

[17] Y. Qin, N. Rahman, and F. Amirabdollahian, "Asymmetrical performance and abnormal synergies of the post-stroke patient wearing script passive orthosis in calibration, exercise and energy evaluation," Adv Robot Autom, vol. 3 (2): 1000122, June, 2014.

[18] A. Basteris, S. M. Nijenhuis, J. H. Buurke, G. B. Prange, and F. Amirabdollahian, "Lag–lead based assessment and adaptation of exercise speed for stroke survivors," Robotics and autonomous systems, vol. 73, 2015, pp. 144–154.

[19] M. A. Oskoei, H. Hu, and J. Q. Gan, "Manifestation of fatigue in myoelectric signals of dynamic contractions produced during playing pc games," in Engineering in Medicine and Biology Society, 2008. EMBS 2008. 30th Annual International Conference of the IEEE. IEEE, 2008, pp. 315–318.

[20] M. A. Oskoei* and H. Hu, "Support vector machine-based classification scheme for myoelectric control applied to upper limb," IEEE Transactions on Biomedical Engineering, vol. 55, no. 8, Aug 2008, pp. 1956–1965.

[21] Myo Armband from Thalmic Labs. [Online]. Available: https://www.thalmic.com/[accessed: 2019-01-7]

[22] H.-P. Huang and C.-Y. Chen, "Development of a myoelectric discrimination system for a multi-degree prosthetic hand," in Proceedings 1999 IEEE International Conference on Robotics and Automation (Cat. No.99CH36288C), vol. 3, 1999, pp. 2392–2397 vol.3.

[23] J. Valls-Solé, J. C. Rothwell, F. Goulart, G. Cossu, and E. Munoz, "Patterned ballistic movements triggered by a startle in healthy humans," The Journal of physiology, vol. 516, no. 3, 1999, pp. 931–938.

You are the Mind of a Robot

Tele-existence for Adults and Children

Vladimir Estivill-Castro and Vladimir Sukhov

School of Information and Communication Technology
Griffith University
Nathan Campus, Brisbane, 4111, QLD, Australia
Email: v.estivill-castro@griffith.edu.au vladimir.sukhov@griffithuni.edu.au

***Abstract*—We carried two experiments of tele-existence. We provide a real-time illusion to humans that they exist in another place. The other place is the real world, although now their new body is a robot. In our experiments, we used virtual-reality to transport the subject to the body of a soccer-playing robot. In this new visions of human-computer interaction, we differentiate the experience between that experimented by adults and that experimented by children. We observed that the experience radically changes the adults' views regarding tele-existence and robotics. On the other hand, children become rapidly transported to the body of the robot.**

***Keywords*–Human-robot interaction; mixed-reality; tele-existence; experiments and applications; virtual reality; immersive environments.**

I. INTRODUCTION

Minsky introduced the term *tele-presence* [1] emphasising the importance of high-quality sensory feedback and suggesting that in the future, human perception and action will be no different from those transferred as from those interacting with the technologies. Since the first robotic-assisted remote tele-presence surgery, its application continues to grow [2]. The iRobot AVA 500 has been heralded now for several years as the first ever self-driving business collaboration robot [3]. The market of robots that can automate or assist in a range of environments, from offices to clinics has seen several companies emerge, such as Anybots, Double Robotics, Mantaro, Revolve Robotics, Vecna, Awabot, Inbot Technology and iRobot. For office work, robots that resemble a tilt-able tablet on wheels are gaining popularity; for example, the products by Amy Robotics, AXYN Robotique, MantaroBot, Suitable Technologies, Double Robotics and Ava Robotics offer video conference and mobility. In 2017, the market value for 2016 was estimated at $1.6 billion [4]. However, how much of these tools create the transportation effect originally suggested by Minsky? Many scholars [5] have pointed out that tele-presence raises fundamental issues about the nature of existence. In particular, one definition of *presence* is

> "*the perceptual illusion of non-mediation [6].*"

Thus, Minsky's tele-presence should be indistinguishable with presence; and the quality of tele-presence is related to the ability to deceive our perceptual system to take for "real" what is not there.

We are interested in how humans consider the possibility of *tele-existence* [7] [8]. There are pioneering studies on how humans attribute social and ethical stance to robots [9] [10]. However, Kahn et al. [9] found the attitude towards robots is fundamentally linked to the anthropomorphism of the robot. Our research here is concerned with the person's simulated immersion in the body of the robot and the effect of this immersion on the person's understanding of possibilities for tele-existence. Moreover, we propose here to explore in children the attribution and transportation of one's body to the body of the robot: the departure of one's own body and accept the body of the robot as our interaction with the world. We suggest this happens remarkably fast when the child is immersed in the environment and controls the body of the robot via mixed reality. Such tele-presence results in children rapidly adopting not only control but a dialogue where children abandon in their language anything related to their own physical body, and they formulate sentences and actions with a semantics that is now grounded in the body of the robot. Note that research in cognitive sciences has revealed language influences thinking and experience and body influence the resolution of ambiguous terms in abstract thought [11].

Although some early work suggested that in a child's world there could be some confusion between reality and fantasy [12], with *tele-existence*, there is nothing more real than the mixed-reality environment and, we argue that their new robotic body is authentic. Our study with adults departs from most tele-presence studies which aim at understanding how to improve tele-presence systems [13]. The dominant approach to facilitate social interaction between humans is Mobile Robotic Tele-Presence Systems (MRTPS) [13]. Typically, such MRTPS could be considered a tablet on wheels; they enable the technologies of computer tele-conference with some mobility. However, the robot (and its pilot) can hardly influence the environment. If the robot is a tele-android system [14], its primary goal is human-to-human reproduction of realistic face-to-face human communication. If the robot has arms [15], the main purpose is gesturing to reinforce human-to-human gesticulation. Here, our robots are Nao robots (humanoids) in the environment of the RoboCup Standard Platform League. Their pilot can navigate them following a ball or to a position in the soccer field. They can kick the ball with a choice of leg and a choice of kick (we ask the reader to reflect on what could "they" stand for, the robots, or the pilots: while the robots physically kick the ball, the pilots command when and how such kick happens). Moreover, our pilots (a person who remotely connects to the robot via a computer interface) have a significantly immersive interface (as opposed to MRTPS). For our pilots, our interface consists of a virtual reality headset and room size tracking technology, giving the pilot an opportunity to experience a simulated environment.

However, in this simulated environment, a large proportion is the streaming video of the robot's cameras. Therefore, our metaphor is that *what the pilot sees is what the robot sees.* We anticipate this forwarding of vision will transport the pilot to the local environment of the robot, and into the robot's body.

We aim to explore and contrast the thesis that our mixed reality achieves a perceptual illusion of no-mediation, and that the interface pragmatically disappears. Thus, our research is probably best identified with the recent emerging term of *tele-existence* [7]. We follow closely the idea of a master pilot commanding naturally a real-world robot [16]. However, rather than fidelity of reproduction of the human motions with arms and feet, we are interested in immersion by orienting the pilot to achieve tasks. The tele-operated robot is no longer an autonomous robot either. The International Federation of Robotics (IFR) and the Australian Robot Association adopted the ISO standard vocabulary (ISO 8373) to describe 'manipulating industrial robots operated in a manufacturing environment'. We suggest here that the proposed tele-existence blurs further the boundary of the machine relative to human. The fundamental robotic characteristic, that after being programmed, a robot operates automatically, is not entirely true for the mixed-reality tele-existence environment of our experiments. Also, those descriptions of a robot that require a control unit typically composed of a computer and software would not adequately apply as the human pilot is significantly the controller and decision maker in our tele-presence world. However, the pilot is liberated of controlling every joint and motor on the robot by significant autonomous behaviours in the robot (if the robot were to fall, it would autonomously get up).

The next section will provide the details of our methods; in particular, how we secured participants, and how we set the experiment; some of it mandated by requirements for ethical approval. Section III gives some insight on how the visual stream for the robot's cameras was placed on the headset (or visor) and how human participants could pilot the robot. We summarise the results of our experiment in Section IV, and we analyse possible validity threats in Section V. Conclusions terminate the paper.

II. THE METHODS

For our experiments, we applied the following method. The research was performed by a series of demonstrations of autonomous Nao robots (designed initially by Aldebaran and now commercialised by SoftBank robotics)., Nao is a humanoid robot 58 cm tall and weighs 4.3 kg wth 25 degrees of freedom, and a relatively large set of sensors that includes two cameras one above the other in the head, four microphones, sonar, and IR and the V5 offers an atom processor. We performed such demonstration on seven different days. These events were six days of special events where participants visited the campus, and the other two days were public displays associated with Australia's Science Week.

We conducted the activities in South-East Queensland, Australia, with the furthest apart being 90km. The demonstrations were conducted to audiences of children and adults. However, we engaged children and adults in different voluntary experiments. We aim to investigate the attitudes of children and adults to tele-existence. For adults, we collected responses to two questionnaires. These questionnaires were a pre-activity questionnaire and a post-activity questionnaire. For children, we conducted specific directed language and measured specific responses, collecting observational data. Table I summarises the presentations and the involvement of participants (we have far more subjects than the 6 participants in a similar setting [7]). Whenever consent was given, photographs of the session were taken. Presentations were set up for approximately six hours long. Although individual participants engaged with the particular activity for strictly less than 2 minutes (nevertheless, the 180 seconds of our immersion is much higher than approximately 30s [7] or 20s [16] of recent research in a similar setting). That is, all session for all participants immersed in the mixed-reality environment lasted 2 minutes. Displays about the activity were available for the full opening hours of the demonstration. There was no reward or any other incentive except the unique opportunity to experience tele-existence (mixed reality, where the human mind drives somehow the body of a robot). No advertisement or fliers were used. The off-campus displays were mostly promotional events on programs and courses offered by Griffith University. Having visitors on campus is part of Griffith University's open doors programs and also the STEM (Science, Technology, Engineering, Mathematics) engagement programs with many local high-schools. These students visit and are involved in educational experiences on campus. All children subjects were 12 years old or older when participating in our experiments.

TABLE I. EXPERIMENT SUMMARY.

Event	*Adult Participants*	*Children Participants*
STEM-6 Day One	0	22
STEM-6 Day Two	0	25
Open Day	23	1
Science Museum	3	1
Pup-Up-Science	0	47
STEM-6 Day Three	0	23
STEM-6 Day Four	0	23
GLO Logan 2018	3	14
Total	29	156

We use virtual reality devices to transport the participant to a virtual world; however, the immersion world reflects the vision of a nearby robot. This setting transports the person into a tele-operator or pilot for the legged robot. During this time, participants tele-operate a robot near a Standard Platform League (http://spl.robocup.org) soccer goal from RoboCup. Figure 1 shows our typical set up of the presentations outside the campus. Our experiments are radically different than the only two experiments we are aware of in a similar setting [7] [16]. While those experiments were concern on the optimal and most loyal reflection of the human pilots' walk and hand motion to the body of the robot in real time, and to the feeding back to the human sensors the images of the robot with maximum fidelity, our work concentrates more on the achievement of a meaningful mission. Thus, our human participants face immediately the task of scoring a goal in an environment with adversaries (those other experiments [7] [16] focus on how precise is the reproduction of a straight walk from the human in the robot, how accurate is a turn by the human pilot on the robot, and how loyal is the imitation of operators' arm movements on the robot). Our approach is rather different, no-one better at executing the kick on the robot's body than the robot itself with its onboard software. Similarly, the best routine to get up from falling is in the

(a) Set up during Science Week.

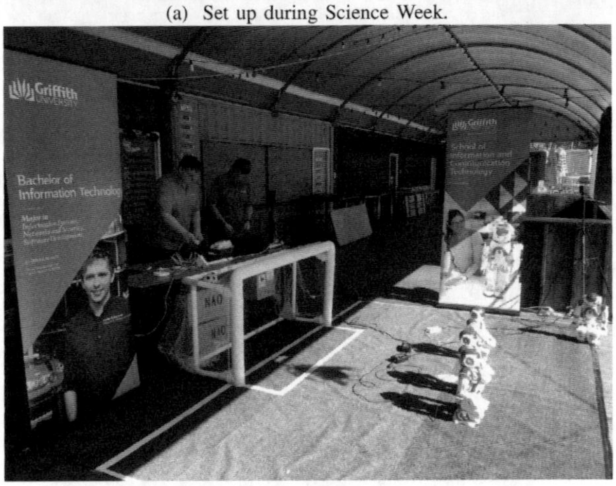

(b) Set up at Pop-Up Science Day.

Figure 1. Typical set-up of a robot soccer field and demonstration of autonomous soccer playing robots.

software on the robot. We do not want human pilots to teach their human bodies how to replicate such get-up motion or kick motion so their surrogate robot can perform these tasks. However, we do believe the humans would find themselves transported to the world of the robot.

During the activity, we requested participants to guide their robot towards the ball, issue kick commands and if possible score a goal (if they were to score the goal, they can chose how to celebrate it, or shall we say, have their robot shall celebrate it). We advised that their objective is to be efficient pilots of the robot, and score as many goals as possible in two minutes. Most of the time, before engaging with the activity, participants had been observing Nao robots playing robotic soccer autonomously. On several occasions, participants had to perform under the competitive circumstance of an autonomous robot also approaching the ball.

Figure 3 shows a sample of the questions used in the pre-activity questionnaire for adults. Figure 4 displays a sample of questions in the post-activity survey.

For children, we will be assessing how rapidly they accept language about the body of the robot as if it was their own

(a) Standing-up adult in indoors environment.

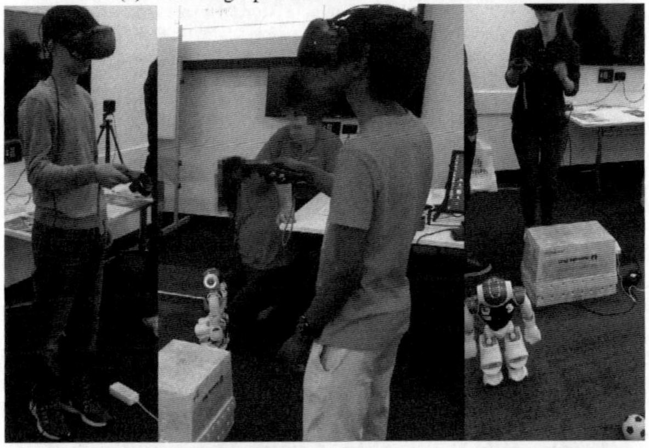

(b) Participant adults in indoors environment.

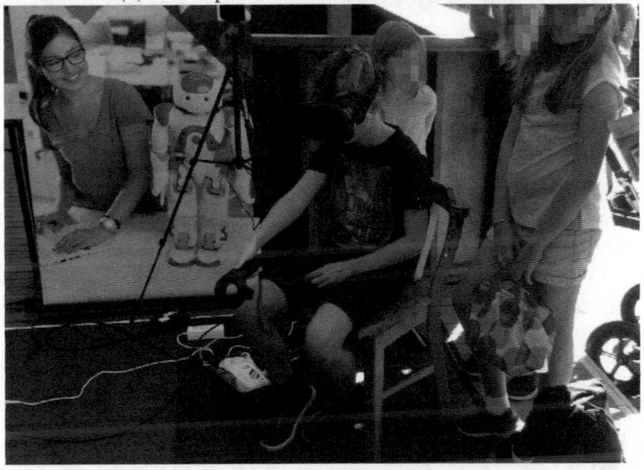

(c) Sitting-down child facing a goal.

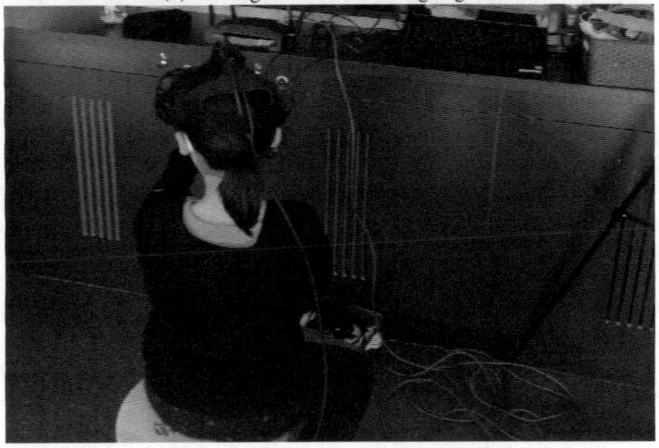

(d) Sitting-down child behind goals of the soccer field.

Figure 2. Adult participants were standing, children participants were sitting. Participants' hearing coincides between virtual world and real world.

1) Have you ever experienced a virtual reality scenario?
2) How often do you play video games?
3) How often do you engage in competitive games against artificial systems where the opponent has no human input (computer chess, XBOX™ alone away from Internet)?
4) How often do you engage in competitive games against other humans (chess, XBOX™ where opponent is piloted by another person)?
5) Rank your interest in engaging in a game with a robot that is the surrogate of another person?
6) Rank your interest in interested in engaging in a game with a robot that is completely autonomous (no human pilot can influence the robot during the game)?
7) Are you familiar with physical presence scenarios such as "reality" TV shows such as *Survivor* and *Big Brother*?
8) In the film *The Truman Show*, Truman (played by Jim Carrey) lives in a television studio manufactured to look like the real world (and he is unaware of this). Do you think this could happen to some person?
9) The film *The Matrix* presents the possibility that although we are in control of our own consciousness, our bodies and the material world that surrounds us are an artificial construction. Do you think it is possible for humans to be immersed in such simulation?
10) Avatar scenarios, such as the popular "life-simulating game" called *The Sims*, are so called because players create characters, profiles and control their lives. Would it be possible to have robots around us that we "control" in such a way?

Figure 3. Sample questions from the pre-activity questionnaire.

body. So, rather than say *"Make the robot kick with its left foot"*, we will evaluate the time it takes for them to accept *"Kick with your left leg"*. For all minors, approval will be requested from parents or guardians as this research was conducted under Griffith University Ethics Reference Number: 2018/846.

The setting could be considered a mix of a computer game with a virtual reality headset and 3D hand-held controllers. We have developed software that renders the camera video stream of the robot to the participant's headset. The 3D hand-held controllers enable pointing at cubes (labelled with icons) in the 3D-virtual environment and triggering an action. To trigger an action, pilots must select a cube. Upon selection, the cube spins in the 3D-virtual environment. The cube changes colour and tilts when triggered (and the chosen action is forwarded). The design of the 3D-virtual world is not a soccer field; it is a pilot's room. Figure 5 illustrates the environment's design.

That is, the human user is still doubled in a controller room, and the cubes offer control to actions that impact the robot's body. The 3-D room has a large screen where the vision of the Nao is presented. The Nao has cameras one above the other (and not side to side as most mammals). So the presentation is an image that reflects such upper and lower camera.

For children and adults, instructions were given regarding the virtual world. We described, prior to placing the headset, the 3D room of Figure 5. Participants were also introduced to the hand-held controllers. These are visible in the virtual world in extremely look-alike objects placed in proportionally the same position relative to the headset in the real world. That is, the hand-held controllers are common element between both worlds. We indicated that the upper button would produce a ray, which does not appear in the real world, but that selects cubes in the virtual world. The trigger under the controller sparks the corresponding action.

At least two assistants support the experiment. One provides instructions to participants, answers their questions, and also plays a role of a bridge between being in the soccer field, and being with the participant in the virtual world by sustaining

1) Did you felt at some point in the experience that your mind was purely confined within the simulated environment and there was no other existence; that is, did it felt for at least an instant that your world was the mixed reality experience?
2) When trying to score a goal, were you aware other opponents were completely autonomous or piloted somehow like your own; that is, did it matter other robots degree of autonomy and simulation?
3) Would you consider other technologies that directly interact with your optical nerve or your senses and connect to your neural hardware for such an experience?
4) As technology improves, would this type of experiences be better if everything was simulated, and no robot in the real world existed, but still felt completely real?
5) After this experience, re-rank your interest in engaging in a game with a robot that is the surrogate of another person?
6) After this experience, re-rank your interest in interested in engaging in a game with a robot that is completely autonomous (no human pilot can influence the robot during the game)?
7) After this experience, and revisiting the hypothesis of the film *The Truman Show*, where Truman (played by Jim Carrey) living in a television studio manufactured to look like the real world (and he is unaware of this). Do you think this could happen to some person?
8) After this experience, and revisiting the hypothesis of the film *The Matrix* (the possibility that although we are in control of our own consciousness, our bodies and the material world that surrounds us are an artificial construction). Do you think it is possible for humans to be immersed in such simulation?
9) After this experience, would you enjoy interacting with avatars (artificial robots that have some control or configuration by humans), for example as receptionists in hotels (and not as boring as vending machines)?
10) Avatar scenarios, such as the popular "life-simulating game" called *The Sims*, are so called because players create characters, profiles and control their lives. After the experience, re-rank your belief that it would it be possible to have robots around us that we "control" in such a way?

Figure 4. Sample questions from the post-activity questionnaire.

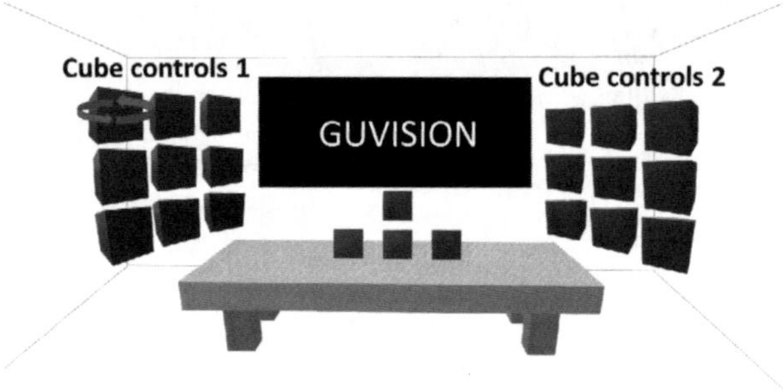

Figure 5. Design of the 3-D worlds the pilot sees.

a dialogue. This first assistant can only see the soccer field as a spectator. The second assistant monitors the execution of the application in a flat monitor with a display similar to Figure 6. The second assistant can monitor the time left, whether all devices (hand-held controller, handset, tracking towers) are operational, whether WiFi link to the robot is operational, and a fraction of the participants view. For example, in Figure 6, we see part of the icon on one of the cubes for waiving (celebrating a goal) and the images of the robot's cameras.

The sessions with a participant consisted of a protocol with the following stages.

1) Demonstration of robotic soccer. The participant encounters a clearly identified soccer field, and humanoid robots dressed in either red or black jerseys engaging in a match that resembles the Standard Platform League setting for RoboCup (refer to Figure 1).

Figure 6. Screen shot of the monitor running the application.

2) Participants are invited to take part in the match. If the participant is an adult, we present ethics information sheet, and pre-activity questionnaire. If the participant is a child, we secure parental consent. Adults are allowed to pilot standing while children are requested to sit (refer to Figure 2).
3) Establishing the control. This stage consists of describing the headset and hand-held controls cloned into the virtual room (in particular, the button used and the trigger). A brief description of what to expect (there are cubes in a room, some to the left, some to the right, some in the middle). A description of the task: to score as many goals as possible in two minutes. The first assistant indicates what robot the human will pilot before setting up the headset (typically, "you are the robot in black jersey 3").
4) Establish the language. From the beginning, the first assistant will purposely engage in a dialogue where it refers to actions on the field by the piloted robot as if it was the body of the person. For instance, "you should be able to see the ball ahead", "walk forward a bit still, the ball is still far from you", "the robot in red will challenge you for the ball". However, on occasion, guidance of the virtual environment would be necessary, with advice such as "the cubes on your right control your motions", "if you want to kick, you must use the cube with the icon of a foot", "if you want to stand-up, you need to activate the higher cube" "if you want to sit down, you need to activate the lower left cube". There will also be perhaps backward situations, such as "after you kicked, you have fallen", and intentionally all celebrations of the goal finish with the robot kneeling down, so the first assistant would say "stand-up, to keep on playing." We record whether the child responds to these commands using their own body, or continues to engage the first assistant as if their body is the robot's body.
5) After two minutes, the activity stops. The headset is removed, and the participant has completed the experience.
6) If the participant is an adult, collect completed post-activity questionnaire.

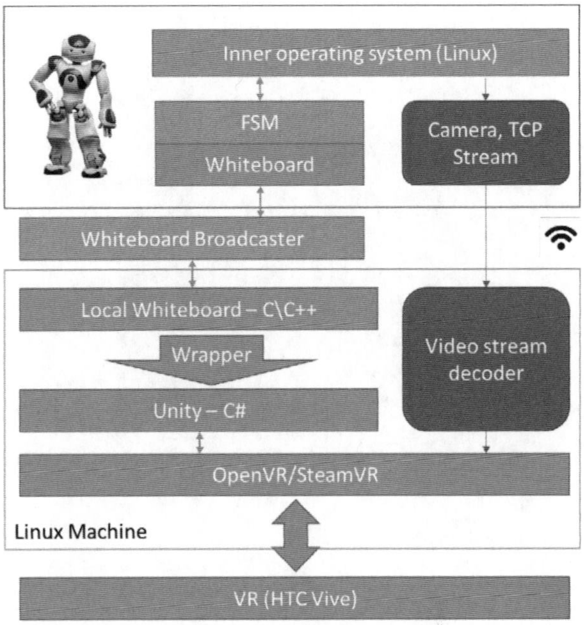

Figure 7. Schema of the components of the application.

III. ARCHITECTURE

Our application architecture displays a pilot's room which may seem a small cinema, where a projection screen is centred and slightly above a theatrical stage. As we explained above, the projection screen renders the video feed of the robot's cameras. Cubes in the centre of the virtual environment are like GUI-buttons for the control of movement on the robot, so that it walks forwards, backwards, spins to the right or to the left. There are some behaviour templates, such as kick with either foot, pass the ball with either foot, kneel and rest, stand up, waive with left or right hand briefly, or wave extensively.

We run our application on a Linux – Ubuntu 16.04LTS WS, and virtual reality equipment of an HTC Vive set, we use Unity 3D 2017.2 BETA Ubuntu, the OpenVR on SteamVR tools set, and other software elements (refer to Figure 7). Unity enabled high-level programming, and facilitated integration with SteamVR, although C/C++ had to be wrapped into C#. However, this wrapping enabled all C++ infrastructure and model-driven behaviour with logic-labelled finite-state machines (LLFSMs) to integrate smoothly [17]. Control commands (captured by Unity) are delivered over the distributed whiteboard, and the distributed object-oriented whiteboard also achieves feedback from sensors in the robot. The local whiteboards are shared-memory middleware that interface well with the concurrent but reliable sequential scheduling of an arrangement of LLFSMs. The distributed middleware operates over idempotent control/status messages over UDP, which has been shown to be more responsive that standards such as ROS [18].

All messages are, therefore, C++ classes, and operate over local whiteboards on the robot and on the host. However, the video feed is a dedicated socket channel of compressed `jpeg` images from the robot to the host. Therefore, the development effort included several technologies, from the

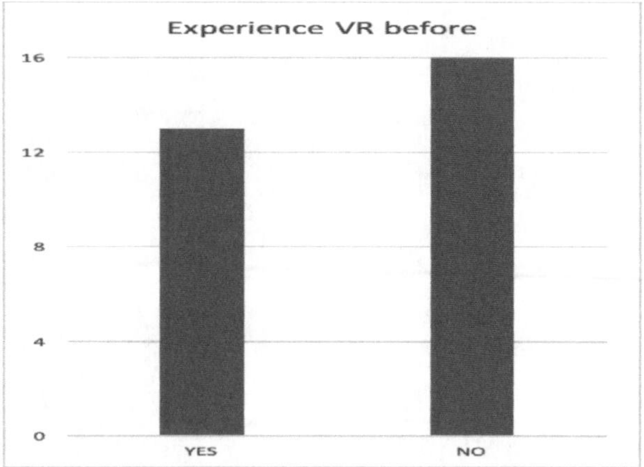

Figure 8. Histogram of responses to first question in pre-activity questionnaire.

programming of C# scripting in Unity, to designing recorded motion gestures in Nao's Choreographe motion composing system, extending the C++ classes/messages known to the whiteboard, and developing finite-state machines that enable behaviours in the robot. Also, some network programming and Open-CV wrapping were required to forward the video stream from the robot to the host.

IV. THE RESULTS

We review the results for adults first and then for children.

A. Adult subjects

The questionnaires were scanned and analysed to compare answers. The first part of the pre-activity questionnaire enables us to judge whether the person is a suitable subject. Griffith University Ethics committee required us to minimise the risk that participants experience adverse reactions to virtual reality exposure (e.g., dizziness, nausea etc.). Therefore, we excluded any individual we suspect was susceptible to a neurological condition (e.g., epilepsy) or that had experienced adverse reactions to virtual reality previously. Side effects of virtual reality exposure are usually associated with long periods of immersion [19]. All our subjects were limited to a period of 2 minutes.

Figure 8 shows that our sample of adult participants (29 individuals) is almost divided evenly (13/16) among those who had previous experience with VR and those who had not.

The pre-activity questionnaire shows that our sample of adult participants holds significant diversity. Figure 9a shows that our subjects are significantly familiar with video games, engaging quite regularly with them. While they have some engagement in competitive games against opponents known to be artificial (Figure 9b), there is a slight predilection for versing other humans (Figure 9c).

The after-experience questionnaire does not show a definite illusion on the subjects that they were transported to a different world. Figure 10a shows that 16 users out of 29 (more than half) felt immersed in another world *on occasions* and although this is more than 50% of the subjects, the other 13 were not definite. We believe this is the participants' perception, and that is one measure which is affected by the lag in the image, and the fact that sounds in the real world have not a perceivable source in the immersed world. However, our experiments with the children, later on, show that children were significantly immersed and one could say even consumed by the task and the activity. Adults also show a slight predilection for experiencing more similar immersions and more accurate and directly reproduced virtual worlds into their senses, with more than a third declaring they would enjoy too much being immersed (Figure 10b). Whether a complete simulation or transportation to another real world is preferable is also undecided (Figure 10c). However, there is a slight preference to have some robot and some reality over a complete simulation.

Now, we report on our analysis of the change in attitude or belief from the adult participant from the pre-activity questionnaire to the post-activity questionnaire. The type of hypothesis we formulate is that the 2-minute immersions results in a positive change towards the technology or to the belief that how humans perceive reality and existence can be opened to new interpretation and possibilities.

Therefore, we start with the re-evaluation offered by Question 5 in both surveys. Our hypothesis is that

> (H) after the experience, participants are more interested in engaging in games with robots on a tele-existence world.

The corresponding null hypothesis is that

> (H_{null}) after the experience participants have no more preference (or potentially less interest) in engaging in games with robots on a tele-existence world.

Since we had a total of 14 responses out of 29 where participants upgraded their interest, 14 maintained the same interest and only one reduced their interest, we observe a prevalence for our hypothesis. The result would not be statistically significant. Nevertheless, when we consider the change in response to Question 6, we have that all participants, that is the 29 of them, preferred to engage in contests challenged by a robot that is totally autonomous. This outcome is naturally a statistically significant result that the experience changed the views of the adult subjects. We also find that the results seem to contrast how our sample of participants engage in competitive games. We note the contrast of Figure 9b with Figure 9c that shows a preference to have humans as opponents, but for this tele-existence, having purely artificially controlled robots is the absolute preference!

If we evaluate the following hypothesis by the change in response to the question regarding the film *The Truman Show*, we also observe a remarkable result. Our hypothesis is that,

> (H) after the experience, participants believe more strongly that human beings can be fooled long-term about the reality they experience.

In this case, responses are such that 25 respondents increased their ranking on the possibility of scenarios like in the film *The Truman Show*. If we make the null hypothesis as follows

> (H_{null}) after the experience participants have no more belief (or potentially even less belief) on the

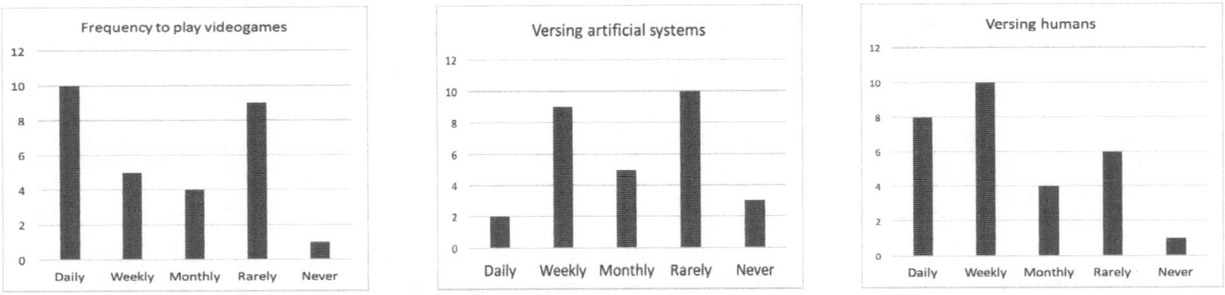

(a) Histogram for usage of video-games.

(b) Histogram for choosing and artificial opponent.

(c) Histogram for selecting a human opponent.

Figure 9. Illustrating the dispersion of personal preferences and habits by adults reflected in the pre-activity questionnaire.

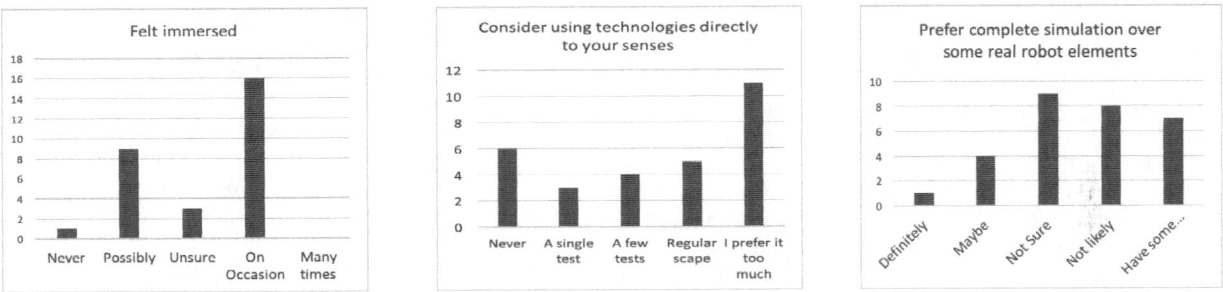

(a) How transported to another world.

(b) Wishing to have more direct and seamless immersion.

(c) Shall we keep a robot and keep it *real* or should it be a complete simulation.

Figure 10. Post-activity histograms on responses showing slight preference for tele-existence experiences.

plausibility of a human being living on a staged reality.

Then, the hypothesis testing using the binomial distribution with 28 degrees of freedom show statistical significance at the 99% level.

Since the thesis of the movie *The Matrix* is a direct illustration of tele-existence, we expect to observe some change on the belief for the plausibility of such a scenario. That is we expect

> (*H*) after the experience, participants believe more strongly that human beings can have their nervous system and brain directly linked to a virtual reality and it would appear a completely real experience.

We found here that 18 out of 29 participants' responses are consistent with the hypothesis. This outcome is not statistically significant. Nevertheless, none of the responses decreased the belief after the experience. It is not methodologically prudent to change the hypothesis after observing the data, but it remains an interesting observation that if we had formulated the hypothesis

> (*H*) participants would increase or maintain their belief in the plausibility of scenarios like in the movie *the Matrix*.

Then, the null hypothesis would be that they would decrease their belief in such plausibility, and the data would have rejected the null hypothesis. It is reassuring that our tele-existence experiment did not have an effect to reduce the chances of people imagining scenarios of tele-existence. That is, our hardware/software immersion is convincing enough to transport adult subjects to a tele-existence that sustains the plausibility of tele-existence scenarios.

Finally, if we look at the change in belief for participants contrasting on the *existence scenario* exemplified by the life-simulating game *The Sims*, we formulated the hypothesis as follows.

> (*H*) Participants would increase their belief in the plausibility of scenarios like in the life-simulating game *The Sims*.

Here 18 out of 29 participants increased their belief, and 11 left it unchanged. This outcome is not statistically significant to reject the null hypothesis. However, if we had formulated the hypothesis as *an increase or maintain*, then the 29 participants would have been consistent with the hypothesis and the result would have been statistically significant. However, this would have the questionable methodological issue of revising the hypothesis after inspecting the data. Nevertheless, it is remarkable that none of the participants decreased their perception that surrogate existence as exemplified by *The Sims* is plausible.

B. Children subjects

Since we will measure how immersed are the children in the tele-existence experience by their reaction to statements like "to play you need to get up", we have in our method a mechanism to establish the baseline. Our approach is derived from the requirement by our ethics approval to have the children sitting during the experiment. For all participants, the robot is always kneeling at the start of the experience.

With participants in the four days of STEM, we had at least 5 different groups in each day. That is, the STEM activities partition the children in the day into 5 groups. Therefore, at most 5 and typically 4 children are introduced to the activity. The first child to sit (from a group) is chosen randomly, and the activity commences immediately with the remark by the first assistant: "to play you need to get up". In total, we had 20 children (5 representatives of a group on 4 days) to which the indication to stand-up was given at the start of the immersion. We iterate that these children had not witnessed the activity, and we suggest the indication is ambiguous as it could refer to the robot's body or the children's body. Our results show that 8 out of 20 children stood up themselves, rather than operate the cube that raises the robot. We take this as a strong indication that early in the activity, the statement "to play you need to get up" is ambiguous.

However, when a child pilot manages to score a goal and celebrate it, the robot will purposely finish kneeling. So, the first assistant gives the indication "to continue playing you need to get up". We only had 44 out of 156 children succeeding in scoring a goal. So, the situation where we evaluate the reaction of children to the indication applies to those 44 participants only. However, 42 children used the control of the virtual world to raise the robot and continue playing for a second goal. Only 2 (two) out of 44 stood up from their sitting position. There was no overlap between the 20 children who received the instruction very early in the activity and the 44 who received it after they succeed in scoring a goal. However, there were 14 children who had witnessed another child participate earlier, scored a goal and not require to stand up themselves, just the robot. So, we exclude those and we are left with 30 children, where 28 used the robot body rather than their own to continue playing. We designed this experiment with the following hypothesis in mind.

> (*H*) The probability that a child participant interprets the ambiguous statement about the body needing to stand up as referring to the robot rather than his own body is larger after being immersed than before being immersed.

Note that our data for interpreting the statement very early in the experience suggest that the probability of interpreting the statement as the robot's body is $\hat{p}_0 = 12/20 = 3/5$ (This is the Maximum Likelihood Estimator (MLE) of the corresponding Binomial distribution). Since we had $n = 20$ trials, the Fisher information is

$$I(p) = \frac{n}{p(1-p)}.$$

Thus, the 95% confidence interval is given by

$$\begin{aligned} \mathrm{CI}_0 &= \hat{p}_0 \pm 1.96\sqrt{\frac{\hat{p}_0(1-\hat{p}_0)}{n_0}} \\ &= \frac{3}{5} \pm 1.96\sqrt{\frac{0.6(0.4)}{20}} \\ &= 0.6 \pm 0.2147. \end{aligned}$$

Now, after scoring a goal, the MLE probability of interpreting the statement as the body of the robot is $\hat{p}_1 = 28/30 = 14/15$. And in this case, the 95% confidence interval is

$$\begin{aligned} \mathrm{CI}_1 &= \hat{p}_1 \pm 1.96\sqrt{\frac{\hat{p}_1(1-\hat{p}_1)}{n_1}} \\ &= \frac{14}{15}1.96\sqrt{\frac{0.9333(0.0666)}{30}} \\ &= 0.9333 \pm 0.0892. \end{aligned}$$

Since the 95% confidence do not overlap, we can say that at the 95% level, we have a statistically significant result for our hypothesis. That is, we reject the null hypothesis at 95% and accept that children interpret the language of *your body* as referring to the robot.

V. Threats to Validity

Analysing the conditions and setting of our experiments we can identify some challenges regarding external validity. The subjects do not represent random samples of adults, neither a random sample of children. The subjects have pre-selected themselves as curious regarding technology, virtual reality or at least robotics. They may be a correlation between the promotion of information technology degrees (being performed during the day), and the belief system of those that approach the display and eventually participated in the activity. The activity is robotic soccer as per the Standard Platform League at RoboCup; it is possible that other challenges or competitive environments of tele-existence deliver different results. There were no awards and perhaps the setting does not constitute realistic pressure on the participants; results could also be different if reaching a specific target of goals would result in receiving a prize. Similarly, if the participant were to perform poorly and a penalty were to be applied, it could cause different behaviour during the activity and different responses regarding the enthusiasm to be involved in competitive settings with physical artificial agents.

While we query about previous experience with virtual environments, it is possible that training and previous practice with the hand-held controllers and familiarity with wearing a VR headset results in skilful tele-operation. Such easy tasks and success with such tasks may impact self-awareness or self-esteem; leading to considering humans more highly, and thus superior than artificial systems.

We also need to consider other aspects of construct validity. Is the pre-questionnaire or post-questionnaire measuring adequately the impact of the exposure to a change in beliefs? Are there other ways by which humans revise their belief system about machines and artificial intelligence? Could the participants (despite answering anonymously) be anticipating what are "normal" responses and trying to please those conducting the research? It is not surprising that people adopt language referring to an avatar as talking about themselves, even for simple video games or massively networked games [20]. However, completely virtual avatars occasionally lead to identity issues [20]. We felt here it was clear to all participants they are the mind for just one body, they could not choose it, and they can not clone it or vary it. All these are elements that are distinctive from the construction of avatars, and would prove interesting avenues to explore in further experimental settings [21].

With respect to statistical validly, challenges could be derived from violations to the statistical assumptions that enable a particular analysis, low statistical power or low effect size. We could have evaluated the results for children using the observed value of the LR statistic [22, Section 12.4, Pages 156-158] and we would establish even stronger (i.e. 99% level) statistical significance. In particular, we reject the hypothesis that assuming the language is about the robot's body is the same before and after scoring a goal. The common MLE for the probability is

$$\frac{12+38}{20+30} = 40/50 = 4/5.$$

Thus,

$$\begin{aligned} D_{obs} &= 2\left(8\log\frac{8}{4} + 2\log\frac{2}{6} + 12\log\frac{12}{16} + 28\log\frac{28}{24}\right) \\ &= 8.42. \end{aligned}$$

and $Prob\{\chi^2_{(1)} \geq 8.42\} < 0.01$. We felt the argument with confidence intervals is more transparent. Thus, we highlighted those results where we could report statistical significance.

VI. CONCLUSIONS

The Oxford living dictionary defines tele-presence as

> *"The use of virtual reality technology, especially for remote control of machinery or for apparent participation in distant events. A sensation of being elsewhere, created by virtual reality technology".*

We believe this definition captures the very distinctive notion of *tele-existence* [7] when it suggests the individual is transported somewhere else. However, we have emphasised here the distinction with a large number of tele-presence products essentially equivalent to a tilt-able tablet on wheels. Such products are closer to tele-conference infrastructure as they offer little capability to influence the world one is transported to. By creating a tele-existence environment with a Nao robot, virtual reality headset and VR-controllers, we have transported adults and children to co-exist with other robots in a soccer match opposing other autonomous robots. We have evaluated adults attitudes to the notion of tele-existence comparing it with some scenarios discussed in the literature and exemplified by some widely known movies or video-games. We found humans attitudes to engaging in competitive matches against robots increased significantly, and our setting does not reduce the belief in humans for the plausibility of such scenarios. In the case of children, they very rapidly adopt the robot's body as the body used in the natural dialogue with the presenter of the activity. Our results open the exploration of the emerging notion of tele-existence to reclaim the definition of tele-presence.

There are many improvement opportunities for furthering our current immersion. The camera relay typically has a lag of at least 1.5s. Such a delay should be reduced. Several situations should relay better feedback to the pilot, such as the robot falling or when the waving of hands is finished (waving actions were included to allow scoring celebrations). There is an open field of how much sensor information to forward to the human, and how. The person must believe they are the mind of the robot.

REFERENCES

[1] M. Minsky, "Telepresence," Omni, vol. 2, no. 9, 1980, pp. 45–52.

[2] G. Ballantyne, "Robotic surgery, telerobotic surgery, telepresence, and telementoring," Surgical Endoscopy And Other Interventional Techniques, vol. 16, no. 10, Oct 2002, pp. 1389–1402.

[3] M. Reid, "Rethinking the fourth amendment in the age of supercomputers, artificial intelligence, and robots," West Virginia Law Review, vol. 119, no. 101, March 16th 2017, pp. 100–126.

[4] E. T. Curtiss and S. Eustis, Telepresence Robots Market Shares, Strategies, and Forecasts, Worldwide, 2017 to 2023. Lexington, Massachusetts: Wintergreen Research, Inc., 2017.

[5] M. T. Jones, M. Lombard, and J. Jasak, "(tele)presence and simulation: Questions of epistemology, religion, morality, and mortality," PsychNology Journal, vol. 9, no. 3, 2011, pp. 193–222.

[6] M. Lombard and T. Ditton, "At the heart of it all: The concept of presence," Journal of Computer-Mediated Communication, vol. 3, no. 2, September 1st 1997, pp. 201–213.

[7] M. Elobaid, Y. Hu, J. Babic, and D. Pucci, "Telexistence and teleoperation for walking humanoid robots," 2018, arXiv:1809.01578.

[8] S. Tachi, "Tele-existence," Journal of Robotics and Mechatronics JRM, vol. 4, no. 1, 1992, pp. 7–12.

[9] P. H. Kahn, Jr., B. Friedman, and J. Hagman, ""I Care About Him As a Pal": Conceptions of robotic pets in online aibo discussion forums," in CHI '02 Extended Abstracts on Human Factors in Computing Systems, ser. CHI EA '02. New York, NY, USA: ACM, 2002, pp. 632–633.

[10] P. H. Kahn, Jr., B. Friedman, D. R. Pérez-Granados, and N. G. Freier, "Robotic pets in the lives of preschool children," Interaction Studies, vol. 7, no. 3, 2006, pp. 405 – 436.

[11] L. Boroditsky and M. Ramscar, "The roles of body and mind in abstract thought," Psychological Science, vol. 13, no. 2, 2002, pp. 185–189.

[12] R. Aylett, Robots: Bringing Intelligent Machines to Life. Woodbury, NY, USA: Barron's Educational Series Inc., 2002.

[13] A. Kristoffersson, S. Coradeschi, and A. Loutfi, "A review of mobile robotic telepresence," Adv. in Hum.-Comp. Int., 2013, pp. 3:3–3:3.

[14] J.-M. Lu, C.-H. Lu, Y.-W. Chen, J.-A. Wang, and H. Y.-L., "TRiCmini - a telepresence robot towards enriched quality of life of the elderly," in First Asia Pacific eCare and TeleCare Congress, vol. 18, June 16th-19th 2011.

[15] S. O. Adalgeirsson and C. Breazeal, "MeBot: A robotic platform for socially embodied presence," in Proceedings of the 5th ACM/IEEE International Conference on Human-robot Interaction, ser. HRI '10. Piscataway, NJ, USA: IEEE Press, 2010, pp. 15–22.

[16] A. Spada, M. Cognetti, and A. De Luca, "Locomotion and telepresence in virtual and real worlds," in Human Friendly Robotics, F. Ficuciello, F. Ruggiero, and A. Finzi, Eds. Cham: Springer International Publishing, 2019, pp. 85–98.

[17] V. Estivill-Castro, R. Hexel, and C. Lusty, "High performance relaying of c++11 objects across processes and logic-labeled finite-state machines," in Simulation, Modeling, and Programming for Autonomous Robots, D. Brugali, J. F. Broenink, T. Kroeger, and B. A. MacDonald, Eds. Cham: Springer International Publishing, 2014, pp. 182–194.

[18] D. Joukoff, V. Estivill-Castro, R. Hexel, and C. Lusty, "Fast mav control by control/status oo-messages on shared-memory middleware," in Robot Intelligence Technology and Applications 4, J.-H. Kim, F. Karray, J. Jo, P. Sincak, and H. Myung, Eds. Cham: Springer International Publishing, 2017, pp. 195–211.

[19] K. Fagan, "Here's what happens to your body when you've been in virtual reality for too long," Business Insider, March 4th 2918, www.businessinsider.com.

[20] Y. B. Kafai, D. A. Fields, and M. S. Cook, "Your second selves: Player-designed avatars," Games and Culture, vol. 5, no. 1, 2010, pp. 23–42.

[21] S.-A. A. Jin, "The virtual malleable self and the virtual identity discrepancy model: Investigative frameworks for virtual possible selves and others in avatar-based identity construction and social interaction," Computers in Human Behavior, vol. 28, no. 6, 2012, pp. 2160 – 2168.

[22] J. G. Kalbfleisch, Probability and Statistical Inference — Volume 2: Statistical Inference, 2nd ed. New York: Springer-Verlag New York, 1985.

Gamified Point System Based On Mobile Devices

Boyang Liu

Graduate School of Information,
Production and Systems
Waseda University
Fukuoka, Japan 808–0135
Email: waseda-liuboyang@moegi.waseda.jp

Jiro Tanaka

Graduate School of Information,
Production and Systems
Waseda University
Fukuoka, Japan 808–0135
Email: jiro@aoni.waseda.jp

***Abstract*—Point system is a system providing points to customers according to the consumption. People can accumulate points and these points can be used to redeem for money off in the next purchase. The purpose of point system is to encourage consumption and maintain the current customers by allowing them to get a sense of satisfaction from accumulating points. However, the reduction in redemption rate increases the difficulty of accumulating points, which leads to a decrease in user interest. The goal of our research is to build a new point system framework to increase user engagement. This paper calls for a multi-player approach based on augmented reality game design to engage users. Compared with existing methods, our system generates engaging gaming experience through multi-player game design.**

Keywords–Gamification; User Interactions; Interface Design; Augmented Reality.

I. Introduction

User engagement is an important research topic in many fields. Loyalty programs are structured marketing strategies designed by merchants to encourage customers to continue to shop at or use the services of businesses associated with each program [1]. Therefore, a lot of research has been conducted to improve customer retention from different perspectives [2]-[3].

Point system is the most common loyalty program methodology [4]. It provides an interesting possibility for retailers in customer relationship management [5]. Customer purchases toward a certain amount of points to redeem their reward. This framework was proved to be revolutionary. For customers, point system can help them reduce the cost of buying. For retailers, they can collect personal data, including demographic data (name, age, gender, postcode, etc.) and individual level purchase data (who bought what, where, when, and at what price) [4]. This data enables retailers to build a customer database, to profile their customers, to target them with tailored incentives, and thus to maximize the profitability of their promotional and pricing strategies. Specifically, a card is used to identify the card holder as a participant in the point system [6]. Typically, it has a barcode or magstripe that can be easily scanned. By giving such a card, purchasers can receive either a discount on the current purchase, or points that they can use for future purchases. With the development of mobile devices, digital point cards are also being used.

In the current system, point is the only feature to engage users and it is no longer as attractive as it used to be. One reason is that the customers perceive the rewards as too difficult to earn. Another reason is that current point systems focus on economic value but ignore other perceived value designs. Kreis et al. [7] divided the perceived value into three dimensions including economic value, interaction value and psychological value. Economic value relates primarily to utilitarian, instrumental benefits. Interaction value is derived from interaction with others and psychological value is derived from recognition.

There are two challenges we need to solve. One challenge is that we need to find a way to increase user engagement without changing the redemption rate. The other is that we need to consider interaction and psychological value to improve user's perceived value.

To address these limitation, we design a new multiplayer gamified point system to engage users. Since current point system is designed for single user, it is difficult to take advantage of user interactions. Our goal is to build a framework for the next generation point system. Important value including interaction value and psychological value should also be considered in the design of new point system. Besides, users desire for user interactions could be combined to increase user engagement. In this system, all users can join the game voluntarily. Users can get mission from our system in mission interface and get value points and experience value as reward in value point & pet interface after completing mission. We explore two variations of user interactions - one is the competition where the users can compete face-to-face with other users and try to win the competition to gain a sense of accomplishment, and one in which users can do non-competitive interaction with their partners to gain happiness. By adding a multiplayer element, users have the opportunity to not only accumulate rewards in the system, but also have the opportunity of compete with opponents or sharing their rewards with friends. It is considered to potentially increase a users motivation to use the system and improve the interaction between users.

The remainder of this paper is organized as follows. Second 2 describes related work. Section 3 and Section 4 describe the design and implementation of our system. Section 5 describes some discussion on our system and current point system. In Section 6, we make a conclusion about our system and come up with some ideas about our future work.

II. Related Work

In this section, we discuss previous research in the areas of point system, social influence, gamification, and augmented reality game.

A. Point System

Enzmann et al. [3] think that users refuse to use point system because they may fear an invasion of privacy. Therefore, they present two variants of a privacy-friendly loyalty system to be used by online vendors for issuing points.

In the study of Coskun et al. [8], the design of Near Field Communication (NFC) enabled loyalty system on smart cards of NFC mobiles and development details are presented. NFC technology is a short-range, high frequency, and low bandwidth wireless technology which occurs between two devices within few centimetres. With this model, loyalty and payment applications share and exchange valuable information through NFC Loyal Database system on smart card.

Lim et al. [9] study online loyalty programs from a searchability perspective. The goal of their research is to explain how searchability can influence participation in loyalty programs.

All above research aims at increasing user engagement through utilitarian motives such as improving the security, convenience and functionality of current point system. Our research focus on enhancing symbolic motives, which are related to needs for self-esteem and social approval.

B. Social Influence

The social impact is particularly significant in commerce. For example, many people read what other people think about products by logging on to social media sites before making a purchase. Social media users trust what their friends, family, and even strangers say online about a brand or product. In-store shopping decisions are also affected, as customers use their mobile devices to look at reviews and ratings to reinforce their purchasing decisions [10].

Lee et al. [11] proposed a multi-phased model for internet shopping, which fully takes the characteristics of the internet and cyber shopping into consideration in their paper. Their results indicate that diverse communication affects the level of trust. If customers share more values with other customers and if they have more diverse means of communication, they would intend to revisit the site more repeatedly.

In the study of Zhu et al. [12], they designed and ran an experiment to measure social influence in online recommender systems. Their results show that social influence could sway peoples own choices significantly.

Li et al. [13] found that emotion played a significant role in the mobile consumption experience in their research. They suggest that attention should be paid on the social communication process between humans to improve consumption experience.

The above research shows that social influence has a positive effect in commerce. Our research is based on the combination of social influences and commerce. Specifically, we have designed two kinds of user interactions in our system to study how different social types affect user engagement.

C. Gamification

Gamification refers to the application of using game design elements and game mechanisms in a non-game contexts to enable users to solve problems and improve the contribution of users [14]. Commonly, gamification employs game design elements to improve organizational productivity, user engagement and more. Lots of research about gamification indicates that a majority of studies on gamification reveal that it exerts good effect on individuals. The gamification techniques are aiming at leveraging peoples natural desires for achievement, competition, socializing or simply their response to the framing of a situation as game or play.

Li et al. [15] design a gamified multiplayer software tutorial system called CADament. Compared with existing gamified software tutorial systems, their system generates engaging learning experience through competitions. Their study shows that their system has an advantage over pre-authored tutorials for improving learners performance, increasing motivation, and stimulating knowledge transfer.

In the paper of Dergousoff et al. [16], they think classic ways of gathering data on human behavior are time-consuming, costly and are subject to limited participant pools. Therefore, they combine both gamification and crowdsourcing techniques into a smartphone-based platform to motivate voluntary participation and provide researchers with a framework that can be used to investigate multiple research questions without the need to develop costly specialized games.

For the purpose of inspiring customers, some ideas of combining game and marketing are proposed to engage customers. Zichermann et al. [17] thought that traditional advertising is losing effectiveness as competition for consumer attention and game playing is on the rise and vying for customers attention.

Gamification is also used in education and health. Arawjo et al. [18] present a puzzle game that builds student understanding of programming concepts. Their results from a lab study demonstrate that novices can learn programming concepts by playing the game and the game was well received. In the paper of Zhao et al. [19], they present the design and findings of a study on the motivational effects of using activity tracker-based games to promote daily exercise. The results of their study show that participants preferred the gamified exercise experience over regular exercises and features related to social factors played a relatively more important role in this game experience.

The above research shows that gamification is a universal and effective means to increase user engagement. Our system incorporates gamification elements to enhance user experience.

D. Augmented Reality Game

In the research of Bai et al. [20], they present an augmented reality system enhancing social pretend play by young children. Observations showed that children are highly engaged with the augmented reality system.

Mulloni et al. [21] present an augmented reality game that strongly exploits mobility and social interaction between players as core gameplay elements. The user study showed a general enthusiasm for their game by young adults with varying interest in gaming. Simple user interface resulted in an enjoyable player experience and users asked for multisensorial feedback and 3D animations.

Baudisch et al. [22] present imaginary reality games that mimic the respective real world sport, such as basketball or soccer. Their game maintained many of the properties of physical sports, such as unencumbered play, physical exertion, and immediate social interaction between players.

III. System Description

To realize the purpose of leveraging user to engage users, we designed and implemented an augmented reality based gamified point system deployed on mobile devices. Our system should be designed based on current system: 1) points will be rewarded if users complete shopping; 2) redemption rate should be consistent with current system.

We present a multi-player approach based on game design in our system to improve user engagement. A theme of raising a pet is chosen in the proposed system because 1) pet reflects user's status; 2) user can get the satisfaction of accumulating value points because redeeming gifts can be much easier in the game; 3) the theme of pet raising can create a relaxing and enjoyable game environment for user interaction.

A. System Structure

In the current point system, shopping is the input and the point is the output. However, points can compensate users for their spending but cannot support value creation in the purchase. For example, an environmental protection enthusiast may be more likely to buy energy-saving lamps because it is for the purpose of protecting the environment rather than accumulating points. Therefore, we designed a new point system on the current point system framework. As shown in Figure 1, the blue line part indicates the current system framework while the red line part is our new design.

Our system can be divided into two modules. One module is the individual module (see Figure 1). In the individual module, new input (mission) is designed. To motivate users to create value from shopping activities, we designed new feedback including value points, pet and food as new output.

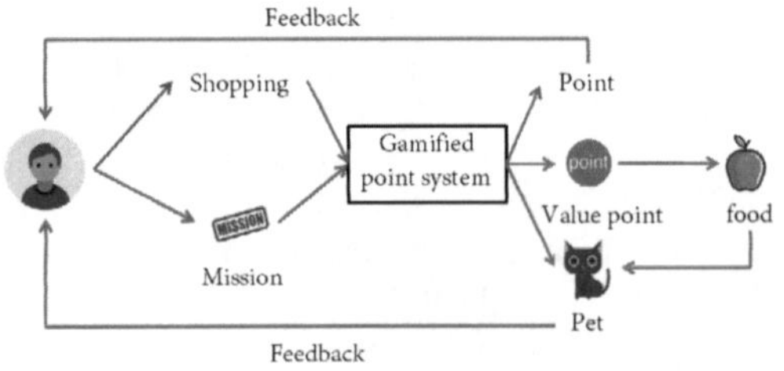

Figure 1. Individual module.

The other module is the user interaction module (see Figure 2). The design of these new feedback increases user engagement by leveraging user interactions including competition and non-competitive interaction. Value point and food are designed to motivate the non-competitive interaction between users. Pet is designed for user competition.

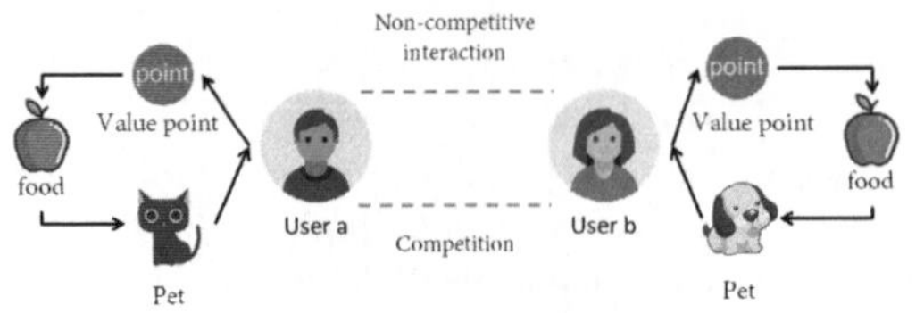

Figure 2. User interaction module.

B. Mission

The mission is designed to remind users of multi-value creation. We developed a set of mission for shopping for our prototype. In an actual deployment, we can create various mission with different value guidance or mission that includes multiple value guidance. Personalized mission could be created based on the purchase information and user information recorded in the point system to provide personalized experience. Previous mission can be easily replaced by new mission and displayed in this interface. The mission could be completed in the purchase. At checkout, mission will be automatically confirmed. For example, a user selects the mission that requires the user to buy low calorie food. The product information will be read automatically by scanning the barcode of the product to confirm whether the mission is completed at checkout. The difficulty of mission could increase gradually and eventually reach a reasonable level. Users can select the mission they want to accomplish in a set of mission.

C. New Feedback

Our gamified points system does not force users to participate. After the users complete the shopping and mission, our system will give feedback to participants to promote their intentions. In our system, users can still earn points from shopping as current system. At the same time, we design some new feedback.

More precisely, there are three new elements:

1) Value Point: We propose a design named value points inspired by the design that users can get points from shopping. Users can get the value points if they complete mission. Value points can be used to buy virtual food to feed pet. Value point is the feedback for mission.

2) Pet: In our system, user can feed a virtual pet. Pet will gain EXP if user completes the mission. If the EXP of pet reaches threshold, the pet will level up. The energy of pet will gradually lose and it will influence the upgrades of pet (if the pet is more energetic, it can get more experience points for the completion of mission). It is designed to motivate users to complete mission continuously. Pet reflects the status of the user.

3) Virtual Food: In this system, user can use value points to buy virtual food. The food can be used to help pet get energy. Users need to get value points continuously to keep their pets in good condition. Food can also be given to other players as gift. The food given to other players can also help the pet get energy. The design of food not only motivates users to accumulate value points, but also encourages them to interact with others.

D. Usage

During shopping, users can start the system deployed on the mobile devices. In the mission interface, users can view the content of mission and select mission. Users can select goods according to the selected mission. At the time of checkout, goods information such will be read and the data will be used to confirm whether the mission selected by the user is completed or not. If purchased is confirmed, user can get points as current system. If mission is confirmed, user can get value points and users pet will get EXP.

E. Game Types

In our design, we leverage user interactions to engage users and help them to create value from purchase. By designing user interfaces, we want to build interactions between users. We explored two different game modes to motivate users, competition and non-competitive interaction.

In competition mode, users can use the point card as an identification of personal status to compete with other users. It will motivate users to continuously improve their personal status to win the competition. Figure 3 shows the assumption scenario where three users participate in the competition. Each of the three users has a mobile phone with a gamified point system installed. Each of them has a digital point card in their client. When three users participate in competition, they put their digital point cards together on the table. The gamified point system on the laptop is running and captures the video stream through the web camera. Based on the level information obtained from the database, the result of competition will be displayed in competition interface.

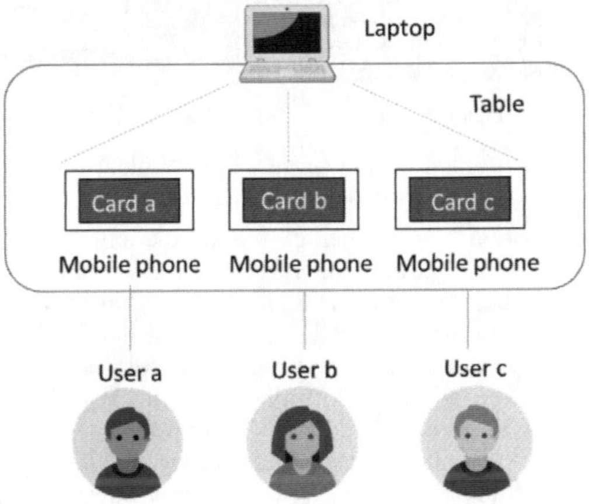

Figure 3. Assumption scenario for competition.

In non-competitive interaction mode, users can interact with other users. Figure 4 shows the non-competitive interaction between two users. Users can get the joy of sharing from giving virtual food to their friends via mobile devices.

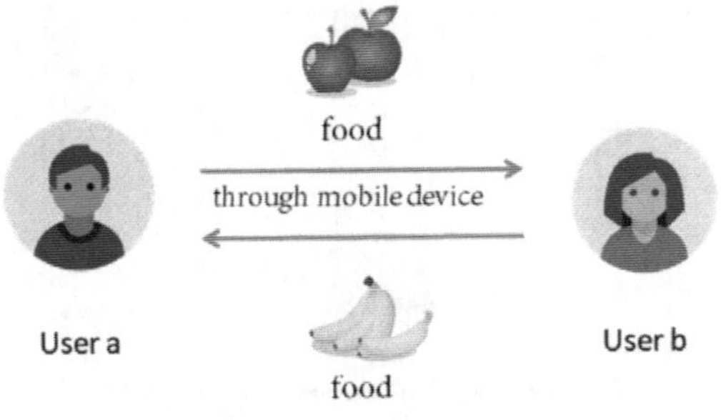

Figure 4. Non-competitive interaction.

Both designs attempt to engage users through interactions between users. In competition mode, users can gain a sense of accomplishment from defeating other users. In non-competitive interaction mode, users can gain the joy of accumulating value points by sharing virtual food with friends.

F. User Interface

In the gamified system, we mainly designed four different user interfaces based on augmented reality visualization.

1) Mission Interface: In the mission interface, user can browse different mission by swiping the screens. The content will be displayed to the user in text form (see Figure 5). Users can click the left arrow and right arrow to view the content of different mission. When users decide to select mission as a shopping target, they can click the choose button. Then, mission information will be stored in the database. It will be confirmed at checkout. If it is confirmed, user can get reward. If it is not finished, it will be deleted from database after checkout.

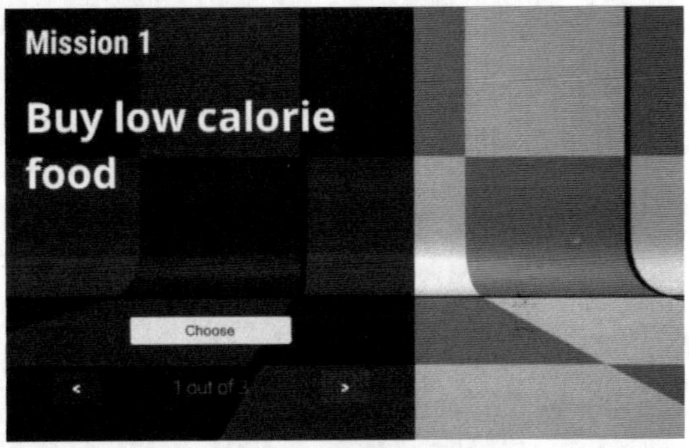

Figure 5. Mission interface.

2) Value Point & Pet Interface: In this interface, we can view the visualization of value points and pet which is superimposed on a digital point card (see Figure 6). If user gets new value points, the volume of value points will increase. This design allows users to get intuitive visual feedback from accumulating value points. The pet will gradually lose energy and the movement of pet will change according to its energy. Therefore, user needs to buy virtual food to help pet recover energy. This design motivates users to complete mission or get food from friends to feed pet. When the user completes a certain amount of mission, users level will increase. This change will be reflected in the size of pet and the level of pet. The level of pet is shown near the pet. Pet needs to research specific level to unlock a new shape.

Figure 6. Value point & pet interface.

3) Competition Interface: We designed a face-to-face competition interface for multiple users. In this interface, users can see their pets. When multiple users put their point cards together, the gamified system deployed on the mobile device will identify their cards and get their level information from the database. Users level information will be reflected in their pets level. In this interface, our system will give ranking results according to the level. For example, the pet with the highest level will stand on the highest podium with a golden crown over its head while the pet with the second highest level will stand on the second highest podium with a magenta crown over its head (see Figure 7).

Figure 7. Competition interface.

4) Non-competitive Interaction Interface: Users can purchase virtual foods with value points in the non-competitive interaction interface. When the value point is spent, the volume of the value point will decrease. The virtual food bought will be displayed in the interface. Users can use virtual food to feed their pets or give food to their friends. If the pet is fed, it will get a certain amount of energy and give motion feedback to the user. If a user receives food from his or her friend, the food will be displayed in the user's interface with a label indicating the sender. This design allows users to socialize with other users by sharing their reward (see Figure 8).

IV. System Implementation

The main hardware devices used for the development of our prototype system include a tablet PC, a webcam and a smartphone. Windows 10 Home Edition is installed in the tablet PC. The processor is Intel(R) Core(TM) i7-6500U CPU @2.50GHz 2.59GHz. The RAM is 8.00 GB. Webcam is connected to the tablet PC to capture real-time video and send video stream to the tablet PC for processing. The development software is Unity 2017.2.0f3 (64-bit), a cross-platform game engine. Unity 3D is used to build and render our three-dimensional system. Vuforia SDK is used for augmented reality implementation, which uses computer vision technology to recognize and track images. After recognizing the image of point card on the smartphone, virtual objects created in Unity 3D will be superimposed on the smartphone. After that, users can see the 3D objects and interact with them. As for the database, we used WampServer Version 3.0.6 32bit consisting of the Apache web server, OpenSSL for SSL support, MySQL database and PHP programming language. Apach and MySQL

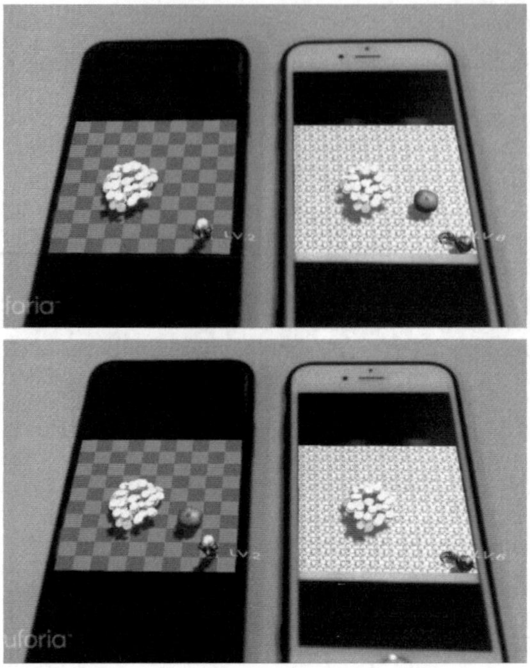

Figure 8. Non-competitive interaction interface.

are always running on the server. Communication between the mobile devices and the server is implemented in PHP.

Our system is implemented based on client-server network structure (see Figure 9). Gamified point system will be deployed on mobile device as a client. The retailers can manage and update user information. Users access data when registering their own information and obtaining their information from database. We use the WWW class and the WWWForm class to send and receive data from Unity. When receiving from the database, the information is converted to JSON format and received. After receiving it on the Unity side, it is decoded into a string format.

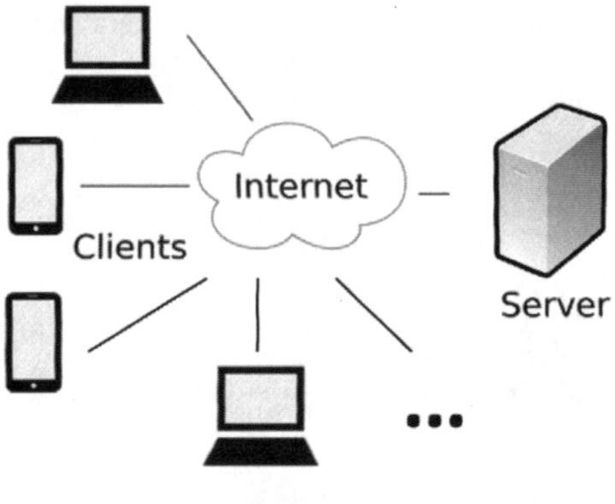

Figure 9. System network structure overview.

V. Conclusion and Future Work

Point system is a system designed to attract consumers. However, due to some problems like the decrease of redemption rate and changes in consumption choice, the attractiveness of system goes down. In this paper, a gamified point system on mobile devices is introduced. Gamified point system presents a method for engaging users using multiplayer game design. As an important advantage over current point system, each user can participate in a game experience to interact with others.

Compared to the current point system, our system has the following advantages:

1) Multi-value shopping guidance by mission.
2) Engaging game experience by four game elements design.
3) User interaction by
    a) Competition.
    b) Non-competitive interaction.

Current point systems only focus on the economic feedback. If users complete the shopping, they can get points as rewards. However, many other value factors should also be considered in consumption such as health and environmental factors. Our system is designed based on current system structure. By adding mission into our system, we remind users of multi-value factors. To motivate users to pay attention to value creation, we design new feedback to improve the system. By adding these game elements, we create a game-like environment for users. Users can get more enjoyable game experience by participating in our system than current system. In order to improve user engagement, two kinds of user interactions are designed with the four game elements. Users cannot only conduct individual mission to get rewards but also can get satisfaction from competition and non-competitive interaction with other users.

Users can choose to participate in the game or not. In the game, there are four game elements. The mission is the task that users need to accomplish. The content of mission combines multiple values. For users that go shopping with the goal to get a particular object and leave the store, we can add some mission related to consumption so that they can also participate in the game. For example, when they spend a certain amount of money, they will also get value points. If users complete the mission during shopping, they can get value points and their pets can get EXP. Users can use value point to buy virtual food which can be used to feed their pets. When the EXP reaches a certain amount, the pet will upgrade. If the pet is not fed for a long time, the pet will become inactive. Therefore, users need to constantly earn value points in exchange for virtual food to keep pets active.

Pet and virtual food are designed for user interaction. In competition interface, users can compete with others with pet. The ranking result will be displayed in the interface according to level of pet. In non-competitive interaction interface, users can buy virtual food and share the food with others. Both of two designs take advantage of users' desire for socializing.

In the future, we would like to investigate other important elements in multiplayer games, such as collaboration and social communities. It would be interesting to further investigate the effect of each game elements. In the future, we would like to further evaluate the effect of our gamified point system by carrying out some experiments. First of all, we will compare gamified point system with the baseline condition to verify that if our system increases engagement by evaluating usage frequency and duration. Then, we will evaluate game elements in our system. We will evaluate three kinds of mission (buy local goods, buy low calories foods and buy recyclable goods) by evaluating mission completion rate. Three kinds of pet (cat, dog, turtle) will be evaluated to understand the impact of pet. Two kinds of user interaction will be evaluated to study the impact of different interaction.

ACKNOWLEDGMENT

We would like to thank the China Scholarship Council for sponsoring Boyang Liu studying at the Waseda University.

REFERENCES

[1] B. Sharp and A. Sharp, "Loyalty programs and their impact on repeat-purchase loyalty patterns," International journal of Research in Marketing, vol. 14, no. 5, 1997, pp. 473–486.

[2] A. Hupfeld and C. Speed, "Getting something for nothing?: A user-centric perspective on loyalty card schemes," in Proceedings of the 2017 CHI Conference on Human Factors in Computing Systems. ACM, 2017, pp. 4443–4453.

[3] M. Enzmann and M. Schneider, "Improving customer retention in e-commerce through a secure and privacy-enhanced loyalty system," Information Systems Frontiers, vol. 7, no. 4-5, 2005, pp. 359–370.

[4] S. G. Magatef and E. F. Tomalieh, "The impact of customer loyalty programs on customer retention," International Journal of Business and Social Science, vol. 6, no. 8, 2015, pp. 78–93.

[5] A. D. Smith and J. A. Potter, "Loyalty card programs, customer relationship and information technology: an exploratory approach," International Journal of Business Innovation and Research, vol. 4, no. 1-2, 2009, pp. 65–92.

[6] C. Mauri, "Card loyalty. a new emerging issue in grocery retailing," Journal of Retailing and Consumer Services, vol. 10, no. 1, 2003, pp. 13–25.

[7] H. Kreis and A. Mafael, "The influence of customer loyalty program design on the relationship between customer motives and value perception," Journal of Retailing and Consumer Services, vol. 21, no. 4, 2014, pp. 590–600.

[8] V. Coskun, B. Ozdenizci, K. Ok, M. Alsadi, and F. Soylemezgiller, "Design and development of nfc enabled loyalty system," in Proceedings of the 6th international conference of advanced computer systems and networks: Design and application, Lviv, Ukraine, 2013, pp. 16–18.

[9] S. Lim and B. Lee, "Online loyalty programs viewed from a searchability perspective," in Proceedings of the 14th Annual International Conference on Electronic Commerce. ACM, 2012, pp. 255–262.

[10] Y. Kim and J. Srivastava, "Impact of social influence in e-commerce decision making," in Proceedings of the ninth international conference on Electronic commerce. ACM, 2007, pp. 293–302.

[11] J. Lee, J. Kim, and J. Y. Moon, "What makes internet users visit cyber stores again? key design factors for customer loyalty," in Proceedings of the SIGCHI conference on Human Factors in Computing Systems. ACM, 2000, pp. 305–312.

[12] H. Zhu, B. Huberman, and Y. Luon, "To switch or not to switch: understanding social influence in online choices," in Proceedings of the SIGCHI Conference on Human Factors in Computing Systems. ACM, 2012, pp. 2257–2266.

[13] M. Li, Z. Dong, and X. Chen, "Factors influencing consumption experience of mobile commerce: a study from experiential view," Internet Research, vol. 22, no. 2, 2012, pp. 120–141.

[14] K. Huotari and J. Hamari, "Defining gamification: a service marketing perspective," in Proceeding of the 16th international academic MindTrek conference. ACM, 2012, pp. 17–22.

[15] W. Li, T. Grossman, and G. Fitzmaurice, "Cadament: a gamified multiplayer software tutorial system," in Proceedings of the SIGCHI Conference on Human Factors in Computing Systems. ACM, 2014, pp. 3369–3378.

[16] K. Dergousoff and R. L. Mandryk, "Mobile gamification for crowdsourcing data collection: Leveraging the freemium model," in Proceedings of the 33rd Annual ACM Conference on Human Factors in Computing Systems. ACM, 2015, pp. 1065–1074.

[17] G. Zichermann and J. Linder, Game-based marketing: inspire customer loyalty through rewards, challenges, and contests. John Wiley & Sons, 2010.

[18] I. Arawjo, C.-Y. Wang, A. C. Myers, E. Andersen, and F. Guimbretière, "Teaching programming with gamified semantics," in Proceedings of the 2017 CHI Conference on Human Factors in Computing Systems. ACM, 2017, pp. 4911–4923.

[19] Z. Zhao, A. Arya, A. Whitehead, G. Chan, and S. A. Etemad, "Keeping users engaged through feature updates: A long-term study of using wearable-based exergames." in CHI, 2017, pp. 1053–1064.

[20] Z. Bai, A. F. Blackwell, and G. Coulouris, "Exploring expressive augmented reality: The fingar puppet system for social pretend play," in Proceedings of the 33rd Annual ACM Conference on Human Factors in Computing Systems. ACM, 2015, pp. 1035–1044.

[21] A. Mulloni, D. Wagner, and D. Schmalstieg, "Mobility and social interaction as core gameplay elements in multi-player augmented reality," in Proceedings of the 3rd international conference on Digital Interactive Media in Entertainment and Arts. ACM, 2008, pp. 472–478.

[22] P. Baudisch, H. Pohl, S. Reinicke, E. Wittmers, P. Lühne, M. Knaust, S. Köhler, P. Schmidt, and C. Holz, "Imaginary reality gaming: ball games without a ball," in Proceedings of the 26th annual ACM symposium on User interface software and technology. ACM, 2013, pp. 405–410.

Line Drawing Perceptual Characteristics for the Number of Strokes Using an Active-Wheel Mouse

Yoshihiko Nomura, Yoshiaki Kashino, Koki Katsuta,
Graduate School of Engineering
Mie University
Tsu, Japan
e-mails: {nomura, y-kashino, katsuta-k}@int.mach.mie-u.ac.jp

Tokuhiro Sugiura
Center for Information Technologies and Networks
Mie University
Tsu, Japan
e-mail: sugiura @ cc.mie-u.ac.jp

***Abstract*—This paper reports perceptual characteristics for multiple line-drawings using an *"active-wheel mouse"* and employing an *"After-Recognition Go"* presentation strategy. The active-wheel mouse is a mouse interface to which a finger-tactile interface is attached. The finger-tactile interface embodies an active wheel being rotatable in any directions, with any speeds and with any time durations, and the rotation provides slippages to users on their fingertip skin. Users are instructed to accept the slippage stimuli as straight-line stroke motions with specific directions, velocities and lengths. A perceptual experiment was conducted: up to seven, straight-line strokes were presented to subjects, i.e., participants by the active-wheel mouse, and the strokes were drawings reproduced by the subjects. Next, the reproduced strokes were evaluated from the viewpoints of lengths, directions, velocities, and time durations. As a result, it made clear that the active-wheel mouse worked well for line drawing presentation.**

Keywords*— *Fingerpad; tactile; interface; stroke; perception

I. INTRODUCTION

Visually impaired persons utilize sensations other than the vision such as skin and proprioceptive sensations. For example, some handy-and-portable devices were proposed. For instructing arm motions, Tsuda et al. [1] and Causo et al. [2] proposed vibrotactile device. Norman et al. [3] proposed skin-stretch device. Gwilliam et al. [4] proposed a skin stretch-based tactile display in conjunction of a joystick-based force feedback, and Koslover et al. [5] combined a skin stretch-based tactile display with vibrotactile and voice guidance. Ion et al. [6] proposed a tactile display to drag a physical tactor across the skin for instructing geometrical shapes. Tsagarakis et al. [7] proposed a slippage display to rotate two cones for instructing 2D directions. Moscatelli et al. [8] proposed other slippage display to rotate a ball for instructing 2D slippages.

They provided motion information with tactors. However, they could not solve following problems: ① the number of physical properties to be presented was restricted in such the way that motion direction can be presented alone, ② the operating range was restricted in several millimeters. As a solution for the problems, the authors have presented an "Active-Wheel Mouse (AWM) [9]" and an "After-Recognition Go (ARG)" presentation strategy [11].

Towards a practical application of the AWM, we should know better the line-drawing perceptual characteristics. The perceptual characteristics can be evaluated by the outcome, that is, the reproduced strokes resulted from a series of processes from the stimulus perception, stroke recognition, and memory-retention. In this study, the perceptual characteristics were examined for multiple-stroke line-drawings up to seven strokes through a psychophysical experiment. The remainder of the paper is structured as follows. The hardware and software of the system employed in this work are explained in Sections II, i.e., the authors' developed AWM, a line-drawing-stroke presenting strategy. Next, a stroke perception experiment follows the system descriptions. Practically, in Section III, perceptual characteristics of simple patterns of 1-, 3-, 5-, and 7-strokes are presented. The paper closes with a conclusion and remarks for further developments.

II. METHOD

This section describes a hardware and software, i.e., a mouse interface and a line-drawing stroke presenting strategy.

A. Active-Wheel Mouse

An "Active-Wheel Mouse (AWM) is a renovated mouse interface: at the front of a mouse interface, a Finger-Tactile Interface (FTI) is attached as shown in Figure 1. In the FTI, a wheel is swiveled and rotated by two stepping motors (M15SP-2N and M25SP-6NK by Mitsumi Electric Co., LTD., Tokyo, Japan) as shown in Figure 2. The rotation and swivel provide a slippage on the user's fingerpad with a velocity and time-duration: the velocity together with the time duration results in a slippage length. The wheel has a diameter of 20 mm and a thickness of 6 mm (see Figure 3). On the wheel peripheral surface, raised dots are formed to enable slippage perception [9]-[11]: as for the raised dots, the height is 0.5 mm, and the diameter of the bottom circle is 1.7 mm. The dot interval was about 10.5 mm so that dots appear one by one on the fingerpad, which makes the slippage perceived [12][13].

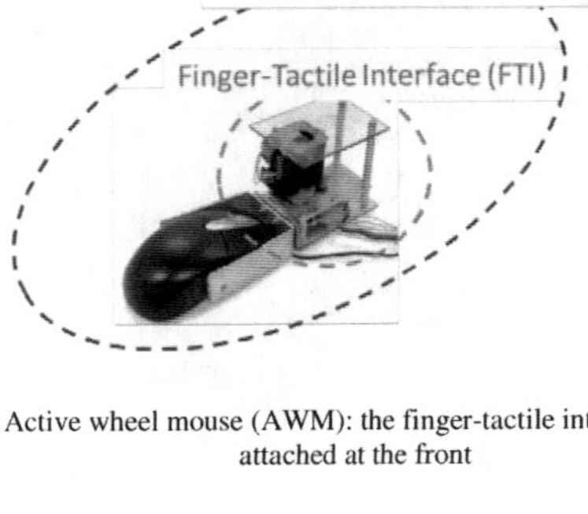

Figure 1. Active wheel mouse (AWM): the finger-tactile interface (FTI) is attached at the front

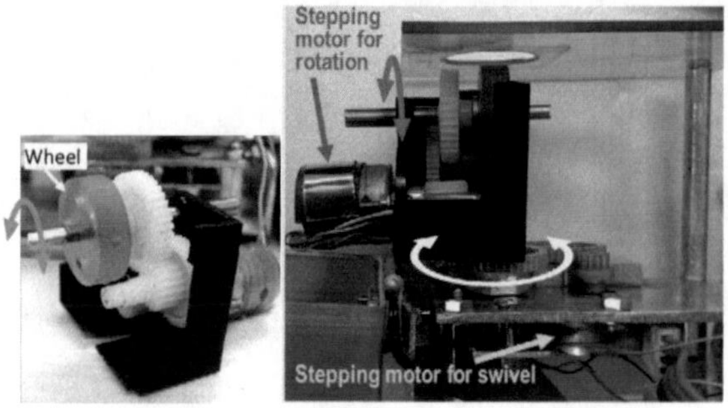

(a) Rotation mechanism (b) Finger-tactile interface in total

Figure 2. Finger-tactile interface: reduction gear ratio for rotation: 6.5, that for swivel: 3.5

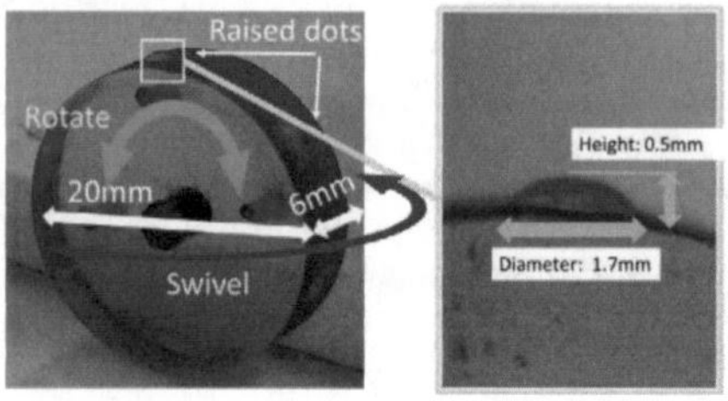

(a) Wheel (b) Raised dot:

Figure 3. Wheel configuration: raised dots were designed, based on the Japanese Industrial Standard (JIS) for tactile graphics

B. *After-Recognition Go Stroke-Presenting Strategy*

Multiple strokes were learned through two recognition stages as shown in Figure 4: (1) the first stage is for whole line segment patterns (i.e., motion loci), and (2) the second stage is for velocity variations (i.e., motion trajectories), in particular, the velocities were changed stepwise. In either case of the first or second recognition stage, the "After-Recognition Go stroke-presenting Strategy (ARG-S)" [14] was employed in presenting each of the strokes as in the following.

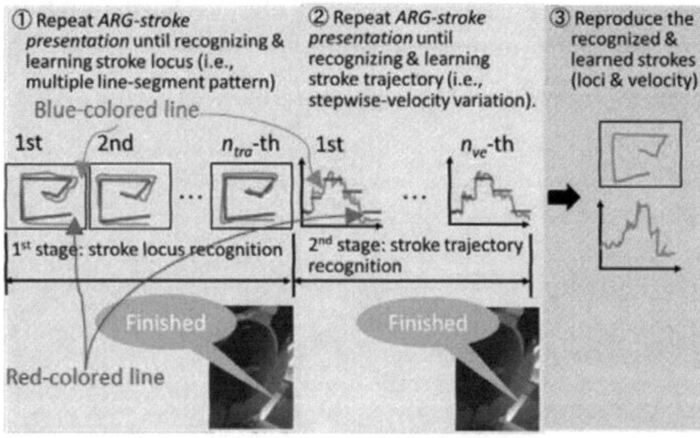

Figure 4. Two recognition stages for learning multiple-stroke loci and velocities.

[Step 1] Subjects hold the mouse in their right hand. Then, they touch the wheel upper peripheral surface from above with their index-fingerpad.

[Step 2] Finger-tactile interface swivels the rotating unit to a given direction and rotates the wheel with a given velocity and time duration: the velocity and the time duration determine a rotation angle. (See Figure 5 ①)

[Step 3] While accepting the slippage stimulus, the subjects recognize the stimulus as a line segment in the 1st stage and as a constant velocity movement in the 2nd stage. (See Figure 5 ②)

[Step 4] The subjects drag the AWM so as to reproduce subjects' recognized motion. (See Figure 5 ③)

[Step 5] The subjects memorize the drag motion as a stroke. (See Figure 5 ④)

[Step 6] Just after memorizing stroke, the subjects send a signal by pressing a button by their left finger.

[Step 7] Return to [Step 2] till all the strokes are presented and memorized.

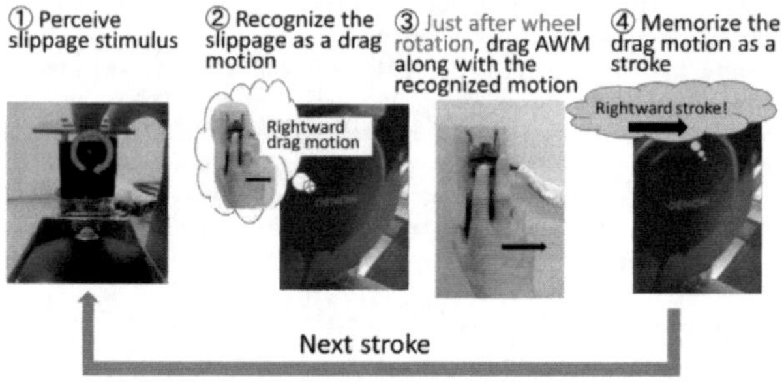

Figure 5. After-Recognition Go stroke-presenting Strategy (ARG-S).

III. Stroke Perception Experiment

This section describes a stroke perception experiment and presents line-drawing perceptual characteristics in relation to the number of strokes.

A. *Experimental Conditions*

Ten healthy right-handed males in their 20s (22~24; mean=22.6; SD=0.9) participated. The line drawings presented were from single to seven straight-line strokes (See Figure 6.). All the strokes were made by constant-velocity straight-line motion. The factors, i.e., the length, speed, direction and stroke-number and the factor-levels are shown in TABLE I. For each of the runs, the factor levels were randomly chosen, provided that corner angles are more than 30 deg.

TABLE I. Factors and factor levels used for Experiment

Factor	Factor level
Subject	10 males
Presentation strategy	After-recognition go
Presented stroke drawing	8 drawings in total: 2 patterns for each of 1-, 3-, 5-, and 7-stroke drawings
Length	50, 66, 83, 100 mm
Speed	12, 25, 37, 50 mm/s
Direction	0, 22.5, 45, ・・・, 337.5 deg

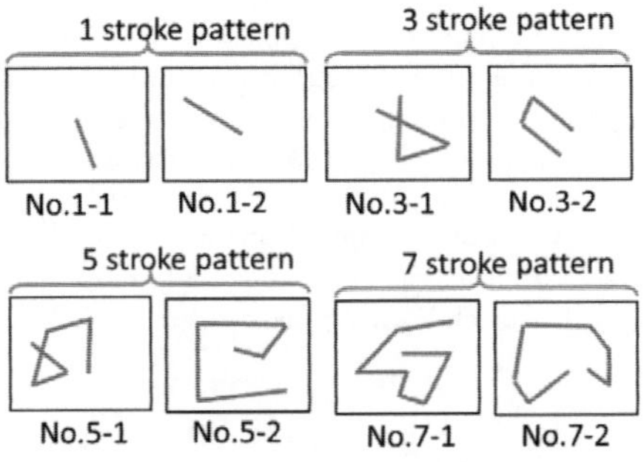

Figure 6. Presented drawings: each stroke is presented as an uniform motion.

B. Evaluation Values

By connecting the start and end point, a secant was obtained for each of the actually reproduced strokes. Then, the length- and angle-differences between the secants and the desired strokes were used as evaluation values (see Figure 7):

$\Delta l = l_{secant} - l_{desired}$

$\Delta \theta = \theta_{secant} - \theta_{desired}$

In addition to these, the velocity difference of the mean velocity from the desired one is also employed as the third evaluation value:

$\Delta v = v_{mean} - v_{desired}$

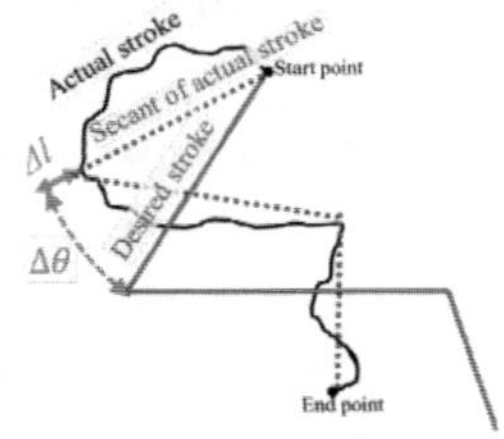

Figure 7. Evaluation values: the differences of lengths and angles between the secants of actual trajectory and the desired trajectory

C. Experimental Result

Some reproduced line-drawings for the drawing No. 7-1 are shown in Figure 8. Even though much improvement is expected, they show a potential for rough sketches. For each of the 1, 3, 5, and 7 stroke drawings and for each of the 10 subjects, the Mean Absolute Errors (MAEs) per stroke for the lengths, angles, and velocities of the reproduced strokes are shown in Figure 9. As the number of strokes increases, the elapsed times and their variances seem to increase. On the other hand, the errors of the length, angle, and velocity per stroke seem to be no difference in this experiment. That is, for the length MAEs (Figure 9 (a)), the angle MAEs (Figure 9 (b)), and the velocity MAEs (Figure 9 (c)), the sample means were calculated for the 1, 3, 5, and 7 stroke drawings, and they are shown by ▭, △, □, and ○, respectively. Then, we applied a statistcal test, ANOVA, to all the residuals (the differences of the perceived values from the actual value). It was confirmed that there were no significant differences between the population means of the 1, 3, 5, and 7 stroke drawings: lengths, $F(3, 309) = 0.73$, $p = 0.54$; angles, $F(3, 309) = 0.47$, $p = 0.70$; mean-velocities, $F(3, 309) = 1.01$, $p = 0.54$.

On the other hand, the sample means of the elapsed times and the number of iterations were plotted by ● and ■, respectively in Figure 10. It is interesting to note that there are linear characteristics of the elapsed time per iteration and the number of iterations. It means that the elapsed times per stroke would not increase as the number of stroke increases (see ○ in Figure 10). Even so, it is also noted that, since there must be some limits for human beings on the amount of information that can be memorized at a time, the elapsed time per stroke may increase in the much more strokes.

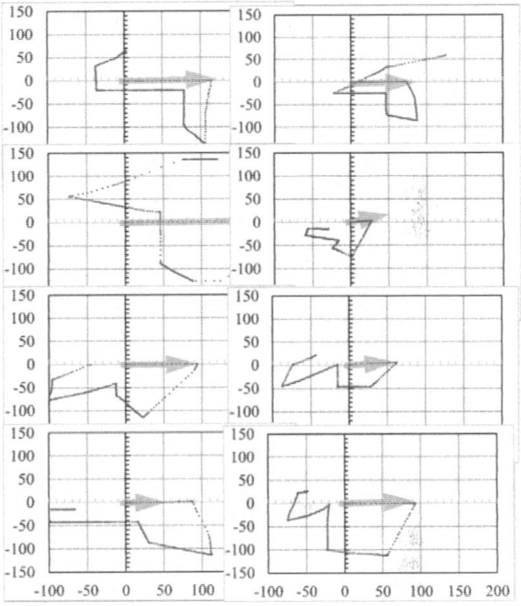

Figure 8. Examples of the reproduced line-drawings: drawing No. 7-1.

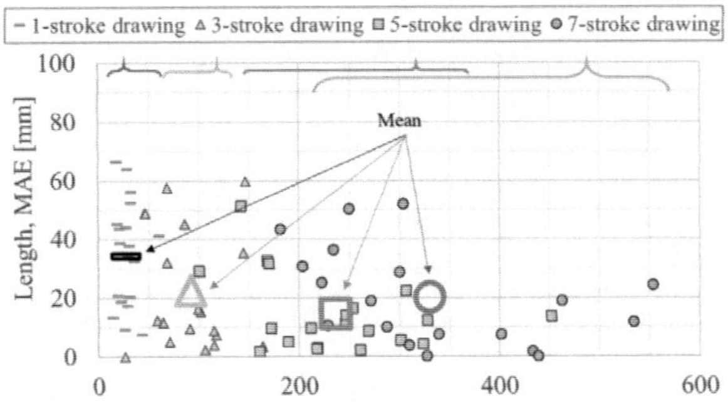

(a) Lengths

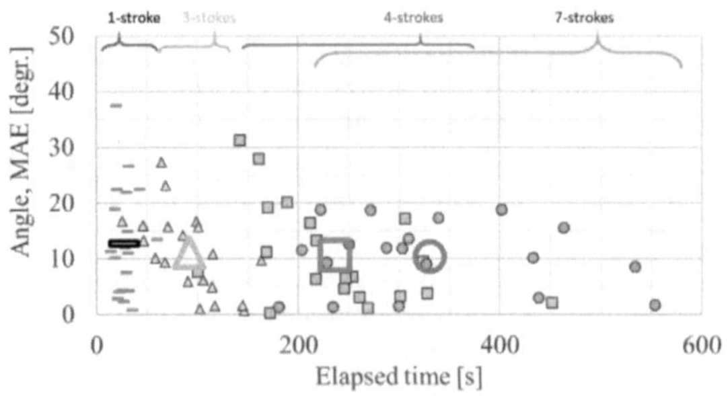

(b) Angles

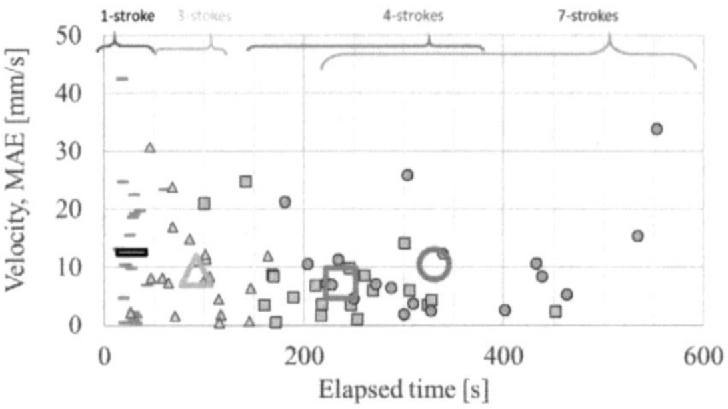

(c) Velocities

Figure 9. Mean absolute errors with respect to the reproduced lengths, angles, and velocities for multi-stroke drawings

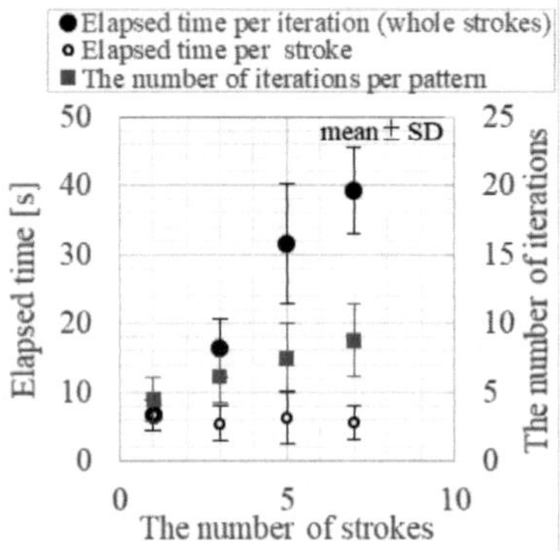

Figure 10. Elapsed times in relationship to the number of strokes

IV. Conclusion

This paper presented multiple-stroke recognition characteristics using a tactile interface, i.e., an active-wheel mouse, and with an after-recognition go strategy. As a result of multiple-stroke recognition experiments using 1- to 7-stroke drawings with less than 100 mm of strokes, the followings were confirmed.

(1) The residuals (the differences of the perceived values from the actual value) of lengths, angles, velocities and elapsed times per stroke did not show significant difference between the 1- to 7-stroke drawings. The means of them were about 20 mm, 10 deg, and 10 mm/s, and 6 sec, respectively.

(2) Elapsed times were proportional to the number of strokes of the presented drawings. It means per-stroke elapsed-times were almost remained unchanged even though the number of stokes increased.

In the future, accuracy and efficiency are to be furthermore improved. Further extension of applicable scope is expected for curved strokes and accelerated strokes.

Acknowledgments

This work was supported by KAKENHI (Grant-in-Aid for Challenging Exploratory Research 15H02929 from Japan Society for the Promotion of Science (JSPS)

References

[1] N. Tsuda, N. Kato, and Y. Nomura, "Instruction of arm motion for calligraphy using vibrotactile stimulations," In Advanced Intelligent Mechatronics (AIM), 2011 IEEE/ASME International Conference, pp. 677-682, 2011.

[2] A. Causo, S. H. Yeo, and I. M. Chen, "Vibrotactile motors on stationary arm as directional feedback to correct arm posture." In Advanced Intelligent Mechatronics (AIM), 2012 IEEE/ASME International Conference, pp. 202-207, 2012

[3] S. L. Norman, A. J. Doxon, B. T. Gleeson, and W. R. Provancher, "Planar hand motion guidance using fingertip skin-stretch feedback.", 2014 IEEE transactions on haptics, vol.7, no.2, pp.121-130, 2014

[4] L. T. Gwilliam, A. J. Doxon, and W. R. Provancher, "Haptic matching of directional force and skin stretch feedback cues," 2013 IEEE World Haptics Conference, pp. 19-14, 2013.

[5] R. L. Koslover, B. T. Gleeson, J. T. De Bever, and W. R. Provancher, "Mobile navigation using haptic, audio, and visual direction cues with a handheld test platform," IEEE Transactions on Haptics, vol. 5, no. 1, pp. 33-38, 2012.

[6] A. Ion, E. J. Wang, and P. Baudisch, "Skin drag displays: Dragging a physical tactor across the user's skin produces a stronger tactile stimulus than vibrotactile," In Proceedings of the 33rd Annual ACM Conference on Human Factors in Computing Systems, pp. 2501-2504, 2015.

[7] N. G. Tsagarakis, T. Horne, and D. G. Caldwell, "Slip aestheasis: A portable 2d slip/skin stretch display for the fingertip," Eurohaptics Conference, 2005 and Symposium on Haptic Interfaces for Virtual Environment and Teleoperator Systems, pp. 214-219, 2005.

[8] Moscatelli, A., Naceri, A. and Ernst, M., "Navigation in the fingertip," IEEE World Haptics Conference, pp. 519-523, 2013.

[9] Y. Nomura, and S. Oike, "Active-Wheel Mouse for Human-Computer Interface: Slippage-Perception Characteristics on Fingerpad," Proc. of 10th International Conference, UAHCI 2016,Part II Part of HCI International 2016, Part II, pp. 54-61, 2016.

[10] Y. Nomura, Y. Kashino, and S. Oike, "Proposal of active-wheel-based finger-tactile interface and its slippage-presenting functions," Transactions of the JSME, vol.83, no.852, pp.1-17, 2017 (in Japanese)

[11] Y. Nomura, Y. Kashino, and T. Sugiura, "Line-drawing presentation strategies with an active-wheel mouse," Proc. ACHI 2018 : The Eleventh International Conference on Advances in Computer-Human Interactions, pp.199-203, 2018.

[12] Y. Nomura, and K. Iwabu, "Length perceptual characteristics on raised-dot slippages," Human-Computer Interfaces and Interactivity: Emergent Research and Applications, IGI Global, pp. 286-308, 2014.

[13] Y. Nomura, and H. Kato, "Raised-dot slippage perception on fingerpad using active wheel device," Recent Advances on Using Virtual Reality Technologies for Rehabilitation, Nova Science Publishers, Inc. New York, pp. 165-172, 2015.

Lifelog Sharing System based on Context Matching

Jiaming Zhang
Graduate School of IPS
Waseda University
Fukuoka, Japan
Email: zhangjiaming777@toki.waseda.jp

Jiro Tanaka
Graduate School of IPS
Waseda University
Fukuoka, Japan
Email: jiro@aoni.waseda.jp

Abstract—**In this paper, we propose a lifelog sharing mechanism based on matching the situation context of audience users and shared lifelogs. Sharing lifelogs can promote information sharing among people and benefit people who face similar situation. However, it is difficult and tedious for audience users to access useful or interesting information from lifelog data taken in chronological order. Our proposed lifelog sharing system pushes appropriate shared lifelogs to audience users by matching the context in real time. Audience users can get information in an unobtrusive way by wearing a head-mounted display. The system also allows audience users to give feedback and customize their preferences. To collect lifelog data, we assume sharing users to capture lifelogs with Autographer and Android smartphone. When uploading captured data to share, sharing users need to set sharing preferences to protect privacy. From the preliminary evaluation, we have obtained a positive feedback.**

Keywords–Lifelog; Wearable camera; Sharing mechanism; Situation context matching; Augmented reality.

I. INTRODUCTION

Lifelogging is the pervasive activity that assists people in recording their daily events in detail. In 1980, Steven Mann built a wearable personal imaging system, which is equipped with head-mounted display, cameras and wireless communications. The prototype system could capture images from first-person perspective [1]. The miniaturization enables devices to be more unobtrusive and gain more social acceptance. More and more commercial wearable devices have been produced and entered the market.

Existing wearable cameras include SenseCam, Vicon Revue and Autographer, which can capture photos passively and continuously. For example, Autographer is a wearable camera that has 6 built-in sensors [2]. The accelerometer measures the change of speed when the camera is moving; the color sensor is used to perceive light and brightness; the passive infrared sensor detects moving objects before the camera; the magnetometer detects the direction in which the camera is facing; the temperature sensor measures environment temperatures; and the integrated Global Positioning System (GPS) locates the camera's position. Autographer will capture photos automatically after certain elapsed time periods, such as 30 seconds. The sensor changes also can trigger the camera.

The lifelog data generated by lifelogging brings new opportunities for many research fields including quantified self, healthcare, memory augmentation and so on. Nowadays, Social Networking Service (SNS) is getting more and more popular, which enables people to communicate and share knowledge with each other. Sharing lifelogs can promote the information sharing among people because lifelogging can record all the details of our daily experiences and one's experience can benefit other people who face similar situation or have common interest. However, current SNS is not suitable for lifelog sharing. For the users who view shared lifelogs, so-called audience users, the accessing method is limited. It is difficult and tedious to access useful or attracting information among the vast amount of lifelogs, because current systems manage shared photos in chronological order mainly, and users can only search photos with hashtags and location. However, the format of hashtags that were added by sharing users are not uniform.

Because the amount of data produced by electronic devices is increasing, recommendation systems are available for users to access relevant information from the vast amount of information [3]. Also, context-aware recommendation system has been researched in various domains, such as e-commerce, multimedia, tourism, to provide a better personalized user recommendation leveraging contextual information. The possibility of using context-aware computing in lifelog retrieving has not been investigated yet.

Some previous research proposed approaches about how to retrieve lifelog more efficiently [4]–[8], but less attention is paid to how to share lifelog and how the users access shared lifelog based on their current situation in real time. For example, you are running outside for exercise and you might want to view other's nearby running record to motivate yourself.

Our target is to propose a lifelog sharing system, which enables audience users to access useful or attracting information easily from shared experiences when they are facing specific situation.

The rest of the paper is structured as follows. In Section II, we describe the goal and approach. In Section III, the sharing mechanism is presented. We provide an overview of the lifelog sharing system in Section IV. Then, we describe user study and results in Sections V. In Section VI, we discuss related work. Finally, conclusion and future work is discussed in Section VII.

II. GOAL AND APPROACH

In this paper, we aim to propose a lifelog sharing system. There are mainly two roles using the sharing system, including sharing user and audience user (Figure 1).

Sharing user uses Autographer and Android smartphone to capture the lifelog data. Autographer is used for taking photos. Android smartphone is used for monitoring activities

Figure 1. Wearable devices for sharing user and audience user.

by analyzing the signals from multiple sensors embedded in the Android device. After recording, sharing user should upload the lifelog data to share. By leveraging computer vision service and location-aware service, our system extracts context within the shared lifelogs automatically, which can be used to match the audience user's situation in real time.

For the audience user, we introduce the Augmented Reality (AR) and context-aware computing technology. Through the head-mounted display, our system presents appropriate shared lifelogs to the audience user by matching the context in an unobtrusive way without interrupting what the user is doing. In this work, we choose Epson Moverio BT-300, which contains smart glass and controller.

III. Sharing Mechanism

We propose a new sharing mechanism for our system: pushing appropriate shared lifelogs to audience user by matching the situation context of user and shared lifelogs in real time. By replaceing explicit request with active push, we aim to save audience user's effort in searching and filtering useful information.

To find out valuable information in describing situation and define the situation context in our research, we summarized some previous work. Dey [9] proposed a generic definition of context. Context is any information that can be used to characterize the situation of an entity. An entity is a person, place, or object. Grubert et al [10] categorized context into three high-level categories, including human factors, environment factors and system factors. Also, our previous research [11] found several cues are important in describing an event, which can help people understand what happened, including where and when the event happened, what object the user interacted with. Therefore, situation context in this research consists of human and environment factors (Figure 2).

Human factors focus on the user, including activity and preferences. *Activity* is the bodily movement, such as walking, running, etc. *Preferences* has a different meaning for lifelogs and audience users. For lifelogs, it means the sharing preferences that are set by sharing user; for audience users, it refers to the objects that audience user prefers or has interest in, such as food, park, etc.

Environment factors describe the surrounding of the user in which the experience took place. *Location* and *time* mean where and when the experience happened. *Object* is what appeared in the user's sight.

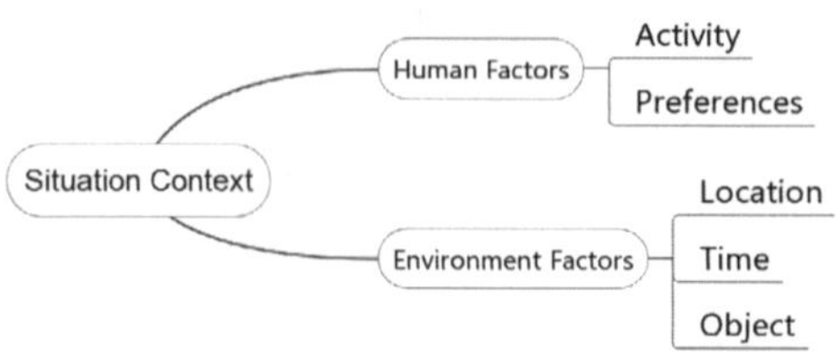

Figure 2. Situation context.

IV. Lifelog Sharing System

In this section, we will describe our lifelog sharing system. We will provide an overview and describe our state of the development.

A. Usage Scenario

- Scenario 1. A person is walking on the street in the morning and approaching a bakery that he has never been in. One other person shared lifelog photos that were taken when he bought bread in this bakery. These photos may be useful for this person. If he has interest or thinks the bread looks delicious, he can go into the bakery and buy some bread for himself.
- Scenario 2. A person is running outside for exercise in the evening. He might feel boring or tired. Some other people also ran nearby and shared photos and running record that were taken when they were running. The person can view the photos and running record such as the running speed of others via the head-mounted display without stopping running, and he may be motivated to run at a proper speed.

B. System Overview

Our proposed system mainly contains two parts (Figure 3). The most important part is for audience users accessing shared lifelogs. The AR-based viewer pushes appropriate shared lifelogs to the audience user by matching the situation context of audience user and lifelogs.

The other part is for sharing users capturing and uploading lifelog data to share to others. The lifelog uploader will extract

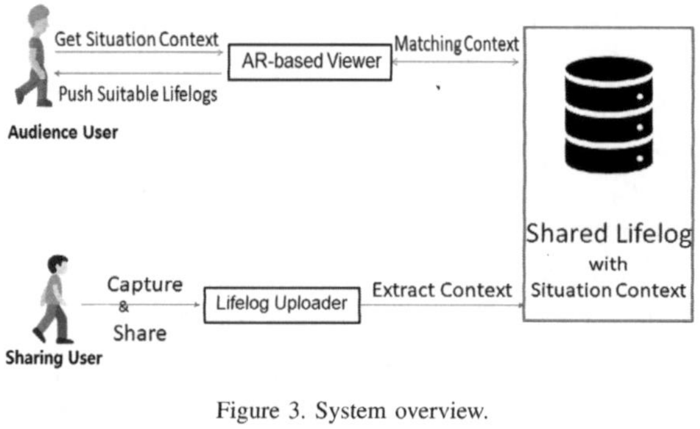

Figure 3. System overview.

situation context, including *location*, *object*, *time* and *activity*, from input data and store them into the database.

C. Sharing User's Part

1) Activtiy Recorder: The activity recorder implemented on Android is used to track and upload share user's activity records.

In our work, we make use of *Moves API* [12]. It can automatically record any walking, cycling, and running the user does and generate daily activity summaries, including step count, distance, duration and consumed calories for each activity.

2) Lifelog Uploader: The web-based lifelog uploader assists sharing users in uploading the photos captured by Autographer (Figure 4). It is implemented based on Browser/Server architecture and mainly uses the combination of the Spring Boot and the Hibernate.

Before sharing, sharing users need to set the sharing preferences, which consider two aspects. One is the scope of visibility, sharing users should choose to share their lifelogs with friends or all users. The other is to choose whether to expose location or object information within the lifelog. For location information, sharing users can set to share location at country, city or street level.

The lifelog uploader extracts situation context from uploaded data according to the sharing preferences set by sharing user by integrating with several existing computer vision service and location-aware service, including *Google Cloud Vision API* and *Google Maps API* (Figure 5). To protect bystanders' privacy, the system blurs the detected faces in lifelog photos using *Marvin Image Processing Framework.*

D. Audience User's Part

For audience users, we develop the AR-based viewer on the Epson Moverio BT-300, which adopts Android as the operating system. The viewer system mainly provides three functions: viewing shared lifelogs, giving feedback to pushed photos and customizing preferences.

1) Viewing Shared Lifelogs: The viewer system displays appropriate shared lifelogs that match the users current situation (Figure 6). When there are more than one pushed lifelog photos, audience users can view more by clicking the Next button. If audience users don't want to view any information at present, they can click the Close button to hide the display panel, which will appear again when the system get new pushed lifelogs.

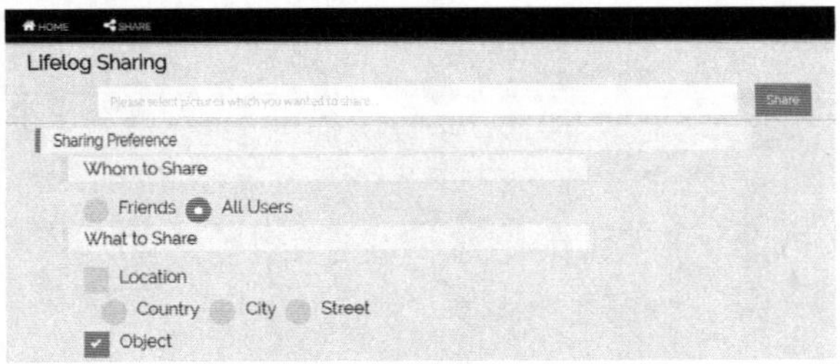

Figure 4. User interface of Lifelog Uploader.

Input: Sharing preferences and lifelog data;
Output: Processing result;
Detect faces within photos with Google Cloud Vision API;
Blur the detected faces using Gaussian Blur;
if Expose *Location* information at *Country* level **then**
    Extract the country address component from the human-readable address got from the location service;
else if Expose *Location* information at *City* level **then**
    Extract the country and city address component from the human-readable address got from the location service;
else if Expose *Location* information at *Street* level **then**
    Keep full human-readable address got from the location service;
else
    Do nothing;
end if
if Expose *Object* information **then**
    Detect objects within photos with Google Cloud Vision API in the object service;
else
    Do nothing;
end if
return results;

Figure 5. Extracting context according to the sharing preferences.

Figure 6. Viewing pushed lifelogs.

To select appropriate lifelogs, we propose a push strategy which pushes appropriate lifelogs to audience users automatically by calculating the situation context similarity between user and shared lifelog data (Figure 7).

The first phase is detecting user's activity to determine the push frequency. The viewer system recognize activities using HARLib, which is a human activity recognition library on Android proposed by Yang et al [13]. For each activity, the push strategy provides a default frequency depending on the average moving speed of the activity. Especially for transport, the system won't push any information considering user's safety because the pushed information may interfere user when he is driving. The second phase will get candidate lifelogs and rank them by calculating the similarity score between user's situation context and lifelog data's situation context, which will be performed once after the time period corresponding to current detected activity. Then, the system will push the lifelogs that have the similarity score over the threshold, which is set to 2.4.

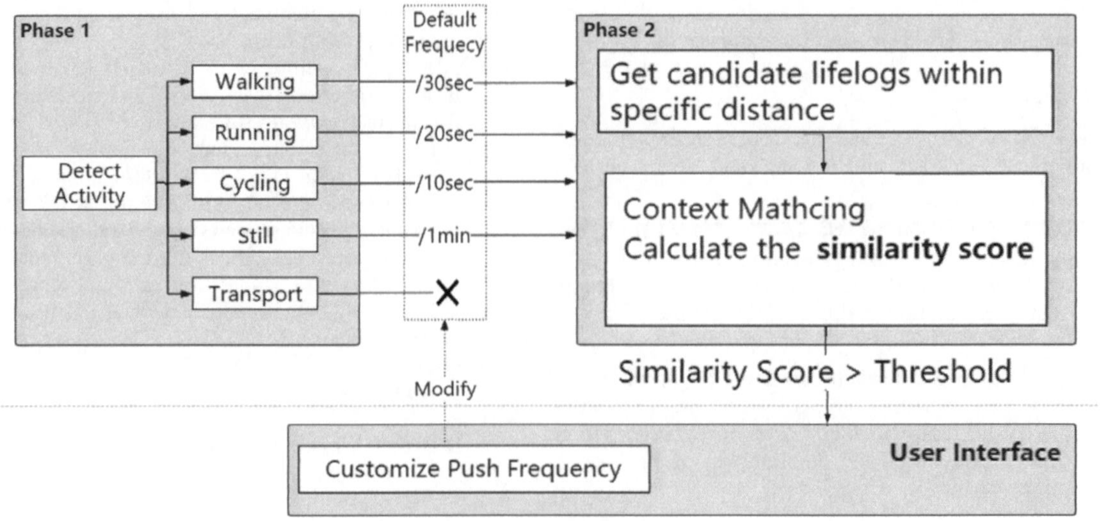

Figure 7. Push strategy.

In order to deal with the huge data volume and improve the query performance, we make use of Haversine formula to filter out lifelogs that are created within 100 meters from the audience user as the candidate lifelogs, and only calculate similarity score for these candidate lifelogs.

The similarity value contains four situation context factors, including *location*, *activity*, *object* and *time*, in the range (0,4]:

$$similarity = locationFit + activityFit + objectFit + timeFit \tag{1}$$

where $locationFit$ is determined by the distance between audience user and lifelog's creation location:

$$locationFit = \begin{cases} 1, & l_u = l_p \\ x, & x = inverseDistance(l_u, l_p) \end{cases} \tag{2}$$

where $inverseDistance$ is a negative exponential function of distance in the range (0,1]. $ActivityFit$ compares audience user's activity and the corresponding activity of lifelog photos:

$$activityFit = \begin{cases} 1, & a_u = a_p \\ 0, & a_u \neq a_p \end{cases} \tag{3}$$

and $objectFit$ evaluates the suitability between lifelogs and user's preferred objects, which is inferred from user's liked photos history in the range [0,1]. The $offset$ is used to solve the cold start problem. When audience user has not given any feedback, the $offset$ will be set to 0.6 to eliminate the impact on the final similarity score, and the value of $offset$ will get smaller with more feedback are given:

$$objectFit = \frac{intersection\_size(o_p, o_{ul})}{size(o_p)} + offset \tag{4}$$

and $timeFit$ evaluates the degree of difference in time in the range (0,1]. We define 6am to 10am as *morning*, 10am to 2pm as *noon*, 2pm to 6pm as *afternoon*, 6pm to 10pm as *evening* and 10pm to 6am as *night*. The closer the time, the higher the $timeFit$ value.

2) Giving Feedback: Audience user can give feedback to pushed lifelog photo by clicking the Like button (Figure 8), which means the user has interest in this photo or the objects that appear in it.

3) Customizing Preferences: The AR-based viewer allows audience users to customize what kind of specific information they want to view and how often they would get new pushed lifelog. The customization panel contains three parts (Figure 9). Audience user can select specific objects to reflect their object preferences. They can also select the activity to view corresponding activity record of the pushed lifelog photo (Figure 10). To provide a better user experience, the viewer system assists audience users in customizing the push frequency instead of the default ones. This feature can adapt to the situations where audience users want view more or less information.

V. PRELIMINARY EVALUATION

We conducted a preliminary user study to verify whether audience users can get useful shared lifelogs easily with our proposed system and evaluate the usability of the system.

Figure 8. Giving feedback to lifelog photos which contain Bread object.

Figure 9. User interface of customizing preferences.

Figure 10. Viewing the lifelog photos with corresponding activity record.

We need to collect lifelog data first. We let 4 people capture lifelogs for one day using Autographer and Android smartphone and they were free to switch off the devices during their private time. After capturing, we let these 4 people set their sharing preferences and upload lifelogs to our system to share. We got 784 lifelog photos in total. After collecting shared lifelogs, the user study can be carried out.

A. Participants

We invited 8 participants to use our system as the audience users, ranging in age from 23 to 25 and including 6 females and 2 males. All of them have regular computer skills and they were given a brief introduction of our system.

B. Method

Each participant needs to use our system to view shared lifelogs by wearing the head-mounted display for at least half an hour. To ensure all participants can get pushed lifelogs, during they use the system, the range of activities of participants should be within the area of shared lifelogs captured places.

After that, the participant will be asked to fill in a questionnaire. The questionnaire has following 4 questions and these questions use the 5-point Likert scale:

1) Do you think pushed lifelogs are useful or interesting?
2) Do you think the preferences customization is helpful in viewing shared lifelogs?
3) Do you think the push frequency customization is helpful in viewing shared lifelogs?
4) Do you think the system is easy to operate?

C. Results

After collecting the questionnaire results from the 8 participants, we calculated the average scores of each question (Figure 11).

Question 1 is used to ask participants about the subjective feelings of the pushed lifelogs. All participants used our system for average 40 minutes and the average score of question 1 is 4.25. The results suggest that the participants generally found the pushed lifelogs are useful or interesting in their specific situation.

Question 2 and 3 are used to judge the design of the customization function in our system and the average scores for these two questions are 4.625 and 4.125. Results of question 2 indicate that each participant thought providing preferences customization is helpful to reflect their interested objects. For question 3, the results show that enabling users to customize the push frequency is helpful. Most of the participants claimed that customizing push frequency makes the lifelog displaying much more flexible.

Question 4 regards the ease of use of our system. It mainly concerns whether it's easy to use the controller to interact with the system. The average score is 3.75. The results prove that the system is easy to operate. Two participants considered that the controller is not hands-free although the glasses can superimpose digital information in an unobtrusive way. It was difficult to operate the system when participants were cycling.

Overall, we got a positive feedback through the preliminary user study.

VI. Related Work

The most similar approach is the work of Memon [14], which proposed a lifelog sharing framework which can identify the target audience users who may find shared lifelogs useful based on locality. Sharing users of the system have to define their sharing strategy by declaring the scope of visibility of their lifelogs, which are, particular city, particular street or location independent. For example, 'particular city' shared logs are visible to the friends who visit that city. Audience users

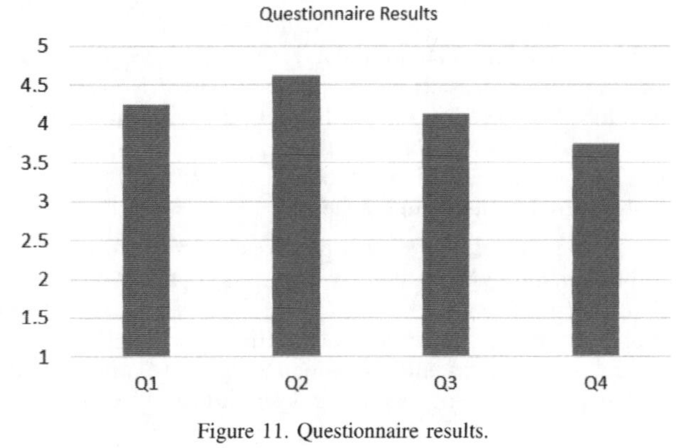

Figure 11. Questionnaire results.

can retrieve friends' shared lifelogs by sending a request to the server with their current location.

This work focused on sharing lifelogs with friends and the sharing strategy is only based on locality. In our work, we consider more specific context by defining the situation context. In Memon's work, Moodstocks API was applied to read barcodes, QR-codes or identify objects. But it needed to previously store the objects' templates at Moodstocks server. Our system makes use of computer vision service for object recognition, which needs no preparation or deployment. Another difference is that our system is presented for the scenario that the audience user is actually being in the specific situation. User can get shared lifelogs in real time without any requests. With augmented reality technology, user don't need to interrupt what he is doing.

Another important related work is the proactivity model for mobile recommendation systems which is proposed by Woerndl et al. [15]. The two-phase model can be used in a proactive, context-aware recommendation system by utilizing the available context information. In the first phase, the system determined whether the current situation needs a recommendation by calculating score of weighted combination of contexts. The second phase dealt with the evaluation of candidate items, and the system would push the items which are considered good enough in the current context to the user. A prototype for the gas station scenario was implemented, in which case that the user context refers to the fuel level, traffic is the temporal context, the geographic context is the nearest gas station and the social context corresponds to the number of persons in the car.

Based on the proactivity model, we defined the push strategy in our system. Different from this work, the contexts defined in our system are more general to meet different scenarios instead of the specific gas station scenario. Our system considers not only adapting the content represented by the system according to the context, but also system's configuration, that is adapting the push frequency according to the user's activity to provide a better user experience.

VII. Conclusion and Future Work

In this work, we propose the lifelog sharing system with the mechanism that matches the situation context of audience user and shared lifelogs.

In our proposed system, there are sharing users and audience users. To collect lifelog data, the sharing users in our system need to use Autographer and Android smartphone. When uploading captured data, sharing users can set the sharing preferences to protect privacy. The AR-based viewer developed on head-mounted display pushes appropriate lifelogs to audience users in real time, which allows audience users to view pushed lifelogs, give feedback to pushed lifelog photos and customize their preferences.

In the future work, the proposed system needs further improvement. For example, we can incorporate other useful contexts in our system and improve the push strategy to give more suitable or desirable shared lifelogs to audience users. So far, the system allows audience users to give feedback to the pushed lifelog photos and sharing users can view the feedback they get. The interaction between audience users and sharer users can be improved to enhance the communication and information sharing between people. After that, we plan to perform user study which involves more participants to get more convincing feedback. We also plan to compare our system to current SNS to justify the performance for retrieving useful lifelogs and displaying to the audience users.

References

[1] S. Mann, "Wearable computing: A first step toward personal imaging," Computer, vol. 30, 1997, pp. 25–32.

[2] K. C. Thoring, R. M. Mueller, and P. Badke-Schaub, "Ethnographic design research with wearable cameras," in Proceedings of the 33rd Annual ACM Conference Extended Abstracts on Human Factors in Computing Systems, ser. CHI EA '15. ACM, 2015, pp. 2049–2054.

[3] e. a. Khalid Haruna, "Context-aware recommender system: A review of recent developmental process and future research direction," Applied Sciences, vol. 7, 2017, p. 1211.

[4] K. Aizawa, D. Tancharoen, S. Kawasaki, and T. Yamasaki, "Efficient retrieval of life log based on context and content," in Proceedings of the the 1st ACM workshop on Continuous archival and retrieval of personal experiences, 2004, pp. 22–31.

[5] L. Zhou, D.-T. Dang-Nguyen, and C. Gurrin, "A baseline search engine for personal life archives," in LTA '17, 2017, pp. 21–24.

[6] e. a. L. Zhou, "Organizer team at ImageCLEFlifelog 2017: Baseline approaches for lifelog retrieval and summarization," in CLEF, 2017, pp. 154:1–154:11.

[7] e. a. D.-T. Dang-Nguyen, "Overview of ImageCLEFlifelog 2017: Lifelog retrieval and summarization," in CLEF, 2017, pp. 10:1–10:23.

[8] D.-T. Dang-Nguyen, L. Zhou, R. Gupta, M. Riegler, and C. Gurrin, "Building a disclosed lifelog dataset: Challenges, principles and processes," in CBMI, 2017, pp. 22:1–22:6.

[9] A. K. Dey, "Understanding and using context," Personal Ubiquitous Comput., vol. 5, 2001, pp. 4–7.

[10] J. Grubert, T. Langlotz, S. Zollmann, and H. Regenbrecht, "Towards pervasive augmented reality: Context-awareness in augmented reality," IEEE Transactions on Visualization and Computer Graphics, vol. 23, 2017, pp. 1706–1724.

[11] J. Zhang, J. Liang, and J. Tanaka, "A lifelog viewer system supporting multiple memory cues," in Human-Computer Interaction. Interaction in Context. Springer International Publishing, 2018, pp. 638–649.

[12] Moves, "Moves api," https://www.programmableweb.com/api/moves/, accessed Dec 25, 2018.

[13] H.-C. Yang, Y.-C. Li, Z.-Y. Liu, and J. Qiu, "Harlib: A human activity recognition library on android," in Proceedings of 11th International Computer Conference on Wavelet Active Media Technology and Information Processing, 2014, pp. 313–315.

[14] M. Memon and J. Tanaka, "Sharing life experiences with friends based on individuals locality," in Design, User Experience, and Usability. Web, Mobile, and Product Design, vol. 8015, 2013, pp. 706–713.

[15] W. Wörndl, J. Huebner, R. Bader, and D. Gallego, "A model for proactivity in mobile, context-aware recommender systems," in RecSys, 2011, pp. 273–276.

A Virtual Shopping System Based on Room-scale Virtual Reality

Chunmeng Lu

Graduate School of Information,
Production and Systems
Waseda University
Kitakyushu, Japan
Email: lcm0113@163.com

Jiro Tanaka

Graduate School of Information,
Production and Systems
Waseda University
Kitakyushu, Japan
Email: jiro@aoni.waseda.jp

***Abstract*—In the Virtual Reality (VR) environment, the user needs to input information and achieves interaction with virtual objects. At present, most VR systems provide some input devices, such as keyboard and controller. However, using such devices is not intuitive, especially in the case of VR shopping system. In the real world, we use our hands to handle objects. In virtual world, using hand gestures to interact with VR shopping store will provide us more intuitive VR shopping experience. According to the needs of the room-scale VR shopping activities, we have introduced a new gesture classification for the gesture set, which has three levels to classify hand gestures based on the characteristics of gestures. We have focused on the gestures in level 3. In our research, we have built a room-scale VR shopping system and applied the new hand gesture set for the interaction in the VR shopping system.**

***Keywords*–Room-scale Virtual Reality; Gesture set; Gesture classification.**

I. INTRODUCTION

Virtual Reality makes it possible for the user to interact with the virtual environment as if he is in the real world. It is a kind of illusion of "being there" [1].

With the development of the computer graphics, 3D technology and electrical engineering, Head Mount Display (HMD) of VR has been gradually improved in the past few years. Some technology companies have introduced their simple and easy-to-use VR devices for the consumer market, such as HTC Vive and Oculus Rift.

A. VR shopping

People can navigate in the virtual environment through a HMD. Shopping is one of the important activities in our daily life. People have already been familiar with e-commerce or online shopping. We can extend online shopping to the virtual environment.

Over the past decades, many VR shopping environments have been presented. Some works aimed at improving VR shopping experience and some works researched on the interaction in virtual shopping environments. Bhatt [2] presented a theoretical framework which showed how to attract customers through a website with the three factors: interactivity, immersion and connectivity. Chen et al. [3] presented a Virtual Reality Modeling Language - Based (VRML- Based) virtual shopping mall. They analyzed personal behavior of customer in the Virtual Shopping Mall System. They also explored the application of intelligent agent in shopping guidance. Lee et al. [4] designed a virtual interactive shopping environment and analyzed whether the interface of virtual interface had positive affects. Verhulst et al. [5] presented a VR user study. In this study, they applied VR store as a tool to find whether the user in store had intention to buy the non-standard food. Speicher et al. [6] introduced a Virtual Reality Shopping Experience model. Their model had three parts: customer satisfaction, task performance and user preference.

The previous researches have shown some good features of VR shopping. Thus, some retail companies and online shopping companies have become interested in VR shopping. IKEA company [7] presented a room-scale VR environment, in which the user could view a virtual kitchen and interact with the furnitures. Another example comes from inVRsion [8], which provided a virtual supermarket shopping system, Shelfzone VR. In the future, there will be more applications on VR shopping.

B. Room-scale VR and Hand Gesture

When a user is moving his view in virtual world with an HMD, he cannot move his physical body in real world. Thus, there is a huge gap between sensorial moving and physical moving. It will reduce the immersion of VR greatly. This gap will also cause motion sickness for some people [6] [9]. If user's walking is synchronous in both virtual world and real world, the experience is much better.

Using controllers in the VR shopping environment is not immersive enough. Users will feel a gap when using controllers to catch the virtual objects which are similar to real objects. Besides, the amount and functions of buttons in the controllers are limited, which limits the interaction when using controllers in the room-scale VR environment. To achieve VR shopping activities, we can use the buttons to design interaction methods in the VR shopping system. Comparing with controllers, using hand gestures can improve the immersion of VR shopping experience and also provide the rich interaction vocabulary for the VR shopping system.

Hand gestures have been widely used in human-computer interface. Gesture-based interaction provides a nature, intuitive communication between people and devices. People use 2D multi-touch gestures to interact with devices like smart phone and computer in the daily life. 3D hand gestures can be used by some devices equipped with camera or depth sensor. The most important problem in hand gesture interaction is how to make computers understand the meaning of hand gestures [10]. Wachs et al. [11] summarized the requirements of hand-gesture interfaces and the challenges when applying hand gestures in different applications. Yves et al. [12] presented a framework for 3D visualization and manipulation in an immersive space. Their works can be used in AR and VR systems. Karam et al. [13] used depth camera and presented a two-hand interactive menu to improve efficiency. These previous researches show that hand gestures have many possibilities for human-computer interaction field.

In Section II, we introduce our goal and approach of our study. In Section III, we show the system design, including VR environment, gesture set and gesture classification. In Section IV, we show the hardware in our system. In Section V, we explain how to achieve gesture recognition in our system. In Section VI, we show how to use the gestures in room-scale VR. In Section VII, we show the preliminary evaluation. In Section VIII, we introduce some related works. Finally, in Section IX, we show our conclusion.

II. Goal and Approach

In this research, we aim to present a new hand gesture set which is suitable for room-scale VR shopping system to replace the controllers. We introduce a new gesture classification to make the gesture set more structural. We apply room-scale shopping system to provide a immersive virtual shopping environment, which is a simulation of physical shopping store. In the room-scale VR shopping environment, the user can walk around in his room to view the virtual shopping environment through an HMD. We design the new gestures for the room-scale VR shopping system. The user can interact with VR environment by the natural hand gestures but not the controllers. We introduce a gesture classification for gestures, which has three levels to classify hand gestures based on the characteristics of gestures. Summarizing the hand gestures, we get a new hand gesture set especially for room-scale VR shopping activities. The hand gesture set will improve the convenience and immersion of the room-scale VR shopping system.

We use VR devices to build the room-scale VR shopping system. In the system, there are two sensor stations installed in the room. The two sensor stations create a walking area for the user. When moving in the walking area, user's motion will be captured by the sensor stations. System will get rotation and three-dimensional coordinates of the HMD worn by user. The view in virtual environment will move synchronously with the HMD. Then we use depth sensor to recognize the hand gestures. In the virtual environment, the user can see his virtual hands moving synchronously with his physical hands. The system can realize the special gestures when the user performing gestures near the depth sensor, and achieve the interaction with virtual environment.

III. System Design

The virtual shopping system is composed of a room-scale VR shopping environment and the gesture-based interaction system.

A. Room-scale VR Shopping Environment

In order to achieve VR shopping activities, we design a VR shopping store as the shopping environment, which is similar to the stores in the real world. We place some desks, shelves and goods in the VR shopping store, as shown in Figure 1.

In the room-scale VR shopping system, we use HTC Vive as the room-scale VR device, as shown in Figure 2. We use Leap Motion [14] as the depth sensor to recognize the hand gesture. Leap Motion is stuck on the HMD.

Figure 1. A VR store

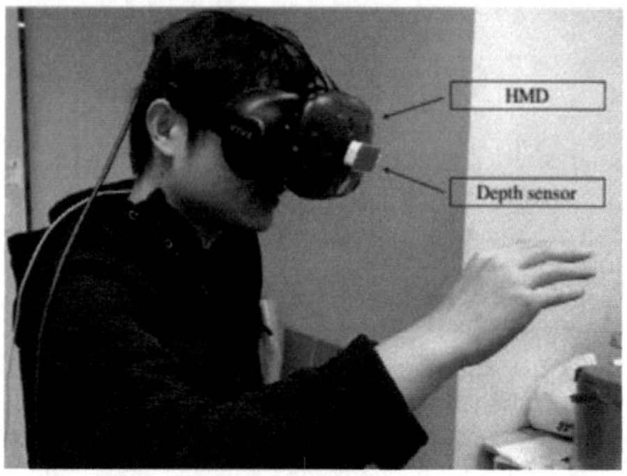

Figure 2. HMD and depth sensor

We prepare an empty area in the real room. The empty area is included in a 3D space. We use two tracking sensors of HTC Vive to capture the motion and rotation of HMD in the 3D space when the user using the VR shopping system. As shown in Figure 3, the length of 3D space is 4 meters, the width of 3D space is 3 meters and the height of 3D space is 2 meters. The 3D space contains walking area of the room.

Figure 3. 3D space and walking area

In the room-scale VR shopping environment, there is also a virtual walking area, as shown in Figure 4. The virtual walking area is same with the area in real room. As the VR shopping store is larger than our real room, the user can change the virtual walking area when view the whole VR shopping store.

B. Gesture Set

In our research, we need to design a series of hand gestures specially for the room-scale VR shopping activities. The hand gestures must provide a natural and suitable interaction for the user and the system. According to the particular activities in room-scale VR shopping system, we design these 14 gestures in our system:

Figure 4. Walking area in VR environment

- (1) pointing, (2) holding, (3) OK gesture, (4) No gesture, (5) push/pull, (6) rotation, (7) drag, (8) waving, (9) click, (10) zoom in/out, (11) opening/closing, (12) grab, (13) two-fingers scroll/swipe, (14) changing area.

These gestures combine a new gesture set for room-scale VR shopping system.

C. Gesture Classification

We present a new gesture classification to classify the hand gestures based on their different characteristics. The gesture classification has three levels:

- Level 1: Core static hand postures are divided into the level 1. In level 1, gestures are just hand shape without hand motion. The classic example is pointing gesture.
- Level 2: Dynamic palm motions are divided into the level 2. In level 2, we just care about the palm movement. We don't care about the shapes of fingers. The classic examples are pull and push.
- Level 3: Combination hand gestures are divided into the level 3. Combination hand gestures combine the features of level 1 and level 2 gestures. In level 3, we care about the motion and shapes of fingers and the motion of palm.

In VR shopping environment, the hand gestures are divided into different levels. In the figures of level 2 and level 3, the red arrows mean the fingers movement trends.

The classification method will make the gesture set more structural. This classification method provides a structure that can also be used in other gesture sets in different VR systems. Based on the systematic structure, researchers can design suitable gestures for their VR systems.

1) Level 1 Gestures: In our system, we use level 1 gestures to give feedback to system. Level 1 gestures are static signals for shopping system. We do not need to care about the motion of fingers or hands. System just needs to detect the hand shapes. Figure 5 shows two level 1 gestures.

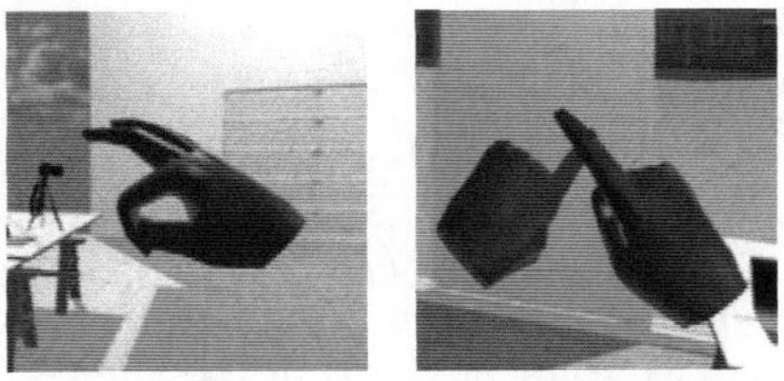

(a) OK gesture (b) NO gesture

Figure 5. OK and NO gestures positive or negative feedback to system

2) Level 2 Gestures: Level 2 gestures are palm motions. After choosing a virtual object, the user can use level 2 gestures to control or interact with it. Figure 6 shows two level 2 gestures and Table I shows the functions of level 2 gestures.

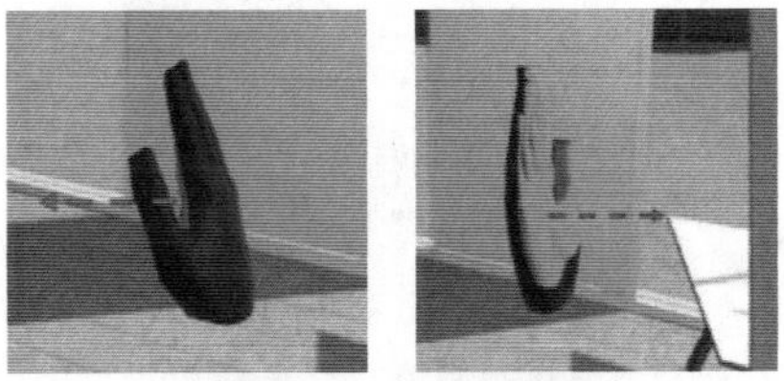

(a) Push gesture (b) Pull gesture

(c) Waving gesture

Figure 6. Level 2 gestures: push, pull and waving

TABLE I. FUNCTION OF GESTURES IN LEVEL 2

Level	*Gesture*	*Function*
2	Push/pull	Push or pull a virtual object with a hand.
2	Waving	Make virtual object return to the original position.

3) Level 3 Gestures: Gestures in level 3 are hand gestures that combine finger shapes and hand motions. These gestures are complex and combine the features of level 1 and level 2 gestures.

Designing a suitable and convenient gesture set for user determines whether the user could have an immersive VR shopping experience. Level 1 and level 2 gestures are simple and a little weak. Thus, level 3 gesture set is the focus of our research.

In level 3, we need to recognize the hand shapes and detect the motions of the fingers and hands at the same time.

The gestures have different usage. Thus, we need to introduce a classification for level 3 gestures. There is the classification:

- The core gesture: pointing gesture
- Gestures for interacting with virtual object: (1) grab gesture, (2) hold gesture, (3) drag gesture, (4) rotation gesture, (5) zoom in/out gesture;
- Gestutes for interacting with menu: (1) click gesture, (2) scroll/swipe gesture, (3) opening/closing gesture;
- Gesture for interacting with space: change area gesture

In the gesture set, pointing gesture is the most important gesture, because we need to choose a target object or button with the pointing gesture before any interaction, as shown in Figure 7 and Table II.

TABLE II. FUNCTION OF POINTING GESTURE

Level	*Gesture*	*Function*
3	Pointing	Point a virtual object with index finger.

Some gestures are mainly used to interact with virtual objects in the VR shopping store, such as moving a virtual

Figure 7. Pointing gesture

object. We design these gestures to achieve it: grab gesture, hold gesture, drag gesture, rotation gesture, and zoom in/out gesture, as shown in Figure 8 and Table III.

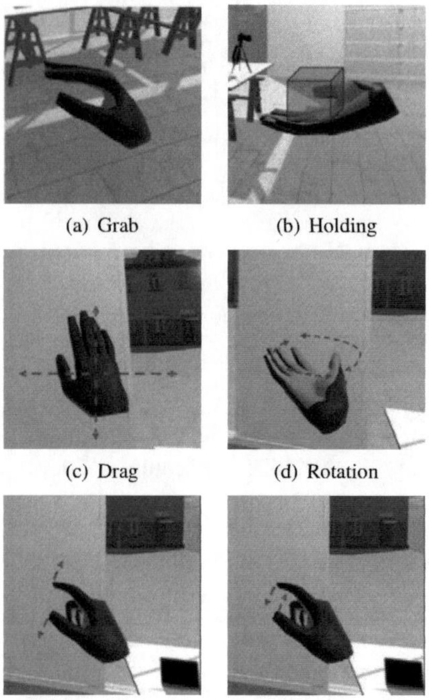

(a) Grab (b) Holding

(c) Drag (d) Rotation

(e) Zoom in (f) Zoom out

Figure 8. Gestures for interacting with objects

TABLE III. FUNCTIONS OF GESTURES FOR INTERACTING WITH OBJECT

Level	*Gesture*	*Function*
3	Grab	Make object move close to hand and grab it with hand.
3	Holding	Hold a virtual object on one hand.
3	Drag	Move virtual object freely with a hand.
3	Rotation	Rotate a virtual object when viewing it with a hand.
3	Zoom in/out	Make a virtual object show a larger or smaller size using relative motion of thumb and index finger.

In some cases, we need to interact with menu to achieve shopping activities. We design these gestures: click gesture, scroll/swipe gesture, opening/closing gesture, as shown in Figure 9 and Table IV.

In room-scale VR shopping system, the user can walk in the real walking area in his own room. However, the room-scale walking area is always smaller than the VR shopping store. Thus, we need to design a gesture for the user to change area in the room-scale VR shopping store. Figure 10 and Table V show the changing area gesture. When performing the changing area gesture, the user needs to extend his index finger and thumb finger. In the system, when the user wants to change area in the VR shopping store, he can point at a position on the virtual floor with the special hand gesture and use thumb to click the index finger to tell system that he wants to move there.

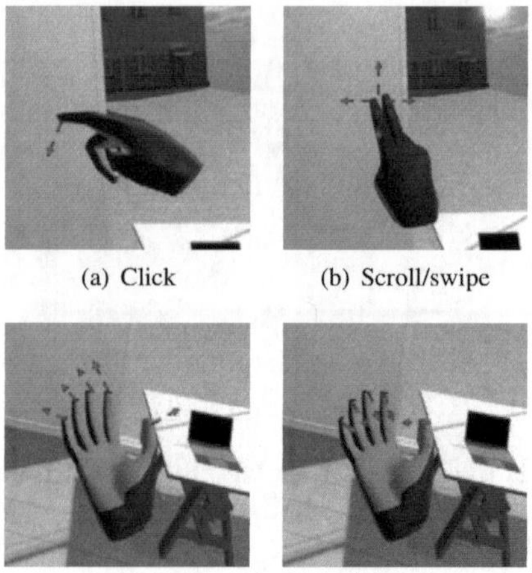

(a) Click (b) Scroll/swipe

(c) Opening (d) Closing

Figure 9. Gestures for interacting with menu

TABLE IV. FUNCTIONS OF THE GESTURES FOR INTERACTING WITH MENU

Level	*Gesture*	*Function*
3	Click gesture	Click the buttons with index finger.
3	Scroll/swipe	Using two fingers gestures to control menus in user interface.
3	Opening	Open five fingers to open the dashboard.
3	Closing	Close five fingers to close the dashboard.

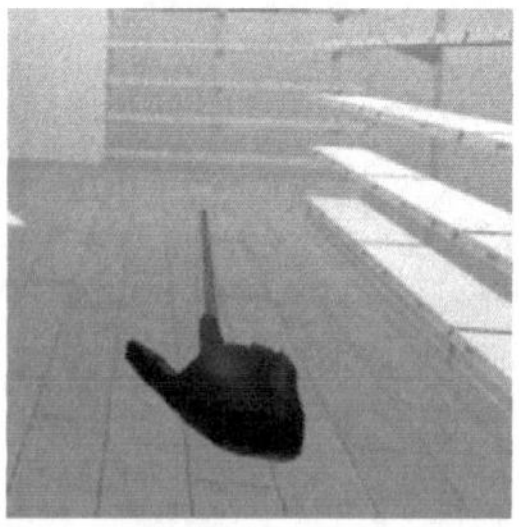

Figure 10. Gesture for changing area in VR environment

TABLE V. FUNCTION OF THE GESTURE FOR CHANGING AREA

Level	*Gesture*	*Function*
3	Changing area	Use index finger to point a new position on the floor and make the thumb click the index finger, then the view in VR will move to the new position.

IV. GESTURE RECOGNITION

In our system, we use Leap Motion as the depth sensor to track the users' hands. Leap Motion can track the joints, fingertips and palm center of user's hands. Meantime, Leap Motion can record the positions of these important points of user's hands in every frame.

With the original position data, we can use machine learning method to recognize the hand shapes. Then combining the hand shapes and motions, we will achieve recognizing the gestures that we design for the room-scale VR shopping system.

A. Hand Shape Recognition

At first, we need to confirm how many hand shapes that we need to recognize. In some cases, several hand gestures have the same hand shape. For example, drag gesture, holding gesture and rotation gesture have the same hand shape. Their differences are the motions of palm. As we have introduced all the 14 gestures we design in Section III, we summary the following hand shapes that we will recognize, as shown in Figure 11.

Besides, the system also needs to recognize whether the user's hands just move naturally without interaction intention. So, we need to recognize the natural hand shape. Therefor, there are 9 hand shapes that we need to realize.

Here is the relationship between 14 hand gestures and 9 hand shapes:

1) OK hand shape (including 1 gestures): OK gesture.
2) Pointing hand shape (including 3 gestures): pointing gesture, NO gesture, click gesture.
3) Extending hand shape(including 5 gestures): pull/push gesture, wave gesture, holding gesture, drag gesture, rotation gestures gesture.
4) Grab hand shape (including 1 gestures): grab gesture.
5) Zoom hand shape (including 1 gestures): zoom in/out gesture.
6) Scroll/swipe hand shape (including 1 gestures): scroll/swipe gesture.
7) Opening/closing hand shape (including 1 gestures): opening/closing gesture.
8) Changing area hand shape (including 1 gestures): changing area gesture
9) Natural hand shape: the hand shape when the user move hands without interaction intention

Then we apply Support Vector Machine (SVM) method in our system to realize these nine hand shapes. So, we need the multi-label classification method in our system. We use open source software, libsvm-3.22 in our system [15]. There are four steps for multi-label classification:

- data collection
- data normalization and scale
- model training
- predicting

1) Data Collection: In a hand, we will capture the end-points of bones and palm center as "key points" to describe the hand structure [16]. As shown in Figure 12, we will track all the position data of the key points in every frame in VR environment.

2) Data Normalization and Scale: We calculate other key point positions relative to palm center. Data normalization follows these steps:

- Move positions to make palm center on the origin coordinate.
- Rotate the points to make palm parallel to the x-z axis plane.
- Rotate the points around the y coordinate axis to make the palm point the –z axis.
- Scale the data to [-1, 1].

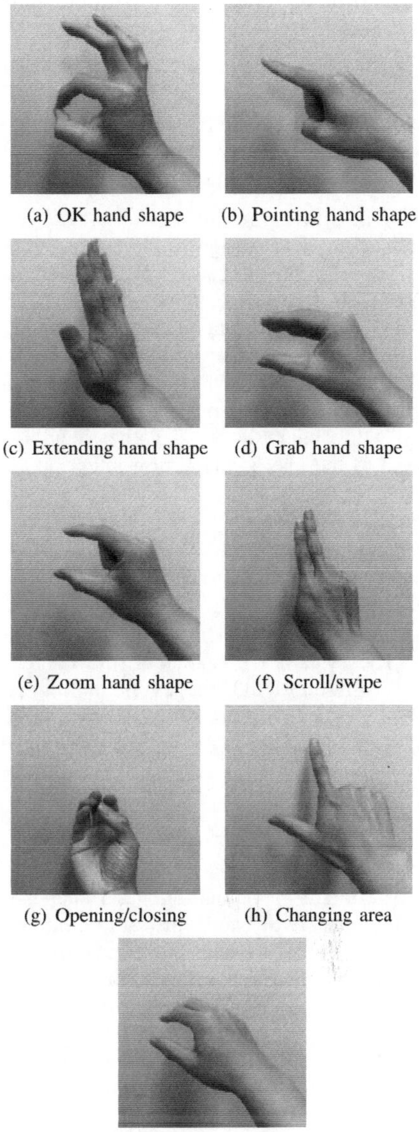

(a) OK hand shape (b) Pointing hand shape
(c) Extending hand shape (d) Grab hand shape
(e) Zoom hand shape (f) Scroll/swipe
(g) Opening/closing (h) Changing area
(i) Natural hand shape

Figure 11. The nine hand shapes

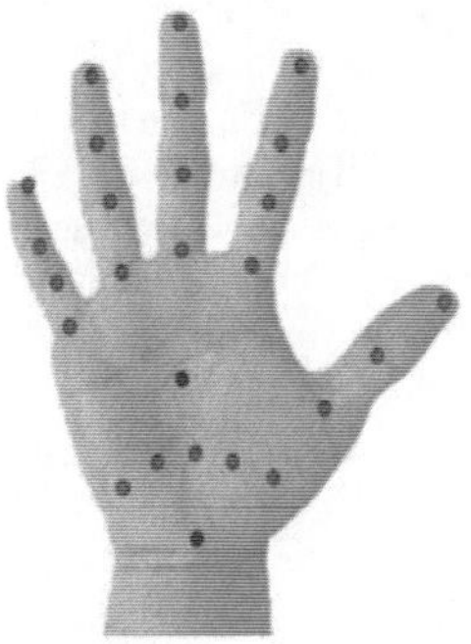

Figure 12. Key Points: two blue points represent the palm center and the wrist joint; red points represent the endpoints of bones in hand

3) Model Training: There are three steps to train the data and get a classifier model:

- Capture 50 groups coordinates of the key points for every hand shape.
- Normalize and scale the data and get 9 groups training sets.
- Through training sets, get the multi-label classifier.

4) Predicting: After getting the classifier, we will use it in VR shopping system to recognize the nine hand shapes. When the user viewing the room-scale VR shopping store, the user moves his hands freely. Depth sensor tracks the hands and gets a group of original data set in every frame. Then, with the classifier, we will get the predicting result. The predicting result will tell the system which hand shape that the user is performing. If the hand shape is natural hand shape, system will not give feedback; if getting other hand shapes, system will respond to the user's interaction intention.

B. Motion Detection

After knowing the hand shape, the system needs motion detection because gestures are defined by both hand shape and motion together.

Once getting the hand shape, the system begins motion detection. The system will calculate the hand data in every frame. For different hand shapes predicting result, system detects hand center or different fingertips to realize gestures.

Based on the hand shapes from label 1 to label 9, there are nine situations when recognize motions.

- **Situation 1**: for OK hand shape, OK gesture is the level 1 gesture and the system does not need to recognize the motion.
- **Situation 2**: for pointing hand shape, if the system finds that two hands are in pointing hand shape, system needs to detect the positions of two index fingertips. If the two index fingertips are close, it shows that the user is performing NO gesture. If only one hand is in pointing hand shape, the system needs to detect the direction and motion of index finger, because we need to use pointing gesture to choose a target or click a button.
- **Situation 3**: for extending hand shape, it is a little complexed. (a) if system detects that the palm center orients to face and moving toward to face, it is pull gesture; (b) if system detects that the palm center orients forward and moving forward, it is push gesture; (c) if system detects that the palm center orients left and moving to left, it is waving; (d) if system detects that the palm center orients to sky, it is holding gesture; (e) if system detects that the palm center orients forward and moving on a vertical plane, it is drag gesture; (f) if system detects that the palm center orients to sky and rotating around the palm center, it is rotation gesture.
- **Situation 4**: for grab hand shape, the system detects the motion of palm center and the target object follows the motion of palm center.
- **Situation 5**: for zoom hand shape, the system detects the motion of index and thumb fingertips. If the fingertips move away from each other, it is zoom in gesture; if the fingertips move closely to each other, it is zoom out gesture. The movement distance will be used to change the size of the target object.
- **Situation 6**: for scroll/swipe hand shape, the system detects the motion of index finger. The movement distance will be used to control menu.
- **Situation 7**: for opening/closing hand shape, the system detects the motion of index, middle and thumb fingertips. If their motions are moving closely to each other, it is closing gesture; if their motion is moving away from each other, it is opening gesture.
- **Situation 8**: for changing area hand shape, system detects the direction of index finger and the motion of thumb fingertip. If index finger points to a position on the floor and thumb fingertip clicks the index finger, it is changing area gesture and the user will move to the target position.
- **Situation 9**: for natural hand shape, system does not need to detect any motion. Because in this situation, the user moves his hands freely in 3D space and does not want to interact with system.

V. Preliminary Evaluation

We apply the gesture set in our VR environment to build the interaction system. We design a typical shopping activity as an example: viewing and buying a laptop.

Firstly, the user can move to the desk with the change area gesture where the laptops are placed in the room-scale VR shopping environment, as shown in Figure 13. In this situation, the desk is a little far away from the user and is out of the original walking area of the user. Then, the user walks near to the desk. He selects one of the laptops with the pointing gesture. Once being selected, the laptop will show a bounce animation, as shown in Figure 14(a). The user can make the laptop move to his hand with the hold gesture, as shown in Figure 14(b). The user can also grab the model. After that, the user can view the details of the laptop with the zoom in/out gesture, as shown in Figure 14(c). Besides, he can also call out the menu to check more information with the open/close gesture and the scroll/swipe gesture, as shown in Figure 14(d) and Figure 14(e). Finally, he can perform the OK gesture to tell the system that he decides to buy it, as shown in Figure 14(f).

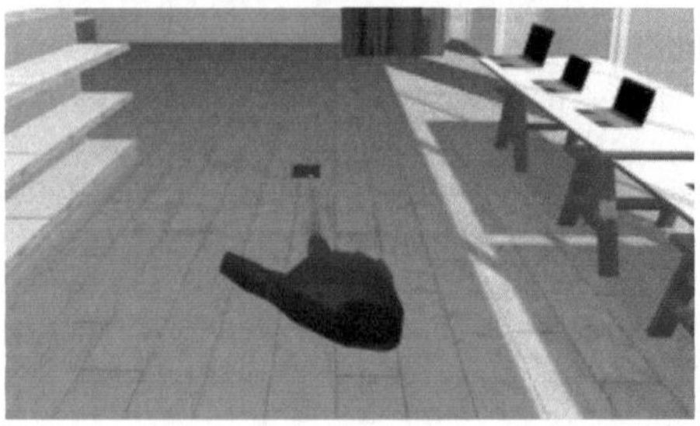

Figure 13. Using change area gesture

We invited 5 students to use our room-scale VR shopping system. The range of their ages is from 19 to 27. They repeated the shopping activity that we designed and performed the nine hand shapes for 50 times respectively. We collected data and found the errors of hand shape classification with SVM method.

Table VI shows the errors of classification of every hand shapes for every user. There are nine hand shapes. So, every

(a) Pointing a product

(b) Hold the product

(c) Zoom in/out the product

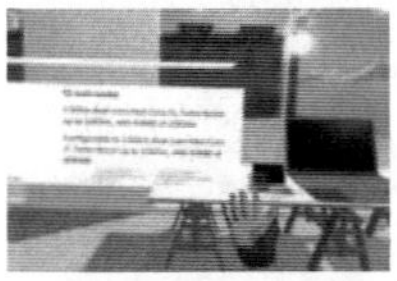

(d) Use Open/close gesture

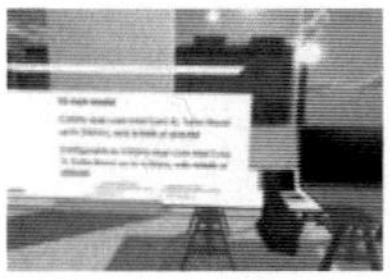

(e) Use scroll/swipe gesture

(f) Use OK gesture

Figure 14. The gestures used in shopping activities

user performs the hand shapes for 450 times in all in our evaluation. Then, we can get the accuracy rate when a user is performing hand shapes in our system, as shown in Table VII.

TABLE VI. ERRORS OF CLASSIFICATION OF NINE HAND SHAPES FOR EVERY USER

Hand Shape	*User 1*	*User 2*	*User 3*	*User 4*	*User 5*
OK	1	0	0	2	1
Pointing	0	0	1	2	1
Extending	3	2	4	5	4
Grab	1	2	2	3	3
Zoom	0	1	1	3	1
Scroll/swipe	1	1	1	2	1
Opening/closing	0	0	1	1	0
Changing area	1	1	1	4	2
Natural	4	3	4	5	4

TABLE VII. THE ACCURACY RATE OF HAND SHAPE RECOGNITION OF 5 USERS

User	*Amount*	*Accuracy*	*Accuracy Rate*
1	450	439	97.56%
2	450	440	97.78%
3	450	435	95.56%
4	450	423	94.00%
5	450	433	96.22%

In Table VI, we can see the relative high error rates of the extending hand shape and the natural hand shape. That is because these two hand shapes are similar when the user performs them in our VR environment. For example, some users often extend their fingers when they perform nature hand shape. Some users sometimes bend their fingers a bit when they use extending hand shape to hold the models. In this situation, system cannot detect which hand shape that they want to perform.

VI. RELATED WORK

With the perfection of VR technology, many researchers and companies try to apply VR technology in e-commerce field and want to find a way to generate economic value. Alibaba is a famous IT company and is known for its great on-line shopping services. Alibaba presented a VR shopping application, called Buy+, running on the smart phone [17]. The Buy+ tried to combine the convenience of on-line shopping and the facticity of physical store shopping. With the simple and cheap VR devices and smart phone, people in China could view an overseas virtual shopping mall and pay for orders on-line.

Some companies use VR technology to create virtual store. IKEA is a famous furniture company. It presented a room-scale VR kitchen to show its beautiful design [7]. In the room-scale VR kitchen, the user could use HTC Vive to view the equal proportion VR kitchen, even could interact with the VR environment like opening the virtual range hood. Comparing with physical furniture stores, the VR environment could provide more functions and interactions. The user could view the kitchen freely in his own room without warring about the crowd in the physical IKEA mall. In the VR kitchen, the user also could change the color of furniture freely, which is impossible in the physical IKEA mall.

A VR technology company, inVRsion, presented a VR supermarket system based on room-scale VR [8]. Their retail space, products and shopping experience VR solutions provide an immersive shopping environment. In the VR shopping environment, businessman could analyze shopper behavior through eye-tracking for extremely powerful market research insights. The system could help sellers to test their category projects, new packaging and communication in the stores before implementation. The users could search their target products more easily than physical supermarket. This system tries to provide a method for people to view a big virtual supermarket in his own room.

In our previous work, we extended 2D multi-touch interaction to 3D space and introduced a universal multi-touch gestures for 3D space [16]. We called these midair gestures in 3D as 3D multi-touch-like gestures.

The previous related works prove the broad application prospect of room-scale VR shopping and gestures. Our work about designing gesture set for room-scale VR can be used in these systems to provide better VR shopping experience.

VII. CONCLUSION

In this research, we built a room-scale VR shopping system and proposed a new hand gesture set for the room-scale VR shopping system. We used the gesture set to replace the controllers of VR device to improve the limitation of controllers in VR shopping activities. Researching on the gesture set, we introduced a new gesture classification. We designed three levels for classification method. The gestures in level 1 were static hand shapes, the gestures in level 2 were movement of palm and the gestures in level 3 combined the features of gestures in level 1 and level 2. The gestures in level 1 and level 2 were simple and were not enough for room-scale VR shopping activities. Therefor, we focused our research on the level 3 gestures.

For the gestures in level 3, we introduced four categories to classify them: core gesture, gestures for interaction with virtual object, gestures for interaction with menu and gesture for interaction with space. The classifications helped us to understand the gesture set in room-scale VR shopping system. Also, the gesture set and 3-level classification method could be transplanted to other VR or AR systems conveniently.

In order to achieve the complex gestures recognition, we applied SVM method in our VR shopping system. In the end, the user could walk around in his room to view the VR shopping store and interact with the system with his natural hand gestures.

In the future work, we will research on two aspects: realizing "natural" hand gesture set and improving the accuracy of hand shape recognition. The gestures we have designed in this paper do not fully reflect the natural hand shapes. Also some hand shapes are very similar and they lowers the accuracy of hand shape recognition. Therefore, we would like to further refine our current gesture set and make our hand gesture more natural and more accurate.

REFERENCES

[1] B. Serrano, R. M. Baños, and C. Botella, "Virtual reality and stimulation of touch and smell for inducing relaxation: A randomized controlled trial," Computers in Human Behavior, vol. 55, 2016, pp. 1 – 8, ISSN: 0747-5632, doi: 10.1016/j.chb.2015.08.007.

[2] G. D. Bhatt, "Bringing virtual reality for commercial web sites," International Journal of Human-Computer Studies, vol. 60, no. 1, 2004, pp. 1–15, ISSN: 1071-5819, [Online]. Available: https://dblp.org/rec/bib/journals/ijmms/Bhatt04 [accessed: 2018-12-14].

[3] T. Chen, Z.-g. Pan, and J.-m. Zheng, "Easymall - an interactive virtual shopping system," in 2008 Fifth International Conference on Fuzzy Systems and Knowledge Discovery, vol. 4, Oct 2008, pp. 669–673, doi: 10.1109/FSKD.2008.124.

[4] K. C. Lee and N. Chung, "Empirical analysis of consumer reaction to the virtual reality shopping mall," Computers in Human Behavior, vol. 24, no. 1, 2008, pp. 88 – 104, ISSN: 0747-5632, doi: 110.1016/j.chb.2007.01.018.

[5] A. Verhulst, J. Normand, C. Lombart, and G. Moreau, "A study on the use of an immersive virtual reality store to investigate consumer perceptions and purchase behavior toward non-standard fruits and vegetables," in 2017 IEEE Virtual Reality (VR), March 2017, pp. 55–63.

[6] M. Speicher, S. Cucerca, and A. Krüger, "Vrshop: A mobile interactive virtual reality shopping environment combining the benefits of on- and offline shopping," Proceedings of the ACM on Interactive, Mobile, Wearable and Ubiquitous Technologies, vol. 1, no. 3, 2017, pp. 102:1–102:31, ISSN: 2474-9567, doi: 10.1145/3130967.

[7] "Ikea vr experience," 2016, [Online]. Available: https://www.ikea.com/ms/en_us/this-is-ikea/ikea-highlights/virtual-reality/index.html [accessed: 2018-12-14].

[8] "Shelfzone vr," 2016, [Online]. Available: https://invrsion.com/shelfzone [accessed: 2018-12-14].

[9] J. J. Lin, H. B. L. Duh, D. E. Parker, H. Abi-Rached, and T. A. Furness, "Effects of field of view on presence, enjoyment, memory, and simulator sickness in a virtual environment," in Proceedings IEEE Virtual Reality 2002, March 2002, pp. 164–171, ISSN: 1087-8270, doi: 10.1109/VR.2002.996519.

[10] P. Garg, N. Aggarwal, and S. Sofat, "Vision based hand gesture recognition," International Journal of Computer, Electrical, Automation, Control and Information Engineering, vol. 3, no. 1, 2009, pp. 186 – 191, [Online]. Available: http://waset.org/Publications?p=25 [accessed: 2018-12-14].

[11] J. P. Wachs, M. Kölsch, H. Stern, and Y. Edan, "Vision-based hand-gesture applications," Communications of the ACM, vol. 54, no. 2, 2011, pp. 60–71, ISSN: 0001-0782, doi: 10.1145/1897816.1897838.

[12] Y. Boussemart, F. Rioux, F. Rudzicz, M. Wozniewski, and J. R. Cooperstock, "A framework for 3d visualisation and manipulation in an immersive space using an untethered bimanual gestural interface," in Proceedings of the ACM Symposium on Virtual Reality Software and Technology, ser. VRST '04, 2004, pp. 162–165.

[13] H. Karam and J. Tanaka, "Two-handed interactive menu: An application of asymmetric bimanual gestures and depth based selection techniques," in Human Interface and the Management of Information. Information and Knowledge Design and Evaluation. Springer International Publishing, 2014, pp. 187–198, ISBN: 978-3-319-07731-4, doi: 10.1007/978-3-319-07731-4_19.

[14] "Leap motion," 2018, [Online]. Available: https://www.leapmotion.com [accessed: 2018-12-14].

[15] "libsvm-3.22," 2016, [Online]. Available: https://www.csie.ntu.edu.tw/ cjlin/libsvm [accessed: 2018-12-14].

[16] C. Lu, L. Zhou, and J. Tanaka, "Realizing multi-touch-like gestures in 3d space," in Human Interface and the Management of Information. Interaction, Visualization, and Analytics, 2018, ISBN: 978-3-319-92043-6, doi: 110.1007/978-3-319-92043-6_20.

[17] "Alibaba buy+," 2016, [Online]. Available: https://twitter.com/AlibabaGroup/status/789086429330575360 [accessed: 2018-12-14].

Usability Evaluation of Augmented Reality as Instructional Tool in Collaborative Assembly Cells

Lea M. Daling, Anas Abdelrazeq, Max Haberstroh, and Frank Hees
Chair of Information Management in Mechanical Engineering (IMA)
RWTH Aachen University
Aachen, Germany
lea.daling@ima-ifu.rwth-aachen.de

Abstract—**The increasing digitalization and customization of the production sector, which is commonly referred to as Industry 4.0, poses new challenges for the qualification of employees. The integration of Augmented Reality (AR) as an instructional tool provides new opportunities to support learning processes close to the workplace. Even though the use of this technology seems promising, there is still little empirically founded knowledge about the performance and fit of the system for collaborative assembly processes. This paper presents an empirical approach for the usability evaluation of a developed AR application, which can be used to assess software and hardware factors separately. In a pre-study, this catalogue was tested in combination with an experimental study design. First results for the evaluation of the developed AR solution and the suitability of different media are presented.**

Keywords-Usability Criteria; Augmented Reality; On the Job Training; Industry 4.0; Human-Robot-Collaboration (key words).

I. Introduction

The distribution of digitalization and networking within the field of 'Industry 4.0' is associated with increasingly individualized and highly flexible production [1]. Thus, fast and efficient training processes will be necessary to prepare both experienced and temporary workers for the respective assembly processes. This becomes particularly important when assembly processes are neither completely manual nor fully automated and take place in cooperation between human and robot [2].

In order to increase the efficiency of training processes, the integration of new technology and digital learning formats is needed to guide employees step by step through assembling processes and to train them flexibly for new use cases. The use of Augmented Reality (AR) as instructional assistant tool is widely expected to be a success factor of digital training programs [3]. However, its adequacy is not yet sufficiently empirically proven [4] .

Since a high degree of usability can be seen as a prerequisite for further performance measures such as increasing effectiveness and reducing the error rate, the aim of our current research is to test the usability of AR in an Industry 4.0 use case [5]. Thus, the presented AR application is designed for the instruction of a collaborative assembly process between human and robot. In Section 2, a brief introduction of the basic functions and application possibilities of AR in the manufacturing context are given. Furthermore, the use case of AR as an on the job instructional tool in a collaborative assembly cell is presented. In Section 3, the methodological approach is presented. We present an overview of relevant usability criteria and our empirical approach to measure usability of an AR application using different instructional media. Finally, section 4 gives an overview of the first results and an outlook on further research.

II. Theoretical Background

The following paragraph gives a brief introduction of the basic functions and application possibilities of AR in manufacturing and the use of AR as an on the job instructional tool in a collaborative assembly cell.

A. *AR in the Manufacturing Context*

An AR system adds virtual objects to the real world, in a way that both virtual and real components homogeneously appear in the user perception. An AR system "combines real and virtual objects in a real environment; runs interactively and in real time and registers (aligns) real and virtual objects with each other"[6]. It can therefore be said that AR systems overlay computer generated objects onto a real world setting, in real time [7].

Within the last 10-15 years, AR systems have shown great improvement and an ability to create solutions to various problems [8]. Using AR, for example, innovative and effective methods can be developed to answer important needs in simulation, assistance and improvement of manufacturing processes. Volvo, for example, is utilizing the Microsoft HoloLens to enable production line workers to digitally view assembly instructions in real-time while working to put together parts of the vehicle [9]. Through such innovative uses, one can minimize the need for improvement iterations, re-works and modifications by 'getting it done the right way' from the start. The use of AR in the current state promises many positive effects, such as constant access to information, lower error occurrences, improved motivation and a synchronized training and performance [10]. For instance, a comparison between paper instructions and AR instructions on a Head Mounted Display (HMD) showed that, although the use of AR in the assembly process gives little "time-advantages", it reduces the assembly errors significantly [10].

Nevertheless, AR systems still face a couple of challenges that prevent the direct implementation of AR solutions in real world problems. The current status, e.g., in display and tracking technology, as well as calibration techniques, still faces many difficulties [10]. Even with those challenges conquered, other questions still arise, like whether or not the implementation of such systems would lead to other problems affecting the overall performance. An over-reliance on the AR generated signals and indications can for example have negative implications on the performance of the user, by disrupting the attention or focusing it all in one direction, leading it away from the surrounding context [11]. Further research and evaluation of the technology is therefore necessary to solve existing problems and expand the spectrum of applications. In the following, an exemplary use case is presented in which AR is to be used as an on the job instructional tool for collaborative assembly processes.

B. *AR as On the Job Instructional Tool*

Since AR is used to add real-time information to a real (working) environment, we expect it to enable “learning on demand” in an on the job training session. To date, there are several approaches that combine learning measures at the workplace with the benefits of new technologies [3]. These on the job learning approaches connect theoretical knowledge with practical application [12]. Further, they provide tailor-made learning processes and can be used time- and learning pace-independent [3]. The use case in which AR is used to enable on the job training consists of a collaborative assembly cell equipped with a robot.

During the assembly process, man and robot are working together to assemble a small gear drive. In collaboration with the UR-5, the participants put together three plates with gear wheels. The human operator performs five steps, while the robot performs a total of four steps. Once the participant has familiarized himself with the cell, he is instructed to position a base plate and rear plate in a holder. The robot inserts four hexagon socket screws and positions the back plate on the base plate, while the human operator assembles two sets of gear wheels. In the final step, these are mounted on the pre-assembled base plate presented by the robot. Previously, the assembly task was guided by a fixed touchscreen with 3-D animations. The use of AR offers the added value of displaying information and work steps directly at the workspace or at the tool required for the respective assembly step. The instructions for the AR application were developed on the basis of the existing work steps and supplemented by virtual objects with real-time animations. Based on fundamental usability heuristics (e.g., visibility of the system status, consistency, aesthetics) [13], we decided to use a minimalistic design, small work steps and an avatar to guide the test persons through the assembly process, which can be seen in Figure 1.

Figure 1. Layout of the AR Application.

However, before the effectiveness of AR and its appropriateness for the use case of human robot collaboration can be tested in an experimental setting collecting quantitative data, the present qualitative pre-study aims at deriving basic implications on the usability of the developed AR application. The evaluation is intended to not only provide feedback on the AR-capable hardware, but also on the AR application software itself. Thus, two AR-capable see-through devices (tablet and Microsoft HoloLens) are used as hardware to test the AR application (software). Using the Microsoft HoloLens as HMD, we intended to enable a hands-free assembly process. Figure 2 shows that the use of the tablet is supported by a desk mount tablet arm. The study design explained below aims to derive implications of the usability of both the respective media and the AR application. For this purpose, relevant usability criteria are evaluated, which are explained in more detail below.

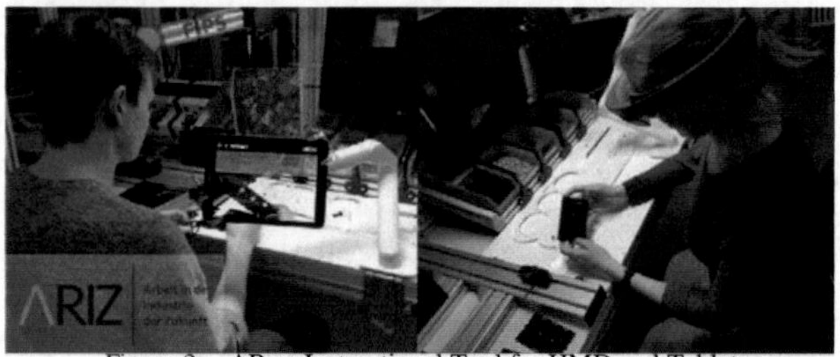

Figure 2. AR as Instrcutional Tool for HMD and Tablet.

C. *Usability Aspects*

Since 1997, DIN EN ISO 9241 has been an international series of standards that defines usability as the extent to which a technical system can be used by certain users in a certain usage context in order to achieve certain goals effectively, efficiently and satisfactorily [5]. Sarodnick and Brau emphasize that usability particularly considers the fit of system, task and user, taking into account the quality of goal achievement perceived by the user [5]. For this reason, it is essential to involve potential users in the evaluation process at an early stage.

Within a survey of Gabbard and colleagues [14] , it was found that in a total of 1104 articles on augmented reality, only 38 (~3%) addressed some aspect of human computer interaction, and only 21 (~2%) described a formal user-based study. Since, as mentioned, the involvement of users in the evaluation process is crucial for the successful development of a product, a user-centered mixed-method approach will be presented in the following.

The most widely used *inductive* approach, which is characterized by the analysis of early versions and prototypes, may be the so called thinking aloud method [5]. Here, test subjects are encouraged to express their cognitions verbally during the test. The advantage of this approach is the explorative acquisition of qualitative data to receive feedback on design and improvement. However, it should be critically noted that the double load of task processing and loud thinking reduces the processing speed. For this reason, this method should not be used in conjunction with a performance measurement. Furthermore, the test conditions in the execution are often few standardized.

Deductive methods, on the other hand, capture the user's perspective on an already developed product. At this point, however, changes and corrections of a system are often time- and cost-consuming. Established evaluation concepts (e.g., IsoMetrics; Isonorm [15]), often make use of the classical questionnaire methodology, which ensures the fulfillment of the quality criteria (validity, reliability, objectivity) to a large extend. The aim of this paper is to combine the advantages of both methods in order to generate feedback on the usability of the AR application based on empirical user surveys - extended by open questions. The thinking aloud method was further used to verbalize and record the impressions, reactions and cognitions of the participants during the work process. The composition of these approaches will be presented in the following.

III. METHOD

The aim of the present usability evaluation is to collect feedback on an AR application prototype that is tested on different media. The chosen mixed-method approach combines inductive qualitative methods with deductive, quantiatively oriented approaches of data acquisition. In 1993, Nielsen stated that a number of 5-6 test subjects were sufficient to detect significant problems [16]. Since not only the AR application but also the usability of the three media used is to be evaluated, we aimed at a minimum N of 15 persons. According to Faulkner, at least 90% to 97% of all known usability problems can be detected with a number of 15 people [17]. Therefore, we decided on a within-subject design in which every test person performs tests on every medium. The study design, the description of the sample and the used questionnaires will be presented in the following section.

A. *Study Design and Procedure*

In addition to the evaluation of the AR application, the usability of the respective instructional media should also be evaluated. Thus, we have set up a within-subject test design, where the participants have to perform three rounds on the assembly cell. Each round was instructed by different instructional media: The AR application is used by two media (the tablet and the HoloLens), so that the evaluation of the AR application can be carried out independently of the medium used. In order to compare these media with previously used media, the touchscreen is also included in the testing. It uses text- and animation-based instructions but is not AR-capable and therefore limited to the dimensionality of the screen. In order to control for repetition and learning effects [18] as far as possible, the order of the instruction media was randomized.

Each participant completed a pre-test questionnaire at the beginning in a paper-pencil format. They were then asked to familiarize themselves with the workstation of the assembly cell. Depending on the randomized condition, the first assembly was instructed by either the tablet, the HoloLens or the touchscreen. The participants had the opportunity to ask the test supervisor for help at any time, but were encouraged to carry out the assembly themselves. After each assembly process, which was completed as soon as the fully assembled gear drive was placed in a box by the robot, there was a post-test questionnaire referring to the medium used. During all three sessions, the subjects were encouraged to express their thoughts aloud. The statements were recorded with a voice recorder. After the third assembly has been completed, participants were asked to fill out the third part of the questionnaire referring to the AR-application itself. The study took about 60 minutes to complete.

B. *Participants*

A total of 8 men and 7 women took part in the study (N = 15). The mean age of the study participants was 25 years (MW = 25.07, range = 20 - 32). The sample consisted of eleven students and four working persons. Seven participants indicated to have high school graduation and/or the general university entrance qualification as highest education degree, the remaining eight already have an academic degree (nBachelor = 4, nMaster = 3, nPhD = 1). Twelve participants have never worked with a robot, the other three have rarely worked with a robot. Only one person had already participated in a study on the collaborative assembly cell.

C. *Questionnaires*

In the following paragraph, the pre- and post-test questionnaires for both "Instructional Media" and the "AR application" are presented.

1) *Pre-Test.*

In addition to the demographic data already reported, the participants were asked about their affinity for technology with five items (e.g., "My enthusiasm for technology is...") on a six-level scale ranging from "very low" to "very high". To complete the data on the participants, we also asked which media (e.g., laptop, smartphone, tablets) are available to them, how often they use them and how easy it is to use the respective medium. In addition, we used the "locus of control for technology" questionnaire (KUT) to assess general control beliefs while dealing with technology [19]. With its eight items (e.g., "Most of the technological problems that I have to face can be solved by myself") on a six-level scale ranging from "not true at all" to "absolutely true" the German questionnaire has a reliability of $\alpha = 0.89$ [19].

2) *Post-Test – Instructional Media.*

The assessment of the usability of the instructional media used is carried out separately from the evaluation of the AR application. Thus, it is possible to separate the findings on software and hardware more clearly. Based on existing usability literature [5]][13][15][20], we decided to select relevant and quantifiable criteria for the task with regard to their face validity in order to determine the suitability of the chosen instructional media.: *a) task load, b) perceived usefulness, c) media self-efficacy, d) perceived enjoyment,* and *e) perceived ease of use.*

a) Task load. The task load was measured by the "NASA Task Load Index (NASA TLX)". It measures subjectively experienced demand using a multidimensional scale that differentiates, for example, between physical and mental strain [21]. The German short version contains six dimensions, namely, mental, physical and temporal demands, as well as performance, effort and frustration. The original scale has 20 gradations from "very low" to "very high". Adapted to the German version, we used a 10-step scale with the poles "little" and "much". Criteria on reliability have been satisfactorily reviewed (Cronbachs α = .68 - .83).

b) Perceived usefulness. The factor perceived usefulness arises from the widespread and empirically well-founded "Technology Acceptance Model (TAM)"[22], which has been incorporated into the development of the usability catalogue. The TAM, currently in its third version, aims at predicting the usage behavior and acceptance of information technologies. To represent the construct, we used four items on a scale from one (strongly disagree) to seven (strongly agree) and adapted them to our application (e.g., "using the instruction medium would improve my work performance"). Cronbach's alpha showed a satisfactory value of α = .91 -.93.

c) Media self-efficacy. Four items from TAM 3's original "Computer Self-Efficacy" scale were used and adapted (e.g., "I would be able to use the instructional medium to do my work if no one were present to tell me what to do"). Since two of these items - presumably due to a misleading formulation – showed a high standard deviation, they were excluded from further analysis. The remaining two items reached a Cronbach's alpha of α = .85 - .95.

d) Perceived enjoyment. This construct is composed of three adapted items from TAM 3 (perceived enjoyment; e.g., "I would enjoy using the instructional medium.") and three other items from the "Modular Evaluation of Key Components of User Experience"(meCue2.0; e.g., "The instructional medium frustrates me."). This questionnaire is based on the analytical "Components of User Experience" model by Thüring and Mahlke [20]. This model distinguishes between the perception of task-related and non-task-related product qualities and includes user emotions as an essential and mediative factor of certain usage consequences. Internal consistency criteria are satisfied for the scale composed in this way (Cronbachs α = .66 - .92).

e) Perceived ease of use. The construct consists of four adapted items from TAM 3 (e.g., "I think the handling of the instructional medium would be clear and understandable for me.") and two further items from the IsoMetrics questionnaire (e.g., "The operating options of the instructional medium support an optimal use of the application."). IsoMetrics was designed for use during the software development process [15]. The focus is set on seven scales, which constitute an operationalization of the seven criteria of the European Committee for Standardization. Here the scale controllability was used to supplement the items from the TAM. Due to its high standard deviation, one item of the IsoMetrics had to be excluded from the analysis. The remaining four items reached a satisfactory internal consistency of Cronbachs α = .56 - .89.

The Post-test on instructional media also contains open questions: "What did you particularly like about the instructional medium you used?", "What would need to be changed in the instruction medium to make the assembly process even easier?", and "Please create a ranking of the instructional media, where 1 is your strongest preference, 2 is your second choice, etc. Please give reasons for your decision."

3) Post-Test – AR application.

The assessment of the usability of the AR application itself was measured by five parameters selected with regard to their fit in terms of early stage evaluation: *(a) perceived usefulness, (b) aesthetic and layout, c) appropriateness of functions,* as well as *d) terminology and terms.*

a) Perceived usefulness. To measure perceived usefulness, the same four items were used as in the instructional media post-test. Only the terms were adapted (e.g., "Using the AR application would improve my performance."). Cronbach's alpha showed a satisfactory value of α = .96.

b) Aesthetic and layout. In order to comprehensively depict this construct, four items from the "Visual Aesthetics of Websites Inventory – Short (VisAWI-S)" were used in the field of aesthetics [23]. The VisAWI-S records how users subjectively perceive the aesthetics of graphical interface. The used short version represents the general aesthetic factor [23]. We adjusted the items in terms of terminology (e.g., "Everything matches within the application") and further added one item from IsoMetrics ("The layout complicates my task processing due to an inconsistent design.") and another from the "Questionnaire for User Interface Satisfaction (QUIS)", which was first published in 1987 to ensure feedback on the font as well [24]. This composed scale reached an internal consistency of Cronbachs α = .60, which is critical for the analysis of this overall scale.

c) Appropriateness of functions. This scale is based on the Task Adequacy Scale of IsoMetrics and with four items (e.g., "The information necessary for task processing is always in the right place on the screen") reaches a Cronbach's alpha of α = .72.

d) Terminology and terms. To illustrate how understandable the terms and instructions used were, we used four items from QUIS (e.g., "On-screen prompts were confusing.")[24]. Furthermore, the transparency of the robot's activities was queried ("The application always informed me about what the robot does."). Two further items (e.g., "Within the AR application, easily understandable terms, descriptions or symbols (e.g., in masks or menus) are used.") for this parameter are taken from the Isonorm questionnaire published in 1993 [15]. Like IsoMetrics, Isonorm is based on the criteria of the European Committee for Standardization and therefore uses the same seven factors. This scale reached in total a Cronbachs alpha of α = .65.

Similar to the instructional media post-test, the post-test for the AR application also contains open questions: "What did you particularly like about the AR application?", "What would need to be changed in AR application to make the assembly process even easier?" Finally, the test persons should decide whether and why they would prefer the AR application to traditional manuals.

D. *Analysis*

The analysis of the collected data was conducted using SPSS. Open questions and the analysis of recorded comments was done using MAXQDA software. Since this is still work in progress, the following is a first insight into the results with a short outlook on qualitative findings. An inferential statistical comparison of the groups is carried out exploratory subsuming the individual test conditions to the media used. Thus, the comparison groups "tablet", "HoloLens" and "touchscreen" are used for the calculations. Due to the small sample, Friedman's ANOVA [18] as a non-parametric test procedure provides an insight into existing group differences, which are further investigated with the help of a post-hoc analysis according to Dunn-Bonferroni [18].

IV. First Results

Section 4 gives an overview of the first results for pre- and post-test questionnaires as well as results of the open questions on "Instructional Media" and the "AR Application".

A. *Pre-Test*

The participants have a mean technical affinity of 4.61 (min = 3.4; max = 5.60; *SD* = 0.71). General control beliefs while dealing with technology is ranging between min = 3.00 to max = 5.75 (*mean* = 4.73; *SD* = 0.72) within the sample. Media as PC (*n* = 7), Laptops (*n* = 11) and Smartphones (*n* = 15) are used daily by the majority of the test persons, while HoloLens (*n* = 12) and the Oculus Rift (n = 13) are used almost never. Only three participants already used the HoloLens before this study.

B. *Post-Test – Instructional Media*

a) Task-load. Descriptive results of the task load (N = 15; Scale: (0) = „low "to (10) = „high") can be seen in Figure 3, where means of each scale are shown as percentages for each media. The mean level of frustration over all tasks and media is 41%, and the highest mean level is reached by the HoloLens with 47%. The lowest mean frustration level is 31% while using the touchscreen. The participants reported to achieve their goal on a mean of 67% and the highest performance was achieved using the touchscreen (73%). On average, 40% effort was needed to fulfill the assembly task. The mean temporal demand ranges from 36% (touchscreen) to 42% (HoloLens). The highest mean of physical demand was reported using the tablet (53%), the highest mean of mental demand was reported using the HoloLens (61%).

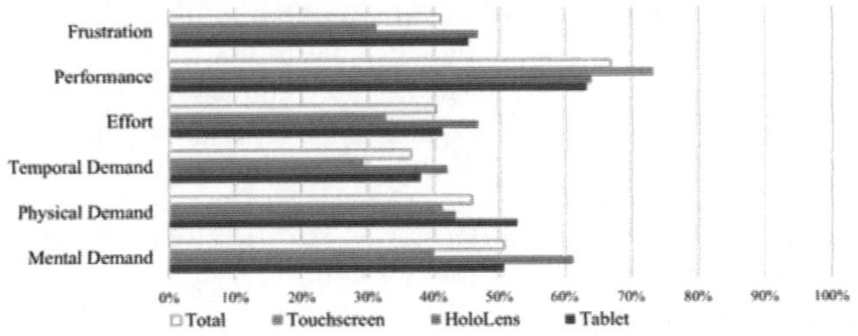

Figure 3. Task Load of Insstructional Media.

b) Perceived usefulness. All descriptive statistics of the following scales can be seen in Table. I. Within Friedman's ANOVA, it is always assumed as null hypothesis that there is no difference between the groups. However, the analysis for perceived usefulness shows a statistically significant difference between the groups (x^2_r (2) = 10.67, *p* = .005, *n* = 15). The subsequently performed Dunn-Bonferroni tests with a corrected alpha = .017 show that both the perceived usefulness between tablet and touchscreen differ statistically significantly (*z* = -2.641, *p* = .008), as well as the perceived usefulness between HoloLens and touchscreen (*z* = -2.548, *p* = .011), indicating that HoloLens and tablet are perceived as less useful as the touchscreen. HoloLens and tablet are not significantly different.

c) Media self-efficacy. Neither mean values nor Friedman's ANOVA show any statistically significant difference between the groups (x^2_r(2) = 4.545, *p* = .103, *n* = 15).

d) Perceived Enjoyment. As in the previous scale, neither mean values nor Friedman's ANOVA show a significant difference between the groups with regard to the perceived enjoyment (x^2_r (2) = 2.980, *p* = .225, *n* = 14).

e) Perceived ease of use. Both mean values and Friedman's ANOVA indicate a statistically significant difference between the groups with regard to the perceived ease of use of the media (x^2_r(2) = 21.088, *p* < .000, *n* = 15). The subsequently performed Dunn-Bonferroni tests with a corrected alpha = .017 show that both the perceived ease of use between tablet and HoloLens differ statistically significantly (*z* = -2.841, *p* = .005), as well as the perceived ease of use between HoloLens and touchscreen (*z* = -3.425, *p* =.001). Tablet and touchscreen also differ statistically significantly (*z* = -2.522, *p* = .012). The results raise an indication that the HoloLens is considered to be the least easy to use, while the touchscreen reaches its highest value.

TABLE I. Descriptive Statistics – Instructional Media

		Descriptive Statistics				
		N	*Mean*	*SD*	*Min.*	*Max.*
Perceived Usefulness	Tablet	15	3.87	.96	2.50	5.75
	Hololens	15	3.85	1.11	2.00	5.50
	Touchscreen	15	4.87	.93	2.25	6.00
Media Self-Efficacy	Tablet	15	4.80	.95	3.00	6.00
	Hololens	15	4.33	1.51	2.75	6.00
	Touchscreen	15	5.10	.96	3.00	6.00
Perceived Enjoyment	Tablet	14	4.29	.88	2.67	6.00
	Hololens	14	4.38	.66	3.33	5.83
	Touchscreen	14	4.98	.66	3.83	6.00
Perceived Ease of Use	Tablet	15	4.60	.60	3.60	5.60
	Hololens	15	3.78	.96	1.80	5.20
	Touchscreen	15	5.17	.59	4.20	6.00

Within the ranking of the instructional tools the touchscreen was chosen ten times as a first choice, the

HoloLens three times, and the tablet two times as a first choice.

The evaluation of the verbal expressions and written comments was done by categorizing them into positive and negative comments for each medium. Individual entries were coded several times. In the following, a brief overview of the most frequently mentioned is given.

Overall, there were 69 positive comments on the media. 33 of these referred to the touchscreen, which was perceived as easy to use and clearly arranged. With the tablet (n = 18) it was positively evaluated that the animations can be viewed on demand. The HoloLens was 18 times positively evaluated - most frequently the intuitive operation and the innovative character were mentioned. In addition, there were 68 negative remarks, 54 of which were verbal and 14 written comments. 38 of these were related to the HoloLens and the lack of wearing comfort or limited vision, e.g., "The HoloLens impairs vision". There were 28 negative comments about the tablet, mainly relating to the difficult positioning of the tablet arm and the resulting limited view of the work surface. The touchscreen had only two negative annotations, namely 'the fixation does not provide orientation at the workstation' and 'animations are not displayed on the work surface'.

C. Post-Test – AR Application

All descriptive statistics of the following scales can be seen in Table. II. The perceived usefulness of the AR application is on a mean of 4.40 which corresponds to an assessment between 'rather agree' and 'agree'. Aesthetics and Layout and Appropriateness of functions (mean = 3.97) corresponds to an assessment of 'rather agree'. Terminology and terms corresponds to an assessment between 'rather agree' and 'agree' with a mean of 4.29.

TABLE II. DESCRIPTIVE STATISTICS – AR APPLICATION

Descriptive Statistics					
	N	*Mean*	*SD*	*Min.*	*Max.*
Perceived Usefulness	15	4.40	1.12	2.25	5.75
Aesthetic and Layout	15	3.97	.67	2.83	5.00
Appropriateness of functions	15	4.00	.93	2.40	5.40
Terminology and terms	14	4.29	.71	3.17	5.67

On the question of whether participants would prefer learning via AR to traditional manuals, 13 out of 15 people said they would prefer AR. Main reasons given were, for example, the active learning process, the small steps, the high degree of interaction, the simplicity of use and the perceived fun. In contrast, comments against included the perceived external control of the technology and the possibility of browsing through manuals at one's own pace.

Open questions and comments. There were a total of 85 positive comments on the AR application. The detailed and vividly visualized animations were mentioned particularly frequently here (29 entries) and are accompanied by the clearly perceived instructions (13 entries). The fun and excitement (20 entries) in the process and the active, goal-oriented learning process (7 entries) were also mentioned. In the 182 negatively coded expressions, there are often remarks about the lack of correspondence between reality and displayed animations (e.g., in color, degree of detail, or positioning; 34 entries), such as: "it's hard to stay focused while the animation moves continuously in the back". In addition, the text instructions were sometimes perceived as cumbersome: "I find it annoying that I always have to read so much text".

V. DISCUSSION AND OUTLOOK

The study reveals first results for the separate evaluation of the usability of different instruction media as well as the developed AR application using a tailor-made usability catalogue. In general, the composition of the usability catalogue from inductive and deductive methods was proven to be a successful approach. A high degree of objectivity could be achieved through the questionnaires. The individual results of the scales could be explained in detail by open comments and verbal statements and were thus made comprehensible afterwards. However, the validation of scales in a larger sample should precede further studies.

The results of the evaluation of the instructional media shows that a high level of frustration occurs when processing the task with the HoloLens, which goes hand in hand with a high cognitive demand. Here, possible connections between the ease of use of the media and the perceived cognitive demand could be an interesting starting point for further research. The touchscreen on the contrary causes a low frustration and is evaluated with the highest performance. The tablet's evaluation usually lies between the other media, but shows the highest physical demand. These findings are supported by the assessment of the usability scales. Here it becomes apparent that HoloLens and tablet are rated with a lower usefulness than the touchscreen. In terms of media self-efficacy and perceived enjoyment, there is no difference between the media tested. In future studies, the possible influence of the high technical affinity of the sample on these variables should be clarified. Both the open questions and the ranking support the impression that the touchscreen convinces users with its simple operation. In addition, it becomes clear that the innovative character of the HoloLens is perceived as enjoyable. Above all, the overlapping of animations with reality still poses a problem, which can be prevented, for example, by using the tablet and moving the holder.

In the evaluation of the AR Application it becomes clear that AR is generally assessed with a relatively high usefulness, which is also supported by the open comments. This shows that especially the clear and small step instructions are perceived as useful. The aesthetics and layout of the application, as well as the appropriateness of functions should be worked on in the further course. It should be considered that images and animations are perceived as helpful, whereas text descriptions are sometimes described as obstructive or misleading.

A main restriction of the study refers to the high academic degree and the young average age of the sample, which is accompanied by a comparatively high affinity for technology. In addition, almost all participants are novices in the field of assembly, which severely limits the transferability of study results. Another limitation refers to the laboratory setting of the study, where no real working conditions (e.g., lighting, noises) occur. The results achieved by such a small number of participants should not be interpreted without caution. Conclusions on the quality of the questionnaire used should not yet be derived, as this requires a larger sample. The items and constructs used here were selected on the basis of the specific use case which limits the transferability of this selection. Further, we only used already established questionnaires and the thinking aloud method but did not include any other usability instruments (e.g., usability cards).

The first impressions of the study should be examined in a real use case within further research. In order to generate a better transferability of the results, a survey of assembly workers is planned for the further course of our investigations. After the revision of the detected usability problems, following studies will be carried out referring to the effectiveness of the use of AR. Hereby, the influence of AR on the general performance, error rate and satisfaction with the work process should be examined. Furthermore, the influence of AR on the acceptance of robots should be investigated within the context of collaborative workspaces.

ACKNOWLEDGMENT

This research and development project is funded by the German Federal Ministry of Education and Research (BMBF) within the "Innovations for Tomorrow's Production, Services, and Work" Program (funding number 02L14Z000) and implemented by the Project Management Agency Karlsruhe (PTKA). The author is responsible for the contents of this publication.

REFERENCES

[1] acatech - Deutsche Akademie der Technikwissenschaften in Kooperation mit Fraunhofer IML & equeo, Ed., *Kompetenzentwicklungsstudie Industrie 4.0: Erste Ergebnisse und Schlussfolgerungen (Industry 4.0 Competence Development Study: First Results and Conclusions)*. München, 2016.

[2] S. L. Müller, S. Stiehm, S. Jeschke and A. Richert, "Subjective Stress in Hybrid Collaboration", in vol. 10652, *Social Robotics*, A. Kheddar et al., Eds., Cham: Springer International Publishing, pp. 597–606, 2017, doi: 10.1007/978-3-319-70022-9_59.

[3] Q. Guo, "Learning in a Mixed Reality System in the Context of Industry 4.0," *Journal of Technical Education*, vol. 3, no. 2, pp. 92–115, 2015.

[4] M. Funk, T. Kosch and A. Schmidt, „Interactive worker assistance", in Proceedings of the 2016 ACM, 2016 UbiComp, pp. 934–939. doi: 10.1145/2971648.2971706.

[5] F. Sarodnick and H. Brau, *Methoden der Usability Evaluation (Methods of Usability Evaluation)*, (2nd. ed). Hans Huber, Hogrefe AG, Bern, 2006.

[6] R. Azuma, Y. Baillot, R. Behringer, S. Feiner, S. Julier and B. MacIntyre, "Recent Advances in Augmented Reality", Naval Research Lab, Washington DC, pp. 34-47, 2001, doi: 10.1109/38.963459.

[7] B. Furht, Ed., Handbook of Augmented Reality, Springer Science & Business Media, 2011, doi: 10.1007/978-1-4614-0064-6.

[8] A. Y. Nee, S. K. Ong, G. Chryssolouris and D. Mourtzis, "Augmented Reality Applications in Design and Manufacturing", *CIRP Annals-manufacturing technology*, 61(2), pp. 657-679, 2012, doi: 10.1016/j.cirp.2012.05.010.

[9] A. Little, *How Automotive Manufacturers are Utilizing Augmented Reality*, August 2018, retrieved January, 08, 2019 fromhttps://www.manufacturingtomorrow.com/article/2018/03/how-automotive-manufacturers-are-utilizing-augmented-reality-/11117.

[10] M. Akçayır and G. Akçayır, "Advantages and Challenges Associated with Augmented Reality for Education: A systematic review of the literature". *Educational Research Review, (20)*, pp. 1-11, 2017, doi:10.1016/ j.edurev.2016.11.002.

[11] A. Tang, C. Owen, F. Biocca and W. Mou, "Comparative effectiveness of augmented reality in object assembly", *In Proceedings of the SIGCHI conference on Human factors in computing systems*, pp. 73-80, ACM, April 2003, doi:10.1145/642611.642626.

[12] A. Ullrich and G. Vladova, "Qualifizierungsmanagement in der vernetzten Produktion - Ein Ansatz zur Strukturierung relevanter Parameter," (Qualification Management in Networked Production - An Approach to Structuring Relevant Parameters) *Lehren und Lernen für die moderne Arbeitswelt*, pp. 58–80, GITO, 2015.

[13] J. Nielsen, Enhancing the explanatory power of usability heuristics. in *Proceedings of the SIGCHI conference on Human Factors in Computing Systems*, pp. 152-158, ACM. 1994, doi: 10.1145/191666.191729

[14] L. Gabbard, J. E. Swan II, D. Hix, S,-J. Kim and G. Fitch, "Active Text Drawing Styles for Outdoor Augmented Reality: a User-based Study and Design Implications", in *Virtual Reality Conference VR'07, IEEE*, pp. 35-42, 2007, doi: 10.1109/VR.2007.352461.

[15] K. Figl, Deutschsprachige Fragebögen zur Usability-Evaluation im Vergleich (German-language questionnaires for usability evaluation in comparison), *Zeitschrift für Arbeitswissenschaft*, *4*, pp. 321-337, 2010.

[16] J. Nielsen, Usability Engineering. London: AP Professional Ltd., 1993.

[17] L. Faulkner, Beyond the five-user assumption: Benefits of increased sample sizes in usability testing. *Behavior Research Methods, Instruments, and Computers*, 35 (3), pp. 379-383, 2003.

[18] A. Field and G. Hole. How to design and report experiments. Sage, 2002.

[19] G. Beier, Kontrollüberzeugungen im Umgang mit Technik: ein Persönlichkeitsmerkmal mit Relevanz für die Gestaltung technischer Systeme (Control Control beliefs in dealing with technology: a personality trait with relevance for the design of technical systems), *Ph.D. Dissertation*, Humboldt-Universität zu Berlin. Available from GESIS database, Record No. 20040112708.

[20] M. Thüring, and S. Mahlke, Usability, Aesthetics and Emotions in Human–Technology Interaction, *International Journal of Psychology*, *42*(4), pp. 253-264, 2007, doi: 10.1080/00207590701396674.

[21] S. G. Hart, NASA-Task Load Index (NASA-TLX); 20 Years Later. *Proceedings of the Human Factors and Ergonomics Society 50th Annual Meeting*, Santa Monica: HFES, pp. 904-908, 2006, doi: 10.1177/154193120605000909.

[22] F. D. Davis, A Technology Acceptance Model for Empirically Testing New End-user Information Systems: Theory and Results, *Ph.D. Dissertation*, Massachusetts Institute of Technology, 1985.

[23] M. Moshagen, and M. T. Thielsch, "A Short Version of the Visual Aesthetics of Websites Inventory", *Behaviour & Information Technology*, 32 (12), pp. 1305-1311, 2013, doi: 10.1080/0144929X.2012.694910.

[24] J. P. Chin, V. A. Diehl and K. L. Norman, "Development of a Tool Measuring User Satisfaction of the Human-Computer Interface",In *Proceedings of the SIGCHI conference on Human factors in computing systems*, pp. 213-218. ACM, 2018.

Suppression of Information Diffusion in Social Network Using Centrality based on Dynamic Process

Eiichi Takazawa and Norihiko Shinomiya

Graduate School of Engineering
Soka University
1-236 Tangi, Hachioji, Tokyo, Japan
Email: shinomi@soka.ac.jp

***Abstract*—Individual activities propagate on social networks and had a large impact on our society. For example, incitement acts such as hoaxes, widely propagated through social media, gave unnecessary confusion and uneasiness to many people. The purpose of this study is to propose an edge centrality index in a network considering the propagation of activities through analysis. Our previous studies have proposed an evaluation method that quantifies the edge importance based on an activity propagation model. The model represents the propagation by an equalization process of the variable amount given to each vertex. This paper experimentally shows that the information diffusion can be suppressed by using the edge importance measure. The experiment verifies that the range of information diffusion becomes smaller than that before deleting some edges from the network based on the importance measure.**

***Keywords*–Centrality; Graph Theory; Information Diffusion.**

I. Introduction

The development and dissemination of information network technologies have accelerated online communications among individuals and dispatch of information at the individual level. In particular, individual activities also have propagated throughout the world due to the advancement in social media. As a result, the impact of individual activities on society has been increasing. For instance, in the so-called Arab Spring, democratization movement spread through social media. That led to huge demonstration activities that occurred in many countries [1]. In the future, it is expected that technological innovation such as blockchain further facilitates interaction among individuals, complicates mutual influence, and makes the scale spread out. Therefore, it is necessary to analyze not only a network itself but also the behaviors of the people connecting to the network.

On the other hand, a variety of *centralities* have been theoretically and experimentally studied in the field of network analysis and graph theory [2]. Each centrality quantifies how important a vertex or an edge is in a graph that abstracts the corresponding network. There are different measures of centrality depending on how to define the criteria on importance. For example, degree centrality [2] is based on the number of edges connected to vertices. As the significance index of centrality, it is assumed that vertices with higher degree strongly contribute to spreading information. Betweenness centrality [3] is defined as a ratio of an edge existing on the shortest path between arbitrary two vertices. It is assumed that information tends to be transmitted along the shortest path. These conventional centralities have been applied in a wide range of fields such as human relationship analysis and information communication network design. However, these measures are defined only based on the *static structure* of the network such as the degree and the shortest path, thereby not suitable for analyzing a *dynamic process* such as activity propagation.

Therefore, the purpose of this study was to propose a new edge centrality index in a network considering the propagation of activities through analysis. The proposed centrality is expected to be used as a clue of prevention on the diffusion of computer viruses, false propaganda, and online flaming, since it can measure the edge importance in propagation. Our study previously has proposed a novel centrality and analyzed its characteristics by comparing it with other centralities [4]. Our centrality index of an edge is defined by the influence on propagation when a link corresponding to the edge is removed. The activity propagation is modeled by an equalization process of exchanging variable amount among vertices.

This paper investigates how the information diffusion can be suppressed by using the proposed centrality. Specifically, the range of information diffusion on a network is compared with that on the transformed network where some edges with higher centrality are deleted. Then, we analyze how much the range of information diffusion becomes smaller after the edges are removed. The results of the numerical experiments on the proposed centrality and betweenness centrality demonstrate that it is possible to reduce the range of information spreading by deleting edges based on the proposed centrality. This fact implies that this centrality is useful as an index to prevent the information diffusion.

The rest of this paper is organized as follows, Section II defines the model that represents how people interact with each other through a network, Section III proposes the new edge centrality based on the propagation model, and Section IV investigates how the information diffusion can be suppressed by using the proposed centrality.

II. Dynamics of Propagation

A. Modeling

This section defines the model that represents how people interact with each other through a network. A given graph $G = (V, E)$ is an undirected and connected graph with vertex set V and edge set E, suppose that each vertex $v_i \in V$ has a variable $W_i(t) \in \mathbb{R}^+$ at a time $t \in \mathbb{N}$, $W_i(t)$ is referred as weight. At each time t, vertices transfer some of their weights to adjacent

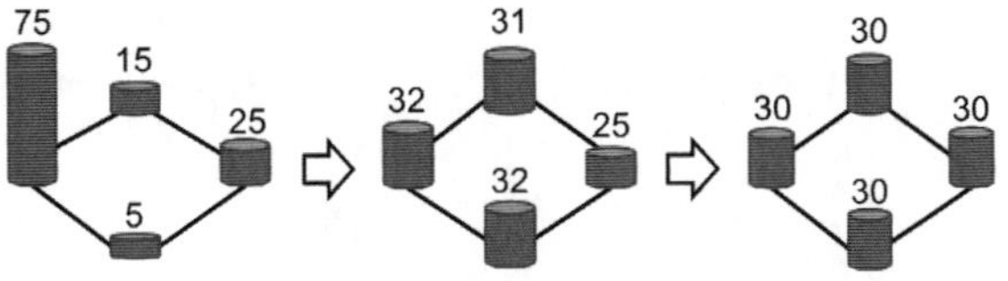

Figure 1. Dynamics of propagation.

vertices, in order to reduce the difference in weights among vertices. The weights are not lost or externally added while transferred, and the total weights of the graph as a whole are conserved (Figure 1). Hence, the sum and ensemble average of all weights is constant and independent of time, and the weight of each vertex approaches the average value over time. If the difference between the ensemble average and each weight of all vertices is less than a threshold ε, this condition says that "the weights have converged". Let the ensemble average of weights be $\langle W \rangle$, the condition of weights convergence can be written by the following equation.

$$|\langle W \rangle - W_i(t)| \leq \varepsilon \quad \forall v_i \in V. \tag{1}$$

In this model, the force trying to synchronize the states at connected vertices works. When there is no state difference between vertices, they are stable and do not mutually influence each other. The force trying to synchronize state with others is seen in various fields such as restoring force in physics, peer pressure in psychology, imitation in sociology. Thus, it is assumed that our model is a universal model describing characteristics commonly included in many models.

B. Propagation Rules

This section shows the rules of weight transfer. If the weight of a vertex is regarded as loads (works), the synchronization process of our model can be thought of as a process of solving the load balancing problem. We define the propagation rules using the simple load balancing algorithm: diffusion algorithm and local equalization algorithm.

1) Diffusion Algorithm: This algorithm determines the rule of weight transfer based on the physical diffusion process such as chemical substances [5]. Specifically, when the vertex v_i transfers some weight to adjacent vertices v_j, the amount of transferred weight can be calculated by the difference between $W_i(t)$ and $W_j(t)$ multiplied by a nonnegative constant A_{ij}. A_{ij} is called the diffusion coefficient and can be interpreted as a parameter representing the ease of transferring weights. When the weight of each vertex at a time t is $W_i(t)$, the weight $W_i(t+1)$ at the next time can be written as follows.

$$W_i(t+1) = W_i(t) + \sum_{v_j:\, neighbor\ of\ v_i} A_{ij}(W_j(t) - W_i(t)). \tag{2}$$

Boillat proposed (3) as a method of choosing A_{ij}. $\deg(v_i)$ expresses the degree of v_i. In the experiment, we assumed the homogeneity of the link for simplicity and set any element of A_{ij} to the inverse of one plus the maximum degree of vertices.

$$A_{ij} = \frac{1}{1 + \max\{\deg(v_i), \deg(v_j)\}} \qquad v_i, v_j \in V. \tag{3}$$

The propagation process based on this rule represents that each node is gradually affected by the surroundings and the influence spreads.

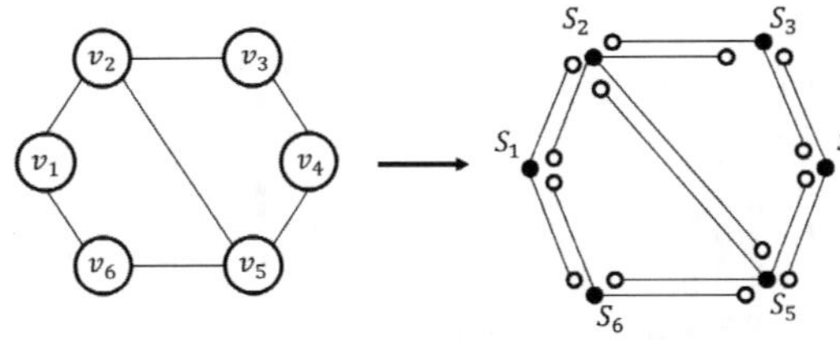

Figure 2. Extracting sub-star graphs.

2) Local Equalization Algorithm: This algorithm repeats the operation of converging the weights locally for each subgraph [4]. First, a sub-star graph S_i centered on each vertex v_i is extracted from the graph G. The sub-star graph S_i is a subgraph induced by one vertex v_i and its adjacent vertices (Figure 2). Since sub-star graphs are extracted for each vertex, the number of elements of the set of sub-star graphs S extracted from the graph G is equal to $|V|$. Next, select the sub-star graph S_i in random order from the sub-star graph set S, and locally converge the weights of the vertices included in S_i. When the local convergence of all sub-star graphs in S is completed, the time t goes to the next. The weight of the vertex v_k included in S_i changes as follows, when converging locally on the sub-star graph S_i.

$$W_j(t+1) = \frac{1}{|S_i|} \sum_{v_k \in S_i} W_k(t) \qquad v_j \in S_i. \tag{4}$$

Unlike the diffusion algorithm, this rule represents the propagation that is very susceptible to mutual influence, because the states are instantaneously synchronized at the surroundings around a node.

III. Edge Centrality Proposal

Using the model of Section II-A, we define the centrality of edge. Here, the time until the convergence of the weights is used as an index of the centrality. In order to define the importance of the edge e, converge the weights of the graph G' obtained by removing an edge e from the graph G. At that time, the weights transmitted along the edge e has to be propagated bypassing e, thus the weights would be difficult to converge. Therefore, the importance of an edge is defined by the difficulty of weights convergence when the edge was removed. Specifically, the importance of the edge e is defined by the ratio of the time to the convergence of the original graph G and the graph G' removed e. The time until convergence depends on the weights $\boldsymbol{W}_0 = \{W_1(0), \ldots, W_n(0)\}$ at the initial ($t = 0$). Hence, the importance is calculated with the initial weights of several patterns, and the average is used as the centrality value. Let $\mathcal{W}_0$ be a pattern set of the initial weights and $T(G, \boldsymbol{W}_0)$ be the time until convergence, the importance $D(e)$ can be written as follows.

$$D(e) = \frac{1}{|\mathcal{W}_0|} \sum_{\boldsymbol{W}_0 \in \mathcal{W}_0} \frac{T(G', \boldsymbol{W}_0)}{T(G, \boldsymbol{W}_0)}. \tag{5}$$

From this definition of importance, if the graph is not connected when an edge is removed, there is a possibility that the weight cannot converge in the propagation model. Therefore, the importance $D(e)$ cannot be defined unless a graph is at least two connected.

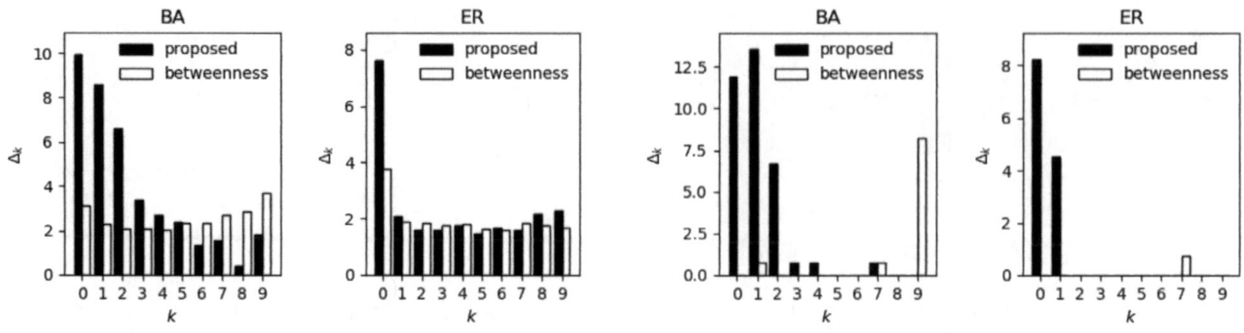

(a) IC model.

(b) LT model.

Figure 3. The value of Δ_k for each k, graph models, and information diffusion models.

IV. EXPERIMENTS

The proposed centrality defines the edge importance by measuring how much the propagation becomes more difficult when an edge is removed. Therefore, it is assumed that the propagation on the network can be suppressed by deleting the edges with high importance in this centrality. In addition, the propagation process expressed by the diffusion algorithm (in Section II-B1) can be used for analysis of the information diffusion [6]. This experiment analyzes how much the range of information diffusion becomes smaller after the edges are removed. These removed edges are chosen in descending order of the importance in our centrality using the diffusion algorithm as the propagation rule.

A. Simulation Setting

1) Information Diffusion Model and Parameter Setting: In order to simulate the diffusion process of information, this experiment uses two popular information diffusion models: Independent Cascade (IC) model [7] and Linear Threshold (LT) model [8]. In these models, each vertex has either *active* or *inactive* state, and active represents a state receiving the information and inactive represents a state which has not yet been received the information respectively. Also, the information diffusion on the network is expressed as the increase of active vertices. In the IC model, the set of active vertices at the beginning and diffusion probability $p_{u,v}$ for each edge (u,v) are given, and active vertex u conveys the information with probability $p_{u,v}$ to its adjacent vertex v. On the other hand, the LT model sets the set of active vertices at the beginning, the weight $\omega_{u,v}$ for each edge (u,v), and the threshold θ_v of each vertex v as initial parameters. The inactive vertex v is affected by all adjacent active vertices u according to $\omega_{u,v}$, and v becomes active when the following equation is satisfied.

$$\sum_{(u,v)\,\in\,E\text{ s.t. }u\text{ is active}} \omega_{u,v} \geq \theta_v \tag{6}$$

Assuming the homogeneity of nodes and links, this experiment set the diffusion probability $p_{u,v} = 0.2$ in the IC model, the weight of edge $\omega_{u,v}$ equals the reciprocal of $\max\{\deg(u), \deg(v)\}$ and the threshold $\theta_v = 0.25$ in the LT model [9]. In addition, the number of active vertices at the beginning is set to $0.25|V|$ for both models.

2) Definition of Indicators for the Information Diffusion Suppression: We simulate the information diffusion by the IC or LT model on a graph $G = (V, E)$, and define $A(G)$ by the expected number of active vertices at the end of that diffusion process. The removed edges are decided as the following. First, we rearrange the element of E by the descending order of the centrality value, that is, the importance of e_i is larger than that of e_j if i is smaller than j. E_k is defined as E divided into $|E|/l$ sets, as in the following equation.

$$E_k = \{e_{kl}, e_{kl+1}, \ldots, e_{kl+l-1}\}, \quad k \in \{0, \ldots, |E|/l - 1\} \tag{7}$$

According to this equation, E_0 is composed of the edges with the highest centrality value. Let G_k be the graph obtained by removing edges included in E_k from G, run the information diffusion model on each G_k to calculate $A(G_k)$. Then, we define $\Delta_k = A(G) - A(G_k)$ as an indicator to how much the information diffusion can be suppressed. This experiment uses the average value obtained by running the diffusion simulation for 1000 times as $A(\cdot)$, and set $l = 0.1|E|$ to investigate the effect of removing the 10 percent edges from the whole.

3) Graph Topology: Graphs generated based on Erdős-Rényi (ER) model [10] and Barabási-Albert (BA) model [11] were used for experiments. The ER model is the simplest random graph. This model generates edges with probability p between arbitrary two vertices. This experiment determines the number of vertices is 180 and the edge generation probability $p = 0.1$. Also, we add some edges randomly to the graph generated by the ER model in order to satisfy the two connectivity, because the proposed centrality can not be defined on the two connected graphs. The BA model generates a graph with scale-free. Many networks in the real world have been reported to be scale-free, for example, social networks and the world wide web. The BA model evolves a graph to add vertices and edges randomly by repetition. In the experiment, the number of vertices of the initial graph is 10, and every time a new vertex is added to the existing graph, 10 new edges are added to that. We add a new vertex until the number of vertices equals 180.

4) Parameter for the Proposed Centrality: Since the value of the proposed centrality varies depending on the initial weight of vertices, we use the average value calculated by 100 samples of the initial weights as the centrality value (that is $|\mathcal{W}_0| = 100$). In addition, as described above, the propagation rule is according with the diffusion algorithm, and the diffusion coefficient A_{ij} of an edge is set by (3).

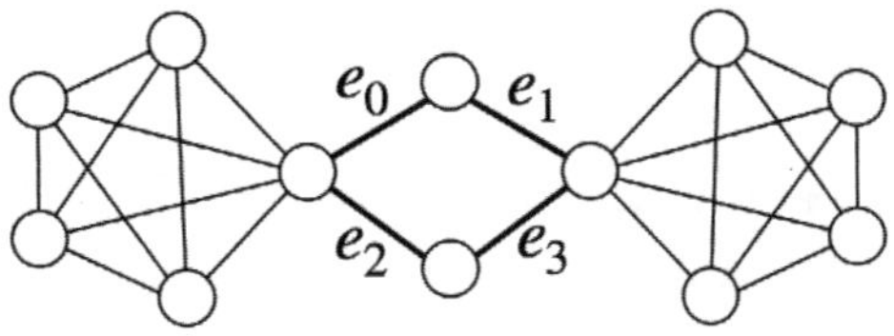

Figure 4. Example of a graph that can not efficiently suppress information diffusion with the proposed centrality

B. Results and Discussion

Figure 3 is a bar chart of the value of Δ_k for each k, graph model, and information diffusion model. For example, the left of Figure 3a represents the simulation result on information diffusion using IC model on a graph generated by the BA model. The smaller the value of k is getting, the more edges with higher centrality values are removed. The experiment uses the proposed centrality using the algorithm in Section II-B1 as a propagation rule and the betweenness centrality [3] for the comparison.

All the charts clearly show that Δ_0 of the proposed centrality is largest in all combinations of information diffusion models and graph models. The number of active vertices after the information diffusion simulation is reduced by elimination of an edge with the higher value in the proposed centrality. This fact suggests that the proposed method is useful to suppress information diffusion as an indicator in comparison with the betweenness centrality.

On the other hand, this result shows that Δ_1 also takes a large value. This fact suggests that there is a possibility that the value of Δ_0 still can be increased by changing the edges in E_k. According to (5), the proposed centrality is defined based on the influence when a single edge is removed, and measures the function of a single edge. Therefore, it is considered difficult to evaluate the influence of removing multiple edges simultaneously like the experiment. Take the case that we remove two edges from the graph in Figure 4 (that is $l = 2$). Let the four edges drawn with bold be the edges with the highest centrality value. In this case, we can divide it into the unconnected graph by removing e_0 and e_2, so it is assumed that the information diffusion can be effectively suppressed. When the two removed edges are chosen based on the centrality value to suppress the information diffusion, since the centrality values of the four bold edges are the same, not $\{e_0, e_2\}$ but $\{e_0, e_1\}$ might be chosen, it is not optimal.

We try to extend the definition of edge importance to consider multiple edges. In fact, it is unlikely that the situation of removing only one edge (corresponding to the link of such as human relations) occurs. Therefore, it is important to consider the influence of removing multiple edges, when applying this method to information diffusion and other propagation phenomena in the real world. In Section III, G' is defined by G without an edge e, and the importance of an edge e is calculated depending on the propagation process on G'. We change the G' in (5) like the following equation in order to calculate the influence of removing multiple edges in a subset E' of E.

$$D(e) = \frac{1}{|\mathcal{W}_0|} \sum_{\boldsymbol{W}_0 \in \mathcal{W}_0} \frac{T(G \setminus E', \boldsymbol{W}_0)}{T(G, \boldsymbol{W}_0)}. \quad (8)$$

This equation measures the influence that the edges in E' are removed from a graph G, so it can evaluate the importance of the multiple edges. However, the number of combinations to select a subset of edges is enormous, and it is necessary to devise an efficient method for calculating them.

V. Conclusion and Future Works

This paper investigates how the information diffusion can be suppressed by using the proposed centrality. The results of the numerical experiments on the proposed centrality and betweenness centrality demonstrate that it is possible to reduce the range of information spreading by deleting edges based on the proposed centrality. We also extend the definition of edge importance to consider the influence for the propagation of multiple edges.

There are future tasks. First, we use only the two type of the ER model and BA model for the experiment, so it is necessary to simulate the real social network topology in the future. In addition, we will analyze the effect when changing parameters for such as graph models, information diffusion models, and the ratio of removing edges, and also add other centralities for comparison. Then, this paper investigated whether the proposed method can be applied to only the information diffusion. However, it is assumed that the proposed centrality can be widely used for analysis of not only for the information diffusion but also the dynamic propagation processes. Therefore, for example, we will investigate whether this method can be applied to such as efficient control of power-flow network for smart grid and design of the communication protocol on mobile ad hoc network.

References

[1] A. Guille, H. Hacid, C. Favre, and D. A. Zighed, "Information diffusion in online social networks: A survey," SIGMOD Rec., vol. 42, no. 2, Jul. 2013, pp. 17–28.

[2] T. E. Ulrik Brandes, Network Analysis: Methodological Foundations. Springer-Verlag Berlin Heidelberg, 2005.

[3] L. C. Freeman, "A set of measures of centrality based on betweenness," Sociometry, vol. 40, no. 1, 1977, pp. 35–41.

[4] K. Hamda, G. Ishigaki, Y. Sakai, and N. Shinomiya, "Significance analysis for edges in a graph by means of leveling variables on nodes," in Proceedings of the 7th International Conference on Computing Communication and Networking Technologies, ser. ICCCNT '16. New York, NY, USA: ACM, 2016, pp. 27:1–27:5.

[5] J. E. Boillat, "Load balancing and poisson equation in a graph," Concurrency and Computation: Practice and Experience, vol. 2, no. 4, 1990, pp. 289–313.

[6] E. Takazawa, K. Hamada, and N. Shinomiya, "Characteristic analysis of the edge centrality based on activity propagation in information networks," in Proceedings of 2018 IEEE International Conference on Systems, Man, and Cybernetics, 2018, pp. 1578–1582.

[7] J. Goldenberg, B. Libai, and E. Muller, "Talk of the network: A complex systems look at the underlying process of word-of-mouth," Marketing letters, vol. 12, no. 3, 2001, pp. 211–223.

[8] M. Granovetter, "Threshold models of collective behavior," American Journal of Sociology, vol. 83, no. 6, 1978, pp. 1420–1443. [Online]. Available: https://doi.org/10.1086/226707

[9] D. Kempe, J. Kleinberg, and E. Tardos, "Maximizing the spread of influence through a social network," in Proceedings of the Ninth ACM SIGKDD International Conference on Knowledge Discovery and Data Mining, ser. KDD '03. New York, NY, USA: ACM, 2003, pp. 137–146. [Online]. Available: http://doi.acm.org/10.1145/956750.956769

[10] P. Erdos and A. Rényi, "On the evolution of random graphs," Publications of the Mathematical Institute of the Hungarian Academy of Sciences, vol. 5, no. 1, 1960, pp. 17–60.

[11] A.-L. Barabási and R. Albert, "Emergence of scaling in random networks," Science, vol. 286, no. 5439, 1999, pp. 509–512.

A Participatory Design *"Method Story"*: The Case of Patients Living With Mild Acquired Cognitive Impairments

Klaudia Çarçani
Faculty of Computer Science
Østfold University College
Halden, Norway
klaudia.carcani@hiof.no

Harald Holone
Faculty of Computer Science
Østfold University College
Halden, Norway
harald.holone@hiof.no

Abstract - **This paper presents a story on how patients with Mild Acquired Cognitive Impairment(s) (MACI) could be actively involved in Participatory Design (PD) sessions. A detailed description of what mild acquired cognitive impairments entitles is given, followed by an overview of PD and how it might be relevant in the design of new Information and Communication Technology (ICT) solutions for this user group. The story on how we applied the method is presented as a description and reflection by the authors involved in redesigning the layout of a document in a rehabilitation hospital. The paper aims to attract the attention of PD practitioners to the MACI user group and trigger discussion and questions about PD techniques for patients with MACI.**

Keywords-Participatory Design; Mild Acquired Cognitive Impairments; Method stories.

I. INTRODUCTION

There is an increase in chronic diseases in our ageing society and ICT is seen as means to cope with the increasing number of these patients. A notable case are individuals with chronic illness affecting cognitive capacities. For this user group, ICT has become a fundamental part of *"their daily lives by providing a wide range of useful services and tools to use at home, work, or anywhere else"* [1]. However, an essential factor for the design of these new ICT solutions is the involvement of users in the design of those solutions that will be used by them in the future. User participation constitutes the core of PD [2], and that is what we will focus on, in this paper.

The user group in focus are people suffering from mild cognitive impairments after an Acquired Brain Injury (ABI). The abbreviation "mild acquired cognitive impairment(s)" (MACI), coined from [1], will be used to refer to the user group further in the paper. Note that this is not an official abbreviation for the clinical condition.

Intensive research is ongoing regarding ICT support for patients with moderate or severe cognitive impairments [3]-[5]. However, less attention has been paid to patients with MACI and their needs, even though mild acquired cognitive impairments are a critical global public health problem and listed among the major causes of permanent impairments [6]-[9]. MACI are usually described as invisible impairments and might include problems with memory, attention, executive functioning, language and fatigue. People suffering from MACI typically have a very challenging daily life, given the invisible nature of the condition.

This paper aims to first bring the attention of PD researchers and practitioners toward this category of patients, by sharing reflections from a PD research project conducted with this user group. Moreover, as Hendriks et al. [10] state, a good way to go forward on a codesign approach for people suffering from some form of impairments is *"facilitating researchers and designers to share experiences, best practices, lessons learned, and so on is considered very valuable"*. This approach aligns with Lee's research [11]. She suggests that the design field *"could reflect and re-specify its research direction for design methods, especially for empathic design methods, that is, not by developing new tools or pinning-down practices into recipes, but rather towards empowering designers to be more sensitive and comfortable with the design-led, local approaches that are essential to empathic design methods"*. Thus, she suggests that designers should start presenting rich descriptions of *as it is* – what they actually did with methods in particular circumstances. She calls these descriptions *method stories*. Lee states that method stories help as a reflection tool for designers as the stories do not strip away the rich contextuality of actual use, including method application in and adaption to a specific context. In this paper, we are not aiming to present a new method and give a clear formula of how to actively involve people with MACI in PD sessions. Instead, we will share what Lee [11] calls a method story from a PD project with patients suffering from MACI. Thus, we will give a detailed description of a project that we did with patients with MACI and present some reflections and meta reflections related to that experience. The next section gives a more detailed overview of the user group, followed by a reflective section on why PD might be important for working with this user group. Further, we describe a project done with this user group in a rehabilitation hospital by the use of designer notes and methodological reflections [12], considering the reflections made before, during and after the workshops. The paper concludes with some meta reflections presented as design recommendation for applying PD with MACI patients.

II. MILD ACQUIRED COGNITIVE IMPAIRMENTS AND THE IMPLICATIONS IN PATIENT'S LIFE

In this section, we will initially describe what it means for a patient to live with MACI. Further, we will define what is cognitive rehabilitation and how this service is offered in a rehabilitation hospital in Norway, where we conducted our research.

A. *What it means to live with Mild Cognitive Impairments (MCI) after ABI?*

Cognition is defined as the individual's capacity to acquire and use information to adapt to environmental demands [13]. Based on Cicerone et al. [14], cognitive impairments may be seen in a) reduced efficiency, b) pace and c) persistence of functioning, d) decreased effectiveness in the performance of routine activities of daily living, and e) failure to adapt to novel or problematic situations. Cognitive impairments may be associated with cognitive decline due to normal ageing, more-serious decline as dementia, or can be the consequence of an ABI. The latest is the category of patients involved in this study.

ABI is brain damage acquired after birth. The causes of ABI can be "*from a traumatic brain injury (i.e., accidents, falls, assaults, etc.) and non-traumatic brain injury (i.e., stroke, brain tumours, infection, poisoning, hypoxia, ischemia, metabolic disorders or substance abuse)*" [15]. It can affect *cognitive*, physical, emotional, social or independent functioning. The consequences vary from mild to severe [16]. Thus, the spectrum of patients which have had an ABI is a mixed etiological group, based on the kind of acquired impairment and the severity of it.

The focus of this research is patients suffering from cognitive impairments after an ABI and with mild severity of symptoms. Eghdam et al. [1] and Nilsson et al. [17] use the term mild acquired cognitive impairment for that category of patients. Eghdam et al. [1] states that "*MACI is a new term used to describe a subgroup of patients with mild cognitive impairment(s) (MCI) who are expected to reach a stable cognitive level over time. This patient group is generally young and have acquired MCI from a head injury or mild stroke.*" In this paper, we borrow this terminology.

Cognitive impairments often persist after the ABI, and they can significantly affect an individual's abilities to perform everyday tasks, fulfil former roles and maintain personal-social relationships [17]-[19]. Thus, patient life becomes challenging based on the severity of their injury. Often the reported symptoms are not related to specific problems. Instead, it can be in the form of a headache, tiredness, irritation, anxiety and memory problems. The patient can experience difficulties in cognitive and emotional processing, while having no or limited movement disorders and being independent in self-care [17][20].

Nilsson et al. [17] referring to the clinical definition of mild acquired cognitive impairment, in line *with the Mild Traumatic Brain Injury Committee of the Head Injury Special Interest Group and American Congress of Rehabilitation Medicine (ACRM)* presented in [21] lists these criteria for classifying a person with MACI:

- *Minor motor dysfunction/no motor dysfunction*
- *Appear to function well in social situations occasionally requiring support*
- *May have some different cognitive disabilities, mostly within the area of attention, concentration and memory*
- *May have some concomitant emotional problems*

In this paper, we will use these four points as criteria for including participants in the research.

B. *Treatment – Cognitive Rehabilitation*

"*Cognitive rehabilitation can be defined as a learning experience aimed at either restoring impaired higher cerebral functioning or improving performance in "the real world" using substitution or compensation techniques.*" [19]. Cognitive rehabilitation is offered in specialised rehabilitation institutions. The case presented in this paper relates to a project that we did with the Cognitive Unit (CU) of a rehabilitation hospital in Norway.

The hospital offers multidisciplinary rehabilitation to people with complex functional impairments following illness or injury. We focused only on the cognitive rehabilitation process. The rehabilitation at the hospital (inpatient) is carried forward by a multidisciplinary team which helps the patient to define realistic and attainable goals for improvement and then define, in collaboration with the patient, a treatment plan based on the predefined rehabilitation goals. This is called the "rehabilitation plan". The rehabilitation plan is imprinted in the "goal plan" document. This "goal plan" document is at the core of the rehabilitation process in the hospital. It coordinates the activities that both the patient and the multidisciplinary team get involved in during the patient's hospitalisation period. In every activity at the hospital both the multidisciplinary team and the patient should refer to the goal plan document. The patient continues with the rehabilitation plan at home and returns to the hospital after 2-6 months for short follow up and further adjustments of rehabilitation goals.

Now that an overview of the patient group symptoms and the rehabilitation process which he/she goes through (specifically the case of the rehabilitation hospital in Norway where we conducted our research), has been presented, we further give a description of PD and how that might be relevant for this user group.

III. PARTICIPATORY DESIGN

PD was established at the end of the 1970s with the aim to democratise both the working life and the design process of new information technologies [15]. PD emphasises the idea that, those who will be affected by the design of new information technologies or digital artefacts, should get involved and have a say during the design process of these technologies [22]. PD considers users as "domain experts" of the realities in which they live, so they must undertake the role of the designers [22].

In Routledge Handbook of Participatory Design, Simonsen et al. [2] define PD as:
"a process of investigating, understanding, reflecting upon, establishing, developing and supporting mutual learning

participants in collective "reflection-in-action". The participants typically undertake the two principal roles of users and designers where the designer strives to learn the realities of users' situation while the users strive to articulate their desired aims and learn appropriate technological means to obtain them."

At the core of PD is the idea of genuine participation in decision making. Genuine participation stands on a political rationale where the voice of marginalised groups is heard in the decision making that will influence them. Thus, designing technologies for patients with MACI require their participation in the design process. Their marginalised voices in a paternalistic healthcare system where the patient follows what the doctors says, should be raised and heard. By applying PD, patients can have a say and genuinely participate in the design of new ICT solutions which will be used by these patients.

PD is applied as a set of general guidelines which should be adapted to the specifics of the project. Equalising power relations and democratised practices, two main principles of PD, arise due to the commitment that PD has in achieving genuine participation. Another important principle in PD is mutual learning. Mutual learning enables the establishment of a common understanding among different actors by finding common ways of working and exchanging knowledge and value [23]. Only through achieving mutual learning we can have genuine participation.

In PD, a lot of research has been done regarding the active participation of people with disabilities in designing new technologies. Significant research has been done with dementia patients or specific severe clinical conditions affecting cognition (examples [10][24]-[26]). Regarding the mild cognitive impairments, the focus is on old adults or people with intellectual disabilities. Little has been done with patients suffering from MACI. Moreover, we are aware of only one paper which focus on the analysis and reflection on the techniques applied for active participation of patients suffering from mild cognitive impairments in design sessions [27].

However, as also stated in Hendriks et al. [10], researchers are adjusting common PD techniques to involve "fragile" groups in PD sessions with the designers and researchers. This requires new techniques and new PD guidelines to be considered and to emerge in the future. Moreover, as a conclusion in their workshop regarding doing PD with people with disabilities Hendriks et al. [10] suggest the sharing of designers' experiences through method stories [11] as the best way of moving forward in the crystallisation of design techniques suitable for people suffering from cognitive impairments. Hence, in this paper, we will share the method story of our project, by giving a rich description of our activities. In order to learn from our experience, we will take a reflective practitioner stand and present a set of reflections on our process.

In this paper, we will use Schön's [28] approach of the reflective practitioner to present some of the reflections-in-action and reflection-on-action of how PD techniques could be applied in the case of patients suffering from MACI.

Reflection-in-action is undertaken in the indeterminate zones of practice. The reflective practitioner *thinks up and tries out new actions intended to explore the newly observed phenomena, test tentative understandings of them, or affirm moves invented to change things for the better. What distinguishes reflection-in-action from other kinds of reflection is its immediate significance for action.* ([28], pp. 28-29). This is also referred to as a reflective conversation with the situation.

Schön's use of the term reflection-on-action refers to the process of making sense of an action after it has occurred. It serves to extend one's knowledge base. We will use reflection-on-action in two layers in this paper, the reflections made after each workshop in order to prepare better for the next workshop and reflection-on-action with the whole project as the analytical perspective. We will use the term meta-reflections for the latest.

IV. PROJECT DESCRIPTION

Above we presented the cognitive rehabilitation process in a hospital in Norway. The structure within the hospital which is specialised on cognitive rehabilitation for patients with MACI is the CU. One of the main working documents at the CU as explained above is the "goal plan" document. With the aim of empowering the patient, the CU wanted to redesign the layout of the document so it would fit more patients' needs and consequently make the patients make more and a better use of the document during their stay at the hospital.

The authors were involved in the project in the role of researchers and designers to investigate patients' needs and together with the patients redesign a new version of the "goal plan" that would fit those needs. Both authors worked in the preparation phase and the reflective analysis presented in this paper, and the first author participated and facilitated the workshops described below.

In collaboration with a project committee with representatives from the multidisciplinary team at the CU, we prepared and conducted three workshops with the patients. The title of the workshops was: Redesign the "goal plan": A patient's perspective. The workshops aim was to get an understanding of what experience the patient has had with the "goal plan" document and discuss ideas on how to redesign that document so that patients can integrate it more in the activities during their rehabilitation period at the hospital. As the document is given to the patient in a paper format, during the workshop we did not put any technological limitations, instead allowing the patient to be free to envision any solution.

A. Preparations

Designing the right workshop for people with mild cognitive impairments has specific challenges and requires thorough preparation. To plan and prepare the workshops, we worked in close collaboration with a multidisciplinary team at the CU. The team was assigned as the leading committee for this project and will be referred hereafter as the multidisciplinary project committee. It consisted of the CU staff members of different professions with high expertise and longtime experience with the patients with MACI. We will refer to these people as the domain experts.

Before planning the patient's' workshop, the first author conducted a PD workshop with the multidisciplinary project committee. The PD workshop aimed to achieve the mutual learning [23] between the researcher designer (the first author) and the multidisciplinary project committee compounded by domain experts. The aim was to trigger a design thinking mindset and make the committee grasp the PD tools and techniques. The designer had expertise on the design methods and the PD approach, but lacked a thorough knowledge of patients' clinical condition, functioning ability, as well as internal procedures and dynamics related to the usage of the "goal plan" in the hospital. On the other side, the domain experts knew the patients and their functioning abilities, but they lacked the knowledge of PD methods and techniques. Indeed, before the authors were involved in the project, the multidisciplinary project committee had planned to do interviews with the patients to map their needs.

It was difficult for the multidisciplinary project committee at the beginning to understand the aim of the workshop, but slowly they started becoming more involved. All the subsequent meetings we had with the committee or specific members of the committee had a PD approach, where everyone was heard, and the common discussion challenged ideas. The domain experts entered a more creative mindset, and the authors in the role of researchers and designers learned more about the patient's group characteristics and the work procedures at the hospital. The participatory meetings were an essential factor in mutual learning.

The multidisciplinary project committee expertise on their patients helped in *"designing"* better workshops. Among the things discussed in the planning phase were:

1) Timing

Based on the committee expertise the optimal workshop duration would be 1 hour, divided into two parts each of 20-30 minutes with a 5-10 minutes break in between. In this way, it would be possible to have the patient concentrated all the time, without fatiguing him/her.

2) Number of participants

The committee suggested that the maximum number of participants for workshops was 4. In this way, the patients would feel more comfortable and had the right space to share their stories and their opinions.

3) Ethical issues

We decided together with the committee that no personal patient data would be recorded. However, the sessions would be audio recorded so we could analyse the data later. The data collected through recordings are considered not anonymous (they are unidentifiable data), so they need to be stored carefully in safe a location. The project agreement was to store all the digital data for the project in a personalised folder at the hospital servers, and that is what we did. Moreover, a consent form including an invitation to the workshop and a description of the project was given to patients by the CU staff members prior to the workshop. The consent form was written in a very simple language to make it easier for the patient to follow. However, it was a detailed and consequently long description, to make sure that all the ethical issues were covered. We agreed with the multidisciplinary project committee about the document. We were aware that the description might be excessive for the patient and could make him/her neglect reading it carefully. To make sure that the patient understood the consent form, one of the staff members at CU would spend time with the patient (that had expressed the willingness to participate) before the workshop, going through the document and provide further explanations where needed.

4) Patients abilities

A thorough review of the literature [6][9] [13][14][18][29][30] about the patients' clinical condition as well as observing the patients in the unit, made clear that it is a very special user group. The symptoms were almost invisible at first sight. Moreover, this is a very diverse user group. When we discussed this with the committee they suggested to focus on the patients' abilities and how to strengthen those during the workshops. The staff highlighted the patients' willingness to share their stories and express themselves both through words and as visual imagery. Writing and visualisation was further combined in workshops.

5) Facilitators

As the number of participants in a session would be maximum four, we decided that only the first author would participate and facilitate the workshops. Discussing the issue of facilitators with members of the committee we considered an extension of the workshop team by someone from the clinical side that knows how to work with the patient group but is not directly involved with the participating patients. The committee suggested a member from the Learning and Mastering Center at the hospital, which was specialised in providing patient with a deeper insight regarding their health. The member might have met the patients during other activities around the hospital but was not part of the CU staff and not directly involved with the patients. We will refer to this as the knowledgeable third-party. The knowledgeable third-party has the right knowledge and expertise to communicate easily with the patient in case help was needed from the first author. We decided that two facilitators (the first author having design skills and the knowledgeable third-party having domain knowledge) would be sufficient in a workshop with four participants. We used the same knowledgeable third-party representative in the three workshops, so we did not need to explain the goal of the project and the methods in each workshop.

B. Workshops

Three patients' workshops with patients suffering from cognitive impairments and hospitalised at CU were organised. In total, ten patients participated. In the first two workshops, we invited patients that had been at the hospital for more than a week, so they were familiar with the document to be redesigned. Four patients participated in the first two workshops. In the last workshop only two patients participated, who were back at the hospital for their follow up week, six months after their discharge.

1) Workshop 1

The workshop was organized in two parts. The first part was "storytelling". The title was "Sharing your experience.". The participants were invited to talk about their experience with the "goal plan" document. They were asked to think and talk about:

- When were they first introduced to the "goal plan" document? How useful was the document in making them better list their goals?
- How had they used the "goal plan" until now, e.g. in a meeting or looking at it in their rooms?
- How had their feelings toward the "goal plan" advanced? How useful was the document to keep them focused on their goals?

The second part was: "What I want my "goal plan" to look like." The technique chosen was drawing and discussion. We asked the patient to think if they had the chance to have a personal "goal plan" document:

- How would they like that to be?
- Think about the kind of information they would want to have there.
- Think about how they could design it a way that could make them look at the document daily.
- Think about how the new design would help them in meetings with the staff members, nurses or doctors. How could the "goal plan" enhance the collaboration?

For the first part, a whiteboard with a print out of the old "goal plan" document in the middle and sticky notes in different colours were provided. The patients could use those to write down keywords to facilitate remembering what they had to say when their turn would come. For the second part, we removed the "goal plan" document and gave each of the participants a white sheet of paper, where they could design their ideal "goal plan".

Reflection-in-action: the patients did not use the sticky notes at all in the first part, and once provided the white sheet of paper for designing, they seemed to step back. Realising the hesitation, the designer and the second facilitator abandoned the drawing idea and started bringing up the questions listed above as discussion points to elicit ideas and needs from the patients. None of the patients designed anything. However, they got the white papers back in their rooms to think about.

Reflection-on-action: Opening the workshop by asking the patients to talk about their experience with the goal plan was problematic. It made the patient focus more on their goals and their specific problems rather than the main project aim, the "goal plan" document layout. Thus, we realised that a narrower approach toward the project aim was needed.

The fear of white paper, the blank page syndrome [31]-[32], was made visible in the second half of the workshop. The patients were good at articulating their needs, but they were not able to create a visual image of their needs and consequently design ideas. They got the white paper with them, and only one of the patients came back the next day with a design suggestion and talked personally to the first author. Joyce [33] in her dissertation discusses the role of open option in creativity and finds how the openness of the design space can constrain creativity. Thus, we needed to provide some boundaries in the alternatives in order to increase the chances for creativity from the patients.

The participants had different MACI, which meant they had different levels of articulation abilities and understanding. We noticed that the patients were more focused on discussing personal goals than contributing to the layout of the document. The reflection-on-action in this issue was that more preparatory work from the staff was needed to reinstate the goal of the project to the patient to make sure the patient would have a clearer understanding of the aim of the workshop before entering the room.

After the workshop, project committee representatives met with the designer and the second facilitator and conducted the reflections-on-action as presented above.

2) Workshop 2

The reflections on action after the first workshop were taken into consideration before the second workshop. Thus, the nurses talked with the patients again in the morning of the workshop day, to make sure the patient understood the scope of the project. The workshop was divided into three parts. In the first part, the patients got a version of the old goal plan. Next, to each of the fields in the document, we added two icons, thumb up and down. We asked the patients to mark with thumb up those fields that they considered important for their rehabilitation. Then they discussed the choices among each other. To structure the discussion, the knowledgeable third-party facilitator started going from one field to another and asking patients for their choice. Thus, was easier for the participants to follow and contribute to the discussion. In the second part, the patients were asked to try to rewrite the fields that they found important, in a way that they thought would be easier to understand and read. The third part was called "rearrange". In this part, the patients were asked to rearrange the fields as they wanted, add new fields or, change the structure of the document. At this point, the patient could use the template of the old "goal plan" or get a white sheet and design on it. Colored sticky notes and pens were provided.

In the third part, the participants were also provided with some examples of design made by the multidisciplinary project committee in the workshop with the designer. The patient could have a look at those sketches for a short period for inspiration.

Reflection-in-action: The workshop went well. The patients liked the task-oriented approach of the workshop and they got engaged in the discussion with each other and the facilitators. They started building on the ideas of each other. If someone brought up a new idea that would also spark the discussion among other participants. We observed that the patient could focus better on the general task, marking thumb up and thumb down of the fields in the goal plan and relate their marking to personal stories. The sharing of the stories was very important because it gave the facilitators an opportunity to ask more questions to elucidate meaning of what the patient just said.

Reflection-on-action: One of the lessons learned was that the workshop approach narrowed down to exactly the scope of the project and helped the patient to stay focused on the aim of the project and contribute significantly. While these reflections are not new, they appear very important in the case of patients with MACI. Moreover, the facilitators observed that more work in the pre-workshop phase was beneficial to prepare the patients better for the workshop and enable them to contribute better.

The workshop was organised as a future workshop as presented by [34]. The future workshops have been widely used in PD. The aim is to make people critically discuss a current situation and then envision possible improvements for the issues critiqued in a fantasy phase. After a phase of envisioning any solution, it comes the realisation phase. In the realisation phase, feasible solutions based on what the technology allows are discussed further.

In this workshop, we had a slightly changed version of the future workshop. In the critique phase our rhetoric was not regarding critique but more on what the patient liked or not. Providing both the thumb up and down options enabled the patient to think that some things needs to be improved but at the same time there are others that are extremely relevant that need to be preserved, so the patient did not enter a negative mindset. The second part of the future workshop is the fantasy phase. It was clear from the first workshop that the patient could not produce much information while moving directly to the fantasy phase. Thus, before jumping in the fantasy phase we introduced a transition phase, by asking the patient to rewrite some of the things that they thought could be better. By doing this, patients could start envisioning a better solution but still connected to the things that they knew, to the goal-plan that they had seen many times. That "teaser of future envisioning" made it easier to get involved in design in the "rearrange" part and be able design something new or on top of the goal plan or on a white paper. The white paper syndrome was defeated. Figure 1 shows some of the design suggestions provided by patients.

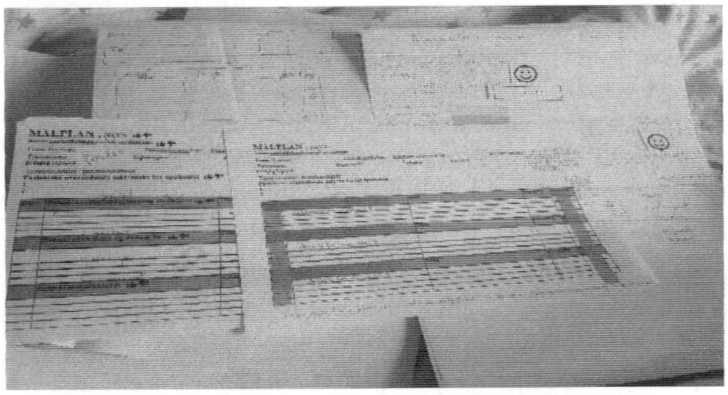

Figure 1. Workshop 2 - Patients' design suggestions

Moreover, the use of exemplars in the "rearrange" part of the workshop, might lead and influence patients' ideas. We were sceptic about the usage of these exemplars, but we wanted to observe what their influence could be and how the patients would react toward that. However, screening the patients' designs did not reveal a noticeable influence from the exemplars presented. Some reflections on this: First the exemplars were presented to the patients in the last part of the workshop, and the patients had already built up a mental vision of their goal plan in the previous phases. Second, the exemplars were exposed only for a short period and were a trigger for possible options of how a goal plan could look like. Integrating exemplars was inspired by research through design and Gaver et al. work with the ludic design [35]-[37]. Finally, looking at the amateur designs from the staff inspired the patients to get the colored pens and sticky notes and start designing, overcoming the fear of the white paper. However, this is a very delicate usage and more investigation of the use of exemplars in design sessions should be considered more carefully.

3) Workshop 3

The lessons learned in the second workshop helped in organising the third. As the third workshop had participating patients that were back at the hospital for a follow-up week, their cognition and understanding of the document was more advanced than the previous patients. We chose to focus more on a long perspective of the rehabilitation process and how the goal plan document could assist in that. The structure of the workshop was the same as workshop two, and the outcomes were comparable.

Refection in-action: The two participants were of different natures. One of them was more expressive, and the other more reserved. Because of this, the facilitator had to make sure that both were getting the same time and attention.

Reflections-on-action on this part where the same as workshop 2.

V. CONCLUSIONS

We will conclude this paper by presenting some meta reflections that we did regarding our experience of doing PD with people suffering from mild cognitive impairments. Through these conclusions we aim to open a discussion in PD regarding the work with this specific user group. Moreover, some of the reflections may also be useful in other contexts.

Based on our refection-in-action and reflection-on-action in each of the workshops our suggestions are:

1) *The role of the multidisciplinary project committee compounded by domain experts* - Working with patients with disabilities can be very demanding. Due to that challenge the patient is typically left out of the design process for technologies aimed for them. While PD promotes the participation of patient in PD sessions the designers and practitioner are aware of the challenges that they might face. Thus, help from domain experts

that know and have a long experience with the patients is vital for the designer. Moreover, the domain experts in most cases lack design knowledge and tends to fall in the trap of surveys as the only method to understand patient's needs. Hence, both designers and domain experts should contribute in preparations of the PD workshops for patients.

2) *The role of the knowledgeable third-party facilitators in PD workshops* – We observed that the presence of a domain expert that has the ability to communicate with the patients but is not directly involved with them had a positive effect. First the patient has someone from the hospital in the workshop so that they can feel safer. Moreover, that someone is not a doctor or anybody from the team that the patient is working with at the hospital, which made the patient feel freer to express themselves. Further, the first author felt more comfortable and in control of the situation with a hospital representative that would smooth any kind of situation that could be presented.
3) *Short workshop duration and Limited number of participants* – Keeping the workshops in one-hour sessions and with up to four participants had positive results in our case. The patients expressed that they enjoyed the participation without fatiguing him/herself.
4) *Avoid the white paper syndrome* – As described by [33], the white paper was a limit in the creativity of the patient. They were not able to envision a new layout. A more task oriented, and creativity evoking technique was needed.
5) *Positive rhetoric and the teasers of future envisioning* – Applying future workshop technique in a more task oriented and transitional way than the original version of Jungk et al. [34] made the participants more engaged during the workshop and later able to design their version of the goal plan as presented in Figure 1. We applied two changes in the future workshop technique. First, we used a positive rhetoric in the critical phase and did not only focus on critique. For instance, we used words like good and better and focused on improvement. The other difference was that we presented what we called a teaser of the future envisioning, were the participants could think about a new version of future changes but keeping that still connected with what they knew, and they were familiar with (in connection with the old "goal plan").
6) *Try out the power of exemplars as a way to enhance creativity* – the usage of examples of designs needs more consideration and further study. However, we can state that it was helpful for our participants which had different MACI. It aided their creativity by making them think out of the box. Moreover, we found that the amateur examples presented helped the participants relate more to them and enhanced their ability to break the white paper syndrome and freely draw their ideas.

Finally, in this paper, we aimed to present a story of how we applied PD with MACI. We used the reflective practitioner approach to present our reflection both in and on action. Moreover, we concluded with some meta-reflections on our process. These meta-reflections can be taken into consideration, discussed and expanded with more insights in other projects in the future.

REFERENCES

[1] A. Eghdam, J. Scholl, A. Bartfai, and S. Koch, "Information and Communication Technology to Support Self-Management of Patients with Mild Acquired Cognitive Impairments: Systematic Review," *Journal of Medical* Internet Research, vol. 14, no. 6, pp. e159, Nov-Dec

[2] J. Simonsen and T. Robertson, "Participatory Design: an introduction," Routledge international handbook of participatory design, pp. 21-38: Routledge, 2012.

[3] S. Lindsay, D. Jackson, G. Schofield, and P. Olivier, "Engaging older people using participatory design." pp. 1199-1208.

[4] J. McGrenere, R. Davies, L. Findlater, P. Graf, M. Klawe, K. Moffatt, B. Purves, and S. Yang, "Insights from the aphasia project: designing technology for and with people who have aphasia." pp. 112-118.

[5] K. Moffatt, J. McGrenere, B. Purves, and M. Klawe, "The participatory design of a sound and image enhanced daily planner for people with aphasia." pp. 407-414.

[6] A. Eghdam, "Understanding how persons with mild acquired cognitive impairment use and experience information and communication technology: an exploratory study," 2016.

[7] B. Roozenbeek, A. I. Maas, and D. K. Menon, "Changing patterns in the epidemiology of traumatic brain injury," *Nature Reviews Neurology,* vol. 9, no. 4, pp. 231, 2013.

[8] M. Majdan, D. Plancikova, A. Brazinova, M. Rusnak, D. Nieboer, V. Feigin, and A. Maas, "Epidemiology of traumatic brain injuries in Europe: a cross-sectional analysis," *The Lancet Public Health,* vol. 1, no. 2, pp. e76-e83, 2016.

[9] C. A. Taylor, "Traumatic brain injury–related emergency department visits, hospitalizations, and deaths—United States, 2007 and 2013," *MMWR. Surveillance Summaries,* vol. 66, 2017.

[10] N. Hendriks, K. Slegers, and P. Duysburgh, "Codesign with people living with cognitive or sensory impairments: a case for method stories and uniqueness," *CoDesign,* vol. 11, no. 1, pp. 70-82, 2015.

[11] J.-J. Lee, "The true benefits of designing design methods," *Artifact,* vol. 3, no. 2, pp. 5-1-5.12, 2014.

[12] D. A. Schön, *The reflective practitioner: How professionals think in action*: Routledge, 2017.

[13] J. Toglia, "Cognitive-perceptual retraining and rehabilitation," *Willard and Spackman's occupational therapy*, pp. 607-629, 2003.

[14] K. D. Cicerone, L. C. Smith, W. Ellmo, H. R. Mangel, P. Nelson, R. F. Chase, and K. Kalmar, "Neuropsychological rehabilitation of mild traumatic brain injury," *Brain Injury,* vol. 10, no. 4, pp. 277-286, 1996.

[15] G. Bjerknes and T. Bratteteig, "User participation and democracy: A discussion of Scandinavian research on system development," *Scandinavian Journal of information systems,* vol. 7, no. 1, pp. 1, 1995.

[16] L. Turner-Stokes, "Evidence for the effectiveness of multi-disciplinary rehabilitation following acquired brain injury: a synthesis of two systematic approaches," *Journal of rehabilitation Medicine,* vol. 40, no. 9, pp. 691-701, 2008.

[17] C. Nilsson, A. Bartfai, and M. Löfgren, "Holistic group rehabilitation–a short cut to adaptation to the new life after mild acquired brain injury," *Disability and rehabilitation,* vol. 33, no. 12, pp. 969-978, 2011.

[18] J. Toglia, "A dynamic interactional approach to cognitive rehabilitation," *Cognition and occupation across the life span: Models for intervention in occupational therapy,* vol. 2, pp. 29-72, 2005.

[19] G. P. Prigatano, *Principles of neuropsychological rehabilitation*: Oxford University Press, 1999.

[20] G. E. Carlsson, A. Möller, and C. Blomstrand, "Managing an everyday life of uncertainty–a qualitative study of coping in persons with mild stroke," *Disability and rehabilitation,* vol. 31, no. 10, pp. 773-782, 2009.

[21] R. M. Ruff, G. L. Iverson, J. T. Barth, S. S. Bush, D. K. Broshek, N. Policy, and P. Committee, "Recommendations for diagnosing a mild traumatic brain injury: a National Academy of Neuropsychology education paper," *Archives of Clinical Neuropsychology,* vol. 24, no. 1, pp. 3-10, 2009.

[22] T. Robertson and I. Wagner, "Engagement, representation and politics-in-action," *The Handbook of Participatory Design, edited by J. Simonsen and T. Robertson*, pp. 64-85, 2012.

[23] J. Greenbaum and F. Kensing, "Heritage: having a say," *Routledge International Handbook of Participatory Design*, pp. 41-56: Routledge, 2012.

[24] D. Corring, R. Campbell, and A. Rudnick, "Cognitive remediation for inpatients with schizophrenia or schizoaffective disorder using "smart" technology in a simulated apartment: a feasibility and exploratory study," in Proceedings of the 9th international conference on Toward useful services for elderly and people with disabilities: smart homes and health telematics, Montreal, Canada, 2011, pp. 286-289.

[25] A. L. Culén and M. van der Velden, "The digital life of vulnerable users: designing with children, patients, and elderly." pp. 53-71.

[26] R. B. Rosseland, "Design and evaluation of an interactive music system for exercise and physical activity with Alzheimer's patients," *SoundEffects-An Interdisciplinary Journal of Sound and Sound Experience,* vol. 6, no. 1, pp. 4-22, 2016.

[27] I. Nakarada-Kordic, N. Hayes, S. D. Reay, C. Corbet, and A. Chan, "Co-designing for mental health: creative methods to engage young people experiencing psychosis," *Design for Health,* vol. 1, no. 2, pp. 229-244, 2017/07/03, 2017.

[28] D. A. Schön, *Educating the reflective practitioner*: Jossey-Bass San Francisco, 1987.

[29] M. C. Greenaway, N. L. Duncan, and G. E. Smith, "The memory support system for mild cognitive impairment: randomized trial of a cognitive rehabilitation intervention," *International Journal of Geriatric Psychiatry,* vol. 28, no. 4, pp. 402-409, 2013.

[30] V. Lichtner, "The everyday ethics of field work research with vulnerable patients," *Studies in health technology and informatics,* vol. 205, pp. 813-817, 2014.

[31] G. A. Price, "Creative solutions to making the technology work: three case studies of dyslexic writers in higher education," *ALT-J,* vol. 14, no. 1, pp. 21-38, 2006/03/01, 2006.

[32] L. Zhu, I. Vaghi, and B. R. Barricelli, "A meta-reflective wiki for collaborative design," in Proceedings of the 7th International Symposium on Wikis and Open Collaboration, Mountain View, California, 2011, pp. 53-62.

[33] C. Joyce, "The blank page: effects of constraint on creativity," 2009.

[34] R. Jungk and N. Müllert, *Future Workshops: How to create desirable futures*: Institute for Social Inventions London, 1987.

[35] B. Gaver and J. Bowers, "Annotated portfolios," *interactions,* vol. 19, no. 4, pp. 40-49, 2012.

[36] W. Gaver, "What should we expect from research through design?." pp. 937-946.

[37] W. W. Gaver, J. Bowers, A. Boucher, H. Gellerson, S. Pennington, A. Schmidt, A. Steed, N. Villars, and B. Walker, "The drift table: designing for ludic engagement." pp. 885-900.

Exploring the Effect of Wordmark in E-Commerce Website Interface Design

Yao Song
School of Design
The Hong Kong Polytechnic University
Hung Hom, Hong Kong SAR
e-mail: yao.song@connect.polyu.hk

Yan Luximon*
School of Design
The Hong Kong Polytechnic University
Hung Hom, Hong Kong SAR
e-mail: yan.luximon@polyu.edu.hk

***Abstract*—Interface design plays a key role for many companies, promoting their business metrics to consumers since it could help companies to enjoy greater benefits by communicating their products or services in a more effective way. Wordmark is one of the most important components in interface design since it is the basic component helping to communicate specific information to consumers. However, the effect of wordmark on consumer's perception in e-commerce website interface appeal has not been studied in detail. This study tries to validate the effect of wordmark on online shopper's perception from interface appeal perspective. An online experiment was conducted to explore and test the perceived edge using three different types of wordmark with a given product. Results indicated that all capital letters and initial capital letter could create a higher level of the perceived edge than the small letters for the given product and website interface design. However, there is no significant difference between initial capital letter and all capital letters scenarios. From the managerial perspective, our research offers implications for marketers and designers to choose the appropriate wordmark for their interface design, improving online shopper's experience.**

Keywords-wordmark; letter; website design; interface; e-commerce

I. INTRODUCTION

Internet, especially website interface design, plays a key role for many companies when promoting their business metrics to consumers since it could help companies enjoy greater benefits through communication of their products or services in a more effective way [1]. However, many of the commercial websites do not communicate and promote as they wish. According to Kearney's research [2], over 80% of people met some problems and did not finish online shopping because the website design did not meet their online-shopping satisfaction and expectation [3]. Although previous research has a long history focusing on the relationship between store's atmosphere and consumer experience, little research has addressed the relationship between web's atmosphere and online shopper's experience [4]. Specifically, the way to improve online shopper's experience through optimizing appropriate website attributes remains ambiguous [5] since it would be inappropriate to directly apply the guidelines of store's atmosphere to interface design [3]. Wordmark, as one of the most commonly used elements in website interface design, plays an important role in influencing users' perception [5]. However, the effect of wordmark has rarely been discussed in previous literature.

In order to address this phenomenon, this study tries to use an experimental method to check whether wordmark could influence people's perception. The rest of the paper is organized as following. Section II discusses the literature review on e-commerce website design and latest trends on interface design research. Section III introduces the experiment-based approach to analyze the effect of wordmark on users' perception. Section IV shows the results of the statistical analysis. Section V discusses the results and limitations of current research, and future research direction.

II. LITERATURE REVIEW

Prior research has long focused on the role of e-commerce website design in IT system building. Even within traditional IT system, e-commerce website design is different from other systems. It highlights the attributes in information exchange (computer factors) and consumer communication (human factors), containing both computer and human interaction from an interface design perspective [6].

While computer factors are task-specific, improving functionality from the technical perspectives, such as website navigation and information presentation, human factors are focused on aesthetic components, meeting consumer's expectation and improving consumer experience [7]. To be more specific, human factors contain six elements of website interface design: consumer satisfaction, cognition attributes, consumer empowerment, trustworthiness, interface appeal and information content [7].

An efficient interface design should be human-oriented and should rely on its framework and aesthetic attributes because the interface design works as the design communication element immediately perceived by consumers [1][8]. An effective interface design could influence consumer behavior, such as perception, decision-making procedure and post-buy evaluation [8] [9]. For example, Carlson and Cass [9] inferred the significant role of consumer perceived comfortability, usability, time-spend and purchase intention in the interface design of e-commerce website. However, this study did not determine the suitability of any particular interface design components.

Compared with the content of the website, the majority of online shoppers would pay more attention to the aesthetic part of the interface that helped to make an efficient interface design [10]. Particularly, online shoppers could have a more positive attitude with human factors than computer factors since it would place them in a user-friendly atmosphere [10]. Actually, the aesthetic part of interface design is a fundamental element in influencing initial perception [11] which contains the arrangement of color, graphics and image selection, wordmark, layout, etc [12].

Several studies have explored the effect of the aesthetic part of interface design on website usability and website evaluation [8][13][14]. The study mentioned color would be more suitable for expressing specific emotion, while shape of different elements in interface design played an important role in recall and memory [8]. Schrott and Gluckler [13] suggested that aesthetic design components, such as main color of interface, photographs themes, wordmark, design harmony and general layout, had a great effect on the usability of a website. In addition, the perceived aesthetics of the website helped to improve interface experience [14]. In other words, better website interface appeal, such as colors, graphics and wordmark, could improve online shoppers' evaluation of website design. However, the inappropriate interface design could have negative effect on users' evaluation. Head and Ivanov [14] suggested that crowed layout and low color saturation might not be helpful in interface design and communicating specific information to users since user would form the initial attitude and perception at the very beginning when they browsed the website.

Although several aesthetic design components have been discussed, previous research has not examined the effect of wordmark on consumer's perception regarding the e-commerce website interface appeal in detail. Wordmark design is tremendously important for interface design [15]. For example, Benchmade [16] and Otario [17] knife companies are using different wordmarks on their websites. While Benchmade knife company uses almost every word or sentence with the capital letters, Otario knife company uses only the initial capital letter in its website design. Prior research on wordmark has discussed how appropriate wordmark influenced consumers' brand perception [18]. For example, the congruence between font and brand perception could improve brand identity building [18]. While the small letter tends to be associated with perceived friendliness, the capital letter tends to be associated with perceived authorities [19]. In addition, compared with the capital letter, the small letter is more frequently used in everyday life [20]. In New York Times, the capital letter was far less utilized than the small letter. Actually in the most common cases, the capital letter is only used in the first letter of a whole sentence, logo design or advertisement [19]. Although there were discussion about sharp cornered font could create tension and represented the attributes of heavy metal [21], this has not been validated with online shoppers' perception from interface appeal perspective.

To sum up, previous research has rarely discussed and emphasized the effect of wordmark on users' perception of the products in interface design of e-commerce website. Regarding the existing theoretical research gap, it is necessary to empirically examine the role of wordmark on users' interface perception. Among all wordmark design elements, the current study tries to focus on improving user interface experience from letter case perspective. Specifically, we would like to investigate whether capital letter would significantly increase people's perceived edge of a given product in a commercial website. Particularly, the research questions are:

Do the different types of wordmark have an impact on interface perception?

What kind of wordmark would increase people's perceived edge?

In order to address the research questions above, an online experiment was conducted to explore and investigate the perceived edge using different types of wordmark with a given product.

III. METHOD

In this section, an online experiment was conducted to empirically analyze the effect of wordmark on people's perceived edge under three scenarios: all capital letters, initial capital letter and all small letters.

A. *Participants*

In order to analyze the relationship, a sample (from Amazon Mechanical Turk) participated in the experiments online. To avoid self-selection and professional survey takers, Qualtrics utilizes by-invitation-only online panel recruitment, thus attracting a cross-section that better generalize the population to a large extent. In total, 139 people were recruited from this online platform (63 males and 76 females; the average age is around 38 years).

B. *Procedure*

There were three wordmark scenarios: all capital letters, initial capital letter and all small letters. One professional interface designer made all scenarios with the same interface layout, a "knife" image at left side and a word description at right side. In order to control the cofounding effect of the position and the size of the knife, all three knives were controlled to be the same size. The length and font size of the description wordmark were also controlled for the same. The first scenario was composed with all capital letters and a knife ("xxx PRODUCT"). The second scenario was composed with the initial capital letter and a knife ("xxx Product"). The third scenario was composed with all small letters and a knife ("xxx product"). All participants were divided into three groups where each group was exposed to one scenario only. In other words, a between-subject experiment was designed in this study. After consenting to participants in this experiment, they were required to look at the product image for 5 seconds and then report their perceived edge of the given product according to a 7-point Likert scale (1 = blunt; 7 = sharp).

IV. Data Analysis and Result

We conducted a one-way ANOVA (Analysis of variance) on the perceived edge with different wordmark scenarios as independent variables. ANOVA is a collection of statistical models and the associated estimation procedures for analyzing the differences among group means in a sample, which is widely used in social science research. Details of the perceived edge for different types of wordmark are shown in Table I.

TABLE I. Descriptives of the Perceived Edge for Different Types of Wordmark

Perceived edge	Different Types of Wordmarks		
	All Capital letters	*Initial Capital letter*	*All Small letters*
Mean	5.5	5.4	4.7
S.D.	1.1	1.1	1.7
Maximum	7	7	7
Minimum	1	1	1

The result of ANOVA showed a significant difference of the perceived edge among these three scenarios ($F(2, 136)=5.5$, $p < 0.05$). The post-hoc Tukey HSD results showed that people in all capital letters scenario gave significant higher perceived edge than those in all small letters scenario (Mean=5.5 vs. 4.7; Tukey HSD, $p < 0.05$). People in initial capital letter scenario perceived also significant higher level of sharpness than those in all small letters (Mean=5.4 vs. 4.7; Tukey HSD, $p < 0.05$). However, there was no significant difference between initial capital letter and all capital letters scenario in terms of the perceived edge (Mean=5.4 vs. 5.5; Tukey HSD, $p=0.98$).

V. Conclusion and Discussion

Interface design is very important for companies to promote their products and services in e-commerce website. This study tries to contribute to interface appeal design literature through investigating the effect of various types of wordmark design on users' perception. The results of the current study showed that wordmark with capital letter (including all capital letters and initial capital letter scenarios) achieved a significantly higher level of the perceived edge than all small letters scenario for an online knife shopping experience. The results were consistent with previous literature that capital letter would be easy to attract people's attention [19]. These results indicated that it would be more appropriate to use all capital letters or initial capital letter wordmark in website interface design when the context is associated with something related with sharpness. However, there is no significant difference between all capital letters and initial capital letter which suggests that merely exposing to the capital letter would be sufficient enough to elicit the perceived edge regardless of all capital letters or only initial capital letter.

By showing appropriate wordmark in the website appeal could affect users' perception, our work contributes to the website design theory from wordmark design perspective. Through the empirical experimental process, we identified the positive effect of the capital letter on the perceived edge and its application in the business field. From practical point of view, as one of the major elements in interface design, wordmark design would act as an efficient tool to communicate specific information to website users compared with other interface design elements [8]. Therefore, the current research results provided some fundamental and useful design references to practitioners. In addition, since previous research has examined the effect of color in the interface design on people's specific perception to some extent [8], it would also be interesting to figure out the interaction between wordmark and color selection in future study.

Some limitations in this study are worth noting. The current study was conducted in the context of a given product related interface design that would potentially influence the generalization of the current finding. Actually, different types of product may interact with wordmark to influence people's perception. In future study, we would use different product contexts to figure out the association between wordmark and specific perception. For example, while the capital letter was more compatible with edge-related stuff, the small letter might be more congruence with stuffed animals.

Acknowledgment

The authors would like to thank the support of the UGC Funding Scheme from the Hong Kong Polytechnic University.

References

[1] S. Lee and R. J. Koubek, "The effects of usability and web design attributes on user preference for e-commerce web sites," Computer Industry, 2010 May, vol. 61, no. 4, pp. 329–341.

[2] H. Ben-Shabet and K. Gada, "Beauty and the E-Commerce," A. T. Kearney Report, 2017 May.

[3] W. C. Chiou, C. C. Lin, and C. Perng, "A strategic framework for website evaluation based on a review of the literature from 1995–2006," Information Management, 2010 Aug, vol. 47, no. 5–6, pp. 282–290.

[4] H. L. O'Brien and E. G. Toms, "The development and evaluation of a survey to measure user engagement," Journal of American Social Information Science and Technology, 2010 Jan, vol. 61, no. 1, pp. 50–69.

[5] J. Song and F. Zahedi, "A Theoretical Approach to Web Design in E-Commerce: A Belief Reinforcement Model," Management Science, 2005 Aug, vol. 51, no. 8, pp. 1219–1235.

[6] A. V. Hausman and J. S. Siekpe, "The effect of web interface features on consumer online purchase intentions," Journal of Bussiness Research, 2009 Jan, vol. 62, no. 1, pp. 5–13.

[7] N. Tractinsky, "Toward the Study of Aesthetics in Information Technology," 2004 Jan, proceeding of Association for Information Systems AIS, pp. 11-20

[8] J. Johonson, "Designing with the mind in mind," Engineering Notes, 2011 Sep, vol. 36, no. 5, p. 52.

[9] J. Carlson and A. O'Cass, "Exploring the relationships between e-service quality, satisfaction, attitudes and behaviours," Journal of Service Marketing, 2010 Apr, vol. 24, no. 2, pp. 112–127.

[10] T. Tullis and B. Albert, "Measuring the user experience : collecting, analyzing, and presenting usability metrics." , Elsevier, 2008 Jan.

[11] O. W. Bertelsen, M. G. Petersen, and S. Pold, "Aesthetic Approaches to Human-Computer Interaction," DAIMI Report Series. 2004 Feb, vol. 33, pp572.

[12] G. Chao, "Human-Computer Interaction: Process and Principles of Human-Computer Interface Design," International Conference on Computer and Automation Engineering, 2009 May, vol 32, no. 9, pp. 230–233.

[13] G. Schrott and J. Glückler, "What makes mobile computer supported cooperative work mobile? Towards a better understanding of cooperative mobile interactions," International Journal of Human Compution Study, 2004 May, vol. 60, no. 5–6, pp. 737–752.

[14] D. Cyr, M. Head, and A. Ivanov, "Design aesthetics leading to m-loyalty in mobile commerce," Information Management , 2006 Dec, vol. 43, no. 8, pp. 950–963.

[15] J. Tselentis, "The graphic designer's electronic-media manual : how to apply visual design principles to engage users on desktop, tablet, and mobile websites. " Rockport Publishers, 2012 Sep.

[16] Benchmade Knife Company, "Benchmade Knife Company." [Online]. Available: https://www.benchmade.com/. [Accessed: 01-Jan-2019].

[17] Ontario Knife, "Online Knife Tool Kit | Buy Knives Online | Hunting, Survival amp; Tactical Knives." [Online]. Available: http://ontarioknife.com/. [Accessed: 01-Jan-2019].

[18] J. R. Doyle and P. A. Bottomley, "Font appropriateness and brand choice," Journal of Bussiness Research, 2004 Aug, vol. 57, no. 8, pp. 873–880.

[19] X. Xu, R. Chen, and M. W. Liu, "The effects of uppercase and lowercase wordmarks on brand perceptions," Marketing Letters, 2017 Sep, vol. 28, no. 3, pp. 449–460.

[20] M. Perea and V. Panadero, "Does Viotin Activate Violin More Than Viocin ?," Experimental Psychology, 2014 Jan, vol. 61, no. 1, pp. 23–29.

[21] E Sadko, "Guide to 10 font characteristics and their use in design," Medium, 2017. [Online]. Available: https://medium.com/@eugenesadko/guide-to-10-font-characteristics-and-their-use-in-design-b0a07cc66f7. [Accessed: 31-Dec-2018].

Supporting Active Participation and Situated Use in Mobile Interaction Design

Susanne Koch Stigberg
Faculty of Computer Sciences
Østfold University College
Halden, Norway
susanne.k.stigberg@hiof.no

***Abstract*—Most mobile applications are designed for interaction only when a user is standing still and able to pay visual and mental attention to the device. New interaction techniques are needed to replace this "stop-to-interact" paradigm. But how can we design for novel non-idiomatic mobile interactions? To inform the mobile interaction design process, I propose a design methodology driven by situated use and active participation. I draw upon a case study co-designing mobile hand gesture interfaces with runners to illustrate how the use of participatory design workshop and field study in a coherent manner can support the design of novel mobile interfaces.**

Keywords-Co-Design; Situated Use; Active Participation; Mobile Interface; Hand Gesture Toolkit.

I. INTRODUCTION

Mobile technology is changing our daily lives. This transformation is less about mobile devices and more about the activities we perform using these devices. That is why Suchman et al. [1] argue that "the study of how new technology emerges should shift from a focus on invention to an interest in ongoing practices of assembly, demonstration, and performance". They request a shift from an analysis in terms of form and function to a performative account. Alike Dourish and Bell [2] call for a deeper understanding of how social and cultural practice is carried out in and around emerging information technologies. They claim that "the vision of ubiquitous computing technologies is already fulfilled", but that we need to pay considerably more attention to just what it is being used to do and its effects. Here, I am especially interested in how mobile technology is used for running and how I can design meaningful mobile interfaces that support runners.

The use of mobile phones for physical activity has become popular. There is a vast amount of mobile health apps available for Android in the Google Play Store. Several research prototypes [3][4] for mobile devices have been developed for investigating the effects of mobile technology on exercise motivation, obesity prevention, and on users' overall fitness. These sport applications operate mainly as digital training diaries collecting performance data on the way, using multiple sensors, such as GPS, heart-rate monitors, and pedometers. They support four essential training functions: performance feedback, navigational means, competition, and entertainment [4]. Before exercising a sport setting must be chosen in the application. Performance feedback is given visually and as audio [3]–[5] directly at the mobile device, forcing the athlete to interact with the device during exercising, which disturbs the running movement [6].

In this paper, I do not present a new sports application, instead I explore how a participatory and situated approach deployed as co-design workshop and field study involving runners during design time and use time can help to understand and design for better mobile interactions. The aim of the study has then been to investigate *how can we apply an approach driven by situated use and active participation to inform the design of mobile non-idiomatic interfaces that support the running experience.* The paper presents a design case of mobile interfaces for runners based on eyes-free hand gestures. Moreover, I discuss the concept of *engaging mobile prototypes* to utilize a participatory and situated approach in mobile interaction design supporting participants' needs, empowering them as co-creators, and studying mobile experiences by integrating their prototypes into their practice. After outlining the challenge for current mobile interaction design (Section 2), I will describe how I responded to that challenge presenting a case study in Section 3. I summarize my findings and discuss the approach and the concept of engaging prototypes in Section 4.

II. A CHALLENGE FOR MOBILE INTERACTION DESIGN

Research in mobile interaction design is concerned with the use of technology while being mobile. So far most mobile systems request the user to "stop-to-interact", designed for interaction only when a user is standing still, paying visual and mental attention to the device [7]. Research has shown that the user's ability to interact with technology in motion is decreased even for simple activities like walking [8][9]. Lumsden and Brewster [10] requested "a paradigm shift in terms of interaction techniques for mobile technology" already in 2003. Since then, mobile technology has been an important theme in HCI research. Liu et al. [11] published a review focusing on keyword analysis of CHI publications to understand how the landscape of the HCI field has evolved. They list mobile phone as the most frequently used keyword between 2004-2013. Still Marshall and Tennent [7] claim that mobile interaction does not exist. They highlight four challenges designing interactions for mobile devices: cognitive load, physical constraints, terrain and other people. So how can we understand and design for mobile interaction?

Löwgren [12] argues that mobile interaction design research explores interaction possibilities outside the established screen idiom, making design methods used for common UIs inadequate. New methods and techniques need to be explored to understand and design for mobile experiences of user-and-technology interplay over time. Moen [13] calls for a non-technological, people-centered point of view in order to create embodied and engaging interaction experiences. Suchman et al. [1] suggest a performative account using working artifacts and Shengdong Zhao [14] requests an interaction shift from device-centric to human-and-environment-centric. I see two major themes from these demands for mobile interaction design: users' active participation and their situated use of technology.

So far, Stigberg [15] describes two common ways of including people in mobile interaction design research, as *informants* at design time and *evaluators* at use time. Work by Ruiz [16], Kim [17], Feng [18] and Pakanen [19] invited participants in early design time, ideating about future interfaces. They stress the importance of participants as *informants* and *co-designers* and explore the design space resulting in design implications, such as end-user inspired gesture sets [16][17], device form factors [18] or design recommendations for wearables [19]. Even though these studies rely on user's participation during early design time, they do not enable participants to experience their imagined mobile technologies in situated use. At use time previous research projects [6][20]–[25] invited participants to evaluate social acceptability [20][23], usability [21][25] or overall device performance [6][22][24] of commercial mobile technologies [6][20][22] and novel prototypes [21][23]–[25]. Participants are seen as *evaluators* of mobile technology most often in a context of use proposed by the researchers. The participants are not able to integrate these prototypes into their exercising practice to afford embodied and engaging interaction experiences. Stigberg's review exposes a gap between, how mobile interaction design research is conducted so far, and what is suggested by Dourish and Bell [2], Suchman [1] or Zhao [14].

III. SITUATED USE AND ACTIVE PARTICIPATION FOR ENGAGING INTERACTION DESIGN.

There is a well-established body of knowledge on situated use to rely on, such as Rogers [26] concepts of a wild theory, or Crabtree's [27] breaching experiments. The outcome of field studies in general demonstrate different results from those arising out of lab studies [28]. They show how people come to understand and appropriate technologies on their own terms and for their own situated purposes. They afford greater motivation for participating - "it is one thing for people to volunteer for a short-term experiment and another for them to integrate a novel technology into their lives" [26]. And the locus of control shifts from the researcher to the participant, making it more difficult to study specific effects. Equalizing power relations between researchers and participants is one of the major principles of participatory design [29]. *Co-design* or *participatory design (PD)* [30] refers to the activity of researchers and people not trained in design working together as equals in the design process. Often workshops and/or toolkits are deployed to engage participants in the design process [31][32]. Examples of PD at use time are less explored. Suchman et al. [1] describe three practices of *design-in-use*: incorporating an artifact into an existing infrastructure; re-configuration and customization of any actual technological solution; as well as co-operative prototyping. Dittrich et al. [33] explore how participatory design can evolve in the wild. They use the term *design-in-use* to "capture practices of interpretation, appropriation, assembly, tailoring and further development of computer support in what is normally regarded as deployment or use" and request new methods for sustainable, distributed co-constructive design processes.

Summarizing I see three approaches from previous work on situated use and active participation to inform mobile interaction design:

- Co-design to engage participants during design time.
- Field studies or breaching experiments to experience technology in practice
- Design-in-use to appropriate technology at use time.

IV. RESPONDING TO THE CHALLENGE: AN EARLY EXPERIENCE

To utilize active participation and situated use, I conducted a case study including a co-design workshop followed by a field study. The co-design workshop included activities for telling, making, and enacting [34]. The participants could tell their mobile interaction story, make their own mobile hand gesture interface, and enact their story using their created artifacts at *design time*. The artifacts are prototypes with working behavior and were used in the participants' everyday workouts during a one-month evaluation period following the workshop. The participants could revise their prototype at *use time* as an ongoing practice of *design-in-use* as suggested by Suchman et al. [1]. In the following I describe toolkit, workshop and field study in more detail.

A. Mobile Hand Gesture Toolkit

The mobile hand gesture toolkit [35] consists of hardware, software and paper tools (Figure 1). A Myo Gesture Control Armband based on surface electromyography [36] can recognize five different hand gestures (Figure 2). The armband communicates via Bluetooth with a LG Nexus 5 mobile phone running Android.

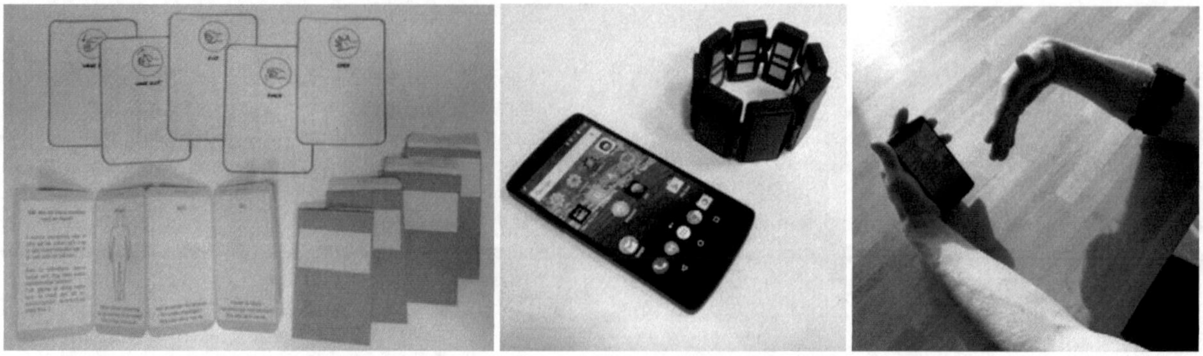

Figure 1. The mobile hand gesture toolkit including (a) Paper tools: invitation and gesture cards, (b) Hardware tools: Myo Gesture Control Armband and LG Nexus 5 phone, (c) Participant performing *Wave In* gesture

The phone has a set of pre-installed applications: *Tasker, Secure Settings, AutoInput, MyoTasker Plugin,* and *MYO Phone App* are software utility tools needed for creating gesture interfaces; *Nike Run Club, RunKeeper, Strava, Spotify, StopWatch,* and *BVR* are software action tools providing desired functionalities for runners. *Tasker* is an application for Android, which performs *tasks* (sets of actions) based on *contexts* (application, time, date, location, event, gesture) in user-defined profiles [37]. Here *Tasker* provides a way of mapping gestures to tasks. I prepared a set of possible runners' tasks in *Tasker* to provide examples, and to reduce the workload for the participants during the workshop. The toolkit is a result of designing the design space: providing possibilities to add new tasks, new devices, and new mappings during the workshop and in future use.

Figure 2. Available hand gestures: Fist, Wave In, Wave Out, Fingers Spread, and Double Tap (from myo.com)

B. *Co-Design Workshop*

I conducted a co-design workshop with four runners (2 male, 2 female) in their twenties to thirties recruited from a local running club in Sweden. All of them used mobile phones for exercising. To inform the participants before the workshop, they received an invitation one week before the date including three questions related to their activity: *what digital equipment do you use; which functionalities do you use from your digital equipment; do you have any problems or limitations with your digital equipment?*

The design workshop was made up off two parts and lasted about 1.5 hours. The first part was a paper-based co-design workshop with three activities using the available paper tools to create a design concept. The use of paper tools was a conscious design choice to lower the threshold for participation and to focus on the participants' experiences and creativity. In the second part of the workshop, I utilized the hardware and software tools and the participants created their functional prototype. I expected this to be the most intense part of the workshop, introducing a new technology, the concept of end-user-development using *Tasker,* and helping participants to create their own working interfaces.

In the first part, we started with a *telling* activity where the participants described a mobile interaction story from running using their notes from the invitation. Each participant defined one scenario that they would like to work on. We continued with a *making* activity there I presented paper cards with pictures of available gestures. Each participant could write functionality that should be accomplished by the illustrated gesture on the card, e.g. "take a picture" written on the fist gesture card. The first part ended with an *enacting* activity there the participants' were asked to demonstrate their designed interface by showing the selected gestures and telling what should happen.

In the second part of the workshop, we utilized the hardware and software tools and the participants created their functional prototype. After I handed out the hardware, I asked the participants to adapt the armband to fit their arm using the included plastic brackets and to try out the *Myo Phone App* to practice hand gestures. Next, I introduced the participants to *Tasker* and I demonstrated how to match gestures to tasks by example (Figure 1). For this *making* activity participants could use the prepared tasks or create new ones. We concluded the workshop with another *enacting* activity there the participants demonstrated their working artifacts. After the workshop, the participants were interviewed about their prototype and their experiences from the workshop.

C. *Field Study*

To support experiencing this mobile technology in practice and explore design-in-use time, I asked the participants to use their prototypes in their everyday practice, at least three times, during one month. They received a how-to sheet for using and altering their prototype and I encouraged them to adapt their interface, if they were unsatisfied. I communicated with the participants through phone calls, text messages and Facebook conversations. I used text messages to remind the participants to use the prototype once a week. The participants were asked to write down short experience notes after each workout and send them to the researcher. Further the participants were able to get technical support throughout the whole time. After one month I collected the prototypes and conducted a second interview with each participant.

D. *Data Analysis*

During design time, I collected data from: 4 completed invitations, 4 sets of completed paper cards, 32 photos taken during the workshop, 6 pages of workshop observation notes, and 51 min audio recordings from interviews. The analysis started after the workshop and has been an on-going process throughout the field study. This continuous process allowed me to refine the questions and directions of the investigation as part of the field study. The collected data from the workshop worked as initial exploration of the domain. I understood what functionality is important to runners during their activity and how they imagine accessing that functionality through an eyes-free hand gesture interface. During the interviews, I reviewed with participants their prototypes. The field study in the wild was a necessity to explore participants' understandings, practices and eventual uses of their prototypes. But it was difficult to observe when and how participants actually used their prototype. The data collection during the field study consisted of: 12 experience notes from participants, and 127 min audio recordings from interviews. All audio recordings were transcribed and together with observation notes and experience notes were analyzed by me and a second researcher using the software TAMS Analyzer. We coded the data regarding three themes: participants' needs for alternative mobile interfaces, their means to co-create a mobile prototype and their experiences from situated use with that prototype. Quotations from the interviews are reported in anonymous form using participant A-D.

E. *Findings*

I retrieved three main insights from the case study, (1) diverse individuals' needs, (2) challenging mobile interactions, (3) the necessity of evaluating mobile interfaces in situated use, are summarized in the following. (1) When designing for mobile interactions, it is important to provide flexibility and tailorability for mobile technology both during design and use time. All four participants created diverse interfaces during the design phase and three of them adapted their interface during use. They appreciated the openness of the mobile hand gesture toolkit. As participant C expresses: "I felt that it gave me a sense of control to design the interface according to my own needs. It felt like, that only my imagination could set the limits. Nor did I feel that it was particularly difficult either."

(2) All four participants identified mobile interactions using the touch screen as problematic. They agreed that minimal hand gesture interactions as probed in this study are a better alternative to control the phone while in motion. Participant A explains: "It is usually not possible to press on the phone screen directly during exercise. Any type of gesture control for the mobile is really needed."

(3) The probed technology based on electromyography is non-optimal for gesture recognition in the wild. The participants felt, that their prototype worked much better during design time sitting down at the workshop compared to use time when they were in motion. Participant D expresses her disappointment: "It works well when you sit with the phone in front of you and you see what's happening. Feedback and technology work well if you sit still and concentrate. When training, everything needs to work straightaway. It must react directly and it did not."

In the following, I present the designed mobile gesture interfaces, findings from the workshop at design time and in the wild at use time.

1) *Mobile Gesture Interfaces*

Four participants created four different personal interfaces. They used expected functionality, such as call management, music and media control as well as activity and performance tracking. But the combination of functionalities into tasks and the mapping from gesture to task was varying between participants.

Participant A created an interface for interval training for biking and running. The participant assumed that *Fingers Spread* gesture would be the only accessible gesture when holding a bike handle so *Fingers Spread* gesture starts a stopwatch application, sets a new lap, and reads out the duration of the last lap.

Participant B's interface is designed for trail running. *Fingers Spread* records 30 sec scenic videos using BVR. *Fist* pauses and resumes activity tracking in RunKeeper. *Double Tap* reads out the current activity time, distance and pace from RunKeeper. *Wave In* skips to previous song and *Wave Out* skips to next song from current Spotify playlist if playing.

Participant C designed an interface for handling calls while runnig. *Fingers Spread* accepts incoming calls and stops current activity tracking in RunKeeper. *Fist* ends a call and resumes current activity tracking in RunKeeper. *Wave In* decreases the volume, and *Wave out* increases the volume.

Participant D plans to use the designed prototype mostly as a music player control. *Fingers Spread* starts the music and activity tracking in RunKeeper. *Fist* pauses music and activity tracking in RunKeeper. *Double Tap* skips to the next song. *Wave In* decreases volume, *Wave out* increases volume.

2) *Design Time*

All four participants provided positive feedback towards the organization of the workshop. Participant C tells about his experience from the workshop: "The workshop worked well. It became clear what we would do. There was no question mark. It was fun to attend. An exciting idea was presented."

I handed out invitations in beforehand to prepare the participants for the workshop. Participants experienced the invitations as important for the success of the workshop. Participant D summarizes it as: "The invitation was easy to fill out. Good with some time for consideration. It's nothing I think of all the time, so it was great to think about that before the workshop."

In the first part of the workshop, we started with a *telling* activity where the participants described a mobile interaction story from running and biking using their notes from the invitation. Each participant defined one scenario without problems. We continued with a *making* activity there I presented paper cards with pictures of available gestures.

a) *Gesture Mappings*

The participants had varying strategies for mapping gestures to tasks. Participant C and D thought that it was easy to come up with meanings. Participant D states: "I immediately came up with how I wanted to control the features. It was easy to write tasks on paper cards. The gestures were clear. It was like using sign language."

She explained her thoughts about the mapping as following: "When you open your hand you start something. That is easy. And then you close your hand, and it will stop."

Participant C agreed that mappings were intuitive to him: "It was quite obvious which task every gesture would have. They were easy gestures for simple tasks, making it easy to remember."

Participant D explained how she connected some gestures to previously known interactions: "I thought of the Apple's headphones when you switch a song you double tap. Easy to remember."

Participant B however felt that none of the mappings were obvious. She said: "There is no gesture task combination that feels completely natural. You just have to choose one."

Participants B, C and D had mappings for four to five gestures. Participant A had a different approach: "I try to use as few gestures as possible. Maybe I add more then. It's important to start with a little thing to remember and see if it works." He felt limited by his bike handle to which gestures he was able to choose from: "Especially with the bike, then I hold the handle bar; I do not want to let go of it to make a gesture."

b) Making the Prototype

In the second part of the workshop, we utilized the hardware and software tools and the participants created their own functional prototype. I introduced the participants to *Tasker* and I demonstrated how to match gestures to tasks by example. For this *making* activity participants could use the prepared tasks or create new ones. Participants felt that it was important to them to learn to create their own interfaces. Participant A states: "It's important to try it out myself and do my own thing. It's always easy to listen to someone else but then often hard to do it myself."

Participant A, B and D felt that it was important to have a workshop. Participant D explains: "I received quite a lot of help from you to create new tasks, so it was easy. If I did it completely by myself, it would have been more difficult."

Participant C disagrees: "Would I sit with that by myself for a while, maybe I would have learned it too. But it was really easy and user-friendly in the workshop."

Participants felt a sense of mastering at the end of the workshop. They were proud that they managed to create their own interface. Participant B says: "I was pleasantly surprised that it actually worked, as I had imagined."

3) Use Time

Participant B reports from a 15km trail run: "Then I was running in some scenic nature I wanted to record and did the double tap gesture to unlock and wave in to record. It vibrated twice and it felt that everything was all right."

The participants exercised with the armband between 5 to 8 times each during one month. They reported back to the researcher after each use with an experience note via Facebook. I conducted final interviews with all participants at the end of the use time to discuss their experiences in more detail. After testing the technology and creating their personal prototype during the workshop participants' expectations were high. Participant A described his experience with the prototype during the final interview: "It works ok, but exercising is delicate it becomes important that it has to work directly. It puts very high demands on technology."

Participant B and D expressed similar thoughts. Only participant C stated that he expected some bugs, and that one cannot assume perfection of a prototype.

a) Breakdowns and Design-in-Use

As anticipated by the researchers the participants experienced issues with the use of the Myo armband in the wild. Sathiyanarayanan and Mulling [38] conclude in a related project from 2015 that Myo has the potential to be used for controlling applications, but needs improvement of physical device as well as gesture recognition optimization. In this study Myo gesture control armband was the available technology to test mobile gesture interfaces and I do not focus on its technical issues. Instead I am interested in findings on how the participants' experienced and coped with experienced breakdowns and how their prototype evolved during use time. I documented two types of breakdowns: when the Myo armband recognized unintentional gestures; and when the Myo armband did not recognize the performed gestures.

Unintentional gesture detection was reported both before and under the workout for all participants. Participants adapted their interfaces and inactivated gestures that were frequently faulty. Participant A describes his experience while getting ready: "It reacts to movements that you haven't thought of, so I started the time unwillingly, because I tied my shoes or pointed at something."

Participant D reports similar problems: "I connected the Myo to the phone without problems. Then I tied my shoes the Myo detected lots of gestures, started Runkeeper, paused, resumed, and went really nuts. So I thought next time I get ready before I connect to the Myo."

Participants reacted on breakdowns by adapting the interface as participant B described: " Then I started running, I started Runkeeper by making a fist and started music by waving out. This worked fine. But I noticed that the Myo armband was vibrating the whole time even though I did not do a gesture. Runkeeper was paused and resumed several times and my tracking status was read up without me doing anything. So after about 500m I stopped and removed Fist and Double Tap gestures from Tasker, so that they would not trigger all the time. I restarted my run and now it was fine."

Participant D changed her interface and removed the double tap gesture that did not work as expected: "I used Myo on Saturday. Run about 5 km on a hilly track. I removed the function to change song (double tap) because it swapped the song unintentionally last time."

Participant C tried to come up with an explanation for these breakdowns: "I think it had problems to disguise my gestures from muscle tension and vibrations caused naturally while running."

Participants A and C were mostly effected by non-respondents from the interface. Participant A reports from his first use: "It worked fine to start the time. Looked at the phone and the time was set. I thought testing the armband when I was almost finished warming up. I did a double tap, but nothing happened."

Participant A found that gesture detection improved when he moistened his arm. After a couple of uses he stated that it gets better the more he uses it. Participant C describes his problems with the armband: "Everything worked great at first, but after a few hundred meters, it stopped working. I tried to reset by flexing out the hand as it should be done, then it vibrated and worked again as it should."

Participant C did not change his interface during use: "I found that all the gestures I chose from the beginning were easy to remember and logical."

While participants B and D removed parts of their functionality during use, participant A came up with new functionality that he added to his interface: "I just had start and stop time. During testing I came across more things I wanted to know, such as distance and cadence and so forth. So I added start and stop tracking in Strava."

V. Revisiting the Challenge

I am aware that this case study only involved four participants. I did not collect enough empirical data to argue for gesture-based interfaces as alternative mobile interactions. However, my goal was to explore how situated use and active participation can be integrated in mobile interaction design to deepen user engagement and to afford a better understanding of what mobile interactions are and how to design for them. The findings reaffirm that mobile interactions are personal and situated, participants' needs are diverse, and their gesture mappings are individual. I have observed that participants' needs can be hidden at design time and emerge during use. I utilized flexible functional prototypes that participants engaged with both during design time and use time. I call them engaging mobile prototypes, they are:

- personal: they are created by the participant
- functional: they are experienced in situated use
- changeable: they can be altered during use

In the following, I discuss how these prototypes can be used to support active participation and situated use and how this approach informed the design of mobile non-idiomatic interfaces supporting the running experience.

A. *The Use of Toolkits in Mobile Interaction Design*

There exist a number of making tools available to support mobile prototyping for programmers and interaction designers in the HCI literature [39]–[41]. Prototyping toolkits that enable non-programmers to design and experience novel interaction interfaces are not yet commonplace. One example is Mogeste [42], a mobile phone tool for users to create rapid, in-situ mobile gestures, however the tool does not support working interaction interfaces, since gestures cannot be coupled to phone functionalities. In this case study, I demonstrate how commercial mobile and wearable technology can be combined to enable non-programmers to be *engaged* in making their own functional prototypes inspired by participatory design toolkits [31] for low-fidelity prototypes. During the workshop the participants create, experience and revise their solution with little help of a researcher.

Unlike mobile prototypes in previous research, the resulting prototypes are personal, created by and for each participant. They enable two dimensions of freedom: the type of support requested during running (functionality); and the mapping of gestures to this functionality. Even though the case study only involved four participants, the findings indicate that both functionality and gesture mappings seem to be personal. Ruiz et al. [16] created a gesture set for common mobile phone functionality using a consensus of user-defined gesture sets. They too, found tasks with poor agreement scores and recommend gesture toolkits to allow end-user customization to support different gesture mappings.

However designers need to balance between complexity of the toolkit and openness of the design space defined by Alan Perlis as the turing tar pit and its inverse [43]. I limited the prototype to five possible gestures for one hand, based on the available hardware. Participants will design different user interfaces having support for more diverse gestures or two hands. Future research can explore alternative hardware components using the toolkit to allow other gesture sets.

B. *Active Participation in Mobile Interaction Design*

The goal of this study was to engage runners in the design and evaluating of a mobile interface based on eyes-free hand gestures. Previous research [24][44] indicated that hand gestures are feasible for running interfaces and I explored what functionality runners would choose, how they would access that functionality through an eyes-free hand gesture interface, and how they experience such an interface integrated into their use practice. I learned that participants answered each of these questions differently. For two participants the gesture functionality mappings were intuitively, the other two just "picked a combination". The co-design workshop enabled all participants to ideate and build their personal engaging prototype despite different technology literacy. This type of active participation supported participants' understanding of technology limitations and made them comfortable handling their prototypes at use time. "It's important to try it out myself and do my own thing" as participant A stated during the first interview. The active participation continued throughout use time. The participants reported on several occasions that they adapted their interfaces during use and explained in detail why and how they did these changes.

C. *Experiencing Mobile Prototypes in Situated Use*

The mobile interface must be meaningful for the runner; otherwise it is a needless gadget. The engaging prototypes contain only functionality that matter to the participants, spanning participants' ideas from design time to use time. But despite creating personal interfaces at design time, situated use cannot be completely anticipated. Participants, at use time, discovered mismatches between their needs and their prototype, and unexpected technology behavior leading to breakdowns [43] and changed requests. Two types of breakdowns were reported: when the Myo armband recognized unintentional gestures; and when the Myo armband did not recognize the performed gestures. These breakdowns were discouraging factors during use time and participants adapted their prototypes to avoid them. Further, one participant uncovered hidden needs during use time and added more gestures to the prototype. One problem was data collection during use time, since the locus of control is shifted from researcher to participant [26]. I collected no use data from the prototypes; instead I relied on experience notes from the participants and interviews with them after the field study, since I was interested how the participants experienced their interface integrated into their use practice. For future research I consider using tools such as AWARE [40] framework, to register additional usage data for more insights during use time.

VI. Conclusion

Marshall and Tennent [7] claim that mobile interaction does not exist, that we are trapped in a "stop-to-interact" paradigm. Löwgren [12] argues that mobile interaction design research should explore interaction possibilities outside the established screen idiom, making common design methods inadequate. Inspired by participatory design and in the wild studies, I studied an approach driven by situated use and active participation to inform the design of mobile non-idiomatic interfaces that support the running experience. At design time, I conducted a co-designing workshop with four runners. They used a hand gesture toolkit to create their own personal mobile prototypes. At use time, I led a one-month field study integrating these prototypes into their running practice. Three of the participants changed their prototypes during use. I found that mobile interfaces ought to be individual and situated; affording different user needs and practices. My suggestion is to provide flexible and functional prototypes that can be experienced in situated use and altered by the participants during use. I believe that an approach of co-designing engaging mobile prototypes can inspire research of non-idiomatic interfaces in other mobile contexts.

References

[1] L. Suchman, R. Trigg, and J. Blomberg, "Working artefacts: ethnomethods of the prototype," *Br. J. Sociol.*, vol. 53, no. 2, pp. 163–179, Jun. 2002.

[2] P. Dourish and G. Bell, *Divining a digital future: mess and mythology in ubiquitous computing*. Cambridge, Mass: MIT Press, 2011.

[3] R. de Oliveira and N. Oliver, "TripleBeat: Enhancing Exercise Performance with Persuasion," in *Proceedings of the 10th International Conference on Human Computer Interaction with Mobile Devices and Services*, New York, NY, USA, 2008, pp. 255–264.

[4] E. Kurdyukova, "Inspire, Guide, and Entertain: Designing a Mobile Assistant for Runners," in *Proceedings of the 11th International Conference on Human-Computer Interaction with Mobile Devices and Services*, New York, NY, USA, 2009, pp. 75:1–75:2.

[5] E. Preuschl, A. Baca, H. Novatchkov, P. Kornfeind, S. Bichler, and M. Boecskoer, "Mobile Motion Advisor — a feedback system for physical exercise in schools," *Procedia Eng.*, vol. 2, no. 2, pp. 2741–2747, Jun. 2010.

[6] M. Seuter, M. Pfeiffer, G. Bauer, K. Zentgraf, and C. Kray, "Running with Technology: Evaluating the Impact of Interacting with Wearable Devices on Running Movement," *Proc ACM Interact Mob Wearable Ubiquitous Technol*, vol. 1, no. 3, pp. 101:1–101:17, Sep. 2017.

[7] J. Marshall and P. Tennent, "Mobile Interaction Does Not Exist," in *CHI '13 Extended Abstracts on Human Factors in Computing Systems*, New York, NY, USA, 2013, pp. 2069–2078.

[8] J. Bergstrom-Lehtovirta, A. Oulasvirta, and S. Brewster, "The Effects of Walking Speed on Target Acquisition on a Touchscreen Interface," in *Proceedings of the 13th International Conference on Human Computer Interaction with Mobile Devices and Services*, New York, NY, USA, 2011, pp. 143–146.

[9] B. Schildbach and E. Rukzio, "Investigating Selection and Reading Performance on a Mobile Phone While Walking," in *Proceedings of the 12th International Conference on Human Computer Interaction with Mobile Devices and Services*, New York, NY, USA, 2010, pp. 93–102.

[10] J. Lumsden and S. Brewster, "A Paradigm Shift: Alternative Interaction Techniques for Use with Mobile & Wearable Devices," in *Proceedings of the 2003 Conference of the Centre for Advanced Studies on Collaborative Research*, Toronto, Ontario, Canada, 2003, pp. 197–210.

[11] Y. Liu *et al.*, "CHI 1994-2013: mapping two decades of intellectual progress through co-word analysis" in Proceedings of the 32nd annual ACM conference on Human factors in computing systems, 2014, pp. 3553–3562.

[12] J. Löwgren, "On the Significance of Making in Interaction Design Research," *Interactions*, vol. 23, no. 3, pp. 26–33, Apr. 2016.

[13] J. Moen, "From Hand-held to Body-worn: Embodied Experiences of the Design and Use of a Wearable Movement-based Interaction Concept," in *Proceedings of the 1st International Conference on Tangible and Embedded Interaction*, New York, NY, USA, 2007, pp. 251–258.

[14] "MUM 2017 - 16th International Conference on Mobile and Ubiquitous Multimedia." [Online]. Available: http://www.mum-conf.org/2017/index.php?web=keynotes. [Accessed: 03-Jan-2018].

[15] S. K. Stigberg, "A Critical Review on Participation in Mobile Interaction Design Research," in *MUM 2017: The 16th International Conference on Mobile and Ubiquitous*

Multimedia, November 26--29, 2017, Stuttgart, Germany, New York, NY, USA, 2017, pp. 161–166.

[16] J. Ruiz, Y. Li, and E. Lank, "User-defined Motion Gestures for Mobile Interaction," in *Proceedings of the SIGCHI Conference on Human Factors in Computing Systems*, New York, NY, USA, 2011, pp. 197–206.

[17] K. Kim, D. Joo, and K.-P. Lee, "Wearable-object-based Interaction for a Mobile Audio Device," in *CHI '10 Extended Abstracts on Human Factors in Computing Systems*, New York, NY, USA, 2010, pp. 3865–3870.

[18] C. Feng, "Designing Wearable Mobile Device Controllers for Blind People: A Co-Design Approach," in *Proceedings of the 18th International ACM SIGACCESS Conference on Computers and Accessibility*, New York, NY, USA, 2016, pp. 341–342.

[19] M. Pakanen, T. Lappalainen, P. Roinesalo, and J. Häkkilä, "Exploring Smart Handbag Concepts Through Co-design," in *Proceedings of the 15th International Conference on Mobile and Ubiquitous Multimedia*, New York, NY, USA, 2016, pp. 37–48.

[20] D. Ahlström, K. Hasan, and P. Irani, "Are You Comfortable Doing That?: Acceptance Studies of Around-device Gestures in and for Public Settings," in *Proceedings of the 16th International Conference on Human-computer Interaction with Mobile Devices & Services*, New York, NY, USA, 2014, pp. 193–202.

[21] E. Costanza, S. A. Inverso, and R. Allen, "Toward Subtle Intimate Interfaces for Mobile Devices Using an EMG Controller," in *Proceedings of the SIGCHI Conference on Human Factors in Computing Systems*, New York, NY, USA, 2005, pp. 481–489.

[22] T. Mulling and M. Sathiyanarayanan, "Characteristics of Hand Gesture Navigation: A Case Study Using a Wearable Device (MYO)," in *Proceedings of the 2015 British HCI Conference*, New York, NY, USA, 2015, pp. 283–284.

[23] J. Rico and S. Brewster, "Usable Gestures for Mobile Interfaces: Evaluating Social Acceptability," in *Proceedings of the SIGCHI Conference on Human Factors in Computing Systems*, New York, NY, USA, 2010, pp. 887–896.

[24] S. Schneegass and A. Voit, "GestureSleeve: Using Touch Sensitive Fabrics for Gestural Input on the Forearm for Controlling Smartwatches," in *Proceedings of the 2016 ACM International Symposium on Wearable Computers*, New York, NY, USA, 2016, pp. 108–115.

[25] J. R. Wiliamson, A. Crossan, and S. Brewster, "Multimodal Mobile Interactions: Usability Studies in Real World Settings," in *Proceedings of the 13th International Conference on Multimodal Interfaces*, New York, NY, USA, 2011, pp. 361–368.

[26] Y. Rogers, "Interaction Design Gone Wild: Striving for Wild Theory," *interactions*, vol. 18, no. 4, pp. 58–62, Jul. 2011.

[27] A. Crabtree, "Design in the Absence of Practice: Breaching Experiments," in *Proceedings of the 5th Conference on Designing Interactive Systems: Processes, Practices, Methods, and Techniques*, New York, NY, USA, 2004, pp. 59–68.

[28] Y. Rogers *et al.*, "Why It's Worth the Hassle: The Value of In-situ Studies when Designing Ubicomp," in *Proceedings of the 9th International Conference on Ubiquitous Computing*, Berlin, Heidelberg, 2007, pp. 336–353.

[29] J. Greenbaum and F. Kensing, "Heritage: having a say," in *Routledge International Handbook of Participatory Design*, Routledge, 2012, pp. 41–56.

[30] C. Mareis, M. Held, G. Joost, "Wer gestaltet die Gestaltung? Praxis, Theorie und Geschichte des partizipatorischen Designs". Bielefeld: Transcript, 2013.

[31] E. B.-N. Sanders, "Generative Tools for Co-designing," in *Collaborative Design*, Springer, London, 2000, pp. 3–12.

[32] D. Svanaes and G. Seland, "Putting the Users Center Stage: Role Playing and Low-fi Prototyping Enable End Users to Design Mobile Systems," in *Proceedings of the SIGCHI Conference on Human Factors in Computing Systems*, New York, NY, USA, 2004, pp. 479–486.

[33] Y. Dittrich, S. Eriksén, and C. Hansson, "PD in the Wild; Evolving Practices of Design in Use," *PDC*, pp. 124–134, Jan. 2002.

[34] E. B.-N. Sanders and P. J. Stappers, "Probes, toolkits and prototypes: three approaches to making in codesigning," *CoDesign*, vol. 10, no. 1, pp. 5–14, Jan. 2014.

[35] S. K. Stigberg, "Mobile Hand Gesture Toolkit: Co-Designing Mobile Interaction Interfaces," in *Proceedings of the 2017 ACM Conference Companion Publication on Designing Interactive Systems*, New York, NY, USA, 2017, pp. 161–166.

[36] "Myo Gesture Control Armband | Wearable Technology by Thalmic Labs." [Online]. Available: https://www.myo.com/. [Accessed: 16-Mar-2018].

[37] "Tasker for Android." [Online]. Available: http://tasker.dinglisch.net/. [Accessed: 20-Mar-2018].

[38] M. Sathiyanarayanan and T. Mulling, "Map Navigation Using Hand Gesture Recognition: A Case Study Using MYO Connector on Apple Maps," *Procedia Comput. Sci.*, vol. 58, no. Supplement C, pp. 50–57, Jan. 2015.

[39] R. Ballagas, F. Memon, R. Reiners, and J. Borchers, "iStuff Mobile: Rapidly Prototyping New Mobile Phone Interfaces for Ubiquitous Computing," in *Proceedings of the SIGCHI Conference on Human Factors in Computing Systems*, New York, NY, USA, 2007, pp. 1107–1116.

[40] D. Ferreira, V. Kostakos, and A. K. Dey, "AWARE: Mobile Context Instrumentation Framework," *Front. ICT*, vol. 2, 2015.

[41] M. Raento, A. Oulasvirta, R. Petit, and H. Toivonen, "ContextPhone: a prototyping platform for context-aware mobile applications," *IEEE Pervasive Comput.*, vol. 4, no. 2, pp. 51–59, Jan. 2005.

[42] A. Parnami, A. Gupta, G. Reyes, R. Sadana, Y. Li, and G. Abowd, "Mogeste: Mobile Tool for In-situ Motion Gesture Design," in *Proceedings of the 2016 ACM International Joint Conference on Pervasive and Ubiquitous Computing: Adjunct*, New York, NY, USA, 2016, pp. 345–348.

[43] G. Fischer and E. Giaccardi, "Meta-design: A Framework for the Future of End-User Development," in *End User Development*, H. Lieberman, F. Paternò, and V. Wulf, Eds. Springer Netherlands, 2006, pp. 427–457.

[44] J. Karlsen, S. Koch Stigberg, and J. Herstad, "Probing Privacy in Practice: Privacy Regulation and Instant Sharing of Video in Social Media when Running," in *Proceedings of the 2016 International Conference on Advances in Computer-Human Interactions*, Venice, Italy, 2016, pp. 29–36.

Discovery and Involvement for an Efficient *Universal Learning Object* Interface

Marina Puyuelo, Mónica Val, Pedro Fuentes-Durá and Hugo Barros da Rocha
Dept. Graphics in Architecture, Universitat Politècnica de València, Spain
e-mail: mapuca@ega.upv.es

***Abstract*— This paper presents a work in progress whose objective is to develop design criteria for the interface of a *Universal Learning Object*, based on an open, free web service. The main purpose of this website is to display different technologies and techniques for discovery learning about architecture and heritage sites. It is central to consider usability and accessibility factors so that this website can target a wide diversity of users. Previously, criteria about the learning method were established. The contents to provide a hands-on pedagogical framework were also defined using 3D production and representation tools. This short paper presents the part of the project pertaining to the definition of a graphic interface for this website, which has to combine contents based on the use of tools and technologies, such as 3D printing or Laser cutting. The main result of the project will be an efficient set of learning tools for learning by making, reaching success through involvement.**

Keywords-Accessibility; Interaction; Requirements; Tools; Usability; Graphic design.

I. INTRODUCTION

Technologies reshape the way we learn and, even more, the societal motivation about learning experiences. The new learning trends are disruptive [1][2] as they increase the diversity and the development of new learning tools and scenarios to learn, and they are faced with the challenge to prove their worth. Massive open online courses (MOOCs) are playing a remarkable role in the autonomous and online learning [3].

The new learning experiences are learner-centered and take on the challenge of participatory design involving different areas (workplace, schools, home, leisure, etc.) and targets. Also, some changes are reducing certain people skills (for instance time management, patience and memory) as dependency on technology increases. Accordingly, several issues regarding participatory design have been explored [4], including the influence of technology on people and the impact of people on technology, the interest in the continuous development of technology, the consequences on wealth and job conditions, and human learning. Some theories support active and efficient participation in the development of learning resources and materials. This is a way to emphasize knowledge acquisition and the relevance of the process, like the multidisciplinary and collaborative work itself.

Some of the most promising technologies since the nineties are Virtual Reality and Augmented Reality (AR/VR), which, combined, produce what is called Mixed Reality (MR) [4]. Both are used frequently nowadays in training simulations, branching scenarios, and serious games. Augmented Reality (AR) focuses on the intersection between two realities and is characterized by the combination of real and virtual elements in an interactive and simultaneous space and time [5]. The use of these technological systems is an established trend in the case of cultural heritage and museums. Displaying historical reconstructions that are impossible to visit, showing their historical timeline and other graphic reconstruction projects aimed at teaching are some examples of its better-known applications [6].

Other platforms promote autonomous and online learning, including various resources and themes. For instance, Khan Academy produces short lessons in the form of YouTube videos, supplementary practice exercises, and materials for educators. All resources are available to the website users and become a set of online tools that help to learn. It has an inviting layout with clear categories for different elements and users. Another kind of learning website is Wolfram Alpha, an online service that answers factual queries directly by computing the answer from externally sourced data. It covers a wide range of topics with minimalistic interface design, and it takes a step further in technical computing systems and encyclopedias [7][8].

A different example of an interface is the National Aeronautics and Space Administration (NASA) education website, very focused on the robust content and the quality of the science, technology, engineering, and mathematics (STEM) learning proposal. The amount of information overwhelms the reader and the layout is cluttered. Navigation is confusing and the black color (space) is not helpful [9].

Pappas [10] has recently published wise and concise guidelines for developing experiential knowledge and learning resources with AR/VR technologies, to make learning more productive, innovative and fun. They are: Understand your target audience to satisfy their needs; Design a memorable story (hypothetical situation or real-life experience) that addresses their concerns and their needs; Present solutions in an effective way; Develop an AR/VR experience by keeping detailed and well-planned product documentation; Care about the post-production stage reusable and adaptable, and arrange the essential minimum equipment to support the e-learning resources (workstations, head-mounted displays, mobile devices, visual and audio.
Although it is a time-consuming development with a costly investment, an online learning object has the potential to boost the learning return on investment (ROI) with more flexibility. Moreover, gaining expertise in this field can now help and in the future of technical tasks and deliverables, especially when using alternate technologies wisely and seamlessly integrating them into the course/web design.
This paper is structured as follow. Section II presents the background of the project. Section III describes usability and accessibility approaches for the website's interaction, some

research on way-finding and graphic communication. It helps to understand the way we see and organize our perception to answer to the stimuli. Section IV describes the basic proposed definition of a standard interface with the conceptual design of the starting wireframes. In the final section, some conclusions and further work are presented.

II. BACKGROUND OF THE PROJECT

Research is carried out by a multidisciplinary team of the Universitat Politècnica de València (Spain) based on the idea of developing a universal learning object to be used in heritage interpretation. In other words, the objective is the design of a learning object which can be accessed in different ways, and also contains built-in opportunities to experiment with the contents, both natural and cultural heritage. The aim is the creation of something new, by the combination of existing concepts and adapting some products to another function.

The proposed design wants to achieve a relevant combination of three merging technological areas, implying disrupting innovation.

First, the development of an open digital platform with virtual elements related to a site or building. The free access to online contents is more innovative than the learning platform itself. This is a crucial point for an ideal integration into different systems and contexts of active learning, e.g. educational centers, cultural interpretation sites, and informal learning.

Second, the use of augmented and virtual reality, both in a real expansion, and the inclusion of digital 3D models in specialized 3D repositories free of charge, in virtual classrooms, or online repositories [11]. Based on graphic representations, this project intends to create new supports and tools, which trigger new relationship models fostering reality and knowledge. These "models" must be researched in the immediate future, as they are new means of communication, for the purpose they symbolize. Simultaneously, these now available means and technologies facilitate an increase in accessibility and interaction with multiple contents within the cultural and heritage scope. Numerous recent studies have identified the benefits of using mixed reality in applications and the gamification principles (use of game design elements in non-game contexts and activities.) This is the central focus of many creative industries, resulting in a new breed of smart education and heritage applications [12]. At the same time, we are witnessing the introduction of (purely virtual) 3D into the consumer market as well, namely stereoscopic television screens, photo frames, games, and tablets.

Third, the assumption of the maker culture (or subculture) as a technology-based extension of *do it yourself* (DIY) culture, with elements of the hacker perspective. Additive and subtractive manufacturing production tools (especially laser cutting) facilitate creating new devices, as well as tinkering with existing ones. That means new opportunities for new teaching practices in a range of subjects and educational settings, from primary education to interpretation and to higher education [13]. There is a fast-growing community of people who use *Rapid Prototyping* to produce things in small numbers at home, using peer-to-peer networks to exchange their prototypes and designs. 3D Printing would provide a more holistic appreciation of the produced objects, but it requires the development of basic guidelines of the 3D offered for printing.

Figure 1 is a generic visual organizer of the learning object contents. The center is the focus (a specific heritage

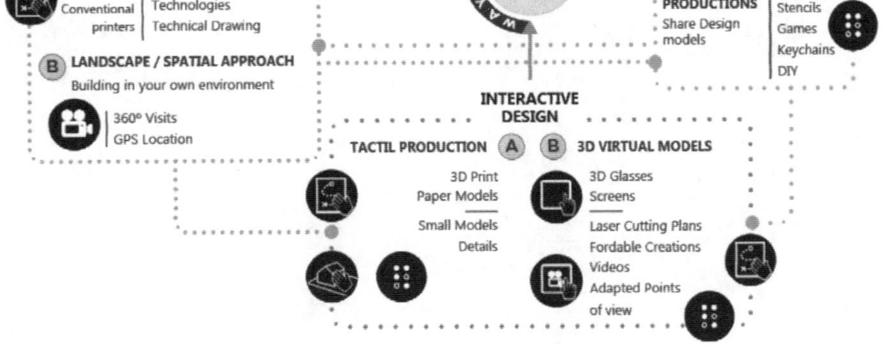

Figure 1. Architecture accessibility contents diagram.

site), and a set of structured resources support comprehension and help understand the rhetoric, where *way-finding* is a primary element. This visual organizer displays the functional elements potentially used. This is interesting because it helps to overcome the challenge of making multidimensional learning formats compatible. This combination of adaptable stimuli facilitates multiple approaches to the educational contents which it offers.

Some experimentation will be necessary to test the quality of the results, the autonomy of the users and the impact on learning. The designs will be tested with user's questionnaires and assessed with the help of experts focus groups. The big point is how to combine activities and specific technologies to obtain tangible outcomes and other exploratory representations. To solve this question, this paper presents a work in progress whose goal is to develop a very intuitive Universal Learning Object website interface for autonomous, varied experiences for a Hands-on approach to knowledge.

III. Usability and Accessibility criteria

The usability is the extent to which a product can be used by specified users to achieve specified goals effectively, efficiently and with satisfaction in a specified context of use. The usability of a system is based on the identification and placement of their components. A clear and simple layout will probably have the right impact on the user. How we move around is defined for the way-finding [14] provided for a specific environment.

From the point of view of website accessibility, it will be essential to make it understandable, usable and practical for all users, which is not an easy task. The guidelines adopted as an International Organization for Standardization (ISO) standard [15], have been updated by the World Wide Web Consortium (W3C) (Web Content Accessibility Guidelines (WCAG) [16] establishing success criteria to be satisfied by web applications or websites. To quantify the accessibility of a website, a standard has been created based on three levels of compliance connected to a list of criteria [17].

Following these criteria, the success of websites can be verified online using evaluation tools. In general, these online evaluation tools are web applications that allow the user to enter the uniform resource locator (URL) of the website to be tested, in order to obtain an assessment report, which includes the verified accessibility requirements, those which are not verified (requiring manual assessment), errors found, and warnings. However, not all the tools have the same way of making available the execution of different activities and of getting particular results. The design of this website interface has to address this.

The aim of this "learning object" is to encourage the general public to approach knowledge for building things and resources, and determining which are better suited to them.

The design and development of this interface to explain a topic should reasonably accommodate a broad range of diverse users, favoring levels of appropriate training, including individuals with disabilities. The design will benefit people with low literacy and new and infrequent users. Following this idea, a preliminary scheme with four phases is proposed (Figure 2), where each tool is independent of the rest, allowing the use of its deliverables and actions separately. A previous phase of general information acts as a door for the other three described below.

Increasingly, more people in society are using and participating via keyboards, screens, telephone handsets, smart cards, etc., so it is possible to communicate efficiently. Young people, people with good manual dexterity, good

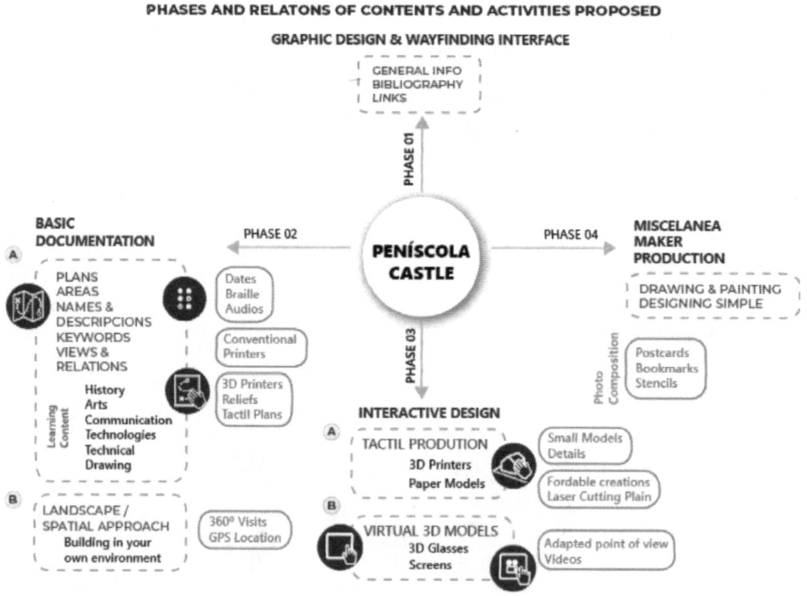

Figure 2. Four phases preliminary scheme.

eyesight and good hearing are daily users of many interfaces. However, for people who have any disability, including dyslexia and other mental limitations, access to this sort of information may not only be difficult, but impossible [18]. As providers of a free system, in order to make significant progress in accessibility, we will need to adopt a 'design-for-all' perspective. Also, it will be necessary to build the prototype to pilot the different utilities with different groups of users.

As designers in this "learning object" we should consider cognitive ergonomics [19] in the product-development process. Cognitive ergonomics analyze the interaction of each person with cognitive artifacts (which demand a mental process) taking into account the cumulative effect of expertise.

Some cognitive processes involved in play activities are very similar to those involved in learning: motivation, meaning, repetition, self-regulation and abstract thinking.

Through design, the website will enable the use of a significant amount of easy-to-do activities and a wide range of interactions while allowing the tailoring of the different learning needs. The preliminary wireframe should immediately show the graphic design, which identifies unmistakably the interface. The areas proposed are the following:

Basic Documentation. Different kinds of representations of general information are presented to the user who wants to approach the topic using multiple tools.

Interactive Design. At this level, there are other sorts of representations: virtual models, animations and tangible elements to be produced. Users may perform in different ways, adapting the format of the available means to support their own experience and knowledge.

Miscellanea Maker production. It includes tools that allow the user to personalize designs and produce functional elements about the topic.

IV. Communication in Learning Platforms. Graphic Design and Wayfinding for Tasks and Tools

As explained at the beginning, there is a growing number of online platforms, and the majority of them expose their functionality through graphics and pictograms. Obviously, the tendency is to offer more functionality using technologies through these websites and, as touchscreens become more common, it is essential that they are designed for everyone's ease of use. Also, the information that the tools include in response to the requests will be more accessible for all or for more cases and formats of the results.

The central aspects of the proposed wireframes for the system will be simplicity and the association between pictograms and results. The main characteristic of this interface is the simplicity to find both the available resources and the goal of the proposed activities. This is crucial because the different working elements are interrelated. Each activity implies two approaches: the analogical technique of constructive tasks and the symbolic logic of graphic representations [20].

Since the point is to show relevant architectures, we raised three types of approaches which are essential for a global comprehension: the contextual presentation as part of a particular landscape; the organization as a space to discover by moving around rooms, levels, etc., and the volumes as in a building site. In all cases, for the sake of simplicity, they are presented using pictograms connected with the result to achieve. In a general sense, we are interested in the "quality" of the visual communication and its relationships with the human experiences as explained by the Gestalt Theory [21]. Gestalt, as a "living thinking" discipline, gives us a series of observations located in experiments with human subjects that could have applications in the design of this Learning Object.

Clearly, it is difficult to combine all these ideas and unify the input parameters to create an interface where the tools are part of the content to learn. Participation in the creation of the results or the resources is part of the process, depending on who is the user. Authors of this paper are working on creating a universal interface proposal, using some graphic technologies, and producing a result with a self-descriptive structure, based on one's own experience [6][11].

The solution proposed here is to include in a knowledge base, at each wireframe, the explicit relation accessibility-result (Figure 3), both visual and tactile, based on semantic and iconographic relations, capable of helping to determine the equivalence between possibilities for knowledge.

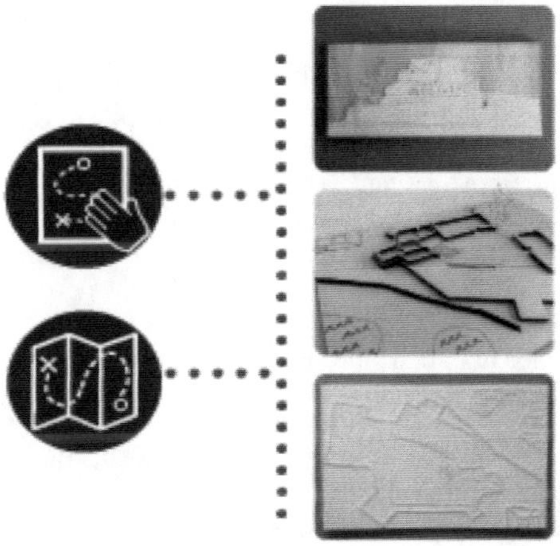

Figure 3. Scheme proposed to develop the wireframe and design of the buttons to establish simple activity-result relations.

Another problem that arises by combining results is the possibility of inconsistencies between the results of different tools for the same accessibility requirement. For example, a tool can determine that the success criterion 1.1.1 is satisfied because all images have alternative text, whereas another more advanced tool could determine that the goal is not satisfied.

V. Conclusions and Further Work

This is a work in progress that intends to provide a design solution to the interface of a learning platform based on the use of different technologies and tools. The site will allow to create and experience tangible models, compositions and resources related to a particular topic. No other learning platform has been found to solve this hands-on approach.

The expected results are in line with the previous work by Kort et al. [22], which highlighted the existence of an interaction between emotion and learning. Their claim, supported by research, is that feelings of amazement, satisfaction, curiosity, hope, and inquiry are good emotions that facilitate a higher level of learning. A hands-on approach also shows that learning improves when using, creating and manipulating tangible elements, and many subjects in education use commonly tactile models in their teaching.

We believe in the impact of positive reaction on individual engagement and multidimensional constructs. It is also expected that this "Learning Object" may be useful to connect different subjects or courses which are often isolated in education programs at school (arts, technology, history, etc.). The variety of activities involved can be seen as a means to create a flow situation when using this learning module. The idea is to increase the learner's participation (not a mere involvement) in design activities and decisions, combining experiences and resources.

All the activities proposed have been developed/applied previously by the authors of this paper. Similar elements have been applied in other areas, such as 3D maps, tactile models, and distributed learning object repositories. This experience is an advantage for the implementation of the proposed architecture for the case of this Universal Learning Object in an accessible website.

The next step will be to build a prototype of the website, including these activities and tools, to make a research-through-design approach, and to use it. Knowledge will always gain from testing. The designs will be tested with users' questionnaires and assessed with the help of experts focus groups.

ACKNOWLEDGMENTS

This paper is part of the research project 'Innovación y Diseño de recursos y contenidos de sustrato gráfico para la interpretación y la educación inclusivas_INDICO", supported by the Generalitat Valenciana in the AICO program (Ref /2017/046).

We would also like to thank our technical assistant María Carrillo, for her work in the design and development of the deliveries from the "Learning Object".

REFERENCES

[1] C. Dygert, "Thinking Out Loud: Disrupting Employee Development," 2017. [Online]. Available: http://dygertthinkingoutloud.blogspot.com/2017/08/disrupting-employee-development.html. [Retrieved: January, 2019].

[2] T. Haak, "6 Trends in Learning and Development | HR Trend Institute," 2017. [Online]. Available: https://hrtrendinstitute.com/2017/12/04/6-trends-in-learning-and-development/. [Retrieved: January, 2019].

[3] D. Otto, A. Bollmann, S. Becker and K, Sander, "It's the learning, stupid! Discussing the role of learning outcomes in MOOCs," Open Learning: The Journal of Open, Distance and e-Learning, vol. 33, nº 3, 2018, pp. 203-220, DOI: 10.1080/02680513.2018.1486183

[4] P. Milgram and F. Kishino, "A Taxonomy of Mixed Reality Visual Displays," IEICE Trans. Inf. Syst., vol. E77–D, 1994, pp. 1321–1329.

[5] R. T. Azuma, "A Survey of Augmented Reality Navigation," Presence Teleoperators Virtual Environ., vol. 6, no. 4, 1997, pp. 355–385.

[6] M. Puyuelo Cazorla, M. Val Fiel, L. Merino Sanjuán, and F. Felip Miralles, "Virtual Representations and Other Technical Resources for Access to Cultural Heritage," EGA Rev. expresión gráfica Arquit., no. 17, 2011, pp. 164–173.

[7] "Khan Academy | Free Online Courses, Lessons & Practice." [Online]. Available: https://www.khanacademy.org/. [Retrieved: January, 2019].

[8] "Wolfram|Alpha: Computational Intelligence." [Online]. Available: https://www.wolframalpha.com/. [Retrieved: January, 2019].

[9] F. Wild, "For Students," 2015. [Online]. Available: https://www.nasa.gov/audience/forstudents/index.html. [Retrieved: January, 2019].

[10] C. Pappas, "How To Develop AR/VR eLearning Resources: A 7-Step Guide - eLearning Industry," 2018. [Online]. Available: https://elearningindustry.com/develop-ar-vr-elearning-resources-step-guide. [Retrieved: January, 2019].

[11] M. Puyuelo Cazorla, P. Fuentes-Durá, and M. Val Fiel, "From information to knowledge. Building new learning strategies in heritage field through graphics and new technologies," in XVI International Forum Le Vie dei Mercanti: World Heritage and Knowledge, 2018, pp. 1108-1117.

[12] M. Ioannides, J. Martins, R. Žarnić, and V. Lim, "Advances in digital cultural heritage: International Workshop", Funchal, Madeira, Portugal, June 28, 2017, Revised selected papers.

[13] L. Armesto, P. Fuentes-Durá, and D. Perry, "Low-cost Printable Robots in Education," J Intell Robot Syst, vol. 81, 2016, pp. 5–24.

[14] D. García Moreno, "Diseño de sistemas de orientación espacial. Design of spatial orientation systems," in Accesibilidad universal y diseño para todos: arquitectura y urbanismo, 2011, ISBN 978-84-88934-47-5, págs. 36-57, Colegio Oficial de Arquitectos, 2011, pp. 36–57.

[15] International Organization for Standardization, ISO/IEC 40500:2012 Web Content Accessibility Guidelines (WCAG) 2.0. 2012, p. 2.

[16] "Web Content Accessibility Guidelines (WCAG) 2.1" [Online]. Available: https://www.w3.org/TR/2018/REC-WCAG21-20180605/. [Retrieved: January, 2019].

[17] N. Fernandes, R. Lopes, and L. Carriço, "An Architecture for Multiple Web Accessibility Evaluation Environments," Springer, Berlin, Heidelberg, 2011, pp. 206–214.

[18] J. M. Gill, Accessibility for Visitors who are Blind or Partially Sighted: How Technology Can Help. London: Royal National Institute of Blind People, 2007.

[19] C. Moreno Muñoz and F. Jeno Hernández, "El aporte de la ergonomía cognitiva perceptual en la comunicación de los productos. The contribution of perceptual cognitive ergonomics in the communication of products," Publicitas Comun. y Cult., vol. 4, 2016, pp. 27–34.

[20] A. Findeli, "Rethinking Design Education for the 21st Century: Theoretical, Methodological, and Ethical Discussion," Des. Issues, vol. 17, no. 1, 2001, pp. 5–17.

[21] J. Moszkowicz, "Gestalt and Graphic Design: An Exploration of the Humanistic and Therapeutic Effects of Visual Organization," Des. Issues, vol. 27, no. 4, 2011, pp. 56–67.

[22] B. Kort, R. Reilly, and R. Picard, "An Affective Model of the Interplay between Emotions and Learning: Reengineering Educational Pedagogy-Building a Learning Companion. In Proceedings of the IEEE International Conference on

Advanced Learning Technologies (ICALT '01). IEEE Computer Society, 2001, 43-46.

International Academy, Research,
and Industry Association (IARIA)
412 Derby Way
Wilmington, DE 19810

ISBN 978-1-5108-8359-8

CURRAN ASSOCIATES INC.
proceedings.com

Tenth International Conference on Emerging Security Information, Systems and Technologies (SECURWARE 2016)

Held at NetWare 2016

Nice, France
24 - 28 July 2016

IARIA